A Writer's Diary

A Writer's Diary

FYODOR DOSTOEVSKY

Volume Two 1877–1881

Translated and Annotated by
KENNETH LANTZ

Northwestern University Press · Evanston, Illinois

Northwestern University Press
Evanston, Illinois 60208-4210

This translation was funded with the assistance of the National Endowment for the Humanities.

First paperback printing 1997
Second paperback printing 2000

Printed in the United States of America

ISBN 0-8101-1517-4

Library of Congress Cataloging-in-Publication Data

Dostoyevsky, Fyodor, 1821–1881
[Dnevnik pisateli͡a. English]
A writer's diary / Fyodor Dostoevsky : translated by Kenneth Lantz : with an introduction by Gary Saul Morson.
v. ; cm.
Translation of: Dnevnik pisateli͡a.
Includes bibliographical references.
ISBN 0-8101-1516-6 (v. 1). — ISBN 0-8101-1517-4 (v. 2).
I. Lantz, K. A. II. Morson, Gary Saul, 1948– . III. Title.
PG3326.A16L36 1992
891.78'307—dc20 92-4604
CIP

The paper used in this publication meets the minimum requirements of the American National Standard for Information Sciences—Permanence of Paper for Printed Library Materials, ANSI Z39.48-1984.

Contents

1877

January

CHAPTER ONE

CHAPTER TWO

February

CHAPTER ONE

April

May and June

July and August

September

November

CHAPTER ONE

CHAPTER TWO

CHAPTER THREE

December

CHAPTER ONE

CHAPTER TWO

---

1 8 8 0

August

CHAPTER ONE

CHAPTER TWO

CHAPTER THREE

---

1 8 8 1

January

CHAPTER ONE

A Writer's Diary

1877

January

1

1. Three Ideas

I shall begin my new year on the same topic with which I ended last year. The final sentence in my December *Diary* said that "almost all our Russian disunities and dissociations have been founded merely on misunderstandings, the crudest sort of misunderstandings, which contain nothing of real substance and nothing that cannot be surmounted." Again I repeat: all our disputes and disunity have arisen only from errors and diverse attitudes of mind but not of heart; and it is this formula that expresses all the essence of our disunity. We may take some consolation in this fact. Errors and quandaries of the mind vanish more quickly and completely than do errors of the heart; their cure is to be found not so much in debate and logical explanation as in the overpowering logic of events of a real, living life, events that very often bear the correct and necessary conclusion within and that indicate the proper path to take; and if this does not happen at once, at the actual moment, then it does happen within a very short time, sometimes even before a new generation appears. The same cannot be said for errors of the heart. Errors of the heart are something terribly significant: they represent the contaminated spirit, sometimes even of the nation as a whole, that very often bears with it a degree of blindness that cannot be cured by facts of any kind, no matter how clearly they might indicate the proper path to take. Quite to the contrary: blindness of this sort modifies the facts to suit its purposes and adjusts them to suit its contaminated spirit; it sometimes even happens that the whole nation deliberately chooses to perish, aware of its blindness but *not wishing* to be cured of it. I hope people will not scoff because I take errors of the mind too lightly and see them as easily corrected. There would be far more cause to scoff at someone—never mind me—who assumed the role of the corrector in this case, firmly and calmly assured that his words could sway or reverse the convictions held by a society at a given moment. I am aware of all that. Nonetheless, one needn't be ashamed of one's convictions, and at the present time one mustn't be ashamed of them; he who has a word to say should say it without fear that he will not be heeded, without fear even that he will be laughed at and that he will produce no impression on the minds of his contemporaries. In that sense *A Writer's Diary* will never stray from its path, will never yield to the spirit of the age or to the force of dominant and prevailing influences so long as it considers them to be unjust, will not fall in line with them or flatter them or try to manipulate them. After publishing for a whole year, we think a statement like that can be made. After all, we fully and quite clearly realized even last year that much of what we wrote with passion and conviction did us only real harm and that, rather, we would have gained far more had we sung with equal passion in unison with others.

We repeat: we think that at present *each one* must say his piece as frankly and as directly as possible, without feeling any shame for naively laying bare certain of his ideas. Indeed, events that are, perhaps, extraordinary and enormous are awaiting us—all Russia, that is. "Some great events may suddenly come to pass and catch our intelligentsia by surprise; then, might it not be too late?" as I said when I closed my December *Diary*. In saying that I had in mind not only political events to come in this "near future," although they, too, cannot help but capture the attention of even the most inferior and "Yiddifying" minds that take no thought for anything beyond their own affairs. Indeed, what is awaiting the world, not only in the remaining quarter of this century, but even (who can tell?) in the current year, perhaps? Europe is restless, of this there is no doubt. But is this restlessness only temporary, a thing of the moment? Certainly not: it is evident that the time is at hand for the fulfillment of something eternal, something millenarian, something that has been in preparation in the world since the very beginning of its civilization. Three ideas rise up before the world and, it seems, are already in their final stage of formulation.

On one side, at the edge of Europe, there is the Catholic idea—condemned and waiting in great torment and perplexity: is it to be or not to be? Is it still to live or has its end come? I am speaking not about the Catholic religion alone but about the entire *Catholic idea,* about the fate of the nations which have formed themselves under this idea over the course of a millennium and which have been entirely permeated with it. In that sense, for instance, France over the ages has seemed to be the most complete incarnation of the Catholic idea; she is the head of this idea, which she inherited from the Romans, of course, and which is in their spirit. This France who, though she has now lost her religion *almost entirely* (Jesuits and atheists are all one and the same thing there), who has closed her churches more than once and who on one occasion subjected God himself to a vote in the Assembly; this France, who developed from the ideas of 1789 her own particular French socialism—i.e., the pacification and organization of human society without Christ and outside of Christ, as Catholicism tried but was unable to organize it in Christ; this same France—in her revolutionary Convention, in her atheists, in her socialists, and in her communards of today—is and continues to be in the highest degree a Catholic nation wholly and entirely, completely contaminated by the spirit and the letter of Catholicism, proclaiming through the mouths of its confirmed atheists: *Liberté, Egalité, Fraternité—ou la mort,* i.e., exactly as the pope himself would have proclaimed had he been compelled to proclaim and formulate a Catholic *liberté, égalité, fraternité* in his style and in his spirit—the actual style and spirit of a pope of the Middle Ages. Today's French socialism itself appears to be a passionate and fateful protest against the Catholic idea by all the people and nations who have been tormented and oppressed by it and who wish, whatever the cost, to go on living without Catholicism and its gods. The protest itself, which to all intents and purposes began at the end of the last century (but in essence much earlier), is nothing other than the truest and direct continuation of the Catholic idea, its most complete and final fulfillment, its fateful consequence elaborated over the course of centuries. For French socialism is nothing other than the *compulsory* union of humanity, an idea that derived from ancient Rome and that was subsequently preserved completely in Catholicism. Thus socialism's idea of the liberation of the human spirit from Catholicism has become incarnated here in the very most restricted of Catholic forms, borrowed from the very core of its spirit, from its letter, from its materialism, from its despotism, from its morality.

On the other side rises up the old Protestantism, protesting for nineteen centuries now against Rome and her idea, against the ancient pagan idea and the renewed Catholic one; against Rome's universal idea of possessing man both morally and materially all the world over, against Rome's civilization; protesting since the time of Arminius and the Teutoburger Wald. This is the German, believing blindly that the renewal of humanity is to be found only in him and not in Catholic civilization. Through his entire history he dreamed only of and longed only for his unification so he could proclaim his own proud idea, an idea that had been powerfully formulated and that had had a unifying effect even in the heresy of Luther; while now, five years after the defeat of France—the foremost, principal, and most Christian Catholic nation—the German is confident in his complete triumph and in the fact that no one can stand in his place at the head of the world and its renewal. He believes in this proudly and unwaveringly; he believes that there is nothing else in the world that is higher than the Germanic spirit and the Germanic word and that Germany alone can utter that word. He finds it absurd even to suppose that there is anything in the world, even if only in embryo, that could contain something that Germany, ordained to lead the world, could not contain. Yet it would certainly not be superfluous to note, though in parentheses, that through all the nineteen centuries of her existence, Germany has done nothing more than to protest; she herself has never uttered her *new word* but has only lived the whole time by rejection and protest against her enemy so that, for example, it is very possible indeed that something as odd as this could happen: when Germany does achieve her final victory and destroys that against which she has been protesting for nineteen centuries, she herself will suddenly have to die spiritually, in the wake of her enemy, for she will have nothing to live for; *she will have nothing to protest against*. This may still be only my chimera, but Luther's Protestantism is already a fact: this faith is one of protest and of mere *denial*, and as soon as Catholicism disappears from the world, Protestantism will also disappear right after it because it will have nothing to protest against; it will be transformed into straight atheism and thus will it end. But that, let's say, is still only my chimera. The German despises the Slavic idea as much as he does the Catholic one, the only difference being that he has always respected the latter as a strong and powerful enemy, whereas he not only had no respect whatever for the Slavic idea, he did not even acknowledge it until very recent times. But lately he has begun to cast a very suspicious eye at the Slavs. Although even now he finds it absurd to suppose that they also could have a goal of some sort and an idea, that there could be some hope there of also "saying something to the world," still, since the defeat of France his unhealthy suspicions have increased, and the events of the past year and of the present can scarcely do much to alleviate his mistrust. Germany's position is now a rather worrisome one: in any case, she has to finish her mission in the West before she can entertain any Eastern ideas. Who can deny that France, still not beaten into submission, does not and did not trouble the German through all these five years after her defeat for the very reason that he had not beaten her into submission? In 1875 that unease reached an extraordinary level in Berlin, and Germany would certainly have rushed to render a final blow to her age-old enemy while there was still time, but certain very powerful circumstances prevented her from doing so. Now, however—this year—there is no doubt that France, which grows ever more powerful materially every year, terrifies Germany even more than she did two years ago. Germany knows that her enemy will not die without a struggle; she knows, moreover, that when that enemy feels he has recovered completely, he himself will begin the battle, so that three or five years hence may be too late for Germany. And so, in view of the fact that the east of Europe has been so completely permeated with its own idea that sprang up suddenly there and that it has too many of its own affairs to look after—in view of that, it may very well happen that Germany, feeling her own hands untied for the moment, will make a final assault on the western enemy, on that terrible nightmare that torments her; and all this may even happen in the very nearest of the near future. On the whole, one can say that though the situation in the east is tense and difficult, Germany herself is perhaps in an even less enviable position. And she may well have even more fears and various anxieties to face, despite her excessively haughty tone. And this, at least, we ought to keep particularly in mind.

And meanwhile, in the East, the third world idea—the Slavic idea, a new idea that is coming into being—has truly caught ablaze and has begun to cast a light that has never before been seen; it is, perhaps, the third future possibility for settling the destinies of Europe and of humanity. It is clear to everyone now that with the solution to the Eastern Question, a new element, a new phenomenon will enter into humanity, one that until now has lain passive and inert and that, in any case and at the very least, cannot but exert an extraordinarily powerful and decisive influence on the fate of the world. What sort of idea is this? What will the union of the Slavs bring? This is all too indefinite at the moment, but that something truly will be contributed and something new will be uttered—that scarcely anyone doubts. And all these three enormous world ideas have come together to be resolved almost at the same time. Of course, this is not simply some idle wish; nor is it a war arising over some legacy or argument between two highly placed ladies, as happened in the last century. This is a matter of universal significance and of ultimate importance; and although it will certainly not resolve *all* human destinies, there is no doubt that it brings with it the beginning of the end of all the previous histories of European humanity, the beginning of the resolution of their eventual destinies, which are in the hands of God and which humans can scarcely foresee, even though they may have forebodings.

And now, the question that cannot help but present itself to every thinking person: can such events be stopped in their course? Can ideas of such dimensions be subordinated to petty, Yiddifying, third-rate considerations? Can anyone postpone their resolution? Is this a useful thing to do? Wisdom, no doubt, must preserve and protect the nations and serve philanthropy and humanity, but there are some ideas that have their own immutable, powerful and all-engulfing force. You cannot hold back with one hand the summit of a cliff that has crumbled away and is falling. Of course, we Russians have two awesome powers that are worth all the others in the world—the intactness and spiritual indivisibility of the millions of our People and their most intimate link with their monarch. The latter, of course, is beyond dispute; but our "pondering Peters" not only do not understand the People's idea, they do not even want to understand it.

2. Mirages. Stundism and the Radstockists

But is it only the "Europeanizers" and the "pondering Peters" who do not want to understand? There are others as well, ones who are much more malignant. The "Peters" at least acknowledge the past year's Popular movement in aid of the Slavs, but these others do not. The Peters even have praise for this movement—in their own way, of course—even though there is much in it that they do not like; but the former reject the movement itself, despite the testimony of the whole of Russia: "There wasn't any movement, and that's all there is to it," they say. "Not only was there no movement, there could never have been one. Nowhere," they say, "did the People cry out and declare that they wanted war." But our People never do cry out and never do make declarations; our People are sensible and calm, and besides, they certainly do not want war, not at all; but their souls and their hearts are filled with deep compassion for their brethren who have been oppressed for the faith of Christ. However, should it prove necessary, should the mighty word of the tsar ring out, then they will all go forth, the entire hundred-million mass of them, and will do everything that such a hundred-million mass can do when it is inspired by a single noble impulse, in accord, as one man. And so such a force of unity, in view of the mysterious, imminent future destinies of all Europe, cannot but be cherished and cannot but be held up for contemplation in our moments of involuntary pondering and conjecture. But enough talk of war; who wants war? Although I would note in parentheses that blood spilled "for the great cause of love" means a great deal; it washes and cleanses many things; it can raise up and restore life to many a thing that theretofore had been devalued and besmirched in our souls.

But these are only "words and thoughts." I said only that there are historical events that draw everything in their wake, events from which we cannot save ourselves either by strength of will or cleverness of mind, just as we cannot forbid the tide to stay its course and turn back. Nevertheless, after the raptures of this summer, this current triumphant cynicism is offensive; this delight in cynicism, a delight in something foul that supposedly has triumphed over people's rapture—this is offensive; offensive are the triumphant speeches of people who not merely scorn but almost entirely reject our whole People and who, as before, it seems, regard them as no more than an inert mass and working hands, exactly as they were regarded for two centuries until the great day of February 19. "Should I model myself on such People? What kind of idea can they have? Wherever did you find it?"—that is what you now hear almost all the time. This disbelief in the spiritual strength of the People is, of course, a disbelief in the whole of Russia as well. No doubt, those who reject are guided by a mixture of various factors; yet—can you believe it?—there is a lot of sincerity in them as well! But above everything else is their complete ignorance of Russia. Can you imagine that some among them are almost happy over Stundism, happy for the People, for their benefit and their well-being? "Still," they say, "this is a little better than the People's former beliefs; still, it might raise them up at least a little." And don't think that these were only rare, isolated opinions. Incidentally, what is this wretched Stundism? A few Russian workers employed by German colonists realized that the Germans lived better than the Russians and that this was because the Germans arranged their lives differently. Pastors who happened to be there explained that this better arrangement of living was the result of a different religious faith. And so groups of Russian "dark people" joined together and began to listen to the interpretation of the Gospel; they themselves began reading and interpreting it; the result was what always results in such cases. A vessel containing a precious liquid is being carried; everyone falls to their knees; everyone kisses and worships the vessel containing this precious, vivifying liquid; and suddenly some people stand up and begin shouting: "You are blind! Why do you kiss the vessel? What is precious is only the vivifying liquid contained within; what is precious are the contents, not the container. But you are kissing glass, simple glass; you worship the vessel and attribute all the sanctity to the glass so that you ignore its precious contents! Idolators! Cast the vessel aside; smash it; worship only the vivifying liquid and not the glass!" And so the vessel is smashed and the vital liquid, the precious contents are spilled on the earth and disappear into it, of course. The vessel has been smashed and the liquid lost. But before all the liquid has disappeared into the earth, a hubbub commences: so as to save what little that remains in a few potsherds, people begin shouting that a new vessel is needed at once; they begin quarreling about how and of what to fashion it. The dispute arises *from the very beginning;* and at once, from the first few words, the letter of the matter becomes the issue. They are prepared to pay homage to this letter even more than they did to the former one, just so long as they can acquire a new vessel; but the quarrel becomes more fierce; people split into warring camps, and each camp carries away in its own particular container of whatever size and shape it can find a few drops of the precious liquid that remains and has no further contact with the other camps. Each wants to be saved through its own vessel, and new quarrels break out in each separate camp. Idolatry increases by as many times as there were fragments of the original vessel. It is an eternal story that began long before Martin Luther; but in accord with immutable historical laws, almost exactly the same thing happened to our Stundists: it is well known that they are already dividing amongst themselves, arguing about the letter of the matter; that each of them takes responsibility for interpreting the Gospels in accordance with his own conscience; and the main thing is that this is happening *from the very beginning*—the poor, wretched, "dark" people! And still, they do this with such pure hearts; they have so many good intentions, so much determination to endure even torture; yet at the same time, how much helpless stupidity, how much petty, pedantic hypocrisy and egotism, how much delight in pride there is among this new category of "saints"—even trickery and chicanery. But the main thing is that it all happened "from the very beginning"—that is, from the very creation of the world, from the questions: "What is man and what is woman?" "What is good and what is bad?" And even: "Does God exist?" And what do you think?—the very fact that they are so helpless and so compelled to begin from the beginning is precisely what appeals to many people, and to a few in particular: "They will start to live using their own minds and so they will certainly arrive at some sort of understanding." What a point of view this is! It means that the precious heritage, acquired over the course of centuries, whose true significance must be explained to this dark people and not thrown on the ground like some worn-out and useless rag from past ages, has in its essence been lost irretrievably to them forever. Development, light, and progress again recede far from their grasp, for now will ensue isolation, dissociation, and the self-enclosed world of sectarianism; and in the place of the "reasonable" new ideas some people expect will arise only the old, ancient, vile idols that everyone knows—and just try to pull them down now! However, there is absolutely no need to fear Stundism, although one may certainly feel sorry for it. This Stundism has no future whatsoever; it will not expand far and will soon stop growing; it will no doubt join one of the dark sects of the Russian People—some Flagellants, perhaps, this most ancient sect in the world, it seems, which certainly has its own significance preserved in two ancient attributes: whirling and prophecy. The Templars themselves were prosecuted for whirling and prophecy, and the Quakers also whirl and prophesy, as did Pythia in ancient times; Tatarinova's group whirled and prophesied, and our Radstockists, very possibly, will end by whirling—it seems that they are prophesying even now. I hope the Radstockists are not offended by the comparison. Incidentally, many people are amused by the coincidence of the appearance of both sects in Russia at the same time: the Stundists among the "dark people" and the

Radstockists among our most fashionable society. Yet there is also a good deal here that is not amusing. As far as the coincidence in the appearance of our two sects is concerned, it undoubtedly came from one and the same ignorance, that is, from complete lack of knowledge of our own religion.

3. Foma Danilov, a Russian Hero Tortured to Death

In the spring of last year all the newspapers reprinted the item that had appeared in *The Russian Veteran* describing the martyr's death of Sergeant Foma Danilov of the Second Turkestan Rifles. Danilov had been taken prisoner by the Kipchaks at Margelan on November 21, 1875, and barbarously murdered by them after long and most refined tortures because he refused to enter their service and accept the Mohammedan faith. The khan himself promised to pardon him and to give him a reward and honors if he would agree to renounce Christ. Danilov answered that he could not betray the cross and, as a subject of the tsar, even though in captivity, had to fulfill his obligation to his monarch and to Christianity. His tormentors, having tortured him to death, marveled at the strength of his spirit and called him a *batyr,* meaning a valiant hero. Although this item appeared in all the newspapers, it aroused little comment in society at the time; the papers themselves, having published it in the form of the usual newspaper *entre-filet,* did not find it necessary to go on about it at any *special* length. In short, the story of Foma Danilov was "inactive," to use the language of the stock exchange. Then, as we know, the Slavic movement began, Cherniaev appeared, and the Serbs, Kireev, the contributions and the volunteers; the tortured Foma was completely forgotten (in the newspapers, that is). And now, quite recently, some additional details have been received to add to the account we already had. There are reports that the governor of Samara Province has made inquiries about Danilov's family, who are peasants of the village of Kirsanovka in the Buguruslan district of Samara Province; it turns out that Danilov has left behind a wife, Eufrosina, aged twenty-seven, and a six-year-old daughter, Ulita, living in destitution. They were aided through a noble initiative of the governor of Samara, who appealed to certain people to help the widow and daughter of a martyred Russian hero; he proposed that the Samara provincial zemstvo assembly support Danilov's daughter as a pupil in a local school. Subsequently, 1,320 rubles were collected, of which 600 were set aside until the daughter reached the age of majority, while the remainder were given to the widow herself; Danilov's daughter was taken into a local school. Apart from that, the chief of the General Staff informed the governor of the emperor's gracious order assigning Danilov's widow a lifetime pension, to be paid from the State Treasury, of 120 rubles a year. Thereupon—thereupon, the matter will probably again be forgotte, in view of the current alarm, political fears, enormous problems awaiting resolution, bankruptcies, and so on.

Oh, I certainly don't mean to say that our society treated this striking action with indifference or as something unworthy of attention. The fact, merely, is that not much was said or, rather, that scarcely anyone spoke about this *in particular*. However, perhaps people did talk about it somewhere, among themselves—among the merchants or the clergy, for example; but this was not the case in society, among our intelligentsia. By the People, of course, this great death will not be forgotten: this hero accepted torments for Christ and he is a great Russian; the People cherish that and will not forget it; indeed, they never have forgotten such deeds. And now already I seem to hear certain very familiar voices: "Yes, of course, there is a force here, to be sure, and we admit it; but still, it is a dark force that manifested itself in such antediluvian, conventionalized forms, so to say; and therefore, what is there *in particular* for us to say? This is not something from our world; a force that manifested itself intelligently and consciously would be another matter. There are others who suffer, and other forces, you see, and there are other ideas which are much, much loftier—ideas of common humanity, for example. . . ."

Despite these sensible and cultured voices, it still seems to me to be permissible and entirely pardonable to say something *in particular* about Danilov; moreover, I even think that our intelligentsia would certainly not have lowered itself had it paid a bit more attention to this fact. What astonishes me more than anything is that there was no astonishment at all, not a bit of astonishment. I am not talking about the People: they have no need for astonishment, and there will be none among them. Foma's act cannot seem unusual to them simply because of their great faith in themselves and in their souls. They will respond to this valorous deed only with great feeling and great tenderness. But were something of the same sort to happen in Europe—i.e., a similar fact manifesting great spiritual power among the English, the French, or the Germans—these peoples would certainly have trumpeted it to the whole world. No, gentlemen, hear me: do you know how this dark, unknown soldier of the Turkestan battalion appears to me? Why, one can say he is the emblem of Russia, of the whole of Russia, of the whole of our People's Russia; he is its genuine image; he is that same Russia in which cynics and our wise men have denied any great spirit and any possibility of the upsurge and manifestation of great thought and great feeling. Listen: you are still not those cynics, after all; you are only cultured, Europeanizing people, i.e., in essence the kindest of people: surely you, too, do not deny that last summer there were places where our People displayed remarkable strength of spirit: people abandoned their homes and children and went to die for the faith, for the oppressed, God knows where and God knows with what means, just as the first crusaders did nine centuries ago in Europe—those same crusaders whose renewed appearance Granovsky, for example, would have considered almost absurd and offensive "in our age of positive objectives and progress." So if this summer movement of ours was, in your opinion, something blind and even unreasonable, a "crusade," so to say, it was still something solid and noble; that you cannot but admit when you take even a slightly broader view of it. It was the awakening of a great idea which elevated, perhaps, hundreds of thousands and millions of souls at once above the apathy, cynicism, debauchery, and ugliness in which those souls had previously wallowed. You know, surely, that our People are still considered to be good-natured and even very capable mentally, yet are seen as a dark, elemental mass, without consciousness, devoted almost to a man to vices and prejudices and almost entirely uncouth. But, you see, I will risk saying something that might even be taken as an axiom—namely: to judge the moral strength of the People and their future capability one must take into account not that depth of vileness to which they—even the majority of them—might temporarily sink; one must take into account only that summit of spirit to which they can ascend when the hour for that ascent comes. For vileness is a temporary affliction, almost always dependent on circumstances that preceded it and which are passing: slavery, centuries of oppression, brutalization; but greatness of spirit is a gift, a perpetual, elemental gift, born with a people and valued all the more if over the course of centuries of slavery, affliction, and poverty it still survives unsullied in the hearts of that people.

In appearance Foma Danilov may perhaps be one of the most ordinary and unremarkable representatives of the Russian People, as unremarkable as the Russian People themselves. (Oh, for many the Russian People are entirely unremarkable!) In his time, perhaps, he was not loath to drink and carouse; perhaps he did not even pray very much, although he never forgot God. And then, suddenly, he's ordered to change his religion, and if he refuses he'll die a martyr's death. And you must keep in mind here what these tortures—these Asiatic tortures—are like! The khan himself stands before him, promises to show mercy; Danilov knows very well that his refusal will certainly provoke the khan and will also provoke the pride of the Kipchaks since, they will think, "how dare the Christian dog bear such scorn for Islam." But in spite of everything that awaits him, this inconspicuous Russian man accepts the cruelest torments and dies, having amazed his tormentors. You know, gentlemen, not one of us would have done such a thing. To make a public display of suffering is sometimes even attractive, but this incident happened in complete obscurity in some out-of-the-way place; not a soul was watching him; and Foma himself could not have thought and could not have supposed that his feat would be proclaimed over the whole of the Russian land. I think that even in the first centuries of Christianity, some of the martyrs, as they endured their tortures, were at least partially comforted and encouraged by their conviction that their deaths would serve as an example for the timid and the wavering and would attract even more people to Christ. Even this great consolation could not have been available to Foma: who would find out? He was alone among his torturers. He was still young; somewhere over there in Russia he had a wife and daughter; never again would he see them, but so be it: "It matters not where I am, I will not act against my conscience; I will bear the torture." This indeed is truth for the sake of truth and not for show! And there was no falsity, no compromise with the conscience: "I'll pretend to accept Islam; I'll commit no sin. No one will see, after all; and later I'll pray for forgiveness. Life is long; I'll give money to the church and do a lot of good deeds." There was none of this; there was only an astounding, primitive, elemental honesty. No, gentlemen, you or I would hardly have done such a thing!

Not for you or me, but for our People, I repeat, Danilov's feat is perhaps not even surprising. And that is precisely the point: that right here we have what amounts to the portrait, the complete picture of the Russian People; and that is why I—and you, too, no doubt—find all this so precious. Precisely in this way do our People love truth for the sake of truth and not for show. They may be coarse and vile and sinful and unremarkable, but when their hour sounds and the cause of the common truth of all the People is to be undertaken, you will be astounded by the degree of freedom of spirit which they will show before the burdens of materialism, passions, the lust for money and possessions, and even before the fear of the cruelest martyr's death. And they will do and show all that simply, steadfastly, demanding neither reward nor praise and not making a display of themselves: "That which I believe I also confess." Here even the most embittered naysayers who speak of the "retrograde nature" of the People's ideals can have nothing to say, for this case has nothing to do with whether an ideal is retrograde or not. It has to do only with the capacity to show the greatest strength of will for the sake of an exploit of spiritual power. (This ridiculous little notion of the "retrograde nature" of ideals I introduced here for the sake of complete impartiality.)

You know, gentlemen, we have to pose the question plainly: I plainly maintain that we have nothing whatsoever to teach a People such as this. This is a sophism, of course, but it sometimes comes to mind. Oh, of course we are more educated than they, but what can we teach them—that's the problem! Naturally I'm not talking about trades and technology and mathematical knowledge—these things can be taught by Germans brought in and paid to do it if we do not; but what do we have to impart to the People? We are Russians, after all, brothers to this People, and accordingly we are obliged to *enlighten* them. Do we have something moral, something sublime to pass on to them, to explain to them, and thus to bring light to their "dark" souls? The enlightenment of the People—that, gentlemen, is our right and our duty; it is a right in the highest Christian sense: he who knows the Good, he who knows the true Word of Life should, is obligated, to convey it to his brother who does not know it and who wanders in darkness; so it is written in the Gospels. But what, then, can we convey to him who wanders that he himself did not know better than we? First of all, of course, that knowledge is a useful thing and that they must study, is that not so? But the People have said even before we did that "Knowledge is light, ignorance is darkness." Destroy prejudices, say, and tear down false gods? But we ourselves have such a host of prejudices and have set up so many false gods that the People will tell us plainly, "Physician, heal thyself." (And our false gods the People can so easily pick out!) Well then, self-respect, a sense of personal dignity? But our People, as a whole, have far more respect for themselves, have a much deeper regard for themselves, and are far more aware of their own dignity than we are. In fact, we have a terrific amount of self-love but no self-respect at all, and there is not the least sense of personal dignity in us, not in any respect. So should we, then, teach the People to respect the convictions of others? Since the time of Peter the Great, our People have shown a respect for the convictions of others, while we, even among ourselves, cannot forgive one another even the slightest deviation from our convictions, and those who are a tiny bit in disagreement with us we plainly consider scoundrels, forgetting that he who is inclined to lose respect for others so easily does not respect himself in the first place. Well, then, should we teach the People faith in themselves and in their own strength? The People have Foma Danilovs by the thousands, while we have no faith at all in Russian strength; and we consider our lack of faith the highest form of enlightenment, almost as a form of valor. And so, finally, what can we teach them? We disdain, almost to the point of anger, everything that our People love and revere and for which their hearts long. What sort of lovers of the People are we? Some may object by saying that the more we love the People, the more we disdain their ignorance, wishing something better for them. Oh, no, gentlemen, this is not it at all: if we in truth and indeed loved the People—and not merely in little articles and books—we would approach them more closely and would concern ourselves with studying that which we now, heedlessly and following European models, are trying to eradicate in them: then, perhaps, we might learn many a thing that now is beyond even our imaginings.

We of the educated classes do, however, have one consolation, one area in which we pride ourselves over our People, and it is that which causes us to despise them so: it is the fact that they belong to a nation and persist in it with all their strength, while we are of cosmopolitan convictions and have set cosmopolitanism as our goal; accordingly, we have elevated ourselves far above them. So this is the cause of all our discord and our split with the People; and I proclaim in plain words: were we to eliminate this one thing, were we to find a point of accommodation, all our differences with the People would end at once. And this point really does exist, and it can very easily be found. Again I stress: even our most radical differences are in essence only a mirage.

But what kind of point of accommodation is it?

2

1. A Conciliatory Dream beyond the Scope of Science

First of all, let me set forth the most controversial and ticklish point and begin with it: "Every great people believes and must believe, if it wants to survive long, that in it and in it alone is contained the means to save the world; that it lives in order to stand at the head of the nations, to bring them all to communion with it and to lead them, in a harmonious choir, toward the ultimate goal for which they are destined."

I affirm that such was the case with all the great nations of the world, both ancient and modern; that this faith and this faith alone elevated them to the possibility, each one, to have in its own time an immense, global influence on the fate of humanity. Such, indisputably, was the case with ancient Rome; such was the case with Rome later, during her existence as a Catholic power. When France inherited her Catholic idea the same thing happened to her, and for almost two centuries France, right up to the time of her recent defeat and depression, indisputably and constantly considered herself at the head of the world—morally, at least, and at times politically; she saw herself as leader of the world's advance and as guide to its future. But Germany, who under the banner of her Protestantism and endless freedom of conscience and enquiry set herself against the universal Catholic idea and its authority, always dreamed of the same thing. I repeat: this is what happens with every great nation, *more or less*, at the zenith of its development. You may say that this is all wrong, a mistake, and may point, for instance, to the *awareness* of these same nations, the awareness of their scientists and thinkers who have been writing specifically about the aggregate significance of the European nations who have participated together in creating and refining civilization; and I, of course, will not deny such awareness. But aside from the fact that such final statements of awareness generally comprise, as it were, the termination of the living life of a nation, I will merely note the following: these same thinkers and people who expressed such awareness—despite what they wrote about the universal harmony of nations—at the same time, and most of the time, *continued to hold* just the same direct, living, and sincere belief as the masses of their own nation: that in the chorus of nations constituting the universal harmony and jointly developing civilization, they (the French, for example) are indeed the head of the entire union; they are in the forefront; they are the very ones destined to lead, while the rest merely follow after them. They believe that if, say, they should borrow something from another nation, it would be still only a little bit, while the other nations borrow everything from them—everything that matters—and can only live by their spirit and their ideas and, indeed, have no choice but finally to come into compliance with their spirit and sooner or later to merge with it. And so today's France, disheartened and spiritually fragmented, now has another idea like this, representing a new but, in our view, completely natural phase of its former universal Catholic idea and its development; and almost half the French believe even now that in this idea is found salvation, salvation not only for themselves but for the world: this idea is their French socialism. This idea—I mean their socialism—is, of course, something false and desperate; yet what matters now is not its quality but that it presently exists, has a living life, and that those who profess it do so without doubt or despair, as is the case in the other huge part of France. On the other hand, look at almost any Englishman of the higher or lower variety—lord or laborer, scholar or uneducated—and you will be convinced that every Englishman tries above all to be an Englishman, to preserve his Englishness in all aspects of his life, private and public, political and cosmopolitan, and even tries to love humanity in no other manner than an English one. You may say that if this were so, if everything really were as I assert, then, still, such self-deceit and self-importance would be degrading for nations as great as these; that their egoism and ridiculous chauvinism would detract from their importance; that their vital force would not be enhanced thereby; that their life, rather, would be damaged and debased from the very beginning. You may say that such mindless and grandiose ideas are worthy not of emulation but, on the contrary, of eradication through the light of reason, which destroys prejudices. Let us suppose that, on the one hand, this is quite true; still, one must be sure to look at the other side of the matter; then we see that not only is it not debasing, but quite the opposite. What significance is there in the fact that a young man who has not yet lived dreams of eventually becoming a hero? Believe me, such arrogant and presumptuous ideas can be far more life-enhancing and useful to this young man than the kind of common sense displayed by a young lad who, at the age of sixteen, puts his faith in the wise old rule that "happiness is better than heroism." Believe me, the life of the former young fellow, even after all his misfortunes and failures, will, on the whole, still be of a higher quality than the placid existence of his prudent childhood friend, even though the latter be destined to live his whole life in luxury. Such faith in oneself is not immoral and is certainly not petty self-glorification. Exactly the same is true of nations: granted there are prudent nations that are honorable and moderate, placid, with no great upsurges of spirit, nations of traders and shipbuilders who live prosperously and in a most orderly fashion. Well, let them be: they still will not go far; they will certainly develop only as some mediocrity that will in no way serve humanity; they lack that energy, they lack that great sense of self-importance, they lack beneath them those three great moving whales on which all great nations stand. The faith that one wants to and *can* express to the world the ultimate word, that one can at last renew the world with the surplus of one's own living force; the faith in the sanctity of one's own ideals; the faith in the strength of one's love and ardent desire to serve humanity—no, such a faith is the token of the very highest life of nations, and only through it will they bring all that benefit to humanity they have been destined to bring; only through it will they bring all that portion of their vital force and organic idea which nature herself, when she created them, destined them to leave as a legacy to future humanity. Only a nation strong in such a faith has the right to the higher life. The ancient knight of legend believed that all obstacles, all specters and monsters, would fall before him and that he would triumph over everything and everyone and achieve all so long as he faithfully kept his vow of "justice, chastity, and poverty." You may say that these are just legends and songs in which only a Don Quixote can believe and that the laws of the real lives of nations are quite different. Well then, gentlemen, you have fallen into the trap I set for you; I will convince you that you yourselves are just such Don Quixotes and that you yourselves have just such an idea in which you believe and through which you wish to restore humanity.

In fact, what do you believe? You believe (and I along with you) in a common humanity, that is, that at some time the natural barriers and prejudices that until now have prevented the free communion of nations through the egoism of national aspirations will someday fall before the light of reason and consciousness, and that only then will peoples begin to live in a single spirit and in accord, as brothers, rationally and lovingly striving for general harmony. Tell me, gentlemen, what can be higher and more sacred than this faith of yours? And the most important thing is that you will no longer find this faith anywhere in the world, not among any people of Europe, for example, where the personalities of the nations are remarkably sharply drawn and where, if this faith exists at all, then it does so only on the level of some sort of metaphysical perception; it may be a passionate, ardent perception, but it is still no more than an academic one. But in you, gentlemen—that is, not only in you but in us, in all us Russians—this faith is a general, living, and dominant faith; all of us believe in this consciously and simply. It is a belief in the world of intellectuals and is a living, instinctual feeling among the common People, whom religion commands to believe this very thing. Indeed, gentlemen, did you think that you among all the Russian intelligentsia were the only "panhumans," while all the rest were only Slavophiles and nationalists? Not at all: the Slavophiles and the nationalists believe in exactly the same thing as you, but believe even more firmly!

Let me take only the Slavophiles: what have we heard proclaimed from the mouths of those who founded, who represent, and who speak for their doctrines? In clear and precise declarations they have stated plainly that Russia, together with the Slavic world and at its head, will pronounce the greatest word the world has ever heard and that this word will be the mandate for the unity of all humanity, and that this will happen not in the spirit of personal egoism which, because of the struggle for existence, now unites people and nations artificially and unnaturally in civilizations in which positive science is used to set moral boundaries on the free spirit and in which, at the same time, people dig pits for one another, spread lies, calumny, and blasphemy about one another. The ideal of the Slavophiles was unity in the spirit of genuine, broad love, without lies and materialism, and resting on the basis of the magnanimous personal example which the Russian People, at the head of a free, all-Slavic union, was destined to provide to Europe. You will tell me that you don't believe this for a moment, that these are all only academic speculations. But the point here is not at all in how one believes but in the fact that all of us in Russia, despite our many discordant voices, still agree and come to this single, definitive, common idea of the unity of all humanity. This is a fact that cannot be denied and is astonishing in itself because, at the level of such a vital and dominant aspiration, no other nation anywhere has such a feeling. If that is the case, then within us—within all of us—resides a steadfast and definite national idea; precisely a *national* one. Accordingly, if the national Russian idea exists, ultimately, only as one of the unity of all humanity, then it follows that the most beneficial thing we all can do is to call a truce to our discord and become Russian and national as quickly as possible. Our entire salvation lies only in not arguing in advance about how to realize this idea and in what form—yours or mine—but for all of us together to leave our writing desks and get directly down to business.

And this is precisely the point.

2. We Are but Useless Wretches in Europe

So tell me, how did you people get down to business? You started a long, long time ago; but just what have you accomplished for the common human cause, for the realization of your idea, I mean? You began with aimless wandering around Europe, full of an ardent longing to be reborn as Europeans, even if only in outward appearance. Through the whole of the eighteenth century we did nothing more than try to change our appearance. We induced ourselves to accept European tastes; we would even eat the worst sorts of muck, trying not to make a face while doing so: "Just see what an Englishman I am; I can't eat a thing without cayenne pepper." Do you think I'm sneering at people here? Not a bit. I know only too well that there was no other way to begin. Even before Peter the Great, still under the Moscow tsars and patriarchs, one young Moscow fop of the time—one of the progressive ones—put on a French suit and buckled on a European sword. We had to begin precisely with contempt for our own things and our own people, and if we remained at this same point for a whole two centuries, moving neither forward nor backward, then, probably, such was the span alloted us by nature. It's true, though, that we did move: the contempt for our own things and our own people kept growing and growing, particularly once we began to understand Europe a bit more thoroughly. However, we were never troubled by the sharp distinctions among nationalities in Europe and by their sharply defined patterns of national character. We began, in fact, by directly "eliminating all the incongruities" and developed the cosmopolitan type of "European"; that is to say, from the very beginning we picked out what was *common*, that which linked them all. And this is quite characteristic. Subsequently, with the passage of time, we grew even more clever; we seized hold of civilization and at once, blindly and devotedly, adopted the creed that it was precisely in civilization that we could find the "universality" destined to unite humanity. Even the Europeans were amazed when they looked at us, aliens and newcomers, and saw our rapturous faith, the more so in that they themselves, alas, had even then already begun, bit by bit, to lose this faith in themselves. We hailed with rapture the arrival of Rousseau and Voltaire; along with the traveling Karamzin, we tenderly rejoiced in the establishment of the *Etats généraux* in 1789; and if later, at the end of the first quarter of the present century, we, along with progressive Europeans, despaired over their defunct dreams and their shattered ideals, then we still did not lose our faith and even consoled the Europeans themselves. Even the "whitest" of Russians at home in Russia at once became "reds" in Europe—another remarkably characteristic trait. Then, in the middle of the present century, some of our worthy generation cast in our lot with French socialism and accepted it, without the least hesitation, as the final answer for the unity of all human beings, i.e, for the realization of the dream which up to that time had entirely absorbed us. In such fashion, to achieve our goal we accepted something that was the acme of egoism, the acme of inhumanity, the acme of economic bungling and disorder, the acme of slander on human nature, the acme of destruction of every human freedom; but this did not trouble us in the least. On the contrary: seeing the despondent perplexity of certain profound thinkers in Europe, with complete nonchalance we quickly labeled them scoundrels and blockheads. We were thoroughly convinced—and we still are—that positive science is entirely capable of defining the *moral* boundaries between individualities and nations (as if science—were it able to do so—could explain these mysteries before *the experiment was completed,* i.e., before the fulfillment of the destinies of humans on earth). Our landowners sold their peasant serfs and traveled to Paris to publish socialist magazines, while our Rudins died on the barricades. At the same time we became so alienated from our own Russian land that we lost all conception of the degree to which such a doctrine is at odds with the soul of the Russian People. In fact, not only did we have no regard at all for the character of the Russian People, we did not even acknowledge that they had any character. We forgot even to think of it, and with complete and despotic equanimity were convinced (without even raising the question) that our People would at once accept everything we told them, i.e., ordered them to believe, in essence. On this topic we always had a number of most amusing anecdotes about the People. As far as their attitudes toward the People were concerned, our cosmopolitans remained complete landowners, even after the peasant reform.

And what did we accomplish? Some strange things: the principal one, that in Europe they look upon us derisively, while the best and indisputably clever Russians are regarded in Europe with haughty condescension. Even emigration from Russia—i.e., political emigration with complete renunciation of Russia—has not spared them this haughty condescension. The Europeans simply did not want to acknowledge us as their own, despite any sacrifices we made and despite the circumstances: *Grattez le russe,* they would say, *et vous verrez le tartare*. And so it remains to the present. We've become one of their proverbs. And the more we tried to please them by despising our own nationality, the more they despised us. We wagged our tails before them, we made servile confessions of our "European" views and convictions, while they haughtily ignored us and usually added, with a polite smile, as if wanting to be rid of us as quickly as possible, that we simply "misunderstood" things in Europe. They were amazed that we, being such Tatars (*les tatares*), had been entirely unable to become Russians; and we never could make them comprehend that we wanted to be, not Russians, but cosmopolitans. It's true that lately they have managed to understand something. They have understood that we want something, something which for them is fearful and dangerous; they have understood that there are many of us—eighty million—that we are aware of and understand all the European ideas and that they are not aware of our Russian ideas; and even if they did become aware of them, they would not understand them; they know that we speak all their languages, while they speak only their own. And many another thing they have begun to realize and suspect. The result is that they have plainly labeled us enemies and future destroyers of European civilization. You see how they have interpreted our passionate goal of becoming cosmopolitans!

And meanwhile we simply cannot renounce Europe. Europe is our second homeland: I am the first to make this ardent affirmation and I have always affirmed it. Europe is *almost* as dear to all of us as is Russia; Europe is the home of the whole tribe of Japheth, and our idea is the unification of all the nations of this tribe and, eventually, in the distant future, of the tribes of Shem and Ham as well. How is this to be done?

First, we must become Russians above all. If cosmopolitanism is the Russian national idea, then each one of us must become Russian above all, that is, we must become ourselves; and then everything will change with the first step. To become Russian means to stop despising our own People. And as soon as the European sees that we have begun to respect our People and our nationality, he will at once begin to respect us as well. And indeed: the more strongly and independently we developed our national spirit, the more strongly and intimately we would speak to the European soul; and once we developed a kinship with that soul, we would at once be better understood by it. Then they would stop turning arrogantly away from us and would hear us out. Even our appearance would become quite different. Having become ourselves, we shall at last acquire the countenance of humans, not monkeys. We shall acquire the appearance of a free being and not a slave, a lackey, a Potugin; then they will consider us as people, not as some international castoffs, not as the useless wretches of Europeanism, liberalism, and socialism. We shall even be able to speak more intelligently to them than we do now because we shall seek out new words among our People and in their spirit, words that will certainly be more comprehensible to the Europeans. And then we ourselves shall also realize that many of the things we despised in our People are not darkness but a source of light, not stupidity but intelligence; and once we understand that, we shall without fail pronounce in Europe such a word as has never been heard there. We shall then know for certain that a genuine social message is borne by no one other than our People; that their idea and their spirit contain a vital aspiration toward the universal fellowship of all human beings, a fellowship that fully respects national individualities and their preservation, that preserves the complete freedom of people, and that shows precisely where this freedom lies—in a union of love *guaranteed* by deeds, by a living example, by the longing, in actual fact, for genuine brotherhood, achieved not by the guillotine, not by millions of severed heads. . . .

However, could I truly have thought to convince anyone? It was a joke. But we all have our weaknesses: maybe some "raw youth," some member of the young generation will read this. . . .

3. An Old Story about the Petrashevsky Circle

At the present moment, as we all know, the trial of the participants in the incident on Kazan Square on December 6 is in progress. My readers probably already know the progress of the trial from the newspaper accounts. But I was struck by a remark made by one newspaper regarding the former members of the Petrashevsky Circle—that well-known illegal organization of the end of the 1840s in which I, too, happened to participate and for which I paid with a ten-year exile to Siberia, including four years of hard labor. The *Petersburg Gazette* made this remark in a heated editorial on the Kazan Square incident. Among other things, the article quoted several excellent passages from the work of Mr. Stronin, *Politics as Science,* which I reproduce here in full. This is a piece of advice to youth who are going "to the People":

> Rather than go to the People, make use of your opportunities; the People can come to you. You have servants, a cook, a maid, a coachman, servant, or janitor. If you want to be a democrat, seat them at your table with you when you are having tea; bring them into your family life. Instead of telling them that there is no God but there are propaganda leaflets, as every silly liberal does when he tries to teach them, tell them, rather, what addition and subtraction are; tell them about grammar and the alphabet. And all the while be honest, attentive, serious, but not familiar with your pupils; and on the whole, provide them with an example of good or at least better moral behavior.

And now about the Petrashevsky Circle in particular. This is what the writer says in his editorial:

> Another idea which the "Kazan Incident" involuntarily brings to mind provides a good deal for comfort to our social consciousness: namely, that the main actors in each new, regrettable incident become steadily more wretched and less worthy of attention, even from hotheads. At one time, fifty years ago, those responsible for political

> crimes in Russia came from the highest, best-educated social milieu (the Decembrists); in the 1840s the Russian political criminal was of a significantly lesser breed (the "Petrashevsky Circle"); at the beginning of the 1860s he had been reduced to the so-called thinking proletariat (Chernyshevsky's group); at the beginning of the 1870s it fell to the level of uneducated school dropouts and low-grade nihilists (the "Nechaev Group"); in the Dolgushin affair some semiliterate riff-raff figure as propagandists; and finally, in the "Kazan Incident," we have not only the semi-literate riff-raff, but also dissolute factory hands and a distinct shading of the Jewish element. Such a gradual degeneration is the best evidence that criminal political propaganda, after all the liberal reforms of the present reign, can no longer count on capturing any sympathy from the educated elements of society; and it can have even less influence on the mass of the People, because the mass has shown how it welcomes its unbidden prophets. . . .

The author's idea of the insignificance of revolutionary propaganda among us is certainly a true one, even though it is not expressed clearly; many things should have been made much more specific here if the cause were to be served. But with regard only to the Petrashevsky Circle, I will observe that the author is quite wrong in using them as an example of the degeneration of the political criminal in comparison with the Decembrists. I might add that I heard this idea of "degeneration" a long time ago; it has been repeated more than once in the press, and that is why I pause to discuss it now, having encountered it at an opportune moment. In my opinion, the radical change in the type of political criminal has occurred among us only in the last twenty years; but the members of the Petrashevsky Circle were still entirely of the same type as the Decembrists, at least in regard to those essential characteristics of the type which the author of the article himself cites. The author says that the Decembrists were people "from the highest, best-educated social milieu." But how were the Petrashevsky Circle any different? Among the Decembrists there really were, perhaps, more individuals having connections to the highest and wealthiest society; but the Decembrists were incomparably more numerous than the Petrashevsky Circle, among whom there were also more than a few individuals with connections and family in the best society, and there were wealthy people as well. Besides, high society had no sympathy at all for the schemes of the Decembrists and did not participate in them even indirectly, so one cannot attribute any special significance to them in this regard.

The Decembrist type was more military than the Petrashevsky-ite, but there were enough military men in the Petrashevsky Circle as well. In short, I do not know where the author finds any difference here. Both groups indisputably belonged entirely to one and the same *gentlemanly,* "*lordly*" society, so to say, and in this characteristic trait of the type of political criminal of the time—in the Decembrists and the Petrashevsky-ites, that is—there was no difference at all. If, indeed, there were a few *raznochintsy* in the Petrashevsky Circle (and very few), then they were there as educated people; and in such a capacity they could have appeared equally well among the Decembrists. Speaking in general, *raznochintsy* and members of the middle classes could not have been present among either the Decembrists or the Petrashevsky-ites in any great number, but only because there were no great numbers of them at the time. Concerning "level of culture" as the quality in which the Decembrists had the advantage over the Petrashevsky Circle, the author is entirely mistaken: the Decembrists were incomparably less educated than the members of the Petrashevsky Circle. Among the Petrashesky-ites were people, in the main, who came from the very best seats of learning—from the universities, from the Alexander Lycée, from the School of Jurisprudence, and from the very best specialized institutions. There were many who taught and who were involved in specialized branches of science. In later years, after their pardons, many of them distinguished themselves in society, and if one takes the whole Petrashevsky Circle—that is, not only those who were exiled to Siberia, but also those whose punishment was exile to various military posts and to the Caucasus or who were sent to work in isolated towns or, finally, who simply remained under police observation—then many, many of them later made contributions of great distinction to science, as professors, as natural scientists, as secretaries of learned societies, as authors of remarkable works of scholarship, as publishers of journals, as very prominent literary figures, poets, and, generally, as very useful and cultured people. I repeat: in regard to level of education, the members of the Petrashevsky Circle were a superior type to the Decembrists.

Of course, those who follow the "degeneration" of the type may find this difficult to believe, also because the Petrashevsky Circle included far fewer people than did the Decembrists; they existed for a very brief period of time and were younger people, in the main, than were the Decembrists.

To conclude, I will say that, on the whole, throughout our century the type of Russian revolutionary is but the clearest possible indicator of the degree to which our advanced, cultured society has torn itself away from the People, has forgotten their true needs and aspirations and does not even want to know what these needs and aspirations are; instead of showing real concern for easing the lot of the People, our cultured class offers the People means that are not at all attuned to their spirit and their natural way of life, means that the People are quite unable to accept, even if they could understand them. Our revolutionaries are saying the wrong things and are wasting their time, and have been doing so for a whole century now. Nowadays, for many and complex reasons, of which we will certainly say a word in one of the future issues of the *Diary*—nowadays, we have a type of Russian revolutionary who is so distinct from the People that each is utterly and completely incapable of understanding the other: the People understand absolutely nothing of what the revolutionaries want, while the revolutionaries have become so out of touch with the People that they are not even aware of their alienation from them (as, for example, the Petrashevsky-ites always were aware). It is quite the contrary: not only do they go directly to the People with the most bizarre message, they go in firm, blissful assurance that the People will unfailingly understand them. This muddle can only end when it plays itself out, and then only when the cycle of our Europeanization is fulfilled and completed and we all return entirely to our own native soil.

With the reforms of the present reign there naturally began an active study and effort to understand the needs of the People, in the context of a living life and not in the "indoor" and abstract manner of former times. In such fashion there appears among the Russian intelligentsia a new, unprecedented stratum that understands the People and their native soil. This new stratum is growing and gathering its strength ever more broadly and firmly, and of this there is no doubt. On these new people rests our entire hope. . . .

4. Russian Satire. *Virgin Soil. Last Songs.* Old Reminiscences

I have been busy this month with literature as well—with belles lettres, I mean—and have read a few things with great interest. By the way, not long ago I read the views of one foreigner about Russian satire—the satire of the present day, that is. These views were expressed in France. What is remarkable here is one conclusion. I have forgotten the exact words, but this is their sense: "Russian satire seems to be frightened of finding a good deed in Russian society. When it encounters such a good deed it becomes upset and does not calm down until it discovers, somewhere at the very basis of that good deed, a scoundrel. Then it at once rejoices and cries out, 'This isn't a good deed at all, and there's no point in being pleased; you can see for yourselves, there's a scoundrel at work here, too!'"

Is that a fair statement? I can't believe that it is. I know only that our satire has its brilliant practitioners who are very popular. Our readers are great lovers of satire, although my conviction at least is that those same readers have incomparably greater love for positive beauty; they long and thirst for it. Count Leo Tolstoy, without a doubt, is the writer most beloved by Russian readers of all stripes.

Our satire, however brilliant it may be, truly suffers from a certain lack of definition: that much, at least, one can say about it. It is sometimes quite impossible to conceive just what our satire wants to say as a whole and in general. It seems that our satire itself has no real foundation; but can this be so? What does it itself believe in? In the name of what does it make its denunciations? All this seems to disappear in the murk of obscurity. There is simply no way to determine what it itself considers to be good.

And so one falls into a strange quandary over such a question.

I have read Turgenev's *Virgin Soil* and am awaiting part two. By the way: I've been writing for thirty years now, and through these entire thirty years I have noticed the same amusing thing many times. All our critics (and I have been following literature for almost forty years), those deceased and those still living—in short, all whom I can remember, either now or in the past—would assume a rather solemn tone as soon as they began to write some survey of current literature (formerly, for example, the journals used to carry regular January surveys of the entire past year) and would always use more or less the same phrase, but always with great delight: "In our time, when literature is in such decline," "In our time, when Russian literature is in such stagnation," "In our sorry state of literature," "Wandering through the deserts of Russian writing," and so on, and so on. One and the same idea in a thousand different variants. But, in fact, over these forty years the last works of Pushkin appeared; Gogol began and ended his career; Lermontov wrote; Ostrovsky, Turgenev, Goncharov, and at least another dozen most talented writers appeared. And this is in belles-lettres alone! One can positively state that scarcely ever in any other literature, over such a short period of time, have so many talented writers appeared as among us; and they appeared one after the other, with no gaps between them. And yet even now, scarcely more than a month ago, I read again of the stagnation of Russian literature and of the "deserts of Russian writing." However, this is only an amusing observation of mine; and, indeed, it is an entirely innocent thing which has no significance at all. Still, one has to chuckle at it.

Of course, I won't say anything about *Virgin Soil*; everyone is awaiting part two. In any case, it is not for me to speak about it. The artistic worth of Turgenev's creations is beyond doubt. I will remark on only one thing: on the top of page 92 of the novel (see *The European Messenger*) there are fifteen or twenty lines in which, I think, are concentrated the entire sense of the work; they seem to express the author's whole view of his subject. Unfortunately, this view is entirely mistaken, and I am in deep disagreement with it. These are a few words spoken by the author about one character in the novel, Solomin.

I read Nekrasov's *Last Songs* in the January number of *Notes of the Fatherland*. Passionate songs and words that do not say quite everything, as is always the case with Nekrasov; but what painful groans of a sick man! Our poet is very sick and—he told me himself—sees his own situation clearly. But I find that difficult to believe.... His is a hardy and percipient organism. He suffers terribly (he has some sort of intestinal ulcer, an ailment which is difficult even to diagnose), but I cannot believe that he will not last until spring; and if he spends the spring at a health resort abroad, in another climate, he will quickly recover, I am certain of it. Strange things happen to people; we rarely saw one another, and there were misunderstandings between us as well, but there was one event in our lives that I can never forget. This was the time we first met. And imagine, not long ago I called on Nekrasov and he, ill and suffering, began at once to tell me that he remembered those days. At that time (that was thirty years ago!) something happened so characteristic of youth, and so fresh and fine—one of those things that remains forever in the hearts of those involved. We were then in our early twenties. I was living in St. Petersburg and had resigned from the Corps of Engineers a year before, not knowing myself why, and with only the foggiest and most uncertain goals. It was May of 1845. At the beginning of the winter, having written nothing previously, I had suddenly begun my first tale, *Poor People*. When I had finished, I didn't know what to do with it and where I should try to have it published. I had no contacts in literature at all, save for D. V. Grigorovich, but he himself had not written anything then except for one little article, "The Organ Grinders of Petersburg," which had appeared in an anthology. As I recall, at the time he was preparing to spend the summer on his country estate and was living for the time being in Nekrasov's apartment. When he stopped by to see me he said, "Bring me your manuscript" (he himself had not read it); "Nekrasov wants to publish an anthology next year, and I'll show it to him." I brought the manuscript, saw Nekrasov for a minute, and we shook hands. I was embarrassed at the thought that I had come with my work and left quickly, having said scarcely a word to Nekrasov. I had few thoughts of success and was apprehensive of that "*Fatherland Notes* party," as people then used to call it. I had been reading Belinsky with great interest for some years, but he seemed to me to be someone awesome and terrible; "He'll make fun of my *Poor People*" was the thought that sometimes came to me. But only sometimes. I wrote the work with passion, almost with tears: "Can it be that all this, all those moments I lived through with pen in hand while writing this story—can it be that all this is a lie, a mirage, counterfeit emotion?" But such thoughts, of course, came only in moments, and my sense of apprehension would quickly return. On the evening of the same day I had handed over the manuscript, I went off to visit an old friend who lived some distance away; we spent the whole night talking about *Dead Souls* and reading the work—I can't remember how many times we had read it before. This is what young people did in those days; two or three would get together: "Why don't we read Gogol, gentlemen!" And they would sit down and read, perhaps all through the night. Many, many of the young people of the day seemed to be filled with a spirit of some sort and seemed to be awaiting something. When I came home it was already four o'clock on a Petersburg "white night," as bright as day. The weather was fine and warm, and when I came into my apartment I did not go to bed but opened the window and sat by it. Suddenly the bell rang, giving me a great start, and then Grigorovich and Nekrasov, in utter rapture and both almost in tears, burst in to embrace me. They had come home early the evening before, taken up my manuscript, and begun to read it to see what it was like: "We'll be able to tell from the first ten pages." But when they had read ten pages they decided to read ten more; and then, without putting it down, they sat up the whole night reading aloud, taking turns as one grew tired. "When he was reading about the death of the student," Grigorovich told me later when we were alone, "I suddenly noticed that at the point where the father was running after the coffin, Nekrasov's voice broke; it happened once, and again, and suddenly he couldn't restrain himself; he slapped the manuscript and exclaimed, 'Ah, the so-and-so!' He meant you, of course. And so we kept on all night." When they had finished (there were 112 pages in all!) the two of them agreed they must come to see me at once: "What does it matter if he's asleep! We'll wake him; *this* matters more than sleep!" Later, when I had a better grasp of Nekrasov's character, I often marveled at that moment: his is a reticent, almost suspicious, cautious, and uncommunicative nature. Such, at least, he always seemed to me; so that this moment of our first meeting was truly a display of the deepest feeling. They spent about a half-hour with me then, and in that half-hour we discussed God knows how many things, one catching the other's meaning before he had finished a word, speaking hastily and with exclamations; we spoke of poetry and of truth and of the "current situation," and of Gogol too, of course, quoting from *The Inspector-General* and *Dead Souls*; but mainly we spoke of Belinsky. "I'll bring him your story this very day, and you'll see; what a man he is, after all, what a man! You'll meet him and you'll see: what a splendid soul he is!" Nekrasov said with delight, both his hands gripping my shoulders and shaking them. "Now, go to bed, we're leaving; you'll come see us in the morning!" As if I could have slept after their visit! What delight, what success, and I clearly remember the main thing: it was the feeling I cherished. "Others have success; people praise them, come to greet them, congratulate them; but these two came running here in tears, at four o'clock in the morning, to wake me up because this matters more than sleep. . . . Ah, how fine!" That is what I was thinking; how could I sleep!

Nekrasov took the manuscript to Belinsky that same day. He revered Belinsky and, I think, loved him more than anyone else he ever knew. At the time, Nekrasov had still not written anything on the scale which he did shortly thereafter, a year later. Nekrasov turned up in Petersburg, as far as I know, at the age of sixteen and completely alone. He also began writing virtually at the age of sixteen. I know little about his acquaintance with Belinsky, but Belinsky perceived his talent from the very beginning and, perhaps, had a powerful influence on the attitudes of his poetry. Despite Nekrasov's youth at the time and the difference in their ages, there certainly must have been some moments between them and some words spoken that had a permanent influence and bound them indissolubly. "A new Gogol has appeared!" cried Nekrasov as he came to Belinsky with *Poor People*. "You find Gogols springing up like mushrooms," Belinsky remarked sternly, but he took the manuscript. When Nekrasov visited him again, in the evening, Belinsky greeted him "plainly excited": "Bring him here, bring him as soon as you can!"

And so (this, then, being on the third day), they took me to Belinsky. I recall that at first glance I was much struck by his appearance, his nose, his forehead; somehow I had imagined him quite differently—"this awesome, this terrible critic." He greeted me with great solemnity and restraint. "Well, I suppose that is as it should be," I thought; but I think not more than a minute passed before everything changed: the solemnity was not that of a great personage, not that of a great critic meeting a twenty-two-year-old novice writer; it came, so to say, from respect for those sentiments which he wished to instill in me as quickly as possible, a respect for those important words which he so hastened to say to me. He spoke ardently, with burning eyes: "Do you, you yourself, realize what it is you have written?" he repeated several times, raising his voice to a shriek, as was his habit. He would always shriek when speaking in the grip of strong emotion. "You, as an artist, could have written this only guided by your God-given instinct; but have you yourself comprehended all the terrible truth that you have shown us? It cannot be that you, with your twenty years, have understood that. This wretched clerk of yours—why, he has been mired in the civil service for so long and has brought himself to the point where his humility will not even allow him to acknowledge his own wretchedness; he considers even his slightest complaint to be a virtual act of freethinking; he does not dare claim even the right to his own unhappiness. And when a good man, his general, gives him those hundred rubles, he is shattered, destroyed from the amazement that 'His Excellency' could take pity on such a one as he. And the button that fell off, and the moment when he kissed the general's hand—why, here it's not a matter of compassion for the poor fellow, it's horror, real horror! The horror is in the fact that he's grateful!

It's a tragedy! You've touched the very essence of the matter; straightaway you've shown the most significant thing. We critics and journalists only talk about such things; we try to explain them in words, but you, an artist, immediately and with one stroke, reveal the very essence in an image that is tangible, so that the most unthinking reader suddenly understands everything! That is the secret of art; that is truth in art! That is how the artist serves the truth! To you, an artist, the truth has been revealed and proclaimed; it has come to you as a gift. So cherish your gift, remain faithful to it, and be a great writer! . . ."

He said all that to me then. He said all that about me later, and to many others who are still alive and could attest to it. When I left him I was in ecstasy. I stopped at the corner of his house, looked at the sky, at the luminous day, at the people passing by, and with my entire being I sensed that there had occurred in my life a solemn moment, an irrevocable turning point, that something quite new had begun, but something I had not anticipated even in my wildest dreams. (And I was a terrible dreamer in those days.) "And can I, in truth, be so great?" I thought diffidently, in a kind of timid rapture. Oh, don't laugh; later on I never thought that I was great, but then—how could I resist it! "Oh, I shall be worthy of that praise. And what people there are! This is where the real people are! I shall earn their praise; I shall strive to become as fine as they are; I shall remain 'faithful'! Oh, but how frivolous I am, and if Belinsky only knew what rotten, shameful things there are within me! And everyone says that these literary men are proud and haughty. But people like him one finds only in Russia; they are alone, but they alone have the truth; and truth, goodness, and authenticity always win and triumph over vice and evil; we will win. Oh, to join them, to be one of their number!"

All these things I thought; I recall the moment with the most complete clarity. And never could I forget it thereafter. It was the most delightful moment of my entire life. Recalling it while in prison used to strengthen my spirit. Even now, I recall it each time with delight. And so, thirty years later, sitting by Nekrasov's sickbed not long ago, I recalled the moment and seemed to relive it once more. I did not remind him of all the details, but only that we had had such moments then; and I could see that he himself was recalling them. I knew that he remembered them. When I returned from prison he showed me one of the poems in his book: "It was you I was writing about then," he told me. And we spent our whole lives apart. On his sickbed he now recalls friends who are no longer:

> Those who, in the flower of their days,
> Fell victim to foul perfidy and hate;
> Whose songs of prophecy remain unsung;
> Whose portraits now *reproach* me with sad gaze. . . .

It's a painful word, this "reproach." Did we remain "faithful?" Did we? Let every one decide this for himself, by his own conscience. But read these suffering songs yourself, and may our beloved and passionate poet be restored! A poet with a passion for suffering! . . .

5. The Boy Celebrating His Saint's Day

Do you remember Count Tolstoy's *Childhood and Youth*? It has a young boy in it, the hero of the whole poem. But he is not just a boy like the other children and like his brother Volodia. He's only about twelve, and his head and heart are already visited by thoughts and feelings unlike those of other children his age. He passionately abandons himself to his dreams and feelings, already aware that it is better to keep them to himself. His shy disposition to purity and his lofty pride prevent him from revealing them. He envies his brother and considers him incomparably higher than he, especially as regards adroitness and good looks; and yet he secretly senses that his brother is far beneath him in all respects; but he drives away this thought, which he considers mean. Too often he regards himself in the mirror and decides that he is repulsively ugly. Through his mind flashes the notion that no one loves him, that people despise him. . . . In short, he is a rather unusual boy, and yet he belongs to that type of upper-middle landowning family that found its poet and historian, fully and completely—and in accordance with Pushkin's behest—in Count Leo Tolstoy. And so some guests arrive at their house—a large, Moscow, family house; it is the saint's day of the boy's sister. Along with the adults arrive children—both boys and girls. Games and dancing begin. Our hero is awkward; he is the poorest dancer of all; he wants to show off his wit, but he fails—and in front of so many pretty girls; he has his perennial notion, his perennial suspicion that he is inferior to all of them. In despair he resolves to do something rash so as to impress them all. In front of all the girls and all those haughty older boys who take no account of him, he, like one possessed, with the feeling of one who hurls himself into a chasm that has suddenly opened before him, sticks his tongue out at his tutor and strikes him with all his might! "Now everyone knows what sort of fellow he is! Now he's made a mark!" He is removed in disgrace and shut up in a storeroom. Feeling that he is ruined forever, the boy begins to dream: now he's run away from home; he's joined the army, and in battle he kills a host of Turks and falls from his wounds. "Victory! Where is our savior?" everyone cries, as they embrace and kiss him. And now he's in Moscow, walking along Tverskoi Boulevard with a bandaged arm; he meets the Emperor.... And suddenly the thought that the door will open and his tutor will come in with a bundle of switches makes these dreams fly away like so much dust. New dreams begin. Suddenly he thinks up a reason why "everyone so dislikes him": very likely he is a foundling, and they've never told him.... His thoughts grow into a whirlwind: now he's dying; they come into the storeroom and find his body: "The poor boy!" says everyone, pitying him. "He was a good boy! You're the one who ruined his life," says his father to the tutor ... and now the dreamer is choked with tears.... This whole episode ends with the boy falling ill with fever and delirium. It is a remarkably important psychological study of the soul of a child, beautifully written.

I had a reason for bringing up this study in such detail. I had a letter from K——v that described the death of a child, also a twelve-year-old boy; and it is quite possible that there was something similar here. However, I shall quote portions of the letter without changing a single word. The *topic* is interesting.

> On the 8th of November, after dinner, the news went round the city that there had been a *suicide: a twelve- or thirteen-year-old lad,* a student in a junior high school, had hanged himself. It happened this way. The teacher, whose lesson the victim had not studied that day, punished him by making him stay after school until five o'clock. The boy kept pacing the floor of the room; he happened to see the cord on a pulley; he untied it, fastened it to a nail on which the honor roll usually hung and which, for some reason, had not been put up that day, and he hanged himself. The janitor, who was washing floors in the other classrooms, spotted the unfortunate boy and ran to get the inspector. The inspector rushed in and pulled the boy from the noose, but they were unable to revive him.... What is the reason for this suicide? The boy had never been rowdy and had shown no signs

> of vicious behavior; on the whole, he had been a good student, but in the period before the suicide he had received a few unsatisfactory marks from his teacher, for which he had been punished. . . . People say that both the boy's father, who was very strict, and the boy were celebrating that day their common saint's day. Perhaps the young lad was dreaming with childish delight of how his mother, father, and little brothers and sisters would greet him at home. . . . But here he is, having to sit all alone and hungry in an empty building thinking about his father's terrible wrath that he will have to face, and about the shame, humiliation and, perhaps, also the punishment he will have to bear. He knew of suicide as an alternative (and in our day what child does not?). One feels terrible pity for the deceased lad, and pity for the inspector, an excellent person and pedagogue who is adored by his pupils; one fears for the school that sees such things happen within its walls. What were the feelings of the classmates of the deceased when they learned of what had happened? And what of the other children who study there, some of whom are only tiny little things in the preparatory classes? Is such training not too stringent? Is there not too much significance given to grades—to "Ds" and "Fs" and to honor rolls from whose nails pupils hang themselves? Is there not too much formalism and arid lack of feeling when we deal with education?

Of course, one feels terribly sorry for the poor young lad who was celebrating his saint's day; but I shall not enter into a detailed commentary on the probable causes for this heartbreaking *incident,* and particularly not on the topic of "grades, 'Ds,' excessive severity," and so on. All those things existed formerly, without suicides, and so evidently the reason does not lie here. I chose the episode from Tolstoy's *Boyhood* because of the similarity between both cases, but there is also an enormous difference. There is no doubt that the young lad, Misha, who was celebrating his saint's day, killed himself not from anger and fear alone. Both these feelings—anger and morbid dread—are too simple and would most likely have been *a result in themselves*. However, the fear of punishment could also really have had an influence, especially given a state of morbid anxiety. But still, even with that, the feeling must have been much more complex, and again, it is very possible that what occurred was something akin to what Count Tolstoy described: that is, suppressed and still unconscious childish questions, a powerful sense of some oppressive injustice, an anguished, precocious and tormenting sense of one's own insignificance, a morbidly intensified question: "Why do they *all* dislike me so?" There is the passionate longing to compel people to pity, which is the same as a passionate longing for love *from them all*—there are these things, and a great host of other complications and subtleties. The fact is that some or other of these subtleties certainly were involved; but there are also features of a new sort of reality quite different from that of the placid, middle-stratum Moscow landowning family whose way of life had long been solidly established and whose *historian* is our Count Leo Tolstoy, who, it seems, appeared just at the time when the former structure of the Russian nobility, established on the basis of old landowners' ways, had arrived at some new, still unknown but radical crisis, or at least at a point when it was to be totally recast into new, not yet manifest, almost entirely unknown forms. In the incident here, of the boy whose saint's day it was, one particular feature comes entirely from our time. Count Tolstoy's boy could dream, with bitter tears of enervated emotion in his heart, of how *they* would come in, find his dead body, and begin to love and pity him and blame themselves. He could even dream of killing himself, but only *dream*: the strict order of the historically configured noble family would have made its mark even in a twelve-year-old child and would not have allowed his *dream* to become *actuality*; the other child *dreamed it, and then he did it*. In pointing this out, however, I have in mind not only the current epidemic of suicides. One senses that something is not right here, that an enormous part of the Russian order of life has remained entirely without any observer and without any *historian*. At least it is clear that the life of the upper-middle level of our nobility, so vividly described by our writers, is already an insignificant and "dissociated" corner of Russian life generally. Who, then, will be the *historian* of the other corners, of which, it seems, there are so awfully many? And if, within this chaos that has gone on for so long and that is particularly prevalent in the life of our society now—a life in which, perhaps, even an artist of Shakespearean proportions cannot find a normative law and a guiding thread—who, then, will illuminate even a little part of this chaos, never mind dreaming of some guiding thread? The main thing is that it seems no one is capable of doing this; it is as if it were still too early even for our greatest artists. One cannot deny that a way of life in Russia is disintegrating; consequently, family life disintegrates as well. But certainly there is also a life that is being formed anew, on new principles. Who will pick these out and show them to us? Who can, even in small measure, define and express the laws of this disintegration and this new formation? Or is it still too early? But have we even taken complete note of what is old and past?

Editor's Note

I.

Despite the categorical statement in my December *Diary*, people continue to send me letters asking whether I will be publishing the new magazine, *Light*; they even enclose postage stamps for my reply. To all who have been enquiring I announce once more, and for the last time, that it is not I who will publish the magazine *Light* but Nikolai Petrovich Wagner, and that I will play no part in editing it.

II.

Miss O. A. An——ova, who wrote to the editor regarding study for her examinations, is requested to supply her correct address. The address on Mokhovaia Street that she provided earlier proved to be incorrect.

February

1

1. Self-appointed Prophets and Lame Coopers Who Continue to Manufacture the Moon on Gorokhovaia Street. One of Russia's Least-known Great Men

As before, the Eastern Question confronts us all at every turn. No matter how we tried to forget about it and divert ourselves with all the things at hand—the pre-Lenten carnival, Turgenev's *Virgin Soil,* bankruptcies, gangs like the "Jack of Hearts"; no matter what a cynical air we tried to assume, assuring everyone, and particularly ourselves, that "absolutely nothing happened, that it was all an invention and a falsification"; no matter how we buried our heads beneath our pillows like little children so as not to see the dreadful apparition—still, the apparition is before us; it has not gone away and stands threatening us as before. Each of us—the malicious cynic, the earnest citizen, the fellow innocently enjoying a spree, the ordinary lazybones—each feels and cannot forget that this something does exist, a something that has certainly not yet been settled and concluded but is urgent and essential, something that will undoubtedly summon us and demand, sooner or later, that it be resolved, and that here, certainly,

> Something surely must be done,
> Somehow surely this be ended.

And, truly, at the very least something must be done and somehow this surely must be ended, and it would be best if it could be ended in the best way. Meanwhile, time passes by; spring is at hand, and what will spring bring us? Some shout that the time has already passed, but this only God knows; there is always a time for a good deed. Indeed, is it not possible that something could be worked out in time for spring? Will not something decisive materialize, something to last at least for a year? No one in Europe these days plans further than a year ahead, the more so because Turkey herself will scarcely hold up for another year. However, the issue here is not Turkey but what will be left after she goes. These decisive solutions that last a year may be advantageous to Europe, but they're not of much use to others; and what will happen to the others, especially to those who lie beyond the Danube? But it is only the Russian People who are thinking about them.

Yes, they are thinking of them, and—say what you will—no matter how hard we tried over the winter to deny our movement of last summer, it has kept going all winter long, in my view, just as it did all over Russia last summer, steadily and faithfully, but now calmly and with hope for a decision by the tsar. And of course it will go on to the very end, despite our prophets who could discern (and specifically this past summer) in the face of Russia nothing more than a vile, slumbering, drunken creature that stretched from the frozen rocks of Finland to the fiery land of Colchis, keeping its grip on a colossal bottle of vodka. In my view, if these prophets of ours cannot even see what Russia lives by, then so much the better for them: they won't be meddling in things and won't get in the way; and if they do meddle, then they will miss their mark. Do you see: the point here is that our Europeanism and our "enlightened" European view of Russia is still that very same moon which that very same lame, itinerant cooper is making on Gorokhovaia Street, the same one he was making before; and he is still doing such a wretched job of it, which he proves continually. And here, just the other day, he proved it again: in future, he'll do an even shoddier job. Well, let him be: he's a German, and lame to boot; you have to have a little compassion.

And indeed, what does Russia care about prophets like these? Nowadays we don't have time to stand around waiting for something to happen; the old days have passed.

There was some mention in the newspapers that over the winter more than one group of poor little orphan children of families destroyed by war in the Slavic lands have been brought to Moscow. They are being placed with various people and institutions. It would be a good thing if this could continue and eventually be organized on the broadest scale all over Russia: and why not?—it's only a good deed, after all, and these children must be cared for; they are all Slavs *of the future*. Incidentally, I've asked myself more than once how on earth the refugees have managed to feed themselves—those several hundred thousand Bulgarians, Bosnians, Herzegovinians, and so on, who fled from their tormenters after massacre and destruction into Serbia, Montenegro, Austria, and wherever. Considering the amount of money needed to feed them, and knowing that neither the Serbs nor the Montenegrins have such money—indeed, they themselves have scarcely anything to eat at present—one can't understand how these hundreds of thousands, with their small children, could feed and clothe themselves over the winter. I've heard that another party of children was brought to Moscow not long ago; these ranged in age from three to thirteen, and the Pokrov Community of the Sisters of Charity took them in. People say that the Pokrov Sisters have housed these little Serbian girls with the Bulgarian girls who came earlier and that one of the sisters who knows Serbian supervises them, so that the children are very happy. Of course the children are comfortable and warm, but not long ago a friend returning from Moscow told me a very revealing story about these same youngsters: the Serbian girls sit in one corner of the room, the Bulgarians in another, and they don't want to play with or speak to one another; and when the Serbs are asked why they don't want to play with the Bulgarians, they answer, "We gave them weapons so they would go with us to fight the Turks, but they hid the weapons and didn't fight." I find that very interesting. If eight- or nine-year-old youngsters speak in such fashion, then they must have picked it up from their fathers; and if the fathers are passing on things like this to the children, then there certainly must be terrible discord among the Balkan Slavs. Indeed, there is eternal discord among the Slavs! They keep it alive in their traditions and preserve it in song; and without a massive center—Russia—to unify them, there will be no accord among the Slavs; indeed, without Russia the Slavs will not survive and will vanish entirely from the face of the earth, despite all the dreams of Serbian intellectuals or various Czechs who've been civilized in European fashion. . . . There are still a lot of dreamers among them. In fact almost all of them are still dreamers. . . .

Do you remember Pushkin's "Song of the Battle at Great Zenitsa" in his "Songs of the West Slavs"? The insurgents, under Radivoj, gathered at Great Zenitsa to go off to fight the Turks.

> And when the Dalmatians espied our host
> They turned up their long mustaches,

Set their caps on askew
And said: "Take us with you."
. . . .
Beglerbei and his Bosnians
Marched against us from Banjaluki;
But as soon as their horses began to whinny
And their curved sabers flashed
In the sun by Great Zenitsa
The Dalmatian traitors fled the field!

By the way, I asked if you remembered "The Songs of the West Slavs," and I shall reply for you all in advance by saying that no one remembers either "The Song of the Battle at Great Zenitsa" or Pushkin's "Songs of the West Slavs" themselves. Well, no one apart from some few specialists, teachers of literature, or the odd person well up in years. I may be badly mistaken, but still I firmly believe that. And yet you know, gentlemen, that "The Songs of the West Slavs" are a masterpiece among Pushkin's masterpieces, to say nothing of the political meaning of these fifty-year-old poems. The fact that these songs appeared among us then is significant: it is a sign of the Russians' presentiment of the Slavs, the Russians' prophecy of future brotherhood and unity. Yet I've never read a single piece of criticism that called these works of Pushkin his masterpieces. They were considered quite ordinary things, yet they are indeed his masterpieces, true examples of high-reaching significance. In my view, we haven't even begun to discover Pushkin yet: he is a genius who moved far in advance of Russian consciousness. He was a Russian, a real Russian; he, through the power of his genius, remade himself into a Russian, while we, even now, are still taking lessons from the lame cooper. He was one of the first Russians who completely sensed the Russian within himself, who summoned up that Russianness within himself, and who demonstrated how the Russian ought to regard his People, his Russian family, Europe, the lame cooper, and his brother Slavs. Never has any Russian had a more humane, more lofty, and more sober outlook. But I don't plan to expand upon this at the moment; and as for the "Songs," I'll say only that, as we all know, Pushkin took them from the French, from Mérimée's little book *La Guzla*, a thing which Mérimée admitted he had written quite casually, without even leaving Paris. This most talented French writer, now deceased, a *sénateur* in later life and virtually a relative of Napoleon III, depicted in this *Guzla* only Frenchmen—and Parisians at that—disguised as Slavs. And they can do no other: for a real Frenchman, nothing exists on earth apart from Paris. Pushkin, after reading the book and sending an inquiry to its author in Paris, used it to compose his songs; in other words, from the Frenchmen depicted by Mérimée Pushkin restored the Slavs. And, of course, now these "Songs of the Slavs" are about real Slavs, Slavs who even are akin to Russians. Such songs do not exist in Serbia, of course; they sing others. But that does not matter: Pushkin's songs are panslavic; they are folksongs that have poured from the Slavic heart, in the spirit and image of the Slavs, with Slavic meaning, customs, and history. I would like to show those highly educated Serbs, many of whom regarded the Russians so suspiciously this past summer, Pushkin's song of "Black George," say, or "The Song of the Battle at Great Zenitsa." These are two masterpieces among the songs, diamonds of the first magnitude in Pushkin's poetry (and it is certainly for that reason that they are completely unknown in our schools, not only among the pupils, but, in all likelihood, among the teachers as well, who now will be astonished to hear for the first time that these, and not "The Captive of the Caucasus" and "The Gypsies" are such masterpieces). Yet it would have been a good thing to have made these songs known in our schools, at least during the past year. However, judging by the course of events, there's little chance the Serbs will soon learn about this least-known of all great Russian men—I think that is how one may define our great Pushkin, about whom thousands and tens of thousands among our intelligentsia still do not know; they do not know that he was a poet and a Russian of such great caliber; we have still been unable to collect money for a monument to him—a thing that will go down in our history. And the Serbs, were they to read these "Songs," would see what we think of their freedom and whether we hold it dear, whether we rejoice in it, whether we want to bring them under our control and deprive them of that freedom. However, enough about poetry. And let people not smile haughtily at me, as if to say, "Look at the trifling things he talks about." This is not a trifle; we must still speak much and at length about Pushkin.

2. Home-grown Giants and a Humiliated Son of a Mountain Village. An Anecdote about Skin Flayed from the Back. The Higher Interests of Civilization, and "May They Be Damned If They Must Be Purchased at Such a Price!"

The Serbian Skupshtina, which assembled last month in Belgrade for a moment (for an hour and a half, as the papers said) so that they could decide whether or not to conclude a peace—this Skupshtina did not display a mood of excessively eager conciliation as people expected, taking into account the circumstances. The talk is that even the agreement to sue for peace came as a result of under-the-table maneuvering and ministerial intrigues. In any case, if there is even the slightest bit of truth in the rumor that the Skupshtina wasn't afraid to continue the war, then—taking into consideration their desperate situation—one cannot help but ask, "Why did we carry on so about the cowardice of the Serbs?" I have been getting letters from Serbia and have spoken to people who have been there; I remember in particular a letter from a young Russian who remained there and who writes of the Serbs with great enthusiasm and with indignation that there are people in Russia who think that they are selfish and cowardly. This enthusiastic Russian emigré even excuses the self-inflicted wounds of the Serbian soldiers who fought with Cherniaev and Novoselov: he claims they are a people so tenderhearted and with such feelings of love for their native villages, where every one of them has left a wife, children, or a mother, sisters, a fiancée, brothers, a horse, and a dog, that they abandon everything, mutilate themselves, shoot off their fingers so as to be declared unfit for military service and returned to their dear, cozy village as soon as possible! Just imagine it. I, too, can understand this tenderness of heart and the whole process; and, of course, we have here a people whose hearts are excessively tender, although, at the same time, they are not very perceptive citizens, since they don't understand what their hearts' desire. I think that in terms of tenderheartedness the Serbian villager is very like those children whom, perhaps, you also can recall from your childhood: suddenly they found themselves in school, having come from a family or from a household that had suddenly broken up or dispersed. Until then, the boy had lived only at home and knew nothing apart from it; and, suddenly, he has about a hundred classmates, new faces, noise, clamor, and it's all entirely different from home. Lord, what torment! At home he may have been cold and hungry, yet they loved him; and even if they didn't love him, still, it was *home*; he was on his own there, but here—not a kind word from his superiors; his teachers are strict; the subjects are so difficult; the corridors are so long; and there are such heartless rapscallions, bullies, and teases; his classmates are merciless: "You'd think they had no heart at all, that they never had a mother and a father!" Until now he's been told that it's terrible and disgraceful to lie and to insult people, but here everyone lies, deceives, insults, and, even worse, they laugh when they see he's shocked. And then they took a dislike to him because he cries for his own cozy little nest and "gives the whole class a black mark." And so they set to pummeling him mercilessly, the whole class, all the time; and they do it just because they feel like it, not from anger, just for diversion. I might say that in my childhood I met quite a number of such unhappy children at various schools—and what crimes of this sort are sometimes committed in our educational institutions of all levels and designations—actual crimes! Should the boy be silly enough to complain, he'll be beaten almost to death (and some are beaten to death); schoolboys beat without mercy and with no regard for the consequences. They'll call him a tattletale for years thereafter; they'll refuse to talk to him and make him a pariah; and how heartless and cruelly indifferent the school authorities are in such cases! I cannot remember a single genuine pedagogue from my childhood and do not think that there are many of them even now: they are all only bureaucrats collecting their salaries. And yet it is these very children, homesick for their families and their own cozy nests when they enter school, who most often turn out to be remarkable people with talents and abilities. But those who, when taken from their families, quickly make themselves at home in whatever new circumstances they find themselves, who get used to everything in the wink of an eye, who never are homesick for anything, and who even become leaders of the others—those most often turn out to be mediocrities or simply bad people, artful dodgers and schemers from the age of eight. I'm generalizing far too much, of course, but still, I think that it is a bad child who does not feel homesick when he goes off to school, unless he has never had a family or has had an extremely bad family.

In the summer, when I read about the Serbian recruits who wounded themselves, I could not help but compare them with such little boys suffering through the first days of school; there was no other way to react to their unfortunate, unthinking, almost animal urge to throw down their rifles and run home as quickly as possible. The only difference was that the Serbian's urge also reveals an amazing, phenomenal insensibility. He seems to have dismissed any consideration that if everyone were to run off as he did, there would be no one left to defend the country, and so the Turks would someday come into his own native village and destroy his dear, cozy nest and slaughter his mother, his fiancée, his sister, his horse, and their dog. Indeed, in so many Serbian hearts, perhaps, this suffering over their native nests has never reached the level of suffering for their native land; and that is a truly odd phenomenon. It is true that now, when their war is over and peace has been concluded, one can also perceive that the hearts of the higher Serbian intelligentsia very often failed to attain a level where they suffered for their native land, but the reason for this was not the same as among the lower people. Among the higher intelligentsia this may be explained, perhaps, by excessive political vanity. Thus, owing to "higher" interests of their native land, these higher hearts had scarcely any time to concern themselves with interests that were lower, related to the people, and quite commonplace. But I think I can still make one rather interesting observation about the lower Serb. One cannot explain his self-inflicted wounds and his flight from the field of battle by tenderheartedness and shortsightedness alone. It seems to me that when he deserted and went home, he knew very well that he was doing something wrong, and it is very likely that he was the first to admit it; but at the same time, he never supposed that his native land would be left without defense and protection if he were to flee: "Oh, the heroes will remain, the Kireevs; Cherniaev will remain, and the Russians; and his own strict Serbian officers; but he—what did he matter? An insignificant little speck, a bit of rubbish, and nothing more; he'll go away and no one will miss him. . . . " In my view, this was exactly what he felt, and it is very interesting and characterizes the people: on top, braggarts, civilized Europeans dreaming of uniting all the Slavs into a single Serbia, even carrying on intrigues against Russia; in short, regular civilized Europeans, these Horvatovićs and Marinovićs—no different from the Moltkes and Bismarcks. On the other side, next to these giants, we have the humiliated son of the mountain village—the *kucha*—humiliated by four centuries of slavery. Because of these centuries of humiliation, he considers himself worthless, a mere speck: "The giants will remain, but no one will notice me. I am so small, and they are such strict masters. . . . " I read somewhere that some of these strict masters, seeing one of the lower Serbs preparing to lay down his arms, directly blew his head off with shots from their pistols: "There. We can also be iron dukes when we have to!" They treat their common people a bit haughtily over there, it seems.

On the whole, these higher Slavs, "with such a glorious future before them," are a remarkably interesting lot in the political, civil, historical, and every other respect.

Now, when Cherniaev has already withdrawn and the volunteers have been sent away, we hear from them—i.e., from their military people—an idea about their military capacity that we never heard before, in the summer. Now they say that their Serb is quite incapable of serving in a regular army in open battle, and that wars fought by the Serbian people are "little wars," meaning partisan wars, fought by small bands in the forests and mountain passes, behind boulders and crags. Well, that might really be so; but since they have already concluded a peace, there is scarcely any way of verifying it now. At least they will have this conviction about their military to hold on to, and it does offer a certain comfort in times of misfortune. Will this peace last for long? But let me make a closing remark about this Serbian war in which we Russians, almost to a man, so invested our feelings: it seems to me that the Serbs are parting from us and from our aid with even more mistrust than that with which they greeted us at the beginning of the war. One can also conclude that their mistrust of us will continue and increase until they themselves grow and develop intellectually; this will take a very long time, and it means that we must simply ignore their mistrust and just do our job as best we can. Where the Eastern Question is concerned, it is essential for us to have one truth constantly in mind: the primary Slavic problem is not only that they be liberated from their oppressors, but that this liberation—though it be done with Russian help (for how else could it be done—they could never manage it without the Russians!)—should be done leaving them indebted as little as possible to the Russians.

Among these Slavic children who have been brought to Moscow (this same friend who has come back from Moscow was telling me), there is one girl of eight or nine who has frequent fainting spells, for which she is being given special care. She faints because of her recollections: last summer, with her own eyes, she watched a group of Circassians flay the skin from her father, and do it completely. The memory of this never leaves her and, most likely, will remain with her forever; as years pass it may grow less terrible, although I don't know if one can speak of something less terrible in a case like this. Oh, civilization! Oh, Europe, whose interests would suffer so were she actually to forbid the Turks to flay the skin from fathers while their children watch! These higher interests of European civilization are, of course, trade, maritime navigation, markets, factories: what can be higher than these things in Europe's eyes? Interests like these cannot be touched, not only by fingers but even by thought, but—but "may they be damned, these interests of European civilization!" These are not my words, these are the words of *The Moscow News,* and I consider it an honor to add my voice to this exclamation: indeed, may they be damned, these interests of civilization; and may civilization itself be damned if its preservation demands the stripping of skin from living people. Yet this is a fact: preserving it demands the stripping of skin from human beings!

3. On Flaying of Skins Generally and Various Aberrations in Particular. Hatred of Authority with Toadyism of Thought

"From human beings? What human beings? From only a tiny number of human beings living in some obscure corner. From some Turkish subjects whom we'd never have known about if the Russians hadn't shouted it far and wide. On the other hand, the rest of the organism—the huge part of it—is alive and well; it flourishes, trades, and manufactures!"

That story of the little Bulgarian girl who kept fainting I heard in the morning; later that same day I happened to be walking along Nevsky Prospect. Between three and four o'clock, mothers and nursemaids were walking their children there. Suddenly an involuntary thought fell heavily on me: "Civilization!" I thought, "who dares to say a word against civilization? No, civilization truly does mean something: at least these children of ours who are peacefully strolling here on Nevsky Prospect will not see the skin flayed from their fathers, and their mothers will not have to watch these children being tossed into the air and caught on bayonets, as happened in Bulgaria. That bit of progress, at least, can be credited to civilization! And what if it does exist only in Europe, i.e., in one little corner of the globe, and in a corner which is rather small in comparison with the surface of the planet (a terrible thought!); but still, it is there, and though it may be only in some little corner, it exists; although the price we pay for it—flaying the skin from our own brothers who live somewhere off on the edge of civilization—is a high one, it exists among us, at least. Just think that in times past, and not that long ago, there was nothing of this sort in solid form even in Europe; and if it now does exist in Europe, then it is for the first time in the history of the planet. No, still, this is an accomplishment and, perhaps, one that will never be reversed; and that is a remarkably important consideration which enters one's soul involuntarily; it is certainly not some small thing unworthy of attention, the more so that the world is still a mystery as before, despite civilization and its gains. God knows what things the world can still engender and what may subsequently happen, even in the very near future."

And so, the moment I felt like exclaiming rapturously to myself: "Long live civilization!" I was suddenly overcome by doubt: "Have we, in fact, achieved even this much, even for these children of Nevsky Prospect? Isn't this, perhaps, entirely a mirage, even here, and aren't we merely deceiving ourselves?"

You know, gentlemen, I ended by thinking that it was a mirage, or, to put it less harshly, virtually a mirage; and if fathers are not skinned alive here on the Nevsky while their children watch, then it is only a matter of chance, so to say, a matter of "circumstances beyond the public's control," and also, of course, because of the policemen standing here. Oh, let me clarify my thought at once: I'm certainly not trying to make up some allegory; I'm not hinting at the sufferings of some proletariat in our present age, nor at some parent who tells his seven-year-old son: "Here is my testament to you: if you steal five rubles, I will curse you; if you steal a hundred thousand, I will bless you." Oh, no; I mean my words to be taken literally. I mean the literal flaying of skin, the same as happened in Bulgaria in the summer and in which, it appears, the victorious Turks are so fond of indulging. And it is that flaying of skin I have in mind when I state: if it does not happen on the Nevsky, then it is only "by chance, through circumstances beyond our control," and, most important, because for the moment it is still against the law; but were it to depend on us, perhaps, nothing would stop us despite all our civilization.

In my view, if one is to be absolutely frank, people are simply intimidated by some sort of habit, some rule taken on faith, almost a prejudice. But if some "expert" were to come up with even the most meager "proof" that there are occasions when flaying the skin from the back of some other person can even be of benefit to the common cause and, though it may be repulsive, still "the end justifies the means"; and if some expert were to say things of this sort using the appropriate style and under the appropriate circumstances, then, believe me, immediately there would be people willing to carry out the idea—very jolly people, even. Oh, let this just be my quite absurd paradox! I'll be the first to set my name to such a description of it and will do so with both hands; nevertheless, I assure you that this is exactly what would happen. Civilization exists; its laws exist; belief in those laws even exists. But all that's needed is for some new fad to appear and hordes of people would instantly be transformed. Not every one, of course, but only such a small handful would be left that even you and I, dear reader, would be astonished; and even we do not know where we would find ourselves: among the flayed or among the flayers? Naturally, people will shout right in my face that this is all a lot of rubbish and that there could never be such a fad and that this, at least, is something civilization did achieve. Gentlemen, how gullible you are! You're laughing? Well, what about France in 1793 (so as not to look into things much more recent)? Did they not affirm that very fad of flaying, and did they not do so even under the guise of civilization's most sacred principles? And this after Rousseau and Voltaire! You may object that this is not what happened at all, and that it was long ago; but note that I resort to history only, perhaps, so as not to speak of the present day. Believe me, the most complete aberration in human hearts and minds is always possible; and in Russia, and specifically in our time, it is not only possible but even inevitable, judging by the course of events. Just look: are there many among us who can agree on what is good and what is bad? And I'm not talking about some "eternal verities" but about the very first question that comes up. And how quickly changes and volte-faces occur among us! What are these "Jack of Hearts" bands in Moscow? It seems to me that they are only a part of that portion of the Russian nobility that was unable to tolerate the peasant reform. They may not be landowners themselves, but they are the children of landowners. The peasant reform left them beggared and down at the heels. Of course, it was not the reform alone that caused this; they simply were unable to cope with "new ideas:" "If all the things we were taught were a lot of prejudices, then there's no point in abiding by them. If there is *nothing*, then we can do *anything*—there's an idea!" Note, please: this is an idea that is unbelievably widespread; nine-tenths of those who follow new ideas profess this one; in other words, nine-tenths of our progressives can't even understand new ideas in any other way. Darwin, for instance, is quickly transformed into a pickpocket in Russia: that's what the "Jack of Hearts" means. Oh, of course, over centuries of experience humanity has accumulated a huge number of rules of humane behavior, some of which are now considered unshakable. But I want only to say that despite all these rules, principles, religions, and civilizations, it is always only the most imperceptible, tiny group of people that is saved by them; true, this is the group that emerges victorious, but only in the final analysis; while in the day-to-day and current course of history, people remain much the same as they were, i.e., in huge majority lacking even any moderately solid concept of duty or sense of honor; and the moment some new fad appears, they immediately go running after it, quite naked and with great pleasure. There are rules, but it is people who are not at all ready to observe them. Some will say that there is no need to be ready; we need only to discover what the rules are! But is that so? And are these rules, whatever they may be, likely to last for long when people are so eager to go running about naked?

This is my view: one can, correctly and immediately, comprehend and feel something deeply; but one cannot, immediately, become a person; one must be formed into a person. It is a discipline. This same relentless discipline over oneself is precisely what our thinkers of today reject: "There's been too much despotism already; we need some freedom." But this freedom leads the huge majority of people only toward toadyism to someone else's ideas, for people are terribly in love with all things they are given ready-made. Moreover, thinkers proclaim general laws, meaning rules that will suddenly make everyone happy, without any need for them to be shaped and formed: it's simply a matter of letting these rules come into force. But even if this ideal were attainable, no rules, not even the most obvious ones, could be implemented with people who *have not been re-formed*. It is through this relentless discipline and unceasing work on himself that our citizen might be born. It is with such a noble process of work on ourselves that we must begin, so as subsequently to turn up our "Virgin Soil"; otherwise there will be no point in turning it up.

Is that not so? But what is good and what is bad—why this, above all, is what we do not know. We have lost all our sense for determining this. All the old authorities have been smashed to bits and new ones have been set up; but anyone who is a bit cleverer than the rest has no faith in the new authorities, while he who is bolder in spirit is transformed from a citizen into a Jack of Hearts. Moreover, he'll start flaying the skin from someone's back, honest to God, he will; and he'll even proclaim that this advances the common cause and so is a sacred act. How, then, and in what sense, can you set to working to refashion yourself when you don't know what is good and what is bad?

4. Metternichs and Don Quixotes

But so as not to speak in abstractions, let's turn to the topic at hand. Now, really, we don't strip the skin from people; moreover, we don't even like that sort of thing (but God alone knows, people who do like that sort of thing often hide themselves; they remain obscure and, for the time being, are embarrassed—"afraid of prejudice"). But if we don't like that sort of thing to go on here and *never do it*, then, really, we should abhor it in others as well. Abhorring it, in fact, is not enough: we should simply not allow anyone to do it; we must simply not allow it. And yet, is that what actually happens? The most indignant people among us are not nearly as indignant as they ought to be. I am not talking even about the Slavs alone. If we are truly so compassionate, then we ought to act by the full measure of our compassion, not by the measure of a ten-ruble donation. You may say that one can't donate all one has, after all. I agree, although I'm not sure why I agree. Why couldn't one give away everything? That's precisely the point here: one has absolutely no understanding even of one's own nature. And all of a sudden the question of "*the interests of civilization*" comes up with enormous authority!

The question is put directly, clearly, clinically, and with cynical frankness. "The interests of civilization"—these are the production, the wealth, the tranquillity required by capital. What is needed is immense, continuous and growing production at reduced prices, in view of the terrible increase in the numbers of the proletariat. In providing the proletarian with earnings, we are also providing him with consumer goods at lower prices. The more tranquil things are in Europe, the lower the prices will be. Accordingly, what is most necessary is a tranquil situation in Europe. The noise of war frightens away production. Capital is cowardly; it will take fright at war and hide itself. If the right of the Turks to flay the skin from the backs of their Christian subjects is to be limited, then a war must be begun; and if a war is begun, Russia will at once step forward; and this might cause complications that could involve the whole world in the war. In that case, say good-bye to production; and the proletarian would be out on the street. And the proletarian is dangerous out on the street. Speeches in various parliaments already declare directly, openly, for the whole world to hear, that the proletarian is dangerous, that he is restless, that he is hearkening to socialism. "No, better let them skin people alive way off there in the wilds. The inviolability of Turkish rights must remain unquestioned. The Eastern Question must be put down; let them skin people. What do these skins matter in any case? Is the tranquillity of Europe worth the hides of some two or three people—or of twenty or thirty thousand people—what's the difference? If we choose to, we won't hear a thing; we'll just plug our ears. . . ."

That's what Europe thinks (perhaps that's what she's decided to do); such are *the interests of civilization*—and, again, may they be damned! And damned all the more in that we are faced with the aberration of minds (and Russian minds above all). The question is plainly put: which is better—for many tens of millions of workers to be thrown onto the street or for a few millions of Christians to suffer at the hands of their Turkish rulers? The numbers are set forth; the figures are used to frighten people. As well as that, the politicians and pundits make their statements: there exists, they say, a rule, a doctrine, an axiom that says that the moral principles of one person—a citizen, an individual—are one thing, and the moral principles of the state are another. Accordingly, what can be considered wickedness on the part of a single individual may, when related to the state, take on the appearance of the greatest wisdom!

This is an ancient and very widespread doctrine, but let it be damned as well! The main thing is that we should not be frightened by figures. Let them do as they like over there in Europe, but let us do things differently. It is better to believe that happiness cannot be purchased with evil deeds than it is to feel happy knowing that you have allowed evil to happen. Russia has never known how to produce her own real Metternichs and Beaconsfields; to the contrary, through the entire period of European life she has lived not for herself but for others, and specifically for "the common interests of humanity." And, in truth, there were occasions during these two hundred years when, perhaps, she did try to copy Europe somehow and acquired a few Metternichs of her own; but somehow it always turned out in the end that the Russian Metternich suddenly proved to be a Don Quixote, something which amazed Europe. Of course, they laughed at the Don Quixote; but now, it seems, the time is at hand, and Don Quixote has begun no longer to amuse people but to frighten them. The fact is that he has certainly comprehended his position in Europe and no longer goes off to tilt at windmills. But yet he has remained a faithful knight, and this is what they find most terrible of all. Indeed, people in Europe shout about "Russian seizure of territory and Russian cunning," but this is only done to strike fear into their own mobs when they need to, while those who do the shouting don't believe it themselves and never did believe it. On the contrary, what troubles and frightens them now in the image Russia presents is rather something upright, something too unselfish and honorable, something that loathes profit and ill-gotten gain. They sense that she cannot be bribed or enticed into a mercenary or violent act by any political advantage. It might be done by deceit; but even though Don Quixote is a great knight, he is sometimes terribly sly, so that he will not allow himself to be deceived. England, France, Austria—is there even one nation there with which we could not have an alliance, at an opportune moment, for political gain and with mercenary, violent intent? We need only not let slip the moment at which the bribed nation can sell herself for the highest price. Russia alone cannot be seduced into an unjust alliance, not at any price. And since Russia at the same time is awfully powerful, and she is obviously growing and maturing at an amazing rate—something that people in Europe see and thoroughly understand (even though they sometimes shout that the colossus has feet of clay)—then why shouldn't they be afraid?

Incidentally, this view on the incorruptibility of Russia's foreign policy and her continual service to the common interests of humanity, even to her own detriment, is borne out by historical fact; and this is something to which we ought to pay attention. This is what makes us distinct from all of Europe. Moreover, this view on the nature of Russia is so little known that even among us there are few who believe it. Of course, Russia should not be held to account for the *errors* in her policy, because the point now is only the spirit and moral character of our policy, not its successes of the recent or distant past. In regard to the latter, there truly were some windmills in times of yore; but, I repeat, I think that their time has passed completely.

But seriously, what is the point of that prosperity purchased at the price of injustice and flaying of people's skin? Let that which is truth for the individual person remain truth for the entire nation as well. Yes, of course, there may be some temporary setback, some short-term loss of income, a loss of markets, a drop in production, and a rise in prices. But in exchange, let the organism of the nation remain morally healthy—and the nation will certainly gain more, even in a material sense. We note that Europe has indisputably reached the point where she places supreme value on her current advantage, on the advantage of the present moment, no matter what the price, because over there they live only from day to day and only for the present moment, not knowing themselves what will become of them tomorrow; we in Russia, however, still believe in something solid which is being created among us, and as a result we seek advantages which are constant and substantive. And therefore we, as a political organism as well, have always believed in an enduring moral system, not in a relative one valid only for a few days. Believe me, Don Quixote also knows where his advantages lie and is capable of calculation: he knows that he will gain in dignity and in awareness of that dignity if he continues to remain a knight; moreover, he is convinced that in following this path he will not forfeit any sincerity in his striving for goodness and truth and that such an awareness will strengthen him in his further pursuits. He is certain, finally, that such a policy is also the best school for the nation. It is essential that no "Jack of Hearts" dare to say to my face: "Everything with you is relative, after all; it's all based on your own self-interest." It is essential that the youthful enthusiast should conceive a love for his own nation and not go off to seek truth and an ideal apart from it and outside society. And he will end by coming to love his nation, once we have passed through this hard, terribly hard, school. Truth is like the sun: it cannot be hidden away; Russia's mission will at last become clear to even the most venal minds, both here at home and in Europe. Why are such intellectual aberrations possible among us now as they are nowhere else? Because under the system that lasted for a century and a half our entire intelligentsia did nothing but become a stranger to Russia; it ended by ceasing to know her altogether and had its dealings with her only via the bureaucrat's office. A new age began with the reforms of the present reign. The work has begun and it cannot be stopped.

And Europe read this fall's manifesto from the Russian emperor and has it fixed in her mind—fixed in her mind not for the present moment alone but for years to come and for future "current moments." We will draw our sword, if need be, in the name of the oppressed and unfortunate, even though it may be to the detriment of our own current advantage. But at the same time, may our faith grow ever firmer that this is precisely where Russia's real mission, strength, and truth lie, and that self-sacrifice, in the name of the interests of civilization, for the oppressed who have been forsaken by everyone in Europe, is real service to the real and true interests of civilization.

No, it is essential that political organisms acknowledge the same truth, the very truth of Christ, that is acknowledged by every believer. That truth must be preserved somewhere, at least; at least one of the nations must cast forth its light. Otherwise, what will happen? Everything will grow dark and confused and will drown in cynicism. Otherwise, you will not be able to keep in check the moral standards of individual citizens, and in that case, how will the whole organism of the state be able to live? Authority is necessary, the sun is necessary so that it can cast forth its light. The sun has appeared in the East, and a new day for humanity is beginning from the East. When the sun shines forth in all its radiance, people will understand what the real "interests of civilization" are. Otherwise, they will only raise the banner carrying the inscription *Après nous le déluge*! Can it be that such a glorious "civilization" will lead the people of Europe to a motto like this and then be done with them? That is what it is coming down to.

2

1. One of Today's Most Important Questions

My readers perhaps have already noted that I, who have been publishing my *Writer's Diary* for over a year now, try to say as little as possible about current things in Russian literature; and if I do permit myself a few words on this topic now and again, then they are expressed exclusively in a rapturously laudatory tone. And yet, what injustice there is in this voluntary abstention of mine! I am a writer, and I put out a *Writer's Diary*; and indeed, I, more than anyone else perhaps, took an interest through the course of this year in the things that appeared in literature: so how, then, can I conceal what may be my most powerful impressions? "You're a writer yourself," I say, "and so every opinion you have about literature, aside from out-and-out accolades, is regarded as showing partiality; unless, of course, you speak of things from the distant past." It was that consideration which kept me from expressing myself.

And yet I will now take the risk of violating this consideration. True, I will not be speaking about anything in a purely literary or critical sense, but will say something "apropos" if the need arises. Such an occasion has arisen now. The fact is that a month ago I happened on a work of current literature which is so serious and so characteristic that I read it in amazement, because it's been a long time since I thought I would find anything of this sort and on this scale in literature. I read a few pages of the work of this writer—an artist in the highest degree and preeminently a writer of fiction—pages that are truly on the topic of the day—all the most important things in our current Russian political and social issues and concentrated in a single point, as it were. And most important, this topic is treated with all the most characteristic nuances of our present moment, precisely in the way in which we now pose the question—pose it and leave it unresolved. I am speaking about a few pages in Count Leo Tolstoy's *Anna Karenina,* which appeared in the January issue of *The Russian Messenger.*

About the novel as a whole I shall say only a few words, and those merely in the form of a most necessary preface. I began reading it, as we all did, very long ago. At first it made a very good impression on me; later, although details of the novel continued to produce this good impression, so that I was unable to put the book down, it appealed to me rather less, on the whole. I kept thinking that I had read this somewhere before, namely in *Childhood and Youth,* by the same Count Tolstoy, as well as in his *War and Peace;* and in these works it was even fresher. Here we have the same story of a noble landowning family, although, of course, the plot is different. Figures such as Vronsky (one of the novel's heroes), who can only speak to one another on the topic of horses and who, indeed, are even incapable of finding any other topic of conversation, were interesting in that one learns about such a type; but they are all the same and represent but one small class. It seemed, for instance, that the love affair of this "stallion in uniform," as a friend of mine called him, could be portrayed only ironically. But when the author began, seriously and without irony, to allow me entry into the inner world of his hero, I found it even rather boring. Then, suddenly, all my prejudices were shattered. There came the scene of the heroine's death (later she completely recovered), and I understood all the essential part of the author's intent. At the very center of this petty and shameless life there appeared a great, everlasting, vital truth, and at once it illuminated everything. These petty, insignificant, and dishonest creatures suddenly became genuine and truthful, worthy of the name of human beings—solely through the power of natural law, the law of human mortality. Their outer shells dropped away and their truth alone was left. The least among them were transformed into the first, while the first (Vronsky) suddenly became the least; they lost their halos and were humbled; but being humbled, they became immeasurably better, worthier, and more genuine than when they had been the first and the eminent. Hatred and lies began to speak in words of forgiveness and love. In place of vapid social conceptions there appeared only a love of humanity. Each one forgave and supported the other. Narrow, exclusive feelings of class suddenly vanished and became unthinkable, and these cardboard figures began to resemble genuine humans! No one was found guilty: each admitted his own guilt without reservation, and in so doing he was at once acquitted. The reader sensed the existence of the truth of life, entirely real and inescapable, a truth which must be believed; he sensed that all our lives and all our problems—both the pettiest and most shameful, as well as the ones we often consider most serious—are for the most part merely the petty, fantastic scramble of life that falls away and vanishes without a struggle before the moment of life's truth. The most important thing here was showing that such a moment truly exists, even though it rarely appears in all its revealing fullness; and in some lives, indeed, it never appears. The poet sought this moment out and revealed it to us in all its awful truth. The poet proved that this truth exists in actual fact, not only as a matter of faith, not only as an ideal, but inescapably, unavoidably, and in plain view. I think that this is precisely what the poet wanted to prove to us when he began his poem. The Russian reader certainly had to be reminded of this everlasting truth: many among us have begun to lose sight of it. The author has done a good deed in reminding us of this, to say nothing of the fact that he has done it as an artist of exceptional power.

Thereafter the novel continued its progress; and then, somewhat to my surprise, I encountered in its part six a scene that reflected the actual topic of the day; most importantly, the scene developed not in any deliberate, tendentious way but sprang from the very artistic essence of the novel. Nevertheless, I repeat that I did not expect this and was somewhat surprised by it: I still did not anticipate such reference to the burning issue of the day. Somehow I did not think that the author would resolve to allow his characters to develop as far as these "Pillars of Hercules." It is true that the entire significance of our lives today lies in these "pillars" and in the drastic conclusions that are drawn; without them the novel would have had an indeterminate air that would be far from corresponding either to immediate or substantive Russian interests: a certain little corner of life would have been portrayed, with deliberate disregard for what is most important and most disturbing in it. However, it seems that I am entering specifically into literary criticism, and that is not my concern. I wanted only to point out this one scene. It is only a matter of two characters depicted from the very aspect that now makes them most characteristic for us;

and in doing that, the author has shown us, in a most interesting way, the present social significance of the category of person to which these two characters belong.

They are both hereditary noblemen and dyed-in-the-wool landowners; the scene in which they are depicted occurs after the peasant reform. They have both been serf landowners, and now the question is: what will remain of those noblemen—in the sense of their status as noblemen—after the peasant reform? Since the type represented by these two landowners is very common and widespread, the question, in part, is answered by the author. One of them is Stiva Oblonsky, an egotist, an urbane Epicurean, an inhabitant of Moscow, and a member of the English Club. Such people are usually regarded as innocent and genial good fellows, affable egotists who do no one any harm, witty, and enjoying their pleasures to the full. Such people often have large families as well; they are kind to their wives and children but give them little thought. They are very fond of easy women, but of the respectable sort, of course. They have scant education, but love refinement and art and love to converse on all subjects. After the peasant reform this type of nobleman at once realized what was happening: he considered and calculated that he would still have something left and, consequently, there was no point in changing his life, and—*après moi le déluge*. He doesn't trouble himself with thinking about the fate of his wife and children. Through connections and the remnants of his estate, he is spared the fate of the "Jack of Hearts"; but should his estate evaporate and were he to find it impossible to receive a salary for doing nothing, he might well become one of this band, though naturally exerting all the powers of his mind (which are at times very sharp) to become as respectable and as well-bred a "Jack" as possible. In the old days, of course, he had to send off some of his serfs to the army in order to provide for his gambling debts or his mistress; but such memories never troubled him, and he has forgotten them altogether. Although he is an aristocrat, he never put much stock in his pedigree; and with the abolition of serfdom such notions disappeared for him forever: the only *people* that mattered for him were *the man whose favor he might win*, the bureaucrat of certain rank, and the rich man. The railway magnate and the banker became forces in society, and he quickly undertook to establish relations and friendship with them. And so the conversation begins with Levin reproaching him—Levin being his relative and another landowner (but one of a completely opposite type who lives on his estate). Levin chides him for visiting railway magnates and attending their dinners and festivities, such people being dubious and harmful in Levin's view. Oblonsky rejects Levin's reproach sarcastically. And, on the whole, once they became related by marriage, their relations rather soured. In our day, in any case, the scoundrel who takes issue with the honest man always has the upper hand because he has the appearance of merit deriving from common sense, while the honest man, trying to be an idealist, looks like a fool. Their conversation takes place on a summer night, while out hunting. The hunters are spending the night in a peasant barn, lying on the hay. Oblonsky is trying to prove that it makes no sense to be contemptuous of railway magnates, their scheming, their quick profits, their wheedling of railway concessions, and their speculation; he claims that they are people like everyone else, working and using their heads, and thus are agents of progress.

> "But any acquisition that doesn't correspond to the work put into it is dishonest," says Levin.
>
> "So who will determine the proper proportion?" Oblonsky continues. "You haven't defined the line between honest and dishonest work. The fact that I receive a higher salary than my chief clerk, even though he knows the job better than I—is that dishonest?"
>
> "I don't know."
>
> "Well, I'll tell you: the fact that your work on the estate brings you, let's say, an extra five thousand, while this peasant, no matter how hard he works, won't get more than fifty rubles is just as dishonest as my earning more than my chief clerk. . . ."
>
> "But wait," Levin continues, "You say that it's unjust for me to get five thousand rubles while the peasant gets fifty: that's true. It's unjust, and I feel it, but. . . ."
>
> "Yes, you feel it, but you won't give him your estate," said Stepan Arkadievich, as if deliberately trying to provoke Levin. . . .
>
> "I won't give away my estate because no one is demanding that I do, and even if I wanted to give it away, I couldn't . . . and there's no one to give it to."
>
> "Give it to this peasant; he won't turn it down."
>
> "Very well, but how should I give it to him? Should I go off with him to execute a deed of purchase?"
>
> "I don't know, but if you're convinced that you don't have the right to. . . ."
>
> "I'm not convinced at all. I feel, rather, that I don't have the right to give it away, that I have obligations to the land and to my family."

"But wait: if you think that this inequality is unjust, then why don't you act accordingly. . . .

"I do act, only in a negative sense, in the sense that I am not going to try to increase the difference in the situation that exists between me and him."

"No, please, excuse me: this is a paradox. . . ."

"That's how it is, my friend. You must choose one or the other: either regard the present order of society as just, and insist on your rights; or admit that you are enjoying privileges that are unjust, *as I do, and take real pleasure in them.*"

"No, if it were unjust you couldn't take real pleasure in these benefits; *at least I couldn't; for me, what is most important is to feel that I am not to blame.*"

2. The Issue of the Day

Such was their conversation. And you have to agree that here we have the issue of the day, in fact, we have everything that constitutes the heart of our issue of the day. And how many characteristic, purely Russian traits we see here! In the first place, some forty years ago all these ideas were barely beginning even in Europe; even there, only a few people knew anything about Saint-Simon and Fourier, the original "idealistic" exponents of such ideas, while here—here scarcely fifty people in the whole country knew of this new movement that had begun in western Europe. And now, suddenly, a couple of landowners out hunting, spending the night in a peasant's barn, begin talking of these "questions," and talking in a most characteristic and knowledgeable fashion, so that at least the negative aspect of the question is already resolved, signed, and sealed by them. It's true that these are landowners from the best society; they have conversations at the English Club, they read newspapers, the follow legal trials from newspaper accounts and other sources; nevertheless, the fact alone that such highly idealistic poppycock is recognized as the most urgent topic of conversation by people who are certainly not professors or specialists but simply society people—Oblonskys and Levins—this fact, I say, is one of the most characteristic peculiarities of the present Russian state of mind. The second very characteristic trait in this conversation conveyed by the author-artist is that the man who is deciding the question of the justice of these new ideas is one who doesn't give a hang for the happiness of the proletariat and the poor; on the contrary, given the opportunity, he would strip them like bark from a linden tree. But with a light heart, and with the pleasure of someone making a pun, he at once affirms the bankruptcy of the entire history of humanity and declares the existing order to be the height of absurdity. "I agree fully with this," he says in effect. Note that it's these very same Stivas who are always the first to agree with such things. With a single stroke he has condemned the entire Christian order, the individual, the family; oh, this costs him nothing. Note also that we in Russia have no science, but these gentlemen—who acknowledge with complete lack of shame that they have no science and that they have begun speaking about this only yesterday, using someone else's ideas to do so—still resolve questions of such magnitude without the slightest hesitation. But here is the third very characteristic feature: this gentleman states frankly: "It must be one or the other: either admit that the present order of society is just and then insist on your rights, *or admit that we are enjoying unjust privileges, as I do, and take full pleasure in them*." In other words, having in essence signed the sentence on the whole of Russia and condemned her, as he has his own family and the future of his children, he declares frankly that this is of no concern to him: "I admit that I am a scoundrel, but I shall remain a scoundrel for my own pleasure. *Après moi le déluge*." The reason he is so calm is that he still has some capital; but should he lose it—why shouldn't he become a "Jack of Hearts"? That would be the most logical step. And so here we have this citizen, this family man, this Russian person—what a very characteristic, purely Russian trait! You may say that he is still an exception. But what kind of exception can he be? Just recall how much cynicism we've seen over these last twenty years, how easily people have made deviations and turnabouts, how lacking they have been in deep-seated convictions, how quick they have been to adopt the first convictions to come along, with the aim, naturally, of selling them for a few pennies tomorrow. There is no moral reserve except *après moi le déluge*.

But most curious of all is that along with this numerous and prevalent type is another—another type of Russian nobleman and landowner who is his direct opposite, his opposite in every way. This is Levin; but there are multitudes of Levins in Russia, almost as many as there are Oblonskys. I am not talking about his personality, the character the artist created for him in the novel; I am talking only about one trait of his essence, but it is the most basic trait; and I maintain that this trait is so terribly widespread among us that it is amazing—I mean given our cynicism and our primitive attitude toward our common task. For some time now this trait has been constantly evident; people with this trait are frantically, almost pathologically striving to find answers to their questions; they are steadfastly hoping and passionately believing, even though they are still able to resolve scarcely anything. This trait is completely expressed in Levin's answer to Stiva: "No, if it were unjust you couldn't take real pleasure in these benefits; *at least I couldn't; for me, what is most important is to feel that I am not to blame*."

And in fact he will not be at peace until he decides whether he is or is not to blame. And do you know how difficult it will be for him to find peace? He will go to the very Pillars of Hercules, and if it is necessary, if it truly is necessary and he proves it to himself, then, in contrast to Stiva, who says: "I may be a scoundrel, but I will go on living for my own pleasure," Levin will turn into a "Vlas," into Nekrasov's Vlas, whose heart melted in a fit of great awe and who gave away his money.

> And, gathering alms, the world he roamed;
> To build God's temple here, he sought.

And if he does not go off to gather alms for building a church, then he will do something on the same scale and with the same zeal. Note this trait, I hasten to repeat once more: there is a multitude, a huge multitude of these new people today, of this new root of Russian people who *must have the truth*, the truth alone, without the lies we unthinkingly accept; these are people who, in order to find this truth, are prepared to give away absolutely everything they have. These people have also made their presence known in the last twenty years, and they are becoming more and more visible, although earlier, even before Peter the Great, it was always possible to anticipate their presence. This is the developing future Russia of honorable people who need only the truth. Oh, there's a lot of intolerance in them as well: through lack of experience they reject every sort of convention and even every attempt at interpretation. But I want only to declare as strongly as I can that they are moved by genuine feeling. Something else very characteristic about them is that they are a terribly long way from coming to terms with one another and still belong to the broadest range of categories and subscribe to the broadest range of convictions: here we have aristocrats and proletarians, men of the cloth and unbelievers, rich men and poor, scholars and the uneducated, old men and young girls, Slavophiles and Westerners. There are immense differences among their convictions, but their striving for honesty and truth is steadfast and constant; and for a word of truth each one of them will give up his life and all his privileges; as I say, he will become a Vlas. People may object that this is a wild fantasy, that such integrity and such a *quest for integrity* does not exist among us. I proclaim that it does exist, side by side with terrible corruption; that I see and sense these people of tomorrow, to whom the future of Russia will belong; that they cannot be seen now; and that the artist who, setting this obsolete cynic Stiva side by side with his new man Levin, juxtaposed this hopeless, corrupt, multitudinous Russian society—which has already ended its life through its own verdict on itself, however—with the society of the new truth, a society that cannot live with the conviction that it is to blame and that will give up everything in order to cleanse its heart of its guilt. Also remarkable here is the fact that our society really is divided almost only into these two categories—so broad are they and so completely do they embrace Russian life—naturally, after one has eliminated the mass of completely lazy, untalented, and indifferent people. But the most characteristic, the most Russian trait of this "issue of the day" to which the author has drawn our attention is that his new man, his Levin, *does not know how* to resolve the question that is troubling him. I mean to say, he has already *almost* resolved it in his heart, and not in his own favor, when he *suspects* that he is *to blame*; but something solid, direct, and real arises from his whole being and still holds him back from pronouncing the final verdict. On the other hand, Stiva, who does not care whether he is to blame or not, can decide without the least hesitation; this is even to his advantage: "If everything is absurd and there is nothing sacred, then one can do anything he likes; I still have some time ahead of me; judgment day isn't tomorrow, after all." It is also interesting that it is precisely the easiest part of the question that has troubled Levin and led him to an impasse; and this is something purely Russian that the author has quite correctly noted: the whole point is that all these ideas and questions among us in Russia are only a matter of theory; they have all come to us from an alien order of things, from Europe, where they have long had their own historical and practical aspects. So what is to be done? Both our noblemen are Europeans, and it is not easy for them to free themselves from European authority; even here they must give Europe its due. And so Levin, the Russian heart, confuses the purely Russian and only possible answer to the question with the European approach to the question. He confuses the Christian solution with historical "right." For the sake of clarity, let us visualize the following little scene:

Levin stands deep in thought after his conversation when hunting with Stiva that night; and, as an honest soul, he has an agonizing longing to solve the question that is troubling him now and that must have been troubling him for a long time previously.

"Yes," he thinks, halfway to a decision. "If one really looks at the matter, then why do we—as Veslovsky was saying the other day—'eat, drink, hunt and do nothing, while the poor man has a life of everlasting toil'? Yes, Stiva is right, I *must* share my estate with the poor and go off to work for them."

Next to Levin stands "the poor man," and he says, "That's truly what you must do; it's your duty to give your estate to us, the poor, and to go and work for us." Levin emerges as completely right, and the "poor man" as completely wrong, at least when they decide the matter in what might be called its higher sense. But this is just where the whole difference in approach to the question lies. For the moral solution must not be confused with the historical one; otherwise there will be hopeless confusion, which is happening even now, particularly in the heads of Russian theoreticians as well as in the heads of the scoundrel Stivas and in the heads of the pure-in-heart Levins. In Europe, life and practice have already posed the question—though absurdly in terms of its ideal solution, but still realistically in terms of its current development, and without confusing the two different views—the moral and the historical—at least insofar as it is possible not to confuse them. Let me continue to explain my idea, though briefly.

3. The Issue of the Day in Europe

Europe had its feudalism and its knights. But over the course of more than a thousand years the bourgeoisie gathered its strength and finally joined battle everywhere; it defeated the knights, drove them out, and then—it set itself up in their place. The truth of the saying "Ote-toi de là que je m'y mette" ("Get out of the way so I can take your place") was demonstrated in practice. But having taken the place of their former masters and taken over their property, the bourgeoisie totally bypassed the people, the proletarian; refusing to accept him as a brother, they transformed him, in exchange for a piece of bread, into a work force for their own well-being. Our Russian Stiva decides privately that he is in the wrong but deliberately chooses to go on being a scoundrel because he has a fine, soft life; the foreign Stiva does not agree with our Russian one and sees himself as being entirely in the right, and of course in his own terms he is more logical, for in his view there is no *right* here at all, there is only *history*, the historical course of events. He has taken the place of the knight because he conquered the knight by force, and he understands very well that the proletarian, who was still insignificant and weak during the struggle of the bourgeois with the knight, may very well gather his strength; indeed, he is gathering it with every day that passes. He can foresee quite clearly that when the proletarian is strong enough, he will push him aside, as the bourgeois once did the knight, and will say the very same words to him: "Get out of the way so I can take your place." There is no question of right here, there is only history. Oh, he would be ready for a compromise, for coming to terms somehow with his enemy; he's even made an attempt at it. But since he has very clearly deduced—and also knows from experience—that his enemy is not at all disposed to make peace, that he does not want to share but wants *everything;* since he knows, moreover, that if he makes any concession, he will only weaken himself—he has decided to yield nothing and is preparing to do battle. His situation may be hopeless, but it is human nature to strengthen one's spirits before battle; he does not despair but, on the contrary, girds up his loins for the fight, using all means at his disposal and exerting all his efforts so long as he has strength; he is weakening his opponent and, for the moment, that is all he is doing.

And so that's the point at which the matter now stands in Europe. It is true that formerly, and not that long ago, there was a *moral* approach to the question over in Europe as well; there were Fourierists and Cabetists, there were questionings, arguments, and debates about various most subtle issues. But now the leaders of the proletariat have put these things aside until the right time comes. They plainly want to do battle; they are organizing an army and marshaling it in their associations; they are raising funds, and they are confident of victory: "And then, after our victory, everything will take shape of itself in a practical fashion, although it's quite possible that this will happen only after rivers of blood have been shed." The bourgeois realizes that the leaders of the proletariat are enticing their followers simply with the prospect of plunder, and that, accordingly, there is no point in raising the moral aspect of the matter. However, even among the vanguard of the proletariat today there are a few ringleaders who also propound the moral rights of the poor. Those who head the movement tolerate these ringleaders specifically for show, so as to enhance their cause and give it an appearance of higher justice. Among these "moral" ringleaders are many schemers, but there are also many ardent believers. They state plainly that they want nothing for themselves but are working only for humanity; that they want to establish a new order of things for the good of humanity. But here the bourgeois can meet them on rather firm ground and point out that they want to compel him to become a brother to the proletarian and to share his property under threat of club and blood. Although this is rather close to the truth, the ringleaders answer that they in no way consider the bourgeoisie capable of becoming brothers to the people and that is why they are simply marching against them in force; they entirely exclude the bourgeoisie from their brotherhood: "Brotherhood will develop later, among the proletarians, but you—you are the hundred million heads condemned to extermination, and nothing more. You must pass from the scene, for the good of humanity." Other ringleaders plainly say that they need no brotherhood at all, that Christianity is nothing more than rubbish, and that the future of humanity will be built on scientific foundations. None of this, of course, can move or convince the bourgeois. He understands and replies that this society on scientific foundations is pure fantasy; that they have an image of humanity that is utterly different from the one nature has created; that it is difficult and impossible for a person to renounce his unconditional right to private property, the family, and freedom; that they demand too many sacrifices from their man of the future, as an individual; that it is possible to fashion such a human being only by means of terrible violence, after subjecting him to a terrible system of spying and continuous control by a most despotic power. In conclusion, the bourgeois challenges them to show him the power that could unite the man of the future into a society based on accord and not on force. In reply, the ringleaders cite utility and necessity, recognized by humans themselves, and the fact that, in order to save themselves from destruction and death, humans will consent voluntarily to make all the concessions demanded of them. The objections made to this point are that utility and self-preservation alone are never enough to engender complete and voluntary unity;

that there is no utility that can replace self-will and the rights of the individual; that these forces and motives are too weak, and that all this, accordingly, remains a matter of conjecture as before. Were the leaders' actions to stem only from the moral aspect of the matter, the proletariat would pay no attention to them; and if they do follow them now and organize themselves to do battle, then it is only because they have been enticed by the promise of plunder and stirred up by the prospect of destruction and battle. In the final analysis, therefore, the moral aspect of the question should be entirely discarded because it will not withstand the slightest criticism; they should simply prepare to fight.

That is how the Europeans approach the matter. Both sides are terribly wrong, and both sides will perish in their sins. I repeat, what is most difficult for us Russians is that even our Levins are pondering these very same questions when the only possible solution to the question, the Russian one—which holds true not only for the Russians but for all of humanity—is the moral, i.e., the Christian approach. Such an approach is unthinkable in Europe, although even there, sooner or later, after rivers of blood and a hundred million heads, it will have to be acknowledged, for only in it is there a way out.

4. The Russian Solution to the Problem

If you have felt it a hard thing only "to eat, drink, do nothing, and go hunting," and if you have really felt this, and if you really feel sorry for "the poor," of whom there are so many, then give them your property; if you wish, donate it to the common good; go and work for all and "you will find your reward in heaven, where they neither hoard nor covet." Go, like Vlas, with

> All the might of his great soul
> Devoted to his Godly cause.

And if you do not want to collect money for God's temple, as Vlas did, then take some concern for the enlightenment of the soul of this poor man; improve him, teach him. And if, indeed, everyone did as you and gave his property to the poor, then all the wealth of the wealthy of the world, divided among all, would be no more than a drop in the sea. And therefore we must take more concern for enlightenment, for education, and for the strengthening of love. Then wealth will grow in actual fact; and it will be genuine wealth, because wealth is not found in golden raiment but in the joy of common unity and in the steadfast hope of each for the help of all others in time of need, to him and to his children. And do not say that you are only a single, weak person and that if you are the only one to give away your property and go off to serve humanity, you will thereby accomplish nothing and make nothing better. On the contrary, if there be but a few such as you, the cause will be advanced. And, really, there is not *necessarily* any need even to give away your property, for any kind of *necessity* here, where love is the issue, will have the air of conformity, regulations, and literal-mindedness. The conviction that one has fulfilled the letter of the law leads only to pride, formalism, and indolence. One must do only that which the heart commands: if it commands you to give away your property, then give it away; if it commands you to go and work for the benefit of all, then go and do so. But even here, do not follow the example of some idealists who at once take up a wheelbarrow and say: "I'm not a nobleman; I want to work like a peasant." The wheelbarrow is only another expression of conformity.

No, it's quite the contrary: if you feel that you will be useful to all as a scholar, then go to university and keep sufficient means to finance your studies. It is not the giving away of your property and the donning of a peasant coat that is obligatory: all that is only literal-mindedness and formalism; what is obligatory and important is merely *your determination to do all for the sake of active love,* all that you possibly can, all that you yourself sincerely believe is possible for you to do. All these efforts to "simplify" one's life are merely the assuming of a disguise, disrespectful to the People and demeaning to you. You are too "complex" to simplify yourself and, in any case, your education will not let you become a peasant. You would do better to elevate the peasant to your level of "complexity." You must only be sincere and open-hearted; this is better than any sort of "simplification." But above all, do not let yourself be frightened; do not quote our proverb: "One man on the field is not a warrior," and so on. Every one who has conceived a sincere desire to find the truth is already awfully powerful. Likewise, do not ape certain phrase-mongers who continually repeat for all to hear: "They won't allow us to do anything; they tie our hands; they fill our hearts with despair and disillusionment!" and so on. All these are only phrase-mongers and characters from some second-rate poem, idlers who are showing off. He who wishes to be useful can, even with hands literally tied, accomplish a mass of good deeds. A real worker who sets out to do something will at once see so many tasks before him that he will not start to complain that he isn't allowed to do anything; he will surely find something and manage to do it. All genuine workers know this. The study of Russia alone will take up so much of our time, because it is only the rarest person among us who knows our Russia. Complaints about disillusionment are utterly stupid: joy at the edifice which is being erected should soothe any soul and assuage any thirst, even though your own contribution to the edifice may have been merely a few grains of sand. Your sole reward is love, should you merit it. Let's suppose you need no reward; still, you are working in the cause of love, and so you cannot help but encourage love. But let no one tell you that you should have done all this even without love, for your own benefit, as it were, and that if you hadn't you would have been forced to do so. No, we in Russia must implant other convictions, and particularly in regard to conceptions of freedom, equality, and brotherhood. The way the world conceives freedom today is as license, whereas real freedom lies only in overcoming the self and the will so as ultimately to achieve a moral condition in which one at each moment is the real master of himself. But giving license to your desires only leads to your enslavement. That is why almost the whole of today's world supposes that freedom lies in financial security and in laws guaranteeing that financial security: "I have money and so I can do whatever I like; I have money and so I will not perish and will not have to ask help from anyone; not having to ask for anyone's help is the highest freedom." Yet in essence this is not freedom but slavery once again, a slavery that comes from money. On the contrary, the very highest form of freedom is not laying up money and seeking security in it, but "dividing up all that you have and going off to serve everyone." If a person is capable of that, if he is capable of overcoming himself to that extent—is he then not free? This is the highest manifestation of the will! And then, what does equality mean in today's civilized world? A jealous watching of one another, conceit, and envy: "He's clever; he's a Shakespeare who takes pride in his talent; he must be humbled, destroyed." Meanwhile, genuine equality says: "What do I care if you are more talented than I, more clever, more handsome? I'm glad of it, rather, because I love you. But though I may be less important than you, I respect myself as a person; and you know this and respect me yourself, and I am happy with your respect. If you, through your abilities, can bring me and everyone else a hundredfold more benefit than I can bring you, then I bless you for it; I marvel at you and thank you, and in no way do I hold my awe for you as something shameful; on the contrary, I am happy that I am grateful to you, and if I work for you and for all in so far as my feeble abilities allow, then it is certainly not to try to balance my account with you, but because I love you all."

If all people speak in this way, then, of course, they will also become brothers, and not merely because of economic benefit but because of the fullness of the joy of life, because of the fullness of love.

Some may say that this is a fantasy, that this "Russian solution to the problem" is the "Kingdom of Heaven" and is possible only in the Kingdom of Heaven. Yes, the Stivas would get very angry if the Kingdom of Heaven were to arrive. But one must take into consideration the fact alone that there is much less fantasy and much more plausibility in this "Russian solution to the problem" than in the European solution. Such people—the "Vlases," I mean—we have already seen and continue to see among all our social classes; we even see them quite often; Europe's "man of the future" we have never yet seen anywhere, and he himself has vowed to come only after wading through rivers of blood. You may say that individuals, and tens of individuals, are of no help and that we must strive for well-known, universal principles and forms of organization. But even if there existed such principles and forms as could organize society without a flaw, and even if it were possible to acquire such principles and forms without trying them in practice—just so, a priori, from heartfelt dreams and "scientific" statistics which, besides, derive from the former social order—then, given people who have not been prepared and fashioned for this new order, no rules could hold up or be put into practice; on the contrary, they would only be a burden. I have unbounded faith in our people of the future and in those who are already beginning now; I was just speaking of them, above, and saying that they had not yet managed to reach any accord, that they seemed very much broken into small groups and camps according to their convictions; yet all of them were seeking the truth before all else and, were they only to learn where that truth could be found, they would be ready to sacrifice all, even their lives, in order to attain it. Believe me, if they set forth on the true path and find this truth at last, they will draw everyone else after them, and not by force but freely. That is what single individuals can do to begin with. And that is the plow with which we can turn over our "Virgin Soil."

Rather than go preaching to people about what they ought to be, show them through your own example. Carry it out yourselves in practice, and everyone will follow you. What is utopian, what is impossible here I do not understand! It's true that we are very corrupt, very fainthearted, and therefore we do not believe and we scoff. But the ones who matter now are scarcely we, they are the people of the future. The People are pure in heart, but they need to be educated. But the pure in heart are rising up in our milieu as well, and that is what truly matters! This is what we must believe above all, and this is what we must learn to discern. And for the pure in heart I have one piece of advice: self-control and self-mastery before taking any first step. Carry it out yourselves before compelling anyone else—herein lies the entire secret of the first step.

An Answer to a Letter

The editor of *A Writer's Diary* received the following letter:

Novokhopersk
February 25, 1877

Dear Fedor Mikhailovich,

On January 12 I sent you two rubles and fifty kopecks with a request that you send me your publication, *A Writer's Diary*. I learned from the newspapers that the first issue came out on February 1; today is already the 25th, yet I still have not received it! It would be extremely interesting to learn the reason for this. I don't know how you feel, but for me such an attitude toward your subscribers seems more than peculiar!

If you do take it into your head sometime to send me your publication, I ask you to address it to Dr. V. V. K——n, Zemstvo Town Hospital, Novokhopersk.

V. K——n

Here is the editor's reply:

Dear Sir,

Unfortunately, complaints about issues of our journal not being received come rather often, and at the beginning of the year in particular. When we check our files we always find that these issues have long been sent off and, accordingly, are being lost en route. The percentage of such losses is, of course, very small in comparison with the number of subscribers, but the losses invariably continue, and with periodicals other than our own as well. Normally, without making excuses and in order to satisfy our subscribers more quickly, we send a second issue: how can we find the one that has gone astray! This matter gets better in mid-year, and by the end of the year there are scarcely any losses.

But you, dear sir, out of all the possibilities as to why your issue did not reach you, unhesitatingly picked one—namely, that the editor was trying to cheat you. This is clear from the tone of your letter and especially from the words: "If you do take it into your head sometime to send me your publication, I ask you . . . ," etc. So you plainly suppose that the editor has deliberately held back your issue and you do not refrain from expressing your doubt that you will ever receive it. In consequence, the editor hastens to return your two rubles and fifty kopecks and requests that you trouble him no further. The editor is compelled to do this owing to an understandable and natural motive which, dear sir, will probably not surprise you.

March

1

1. Once More on the Subject That, Sooner or Later, Constantinople Must Be Ours

In June of last year, in the June issue of my *Diary*, I said that Constantinople "sooner or later, must be ours." It was an impassioned and a glorious time then: all of Russia had risen up in heart and spirit, and the People were going "of their own accord" to serve Christ and Orthodoxy against the unbelievers for the sake of our brethren in faith and blood, the Slavs. The article I wrote then may have been called "The Utopian Conception of History," but I myself believed strongly in my own words and did not consider them utopian; indeed, even now I am prepared to confirm them literally. This is what I wrote about Constantinople then: "Yes, the Golden Horn and Constantinople—all that will be ours. . . . and in the first place, it will happen of its own accord precisely because the time has come, and if the time has not yet arrived just now, then it is truly at hand, as all the signs indicate. This is a natural result; this is something decreed by Nature herself, as it were. If this has not happened before, it was simply because the time was not yet ripe."

Thereafter I explained my thought as to why the time was not yet ripe and could not have been ripe formerly. "Had Peter then hit upon the notion of seizing Constantinople rather than founding Petersburg," I wrote:

> then it seems to me that he would have abandoned the idea after some thought, even if he had had sufficient strength to crush the Sultan, precisely because the matter was still inopportune and might have even led to Russia's ruination.

> If in Finnish Petersburg we couldn't avoid the influence of neighboring Germans (who, despite their usefulness, paralyzed Russian development before its true path had been clearly revealed), then how, in the huge and distinctive city of Constantinople with its remnants of a mighty and ancient civilization—how could we have avoided the influence of the Greeks, a nation far more subtle than the coarse Germans, a nation with whom we have much more in common than the Germans, who are utterly unlike us? The Throne would have at once been surrounded by crowds of courtiers; they would have become educated and learned sooner than the Russians; they would have enchanted Peter himself, not to mention his immediate successors, exploiting his weak point by demonstrating their knowledge and skill in seamanship. In short, they would have gained political power in Russia; they would have at once dragged her off on some new Asiatic road, into another sort of seclusion, and of course Russia of that time would not have survived it. The development of Russia's strength and her sense of nationhood would have been halted in their course. The mighty Great Russian would have remained in isolation in his gloomy and snowy North, serving as no more than raw material for the renewal of Tsargrad and ultimately, perhaps, the Russian would have found it unnecessary even to follow Constantinople. The South of Russia would have fallen entirely into the clutches of the Greeks. Orthodoxy itself might even have divided into two entirely separate worlds: one in a renewed Tsargad, the other in old Russia. . . . In short, the matter would have been most untimely. Now, however, things are quite different.

Now (I wrote), now Russia can take possession of Constantinople and do so without transferring her capital there, something that would have been impossible to avoid in Peter's time and even long after him. Now Tsargrad could be ours, and not as the capital of Russia but (I added) also not as the capital as Slavdom as a whole, as some people envisage: "Slavdom as a whole, without Russia, would exhaust itself there in struggling with the Greeks, even if it could manage to create some sort of political unity from its various entities. But to leave Constantinople as a legacy to the Greeks alone is now utterly impossible: we must not give them such a critical point on the globe; this would be altogether too generous a gift to them."

But in the name of what, in the name of what *moral* right could Russia make a claim on Constantinople? What lofty purpose could we use as a basis to demand it from Europe?

> On just this lofty purpose: as leader of Orthodoxy, as its protector and guardian, a role set out for Russia since Ivan III, who placed as an emblem the double-headed eagle of Tsargrad above the ancient coat of arms of Russia, but a role revealed clearly only after Peter the Great, when Russia realized that she had the power to fulfill this mission and in fact became the actual and only guardian both of Orthodoxy and of the nations who profess it. This is the reason and the *right* to ancient Tsargrad, one that would be clear and inoffensive even to the Slavs who guard their independence most jealously, or even to the Greeks themselves. This would be the means to reveal the essence of the political relationships that must inevitably ensue in Russia toward all the other Orthodox nationalities, Slavic and Greek alike: Russia is their protector and even, perhaps, their leader, but not their ruler; she is their mother, but not their mistress. And if she should become their sovereign at some time, then it would only be because they would have proclaimed her so, allowing themselves to keep all those things by which they would define their own independence and individuality.

Of course, I conceived all these considerations in my June article last year as by no means bound to immediate fulfillment, but only as things that certainly must come to pass when their historical moment and destined time arrive and whose proximity or remoteness, though impossible to predict, may nonetheless be sensed. Nine months have passed since then. There is no need, I think, to recall those nine months: we all are aware of this exuberant period, initially full of hopes and then strange and disturbing, a period that has by no means yet come to an end, so that God alone knows (I think this the only way one can express it) what its resolution will be: will we draw our sword, or will the matter once more be dragged out endlessly by some compromise? But whatever may happen, I felt that at this particular moment, somehow, I must say a few supplementary and explanatory words to my June musings on the fate of Tsargrad. Whatever may happen there now—whether it be peace or concessions once again from Russia—sooner or later Tsargrad will be ours. That is what I want to reaffirm at this particular time, but now from a rather different point of view.

Yes, the city must be ours, not only because it is an illustrious port, because of the straits, because it is "the focus of the universe," "the earth's navel"; not because of the long-acknowledged need for such an enormous giant as Russia to emerge at last from his locked room in which he has already grown to reach the ceiling—

to emerge into open spaces where he can breathe the free air of the seas and oceans. I want to set before you only one factor, also of the very greatest importance, that makes it impossible for Russia to avoid Constantinople. I set this factor before the others because, as it seems to me, no one now is taking it into account or, at least, they have long forgotten to take it into account, whereas it may be among the very most important ones.

2. The Russian People Have Completely Matured to a Sane Conception of the Eastern Question from Their Own Standpoint

It may seem ridiculous to say it, but the four centuries of Turkish oppression in the East was, on the one hand, even beneficial to Christianity and Orthodoxy there—in a negative sense, of course, yet it worked to strengthen them and, most important, to unite them and make them one, in just the same way that the two centuries of Tatar domination also once worked to strengthen the church here in Russia. The oppressed and harassed Christian population of the East saw Christ and belief in Him as their only consolation and the church as the single and final remnant of their national personality and particularity. This was their last and only hope, the last plank left from their wrecked ship; for still, the church preserved these populations as a nationality, while faith in Christ prevented them—or parts of them, at least—from merging entirely with their conquerors, forgetting their heritage and their past. The oppressed nations themselves sensed all this and understood it very clearly; and they huddled more tightly around the cross. On the other hand, from the very conquest of Constantinople, the peoples of the whole immense Christian East involuntarily and suddenly turned their prayerful gaze toward distant Russia, which only then had emerged from enslavement to the Tatars, and seemed to foresee her future might and their future, all-uniting center of salvation. Russia quickly and unhesitatingly took up the banner of the East and placed the double-headed eagle of Tsargrad higher than her own ancient crest; and in so doing, as it were, she took up her obligations toward the whole of Orthodoxy: to preserve it and all the peoples who profess it from final destruction. At the same time, the entire Russian People as well completely endorsed the new mission of Russia and their tsar in the future fates of the entire Eastern world. Since that time the People have firmly and unwaveringly given as the principal, beloved appelation of their tsar the word "Orthodox," "Orthodox Tsar"—and so they still see him. Having thus named their tsar, the People thereby essentially acknowledged his mission as well—his mission as guardian and unifier and, when God's commandment thunders forth, as liberator of Orthodoxy and of all Christendom professing it, from Mohammedan barbarism and Western heresy. Two centuries ago, and beginning with Peter the Great particularly, the beliefs and the hopes of the peoples of the East began to be realized in fact: the sword of Russia had already shone forth more than once in defense of the East. It was evident that the peoples of the East as well could not fail to see the tsar of Russia as a liberator and also as their own future tsar. But in the course of these two centuries European education and European influence appeared among them as well. The upper, educated portion of the people, their intelligentsia, little by little grew more indifferent to the idea of Orthodoxy, as did the intelligentsia in Russia, and even began to deny that in this idea lay the renewal and resurrection into a new, grand life for both the East and Russia. In Russia, for instance, a huge portion of the educated class stopped regarding this idea as Russia's principal mission and the pledge of her future vital force; instead they began to find her mission in new areas. Many, in Western fashion, began to see in the church no more than dead formalism, peculiarity, ritualism, and, since the end of the last century, even prejudice and bigotry: the spirit, the idea, the living force was forgotten. There appeared economic ideas of Western character, there appeared new political doctrines, there appeared a new morality that strove to correct the old one and to stand above it. There appeared, at last, science, and it could not help but introduce unbelief in the former ideas. . . . Apart from that, and as a most important factor, ideas of nationality began to be born among the peoples of the East: the fear suddenly arose that once liberated from the Turkish yoke they would fall under the yoke of Russia. Yet in the minds of the many millions of our simple People and in their tsars the idea of the liberation of the East and the church of Christ never died. The movement that caught up the Russian People last summer proved that the People had forgotten none of their former hopes and beliefs; the movement even astonished the immense portion of our intelligentsia to the point where they plainly could not accept it, regarded it skeptically and mockingly, began assuring everyone—and themselves above all—that this movement had been invented and falsified by some disreputable people who wanted to push themselves ahead into prominent positions. In fact, in our time, who among our intelligentsia—apart from a small group that has separated itself from the general chorus—could admit that our People might be capable of *consciously* understanding their political, social, and moral mission? How could they have admitted that this coarse, dark mass, enserfed until only recently and now drinking itself to death, could know and be certain that its mission was the service of Christ, and that of its tsar was the guardianship of Christ's faith and the liberation of Orthodoxy? "Granted, this mass never called itself other than Christian, yet it had no concept either of religion or even of Christ; it doesn't know the commonest prayers." That is what usually is said of our People. Who says this? You may think it is the German pastor who cultivated our Stundism, or some visiting European, the correspondent of a political newspaper, or some educated Jew of the higher orders—one of those who does not believe in God and whose numbers have now suddenly multiplied in our midst—or, finally, one of those Russians who have settled abroad and whose image of Russia and her People is merely a drunken peasant woman holding a vodka bottle. Oh, no, this is how the enormous portion of our own Russian and very best society thinks; and they don't even suspect that although our People may not know their prayers, the essence of Christianity, its spirit and its truth, has been preserved and reinforced within them more firmly, perhaps, than within any of the other peoples of this world—and this despite all their flaws. However, the atheist or the Russian European indifferent to matters of religion sees religion only as formalism and bigotry. They find nothing like bigotry among the People, and so they conclude that the People comprehend nothing of religion; they pray, when they need to, to a wooden plank, but are essentially indifferent, and their spirit is crushed by formalism. They can find no Christian spirit in them at all, perhaps because they themselves have long since lost this spirit and do not even know where it is to be found and where it is wafting. These "depraved" and dark People of ours, however, love the humble man and "the fool in Christ": in all their traditions and their legends they preserve the belief that the weak and the oppressed, who suffer unjustly and wrongfully for the sake of Christ, will be raised above the exalted and the powerful when God's judgment and pronouncement are heard. Our

People also love to tell the story of the grand and glorious life of their great, chaste, and humble Christian hero Ilya Muromets, fighter for truth, liberator of the poor and the weak, humble and unassuming, faithful and pure in heart. And having, honoring, and loving such a hero, can our People not believe in the triumph of the now oppressed nations, our brethren, in the East? Our People honor the memory of their great and humble religious hermits and saintly men; they love to tell their children stories of the great Christian martyrs. They know these stories and have learned them by heart; I myself first heard them from the People, told with perception and reverence, and they have remained in my heart. Aside from that, every year our People themselves provide from their midst great repentant "Vlases" who give away all they own and go with tender feeling to perform the humble and great feat of truth, work, and poverty. . . . However, I will speak of the Russian People later; someday they will manage to make others begin to understand them or, at least, to take them into account. Others will realize that the Russian People indeed do count for something. They will realize, at last, this important factor as well: that not even once in the great, or even in the barely important moments of Russian history, could Russia manage without her People; that Russia is *of the People;* that Russia is not Austria; that in every significant moment of our historical life, the matter was always resolved in the spirit of the People and from their viewpoint, by the tsars of the People acting in the greatest degree of unity with them. Our intelligentsia usually passes over this remarkably important historical factor with scarcely a glance, and it is always brought to mind suddenly, somehow, when some new fateful moment in history looms ahead. But I've strayed from the topic; I began speaking of Constantinople. . . .

3. The Most Appropriate Thoughts for the Present Time

Through all four centuries of its enslavement, the Eastern church, its officers, and the ecumenical patriarch lived peacefully with Russia and among themselves—in matters of the faith, that is: there were no great disturbances, heresies, or schisms; there were more important things to think about. But here in the present century, and especially in the last twenty years, after the Crimean War, one seemed to smell among them the putrescent odor of a decaying corpse: a sense of the death and decay of the "sick man" and the end of his kingdom has become the dominant and essential feeling. Oh, of course, the final liberation could still be accomplished only by Russia, that same Russia which even now, and at the present moment of general discussions about the East, is still the only one who speaks up for them in Europe, whereas all the other peoples and kingdoms of the enlightened European world would, of course, be happy if all of them—these oppressed peoples of the East—were simply to vanish from the face of the earth. But, alas, though almost all the intelligentsia of the Christian population of the East calls for Russia's help, they fear her as much, perhaps, as the Turks: "Though Russia will liberate us from the Turks, she will swallow us up just as the 'sick man' did and will not allow our national entities to develop"—that is the idée fixe that infects all their hopes! And beyond that, national rivalries even now are being more and more inflamed among them; these began almost as soon as the first rays of the light of education touched those peoples. The very recent discord between the Greek and the Bulgarian churches was, of course, no more than a national dispute in the guise of an ecclesiastical one, and it provides a certain promise of things to come. The ecumenical patriarch, censuring the Bulgarians for disobedience and excommunicating them and the exarch they had elected on their own accord, made it very plain that in matters of faith one must not sacrifice the statutes of the church and church discipline to "the new and pernicious principle of nationality." Meanwhile, he himself, being a Greek and pronouncing his excommunication to the Bulgarians, was doubtlessly serving that same principle of nationality, only in favor of the Greeks against the Slavs. In short, one can predict with some probability that should the "sick man" die, there would at once commence among them disarray and discord which, at first, would have an ecclesiastical nature and which would certainly inflict damage even on Russia herself; damage would be done even if Russia were to exclude herself entirely, or be excluded by circumstances, from participating in solving the Eastern Question. Moreover, these disorders might well be felt even more painfully in Russia should she exclude herself from active and prominent participation in the destinies of the East. And here, suddenly, people will cry out (and not only Europeans, but many leading political thinkers in Russia as well) that should the Turks happen to die off as a state, then Constantinople must be reborn in no way other than as an "international" city, that is, as something intermediate, common, and free so that there should be no disputes over it. A more mistaken idea is impossible to invent.

First of all, there is the very fact that such a magnificent spot on the globe simply will not be allowed to become international, that is, to belong to no one; the English, say, would certainly appear at once with their fleet, in the capacity of friends, specifically to preserve and protect this very "internationality," but in essence to gain possession of Constantinople for their own benefit. And once they've settled in a spot, it's hard to get rid of them; they're a tenacious lot. Moreover, Greeks, Slavs, and Moslems would call in the English themselves, fasten on to them with both hands, and not let them go, the reason being, once again, that same Russia: "They'll defend us from Russia, our liberator," they would say. And this might be all very well had they not seen and understood what the English, and Europe in general, meant for them. Oh, even *now* they know better than anyone that the English (and, indeed, no one in Europe apart from Russia) haven't the least concern about their happiness—the happiness of the whole Christian population of the area, that is. All these Christians know very well that if it were possible to repeat the Bulgarian atrocities of the summer (and this, it seems, is quite possible) quietly and on the sly, somehow, then in Europe the English would be the first to want these murders to be repeated even tenfold—and not from bloodthirstiness, by any means: the peoples over there are humane and enlightened—because such murders, were they multiplied ten times, would exterminate the Christians utterly, would exterminate them to the point that there would be no one on the Balkan peninsula to undertake uprisings against the Turks. And this is the whole essence of the thing: only the dear Turks would remain, and Turkish securities would at once rise on all the European stock markets, while Russia, "with her ambition and plans for conquest," would have to pull up stakes and withdraw more deeply into her own lands for lack of anyone to protect. The Balkan Christians know all too well that these are the only sentiments they can now expect from Europe. But the situation would change entirely in an instant were the "sick man" somehow finally to die, either on his own or from Russia's sword. The whole of Europe would at once commence to glow with the tenderest of love for the reborn peoples and would at once rush off "to save them from Russia." One has to believe that Europe would be the first to bring this idea of "internationality" into her new order. Europe will realize that around the corpse of the "sick man," disorders, disputes, and rivalries would immediately erupt among the liberated nations, and this is just what she wants: a pretext for intervention and, principally, a pretext to rouse them against Russia, who certainly will not wish to let them quarrel over the "sick man's" legacy. And there is not a piece of slander which Europe would not circulate against us. "Because of the Russians we didn't help you fight the Turks," the English would tell them then. Alas, the nations of the East even now realize this full well and know that "England will never take part in their liberation and will never give her agreement to it if such were considered necessary, because she hates these Christians for their spiritual ties to Russia. England needs the Eastern Slavs to hate us with all the strength of the hatred she herself bears toward us . . ." (*Moscow News*, No. 63). This is what these peoples know and, for the moment, hold in their memory, and this is what they have now charged to Russia's future account. And we think that they adore us.

In an international city, aside from the protection of the English, the Greeks—the original masters of the city—will still be the masters. The Greeks surely regard the Slavs with even more scorn than the Germans do. But since the Greeks will also fear the Slavs, their scorn will change to bitterness. They will not, of course, be able to wage war against one another or declare war on one another, because the protectors will not permit them to go that far, at least not in any serious way. But precisely because of the impossibility of any open and earnest conflict between them, all sorts of other disputes will start, and these will assume primarily the aspect of religious disorders. That is how it will begin, because it is the readiest pretext of all; and that is what I wanted to point out.

I say this because the program has already been announced: the Bulgarians and Constantinople. From this point of view the Greeks are strong, and they know it. And yet there is nothing in the future that can be more frightening for the entire West, and for Russia as well, than just such ecclesiastical strife that is so possible should Russia even for an instant withdraw her protection and strict supervision. Although this is only a matter of the future, and a matter of guesswork at that, it would still be unpardonable to overlook it, even as mere guesswork. Should we, too, in fact, be wishing for the continuation of Turkish rule and the health of the "sick man"? Should we, too, go that far? Is it really not clear that should this "sick man" die and, most important, should Russia even retreat halfway from exercising ultimate and prevailing influence on the destinies of the East, should she make this concession to Europe, it is more than probable that the centuries-long unity of the church on the Balkan peninsula will be shaken and, perhaps, shaken in areas farther to the east as well. One can even say this: whether this strife breaks out or not, should the "sick man" die, it is highly probable that there may, *in any case,* be no avoiding a great ecclesiastical *sobor* for settling the affairs of the newly reborn church. Why could this not have been foreseen? During these four centuries of persecution and oppression, the officials of the Eastern church always heeded Russia's advice; but should they free themselves from Turkish oppression tomorrow, and should Europe offer them her patronage to do so, they would at once display a different attitude toward Russia. The moment Russia took the side of the Slavs, the officials of the Eastern church—i.e., mainly Greeks—would at once, perhaps, want to make clear to her that they have no more need of her and her advice. They would be anxious to make that clear precisely because for four centuries they have looked at her with their hands folded in prayer. And Russia's situation would be almost the most difficult one of all. Those same Bulgarians would at once cry out that a new Eastern pope has ascended the throne in Constantinople and—who knows?—they might be right. An international Constantinople actually could serve, at least for a time, as a pedestal for a new pope. In that case, for Russia to support the Greeks would mean losing the Slavs, while to support the Slavs, in this future and so probable strife between them, would mean taking on, perhaps, some most unpleasant and most serious ecclesiastical problems. It is clear that all this can be avoided only by Russia adopting in advance a steadfast attitude to the Eastern Question and by her following unswervingly the grand traditions of our ancient, centuries-old Russian policy. We must concede nothing in this matter to any sort of Europe, not for any considerations, because this matter is our life and death. Constantinople must be ours, sooner or later, even if only to avoid the painful and appalling ecclesiastical disorders that could so easily arise among the young and inexperienced peoples of the East and whose example we have already seen in the dispute of the Bulgarians and the ecumenical patriarch, a dispute that ended so badly. Once we take possession of Constantinople, nothing of this sort can happen. The peoples of the West, who watch Russia's every move so jealously, at the present moment still do not know and do not suspect all these new possibilities which are still fanciful but all too probable. If they really were to learn about them now, then they would not understand them and would not attribute any special significance to them. But later, when it is already too late, they will understand and will attribute significance to them. The Russian People understand the Eastern Question in no other way than as the liberation of all Orthodox Christianity and the great future unity of the church; but if, to the contrary, they see new disorders and a new discord they will be deeply shaken, and any new solution to the matter, perhaps, will have a profound effect both on them and on their whole way of life, particularly if the matter ultimately takes on a predominantly ecclesiastical character. And so, for this reason alone, we can in no way abandon or weaken the level of our age-old participation in this great question. It is not only the magnificent port, not only the access to the seas and oceans, that binds Russia so closely to the resolution of the destinies of this fateful question, nor is it even the unification and the regeneration of the Slavs.... Our goal is more profound, immeasurably more profound. We, Russia, are truly essential and unavoidable both for the whole of Eastern Christendom and for the whole fate of future Orthodoxy on the earth, for its unity. This is what our People and their rulers have always understood.... In short, this terrible Eastern Question is virtually our entire fate for years to come. It contains, as it were, all our goals and, mainly, our only way to move out into the fullness of history. It contains as well our final collision with Europe and our final uniting with her, but now on new, powerful, productive principles. Oh, how is Europe now to grasp all the fateful, vital significance the solution of this question has for us! In short, whatever the result of the current and, perhaps, so essential diplomatic agreements and discussions in Europe, sooner or later *Constantinople must be ours,* even if it be only in the next century! This we Russians must always keep in mind, and keep in mind continually. This is what I wanted to state, particularly given the present moment in Europe....

2

1. "The Jewish Question"

Oh, don't think that I'm really planning to raise "the Jewish question"! I wrote the title as a joke. Raising a question of such magnitude as the position of the Jew in Russia, and the position of Russia, who numbers three million Jews among her sons, is too much for me. This question is beyond my limits. But I still can have some opinion of my own, and it turns out that some Jews have suddenly begun to take an interest in my opinion. I have been getting letters from them for some time now; they reproach me severely and bitterly for "attacking" them and for "hating the Yids," hating them not for their flaws, "not as an exploiter," but specifically as a race, supposedly because "Judas betrayed Christ." Such things are written by "educated" Jews, i.e., by those who (I have noted this, but I am in no way making a generalization—this I wish to point out in advance) always seem to try to let you know that they, with their education, have long ceased to share the "prejudices" of their nation; that they no longer carry out their religious rites as do other petty Jews; that they consider this beneath the level of their enlightenment; that, moreover, they do not even believe in God. I note, apropos of this and in parentheses, that all these gentlemen from the "higher Jews" who defend their nation in this way find it too great a sin to ignore their forty-centuries-old Jehovah and to renounce him. And it is a sin, not only because of feelings of nationality, by any means; there are also other reasons of very great importance. It's an odd thing, indeed: a Jew without God is somehow unthinkable; one can't even imagine a Jew without God. But this is one of those immense topics, and we will drop it for the moment. What surprises me most is how and why I could be placed among the haters of the Jews as a people, as a nation. Even these gentlemen themselves permit me, to some extent, to condemn the Jew for some of his flaws and for being an exploiter, but—but this is only in words: when it comes to deeds, it is difficult to find anything more irritable and punctilious than an educated Jew and more ready than he to take offense—as a Jew. But once again: when and how did I declare my hatred for the Jews as a people? Since there was never any such hatred in my heart—and those Jews who are acquainted with me and who have had dealings with me know this—I, from the very outset and before saying anything else, reject this accusation once and for all so as not to make special mention of it later. Might they not be accusing me of "hatred" because I sometimes call the Jew a "Yid"? But in the first place, I never thought this was so offensive, and in the second place, as far as I can recall, I always used the word "Yid" to denote a well-known idea: "Yid, Yid-ism, the Kingdom of the Yids," etc. These designated a well-known concept, a tendency, a characteristic of the age. One can argue with that idea, one can disagree with it, but one should not take offense at a word. I shall quote one portion of a letter from one highly educated Jew who wrote me a long and, in many respects, a beautiful letter that aroused great interest in me. It is one of the most characteristic accusations of me of hating the Jews as a people. It goes without saying that the gentleman who wrote me this letter will remain strictly anonymous.

> ... but I intend to touch upon one subject which I truly cannot explain to myself. This is your hatred of the "Yid," which reveals itself in virtually every issue of your *Diary*.
>
> I would like to know why you rise up against the Yid and not against the exploiter in general; I can tolerate the prejudices of my nation no less than you—I have suffered from them in no small measure—but I will never agree that shameless exploitation lives in the blood of this nation.
>
> Can it be that *you* are incapable of rising to the basic law of all social life: that *all* citizens of a state, without exception, so long as they bear all the obligations essential for the existence of the state, must enjoy *all* the rights and privileges of its existence, and that those who do not abide by the law, the noxious elements of society, must be subject to one and the same measure of penalty, common to all? ... Why, then, must the rights of all Jews be limited and why must there be special punitive laws for them? In what way is foreign exploitation (Jews, after all, are Russian subjects)—by Germans, Englishmen, and Greeks, of whom there are such numbers in Russia—

better than exploitation by Yids? In what way is the Russian Orthodox kulak, the peasant exploiter, the tavern keeper, the one who preys on the peasant and sucks his blood and who has so proliferated over *the whole of* Russia—in what way is he better than those Yids who, still, operate within a limited sphere? In what way is the one better than the other? . . .

(At this point my worthy correspondent compares several well-known Russian kulaks with European ones to show that the Russians do not take second place. But what does this prove? We don't boast about our kulaks, after all; we don't display them as models to be emulated; on the contrary, we agree completely that both types are bad.)

I could pose thousands of such questions to you.

Meanwhile, when you speak of the "Yid," you include in this concept the entire, terribly impoverished mass of the three million Jewish population of Russia of which 2,900,000, at least, are waging a desperate struggle for a wretched existence, who are morally purer not only than other nationalities but even purer than the Russian People whom you deify. In this term you also include the honorable numbers of Jews who have received higher education, who have distinguished themselves in all fields of the life of the state; take, for example . . .

(Here again there are several names which, apart from Goldstein's, I do not consider myself entitled to publish because some of them, perhaps, might be displeased to read that they are of Jewish descent.)

. . . Goldstein (who died heroically in Serbia for the Slavic idea) and who worked for the benefit of society and humanity? Your hatred for the "Yid" extends even to Disraeli . . . who, probably, did not know himself that his forebears were once Spanish Jews and who, of course, does not regulate English Conservative policy from the point of view of a "Yid" (?) . . .

No, unfortunately, you known neither the Jewish *people,* nor their life, nor their spirit, nor, finally, their forty centuries of history. Unfortunately—because you, in any case, are a sincere and absolutely honorable person; but you are unconsciously doing damage to an enormous mass of impoverished people, while the powerful "Yids" who receive in their salons the powerful people of this world are, of course, afraid neither of the press nor even of the impotent rage of the exploited. But enough of this subject! I will scarcely be able to

> persuade you to my view, but I would very much like you to convince me.

That's the excerpt. Before I make any reply (for I do not want to accept so serious an accusation), I will note the intemperance of the attack and the degree of touchiness. During the entire year of publishing my *Diary* there positively was no article of such dimensions against the "Yid" as could justify an attack of such vehemence. In the second place, one cannot help but note that the honorable correspondent, when he touches on the Russian People in these few lines, could not restrain himself and could not resist treating this poor Russian People with rather excessive contempt. It's true that in Russia even the Russians themselves haven't left a single spot unspat upon (as Shchedrin expressed it), so it's all the more excusable for a Jew. But in any case, this bitterness clearly testifies to the way the Jews themselves regard the Russians. This was written, indeed, by an educated and talented person (only I think he is not without prejudices); so, after that, what can we expect from the uneducated Jew, of whom there are so many? What feelings must they have toward the Russians? I say this not in accusation: this is all natural; I want only to point out that when it comes to motives for our alienation from the Jew, it is, perhaps, not only the Russian People who are at fault and that these motives have accumulated, naturally, on both sides, and that one still does not know which side has more of them. Having noted that, I will say a few words in my defense and, generally, on how I regard the matter. And even though, I repeat, this question is too large for me to cope with, I still can express a thing or two about it.

2. Pro and Contra

Granted, it is very difficult to learn the forty centuries of history of a people such as the Jews; but one initial thing I do know is that certainly no other people in the whole world have complained so much about their fate, complained constantly, at their every step and every word, about their oppression, their suffering, their martyrdom. One would think that it is not they who rule in Europe, not they who at least control the stock exchanges there and, accordingly, the policy, the internal affairs, and the morality of the states. The noble Goldstein may die for the Slavic idea. But still, were the Jewish idea not so powerful in the world, that same

"Slavic" question (last year's question) might well have been solved long ago in favor of the Slavs, not the Turks. I am prepared to believe that Lord Beaconsfield himself, perhaps, has forgotten about his descent, some time ago, from Spanish Yids (however he certainly hasn't forgotten); but that he "regulated English Conservative policy" over the last year *in part* from the viewpoint of a Yid—in this, I think, there can be no doubt. That this happened "in part" is impossible not to admit.

But let all this be my idle talk that proves nothing, merely my casual tone and casual words. I grant that. Yet I am still unable to believe completely the cries of the Jews that they are so downtrodden, tormented, and oppressed. In my view, the Russian peasant, and the Russian commoner generally, bears burdens that are almost greater than the Jews'. My correspondent writes me, in another letter:

> First of all it is *essential* to grant them (the Jews) all the civil rights (just think that they are still deprived of the most basic right: that of free choice of place of residence, which results in a host of terrible restrictions for the whole mass of the Jews) that are enjoyed by all other non-Russian nationalities in Russia, and only then demand from them that they fulfill their obligations to the state and to the native population.

But you, Mr. Correspondent—you who tell me in this same letter, on the next page, that you "have a lot more love and pity for the toiling masses of the Russian People than for the Jews" (which, for a Jew, is surely too strongly stated)—you must keep in mind that while the Jew "was enduring the consequences of his lack of free choice of place of residence," at the same time twenty-three million of the "Russian toiling masses" were enduring serfdom, which, of course, was a bit more painful than "choice of place of residence." And so, did the Jews take pity on them then? I don't think so; people on the western frontier of Russia and in the south will give you a detailed answer to that. No, even then they were crying in just the same way about rights that the Russian People themselves did not have, crying and complaining that they were downtrodden and martyrs and that once they were given more rights, "then demand from us the fulfillment of obligations to the state and to the native population." And so the liberator came and liberated the native People; and who do you think were the first to fall upon them as on a victim? Who was foremost in taking advantage of their weaknesses? Who, in their eternal pursuit of gold, set about swindling them? Who at once took the place, wherever they could manage it, of the former landowners—with the difference that though the landowners may have thoroughly exploited people, they still tried not to ruin their peasants, out of self-interest, perhaps, so as not to wear out the labor force, whereas the Jew doesn't care about wearing out Russian labor; he takes what he can and he's gone. I know that when they read this the Jews will at once cry out that it's untrue, that it's a slander, that I am lying, that I believe all these stupid remarks, that I "do not know the forty centuries of history" of these immaculate angels who are incomparably "morally purer not only than other nationalities but even purer than the Russian People whom I deify" (according to my correspondent—see above). But I'll grant that; let them be morally purer than all the other peoples of the world, and purer than the Russians, naturally; yet I have only just read in the March issue of the *European Messenger* the news that the Jews in America, in the Southern states, have already thrown themselves en masse on the many millions of liberated Negroes and have already got them in their clutches in their usual style via the well-known and eternal "pursuit of gold" and by taking advantage of the inexperience and weaknesses of the exploited people. Imagine that when I read this I at once recalled that five years ago the very same thing had occurred to me—namely, that now the Negroes have been liberated from their slavery, they still won't come off unscathed because the Jews, who are so numerous in the world, will at once fling themselves on this fresh little victim. That is what I thought and, I assure you, several times thereafter in those days it occurred to me: "Why is it that we hear nothing of the Jews over there? Why don't the papers write about it? Why, these Negroes are a treasure trove for the Jews; surely they won't pass that up?" And so I waited, and the papers did write about it; I read it. And some ten days ago I read in *New Times* (no. 371) a report from Kovno, a most characteristic one, that says "the Jews have made such an onslaught on the local Lithuanian population that they have almost destroyed all of them with vodka, and it was only their Catholic priests who managed to save the poor drunkards by threatening them with the torments of hell and organizing temperance societies among them." The enlightened correspondent, it's true, blushes with embarrassment for his compatriots, who still believe in priests and the torments of hell, but he adds here that some enlightened local economists have risen up in the wake of the priests and have begun to organize rural banks, specifically to save the people from the money-lending Jew, as well as rural markets so that "the poor toiling mass" can acquire the necessities of life at proper prices, not the ones set by a Jew. Well, I've read all that and I know that at once people will begin shouting at me that none of this proves anything; that it happens because the Jews themselves are oppressed and poor; that all this is merely the "struggle for survival"; that only an idiot would be unable to figure that out; and that if the Jews themselves were not so poor but, rather, could enrich themselves, then they would at once show their humane side so that the whole world would be astonished. But, of course, all these Negroes and Lithuanians are even poorer than the Jews who are squeezing them dry, and yet the former (just read the news item) disdain the sort of trade for which the Jew is so avid. In the second place, it's not hard to be humane and moral when you're happy and rolling in money, but once it's a question of "struggle for survival"; then you'd best keep your distance. As far as I'm concerned, that's not such an angelic quality; and in the third place, I'm not, after all, setting forth these two stories from *The European Messenger* and *New Times* as absolutely fundamental facts that explain everything once and for all. If one begins to write the history of this worldwide tribe, one can at once find a hundred thousand such facts, and ones even more significant than these, so that one or two extra facts will not add anything in particular; yet there's something curious here: it's curious that just as soon as you need some information about the Jew and his dealings—whether it be for an argument or simply in a moment of your own ponderings—you needn't go to a public library; you needn't go rummaging in any old books or in your own old notes; you needn't make an effort, you needn't search, you needn't strain yourself; you needn't move, you needn't even get up from your chair: just reach over to the first newspaper that happens to by lying next to you and take a look at the second or third page: you'll certainly find something about the Jews and certainly something that interests you; certainly it will be something most characteristic and certainly it will be the same old thing—the same old exploits, I mean! And so you have to agree that this really does mean something; it does indicate something; it does reveal something to you, even though you may be a total ignoramus about the forty centuries of history of this tribe. Naturally, people will tell me that everyone is obsessed with hatred and so everyone lies. Of course, it could well be that everyone, to the last man, is lying, but in that case a new question arises: if everyone, to the last man, is lying and is obsessed with such hatred, then this hatred must have stemmed from something; this universal hatred must mean something, after all; "the word *everyone* means something, after all!" as Belinsky once exclaimed.

"Free choice of place of residence!" But is the "native" Russian person really so absolutely free in his choice of place of residence? Do not the former restrictions on completely free choice in the place of residence—restrictions that are undesirable survivals from the time of serfdom and have long been an object of the government's attention—continue to exist for the Russian commoner as well, right up to the present day? But as far as the Jews are concerned, it's obvious to everyone that their rights in choice of place of residence have broadened immensely over the last twenty years. At least they have appeared in Russia in places where they were never seen formerly. But the Jews keep on complaining about hatred and restrictions. I may not have the most thorough knowledge of Jewish life, but there is one thing I do know for certain and am prepared to argue about with anyone: namely, that among our common People there is no preconceived, a priori, obtuse, religious hatred of the Jew, supposedly based on the notion that "Judas betrayed Christ." If one does hear this from some little urchins or drunkards, still the whole of our People regard the Jew, I repeat, without any preconceived hatred. I have seen this over the course of fifty years. I even happened to live among the People, among a mass of them, in the same barracks, and sleep on the same bunks as they. There were several Jews there, and no one *hated* them, no one excluded them or persecuted them. When they prayed (and the Jews pray with loud exclamations, wearing a special garment), no one found this strange or hindered them or laughed at them, something, however, which was just what one would expect from such a coarse (as we see it) People as the Russians; on the contrary, when they looked at them they would say: "That's the sort of faith they have; that's how they pray"—and they would pass by peacefully and almost approvingly. And yet these same Jews shunned the Russians in many respects: they did not want to eat with them; they regarded them almost haughtily (and this, of all places, in prison!); and, in general, they showed loathing and aversion toward the Russians, these "native" People. Exactly the same things happen in soldiers' barracks, over the whole of Russia: just pay a visit and ask whether a Jew in the barracks is abused as a Jew, as a *Yid*, because of his customs and his faith. Nowhere is he abused, and this is the case among the People everywhere. On the contrary, I assure you that in the barracks and everywhere else the Russian common person sees and understands all too well (and, indeed, the Jews themselves don't hide it) that the Jew does not want to eat with him, turns up his nose at him, avoids him, and does his best to build a wall between them; and yet, instead of taking offense at this, the Russian common person calmly and clearly says, "That's the sort of faith they have; it's because of his faith that he won't eat with us and keeps to himself" (not because he is hostile, that is), and having understood this great reason, he forgives the Jew with all his heart. Yet at times, a wild notion would come into my head: what if it weren't the Jews who numbered three million in Russia but the Russians; and what if there were eighty million Jews? Now how would they transform the Russians, and how would they treat them? Would they allow them to become their equals in rights? Would they allow them to pray freely in their midst? Would they not turn them directly into slaves? Even worse: would they not strip them utterly bare? Would they not massacre them altogether, exterminate them completely, as they did more than once with alien peoples in times of old in their ancient history? No, ladies and gentlemen, I assure you that there is no preconceived hatred of the Jew in the Russian People, although there is, perhaps, an antipathy, in certain areas particularly, and even a very strong antipathy, perhaps. Oh, this can't be avoided; it exists, but it certainly does not arise from the fact that he is a Jew; it is due neither to racial nor religious hatred of any sort but comes from other motives, for which it is not the native people but the Jew himself who is responsible.

3. *Status in Statu*. Forty Centuries of Existence

Hatred, and hatred caused by prejudice—that is the accusation the Jews make against the native population. But since we've begun on the topic of prejudices, then what do you think: does the Jew harbor fewer prejudices toward the Russian than the Russian toward the Jew? Doesn't he have a few more of them? I just gave you some examples of how the Russian common person regards the Jew; but I have before me letters from Jews, not common people but educated Jews, and how much hatred these letters express toward the "native population"! What's most important is that they don't notice the hatred contained in what they write.

You see, in order to exist on the earth for forty centuries, i.e., for almost the entire historical period of humanity, and to exist in such a close and indissoluble unity; in order to lose so many times their territory, their political independence, their laws, almost even their religion—to lose these things and each time to unite once more, to be reborn once more *in their old idea,* even though in another form, and to create themselves, their laws, and almost their religion once more—no, a people of such vitality, a people so unusually strong and energetic, a people so unprecedented in the world cannot exist without *status in statu,* something they have maintained always and everywhere during their most awful, thousand-year-long Diaspora and persecution. When I speak of *status in statu* I am certainly not making any accusation. But still, what is the meaning of this *status in statu;* what is its centuries-old, unchanging idea, and where does the essence of this idea lie?

To expound this would take a long time and, indeed, would be impossible in a short little article; it would also be impossible because, despite the forty centuries that have elapsed, *all the times and the seasons* have not yet arrived, and the final word of humanity about this great tribe still remains to be said. But without entering into the essence and the depth of this subject, one can outline at least some of the characteristics of this *status in statu,* even if only superficially. These characteristics are: alienation and estrangement on the level of religious dogma; no intermingling; a belief that there exists but one national individuality in the world—the Jew, and though there may be some others, one still has to think of them as nonexistent, as it were. "Go forth from the other nations, form thine own entity and know that henceforth thou art *the only one before God;* destroy the others or enslave them or exploit them. Have faith in thy victory over the whole world; have faith that all will submit to thee. Shun everyone resolutely, and have no communion with any in thy daily life. And even when thou art deprived of thy land, thy political individuality, even when thou are scattered over the face of the earth and among all the other peoples—pay no heed; have faith in all these things that have been promised unto thee; believe, once and for all, that all this will come to pass; and meanwhile thou must live, shun, cling together, exploit and—wait, wait. . . ." That is the essential idea of this *status in statu;*

and then, of course, there are the internal and, perhaps, mysterious laws that preserve this idea.

Gentlemen—you educated Jews and opponents—you say that this is all nonsense and that "if there really is a *status in statu* (i.e., that there was, but now, supposedly, there remain only the weakest traces of it), then it is only because the persecutions have led to it; persecutions have given birth to it, religious persecutions from the Middle Ages and earlier; and this *status in statu* has arisen exclusively from a sense of self-preservation. If it does continue, particularly in Russia, then it is because the Jew still does not have rights equal to those of the native population." But this is how it seems to me: even if the Jew really did have equal rights, he would still never give up his *status in statu*. Moreover, to attribute the *status in statu* only to persecutions and a sense of self-preservation is insufficient. Indeed, the tenacity in self-preservation would not have lasted forty centuries; the Jews would have grown tired of trying to preserve themselves over such a period. Even the mightiest of the world's civilizations never lasted half of forty centuries and lost their political force and their tribal characteristics. It is not self-preservation alone that is the main reason here, it is a certain idea that has a motive power and an attraction; it is a certain something, universal and profound, on which, perhaps, humanity is still incapable of pronouncing its last word, as I said above. That we have something here which has a predominantly religious character—that is beyond doubt. That their Providence, under the former, original name of Jehovah, with his ideal and his covenant, continues to lead his people to a fixed goal—that is certainly beyond doubt. Besides, it's impossible, I repeat, even to imagine a Jew without God; moreover, I don't believe that there are godless people among educated Jews either: they are all of the same essence, and Lord only knows what the world can expect from these educated Jews! Even in childhood I read and heard the legend about the Jews that told how they were all faithfully awaiting the Messiah, every one of them, from the very lowest Yid to the very highest and most learned among them, the philosopher and cabalist-rabbi; that they all believe the Messiah will gather them together in Jerusalem once more and will use his sword to bring down all the other peoples to sit at their feet; that for some reason the Jews, at least the overwhelming majority of them, prefer but one profession—the trade in gold or, at least, the working of that metal; and they do this, supposedly, so that when the Messiah appears they will not have a new fatherland and not be attached to an alien land, which they would own, but will possess everything only in the form of gold and jewels that will be easier to take away when

> The ray of dawn casts forth its glow:
> The cymbal, flute, and tambourine,
> The silver, gold, and holy shrine,
> We shall bring to our ancient home,
> Our much beloved Palestine.

I heard all this, I repeat, as a legend, but I believe that the essence of the thing exists without a doubt, particularly among the great mass of Jews, in the form of an instinctive and irresistible predilection. But in order for such an essence to be preserved, it's essential, of course, that the strictest *status in statu* be preserved as well. It is being preserved. And so it is not only persecution that was and is the motive here, but another *idea*. . . .

If the Jews truly do have such a special, strict, internal makeup that binds them into something integral and particular, then one might almost give some thought to the question of granting them *rights* that are equal in all respects to the rights of the native population. Naturally, everything required by humaneness and justice, everything required by compassion and Christian law—all this must be done for the Jews. But if they, fully equipped with their particularity and their own special makeup, their racial and religious segregation; if they, armed with laws and principles entirely opposed to the idea by which the entire European world has developed until now, at least—if they should demand complete equality of *all possible* rights with those of the native population, then will they not receive something more, something extra, something beyond that of even the the most native of native populations? Here, of course, the Jews will point to other alien peoples: "These people, now, have been given equal or almost equal rights, while the Jews have fewer rights than any aliens; and that's because they're afraid of us, the Jews, because we're supposedly more harmful than other aliens. Yet how is the Jew harmful? If, indeed, the Jewish people have some bad qualities, then it's only because the Russians themselves encourage these through their own Russian ignorance, through their own lack of development, through their own incapacity for independence, through their own economic backwardness. The Russians themselves ask for an intermediary, a leader, someone to look after their economic affairs, a creditor;

they themselves call for this and they themselves submit to him. On the other hand, just look at Europe: the peoples there are strong and independent of spirit; they have a strong sense of nationality; they have long been used to working and know how to work; and so over there they aren't afraid of giving all rights to the Jew! Have you ever heard anything in France about the harm from the *status in statu* of their Jews?"

On the surface, this is a powerful argument; first of all, though, one envisions, in parentheses, one observation—namely, "It follows, then, that Jewry thrives in places where the people are still ignorant or not free or economically backward—that's just where they're in clover!" And instead of using their influence to raise the level of development, to encourage knowledge, to give rise to economic competence among the native population—instead of this, the Jew, wherever he has settled, has humbled and corrupted the people even more; humaneness in such places declined even further; the level of education fell still lower; hopeless, inhuman poverty spread even more abominably, and with it, despair. Ask the native population in our border areas: what is it that drives the Jew and what is it that has driven him for so many centuries? You will always get the same answer: *mercilessness;* "They've been driven for so many centuries by their mercilessness to us, solely by their thirst for our sweat and our blood." And, in truth, the entire activity of the Jews in these border areas of ours has consisted only in making the native population as hopelessly dependent on them as possible by *taking advantage of the local laws*. Oh, in this case they have always found the possibility of taking advantage of *rights and laws*. They have always known how to maintain friendship with those on whom the people depended, and it was certainly not for them to grumble, at least in this regard, about *their limited rights in comparison with the native population*. They've received from us quite enough of these rights over the native population. The history of our border regions bears witness to the fate of the Russian People, over decades and centuries, in areas where the Jews have settled. And what do we see? Just point out any other tribe among Russia's aliens that could compete in this sense with the terrible influence of the Jew. You will not find any; in this sense the Jew preserves all of his distinctiveness compared with Russia's other aliens, and the reason for it, of course, is his *status in statu,* whose spirit is imbued precisely with this merciless attitude toward everyone who is not a Jew, this disrespect for every tribe and nation and for every human creature who is not a Jew. And how can that be justified by saying that in the west of Europe the peoples have not allowed themselves to be overcome and so, accordingly, the Russian People themselves are to blame? Because the Russian People in Russia's borderlands proved to be weaker than the European peoples (and solely as a result of their harsh, centuries-long political circumstances), must they, for that reason alone, be utterly crushed by exploitation and not be helped?

And if people are going to point to Europe—to France, for example—then it is hardly the case that the *status in statu* has been harmless there either. Of course, Christianity and its idea have declined and continue to decline there not through fault of the Jew but of the Europeans; yet there, too, one cannot fail to note the effective triumph of Jewry which has replaced many of the old ideas with its own. Oh, of course human beings always and at all times idolized materialism and tended to see and understand freedom only as safeguarding one's self with wealth accumulated with one's every effort and hoarded by every possible means. But never before have these strivings been elevated so openly and held up as a higher principle as in our nineteenth century. "Every man for himself and only for himself; all communion among people only for oneself"—such is the moral principle of the majority of today's people,* and not even of the bad people but, on the contrary, of those who labor and who do not rob and murder. But mercilessness to the lower masses, the decline of brotherhood, the exploitation of the poor by the rich—oh, of course, all these things existed before as well, and they always did, but—but they were not elevated to the level of higher truth and science; they were condemned by Christianity, while now, on the contrary, they are elevated to a virtue. And so it is not without significance that the Jews reign over all the stock exchanges there; it is not without significance that they control the credit, and not without significance, I repeat, that they are the ones who control the whole of international politics as well; and what will happen hereafter is, of course, known to the Jews themselves: their reign, their complete reign, is drawing nigh! Coming soon is the complete triumph of ideas before which feelings of love for humanity, the longing for truth, Christian feelings, the feelings of nationhood and even of national pride of

*The basic idea of the bourgeoisie which, at the end of the last century, replaced the former world order and became the main idea of the entire present century throughout entire the European world. [Dostoevsky's note]

Europe's peoples must give way. What lies ahead, on the contrary, is materialism, a blind, carnivorous lust for *personal* material security, a lust for personal accumulation of money by any means—it is this, and not the Christian idea of salvation only through the closest moral and brotherly unity of people, that is acknowledged as a higher goal, as something rational, as representing freedom. People will laugh and say that this is certainly not caused by the Jews over there. Of course, it is not only because of the Jews, but if the Jews have had their complete triumph and have flourished in Europe precisely when these new principles have triumphed there, even to the point of being elevated to a moral principle, then one cannot help but conclude that the Jews have also exerted their influence. Our opponents will point out that the Jews, on the contrary, are impoverished, impoverished everywhere, even, and in Russia particularly; that only the very top level of the Jews are wealthy—the bankers and the kings of the stock market—while almost nine-tenths of the rest of the Jews are, literally, beggars who rush about looking for a crust of bread, offering their services as middlemen, looking for a place to pick up a kopeck for bread. Yes, that's true, it seems, but what does it signify? Does this not mean precisely that in the very work of the Jews (I mean in the work of the overwhelming majority of them, at least), in their very exploitation, there is something wrong, abnormal, something unnatural that bears its own punishment within it? The Jew offers his services as intermediary and trades in the labor of another. Capital is accumulated labor; the Jew loves to trade in the labor of another! But none of this changes anything for the moment; yet the top level of Jews gains a stronger and surer hold over humanity and strives to mold the world to its image and its essence. The Jews keep shouting that there are good people among them as well. Oh, heavens! Is this really the point? We aren't even talking about *good* or *bad* people now. And surely there are good people among them. Wasn't the late James Rothschild of Paris a good man? We are talking about the whole and its idea; we are talking about *Yidism* and about the *idea of the Yids,* which is creeping over the whole world in place of "unsuccessful" Christianity. . . . .

4. But Long Live Brotherhood!

But what am I talking about, and why? Or am I, too, an enemy of the Jews? Can it be true, as one Jewish girl who is—of this I have no doubt—most honorable and educated (that's quite evident from her letter and from the sincere, ardent feeling expressed in it)—can it be true that I, too, am (in her words) an enemy of this "unfortunate" race which I "seem to attack so cruelly at every opportune moment"? "Your scorn for the race of Yids which 'thinks of nothing but itself,' etc., etc., is obvious." No, I will speak up against this "obviousness" and deny even the fact itself. On the contrary, I say and write specifically that "everything required by humaneness and justice, everything required by compassion and Christian law—all this must be done for the Jews." I wrote these words above, but now I will add that, despite all the considerations I have already set forth, in the end I still stand for the full extension of rights to the Jews in formal legislation and, if such is possible, also for the fullest equality of rights with the native population (N.B.: although in some instances, perhaps, they already now have more rights or, to put it better, more *possibility to exercise them,* than the native population itself). Of course, a fanciful picture like the following occurs to me: what if, for some reason, our rural commune, which defends our poor, native peasant from so many evils, should collapse? What if the Jews should descend like a horde upon that liberated peasant who has so little experience, who is so little able to restrain himself from temptation and who, until now, has been watched over by the entire commune? Why, that would be the end of him at once: all his possessions, all his strength would tomorrow pass into the hands of the Jew, and an era would begin that could not be compared with serfdom, or even with the Tatar yoke.

But despite all the "fanciful pictures" and despite everything that I wrote above, I still stand for complete and conclusive equality of rights—because this is Christ's law, because this is a Christian principle. But if that is so, then why on earth did I fill so many pages with writing, and what point did I want to make if I *contradicted myself* in such a fashion? Precisely this: that I am not contradicting myself and that from the standpoint of the Russians—the native population—I can see no obstacles to broadening Jewish rights; yet I do contend that there are many more of these obstacles on the Jewish side than on the Russian, and that if this thing so wholeheartedly desired has still not come to pass, then the Russian is much, much less to blame for it than the Jew himself. What I indicated about the common Jew—who did not want to associate and eat with the Russians, while they not only did not get angry at him and reply in kind but, rather, immediately understood the situation and forgave him, saying, "That's because of his religion"—in just the same way as in this common Jew we very often see the same boundless and arrogant anti-Russian prejudice in the educated one as well. Oh, they shout that they love the Russian People; one of them even wrote to me along those lines, saying that he was grieved that the Russian People were without a religion and understood nothing of their own Christianity. This is too strongly said for a Jew and only gives rise to the question as to whether this highly educated Jew himself understands anything about Christianity. But self-importance and arrogance are traits of the Jewish character that are very painful for us Russians. Which of us, the Russian or the Jew, is less able to understand the other? I avow that I would rather vindicate the Russian: the Russian, at least, has no (absolutely no) religious hatred for the Jew. And who has more of the other prejudices, and on which side are they? Now we hear the Jews shouting that they have been oppressed and persecuted for so many years, that they are oppressed and persecuted even now, and that the Russian must at least take this into account when he makes judgments on the Jewish character. Very well, we do take that into account and can prove it: among the educated classes of the Russian people voices have been raised in favor of the Jews on more than one occasion. Now what about the Jews: have they ever, and do they now, when they complain and make accusations against the Russians, take into account the many centuries of oppression and persecution the Russian People themselves have endured? Can one really claim that the Russian People have endured fewer misfortunes and evils "in their history" than the Jews, in any place you care to mention? And can one really claim that it was not the Jew who, so very often, joined with the oppressors of the Russians, who indentured the Russian People and became their oppressor himself? All this happened, after all; such things went on; this is history, historical fact, but we've never heard anywhere that the Jewish people have repented for it, yet they still accuse the Russian People of having little love for them.

But still: "Let it come to pass! Let it come to pass!" May there be a complete and a spiritual union of the tribes and no disparity in their rights! And to this end I first implore my opponents and Jewish correspondents to be, on the contrary, a bit more indulgent and fair to us Russians. If their arrogance, if the perennial "resentful affliction" of the Jews toward the tribe of Russians is only a prejudice, a "historical tumor," *and is not buried among some far deeper mysteries of their law and their makeup,* then may all this disappear as quickly as possible and may we all join together in a single spirit, in complete brotherhood, for mutual help and for the great cause of service to our land, our state, and our fatherland! May the mutual accusations be softened; may the perennial intensification of these accusations, which stands in the way of a clear understanding of things, vanish away. But one can vouch for the Russian People: oh, they will accept the Jew in complete brotherhood, despite the difference in religion, and with complete respect for the historical fact of this difference; nevertheless, for brotherhood, for complete brotherhood, *brotherhood is needed on both sides.* Let the Jew himself show the Russian even a little brotherly feeling so as to encourage him. I know that among the Jewish people even now one can find enough individuals who seek and long for the misunderstanding to be dispelled; these are humane people as well, and I will not be the one to ignore that fact and hide the truth. It is specifically in order that these useful and humane people should not grow despondent and lose courage, that their prejudices might be weakened in some small measure and that they might thus find it easier to begin to act—it is for these reasons I would like to see the complete broadening of the rights of the Jewish race, as far as is possible, at least, precisely in so far as the Jewish people themselves demonstrate their capacity to accept and to use these rights without damaging the interests of the native population. It might even be possible to make some concessions in advance, to take still more steps forward on the Russian side. . . . The only question remains: will the new, good people among the Jews manage to do this, and to what extent are they themselves capable of serving the new and beautiful cause of *genuine* brotherly unity with people who are alien to them by religion and by blood?

3

1. The Funeral of "The Universal Man"

There are a lot of things I wanted to talk about in this March issue of my *Diary*. And here again it somehow happened that the thing I wanted to say only a few words about took up all the space. And there are so many topics I've been planning to discuss for a whole year, yet I just don't manage to get to them. There are certain things, particularly, about which a lot needs to be said, but since it very often happens that it's impossible to say a lot, one just doesn't take up the topic.

Apart from all these "significant" topics, I also wanted to say a few words this time about art, if only in passing. I saw Rossi in *Hamlet* and came to the conclusion that instead of Hamlet I had seen Mr. Rossi. But I'd better not begin that topic if I don't intend to say everything. I would like to say something (just a little) about Semiradsky's painting, but most of all I'd like to put in even a few words about idealism and realism in art, about Repin and about Mr. Raphael—but, obviously, all that will have to be put off to a more convenient moment.

And then I wanted to write, and at somewhat greater length, about a few of the letters I have received during the whole time I have been publishing my *Diary*, and about the anonymous letters in particular. Generally, I'm not able to answer all the letters I receive, and naturally not the anonymous ones, yet in the course of these nearly eighteen months these letters (on topics that concern all of us) have led me to make a few observations that are, perhaps, interesting—in my view, at least. At least one can make a few special remarks, based on experience, regarding today's intellectual mood in Russia; on the things that interest our active minds and the direction in which these minds are moving; on just who our active minds are; and in this regard, some very interesting traits emerge regarding age, sex, social class, and even one or another locality in Russia. I think that I might set aside a few places in some future issue of the *Diary* to take up at least a few of these anonymous letters and look at their characteristics, and I don't think that it would be all that boring, because there's a great range of views here. Of course, one can't talk about everything and convey it all—not even, perhaps, the most interesting things. And therefore I'm afraid to undertake it, not knowing whether I'll be able to manage the topic.

However, I do want to cite one letter now, and not an anonymous one; it is from a Miss L., a very young girl, a Jew, whom I know very well and whom I met in Petersburg and who now writes to me from the city of M——. I scarcely ever spoke to the respected Miss L. about "the Jewish question," although it seems that she is one of the strict and serious Jews. I can see that, oddly enough, this letter fits with the whole chapter on the Jews that I have just written. It would be too much to keep going on about the same topic. But the letter is on a different topic; and if it does, in part, concern the Jewish question, then it shows, as it were, an entirely different and quite opposite side of the question, and even something that might hint at its solution. I hope that Miss L. will graciously forgive me for my permitting myself to quote her words from that whole part of her letter on the funeral of Dr. Hindenburg in the city of M——; it was under the immediate impression of this funeral that she wrote these lines, so sincere and touching in their truth. I also did not want to conceal the fact that this was written by a Jew and that these feelings are the feelings of a Jew. . . .

> I am writing this under the fresh impression of a funeral march. Dr. *Hindenburg* was buried at the age of eighty-four. He was a Protestant, so his body was first taken to the church and only then to the cemetery. Never before at a funeral had I seen such sympathy, such ardent tears, or heard such words that came straight from the heart. . . . He died in such poverty that he lacked the means to pay for his burial.
>
> He had been practicing in M—— for fifty-eight years, and what an amount of good he did during that time. If only you knew what sort of man he was, Fedor Mikhailovich! He was a doctor and an obstetrician; his name will be preserved for posterity here; legends have already grown up around him; all the common people called him "father," and loved him, adored him; and only with his death did

they realize what they had lost in this man. While he still lay in his coffin (in the church), there was not a single person, I think, who failed to go and shed tears over him and kiss his feet; and, in particular, the poor Jewish women whom he helped so much, wept and prayed for him to go straight to heaven. Our former cook, an awfully poor woman, came to us today and said that when she gave birth to her last child, he saw that she had no food at home and gave her thirty kopecks to make herself some soup; after that he used to come every day and leave her twenty kopecks; and seeing that she was making her recovery he sent her a pair of partridges. In the same way, when he was called to one terribly poor woman who was about to give birth (these were the kind of women who would call him), he saw that she had nothing with which to clothe the child and took off his outer shirt and handkerchief (he wore a handkerchief tied round his head), tore them up and gave them to the woman.

He also cured one poor Jew, a wood-cutter; then the man's wife fell ill, and then his children; twice every single day the doctor would call on them, and when he had set them all on their feet again he asked the Jew: "How are you going to pay me?" The Jew replied that he had nothing at all except for a goat that he would sell that same day. And so he did; he sold the goat for four rubles and brought the money to the doctor; and then the doctor gave his servant twelve rubles in addition to the four and sent him off to buy a cow, and told the wood-cutter to go home. An hour later the servant brought the cow to the wood-cutter and said that the doctor believed that goat's milk was not good for them.

And so he lived all his life. There were cases when he left thirty or forty rubles with poor people; he would also give money to poor peasant women in the villages.

And in return they buried him like a saint. All the poor people closed up their shops and ran after the coffin. Among the Jews it is the custom to have boys who sing psalms at funerals, but it is forbidden to sing such psalms at the funeral of a non-Jew. This time the boys marched in the procession, ahead of the coffin, and sang these psalms. Prayers were said for his soul in all the synagogues, and the bells of *all* the churches were rung all during the procession. There was a military band, and Jewish musicians as well called on the son of the deceased to request, as an honor, permission to play during the procession. All the poor people donated something—five kopecks or ten—while the wealthy Jews gave a great deal and provided a magnificent, enormous wreath of fresh flowers with black and white ribbons at its sides on which, in gold letters, his major public services were listed—for instance, setting up a hospital, and so on—I couldn't make out what else was there; in any case, is it really possible to list all the good things he did?

A pastor and a Jewish rabbi spoke at his graveside, and both wept; but he just lay there in his old, worn uniform coat with an old handkerchief tied around his head—that dear head; and it seemed that he was sleeping, so fresh was the color of his face. . . .

2. An Isolated Case

An isolated case, you may tell me. Well, gentlemen, what can I say? Once more I'm guilty: once more I see in an isolated case almost the beginning of the solution to the whole question . . . well, at least to that same "Jewish question" I used as title for my second chapter of this *Diary*. By the way, why did I call this old doctor "the universal man"? He was not a universal man but, rather, a common man. This city of M—— is a large provincial town in our western region and many Jews live there; there are Germans, Russians, of course, Poles, and Lithuanians—and all of them, all these nationalities recognized the righteous old man as one of their own. He himself was a Protestant and a German, very much a German: his way of buying a cow and sending it to that poor Jew was an example of purely German *Witz*. First he confounded him: "How are you going to pay me?" And, of course, when the poor fellow sold his last goat to pay his "benefactor," he didn't grumble in the least but, rather, was deeply pained because the goat was worth only four rubles, while "this poor old man who's working for all us poor folks has to live, too, and what's four rubles for all the fine things he's done for the family?" And the old fellow's a sly one: he chuckles, but his heart is full: "Now I'll show that poor down-and-out some of our German *Witz*!" How he must have laughed to himself when the cow was brought to the Jew; how his spirits must have been strengthened; and perhaps he spent all of that night in some wretched hovel fussing over a poor Jewish woman who was giving birth. And an eighty-year-old man would be happy to get a bit of sleep at night and give some rest to his tired old bones. If I were a painter I would paint just such a "genre" picture, that night at the bedside of the new Jewish mother. I'm awfully fond of realism in art, but some of our contemporary realists have *no moral center* in their paintings, as one mighty poet and refined artist expressed it the other day when he was speaking to me of

Semidradsky's painting. Here, in this subject I propose for a "genre," there would be such a center, I think. And it's a lavish subject for an artist. In the first place, there's the absolute, incredible, stinking misery of a poor Jewish hut. One could even show a lot of humor here, and it would be awfully apropos: humor, after all, is the wit of deep feeling, and that definition appeals to me very much. Using refined feeling and intelligence, an artist can do a lot simply by reassigning the roles of all these wretched objects and household articles in the poor hut, and with this *amusing* reassignment he can touch your heart deeply at once. Even the lighting could be made interesting: a guttering tallow candle is burning out on a crooked table, while through the single, tiny window, covered with ice and hoarfrost, there glimmers the light of a new day, a new day of toil for the poor people. Women who have difficulty in giving birth often do so at dawn: they suffer the whole night through and give birth toward morning. And here's the tired old man, who's left the mother for a moment, looking after the child. There's nothing to wrap it in, there are no swaddling clothes, there's not even a rag (such poverty exists, gentlemen, I swear it does; this is realism of the purest sort, a realism that approaches the fantastic, so to say), and so the righteous old man has taken off his own wretched, worn uniform coat, has taken off his own shirt and is tearing it up to make swaddling clothes. His face has a severe, concentrated expression. The poor, newborn little Jewish baby is squirming on the bed before him; the Christian takes the little Jew in his arms and wraps him with the shirt taken from his own back. The solution to the Jewish question, gentlemen! The eighty-year-old torso of the doctor, naked and shivering from the morning damp, could take up a prominent place in the painting, as well as the face of the old man and the face of the worn-out, young mother who is looking at her newborn and at what the doctor is doing with it. Christ sees all this from on high, and the doctor knows it: "This poor little Yid will grow up and, perhaps, he himself may take the shirt from his back and give it to a Christian when he recalls the story of his own birth," thinks the old man to himself with naive and noble faith. Will this come to pass? Most likely it will not, yet it could come to pass; and on earth one can do nothing finer than believe that this *can* and *will* come to pass. And the doctor has a right to believe it, because in him it already has come to pass: "I did it, and another will as well; am I any better than another?"—he reassures himself with such a line of reasoning. A tired, ragged old Jewish woman, the mother of the one who gave birth, is busy fussing at the stove. A Jew who has gone out for a bundle of kindling opens the door of the hut and a cloud of frozen vapor bursts into the room for a moment. Two little boys are asleep on the floor on a felt blanket. In short, the background details could be very effective. Even thirty copper kopecks on the table, which the doctor had laid there for soup for the mother, could provide another touch: a copper stack of three-kopeck pieces, methodically piled up and not just thrown down. There could even be some mother-of-pearl, as in Semiradsky's painting, where a piece of mother-of-pearl is amazingly rendered: doctors are sometimes given such pretty little things, after all (so as not to pay much in cash); and so the doctor's little mother-of-pearl cigar case is lying here next to the stack of kopecks. Yes, indeed, the little picture would come off with a "moral center." I invite someone to paint it.

An isolated case! A couple of years ago, from somewhere in the south of Russia (I've forgotten where) there came news of some doctor who, on the morning of a hot day, had just emerged from his bathing cabin, refreshed, invigorated, and in a hurry to get home to have his coffee and therefore unwilling, despite the urgings of a crowd, to help a drowned man who had only just been pulled from the water at that same spot. I think he was taken to court for this. And yet he was, perhaps, an educated man with new ideas, a progressive, but one who "rationally" demanded new, common laws and rights for all and who paid no heed to isolated cases. He may well have supposed, rather, that isolated cases damage the cause by postponing general solutions to the question, and so as far as isolated cases are concerned, "the worse, the better." But without isolated cases, common rights cannot be put into effect. This common man of ours, though he may have been an isolated case, brought the whole city together around his grave. Together those Russian peasant women and poor Jewish women kissed his feet in his coffin; together they crowded around him; together they wept. Fifty-eight years of service to humanity in this city, fifty-eight years of ceaseless love united them all, if only once, over his coffin in a common rapture and common tears. All the town comes out for his funeral; the bells of *all* the churches peal; prayers are sung in all the languages. The pastor, in tears, gives his speech over the open grave. The rabbi stands off to one side, waiting, and when the pastor has finished he takes his place and gives his speech and sheds the same tears. Why, at that moment this very "Jewish question" had almost been solved! The pastor and the rabbi were united in common love; why, they almost embraced over this grave in the presence of Christians and Jews. What does it matter that, when the crowd dispersed, each one took up his old prejudices? Drops of water wear away even the stone, as the proverb says, and these "common people" conquer the world by uniting it; prejudices will pale with every isolated case, and finally they will disappear altogether. Legends will grow up around the old man, writes Miss L., who is also a Jew and who also wept over the "dear head" of this lover of humanity. And legends—they are the first step toward action, they are a living recollection and a ceaseless reminder of these "conquerors of the world," to whom the earth belongs. And once you believe that these really are conquerors and that such people truly will "inherit the earth," you have already almost become united in everything. All this is very simple; only one thing seems complicated: just to become convinced that without these same isolated instances you will never arrive at a total; everything may be about to fall apart, but it is these people who can bring it together. They are the ones who inspire ideas; they are the ones who give us faith; they provide a living example, and so a proof as well. And there's certainly no need to wait until everyone, or at least very many people, are as good as they are: we need very few such people in order to save the world, so powerful are they. And if such is the case, then how can we not hope?

3. To Our Correspondents

Novocherkassk. Iu. G. On the Stundists. Please send it.

Mrs. N.N., who proposed to send information on events from peasant life and the work of the *zemstvo* in her region, is asked to proceed to do what she promised.

Humble apologies to all who sent us announcements of their publications for inclusion in the *Diary:* we were unable to fulfill their requests due to lack of space.

April

1

1. War. We Are Stronger Than the Others

"It's war! War has been declared!" Such were the shouts we heard two weeks ago. "Is it to be war?" asked others when they heard. "It's true, it's been declared!" was the reply. "It may have been declared, but will it happen?" the others kept asking. . . .

And, truly, questions such as these were asked; perhaps they are being asked even now. And it's not only the drawn-out diplomatic dawdling that has made people so skeptical; it's something else, an instinct. Everyone senses that something decisive has begun, that there is somehow going to be a resolution of an issue from the past—a long, drawn-out issue from the past—and that a step is being taken toward something quite new, toward something that means a sharp break with the past, that will renew and resurrect the things of the past for a new life and . . . that it is Russia who is taking this step! This is just the thing that makes our "wise" people so skeptical. There is an instinctive premonition, yet the skepticism continues: "Russia! But how can she? How does she dare? Is she ready? Is she ready inwardly and morally, never mind materially? That's Europe over there, and Europe is no small matter! While Russia . . . well, what is Russia? And to take such a step?"

But the People believe that they are ready for a great, new, and regenerating step. It is the People themselves who rose to go to war, with the tsar at their head. When the word of the tsar rang out, the People rushed into the churches, and this happened all over the Russian land. When they read the tsar's manifesto the People crossed themselves and everyone *congratulated* each other on the war. We have seen this with our own eyes and heard it, and all this is happening even here in Petersburg. And once more the same activities have begun and the same facts come to light as last year: peasants in rural districts are donating money, as their means allow, and sending carts; and suddenly these thousands of people exclaim as one, "Donations and carts are little enough; we will all go off to fight!" Here in Petersburg we see people giving money for wounded and sick soldiers; they give sums of several thousand and ask that they be listed *anonymously.* There is a host of such facts; there will be tens of thousands of similar ones, and no one will be surprised at them. They signify only that the entire People have risen up for the truth, for a sacred cause, that the entire People have risen up to go to war and are on their way. Oh, the wise men will deny these facts as well, as they did last year's; the wise men still laugh at the People, as they did even recently, although they have plainly lowered their voices. Why do they laugh? From where do they draw so much faith in themselves? They continue to laugh precisely because they still see themselves as a power, that very power without which nothing can be achieved. And meanwhile, their power is drawing to its end. They are approaching a dreadful collapse, and when the pieces start to fall on their heads they, too, will begin talking in a different language, but everyone will see that they are only mumbling someone else's views and echoing someone else's voice; and everyone will turn away from them and invest their hopes in the tsar and his People.

We also need this war for ourselves; we rise up not only for our "brother Slavs" who have been suffering at the hands of the Turks but for our own salvation as well: war will clear the air we breathe and in which we have been suffocating, helplessly decaying within our narrow spiritual horizons. The wise men shout that we are perishing and suffocating from our own internal disorganization and that therefore we should seek not war but, rather, a prolonged peace so that we may be transformed from beasts and blockheads into real people and learn about order, honesty, and honor: "And then go off and help your brother Slavs," they conclude, singing in close harmony. In such a case, it would be interesting to know how they conceive the process by which they would become better. And how could they acquire any honor for themselves through a clearly dishonorable act? It would be interesting, finally, to know how and with what they would justify their refusal to share the feeling we find everywhere among the People. Yes, evidently it's right that the truth is purchased only at the cost of martyrdom.

Millions of people are moving and suffering and passing away without a trace, as if destined never to comprehend the truth. They live by the ideas of others; they seek the ready-made word and example and latch onto causes suggested by others. They shout that the authorities are on their side, that Europe is on their side. They jeer at those who do not agree with them, at all who despise flunkyism of thought and who believe in their own and their People's independence. And, indeed, these masses of shouting people are destined to serve only as a passive means for a scant few individuals among them to draw a little closer to the truth, or at least to get some slight premonition of it. It is these same individuals who later lead all the others, who take control of the movement, who give birth to an idea and leave it as a legacy to the teeming masses of people. We have already had such individuals among us. Some of us—even many of us—already understand them. But the wise men still continue to laugh and believe that they are a great power. "They'll have a little spree, and then they'll come home"—that's what they are now saying about our forces that have crossed the border; they even say it aloud. "There won't be a war—what war? How can we go to war? It's just a military review and some manoeuvres, at the cost of some hundreds of millions, so as to bolster our honor." That is the private view of the matter. But is it really only a private war?

Indeed, if we should be beaten, or if, after beating the enemy, we still were pressured by circumstances to come to terms cheaply—oh, then, of course, the wise men would be triumphant. And what dreadful jeering and racket and cynicism we'd have for years to come; what a bacchanalia of self-contempt, face slapping, and jeering at ourselves there would be again—and it would not be a summons to resurrection and strength but specifically to celebrate their own lack of honor, personality, and strength. And a new nihilism would begin, absolutely the same as the old one, with a rejection of the Russian People and their independent view. And the main thing is that is would acquire such force and become so strong that it would certainly begin, even openly, to ride roughshod over Russia's most sacred values. And young people would again spit upon their homes and families and flee from their elders, mindlessly repeating the endless platitudes and boring old words about the grandeur of Europe and our duty to be as lacking in personality as possible. And the main thing is—the same old song, the same old words, and nothing new for a long time! No, we need the war and the victory.

With war and victory will come a new word, and a living life will begin, not merely the mind-numbing twaddle we used to hear—what do I mean, we used to hear? That we hear to this day, gentlemen!

But we must be ready for everything; and indeed, if we assume even the worst, even the impossibly worst outcome for the war that has now begun, then, although we may endure much of that disgusting old misery that has sickened us all to death, the colossus will still not be shaken and, sooner or later, will take all its due. This is not merely a hope; it is a comlete certainty, and in this impossibility of shaking the colossus lies our entire strength over Europe, where now virtually everyone fears that their old edifice will be shaken and the ceilings will crash down upon them. This colossus is our People. And the beginning of the current *People's* war, and all the recent circumstances that preceded it, have merely made it patently obvious to everyone who knows how to look that the People truly are one, that we are fresh, and that our People's strength has not been touched to any real extent by the decay that has spoiled our wise men. And what a service these wise men have rendered us in our dealings with Europe! Only recently they were still shouting to the whole world that we were poor and insignificant; with a jeer they assured everyone that there was no spirit whatsoever among our People because there were no *People* whatsoever, since our People and their spirit were mere products of the fantasies of homegrown Moscow dreamers; that eighty million Russian peasants were nothing more than millions of inert, drunken taxation units; that there was no unity between tsar and People; that this was only some copybook maxim; that, on the contrary, everything had been shaken and corroded by nihilism; that our soldiers would throw down their arms and run like sheep; that we had neither cartridges nor provisions; and finally, that we ourselves could see that we had been merely talking to keep our spirits up and had gone too far, and now were only looking anxiously for any pretext to retreat without the ultimate disgrace of having our face slapped—something that "even we would be unable to endure"—and were praying for Europe to invent such a pretext for us. This is the sworn testimony of our wise men and, indeed, one can scarcely get angry at them; this is their view and their understanding, their utterly sincere view and understanding. And truly, yes, we are poor; yes, we are pitiful in many respects; yes, there really is so much wrong with us that the wise man, and particularly if he is one of *our* wise men, cannot "betray" himself and cannot help but exclaim, "Russia is *kaputt* and we needn't feel sorry about it!" And so it is these heartfelt ideas of our wise men that have flown around Europe, particularly through the channel of European correspondents who flocked here on the eve of the war to study us at first hand, to examine us from their European viewpoints and to measure our strength by their European yardstick. And it goes without saying that they have been listening only to our "most wise and sensible" people. All of them have overlooked the strength of the People, the spirit of the People, and the news has flown around Europe that Russia is perishing, that Russia is nothing—she was nothing, she is nothing now, and she will be brought to nothing. The hearts of our age-old enemies and Russophobes, whom we have annoyed in Europe for two centuries now, started to quiver; the hearts of many thousands of European Yids, along with the hearts of millions of "Christians" who practice the Yiddish trade along with them, also began to quiver; Beaconsfield's heart quivered: he had been told that Russia would endure everything, right to the most disgraceful and final slap in the face, but would not go to war—such, he was told, was the strength of her "peaceable nature." But God saved us, having sent blindness upon them all; they have put far too much faith in the ruination and the insignificance of Russia and have overlooked the very most important thing. They have overlooked the entire Russian People as a living force and have overlooked a colossal fact: the union of the tsar with his People! It's *only this* they have overlooked! Besides, they simply could not comprehend and believe that our tsar truly is peaceable and truly does regret the blood that will be shed: they thought that all this was merely "politics." And even now they see nothing: they shout that suddenly, after the tsar's manifesto, "patriotism" has reared its head among us. But is this patriotism? This is where our main strength lies: that they do not understand Russia at all, that they understand nothing in Russia! They do not know that nothing in the world can conquer us, that we may, perhaps, lose battles but will still remain unconquerable precisely because of the unity of our People's spirit and by our People's consciousness; that we are not France, which is entirely in Paris; that we are not Europe, which completely depends on the stock markets of its bourgeoisie and on the "placidity" of its proletariats, a placidity purchased by the last resorts of their governments there—and this only for an hour. They do not understand and do not know that if such is our *will*, we will not be conquered by all the Yids of Europe taken together, nor by the millions of their gold, nor by the millions of their armies; that if such is our will, we cannot be compelled to do that which we do not wish to do, and that there is no power on earth that could compel us. The only problem is that people not only in Europe but in Russia as well will laugh at these words, and that not only our wise and sensible people but even genuine Russian people of our educated class will laugh as well—such is our lack of understanding of ourselves and our age-old strength, which, thank God, has not yet been broken. These good people do not understand that in Russia, in our vast, unique, utterly un-European land, even military tactics (so common a thing as that!) can be quite unlike European ones, that the bases of European tactics—money and the scientific organization of six-hundred-thousand-man invading armies—may stumble in our land and fall against what for them is a new and unknown power, whose bases lie in the nature of the endless Russian land and in the nature of the all-uniting Russian spirit. But never mind that, *for the time being,* so many good people among us still do not know this (they do not know and are hesitant). Yet our tsars do know it, and our People sense it. Alexander I knew about this unique power of ours when he said that he would let his beard grow and go off into the forest with his People, but would not lay down his sword and submit to the will of Napoleon. And, of course, should the whole of Europe come up against such a force, it would all be shattered, because they have neither the money nor the unified organization to conduct such a war. When all our Russians realize that we are that strong, then we shall have reached a point where we shall no longer have to wage war; then people will believe in us and will *discover* us for the first time, as Europe once discovered America. But for that to happen we must discover ourselves before they do, and our intelligentsia must understand that it can no longer remain isolated and estranged from its People. . . .

2. War Is Not Always a Scourge; Sometimes It Is Salvation

But our wise men have seized upon yet another aspect of the matter: they preach benevolence and humaneness, they grieve over the blood to be shed and over the fact that we will become even more bestial and defiled in a war and thereby move even further away from our goal of domestic well being, from the true path, from science. Yes, war, of course, is a misfortune, but there is also much that is wrong in these arguments; and the main thing is that we have had enough of this bourgeois moralizing! The feat of sacrificing our blood for all that we consider sacred is, of course, more moral than this entire bourgeois catachism. The nation's surge of spirit for the sake of a noble idea—that is an impulse toward progress and not bestialization. Of course, we may be mistaken in what we regard as a noble idea; but if the thing we consider our holy of holies is shameful and flawed, then we will not escape punishment from Nature herself: that which is shameful and flawed bears death within it and sooner or later will exact its own punishment. For instance, a war fought to acquire wealth, for the demands of the insatiable stock market, may arise from the same law of development of national personality common to all nations, yet there is a limit to this development that must not be crossed and beyond which every acquisition and every development means excess; it bears a disease within it, a disease that ends in death. So it is that England, should she take the side of Turkey in this current conflict in the East, having utterly ignored the groans of tormented humanity for the sake of her commercial interests, would surely be raising her sword against herself, a sword that, sooner or later, will fall on her own head. On the other hand, what is more sacred and pure than the feat of a war such as Russia is presently undertaking? People will say: "But though Russia, too, may truly be setting out only to liberate the oppressed peoples there and to restore their independence, in so doing she will acquire future allies in these same peoples and, accordintly, acquire power; and so it is all just another example of this same law of development of national personality toward which England is also striving. And since the colossal scope of this proposed 'panslavism' may truly frighten Europe, then the same law of self-preservation certainly entitles Europe to stop us; on the same basis, however, we are entitled to go ahead, paying no heed to her fears and guided in our movement only by political foresight and prudence. Thus there is nothing here either sacred or shameful; there is only the age-old life instinct of peoples to which all of the earth's insufficiently and improperly developed tribes respond without differentiation. Nevertheless, as consciousness, science, and humaneness accumulate, sooner or later the age-old and bestial instinct of improperly developed nations must weaken and inspire, rather, a desire for peace, international unity, and humane development in all peoples. Accordingly, one must still preach peace, not blood."

Holy words! But in the present instance they somehow do not apply to Russia, or, to put it even better—Russia, at the present historical moment of Europe, is a kind of exception, and this is really so. In fact, if Russia, who has so selflessly and justly now taken up arms for the salvation and renewal of the oppressed tribes, should later increase her power through them, then in such a case she is still a most exceptional example that Europe, who measures by her own yardstick, simply cannot anticipate. If Russia is strengthened, even excessively, through her alliance with the tribes she has liberated, she will not fall upon Europe with a sword, will not seize and take away anything from her, as Europe certainly would do should she find the opportunity to unite herself once more against Russia, and as all the nations of Europe have been doing all their lives, the moment they found the opportunity to increase their strength at the expense of their neighbor. (And this has been going on from the most savage, primordial times of Europe right up to the modern and so recent Franco-Prussian War. And what became of all their civilization then? The most educated and enlightened of all nations attacked another nation, just as educated and enlightened and, taking advantage of the opportunity, tore the life out of it like a wild beast, drank its blood, squeezed the juices out of it in the form of billions in reparations, and cut off its whole side in the form of two of its best provinces! Yes, in truth, can Europe be blamed if, after that, she cannot understand Russia's mission? How can they, proud, educated, and strong, understand and admit, even in their wildest fantasies, that Russia is predestined and created, perhaps, for their salvation as well and that only she, perhaps, will at last pronounce this word of salvation?) Oh, yes, yes, of course, not only will we seize nothing from them and take nothing away, but the fact that we will be vastly strengthened (through an alliance of love and brotherhood, not through seizure and violence) will at last allow us not to bare our sword but, rather, in the calm assurance of our strength, to give an example of sincere peace, international unity, and selflessness. We shall be the first to declare to the world that it is not by suppressing the national personalities of other tribes that we strive to achieve our own well-being; on the contrary, we see that well-being only in the freest and most independent development of all other nations and in fraternal unity with them, each one enhancing the other, grafting their organic features onto ourselves and giving them our branches to graft onto themselves, communing with them in soul and in spirit, learning from them and teaching them; and so it will be until such time as humanity, having achieved universal unity through the communion of nations of the world, will, as a great and magnificant tree, cast its shade over the happy earth. Oh, let today's "universal men" and those full of contempt for their own People laugh at these "fantastic" words, but we cannot be blamed if we believe these things, that is, if we go hand in hand with our People who believe precisely these things. Ask the People; ask the soldier; why do they rise up, why do they go to war, what do they expect from the war that has just begun? They will tell you, as one man, that they are going to serve Christ and to liberate their oppressed brethren, and not a single one of them is thinking about seizing territory. Indeed, it is precisely here, in this present war, that we shall demonstrate our whole idea about Russia's future mission in Europe and demonstrate it precisely by the fact that when we do liberate the Slavic lands, we shall not acquire a single inch of them for ourselves (as Austria now has visions of doing); we shall, rather, watch to see that they live in mutual harmony and shall defend their freedom and independence, from the whole of Europe if need be. And if such is the case, then our idea is sacred, and our war is not at all "the age-old and bestial instinct of improperly developed nations," but is precisely the first step toward attaining that eternal peace in which we are fortunate enough to believe, toward attaining international unity *in truth,* and a humane state of well-being *in truth!* And so, one need not always preach only peace, and it is not in peace alone, despite everything, that salvation is to be found; sometimes it is also in war.

3. Does Shed Blood Save Us?

"But the bloodshed; we are talking of bloodshed, after all," the wise men kept repeating, and truly, all these official phrases about bloodshed are often nothing more than a collection of most insignificant, high-sounding words spoken with a definite purpose in mind. Stock-exchange operators, for instance, are extremely fond of talking about humaneness. And many of those who now talk of humaneness are nothing more than traders in it. And yet, even more blood might be shed without a war. Believe me, in some instances, if not in almost all instances (except in those of civil wars), war is the process *precisely* through which international peace is achieved with the least amount of bloodshed, the least amount of misery, the least expenditure of effort, and in which at least some approximation of normal relationships between nations are worked out. Of course, it's a sad thing, but what can be done if such is the case? It's better, after all, to draw the sword than to suffer endlessly. And in what way is the current peace among civilized nations better than war? On the contrary, it is not war but peace, a prolonged peace, that bestializes and hardens people. A prolonged peace always gives rise to cruelty, cowardice, and coarse, bloated egoism and, above all, to intellectual stagnation. During a prolonged peace only the hangman and the exploiters of peoples grow fat. We hear again and again that peace generates wealth, but this is true only for a tenth of people, and this ten percent, having become infected with the diseases of wealth, pass on the infection to the remaining ninety percent, although they do not pass on the wealth. The former become infected with vice and cynicism. An excessive accumulation of wealth in the hands of a few generates coarseness of feeling in the possessors of that wealth. The sense of refinement is transformed into a thirst for frivolous luxuries and abnormality. There is a terrible spread of voluptuousness. Voluptuousness generates cruelty and cowardice. The bloated and coarse soul of the voluptuary is more cruel than any other—even one with many flaws. A voluptuary who faints at the sight of blood from a cut finger will not pardon some poor wretch and will have him sent to prison for a tiny debt. Cruelty, in turn, generates an intensified and most cowardly anxiety over one's own safety. This cowardly anxiety over one's security is always ultimately transformed, during a prolonged peace, into a kind of panic fear for oneself, and that spreads through all levels of society; it generates a terrible greed for the acquisition and accumulation of money. Faith in human solidarity, in human brotherhood and in the help of society, is lost; the slogan Every Man for Himself is loudly proclaimed; the poor man sees all too clearly what the wealthy man is and what sort of brother he is to him, and so each one isolates himself and dissociates himself. Egoism kills noble feelings. It is only art that still supports the higher life in society and awakens the souls that have fallen into slumber during periods of prolonged peace. And that is why people have conjured up the notion that art can flourish only in a time of prolonged peace, yet there is an immense error here: art, I mean *genuine* art, develops during a prolonged peace precisely because it is at odds with the heavy and immoral slumber of souls; in such periods the creations of art always invoke an ideal, generate protest and indignation, rouse society, and often cause suffering for those who long to awaken and climb out of the stinking pit. Ultimately, the result is that a prolonged, bourgeois peace almost always generates an urge for war; this is its miserable consequence, and it is not a war for a grand and just purpose, worthy of a great nation, but for some wretched bourgeois interests, for new markets needed by the exploiters, for acquiring new slaves essential to those who own the sacks of gold—in short, for reasons that are not justified even by the need for self-preservation but, rather, for reasons that testify to the frivolous, pathological state of the natnional organism. These interests, and the wars that are undertaken to support them, corrupt and even utterly destroy nations, whereas a war for some noble purpose, for the liberation of the oppressed, for the sake of a selfless and sacred idea—such a war can only clear the air befouled by accumulated miasmas, cure the soul, drive out shameful cowardice and laziness, declare and set forth a firm goal, provide and clarify an idea that this or that nation is summoned to put into effect. Such a war strengthens every soul with the awareness of self-sacrifice, and the spirit of the entire nation with the awareness of the mutual solidarity and unity of all the members that constitute it. And the most important thing is the awareness of a duty fulfilled and of a good deed accomplished: "We have not entirely fallen and become corrupt; there remains something human even in us!" And just look at how these proponents of peaceableness and humaneness began their preaching so recently: they began directly with the most inhuman cruelty. They themselves did not want to help the martyrs who were calling out to us, and they restrained others from doing so. These people, evidently so humane and so sensitive, cold-bloodedly and mockingly denied our need to sacrifice ourselves and accomplish a great spiritual deed. They sought to push Russia onto the lowest and most unworthy path for a great nation; and beyond that, there was their contempt for the People who saw the Slavic martyrs as their brothers and, consequently, their haughty alienation from the will of the People, above which they placed their own false "European" enlightenment. Their favorite slogan was Physician, Heal Thyself. "You go off to heal and to save others, but you haven't even built schools of your own"—such was the evidence they provided. "Well, and what of it? that's why we are going—to heal ourselves. Schools are an important thing, of course; but schools need a spirit and a direction—and that's why we're going now: to gather up some spirit and to acquire a proper direction. And we will acquire these things, particularly if God sends us a victory. We shall return with the awareness of the selfless deed we have accomplished, with the awareness that we have gloriously served humanity with our blood, with the awareness of our renewed strength and energy—and all of this in place of our so recent shameful infirmity of purpose, in place of the deathly stagnation of our mindlessly borrowed Europeanism. And the most important thing is that we shall commune with the People and unite ourselves more firmly with them—for in them and in them alone shall we find the cure for our two-hundred-year-old ailment, for our two-hundred-year-old unproductive impotence."

Indeed, one can say generally that if society is unhealthy and infected, then even such a fine thing as a prolonged peace can, instead of benefiting society, be harmful to it. One can even apply this to all of Europe generally. It is not without reason that no generation has passed in the history of Europe, as far as we can remember it, without a war. And so, evidently, even war is essential for something; it is healing; it relieves humanity. This is shocking if one thinks in abstract terms, but in practice it turns out that way, it seems, and precisely because in an infected organism even such a fine thing as peace is transformed into something harmful. But still, the only useful war is one undertaken for a grand idea, for a higher and noble principle and not for material interests, not for greedy seizure of territory, not for contemptuous violence. Wars of that sort have only led nations along wrong paths and have always destroyed them. If not we, then our children, will see how England ends. Now, for everyone in the world, "the time is at hand." And about time, too.

4. The Opinion of the "Most Serene" Tsar on the Eastern Question

I have been given an excerpt from a book published in Kiev last year: *The Moscow State under Tsar Alexis and Patriarch Nikon, from the Records of Archdeacon Pavel of Aleppo,* by Ivan Obolensky, Kiev, 1876, pp. 90–91. This is a page from someone else's work, but it is so characteristic and so interesting at our present moment, and the work itself probably so little known to the general public, that I decided to include these few lines in the *Diary.* The passage reveals the opinion on the Eastern Question of Tsar Alexis—also a "most serene" tsar—and his lament that he was unable to be a tsar-liberator.

> It was said that Easter in the year 1656 the sovereign, exchanging Easter greetings with some Greek merchants who were visiting Moscow, asked them, "Is it your wish and expectation that I liberate and ransom you from captivity?" And when they replied: "How could it be otherwise? How could be not wish it?"—he added, "So therefore, when you return to your lands, ask all the monks and bishops to pray to God and to hold services for me so that through their prayers I may be given strength to cut off the head of their enemy." And having shed many tears over this, he then addressed the nobles, saying: "My heart is filled with grief over the enslavement of these poor people who suffer in the clutches of the enemies of our faith; God will call me to account on judgment day *if, having the power to liberate them, I neglect my duty.* I do not know how long government affairs will continue in such a lamentable state, but since the time of my father and his predecessors we have been visited unceasingly by patriarchs, bishops, monks, and ordinary poor people bearing complaints of their conqueror's oppression, and not one of them has come save because he was burdened with most bitter sorrow and was fleeing from the cruelty of his masters. *And I dread the question the Creator will put to me on that day: and I have resolved in my mind, should it please God, to use all my armies and my treasury, and shed my blook to the last drop, yet will I strive to liberate them."* To all this the nobles replied, "*O Lord, grant thy heart's desire.*"

2

The Dream of a Ridiculous Man: A Fantastic Story

1

I'm a ridiculous man. Now they call me a madman. It would have been a promotion if I hadn't remained just as ridiculous in their eyes as before. But now it doesn't bother me; now they're all dear to me, and even when they laugh at me—even then there are things that make them especially dear. I'd laugh along with them—not at myself, but loving them—if I didn't feel so sad when I look at them. I feel sad, because they don't know the truth, while I know the truth. Ah, what a hard thing it is to be the only one who knows the truth! But they won't understand that. No, they won't understand.

But in times past I used to worry a good deal because I seemed a ridiculous man. Not seemed: I was. I was always a ridiculous man, and I've known it, I suppose, ever since I was born. Perhaps I knew it already at the age of seven. Then I went to school, and then to university, and what do you think? The more I studied, the more I came to realize that I was a ridiculous man. So as far as I was concerned, the more deeply I became involved in my university studies, the more its ultimate purpose seemed only to prove and make clear to me that I was a ridiculous man. My life followed the same pattern as my studies. With every year the same awareness—that I looked like a ridiculous man in every respect—grew and strengthened within me. Everyone always laughed at me. But not one of them knew or suspected that if there was one person on earth who knew better than anyone that I was a ridiculous man, then that person was I myself; and this was just the thing that was most painful to me—that they didn't know it. But that was my own fault: I was always so proud that I could never have admitted this to anyone. This pride grew inside me over the years, and if there had ever come a time when I permitted myself to admit to someone that I was a ridiculous man, then I think that at once, that very same evening, I would have blown my head off with a revolver. Oh, the pains I suffered in my adolescence, thinking that I might give in and suddenly somehow confess to my comrades. But as I grew to manhood, for some reason I became calmer, even though with every year I became more and more aware of my awful quality. I say "for some reason" because even now I can't explain why. Perhaps it was because in my soul there kept growing a terrible ache caused by one thing that was infinitely beyond anything in my own self—namely, the conviction that everywhere on earth *nothing mattered.* I had sensed this long before, but the complete conviction somehow suddenly struck me in the last year. I suddenly sensed that, as far as I was concerned, *it wouldn't matter* whether the world existed or whether there were nothing anywhere. I began to sense and feel with all my being that *nothing existed around me.* At first I kept thinking that a good many things used to exist in the past; then I conclusded that even in the past there had not been anything, but that for some reason it had only seemed as if there had been something. Little by little I became convinced that there would never be anything in the future either. At that point I suddenly stopped being angry at people and almost ceased to notice them. It's true that this showed itself even in the most trivial things: for instance, I'd be bumping into people as I was walking along the street. And this wasn't because I was deep in thought: what did I have to think about? At that point I'd stopped thinking altogether; it didn't matter to me. It would have been very well if I'd answered my questions; oh, but I hadn't answered a single one, and yet how many of them were there! But I began to feel that *nothing mattered,* and all the questions vanished.

And so, just after that, I discovered the truth. I discovered the truth last November, on the third of November to be precise, and I can recall every moment of my life since then. It happened on a gloomy evening, the gloomiest evening there could ever be. Some time after ten o'clock I was going back home, and I recall thinking specifically that there could be no gloomier time than this. Even in a physical sense. Rain had been pouring down all day, and it was the coldest and gloomiest rain, even a sort of menacing rain,

I recall, with an open hostility toward people; and then, suddenly, towards eleven o'clock it stopped and a horrible dampness set in—damper and colder than when the rain was falling, and a kind of vapor rose from everything, from every stone on the pavement and from every side street, if you peered down to its farthest recesses. I suddenly imagined that if they were to shut off the gas everywhere it would be more cheerful, but one's heart was heavier with the lights on, because they illuminated everything. I had scarcely had any dinner that day and had spent the whole evening visiting an engineer, who had two of his friends there as well. I never opened my mouth the whole time and, I imagine, must have got on their nerves. They were discussing some controversial topic and suddenly even grew excited. But I could see that it really didn't matter to them and that they were excited just for form's sake. And suddenly I told them so: "Gentlemen," I said, "this really doesn't matter to you, does it?" They didn't take offense, and they all laughed at me. That was because I said what I did with no reproach and simply because it didn't matter to me. They saw very well that it didn't matter to me and were amused.

When the thought about the gaslight occurred to me out on the street, I looked up at the sky. The sky was awfully dark, but you could clearly make out some tattered clouds and bottomless black depths among them. Suddenly I noticed a tiny star in one of these depths and began looking at it intently. That was because this tiny star had given me an idea: I resolved that night to kill myself. I had made such a firm resolution even two months before, and despite my poverty I had bought a beautiful revolver and had loaded it that same day. Two months had passed, and it was still lying in my drawer; but so little did it matter to me that I wanted, at last, to catch a moment when it might matter, even just a little—for what reason, I don't know. And so it was that every night for these two months I came home thinking I would shoot myself. I kept waiting for the right moment. And now this tiny star had given me the idea, and I resolved that it would *definitely* happen on this very night. Why the tiny star gave me that idea I don't know.

And so, just as I was looking up at the sky, this little girl suddenly seized me by the elbow. The street was already deserted and there was scarcely a soul about. Off in the distance a cabbie was dozing in his droshky. The girl was about eight, wearing a kerchief and only a wretched little dress, and was soaked to the skin; but I particularly noticed her tattered boots, and remember them even now. The boots struck me particularly. She suddenly began tugging at my elbow and calling me. She wasn't weeping, but kept jerkily crying out some words that she couldn't pronounce clearly because she was all atremble from the cold. She was terrified of something and kept crying out desperately, "Mamma! Mamma!" I considered turning to face her, but said not a word and went on my way; but she ran after me and plucked at my sleeve, and I could hear in her voice the note that in very frightened children means despair. I know that sound. Although she didn't say so in wordss, I understood that her mother lay dying somewhere, or something had happened to them there and she had run out to call someone or find something to help her mother. But I didn't follow her and, on the contrary, suddenly got the notion to drive her away. First I told her that she should find a policeman. But she suddenly folded her tiny hands and, sobbing and choking, kept running alongside me and would not leave. At that point I stamped my foot and shouted at her. She only cried out, "Sir, oh sir!..." But suddenly she left me and rushed across the street: some passerby had appeared there, and she rushed over to him.

I went up to my fifth floor. I rent a place in a rooming house. My room is wretched and small, with a semicircular garret window. I have an oilcloth sofa, a table with some books on it, two charis and a comfortable armchair, a very ancient thing but a "Voltaire one," for all that. I sat down, lit a candle, and fell to thinking. In the room next door, behind the partition, the row was still going on. They'd been at it for three days now. A retired captain lived there, and he had visitors—six or more good-for-nothings who were drinking vodka and playing faro with some old cards. Last night there had been a brawl, and I know that two of them spent a long time tearing at each other's hair. The landlady wanted to complain, but she's awfully afraid of the captain. The only other lodgers in our place are a short, skinny lady—an army officer's wife from out of town—with three small children who have already fallen ill since coming to live here. She and the children are deathly afraid of the captain and spend their nights trembling and crossing themselves; the smallest child was so afraid he had a fit of some kind. I know for certain that this captain sometimes stops passersby on the Nevsky and begs money from them. They won't take him into the civil service, yet the strange thing is (and this is why I'm telling you this), the whole month the captain has been living here he hasn't caused me the least bit of annoyance. From the very beginning, of course, I shied away from any acquaintance with him, and in fact he was bored with me from our first meeting; but no matter how much shouting went on behind the partition and no matter how many of them there were, it didn't matter to me. I sit up all night long and, truly, I don't hear them—that's how well I'm able to ignore them. I never get to sleep until dawn, you see, and it's been that way for a year now. I sit by the table in my armchair all night long and do nothing. Books I read only during the day. I sit, not thinking about anything in particular, just like that; vague thoughts wander through my mind, and I let them flow as they please. A whole candle burns up during the night. I sat down quietly by the table, took out the revolver and put it down in front of me. I recall asking myself as I put it down, "Is this how it is to be?" And I answered myself absolutely affirmatively, "Yes, it is." That's to say, I'll shoot myself. I knew that I would certainly shoot myself that night, but how much longer I would go on sitting by the table—that I didn't know. And of course I would have shot myself had it not been for that little girl.

2

You see, even though it didn't matter to me, I could still feel pain, for instance. If someone were to strike me, I would feel pain. It was just the same way in a moral sense: if something very sad were to happen, I would feel pity, just as before, when things in life still did matter to me. I had felt pity earlier that evening: I would certainly have helped out a child. So why didn't I help the little girl? It was because of a thought that came to me then: when she was tugging at my sleeve and calling me a question suddenly arose in my mind, and I wasn't able to answer it. It was an idle question, but it made me angry. I got angry because if I had already decided that I would kill myself that same night, then nothing on earth ought to matter to me, now more than ever. Why was it, then, that I suddenly felt that I was not indifferent to everything and pitied the little girl? I recall that I felt a great deal of pity for her, to the point even of a strange pain, even an improbable pain, given my situation. Truly, I don't know how better to convey that fleeting sensation I had then, but the sensation continued at home as well, when I had taken my seat by the table, and I was very irritated, as I hadn't been for a long time. One train of thought followed another. It seemed clear that if I were a human being and not yet a nonentity—and until such time as I became a nonentity—I was living, and accordingly could suffer, get angry, and feel shame for my actions. Granted. But if I were going to kill myself in two hours, say, then what should I care about this girl and about shame and about anything on earth? I was going to be transformed into a nonentity, an absolute nonentity. Could it be that the awareness of the fact that shortly I would *absolutely* cease to exist and that, accordingly, nothing else would exist—could that not have had the least influence either on the feeling of pity for the little girl or on the feeling of shame after the vile thing I had done? After all, that was the reason I had stamped my foot and shouted in a savage voice at the unfortunate child—that I could think "not only do I feel no pity but I can permit myself to commit some inhuman, vile deed because in two hours everything will be extinguished." Can you believe that this was why I shouted? Now I'm almost convinced of it. It seemed clear that from this point life and the world were dependent on me, as it were. I can even say that now the world had been created for me alone, as it were: I'll shoot myself and the world will exist no longer, at least as far as I'm concerned. To say nothing of the possibility that, perhaps, nothing really would exist for anyone else after me and that as soon as my consciousness was extinguished, the whole world would be extinguished with it, like a mirage, like a product of my own consciousness alone; and it would be done away with because this entire world and all these people were, perhaps, nothing more than myself. I recall that as I sat there thinking this out, I gave all these new questions that were crowding into my mind one after the other an entirely different twist and conceived something quite new. For example, I suddenly had the following strange notion: suppose I had formerly lived on the moon or on Mars and had committed there the most disgraceful and dishonorable act one can imagine for which I had been defamed and dishonored to an extent one can imagine only in some dream or nightmare; and, if I had later found myself on earth, still with the awareness of what I had done on the other planet, and knew, as well, that I would never ever return there, then would I, as I looked from the earth to the moon, feel as if *it didn't matter?* Would I have felt shame for my act or not? These were idle, unnecessary questions, since the revolver was lying on the table before me, and I knew with all my being that *it* would certainly happen; yet they excited me and worked me into a frenzy. It seemed I could not die now without having first resolved something. In short, that little girl saved me because the questions led me to put off shooting myself. Meanwhile, everything began to quiet down in the captain's room: they finished their card game and were settling down to sleep, still grumbling and lazily abusing one another. And at this point I suddenly dropped off to sleep in my chair by the table, something that had never happened to me before. I didn't notice falling asleep at all. Dreams, as we know, are extraordinarily strange things: you'll have one that has an awful clarity, with all its details presented with lapidary precision, while in another you don't even notice how you swoop through time and space. Dreams, I think, are governed not by reason but desire, not by the head but the heart; and yet what crafty tricks my reason sometimes plays on me in dreams! Furthermore, some quite incomprehensible things happen to my reason in sleep. My brother, for instance, died five years ago. I sometimes dream of him: he takes part in my affairs; we are deeply involved with one another, yet throughout the dream I know and remember full well that my brother is dead and buried. How is it that I'm not amazed at the fact that even though he's dead, he's still right here beside me, concerning himself with my affairs? Why does my reason accept all this so completely? But enough. I'll get back to my dream. Yes, this is the dream I had then, my dream of the third of November. They tease me about it now, saying that it was only a dream, after all. But surely it doesn't matter whether it was a dream or not since this dream revealed the Truth to me. If once you've recognized the truth and have seen it, then you surely know that it is the truth and that there is not and cannot be any other, whether you are asleep or awake. Well, it was a dream—let it be so; yet I was going to put an end to this life which you make so much of, but my dream—oh, my dream revealed to me a new life, renewed, intense, and majestic!

Listen.

3

I said that I drifted off to sleep without noticing it and even went on mulling over those same matters, as it were. Suddenly I dreamed that I took up the revolver and, still sitting in my chair, was aiming it right at my heart—at my heart and not my head; earlier I had decided that I would definitely shoot myself in the head, in the right temple, to be specific. With the revolver pointed at my chest I hesitated for a second or two, and suddenly my candle, the table, and the wall before me began to move and sway. Quickly I fired.

In dreams you sometimes fall from a great height or are being stabbed or beaten, but you never feel any pain unless you somehow bump yourself against the bedpost; then you feel pain and almost always wake up. So it was in my dream: I felt no pain, but it seemed that after my shot everything within me was shaken, and suddenly everything went blank and there was an awful blackness all around me. I seemed to be blind and mute and was lying on my back, stretched out full-length on something hard, seeing nothing, and unable to make the least movement. All around me people were walking and shouting; the captain rumbled and the landlady screeched—and suddenly there was another quiet interval, and now I was being carried in a closed coffin. And I could feel the coffin swaying and was thinking about that; and suddenly for the first time I was struck by the thought that I was dead, quite dead, and knew it without a doubt; I could not see and could not move, yet I could feel and think. But I quickly become resigned to that and, as usual in a dream, accepted the facts with no argument.

And so they were burying me. Everyone went away, and I was alone, completely alone. I made no move. Formerly, whenever I used to imagine what it would be like to be buried, the only sensation I would associate with the grave was cold and damp. And so it was now: I felt very cold, especially the tips of my toes; but I felt nothing more than that.

I lay there and, strangely enough, expected nothing, accepting without demur that a dead man had nothing to expect. But it was damp. I don't know how much time passed—an hour or a few days or many days. But suddenly a drop of water that had seeped through the lid of the coffin fell on my left eye, which was closed; a minute later there was another one, and a third minute later; and so it continued, a drop every minute. Deep indignation suddenly welled up in my heart, and suddenly I felt a physical pain there: "That's my wound," I thought, "it's the shot, there's a bullet there. . . ." and the drops kept falling every minute, directly on my closed eyelid. And suddenly I called out—not with my voice, for I could not move, but with my whole being—to the One who governed all that was happening to me: "Whoever Thou may be, but if Thou art and if there does exist anything more rational than what is now coming to pass, then grant that it happen here as well. But if Thou art taking vengeance upon me for my unwise suicide, through the ugliniess and absurdity of life after death, then know that no torment that might ever befall me could compare with the contempt that I shall always feel in silence, though it be through millions of years of martyrdom! . . ."

I cried out and fell silent. A profound silence continued for almost a whole minute, and one more drop of water even fell; but I knew, I knew and believed infinitely and unshakably that now everything must certainly change. And then suddenly my grave opened wide. I mean to say, I don't know whether all the earth had actually been dug away, but I was taken up by some dark and unfamiliar creature and we found ourselves in open space. I suddenly recovered my sight: it was the depths of night, and never ever had there been such darkness! We were flying through space, and the earth was already far behind us. I did not ask anything of the one who bore me; I waited, proud. I assured myself that I was not afraid and was dizzy with delight at the thought that I was not afraid. I don't recall how long we flew and can't even imagine it: everything happened as it always does in dreams, when one leaps through space and time and over the laws of existence, stopping only where one's heart longs to stop. I recall that I suddenly caught sight of one tiny star in the darkness. "Is that Sirius?" I asked, suddenly unable to hold back, for I had decided not to ask about anything. "No," answered the creature who bore me, "it is that same star you saw among the clouds when you were coming home." I knew that the face of the creature was in the likeness of a human. But, strangely enough, I did not like that creature and even felt a deep aversion toward it. I had been expecting complete nonexistence, and with that in mind had shot myself in the heart. And now I was in the hands of a creature which was not human, of course, but which *was*, which existed. "And so there is a life beyond the grave!" I thought, with the bizarre frivolity of dreams, but the real essence of my heart remained unchanged: "And if I must *be* once more," I thought, "and live again by someone else's intractable will, then I will not be vanquished and humiliated!"

"You know that I am afraid of you, and therefore you despise me," I said suddenly to my companion, unable to resist a humiliating question that held an admission and sensing the humiliation in my heart like a pinprick. He did not answer my question, but I suddenly sensed that I was not despised and that I was not being laughed at, that I was even being pitied, and that our journey had a goal, unknown and mysterious and concerning only me. Fear welled up in my heart. Something was passing from my silent companion to me, mutely but agonizingly, and it seemed to pierce to the core of my being. We were rushing through dark and unknown regions of space. I had long lost sight of the constellations familar to me. I knew that there are such stars in the vastness of the heavens whose rays reach the earth only after thousands and millions of years. Perhaps we were already flying through these spaces. I was expecting something, in a terrible agony that gripped my heart. And suddenly I was shaken by a familiar and most nostalgic feeling: I suddenly caught sight of our sun! I knew that it could not be *our* sun that had given birth to *our* earth and that we were an infinite distance from our sun, but somehow I realized, with all my being, that this was just the same kind of sun as our own, its duplicate and twin. A sweet, welcoming feeling roused an ecstasy in my soul: the old, familiar power of the light, the same light that had given me life, made my heart respond and restored it, and I sensed life, the former life, for the first time since my burial.

"But if this is the sun, if this is exactly the same sun as ours," I cried, "then where is the earth?" And my companion pointed to a little star that glittered in the darkness with an emerald light. We were rushing directly toward it.

"And are such duplicates really possible in the universe? Is there really such a law of nature? . . . And if that is the earth over there, then is it really the same kind of earth as our own . . . just the same—unhappy, wretched, yet dear and eternally beloved, one that engenders as painful a love in its most ungrateful children as does our own?" I cried, trembling with irresiistible, rapturous love for that once native earth I had abandoned. The image of the wretched little girl whom I had offended flitted before me.

"You shall see it all," answered my companion, and there was a kind of sorrow in his words.

But we were quickly drawing near the planet. I could see it seeming to grow in size; I could already make out the ocean, the outlines of Europe; and suddenly a strange feeling of some tremendous and sacred journey began to burn in my heart: "How can there be such a duplication, and why? I love—I can love only the earth I have left behind, which I have spattered with my blood when I, ungrateful wretch, extinguished my life with a bullet in my heart. But never, never did I cease to love that earth, and even on the night I parted with it I loved it, perhaps, more agonizingly than ever. Does suffering exist on this new earth? On our earth we can truly love only with suffering and only through suffering! We know not how to love in any other way, and know no other love. I want to suffer in order to love. This very instant I want, I long, to kiss and to water with my tears the one and only earth I have abandoned, and I do not want and do not accept life on any other! . . ."

But my companion had already left me. Suddenly, without really knowing how it happened, I was standing on this other earth in the sunny brightness of a day as lovely as paradise. I think I was on one of those islands that on our earth form part of the Greek archipelago, or somewhere on the mainland coast adjacent to that archipelago. Oh, it was all just the same as it is on our earth, but everything seemed to have a festive glow, as if some glorious and holy triumph had at last been achieved. The friendly emerald-green sea lapped quietly against the shore and kissed it with a love that was unmistakable, visible, almost conscious. Tall, beautiful trees stood in full splendor, and their countless little leaves—I'm convinced of it—welcomed me with their gentle, calming rustle and seemed to be whispering words of love. The meadow was ablaze with bright, fragrant flowers. Flocks of little birds wheeled through the air and landed unafraid on my shoulders and hands, beating joyfully at me with their dear little fluttering wings. And at last I met and came to know the people of this happy land. They came to me themselves, gathered around me, and kissed me. Children of the sun, children of their sun—and oh, how beautiful they were! Never on our earth have I seen such beauty in people. Perhaps only in our children of tenderest age could you find a distant, though pale reflection of this beauty. The eyes of these happy people shone with a clear light. Their faces radiated wisdom and a consciousness that had attained serenity, but their faces were happy: the voices and words of these people rang with childlike joy. Oh, at once, the moment I looked at these faces, I understood everything, everything! This was an earth that had not been defiled by sin; on it lived people who had not sinned, who lived in just such a paradise in which our fallen ancestors had once lived, according to the traditions of all of humanity, the only difference being that the entire earth here was one and the same paradise. These people, laughing joyously, crowded around and caressed me; they took me to their dwellings, and each one of them was anxious to comfort me. Oh, they did not question me about anything but seemed to know everything already and wanted quickly to banish suffering from my face.

4

Now, I'll say it once more: what would it matter if it had been only a dream! Still, the feeling of the love of these innocent and beautiful people has remained ever within me, and I feel that their love comes pouring down on me even now. I saw them myself, came to know them, and became convinced; I loved them and I suffered for them afterward. Oh, even then I realized at once that there were many things about them I would never understand; for instance, I, a modern Russian progressive and wretched inhabitant of Petersburg, found it inexplicable that they, who knew so much, had none of our science. But I soon realized that their knowledge was supplied and nourished by insights different from those on our earth and that their aspirations were also quite different. They had no desires and were content; they did not strive for knowledge of life as we strive to comprehend it, because their lives were complete. But their knowledge was more profound and more elevated than our science; for our science seeks to explain what life is and itself strives to comprehend it so as to teach others how to live, while they knew how to live even without science; I realized that, but could not understand their knowledge. They showed me their trees, and I could not understand the intensity of love with which they regarded these trees: it was just as though they were speaking to creatures like themselves. And, you know, I may not be wrong in saying that they spoke with them! Yes, they had found their language, and I am convinced that the trees understood them. They regarded the whole of nature in the same way—the animals, which lived peaceably with them and did not attack them, conquered by their love. they showed me the stars and told me something about them that I was unable to grasp, but I am convinced that they were able somehow to make contact with these heavenly stars, not only through thought but in some living way. Oh, these people did not strive to make me understand them, they loved me without that; and yet I knew that they would never understand me either, and therefore I scarcely ever spoke to them of our earth. I merely kissed the earth on which they lived, in their presence, and adored them wordlessly; and they saw this and let me adore them, unashamed that I was doing it because they themselves deeply loved me. They felt no pain for me when I, in tears, would kiss their feet, for in their hearts they joyously knew the strength of love with which they would return my feeling. At times I would ask myself in amazement how they managed never to offend a person like me and never to make me feel any jealousy or envy. Many times I asked myself how I, a braggart and liar, could refrain from speaking of the things I knew, things of which they, naturally, hadn't the least conception. How could I not want to astonish them with my knowledge, even if only out of love for them? They were as full of life and joy as children. They wandered through their magnificent groves and forests; they sang their beautiful songs; they ate but lightly, of the fruits of their trees, the honey of their forests, and the milk of their devoted animals. Acquiring food and clothing cost them little and easy toil. They loved and begot children, but never did I see in them the outbursts of *cruel* sensuality that befall almost everyone on our earth—each and every one—and serve as the single source of almost all the sins of our human race. They rejoiced in their newborn children as new participants in their bliss. There were no quarrels and jealousy among them, and they did not even understand what these things meant. Their children were the children of all because they all were part of one family. They had scarcely illnesses, although there was death; but their old people died peacefully, as if sinking into slumber, surrounded by people who had come to bid them farewell, blessing them, smiling at them, and departing life accompanied by the radiant smiles of others. I saw no grief or tears on these occasions, only a love that seemed to multiply to the point of rapture, but a rapture that was calm, contemplative, and complete. There was reason to think that they were able to keep in touch with their dead even after death and that the earthly union among them was not broken by death. They could scarcely understand me when I asked them about eternal life, but apparently they were so utterly convinced of it that it was not even a question for them. They had no temples, but they did have a kind of essential, living, and continuous union with the Totality of the universe; they had no religion; instead they had a certain knowledge that when their earthly joy had fulfilled itself to its limits there would ensue—both for the living and for the dead—an even broader contact with the Totality of the universe. They awaited this moment joyfully but unhurriedly, not with painful longing but as if their hearts held a presentiment of it that they communicated to one another. Before going to sleep in the evenings they loved to sing in harmonious and melodious chorus. In these songs they expressed all the feelings the passing day had brought them; they sang praise to the day and bade it farewell. They sang praises to nature, the earth, the sea, the forests. They loved to compose songs to one another and heaped praises on each other like children; these were the simplest of songs, but they came from the heart and moved the heart. And not only their songs but, it seemed, their whole lives were devoted only to admiring one another. It was a kind of complete, all-encompassing devotion to one another. Yet some of their songs were solemn and ecstatic, and I could scarcely understand them at all. While understanding the words, I could never comprehend their full meaning. That remained inaccessible to my mind, as it were, yet my heart seemed more and more to grasp instinctively its essence. I often told them that I had had a presentiment of all this long ago, that all this joy and glory had affected me while still on our earth by evoking a longing that at times reached unbearable sorrow; that the dreams of my heart and the fancies of my mind had given me a presentiment of all of them and their glory; that on our earth I often could not look upon the setting sun without tears.... That my hatred for the people of our earth was always touched with anguish: why could I not hate them without loving them? why could I not help but forgive them? And in my love for them there was anguish: why could I not love them without hating them? They listened, and I saw that they could not comprehend what I was telling them; but I did not regret telling them of this: I knew that they understood the full force of my anguish over those I had left behind. And, indeed, when they looked at me with their tender gaze so filled with love, when I sensed that in their presence my heart as well was becoming as innocent and as honest as theirs, then I was not sorry I could not understand them. The sensation of the fullness of life almost took my breath away, and I could only worship them in silence.

Oh, how everyone laughs in my face and tells me that it's impossible to dream all of these details I'm telling you here; they say that in my dream I saw or felt only some sensation that my own heart engendered in a fit of delirium, while I invented all the details after I woke up. And when I admitted that, perhaps, this is really how it was—Lord, how they laughed in my face and what entertainment I provided them! Oh, yes, of course, I was overcome only by the sensation of that dream, and it alone survived in my wounded and bleeding heart; yet the actual images and forms of my dream—I mean those things I actually saw during the very time of my dreaming—were so filled with harmony, were so filled with charm and beauty, and were so filled with truth, that when I awakened I was naturally unable to embody them in our feeble words, so they were bound to become blurred in my mind; and so I may very well have been unconsciously forced to invent some of the details afterward and, of course, I distorted them, especially in my passionate longing to express them in some way or other as quickly as possible. And yet, how can I not believe that all this happened? That it happened, perhaps, a thousand times better, more brightly and joyously than I am telling it? Let it be a dream, but all of this had to have happened. You know, I'll tell you a secret: this whole thing, perhaps, wasn't a dream at all! For at this point something happened, something so awfully true that it could not have been the product of a dream. Let's suppose that my heart did give birth to my dream; but could my heart alone have been able to give birth to that awful truth that befell me then? How could I alone have invented it? How could it have been a product of my heart's fancy? As if my petty heart and my frivolous, trivial mind could have risen to such a revelation of the truth! Oh, judge for yourselves: I've kept this from you until now, but now I shall tell you this truth as well. The fact is that I... I corrupted them all!

5

Yes, yes, it ended in my corrupting them all! How it could have happened I don't know, I don't remember clearly. The dream encompassed thousands of years and left me merely with a sense of the whole. I know only that the cause of their fall into sin was I. Like some filthy trichina, like some atom of the plague that infects entire countries, so I infected that whole happy earth which had been sinless until my coming. They learned to lie, they came to love falsehood and to know the beauty of the lie. Oh, it may well have begun *innocently*, with a joke, with a bit of flirtation or amorous play, or it may really have been from an atom, but this atom of falsehood penetrated their hearts and pleased them. And then it was not long before sensuality was born; sensuality gave birth to jealousy, jealousy to cruelty.... Oh, I don't know, I can't remember, but soon—very soon—the first blood was shed: they were astonished and horrified and began to separate from one another and lose their unity. Alliances were formed, but now they were against one another. Recriminations and reproaches began. They came to know shame and elevated shame as a virtue. The concept of honor was born, and its banner was raised in each of the alliances. They began to abuse the animals, and the animals fled from them into the forests and became their enemies. There began a struggle for separation, for dissociation, for individuality, for "mine" and "thine." They began to speak in different languages. They tasted of sorrow and came to love it; they longed for suffering and said that Truth was attained only through suffering. At that point science made its appearance among them. When they had become wicked, they began to speak of brotherhood and humaneness and understood the meaning of these ideas. When they had become criminal, they invented justice and prescribed entire codes of law in order to maintain it; and to enforce these codes they set up a guillotine. They could scarcely remember what they had lost, and did not even want to believe that they had once been innocent and happy. They even laughed at the thought that they had once been happy and called it an idle fancy. They could not even imagine it in specific forms and images, yet the strange and marvelous thing was that though they had lost all faith in their former happiness and called it a fairy tale, they wanted so much to be innocent and happy again that, like children, they succumbed to the desires of their hearts and deified those desires, built temples and began to worship this idea of theirs, these "desires" of theirs, even while believing fully that these desires would never be fulfilled or achieved; still, they worshiped them in tears and bowed down to them. And yet, had it become possible for them to return to the innocent and happy state that they had lost, and should someone have suddenly shown it to them again and asked whether they wanted to return to it, they would certainly have refused. They told me: "We may be deceitful, wicked, and unjust; we *know* this and we lament it and torment ourselves over it; we inflict more punishment and torture on ourselves, perhaps, than will that merciful Judge who will weigh our sins and whose name we know not. But we have science, and with its help we shall again find the truth, but now we shall accept it consciously. Knowledge is higher than feelings, consciousness of life is higher than life. Science will give us true wisdom, wisdom will reveal the laws, and a knowledge of the laws of happiness is higher than happiness." That is what they said, and after saying it each one began to love himself more than he loved the others; and, indeed, they could not do otherwise. Each one became so jealous of his own individuality that he tried with all his might only to humiliate and belittle the individuality of others; and therein he saw the very purpose of his life. Slavery appeared, even voluntary slavery: the weak eagerly submitted to the strong merely so that the strong could help them crush those who were still weaker than they. Righteous men appeared, and they came to these people in tears and spoke to them of their arrogance, of their loss of measure and harmony, of their loss of shame. But the righteous men were mocked or stoned. Sacred blood was spilled on the porches of the temples. Then there appeared people who began trying to find some manner in which all might be united once again so that each, without ceasing to love himself more than everyone else, might at the same time not interfere with anyone else, so that they all might live in a harmonious society. Entire wars were waged for the sake of this idea. At the same time, all the warring parties believed that science, true wisdom, and a sense of self-preservation would at last compel humanity to unite in a harmonious and rational society; and so in the meantime, to speed the matter, the "wise" attempted as quickly as possible to annihilate all the "unwise" who did not understand their idea, so that the latter should not stand in the way of its triumph. But the sense of self-preservation began quickly to weaken; proud men and sensualists appeared who flatly demanded, "All or nothing." To achieve everything they wanted they resorted to crime and, if that failed, to suicide. Religions appeared with a cult of nonexistence and self-destruction for the sake of eternal peace in nothingness. At last, these people tired of their senseless labor and suffering appeared on their faces; and they proclaimed that suffering was beauty, for in suffering alone was there thought. Their songs were hymns to suffering. I walked among them wringing my hands, and I wept over them, yet I loved them even more, perhaps, than I had before, when suffering had not yet been written on their faces, when they were innocent and so beautiful. I came to love the earth they had defiled even more than when it had been a paradise, solely because grief had made its appearance on it. Alas, I have always loved grief and sorrow, but only for myself, only for myself, while I wept over them in pity. I stretched out my arms to them, accusing, cursing, and despising myself in despair. I told them that I had done all this, I alone, and that it was I who had brought them corruption, contamination, and falsehood! I implored them to crucify me; I taught them how to make a cross. I could not, I did not have the strength to kill myself, but I wanted to suffer at their hands; I longed for suffering, I longed for my blood to be spilled to the last drop in these sufferings. But they only laughed at me and at last began to consider me a holy fool. They tried to defend me, saying that they had taken only that which they themselves desired and that everything that now was happening could not have been otherwise. At last they declared that I was becoming a danger to them and that they would put me into a madhouse if I did not keep silent. Then sorrow entered my soul with such force that my heart contracted and I felt that I would die, and then . . . well, and then I woke up.

It was already morning; I mean, it wasn't daylight, but it was about six o'clock. I awoke in my same armchair, my candle had already burned itself out; everyone in the captain's room was asleep, and all around there was a silence that is rare in our house. I at once jumped to my feet in extreme amazement; nothing like this had ever happened to me before, even so far as the little details were concerned: I had never fallen asleep this way in my armchair, for instance. Then suddenly, while I was standing there coming to my senses, I caught sight of my revolver lying in front of me, loaded and ready—but in an instant I pushed it away! Oh, now I wanted life, and more life! I raised my arms and called out to eternal Truth; or rather, I did not call out but wept; rapture, infinite rapture elevated my entire being. Yes, life and—preaching! I decided on preaching at that very moment and, of course, to go on preaching for my whole life! I am going off to preach; I want to preach, but what? The Truth, for I have beheld it, beheld it with my own eyes, beheld all its glory!

And since then I have been preaching! What's more, I love all those who laugh at me, love them more than all the others. Why that is so I do not know and cannot explain, but so be it. People say that even now I'm confused, and that if I'm so confused now, what will happen in the future? It's absolutely true: I am confused, and perhaps in the future it will be even worse. And of course I shall get confused a few times before I find out how to preach—I mean to say, which words to use, and which deeds, because this is a very difficult thing to do. Why, even now I see it all as clear as day, but listen: who doesn't get confused? And yet we're all moving toward the same thing, at least we're all striving toward one and the same thing, from the wise man to the meanest bandit, only we're traveling by different roads. It's an old truth, but here's what's new: even I can't be all that confused, you know. Because I've seen the truth, I've seen it and know that people can be beautiful and happy without losing their capacity to live on the earth. I don't want to believe, and can't believe, that evil is man's normal state. And yet they all just laugh about that belief of mine. But how can I not believe it: I have seen the truth—it was not some invention of the mind; I saw it, I truly saw it, and its *living image* has filled my soul forever. I saw it in such consummate wholeness that I cannot believe it could not exist among people. And so, how will I get confused? I'll stray from the path, of course, and do so more than once, and I may even speak with someone else's words, although not for long: the living image of what I saw will always be with me and will always correct and guide me. Oh, I am of good cheer and full of strength, and I am on my way, though the trip may take a thousand years. Do you know, at first I even wanted to hide the fact that I had corrupted them all, but that was a mistake—my first mistake already! But truth whispered to me that I was *lying* and preserved and guided me. But how we are to build paradise I do not know, because I do not have the words to express it. I lost the words after my dream. At least all the main words, the most essential ones. But never mind: I shall go off and shall keep talking tirelessly, for I have indeed seen it with my own eyes even though I do not know how to tell of what I saw. But this is just what the scoffers do not understand: "He had a dream," they say. "It's just ravings and hallucinations." Well! How wise is that? And they're so proud of themselves! A dream? What's a dream? Is our very life not a dream? I'll say even more: suppose this never comes to pass, suppose paradise never is realized (that much I do understand, after all)—well, I shall still go on preaching. And yet it could happen so easily: in a single day, *in a single hour*—everything could be established at once! The main thing is that you must love others as you love yourself; that's the main thing, and that's everything, and absolutely nothing more than that is needed: you'll at once find a way to build paradise. And yet this is only an old truth that has been read and repeated a billion times, but it has still not managed to take root! "Consciousness of life is higher than life, knowledge of the laws of happiness is higher than happiness"—that's what we need to fight against! And I shall. If only we all want it, everything will be arranged at once.

And I've found that little girl. . . . And I shall go on! Yes, I shall go on!

The Defendant Kornilova Is Freed

On April 22 of this year the defendant Kornilova was tried a second time in the local circuit court by new judges and jurors. The former verdict, pronounced last year, was quashed by the Senate on the grounds that the medical evidence produced was insufficient. Most of my readers, perhaps, remember this case well. A young stepmother (who at the time had still not reached the legal age of maturity), pregnant, angry at her husband who kept citing the example of his first wife to reproach her, and after a bitter quarrel with him, threw her six-year-old stepdaughter (her husband's daughter by his former wife) from a fourth-floor window, nearly forty feet above the ground; a near-miracle occurred: the girl was not dashed to pieces, she sustained no fractures or other injuries, and quickly regained consciousness; she is now alive and well. The young woman's bestial act took place within the context of her other actions, so senseless and mysterious that one could not help but wonder whether was she acting in her right mind. Was she not, at least, in a state of temporary derangement caused by her pregnancy? When she woke up in the morning, after her husband had gone off to work, she let the child sleep; then she dressed the little girl and gave her some coffee. Then she opened the window and threw the girl out of it. Without even bothering to look down to see what had happened to the child, she closed the window, got dressed, and set off for the police station. There she stated what had happened and answered questions rudely and strangely. When she was told, several hours later, that the child had survived, she displayed neither joy nor chagrin and remarked, quite indifferently and cold-bloodedly, as if deep in thought, "She's got the lives of a cat." For nearly a month and a half thereafter, in the two prisons where she happened to be confined, she continued to be sullen, rude, and uncommunicative. And suddenly all these traits disappeared at once: through all the four months that remained until her delivery, and through all her trial and after it, the wardress of the women's section of the prison could not say enough in her praise: her disposition became stable, calm, kind, and serene. However, I have described all this before. In short, the former verdict was quashed, and then on April 22 a new verdict was rendered by which Kornilova was acquitted.

I was in the courtroom and took away many impressions. It is a pity, though, that I'm quite unable to pass them on to you and am literally compelled to limit myself merely to a very few words. Besides, I am discussing this case only because I wrote a good deal about it earlier and so I feel that it is not superfluous to inform the readers about its outcome. The trial went on twice as long as the former one. The composition of the jury was particularly noteworthy. A new witness was called—the wardress of the women's section of the prison. Her testimony about Kornilova's character weighed heavily in the defendant's favor. The testimony of Kornilova's husband was also quite remarkable: he spoke with extraordinary frankness and hid nothing—neither the quarrels nor the things he had done to abuse her; he spoke from the heart—directly and openly. He is still only a peasant, though it's true he's dressed in European style, reads books, and has a monthly salary of thirty rubles. Then came the assortment of expert witnesses, which was also remarkable. Six people were called, all of them well-known luminaries of medical science; five of them gave testimony: three of them declared unequivocally that the pathological condition peculiar to a pregnant woman certainly *could have* had an influence on the crime that had been committed in this instance. Only Dr. Florinsky was not in agreement with this opinion, but fortunately he is not a psychiatrist and his opinion was not given any particular weight. The last to testify was our well-known psychiatrist, Diukov. He spoke for almost an hour, answering questions from the prosecutor and the presiding judge. It's hard to imagine a more subtle understanding of the human soul and its pathological states. The wealth and variety of his extraordinarily interesting observations, culled over many years, was also striking. As for me, I listened to parts of the testimony of this expert with real admiration. The opinion of this expert witness was entirely in favor of the defendant; he stated *positively* and *conclusively* that, in his opinion, when the defendant had committed the crime she was in pathological mental state.

The result was that the prosecutor himself, despite his formidable speech, withdrew the charge of premeditation, i.e., the most serious aspect of the indictment. Lustig, the defense attorney, also very skillfully countered several accusations; one of the most damaging ones—the stepmother's alleged long-standing hatred for her stepdaughter—he discredited entirely by clearly showing it was no more than backstairs gossip. Then, after a lengthy speech by the presiding judge, the jury retired and in less than a quarter-hour brought back an acquittal, which produced near delight among the large crowd of spectators. Many crossed themselves, some congratulated each other and shook hands. The husband of the acquitted took her home that same evening, after ten o'clock; the happy woman entered her own home again after nearly a year's absence, with the impression of the enormous lesson she had learned, a lesson that would last for her whole life, and an impression of the clear intervention of the hand of God in this case—beginning with the miraculous sparing of the child, to take but one example.

To My Readers

I crave the forbearance of my readers. Last year, because of my summer trip to Ems to be treated for an illness, I was compelled to publish the July and August issues of my *Diary* as a single issue, on August 31, but of course with double the number of pages. This year, because of the increasingly serious nature of my illness, I am compelled to publish the May and June issues together, under one cover, at the end of June or the very first part of July. Then the July and August issues will be published again in August, as they were last year. Beginning in September, the *Diary* will again be published regularly on the last day of each month.

Leaving Petersburg on the advice of doctors, I wish to say that although the editorial office in Petersburg will be closed until September, all out-of-town subscribers and readers, *as well as those living in the city*, can, if need be, still contact the editorial office *by mail*, exactly as they did before. These letters will be promptly forwarded by the manager of the office, and each complaint, misunderstanding, etc., will, as in the past, be seen to as quickly as possible. All letters addressed to me will be promptly forwarded in the same manner. Quite specific arrangements for this have been made by the editor. Subscriptions will be maintained as before: new subscribers will be promptly taken care of.

I trust that those who read and subscribe to my *Writer's Diary* will excuse me. Given such unforeseen circumstances as the complication of an illness, it was difficult to anticipate all this. I know, on the basis of valid facts, that until now the vast majority of my readers have treated me in a most benevolent manner. I venture to anticipate their kindness on this occasion as well.

May and June

1

1. From the Book of Predictions of Johann Lichtenberger, 1528

I have been given a most curious document. It is a very ancient prediction, murky and allegorical, to be sure, of current events and the present war. In the Royal Library in London one of our young scholars found a very old *folio*, a "book of predictions" of Johann Lichtenberger, published in Latin in 1528. It is a rare copy and may even be the only one extant. The book depicts the future of Europe and of humanity in murky images. It is a mystical book. I shall cite only those lines that were provided to me, *and merely as a given*, not without a certain interest.

After predictions of the French Revolution (1789) and Napoleon I (who is called the "great eagle" [*aquila grandis*] in the book), the following is said about future events in Europe:

"Post haec veniet altera aquila quae ignem fovebit in gremio sponsae Christi et erunt tres adulteri unusque legitimus qui alios vorabit." (After this will come another eagle who will kindle a fire in the bosom of the bride of Christ, and there will be three natural children and one legitimate, who will devour the others.)

"Exsurget aquila grandis in Oriente, aquicolae occidentales moerebunt. Tria regna comportabit. Ipsa est aquila grandis, quae dormiet annis multis, refutata resurget et contremiscere faciet aquicolas occidentales in terra Virginis et alios montes Superbissimos; et volabit ad meridiem recuperando amissa. Et amore charitatis inflammabit Deus aquilam orientalem volando ad ardua alis duabus fulgens in montibus christianitatis." (The great eagle shall arise in the East, and those who dwell in the islands of the West shall wail. He shall seize three kingdoms. This is a great eagle who shall sleep for many years; though wounded, he shall rise up and make tremble those who dwell by the waters in the West in the land of the virgin and the other proud summits; and he shall fly to the South to recover that which has been lost. And God shall kindle a love of charity in the eagle of the East, that he may fly to this arduous task, his two wings flashing on the heights of Christianity.)

Of course, this is rather obscure, yet you must agree that "the great eagle of the East, who sleeps for many years and *though wounded* [N.B., does this not refer to our war with Europe twenty-two years ago?] shall rise up and make tremble those who dwell by the waters in the West"—you must agree that this seems rather similar to what is now happening—that is, of course, provided you take no account of our Europeanizing wise men, who seem to be still trembling before "those who dwell by the waters," contrary to the prophecy, whereas the eagle has already taken flight, "his two wings flashing." But only the wise men tremble, not the eagle. Further, if one applies Lichtenberger's prophecy to contemporary events, then the phrase "those who dwell by the waters in the West in the land of the virgin" evidently refers to England. But in that case, why does he say "in the land of the virgin"? In 1528 Queen Elizabeth had not yet begun her reign. Does Lichtenberger's allegory not mean a land (the islands of Great Britain) that has never once been invaded, in the same sense as Napoleon once said of the European capitals that he had invaded, "A capital that has been invaded is like a girl who has lost her virginity." But the eagle, according to the prophecy, will cause the other "proud summits" to tremble as well, and will fly to the south to recover that which was lost; and what is most remarkable, "God shall kindle a love of charity in eagle of the East, that he may fly to this arduous task, his two wings flashing on the heights of Christianity." You must agree that this is something really quite appropriate. Did our eagle not take flight, enkindled with the love of charity for the oppressed and the suffering? Was it not the charity of Christ that moved our entire People to "this arduous task," both last year and this? Who shall deny that? This People, these soldiers recruited from a People who did not even know their prayers very well, would still pick up wounded Frenchmen in the Crimea, at Sevastopol, and take them to be treated *before* their own Russians: "The Russians can lay there a bit and wait; anybody will pick up a Russian, but the Frenchie's a foreigner and you've got to take care of him first." Is this not Christ? Is it not the spirit of Christ we hear in these simple-hearted, noble words, spoken playfully? And so, is the spirit of Christ not present among our People—a People backward but good, ignorant but not barbaric? Indeed, Christ is their strength, our present Russian strength, now that the eagle has flown off "to this arduous task." And what does a single such anecdote about some little soldier at Sevastopol mean in comparison with the thousands of manifestations of the spirit of Christ and the "fire of charity" among our People, in actuality and in plain view in our time, even though our wise men still try with all their might to suppress the idea and to bury the fact of our People's participation, in spirit and in heart, in the current fates of Russia and the East? And don't bother to point to the "bestiality and obtuseness" of the People, to their ignorance and backwardness which, supposedly, make them incapable of understanding what is now going on. They understand full well the essence of the matter, rest assured of it; they have understood it for four centuries now. Today's diplomats they wouldn't understand at all, were they to learn about them; but then who can understand them? Yes, our great People have been raised like animals; they have suffered torments from the very time of their origins, for all their thousand years of existence, torments such as no single nation of the world could have borne without disintegration and annihilation; but our People only grew in strength and solidarity in the course of these torments. Do not reproach them for "bestiality and ignorance," you respected wise men, because you—you specifically—have done nothing for them. To the contrary, you went away from them two hundred years ago; you abandoned them and detached yourselves from them; you transformed them into a unit for paying poll tax and an entity for paying you quitrent; and, my dear, enlightened, European gentlemen, the People have grown up, ignored and oppressed by you, driven by you like a beast into his den; but Christ was with them, and with them alone has He lived until the great day, twenty years ago, when the northern eagle, enkindled with the fire of charity, beat his wings and stretched them forth over the People.... Yes, there is much bestiality among the People, but there is no need to point it out. This bestiality is the grime of centuries; it will be washed clean. And the misfortune is not that bestiality exists; the misfortune is when bestiality is elevated as a virtue. I have seen even robbers who had committed terribly many bestial deeds and whose depraved and enfeebled wills had brought them lower than the lowest depths; but these depraved animals who had fallen so low still knew, in their hearts at least, that they were animals, and they were aware of how low they had fallen; and in the pure, bright moments that God sends even to animals they could pass judgment upon themselves, even though they often had no more strength to raise themselves up. It is another thing when bestiality is raised above everyone like an idol and people bow down to it, thinking themselves virtuous precisely for doing so. Lord Beaconsfield, and all the other Beaconsfields after him, both our own and those of Europe, have stuffed up their ears and closed their eyes to the bestialities and tortures being inflicted upon entire tribes of people; and they have betrayed Christ for "the interests of civilization," and because these tormented tribes are called Slavs, i.e., because they bear within them something new; accordingly, there is all the more reason for them to be struck down to the very root, again for the interests of a rotten old civilization. That, now, is bestiality—developed and elevated like a virtue, and people in the West and here in Russia bow down to it as if it were an idol. And "the most beatific pope, God's infallible vicar," while preparing to meet his maker during his last days on earth—did he not long for a victory of the Turks and the tormentors of Christianity over the Russians who rose up for Christianity in Christ's name—for the sole reason that by his *infallible* definition, the Turks were nonetheless better than the Russian heretics, who did not recognize the pope? Is this not bestiality? Is it not barbarity? Indeed, the prediction of Johann Lichtenberger is truly appropriate to the present moment. And should we not see the pope as well among the other "proud summits" that the beating wings of the eagle will cause to tremble? By the way, to finish with these predictions: what did Johann Lichtenberger mean when he said that "there shall come an eagle who will kindle a fire in the bosom of the bride of Christ, and there will be three natural children and one legitimate, who will devour the others"? In religious and mystical language the expression "the bride of Christ" has always meant the church in general. Who, then, are the three natural children and the one legitimate? I should think this means—that is, if we are to take Lichtenberger as a prophet—the three religions: Catholicism, Protestantism, and . . . which is the third illegitimate one? And which one is legitimate?

But let us leave Johann Lichtenberger. It's difficult to speak seriously about all this; it's only some mystical allegory, even though it is somewhat close to the truth.

And aren't there more than a few coincidences? True, it was all written and published in 1528, and that is very interesting. At that time, it would seem, such works often appeared; and although the wars of the great Protestant Reformation had not yet happened, there were still plenty of protestants, reformers, and prophets. We also know that later on, especially in the Protestant armies, there were always ecstatic "prophets," prognosticators, and convulsionaries among the warriors themselves. If I published this Latin quotation from an old book (and, I repeat, the book certainly does exist), then it was only as an interesting given fact. It was not as some miracle; besides, it is not only miracles that are miraculous. What is most miraculous are very often the things that happen in the reality around us. We see reality almost always in the way we *want* to see it, as we ourselves, *in a preconceived manner,* wish to interpret it to ourselves. If once in a while we suddenly analyze it and see in the visible not the things we wished to see but the things that exist *in actual fact,* then we at once take what we have seen as a miracle; and this happens not rarely, and once in a while, I swear, we would sooner believe in a miracle and an impossibility than in reality, than in the truth *we did not wish to see.* And so it always happens on earth; in this is the whole history of humanity.

2. On Anonymous Abusive Letters

I did not go abroad and am now in the province of Kursk. When my doctor learned that I had a chance to spend the summer in the country, and especially in such a province as Kursk, he prescribed Essentuki water and added that this would be far more beneficial to me than Ems, whose waters I had supposedly grown accustomed to. I feel obliged to state that I have received very many letters from my readers expressing sincerest concern over my illness. And in general, by the way, all the while I've been publishing my *Diary* I have received and continue to receive many letters, both signed and anonymous, that are so flattering and so supportive and approving of my work that, frankly speaking, I never counted on such widespread sympathy and never considered myself deserving of it. I shall keep these letters as something precious, and—can it be mawkish to mention it in print? Can it be a bad thing that I value and treasure widespread attention? But some may say that I'm praising myself and boasting now. Let them say it: I know in my heart that this is not boasting, that I am only stating my gratitude, my sincere feeling; and I've lived long enough to know that I'm irritating certain gentlemen with my statement. But even these gentlemen, I think, are not all that numerous. Out of the several hundred letters I have received over these eighteen months of publication of the *Diary,* at least a hundred (but very likely more) were anonymous; but of these hundred anonymous letters only two were absolutely hostile. There are people who do not agree with my convictions, and they frankly set forth their objections, but always do so seriously, sincerely, without the least personal reference; and this is true of both signed and anonymous letters. I only regret that because of the large numbers of letters I receive, I simply cannot reply to them all. But these two letters are exceptions and were written not to object to my views but to abuse me. And so it is the gentlemen who composed these letters who will be angered at my expression of gratitude. The second of these two letters, in fact, deals with my announcement of my illness. My anonymous correspondent was genuinely angry: how, he says, did I dare to make a statement in print about such a private, personal matter as my illness, and in his letter to me he wrote a quite indecent and crude parody of my announcement. But setting aside the main purpose of the letter—abuse, I could not help but be intrigued by the following question: if, through ill health, I found it necessary to go away for treatment and was thus compelled to publish the May issue of the *Diary* late, along with the June issue; and if in each issue of the *Diary* I have always announced the time of publication of the next issue—then it seemed to me that a direct, unadorned statement, with no explanation at all, that the next issue of the *Diary* would come out together with the June issue, would have been somewhat impolite; and why should I not announce the reason this was to happen? And did I, in my announcement, really go on at such length about my illness? But these are all trifles, of course, and were it simply a matter of a person whose sense of literary and social decorum had been deeply violated, then we would have had a curious, though perhaps partly honorable, specimen of a gentleman who may stand outside the ranks of literature, yet because of his disinterested love for it is, so to say, burning with the worthy desire for the observance of literary decorum; and though his intentions have been taken to the point of punctiliousness, he nevertheless derives them from a worthy and interesting source; and so I, from a sense of courtesy alone, could not deny such an anonymous letter a kind of respect. But the abuse spoiled everything: it was clear that this was the whole point of the letter. And certainly it would not have been worth bringing up all this here, but I have long been wanting to say a few words about anonymous letters in general—I mean about abusive anonymous letters particularly—and I am pleased I have come upon an opportunity to do so.

The fact is, I have long thought that in our age, an age so unstable, so transitional, so filled with changes, and so little able to satisfy anyone (and so it must be)—there absolutely must be a great proliferation of people who have been passed over, as it were—people who have been forgotten or neglected and who are irritated: "Why are *they* everywhere, while I am nowhere? Why they don't pay some attention to me as well?" This state of personal irritation and, as it were, frustrated ideals, is so painful that a certain kind of gentleman is ready, at times, to take a match and go off to set fire to something. I understand this very well, and if one is to condemn it, one must be armed with humaneness rather than indignation. But setting fire to things is an extreme measure and is, so to say, the role assigned to mighty, Byronic characters. Fortunately, there are less terrible outlets for characters who are not so mighty. Such an outlet is simply to sling mud, to malign, to spread lies and gossip, or to send off an anonymous, abusive letter. In short, I have long suspected and still suspect that though our age is certainly one of great reforms and events—of that there's no doubt—it is at the same time an age of increasing numbers of anonymous letters of an abusive nature. As far as literature is concerned, there's not a shadow of doubt: anonymous abusive letters comprise, one might say, an integral part of contemporary Russian literature and accompany all its various tendencies—and who among writers and publishers does not receive them? I have even checked with a few periodicals and at one of them—specifically in one that sprang up suddenly, made a quick and unexpected impression, and pleased the public to an extent the publishers themselves never anticipated—one of the most active contributors told me that they receive such a mass of anonymous abusive letters that they do not even bother to read them, just open them. He was about to give me the details of some of these missives, but with his first words he burst into unrestrained laughter. And so it should be; our inexperienced, anonymous correspondents still do not even suspect, I think, that the more abusive their letters, the more innocent and harmless they are. This is a good thing: it signifies that though our anonymous correspondents are passionate, they still lack restraint and do not realize that the more polite and dignified the tone of a spiteful anonymous letter, the more malicious it will be and the stronger effect it will have. It follows that this Jesuitical trait has still not developed among us; that the thing has still not entered into its second, *higher* phase, and so is still in its very infancy; and consequently, it is no more than the fruit of the initial, unbridled fervor and not the fruit of deliberate, meticulously developed malice. It's not what one might call Spanish revenge, with its studied restraint and its readiness even to make great sacrifices to achieve its goal. Our anonymous abuser is far from that mysterious stranger of Lermontov's play *Masquerade*—a colossal figure who once was slapped in the face by some little officer and who went off to the wilderness for thirty years to plot his revenge. No, what's at work here is still that same Slavic nature of ours, a nature given to expressing abuse in haste and so to have done with it (and, for all I know, to make up right then and there); and you must agree that in one sense this is all good news, for here, too, it indicates, so to say, youth, immaturity, freshness, almost the very springtime of life—although I must confess it's a very nasty spring indeed. I feel obliged to add one more observation: I think that our young generation, I mean our very young "raw youths," do not write anonymous abusive letters. I receive many letters from young people, and all of them are signed. Only those that express rather excessively friendly feelings are unsigned. But young people who do not agree with me on something always sign their names. (One can tell all too easily, from various signs and devices used, when an anonymous abusive letter is not from a member of the young generation, not from some young "raw youth.") And so our young people obviously realize that, first, one can write even a very sharp letter but that a signature under it adds extraordinary weight to the thoughts expressed, and that the whole nature of such a letter will change for the better with a signature, which gives it a spirit of frankness, courage, and readiness to stand up and answer for one's convictions; indeed, the very sharpness of the wording shows only the passion of the convictions and not the desire to offend. And so it's clear that the abuser who does not sign his name wishes mainly to express his abuse in the language of the gutter and wishes to afford himself this particular satisfaction above all, and has no other purpose in mind. Why, he knows very well that he's doing a nasty thing and is damaging himself—damaging the effect of his letter, that is; yet such is the urge for name-calling. This feature—I mean this urge—must be noted, for it still predominates among our educated society. And you needn't be amused at me for believing that this feature *predominates* among us; I'm convinced that I'm not exaggerating and that we are now standing precisely at this point in the development of our society as a whole. Furthermore, consider also the fact that one can live one's whole life without writing a single anonymous abusive letter and yet carry within, all life long, the soul of the anonymous abuser; and this, too, is an important consideration. And what of the fact that I, over eighteen months, have received only two abusive letters? This proves only that I am innocent of blame and not very noteworthy, just as it proves the small sphere of my activity; and it proves above all that I am dealing only with decent people. Other figures, more worthy of note than I (and, accordingly, that alone makes them more to be blamed than I) and who, beyond that, are compelled by the very nature and character of their publications to act in a much broader sphere, receive not two, but perhaps two hundred anonymous letters in a year and a half. In short, I'm convinced that European civilization has instilled very little humaneness in us, and that the number of people among us who wish to shout out their abuse immediately and directly whenever they find something even mildly distasteful may be so significant that one is frightened to admit it; and the number of those who wish to shout abuse with impunity—anonymously and safely from behind the door—is still greater; and so the anonymous letter is just the thing that gives them this opportunity: you can't give a letter a thrashing, and a letter doesn't blush.

In times of old we had no notion of European honor; our boyars shouted their abuse and even fought openly with one another, and a smack on the face wasn't thought of as any great and ultimate violation of one's honor. Yet they had their own sense of honor, and though it wasn't in European form it was still no less sacred and serious than Europe's; and for the sake of this honor the boyar sometimes gave up everything—his estate, his position at court, even the favor of the tsar. But with the change of costume and the introduction of the European rapier came a new, European honor, and for two centuries it has not managed to take hold properly, so that the old ways have been forgotten and despised, while the new has been accepted only suspiciously and skeptically. We have accepted it mechanically, as it were, but spiritually we have forgotten what honor means and we've lost the heartfelt need for it; and, dreadful as it is to admit, this is the case, apart from perhaps only a very few exceptions.

During these two centuries of our European and, so to say, "rapier" period, honor and conscience—strange to say—were best preserved and even entirely preserved among our People, who were all but untouched by the rapier period of our history. Our People may well be filthy, ignorant, barbaric; you well may laugh at my proposition without the least indulgence; still, for my whole life long, I have held the conviction that our People are incomparably purer in heart than our upper levels of society and that their minds are not split to the extent that they can have the most radiant idea and, at the very same moment, cherish its most vile antithesis, as is the case everywhere among our intelligentsia; indeed, the latter can entertain both these ideas, not knowing which of them to believe and which to prefer in practice, while calling this state of mind and soul of theirs "abundant development," "the boons of European civilization"; and though they may die of boredom and disgust with such abundance, they still pour out fierce ridicule on our simple People, as yet untouched by foreign civilization, for the naivete and straightforwardness of their beliefs. . . . But this is a broad topic. I will simply say: the coarsest person among our People would be ashamed of certain thoughts and impulses of certain of our "higher people," I am convinced of it; and they would turn away in disgust from most of the actions of our educated people. I am convinced that our People do not understand, and will not understand for a long time, that if one is alone, behind closed doors, with no one watching, one may privately commit the foulest deeds and consider them completely permissible and morally tolerable only because there are no witnesses and no one is watching; and yet this is something that is practiced with fearful frequency among our educated classes and is done without the slightest pangs of conscience; on the contrary, it is very often done with the greatest of satisfaction of the mind and the higher qualities of an enlightened spirit. As far as the People understand it, what is vile in public is just as vile behind closed doors. Meanwhile, we look upon the People as a foul-mouthed, degenerate, reactionary lot who find their only enjoyment in shouting out abuse. It's apropos to recall something in this regard, the more so as it is from days long past and things have changed. In the time of my youth there was a conviction among the vast majority of military people that the Russian common soldier, as one who came from the People, was terribly fond of obscenities, abusive and ribald language. Consequently, so as to win popularity, certain commanding officers permitted themselves, during drills, for example, to curse with such vigor, with such finesse and such turns of phrase, that the soldiers literally blushed at them; later, in their own barracks, trying to forget what they had heard from their officers, the whole group of them would shout down any fellow who repeated them. *I witnessed this personally.* Yet the commanders were so pleased with themselves, thinking that now they had managed to imitate the spirit of the Russian soldier! Indeed, even Gogol, in his *Correspondence with Friends*, advised his friend, when giving a public scolding to a peasant serf, to be sure to use strong language and even provided examples of the sort of words to use: that is, specifically ones that were most biting, that carried, so to say, obscenity more moral than overt, so that there should be a maximum of finesse in the abuse. Meanwhile, though the Russian People do, unfortunately, use some very obscene language, this is by no means true of all of them—far from it—but only of a very insignificant part of them (will anyone believe that?); and the main thing (of which there is no doubt) is that they use foul language mechanically rather than with moral finesse, by habit rather than deliberation; and this last thing—the deliberation, I mean—happens only in very rare specimens, among tramps, confirmed drunkards, and good-for-nothing layabouts whom the People despise. The People may use foul language from habit, but they themselves know that it is a bad habit and condemn it. And so, breaking the People of this habit of foul language is, in my opinion, simply a matter of mechanical disuse and not of moral suasion. On the whole, this notion of our People as lovers of low, foul language took root among our educated classes—in my opinion, mainly after they had made their final, moral break with the People, a break which, as we know, resulted in their absolute misunderstanding of the People. That was the time when all sorts of other mistaken notions of our People appeared as well. You may not believe me when I say that our People are not such lovers of abusive language as they have been described and pictured until now, but so be it: I am still convinced that what I've said is justified. The same hopes I invest in the People, I also invest in our young generation. Our People and the young generation of our intelligentsia will suddenly come together and understand one another in many things, and much more closely and readily than was the case in our day and in our generation. There is a seriousness among our young people, and may God grant that it be directed in the most sensible manner. About young people, by the way: one very young man sent me a letter not long ago with a very sharp objection to a certain topic—I won't mention which one—and signed this sharp (but by no means impolite) letter with his full name and even included his address. I invited him to come and see me to clear things up. He came and impressed me with the passion and seriousness of his attitude toward the matter. He agreed with me in certain things and left deep in thought. I will also note that, as it seems to me, our young generation knows far better how to argue than do our elders, I mean in their manner of disputing in particular: they hear you out and let you speak, and this is precisely because clarifying the matter is more important to them than their vanity. As he was leaving the young man expressed regret over the sharpness of his letter and did so with genuine dignity. Our young people have no one to guide them, that's the point! And how badly they need guides, how often they have rushed off enthusiastically to follow people unworthy of their enthusiasm and scarcely even sincere! And what should these future guides be like—whoever they might be? In fact, will our Russian destiny still send us any such people? These are questions!

3. A Plan for a Satirical Novel of Contemporary Life

I still haven't finished with the anonymous abuser, though. The fact is, such a person can become a very significant literary type for a novel or tale. The main thing is that one can and must approach the thing from a different point of view, a broad, humane viewpoint, harmonizing it with the Russian character generally and with the contemporary factors that now cause this type in particular to appear among us. In fact, no sooner do you begin to elaborate such a character than you immediately realize that we simply cannot help but have such people or, to put it more properly, that in this age of ours such people are the very ones that we should expect above all, and that if there are comparatively few of them as yet, it is due specifically to the particular grace of God. In fact, these are all people who have been raised in the unstable families we have had of late, with discontented, skeptical fathers, who have passed on to their children nothing but indifference to everything most vital and little more than a kind of vague apprehension over some future which is terribly fanciful but in which even these so-called *ready-made* realists and cold-blooded enemies of our present put their faith. And beyond that, such fathers passed on to their children their skeptical, impotent mockery, scarcely conscious but always utterly complacent. Were there only a few children who grew up in the last twenty or twenty-five years among such vile, envious people who had run through the last of their redemption money and who bequeathed their children poverty and a precept of baseness—were there only a few such families?

And so, let's suppose a young person takes up a job. He doesn't cut a fine figure; he "lacks wit"; he has no connections at all. He has his native-born intelligence, however, everyone else has that too; but since that intelligence was developed predominantly through the aimless sneering that we have taken as liberalism for twenty-five years now, our hero naturally and immediately takes his intelligence for genius. For heaven's sake, when a person has grown up without the least moral support, could you expect anything other than boundless egoism? At first he puts on a terrific show, but since he does have some intelligence, after all (and I prefer my type to be somewhat more intelligent than average rather than have him more stupid, for it is only in these two variants that such a type can appear), he soon figures out that his sneering is only something negative and certainly cannot lead him to anything positive. And if sneering was enough for his daddy, then it was because daddy was just an old duffer, though a liberal fellow, while he, the young lad, is a genius, after all, and has only been having some temporary problems proving his talents. Oh, of course in his soul he's ready to commit any of the meanest acts, "for why shouldn't one resort to meanness to get something done? And anyway, in times like these, who can prove that meanness is meanness?" etc., etc. In short, he's been raised with a stock of these ready-made questions. But he soon realizes that these days even resorting to some mean trick to get something done means a long wait in line, and besides, even a person like him may see that it's a long way from the moral readiness to employ a mean trick to the deed itself, and that first he must take some practical measures to get himself into the line. Well, of course if he were a bit less clever he'd arrange things in a moment: "To hell with these feeble impulses toward higher things; I'll just change myself to suit Mr. A. or Mr. B. and follow in his wake, settle submissively and confidently into the daily grind, and sooner or later I'll make a career for myself." But his egoism, this conviction of his own genius, still stands in his way: even in his own mind he cannot merge the glorious fate he had conjured up for himself with the fate of Mr. A. or Mr. B. "No, sir, we're still in opposition, and if they want me, let them come to me on their knees." And so he keeps waiting for someone to come to him on his knees, waiting full of malice and spite; and meanwhile, right beside him, some other fellow has managed to get a step ahead of him; another one has settled in nicely, while a third has already become his boss—this third being the very fellow for whom he had invented a nickname when they studied together in their "higher school" and about whom he'd written an epigram for the school magazine when he edited it and was thought to be a genius. "No, sir, that's an insult! Why was it he and not I? And wherever you look the places are taken! No," he thinks, "my career isn't here. What's the point of working in the civil service? Only numskulls serve. My career is literature." And so he begins sending his works around to various editors, at first incognito and then giving his full name. He gets no reply, of course; impatient, he sets to haunting the thresholds of editors' offices. On the occasions a manuscript is returned to him, he even permits himself to make jokes about it and sneer biliously, giving vent to his rage, as it were; but none of this helps. "No, it's obvious that all the places are taken here, too," he thinks with a bitter smile. The main thing is that he is continually tormented by the fatal need to seek out, always and everywhere, as many people he can find who are worse than he. Oh, he could never understand how anyone could rejoice in the fact that there are people better than he! And it's at this point that he first hits upon the notion of sending some nasty little unsigned letter to an editor, and to an editor who had insulted him most deeply. He writes it, sends it, and then he does it again—it pleases him. Still, it brings no results; everything around him is deaf, dumb, and blind as before. "No, this is no kind of career," he decides, once and for all, and decides to "settle in" at last. He selects a *personage*—his boss, the director, to be precise;

here, perhaps, a bit of luck and a few minor connections help him out. Gogol's Poprishchin, after all, began by distinguishing himself in sharpening pens and was summoned for that purpose to the apartment of His Excellency, where he saw the director's daughter and sharpened two pens for her. But Poprishchin's time has passed, and anyway, these days pens don't need sharpening; besides, our hero can't change his nature: it's not pens that are on his mind but the most daring thoughts. Briefly, then, in the shortest time he becomes convinced that he has captivated the director's daughter and that she is pining for him. "Well now, here's a career," he thinks, "and in any case, what good are women if a clever man can't use them to make a career; that, in essence, is the whole woman question, if one judges it realistically. And the main thing is that it's not shameful: more than a few careers have been launched by women." But—but at this point, just as with Poprishchin, a new assistant turns up! Poprishchin reacted characteristically: he went out of his mind over his notion that he was the king of Spain. And how natural that was! What else was left for the mortified Poprishchin, with no connections, no career, no fortitude, and no initiative whatsoever, particularly during the Petersburg period; how could he help but plunge into the most desperate fantasies and believe in them? But our Poprishchin, our contemporary Poprishchin, is utterly incapable of believing that he's the very same as the original Poprishchin, only duplicated thirty years later. His soul is full of regular fireworks, contempt, and sarcasm and—and so he also plunges into fantasy, but of a different sort. He recalls that there are such things on earth as anonymous letters and that he has already resorted to them once; and so he risks writing his little missive, but this time not to an editor; this one is something finer, if you please: he feels that he is entering a new, practical phase. Oh, how he shuts himself up in his little room, away from his landlady; how he trembles lest someone look in on him; but he scribbles line after line, changing his handwriting, and composes four pages of slander and abuse; he reads it over with relish; and, having sat up the whole night, in the morning he seals up the letter and addresses it to the fiancé, the assistant. He's changed his handwriting, so he's not afraid. And now he counts the hours; and now the letter ought to be arriving—it's to the fiancé about his intended; and the fiancé, naturally, will turn her down; he'll take fright; why, it's not a letter, it's a masterpiece! And our young friend knows full well that he's a mean little wretch, but that only pleases him: "These are the days of bipartite thinking, a breadth of approach; these days a straight-line approach gets you nowhere."

Of course the letter had no effect and the wedding took place; but a beginning had been made, and our hero seemed to have hit upon his career. He was seized by a kind of illusion, just as Poprishchin was. He plunges feverishly into this new activity of writing anonymous letters. He dredges up information about the general, his boss; he calculates, he pours out all the things that have accumulated inside him over whole years of unsatisfying service, wounded vanity, bile, and envy. He criticizes the general's every action, he ridicules him in the most merciless fashion, and he does so in a number of letters, a whole series of them. And how pleasing this is at first! The actions of the general, his wife, his mistress, and the stupidity of their whole department—he's depicted every bit of it in his letters. Little by little he even ventures into matters of state; he composes a letter to the minister in which he proposes to reform Russia in quite unceremonious fashion. "No, the minister cannot help but be impressed; the genius of the thing will impress him, and the letter may be passed on to . . . passed on to such a personage who. . . . In short, *courage, mon enfant;* and when they start to look for the author, I'll declare myself, so to say, with no more shyness." In short, he revels in his compositions and continually imagines his letters being opened and the effect they then produce on the faces of those people. . . . In such a frame of mind he sometimes even permits himself a bit of mischief: as a joke he writes even to some quite ridiculous people, not overlooking even some Egor Egorovich, his old head clerk, whom he nearly drives out of his mind by anonymously telling him that his wife has become involved in a love affair with the local police officer (the most important thing is that half of it could be true).

And so, some time passes, but . . . but suddenly a strange idea dawns on him: that he, in fact, is Poprishchin, nothing more than Poprishchin, that very same Poprishchin, only a million times more base, and all these libels from around the corner, all this anonymous might of his is essentially only a mirage and nothing more, and the vilest kind of a mirage besides, the nastiest and most disgraceful, worse, even, than the dream of the Spanish throne. And at this very point something serious happens—not something disgraceful. "What's disgrace? Disgrace is nonsense. Nowadays only pharmacists are afraid of disgrace." But this is something really and truly terrible. The fact is that although he had a clear head, he still was unable to restrain himself, and during his period of rapture over his new career—specifically, after his little missive to the minister—he let something slip about his letters, and to whom?—to his German landlady. Of course he didn't tell her everything; she wouldn't have understood everything, of course; just a bit, just in passing, because his heart was so full; but imagine his astonishment when, a month later, the meek little clerk from another department, who rented a tiny room in an out-of-the-way corner of this same landlady's establishment, a spiteful and uncommunicative little fellow who, when he suddenly got angry over something, suggested as he passed by our hero in the corridor that he—this same meek little fellow, that is—was "a man of morals and did not write anonymous letters in the manner of certain gentlemen." Imagine! At first he did not get so frightened; moreover, after questioning the clerk—for which he deliberately and even humiliatingly had to make up with him—he was convinced that the fellow knew scarcely anything. But . . . well, what if he does know? Besides, the rumor had begun in the department a long time ago that someone was sending abusive letters to the superiors via the local mail and that this must certainly be someone who worked there. Our unhappy hero sets to thinking and can't even sleep at night. In short, one could show his inner torment with particular vividness—his morbid doubts, his mistakes. At last, he is all but convinced that everyone knows everything, that they're just holding off telling him; and as far as his dismissal from the service is concerned, that's already been decided, though it won't only be dismissal, of course—in short, he almost loses his mind. And so, one day he's sitting in the department and his heart is seized with an almost boundless indignation toward everything and everyone: "Oh, you wicked, damned people," he thinks, "how can you put on such a show of pretense! They know very well that *it's I,* every last one of them knows it; they whisper about it to each other when I pass by; they even know about the document that's been drawn up about me in the office there and . . . and they're all pretending! They all hide it from me! They want to enjoy it, they want to see me being dragged off. . . . But it won't happen! It won't happen!" And so an hour later he chances to deliver some document to His Excellency's office. He enters, places the document respectfully on the desk; the general is busy and pays no attention; our hero turns to leave silently, grasps the door knob, and—suddenly, as if falling into an abyss—he flings himself at His Excellency's feet, though a second earlier he hadn't even suspected he would do so: "All the same, I'm finished; it's better I confess on my own!" "Just be calm, Your Excellency; let's please be quiet, Your Excellency! I'll tell you everything, absolutely everything, but I don't want anyone else to hear!" So, like a madman, he implores the bewildered excellency, clasping his hands foolishly in front of him. And so, in broken, incoherent phrases, all atremble, he stupidly confesses everything, to the utter amazement of His Excellency, who never suspected any of it. But yet, even here our hero fully lives up to his character, for why does he fling himself at the general's feet? Of course, it's his illness, his morbid doubts, but *mainly* it is because he, frightened, humiliated, blaming himself for everything, still dreams as before, like a little fool intoxicated by his own conceit, that His Excellency, having heard him out but nonetheless struck by his genius, so to say, may stretch out his hands, with which he signs so many papers for the benefit of his fatherland, and take him into his embrace: "Oh, you unfortunate but gifted young man, have you really been driven to such lengths! Oh, it is I, I who am to blame for everything; I have overlooked you! I take the entire blame on myself. My God, the things our talented young people are compelled to do by fault of our antiquated procedures and prejudices! But come, come to my bosom and share my post with me, and we . . . we shall revolutionize the department!"

But it did not happen that way, and later—much later, in disgrace and humiliation, recalling the kick from the tip of the general's boot that he happened to receive full in the face, he almost sincerely put the blame on fate and other people: "For once in my life I opened myself fully to people, and what did I get in return?" One could invent some very natural and contemporary finale for him; for example, now kicked out of the service, he is hired for a hundred rubles to take part in a fictitious marriage; after the ceremony, he goes one way and she another, to her flour dealer. "Sweet and noble," as Shchedrin's policeman expresses it in a similar instance.

In short, I think that the type of an anonymous abuser is not at all a bad subject for a short novel. And it's a significant subject. We'd need a Gogol here, of course, but. . . . I'm glad at least that I happened to come upon this idea. Perhaps I may actually try to include it in a novel.

2

1. Former Farmers—Future Diplomats

But how far have I strayed from my topic? I began by saying that I was in the country and happy to be so. It's been a long time since I've lived in the country in Russia. But I'll talk about the country later; for now I'll mention only that one of the reasons I'm happy to be in the country rather than abroad is that I won't see our Russians who hang around over there. In fact, in this time of ours, with its deep feelings of nationality, unity, and patriotism, when we are searching specifically for Russians here at home, waiting for Russians, longing and needing Russians—at such a time, it is too painful to see, abroad, where for twenty years now our intelligentsia has been annually expatriating themselves and setting up colonies, the transformation of purely Russian, raw, and, perhaps, excellent material into some wretched international rubbish, deprived of personality, devoid of character and nationality, and without a country to call their own. I'm not talking about the fathers—the fathers are beyond help, and we can forget about them; I mean their unhappy children, whom they are ruining abroad. The fathers themselves are finally beginning to look ridiculous, even in the eyes of our most dyed-in-the-wool Russian Europeans. Mr. Burenin, who went off as a war correspondent, tells in one of his letters of an amusing encounter in a railway carriage with one of our Europeans of the 1840s, a man with "respectable gray curls," who lived permanently abroad but who had come specially to have a look at the war, at the "spectacle of battle" (from a most respectable distance, of course) and who poked fun at everything these gentlemen have been poking fun at for forty years now, i.e., the Russian spirit, the Slavophiles, etc. He lived abroad, he claimed, because here in Russia "a serious and decent man still has nothing to do." (N.B.: I am quoting from memory.) One of his best witticisms was that "in view of the entry of our forces into Bulgaria and the rebirth of Slavdom, arrangements have already been made with the railways for a special car to bring in the ghost of Khomiakov." But one might have remarked to this gray-haired gentleman that he himself was also very like the ghost of some, perhaps highly respectable, liberal-Westernerizer windbag of the 1840s; but now, after the passage of so many years and the graying of his hair, were he still repeating the same things he had stopped at in his forties, even if he were Granovsky himself, he would certainly look just the sort of buffoon as this did gentleman, relating the story of delivering Khomiakov's ghost by rail to the theater of war and claiming that in our Russia a decent man still has nothing to do.

Twenty years ago it was mainly landowners who emigrated (and I want that word to be remembered) from Russia, and since then the emigration has continued year by year. Of course, there are many in that number who are not landowners; there have been all sorts of people; but the vast majority of them, if not all of them, have more or less hated Russia, some of them on moral grounds, on the conviction that "in Russia there's nothing to do for such decent and intelligent people as they," others simply hating her without any convictions—naturally, one might say, physically: for her climate, her fields, her forests, her ways, her liberated peasants, her Russian history; in short, hating her for absolutely everything. I note that such hatred may be quite passive as well, very quiet and indifferent to the point of apathy. And just at this point they found their hands full of redemption money, and beyond that it dawned on a terrific lot of them that with the liberation of the peasants everything was lost—the countryside, landownership, the nobility, and Russia. It's also true that with the liberation of the peasants, rural labor was left with insufficient organization and security, and the body of individual landowners lost heart and grew confused as they had in no historical revolution of the past. And so the landowners began selling off their lands, and a part of them (not a small part) went rushing abroad. But whatever evidence they might provide in their defense, they still could not hide from their fellow countrymen and their children the fact that another major reason for their emigration was the attraction of egoistic "do-nothingness." And since then individual Russian landownership has been in total chaos; land is being bought and sold, its ownership changing by the minute; the very appearance of the land is changing; it is being deforested—and how will it be transformed? Who will ultimately own it? Who will ultimately comprise the new Russian landowning class? What form will it at last assume? All these things are difficult to predict, and yet these are the principal questions of the Russian future, if you please. It's something of a law of nature, after all, not only in Russia but all over the world: the people who own the land in a country are the masters of that country, in all respects. So it has been always and everywhere. But, people will tell me, we have the rural commune in addition, and so they are the masters. But . . . is the question of the commune really one that we have finally resolved? Didn't that question enter a new phase of development here fifteen years ago, as did everything else? But I'll talk about all this later; meanwhile, let me conclude my idea without any substantiation: if landownership in a country is managed *seriously,* then everything else in that country will be done seriously, in all respects, I mean, both in the most general and in the particulars. People in Russia are now concerned about education, for instance, about peasant schools; yet I believe that a serious and fundamental system of schools will become entrenched in Russia only when we have a serious and fundamental organization of landownership and agriculture, and that we are less likely to get proper agriculture from schools than we are to get proper schools from agriculture (I mean from productive agriculture), and it will never happen before that. Everything else runs parallel to this example: customs, laws, morality, and even the very mind of the nations; and finally, every proper function of the national organism can be organized only after a solid system of landownership has been firmly established. The same can be said of the character of landownership: let it be aristocratic or let it be democratic, but the character of landownership determines the entire character of the nation.

But now our former landowners are still wandering around abroad, through all the cities and spas of Europe, causing a price rise in the restaurants and, like rich men, dragging behind them governesses and nurses for their children, who are decked out in laces and English clothes, exhibiting their bare legs to Europe. And Europe looks on in wonder: "What a lot of wealthy people they have over there; and, above all, what educated people, so eager for European enlightenment. Because of their despotic system they weren't allowed foreign passports until now; and suddenly, what a lot of landowners and capitalists and retired investors they have—

even more than in France, where there are so many living on investments!" And just tell Europe, just try to explain to her that this is a purely Russian phenomenon, that these aren't investors at all but, on the contrary, are people who are gobbling up their basic capital, who are burning the candle at both ends; Europe, of course, wouldn't believe such a thing, which would be impossible there, and wouldn't understand it at all. And the main thing, after all, is that these sybarites loafing in German spas and on the shores of the Swiss lakes, these Luculluses who run through their fortunes in the restaurants of Paris—these people themselves know and can sense, even with some pain, that eventually they will eat up their capital and that their children, these very same little cherubs in English dresses, may have to go begging in Europe (and they will go begging!) or will become French or German workers (and they will become French or German workers!). But, they think, "*après nous le déluge* and, in any case, who's to blame? It's still those same Russian ways of ours that are to blame, it's our clumsy Russia, where even now a decent man has nothing to do." That's how they think, and the more liberal ones among them, those who can be called the higher and purist Westernizers of the 1840s, will also say, perhaps only to themselves: "Well, what does it matter that my children will be left without any assets; instead they'll inherit an idea, the noble leaven of true and sacred views. Brought up far from Russia, they will know nothing of priests and the ridiculous word 'fatherland.' They will realize that 'fatherland' is a prejudice, even the most pernicious prejudice that exists in the world. From them will come noble, cosmopolitan intellects. We, and only we, the Russians, will lay the basis for these new intellects. It is precisely by squandering our redemption money abroad that we are laying down a foundation for the new, future international citizenship that, sooner or later, will renew Europe, and we deserve full honors for this because we were the ones who first began it." However, only the ones with "gray curls" speak thus, i.e., only a very few, for are there many such "advanced" people? The more practical ones, even among those with "gray curls," those who *are not so noble*, ultimately still put their trust in "connections": "We're squandering our money here, it's true, but yet we're still picking up something—acquaintances, say, connections that will come in handy later on, back in the 'fatherland.' Besides, even though our youngsters are being brought up in a liberal spirit, they're gentlemen just the same—and that's the main thing, after all. They'll be dwelling in higher, exclusive spheres, and liberalism in higher spheres in Russia has always meant and has gone together with gentility, for genteel liberalism is useful also for the 'higher' conservatism; people have always been able to make that distinction in Russia. And so what if we are bringing up our children abroad—that just means we are preparing them to be diplomats. What a lot of delightful posts there are in all these embassies and consulates! What countless numbers of delectable little posts, and how exquisitely they're subsidized! They'll do nicely for our youngsters: they're quiet, fine, well paid, and secure, and the service always puts you in the public eye. And it's a service that's clean, for well-dressed people, for gentlemen; and as for the work involved, well, it's not taxing: you have to know how to make acquaintances with Russians abroad, at least with the more respectable ones; but those who get into mischief and ask their consul for protection—those we'll haughtily turn away in proper magesterial fashion and won't even listen to them: 'We don't believe you; you're responsible for the trouble; you still think you're back in your dear fatherland, but this is a clean place. There may be some unpleasantness because of you; and in any case, is it worth troubling foreign authorities over someone like you? Take a look at yourself in the mirror; look at what you've come to!' And that's the whole essence of the service! In short, our youngsters as well will know how to make their way in the world; yes, sir, you have to have connections—that's what the heart of a parent has to keep foremost, and all the rest will be added when the need arises."

And so, all the not-so-noble ones who are squandering their money abroad are more or less relying on connections. But what are connections, in fact? Well, even though they do mean something, this *fabric* still wears thin awfully quickly. And it would certainly not hurt to equip oneself, apart from connections, with, say, even a little awareness of Russia and a mind of one's own, just in case. Particularly these days, in an era of reforms and new approaches, everyone in Russia makes a deliberate effort to live by the dictates of his own mind; everyone wanted to do that, and there's no doubt that it's an enlightened idea, but the problem is that never before in Russia have we had so little independent thought as now, in the midst of this general desire to have it. I won't venture to say why this is, and it would be difficult to do so in any case; but there's one reason, which I know for sure, why our little cherubs will certainly turn out to be fools, and though it's an old one, I still want to point it out. And yet it's the very same thing I was talking about last year. The reason is the Russian language—I mean the lack of the native, Russian language caused by being raised abroad, with foreigners as governesses and maids. This has always been our practice, even formerly—I mean this lack of Russian—but never as much as now, when so many little cherubs are being raised abroad. Let's suppose that they are being prepared for the diplomatic service, and the language of diplomacy, as we know, is French; it's enough to know Russian only grammatically. But is that so? Although this question is so old as to have become a cliché, yet it still remains unresolved, so that not long ago it was even taken up in the press again, though indirectly, apropos of Mr. Turgenev's works written in French. Someone even expressed the view "does it really matter whether Mr. Turgenev writes in French or in Russian, and can anyone make any prohibitions here?" There is no prohibition at all, of course, and particularly for such a great writer and master of the Russian language as Turgenev; and if he has such a fancy, then why shouldn't he write in French, particularly if he knows French almost as well as Russian? And so I won't say a word about Turgenev, but . . . but I see that I am certainly repeating myself and certainly said the same thing last year on the same topic when I was abroad last summer and was having a talk with our Russian expatriate mamma about the harm the French language can do to her little cherubs. But now mamma is preparing her little cherubs for the diplomatic service; and so I'm going to talk only about diplomacy in particular; and though it's not nice to repeat oneself, still I'll risk saying another word or two to her.

"But French is the language of diplomacy, you see," mamma interrupts this time, without even giving me a chance to begin. Alas, she's been ready for me since last year and treats me somewhat haughtily. "Indeed it is, madam," I reply. "You have a strong argument, and I agree with you completely. But, in the first place, what I said about knowledge of Russian must be equally applied to French, isn't that so? In order to express in French the whole wealth of your being, you must master French as well, in all its subtleties. Well, you must know that there exists such a riddle of nature, her law, by which you can master perfectly only the language with which you were born, the language spoken by the people of whom you are a part, that is. You're frowning; I've offended you; you're giving me a mocking look. You wave your dainty hand and assure me that you heard this even last year and that I'm repeating myself. Very well, I'll concede that; in any case, this isn't a *ladies'* topic. I'll concede to you, plainly and simply, and agree that a Russian can also master French perfectly; but I'll concede with one very large reservation: that he be born in France, grow up in it from the first hour of his life, and be transformed into a Frenchman. Oh, now you're enjoying this; you're already smiling; but keep in mind, madam, that it's not entirely possible even for you to do such a thing for your little cherub, despite all the conveniences such as emigration, redemption money, a Parisian nurse, and so on. You also have to take into account innate gifts, so to say, because in that regard you can't compare Mr. Turgenev with your own little cherub, for instance. There aren't a lot of these Turgenevs born, after all. . . . Ah, but no—what am I saying! I've made another mistake, a slip of the tongue: your little cherub will certainly turn into a Turgenev, or even three Turgenevs at once; let's leave this topic; but. . . ."

"But," you interrupt me again, "these diplomats are all clever anyway, so why must we worry so much about intellect? Believe me, all you need are connections. *Mon mari*. . . ."

"You're absolutely right, madam," I quickly interrupt, "all you need are connections, and leaving your husband aside as far as possible, I still want to add that a little bit of intelligence is not a bad thing to have along with the connections. And, in the first place, diplomats are certainly not clever simply because they are diplomats but only because they were clever people even before they entered the diplomatic service; and believe me, there are even a surprising number of remarkably unintelligent diplomats."

"Oh, no; excuse me," you interrupt impatiently. "All diplomats are always intelligent, and they all occupy excellent positions; it's a most noble service!"

"Madam, madam," I exclaim, "you say: connections and a knowledge of languages, but connections only get you the post, and then, later on. . . . Well, just imagine: this little cherub of yours grows up in the restaurants of Europe; he sows his wild oats with fashionable courtesans in the company of foreign viscounts and Russian counts, but then later on. . . . Now he knows all the languages, and for this reason alone he doesn't know any of them. Not having his own language, he naturally seizes on fragments of the thoughts and feelings of all nations; from the time of his youth, his intellect is, so to say, churned up into some wishy-washy mixture and he becomes an international creature, neither fish nor fowl, with narrow, unfulfilled little ideas and a dull, straight-line way of thinking. He's a diplomat, but as far as he's concerned the history of nations isn't much more than a vaudeville performance. He doesn't see, and doesn't even suspect, the things that nations and peoples live by, what laws govern their organism, and whether there is anything integral in these laws, whether some general international law can be perceived in them. He's ready to conclude that all the events of the world deduce only from the fact that, say, a queen angered the favorite of some king or other and so a war broke out between the two kingdoms. Allow me, please, to look at it from your point of view. Let him have his connections.... But yet, in order to acquire connections he needs character; he needs, so to say, goodness of character, gentleness, kindness, and at the same time soundness and perseverance.... A diplomat has to be charming, after all; he has to captivate, so to say, and to conquer, isn't that so? Well, I don't know whether you'll believe me when I tell you frankly and most definitely that without a knowledge of one's natural language, without mastering it, one can't even shape one's character, particularly if the little cherub has been well and truly blessed by nature: in due time he'll begin to have thoughts, ideas, and feelings; these thoughts and feelings will begin to press on him from within, so to say, as they seek and demand to be expressed; but without ample, ready forms of expression assimilated since childhood—that's to say, without the language, without its cultivation, without its refinement, without mastery of its nuances—your son will be dissatisfied with himself: he will no longer be satisfied with fragments of thought; the material that collects in his mind and in his heart will demand to be expressed in thorough fashion.... The young man will become preoccupied, absent-minded, vaguely pensive, and then grumpy and impossible to live with; and then his health will be undermined and even, perhaps, his digestion; believe me....

"But now I can see you've burst out laughing; I've been carried away again, it's true (and yet, my Lord, what I'm saying is the truth!); but let me finish, let me remind you that I conceded something to you a moment ago and agreed, for appearance's sake, that diplomats are still clever people; but, madam, you've reduced me to the point where I must now no longer hide from you the most secret, underlying reason for my view on this subject. As ill luck would have it, madam, several times in the course of my life the thought has occurred to me that among diplomats—I mean within the diplomatic service generally, of all the nations and throughout the nineteenth century—there have in fact been extraordinarily few clever people. It's striking, even. On the contrary, the poverty of intellect of this class of people in Europe over the present century . . . what I mean to say is that they're all clever, more or less, that's beyond dispute; they're all witty, but just look at the sort of cleverness they show! Has even one of these clever minds managed to penetrate to the essence of things? Has he realized, has he sensed the mysterious laws that are leading Europe toward something, toward something unknown, strange, and terrible but which now is evident and is happening almost before the very eyes of those who ought to be able to have at least some presentiment of it? No, ma'am, one can positively affirm that there has not been even a single such diplomat, nor a single such clever mind among this so respectable and privileged class! (When I say this, of course, I am excluding Russia and everything on the home front because we, by our very essence, are a 'special case' in this matter.) On the contrary, all through the century there have been, to be sure, some most cunning diplomatic minds, masters of intrigue who claimed to have a most practical understanding of things, and yet not a single one of them was able to see beyond his own nose and his current interests (and even the most superficial and mistaken interests at that). To tie up the loose ends somehow, to stick a little patch over the hole, 'to jack up the price, and give the thing a fresh coat of paint so it looks like something new'—that's our job, that's what we do! And there are reasons for all this, the main one being, in my view, two alien sets of principles, alienation from the People and the dissociation of diplomatic minds in a sphere that is, one might say, overly fashionable and remote from humanity. Take Count Cavour, for instance: now wasn't his a great mind, and wasn't he a real diplomat? I take him because he has already been accepted as a genius, and also because he is dead. But just look at what he accomplished: oh, he achieved his aim; he united Italy; and what was the result? For twenty-five hundred years Italy has borne within her a universal and unifying idea—not some abstract idea, not some speculations of a bureaucratic mind, but something real and organic, the fruit of the life of a nation, the fruit of life in the world: this was the unification of the entire world, first the ancient Roman unification, and then the papal one. The peoples who sprang up and disappeared in

Italy during these two and a half thousand years realized that they were the bearers of a universal idea, and those who did not realize it still felt and sensed it. Science, art—everything was invested and imbued with this universal significance. Oh, yes, we have to admit that this universal idea over there at last wore itself out and was expended (although can that really be so?); but what was it that ultimately emerged in its place? What do we have to congratulate Italy about now? After Count Cavour's diplomacy, what did she achieve that was better? What did appear was a united, second-rate little kingdom that had lost every last one of its universal ambitions, that had exchanged them for the most worn-out bourgeois principle (the thirtieth time this principle has been repeated since the first French Revolution); a kingdom that is utterly satisfied with its unity, which signifies absolutely nothing, with its mechanical but not spiritual unity (not the former universal unity, that is); and, on top of this, that has debts it can never pay and, on top of this, that is utterly satisfied with its own second-rateness. That's what emerged, that's the creation of Count Cavour! In short, today's diplomat is precisely 'a mighty beast for petty deeds.' Prince Metternich was regarded as one of the most profound and subtle diplomats in the world, and certainly his influence extended all over Europe. And yet, what idea did he have and how did he understand his own age, which was only beginning in his lifetime? How did he foresee the future? Alas, he decided to use police measures to deal with all the fundamental ideas of the century that was beginning, and he was completely confident of success! Now let's look at Prince Bismarck; there's no disputing his genius, but. . . ."

"*Finissons, monsieur,*" mamma interrupts me sternly, with a haughty air of profoundly wounded dignity. Naturally, I'm at once terribly frightened. And, of course, I haven't been understood; one still can't take up such topics with mammas nowadays, and I've made a dreadful faux pas. But with whom, then, can one now take up the topic of diplomacy?—that's the question. And yet it's such an interesting topic, particularly in our time! But. . . .

2. Diplomacy Facing World Problems

And what a serious topic it is! For what is our present time? Everyone endowed with any wisdom says that our time is primarily one of diplomacy, a time of resolving all the fates of the world by diplomatic means alone. People maintain, for instance, that we supposedly have a war going on somewhere now. And I've even heard that there's a war, but people tell me, and I read everywhere, that if there really is something like a war going on over there, then we have no proper understanding of it. . . . At least it has been decided that this war will not stand in the way of anything; that is, it will not stand in the way of the healthy workings of the nation which, in accordance with the latest views of everything that is generally called "higher wisdom," coincides primarily and even exclusively with diplomacy alone; and that all these military excursions, maneuvers, and so on, though always necessary, constitute in the true sense of things no more than one of the phases of higher diplomacy and nothing else. So we must believe. For my part, I am very much inclined to believe it, for it's all very reassuring; still, this is what is curious and what really stands out: the Eastern Question flared up among us, for example; at the same time, and even earlier, it flared up all over Europe, and it's very easy to understand why: everyone, even the nondiplomats (and even particularly the nondiplomats)—everyone has known for a long, long time that the Eastern Question is, one might say, one of the world questions, one of the principal *divisions* of the worldwide and imminent resolution of the fates of humanity, their new and approaching phase. We know that this matter concerns not only the East of Europe, not only the Slavs, the Russians, and the Turks, or, specifically, some Bulgarians over there, but that it concerns also the whole of the West of Europe, and not only in relation to the seas and the straits, access and egress, by any means; it is much deeper, more fundamental, more elemental, more necessary, more essential, more primary. And therefore one can understand that Europe is alarmed and that diplomacy has so much business. But really, what is the business of diplomacy?—that's my question! What is it doing (now, primarily) on the Eastern Question? The business of diplomacy (and otherwise it would not be diplomacy)—its business now is to lay hold of the Eastern Question in all respects and to assure everyone, involved and uninvolved, as quickly as possible, that no question whatever has come up, that these things are nothing more than some little excursions and maneuvers and even—if at all possible—to assure everyone that not only has the Eastern Question not come up but that there never was such a thing at all, that it never existed but is only a fog that was spread a hundred years ago for certain reasons (diplomatic ones as well), and that this unexplained fog persists to this day. Frankly speaking, even this could be believed were it not for one riddle, no longer a diplomatic one (that's the problem!), for diplomacy never ever tackles such riddles; moreover, it turns scornfully away from them, for it considers them mere fantasies unworthy of superior intellects. One might formulate the riddle in this way: why does it always happen, and particularly lately—I mean from the middle of the nineteenth century, and the more recently, the more obviously and tangibly—that the moment some issue in the world touches on something general and universal, *all the other* world problems at once rise parallel to it? For instance, in Europe it's now not enough to have just one world problem, the Eastern Question; no—in France, Europe suddenly and unexpectedly raises another question of world importance—the Catholic one. And the Catholic question is there, not because the pope, supposedly, is soon going to die so that France, as the representative of Catholicism, must see to it that nothing disappears and changes in the organization of Catholicism established over the centuries, but also because it has been accepted here that Catholicism is the common banner under which to unite the whole old order of things, the order established over the last nineteen centuries—to unite it against something new and imminent, vital and fateful, against the renewal of the macrocosm by a new order of things, against the social, moral, and radical revolution in all of Western European life or, at least, should this renewal not be accomplished, against the terrible trauma and colossal revolution that certainly threatens to shake all the kingdoms of the bourgeoisie all over the world, where they have been organized and have flourished on the French pattern of 1789, a revolution that threatens to overthrow them and to take their place.

By the way, let me depart from my topic for a moment and make one indispensable nota bene, for I sense how absurd it will seem to certain wise men, liberal ones in particular, that I, in the very midst of the nineteenth century, call France a Catholic power, the representative of Catholicism! And therefore, in explaining my idea I make an unsubstantiated (for the moment) declaration that France is precisely the country which, should it hold not a single person who believed in the pope or even in God, would still continue to remain primarily a Catholic country—the representative, one might say, of the entire Catholic organism, its banner—and so it shall continue there for a very long time, even for an incredibly long time, until such time, perhaps, as France ceases to be France and changes into something else. Moreover, socialism itself will begin there on the Catholic pattern, with a Catholic organization and a Catholic infusion, and in no other way—such is the degree to which this country is a Catholic country! At the moment I will not set about trying to prove this in any detail, but for the time being will merely point to the following as an instance: what was it that suddenly prompted Marshal MacMahon to raise and stir up, just out of the blue, the Catholic question specifically? This brave general (who, however, lost almost all his battles and who distinguished himself in diplomacy only by the brief phrase "*J'y suis et j'y reste*")—this general is certainly not one of those figures who could *consciously* raise a question of this sort. Yet he did; he raised the most fundamental of all the old European questions, and did so precisely in the form in which he had to raise it—but the main thing is why: why raise it at that precise moment, when at the other end of the world another universal question, the Eastern Question, had flared up? Why does one question impinge upon the other? Why does one evoke the other when, it would seem, there is no link between them? And, indeed, it's not only these two questions that were raised at the same time: along with the Eastern Question came still others, and more and more of them will be raised if the Eastern Question develops properly. In short, all the most important questions of Europe and humanity generally in our age are always raised simultaneously. And this very simultaneity is striking. The condition whereby all these questions appear simultaneously is what constitutes the riddle! But why am I saying all this? It's precisely because diplomacy regards such questions scornfully. Not only does it not acknowledge such coincidences, it does not even wish to think about them. Mirages, it calls them—trivial nonsense. "There's nothing in this at all; it's just that Marshal MacMahon, and his wife even more, got a certain notion, and that's how it all happened." And therefore, despite the fact that when I began this section of the chapter, I proclaimed that our time was primarily a diplomatic one, while everything else was a mirage, still I am forced to be the first to disbelieve this. No, there is a riddle here! No, it is not only diplomacy that decides the matter, but something else as well. And, I confess, I am extremely baffled by this outcome; I was so inclined to put my trust in diplomacy, but all these new questions are merely new fuss and bother, nothing more. . . .

3. Never Has Russia Been as Powerful as Now—A Nondiplomatic Judgment

In fact, I've just posed a question and so far have only discussed it without any supporting evidence. But even long before the current question (i.e., the question of why all these world problems come up at the same time the moment any one of them is raised), one other question always presented itself to me; this one is incomparably simpler and more natural but, precisely because it is so simple and natural, men of wisdom pay almost no attention to it. This is the other question: very well, diplomacy may have been and still is, always and everywhere, the thing that resolves all the fundamental and crucial questions of humanity, and will do so in the future; still, will the final resolution of European problems always depend on diplomacy? Is there not, on the contrary, such a phase, such a point in every question when it can no longer be resolved by all the usual, soothing diplomatic means—by applying little patches to it, that is? And although it's undeniable that all world problems—from the diplomatic point of view and accordingly from the commonsensical point of view—are always explained as merely the fact that some state or other got the urge to expand its borders, or such and such a brave general personally got the urge to do something, or some prominent lady was displeased by one thing or another, etc., etc. (that may be beyond dispute; I'll already grant you that, for it's the wisdom of the wisest)—but still, even given these very down-to-earth reasons and explanations, isn't there at a given moment such a point in the course of events, such a phase when there suddenly appear some strange new forces—incomprehensible and mysterious ones, let's assume—that suddenly take hold of everything, that at once seize everything as a whole and draw it away irresistibly, blindly, as if down a slope or, perhaps, into an abyss? Essentially, I would only like to find out: does diplomacy always place such reliance on itself and on its own resources that it has no fear whatever of such forces, points, and phases and perhaps doesn't even assume that they exist? Alas, it seems this is always so, and therefore: how can I believe and trust it, and how can I accept it as the final arbitrator of the fates of a still so capricious and dissolute humanity!

Alas, in Kaidanov's voluminous history there is one magnificent sentence. It is found at the point where, in his *Modern History,* he sets about describing the French Revolution and the appearance of Napoleon I. This sentence begins a chapter, and it has remained in my memory all my life: "A profound silence reigned throughout Europe when Frederick the Great closed his eyes forever; but never had a similar silence preceded such a great storm!" Now tell me, do you know any finer sentence than that? In fact, who then in Europe—I mean at the time when Frederick the Great closed his eyes forever—could foresee, even in the remotest fashion, what would happen to the people of Europe in the course of the following three decades? I'm not talking about some ordinary educated people, or even about writers, journalists, and professors. All of them, as we know, were completely taken aback: Schiller, for instance, wrote a dithyramb on the opening of the National Assembly; the young Karamzin, who was then traveling in Europe, looked at the event with a tender quivering in his heart, while even well before that our own Petersburg had been graced by a marble bust of Voltaire. No, I am addressing a question directly to the very wisest among the wise, directly to those who resolve all human destinies—I mean to the diplomats themselves: did they then foresee anything at all of what was to occur over the next three decades?

But this is what is really terrible: if I were to ask the diplomats this (and note that almost all European diplomats studied Kaidanov's textbook—the "Kaidashka," as it was called), and if they were to pay me the honor of listening, then they would certainly have replied with a haughty laugh that "*matters of chance* are impossible to foresee and that the whole of wisdom consists only in being prepared for any matter of chance."

Well, what about that! No, I'll tell you: this is a typical answer, and although I thought it up myself—because I haven't bothered even one diplomat with my questions (and I wouldn't dare to)—still, what I find so awful is that I'm certain that this would be exactly the reply, and that is why I called it a typical answer. For in the eyes of diplomats, what, please tell me, were these events at the turn of the last century if not *matters of chance*? They were and they are. And Napoleon, for instance—he was a matter of chance par excellence, and had he not appeared, had he died over there in Corsica of scarlet fever at the age of three, the *tiers état* of humanity, the bourgeoisie, would not have streamed forth with their new banner in hand to change the face of the whole of Europe (a process that continues even to this day) and would have just gone on sitting at home in Paris and, indeed, might well have died off at the very beginning!

The point, it seems to me, is that the present age as well will end in Old Europe with something colossal; that's to say, with something that may not literally resemble the ending of the eighteenth century, perhaps, but that will still be colossal enough—elemental and dreadful, and also changing the face of this world—at least in the West of Old Europe. And so, if the wisest of our wise will state that they can't foresee *matters of chance*, and so on; and, besides, if nothing about such a finale has even entered their heads, then. . . .

In short, patches, little patches, and more little patches!

Well, then, let's be prudent; let's wait. Little patches are, if you like, also essential and useful, prudent and practical things. The more so that little patches, you see, can deceive the enemy. Here we are at war, and if Austria should make a hostile move against us, then we could at once deceive her with "little patches," and she would readily fall into the trap, because what is Austria. She herself is practically breathing her last gasp, about to collapse, and is just such a "sick man" as Turkey—maybe even sicker. She is an example of every sort of dualism, every sort of internal, hostile mergings, nationalities, and ideas; she contains every sort of discord and conflicting tendency; here we have Hungarians and Slavs and Germans, and here we have the kingdom of the Yids. . . . Well, and now, thanks to diplomacy's courting of her, she might really get the notion that she is a power that truly does mean something and that she is able to do a good deal in settling fates generally. Such a delusion, inspired specifically by the others' courting of her and the little patches applied to resolve the fates of the Slavs, is useful because it can draw off the enemy for a time, and when the moment of decision comes and he suddenly sees that no one is afraid of him and that he's not a power at all, he may be disheartened and simply confused. England is another matter: she is something rather more serious and, besides, is terribly absorbed in her own fundamental undertakings. She's not one to be lulled to sleep by little patches and courtship. Whatever you try to tell her, she simply will never believe that an enormous nation, now among the great powers of the world, that has drawn its mighty sword and unfurled the banner of a grand idea and has already crossed the Danube, can in fact wish to solve the problems that it has taken on to its own obvious detriment and solely to England's benefit. For every improvement in the lot of the Slavic nations is *in any case* to England's obvious detriment, and in this case little patches are no good at all for coaxing anyone: they won't believe you!—people in England simply won't believe any of it. And, indeed, what arguments could convince her? "I'll *start* the thing off, just a bit, but I won't finish it." But in politics, the beginning is everything, after all, for the beginning, naturally, sooner or later will lead to the end. What does it matter that the ending will not take place today?—it will still take place tomorrow. In short, they won't believe it, and so we, too, shouldn't believe the English, or should believe them as little as possible, but keep it to ourselves, of course. It would be good if we could also realize that at the moment England is in the most critical situation it has ever been in. This critical situation of hers can be formulated most accurately in a single word: *isolation,* for never before, perhaps, has England found herself in such terrible isolation as now. Oh, how happy she would be now to find an alliance in Europe, some sort of *entente cordiale.* But her problem is that there has never yet been a moment in Europe in which it was more difficult to put together an alliance. For it is precisely now that everything in Europe has risen up simultaneously, all the world problems at once, and with them all the world contradictions, so that every people and state have *more than enough to do in handling their own domestic affairs.* And since England's interest is not a world interest but one that has long isolated itself from everything and is concerned with England alone, then at least for a time she will remain in total isolation. Oh, of course, for the sake of mutual benefit she could come to terms even with those who are pursuing aims quite different from her own: "I'll let you have this, and you'll let me have that." But given the nature of the current troubles in Europe, it is difficult to put together an *entente cordiale* of this sort, at least at the present moment, and she will have to wait a long time until, eventually, as things develop in the future, she will find such a moment when she too will cling on somewhere with her alliance. Moreover, England above all needs a profitable alliance, meaning one in which she will take everything and will herself, if at all possible, pay out *nothing at all.* Now that's just the sort of profitable union that can't be seen anywhere on the horizon, and England is in isolation. Oh, if only we had the skill to take advantage of that isolation! But now we hear another exclamation: "Oh, if only we were less skeptical and could believe that there are problems of world importance and that they are not a mirage!" The main thing is that here in Russia a very large part of our intelligentsia has always seen and accepted Europe unrealistically, not as she now is but always with a kind of hindsight, looking at her as she once was. They don't look into the future, but are inclined to judge more by the past, even by the distant past.

But still, these world problems really do exist, and how can we—we especially—not believe in them? Two of them have already arisen and are now being moved not by human wisdom but by their own elemental force, by their own fundamental, organic need; and they can no longer remain unsolved, despite all the calculating of the diplomats. But there is also a third question, and it is also a world one, and is also rising up and has almost fully arisen already. This question may in part be called the German one, but in essence, as a whole, it is above all a pan-European one, and it is completely and organically a part of the fate of the whole of Europe and of all the other world questions. On the surface, however, it would appear that nothing could be more peaceful and less turbulent than Germany is now: in the calm assurance of her awesome strength, she watches, observes, and waits. Everyone, more or less, needs her; everyone, more or less, depends on her. And yet . . . all this is a mirage! And that's just the point: everyone in Europe now is busy with his own affairs; everyone has found his own question of ultimate importance, a question almost as important as his own existence, a question like "to be or not to be": and it's that sort of question that has come up in Germany as well, just at the time the other world questions have arisen—and it's this particular state of affairs in Europe, I might add, getting ahead of myself, that is absolutely the most useful thing for Russia at the present moment! For never has she been so necessary to Europe, nor so powerful in Europe's estimation, and yet so isolated from the most fundamental and terrible questions that are arising in this Old Europe—questions that belong to Old Europe, that are hers alone, and not Russia's. And never has an alliance with Russia been more valued in Europe than now; never before could she have more joyfully congratulated herself that she is not the Old Europe but the New; that she, in herself, is a separate and powerful world whose moment has just now arrived to enter into a new and higher phase of power and, more than ever, to become independent of other, *their,* fateful questions with which dilapidated Old Europe has bound herself!

3

1. The German World Problem. Germany— A Protesting Country

But we have taken up the topic of Germany, her present objective, her present fateful problem, which is at the same time a world problem. What is this objective of hers? And why is this objective only now becoming such a troublesome problem for Germany, and why did this not happen before, some time back, a year or even two months ago?

Germany's objective is one; so it was before, and so it was always. It is her *Protestantism*—meaning not just the expression of the Protestantism that took shape in Luther's time but her chronic protestantism, her chronic tendency to *protest*—against the Roman world, beginning with Arminius; against everything that was Rome and Roman in its objective; and then against everything that was passed on from ancient Rome to the new Rome and to all those peoples who took the idea of Rome, the Roman formula and fundamentals, against the heirs of Rome and everything that makes up this legacy. I am convinced that some readers, as they read this, will shrug their shoulders and laugh: "Come now, can one talk about Catholicism and Protestantism in the nineteenth century, an age of new ideas and science, as if we were still living in the Middle Ages! And if, perhaps, there still exist some religious people and even fanatics, then they've been preserved like archaeological relics; they persist only in certain specific places and little corners and are condemned and ridiculed by everyone; what really matters is that there are so very few of them, just an insignificant, miserable little collection of backward people. And so, can we really regard them as counting for anything in as lofty a matter as world politics?"

But I what have in mind is not a religious *protest;* I don't wish to dwell on the temporary expressions of the ancient Roman idea any more than on the age-old Germanic protest against it. I am taking only the basic idea, which began two thousand years ago and which has not died out to this day, even though it has continually been reincarnated in various guises and expressions. Nowadays it is precisely this whole extreme western European world—precisely the world that inherited the Roman legacy—that is in the throes of giving birth to a new incarnation of this ancient idea; and for those who know how to look, this is so obvious that it needs no explanation.

Ancient Rome first gave birth to the idea of the universal unity of people and first thought of (and firmly believed in) putting it into practice in the form of a worldwide monarchy. But this formula fell before Christianity—the formula, but not the idea. For this idea is the idea of European humanity; their civilization was put together on the basis of this idea; they live only for this idea. What was defeated was only the idea of the universal *Roman* monarchy, and it was replaced by a new ideal of universal union in Christ. This new ideal split into an eastern one, meaning an ideal of the complete spiritual union of people, and a western European one, Roman Catholic and papal, the complete opposite of the eastern one. This western, Roman Catholic incarnation of the idea was achieved in its own way, but only after it lost its Christian, spiritual foundation and took on instead a part of the legacy of ancient Rome. The Roman papacy proclaimed that Christianity and its idea cannot be realized without worldwide dominion over lands and peoples—and not spiritual but political dominion; in other words, Christianity and its idea are unrealizable without the implementation on earth of a new, worldwide Roman monarchy headed, not by a Roman emperor, but by the pope. And so began another attempt to establish a worldwide monarchy entirely in the spirit of the ancient Roman world, but now in a new form. Thus, the eastern ideal places first the spiritual union of humanity in Christ, and only then, on the strength of this spiritual union of all in Christ and as an inevitable product of it will come a just political and social union; the Roman interpretation, however, it is the reverse: first a solid political union in the form of a worldwide monarchy must be secured, and only then, perhaps, will come a spiritual union under the direction of the pope, as lord of this world.

Since then, this endeavor has gone ahead in the Roman world, and its form has changed continually. As it progressed, the most essential part of the Christian principle was almost entirely lost.

Having at last rejected Christianity in spirit, the heirs of the ancient Roman world rejected the papacy as well. The terrible French Revolution burst forth, a revolution that in essence was no more than the latest metamorphosis and reincarnation of this same ancient Roman formula of worldwide unity. But the new formula proved to be insufficient; the new idea was not realized. There was even a moment when all the nations that had inherited the ancient Roman mission almost despaired. Oh, of course, the portion of society that won political leadership in 1789—the bourgeoisie, that is—was triumphant and declared that there was no need to go any further. But all those minds which by the age-old laws of nature were condemned to remain everywhere endlessly restive, to search for new formulations of the ideal and a new word essential to the growth of the human organism—all those minds hastened to all the humiliated and bypassed, to all those who had not received a share in the new formulation of universal unity proclaimed by the French Revolution of 1789. Now they proclaimed their own new word, namely the need for the unity of all people, no longer looking to assign equality and rights to some mere quarter of humanity, leaving the rest only as raw material and as a means to be exploited for the happiness of this quarter; on the contrary, they wanted a worldwide union of people on the basis of universal equality, with each and every one enjoying his share of the blessings of this word, whatever those blessings might prove to be. They resolved to resort to *any* means to put this idea into practice—not the means of Christian civilization, that is—without stopping at anything.

What role has Germany been playing here through all these two thousand years? The most characteristic, most fundamental trait of this great, proud, and distinct people, from the very first moment of their appearance on the historical scene, has been that they have never wanted to unite, in terms of their mission and their principles, with the extreme western European world, meaning with all the heirs of the ancient Roman idea. They *protested* against this world for the whole two thousand years, and although they did not manage to express (and have never yet expressed) their "word," their strictly formulated ideal to take the place of the ancient Roman idea, it seems that they were always inwardly convinced that they had the capacity to express this new word and to have humanity follow in their wake. They had struggled with the Roman world even in the time of Arminius; and then, in the time of Roman Christianity, they struggled more vigorously than anyone for supreme power over the new Rome. Finally, they protested in the most forceful and powerful manner, deriving their formula for protest from the very elemental, spiritual bases of the Germanic world: they proclaimed freedom of inquiry and raised up the banner of Luther. The break was terrible and of world importance; the formula of protest had been found and given content, even though it was still a negative formula, even though a new and a *positive* word had not yet been pronounced.

And so the Germanic spirit, having spoken its new word of protest, seemed to come to a standstill for a time, and this happened absolutely parallel to a similar weakening of the former strictly formulated unity of forces in its opponent. The westernmost world, under the influence of the discovery of America, the new science and new principles, sought its rebirth into a new truth and a new phase. When the first attempt at this reincarnation came during the French Revolution, the Germanic spirit was in great confusion and for a time seemed even about to lose its individuality and its faith in itself. It could say nothing to oppose the new ideas of the westernmost European world. Luther's Protestantism had long outlived its time; the idea of free inquiry had long been accepted by world science. Germany's immense organism sensed more than anyone that it did not have, so to say, the flesh and the forms to express itself. And at that point there was born the urgent need to close its ranks, even if only externally, into a single, harmonious organism, in anticipation of the coming new phases of its eternal struggle with Europe's westernmost world. Here I should note a most curious coincidence: both the eternally hostile camps, both of those contesting in old Europe for predominance within her, at one and the same time (or almost) take up and carry out a very similar objective. The new, future formula that in the westernmost world is still a dream—the renewal of human society on new social principles—this formula, which through almost the whole of our century has been proclaimed only by dreamers, by its scholarly representatives, by idealists and fantasists of all sorts, in recent years suddenly assumed a new guise and course of development; and it resolved: to abandon for the moment the theoretical definition and reconstruction of its objective and to take directly, in advance of any fantasizing, a practical step toward the objective—to initiate the battle directly, that is, and for that purpose to make a start at uniting into a single organization all the future warriors for this new idea, i.e., the whole *fourth* estate, the people who had been bypassed in 1789, all the workers, all the needy; and having set up this union, to raise the banner of a new and unprecedented world revolution. There appeared the International; there were international links among all the poor people of the world; there were meetings, congresses, new regulations, laws—in short, *all over the old western Europe* a foundation was laid for a new *status in statu* intended to swallow up the old order that had prevailed in the westernmost part of Europe. And so, while this was going on among the enemy, the Germanic genius realized that it was the German task—before any other undertaking or initiative, before any attempt to pronounce a new word to counter the idea of the enemy reincarnated from the old, ancient Catholic idea—to achieve its own political unity, to complete the creation of its own political organism and, having created it, only then to stand face-to-face with its age-old enemy. And so it happened: having completed her unification, Germany flung herself on her enemy and entered into a new period of struggle with it, having begun the struggle with blood and iron. In terms of iron the matter has been finished; now it needs to be finished spiritually and in essence. But now Germany is suddenly faced with a new concern; there is a new, unexpected turn of events that complicates her objective terribly. What, then, is this objective, and what is this new turn of events?

2. One Brilliantly Suspicious Man

This objective, this new, *sudden* concern for Germany, if you like, has long been trying to emerge, but now the whole problem is that it has leapt onto center stage as a result of the sudden clerical upset in France. Germany's worry can be expressed, in part, by the following statement of doubt: "Has the Germanic organism in fact been united into a single whole? Is it not, rather, fragmented as before, despite the brilliant efforts of Germany's leaders over the last twenty-five years? Moreover, has it even been united politically? Perhaps this, too, is a mirage, despite the Franco-Prussian War and the new, unprecedented German Empire proclaimed after the war?" Such is the complex question.

The whole complexity of this question lies mainly in the fact that until almost recently no one even supposed it existed, at least no one among the vast majority of Germans. After the Franco-German War vainglory, pride, and utter faith in their own boundless strength virtually intoxicated the Germans to a man. A people who have so very rarely been conquerors but who, strangely, have been so often conquered—this people suddenly conquered an enemy who had almost always conquered them! And since it was clear that they could not help but conquer, as a result of the exemplary organization of their innumerable army and its unique reconstitution on entirely new principles and its having, besides, so many brilliant leaders to head it, the Germans naturally could not help but grow proud to the point of intoxication. There's no need here even to take into account the eternal self-satisfied boastfulness of every German—that age-old trait of the German character. On the other hand, when a harmonious whole suddenly appeared out of a political organism that so recently had still been fragmented, the German could not doubt, and was fully convinced, that the unification had been accomplished and that the German organism was entering into a new, brilliant, and grand phase of development. And so, not only pride and chauvinism appeared, but also an almost light-minded attitude as well; and what kind of doubts could arise, not only in the mind of some pugnacious shopkeeper or shoemaker, but even in the mind of a professor or a cabinet minister? Yet there was still a little group of Germans who, very soon, almost immediately after the Franco-Prussian War, began to doubt and ponder. At the head of the most remarkable members of that little group stood, unquestionably, Prince Bismarck.

The German forces had not yet managed to withdraw from France when Bismarck already saw clearly that too little had been achieved with "blood and iron" and that, considering the extent of his aims, he should have taken advantage of the situation and done twice as much at least. It's true that the German side has gained incalculably more military advantages and that this will be so for a long time to come. After giving up Alsace and Lorraine, France, in terms of territory, has become such a small country for a great power that in the event of a new war, Germany needs to win only two or three battles and the German forces will at once be in the center of France, and in strategic terms France will be lost. But yet, are these victories certain? Can they fully count on these two victorious battles? In the Franco-Prussian War it was not the French themselves whom the Germans conquered, it was only Napoleon and his system. The French forces will not always be so badly organized and so poorly led; neither will there always be usurpers who, from dynastic reasons, need generals and civil servants and be compelled to tolerate the lamentable shortcomings that make the maintenance of a proper army impossible. There will not always be repetitions of Sedan either, for Sedan in essence was only an accident and happened only because Napoleon could no longer return to Paris as emperor other than by the grace of the king of Prussia. There will not always be generals of such little competence as MacMahon or such traitors as Bazaine. Intoxicated by the utterly unprecedented nature of their triumph, the Germans—every last one of them, of course—could come to believe that everything they achieved had been achieved by their talents alone; but the little group of doubters might think otherwise, particularly after the conquered enemy, still so shaken and disorganized, could suddenly pay off three billions in reparations at once and not even frown about it. Prince Bismarck, naturally enough, was much grieved by this.

On the other hand, the little group of doubters faced another and perhaps still more important question: had the political and civil unification within the organism been entirely completed? For almost everyone in Europe and, it seems, for us in Russia in particular, this has not yet been a matter of doubt. On the whole, we Russians have accepted everything that has happened in Germany over the last ten or fifteen years as something final, as something by no means accidental but quite natural, as something that now must not change. The things that have occurred have inspired us with unusual respect. And yet such brilliant people as Prince Bismarck hardly believe that everything has assumed its final and stable form. That which might seem solid now is, perhaps, still no more than a fantasy. It's difficult to believe that such a long habit of political disunity has vanished among the Germans as quickly as one can drink a glass of water. The German is stubborn by his very nature. The present generation of Germans, besides, has been bribed by successes, intoxicated by pride, and restrained by the iron hand of its leaders. But in the very near future, perhaps, when those leaders have gone on to their reward and have yielded their places to others, it is possible that questions and instincts that have been temporarily suppressed will surface. It is also highly probable that then the energy of the first upsurge of feeling for unification will run out and that, rather, there will be a new intensity of opposition that will unsettle the things that have been achieved. A tendency toward disintegration and dissociation will appear, and just at the point when in the West the terrible enemy is quite recovered from the blow he has been dealt, the enemy who even now is not sleeping or slumbering, and who will begin even with something we might anticipate. And besides this, there is what we might call a law of nature: Germany is still a *middle* country in Europe; no matter how powerful she is, she has France on one side and Russia on the other. It's true that the Russians are polite for the moment. But what if they suddenly figure out that it is not they who need an alliance with Germany, it is Germany who needs an alliance with Russia: *that dependence on an alliance with Russia is, evidently, Germany's fatal destiny, particularly since the Franco-Prussian War.* Now that's just the point: even one as convinced of his own strength as Prince Bismarck is incapable of believing in Russia's profound respect. It's true that until the latest unexpected escapade in France, which suddenly changed the whole appearance of the matter, Prince Bismarck was still hoping that Russia's extraordinary politeness would remain constant for a long time to come; and then, suddenly, there's this escapade! In short, something unusual happened.

Unusual for everyone, but not for Prince Bismarck! Now it seems that his genius had foreseen this whole "escapade." Tell me, was it not his genius, was it not his brilliant eye that so long ago picked out his principal adversary? Why, specifically, did he develop such a hatred for Catholicism? Why has he persecuted and oppressed everything emanating from Rome (from the pope, that is) for so many years now? Why did he, with such foresight, enlist the support of an Italian *alliance* (one can put it that way) if not so as to stamp out the papal principle in the world, with the help of the Italian government, when the time comes to elect a new pope? It was not the Catholic religion he was persecuting, it was the Roman principle of this religion. Oh, there's no doubt that he was acting as a German; as a Protestant he was acting against the fundamental element of the western edge of the European world that was always hostile to Germany; but yet very, very many of the most brilliant and liberal thinkers of Europe regarded this campaign of the great Bismarck against such an insignificant pope as a battle between an elephant and a fly. Some of them explained it even as the quirk of a genius, the caprices of a brilliant man. But the fact is that this brilliant politician, perhaps alone among the politicians of the world, *was able* to judge how much strength the Roman principle still had within itself and among Germany's enemies and to see how it might serve as a terrible cement to hold all those enemies together. He was able to perceive that perhaps only the Roman idea could provide the banner around which, at the fateful (and in

Bismarck's eyes the inevitable) moment, all Germany's enemies, which he had already crushed, could rally. And so this brilliant hunch suddenly proved true: in defeated France all the parties that could have begun a movement against Germany were fragmented; not one of them could prevail and seize power in France. Neither were they able to unite in any way, since each of them had in mind aims that were contradictory to those of the others—but suddenly the banner of the pope and the Jesuits brings everything together. The enemy rose up, and this enemy is no longer France but the pope himself. It is the pope who leads everything and everyone; it is the pope who has inherited the Roman idea and who goes forth to assault Germany. But so as to set forth more clearly what has happened, let us look more closely into the camp of Germany's enemies.

3. Both Angry and Strong

The pope is dying. He will very soon pass away. The whole of Catholicism, which accepts Christ in the form of the Roman idea, has long been in terrible turmoil. The fateful moment is approaching. There mustn't be a slip, for that would mean the end of the Roman idea. It could just happen that the new pope, under the pressure of the governments of all Europe, will be elected "not freely," and once proclaimed pope, will agree to renounce, forever and in principle, earthly dominions and the rank of earthly sovereign which Pius IX refused to renounce. (On the contrary, at the fateful moment, when Rome was taken from him and the last scrap of land remaining as his property was the Vatican, he, as if deliberately, proclaimed his infallibility and along with it the following thesis: that without earthly dominions Christianity cannot survive on earth, i.e., in essence he proclaimed himself the sovereign of the world and gave Catholicism, now as a dogma, the direct aim of worldwide monarchy and ordered it to strive to this end for the glory of God and Christ on earth.) Oh, of course, he gave a good laugh to all the sharp-minded people of the time: "He's angry but not strong—Khlestakov's brother." And now, suddenly, should the newly elected pope be bribed, and should even the conclave itself, under pressure from all of Europe, be compelled to enter into an agreement with the opponents of the Roman idea—well, that will be the end of it! For once a pope, duly elected and therefore infallible, renounces in principle the title of earthly sovereign, then it follows that this will remain so forever and ever. On the other hand, should the pope newly elected by the conclave declare firmly and *urbi et orbi* that he has no intention of renouncing anything and will hold entirely to the former idea and begin with an anathema to all the enemies of Rome and Roman Catholicism, then the governments of Europe may not recognize him and, accordingly, here too there may be occur within the Roman church a turmoil so fateful that its consequences may be incalculable and unforeseeable.

Oh, the politicians and diplomats of almost the whole of Europe find all this highly amusing and inconsequential, do they not? In recent years, the pope, reduced in stature and shut up in the Vatican, was such a nonentity in their eyes that it was embarrassing to have any dealings with him. That was how an immense number of Europe's leading people thought, particularly the more sharp-witted and liberal ones among them. As far as they were concerned, the pope, issuing allocutions and syllabuses, receiving pilgrims, damning and dying, was like a buffoon performing for them. The thought that one of the most enormous ideas of the word, an idea that came from the mind of the devil when he was tempting Christ in the wilderness, an idea that has lived organically in the world for a thousand years now—that this idea would just simply die in an instant was accepted without a qualm. The error here, of course, lay in the religious significance of this idea, in the fact that two meanings had been mixed together: "Since it's so rare to find anyone who believes in God, especially in the Roman version of Him, and in France even the common people don't believe in Him, while the upper classes . . . well, even they don't believe but only try to look as if they do—then what power can the pope and Roman Catholicism have in our enlightened age?" That's what sharp-witted people believe even now. But the religious idea and the papal idea are different in essence. And now that same papal idea suddenly, in our day, only two months back, at once showed such tenacious vitality and such strength that it provoked in France a most radical political upset, put a bridle on the whole of France, and led her away like a slave.

In France in recent years, the majority in parliament have been republicans and they have carried on their affairs decently, fairly, and without commotions. They have improved the army and allotted enormous sums for it without any dispute; but they had no thought at all of war, and everyone, both in France and in Europe, realized that if there is a party that stands fully for peace, then of course it is they, the republicans. Their leaders were marked by restraint and unusual good sense. In essence, however, they are all idealists and men of abstraction. They are has-beens and terribly weak people. They are liberal, gray-haired old fellows trying to make themselves look young and imagining that they are still youngsters. They have gone no further than the ideas of the first French Revolution, i.e., the triumph of the *tiers état*, and are an incarnation of the bourgeoisie in the full meaning of the word. They are exactly that same July monarchy, the only difference being that it was called a republic and there was no king (that's to say, of course, no "tyrant"). The only new thing they introduced was the proclamation in 1848 of universal sufferage, something the government of the July monarchy so feared and that resulted in nothing dangerous but, rather, even a great many useful things for the bourgeoisie. Later on this idea also proved most useful for the government of Napoleon III. But the little old men were as pleased as could be with it and as delighted as children at being republicans. In their mouths the word *republic* is comically idealistic. It would seem that this innocent party would fully satisfy France, meaning the urban bourgeoisie and the landowners. But it proved to be just the contrary. Indeed, for that reason the republic has always seemed to be an unreliable government in France. And if the republicans were not always hated, they were always despised for their impotence by the vast majority of the bourgeoisie. If they were not plainly despised, they were never respected. The common people almost never trusted them either. The fact is that every time a republic has been installed in France, everything in France has seemed to lose its solidity and self-confidence. Until now the republic has always been merely some sort of temporary middle ground—between social endeavors of the most terrible scope, on the one hand, and, on the other, some usurper, occasionally a most brazen one. And since this almost always happened, society grew accustomed to regarding a republic in this way; and the moment a republic came into being, everyone always began to feel he was living in some sort of interregnum; and no matter how prudently the republicans governed, the bourgeoisie were always certain that sooner or later a red rebellion would burst out or some new monarchy or other would be proclaimed. The result was that the bourgeoisie became much fonder of a monarchical form of government than of a republic, despite the fact that a monarchy, such as that of Napoleon III, for example, even seemed to be making some attempts to enter into an agreement with the socialists, whereas no one on earth can be more hostile to the socialists than pure republicans: for the republicans, the word *republic* would be enough, while the socialists are looking not for words but for deeds alone. According to socialist principles it's all the same—whether it's a republic or a monarchy, whether they'll be French or become Germans, and, truly, even if it somehow were to transpire that they could make use of the pope himself, then they would hail the pope as well. They are seeking first of all to advance *their own cause*, meaning the triumph of the fourth estate and equality in the assignment of rights and the enjoyment of the blessings of life; and this can happen under any banner at all, even the most despotic—it makes no difference.

It's worth noting that Prince Bismarck hates socialism no less than papacy and that the German government, particularly in most recent times, has begun somehow to be excessively fearful of socialist propaganda. Without a doubt, this is because socialism depersonalizes the national principle and eats away at the very root of nationality, whereas the principle of nationality is the fundamental, leading idea of the whole German unification and of all that has taken place in Germany in recent years. But it is very possible that Prince Bismarck is looking even more deeply into the matter, i.e.: that socialism is the force of the future for the whole of western Europe, and if papacy should someday be abandoned and cast aside by the governments of this world, then it really and truly could be thrown into the embrace of socialism and merge completely with it. The pope, on foot and barefoot, will go forth to all the poor and will say that everything the socialists teach and all they desire has long been found in the Gospels; that hitherto the time had not yet come for them to learn about this, but that it has now come and that he, the pope, will turn Christ over to them and that he believes in the ant heap. Roman Catholicism (and this is all too clear) needs not Christ but universal dominion: "What you need is unity in the face of the enemy," it will say. "So join together under my power, for I alone among all the powers and sovereigns of the world am *universal;* let us go together." Prince Bismarck probably can foresee this picture, for he alone among all the diplomats was keen-sighted enough to foresee the tenacious vitality of the Roman idea and all the energy it is prepared to use to defend itself, whatever the means. It has an infernal desire to live, and it is as hard to kill as a serpent! That is what Prince Bismarck alone, the chief enemy of papacy and the Roman idea, understands with every fiber of his being!

But the little old men trying to be young, the French republicans, were incapable of understanding this. Their liberalism alone made them hate clericalism, but they regarded the pope as powerless and despicable and the Roman idea as having entirely outlived its time. It never even occurred to them to try to get along with the dreadful clerical party, even if only politically, so as to give themselves more solidity. At the very least, they did not have to irritate the clerical party for the time being; they did not have to go so far out of their way to offend them and could even have promised them some cooperation in the near future in electing the new pope. But they did just the opposite of all that—either because of some idealistic sense of the honor of their convictions or simply from light-mindedness. Lately they have begun particularly to oppress the clericals, and just at the moment when the papacy has only France to support it and runs the terrible risk of dying along with Pius IX. For who in Europe, should the need arise, could bear the sword for "freedom" in the election of the pope and for the freedom of the elected pope? And this must be a strong and mighty sword indeed. There is no other candidate besides France and her million-strong army. And now France is at the head of the enemies! It's true that Marshal MacMahon is obedient, but his hands are tied and he can't get loose: the majority of the Chamber is republican and liberal, and none of the other parties is able to replace it. In short, it's impossible to overthrow the republican majority, and here, suddenly, the clericals—those despised and impotent clericals—come to the rescue of Marshal MacMahon and display to the whole world a power such as no one expected from them anymore. They are letting the other parties know that they can unite only under the banner of clericalism, and the others, struck by the obviousness of it, at once agree. In fact, both the legitimists and the Bonapartists still have as their main and closest enemy that same republican majority. If each of these parties is going to work for itself, apart from the others, then it will achieve nothing; but if they join together, these parties can constitute a force, overcome everything, and drive out the republicans. And then, when they have crushed the republic, each party can worry about itself; and, of course, each of them will have all the more chance of success the more it pleases the clericals. The clericals have figured all this out mathematically; the union has taken place, and the clerical majority of the Senate allowed MacMahon to drive out the republicans.

4. The Black Army. The Opinion of the Legions as a New Element of Civilization

Having displayed such sudden strength and deftness, the clericals will certainly go further: at a moment that will be decisive for them, they will declare war on Germany—and that is what Prince Bismarck grasped very quickly! The main thing they have already achieved: MacMahon has already agreed to launch France on a policy of adventure. Now will the clericals hesitate at even greater things? They don't care about France; they need France, as they do everything else on earth, only as long as she is useful to them. Oh, they should have cared about her: this country is their only hope and has served them for so many centuries! But now they are facing the very most fateful moment in a whole millennium, and if France is available, why not suck the juices out of her as well, even if it kills her? Why not risk her very existence? They have to take from her everything she can give, and the main thing is not to dillydally: a few moments more and it will certainly be too late for them. So it's right now that they must try to turn back Bismarck, for if there is anyone who can do harm at the election of the pope then of course it is he. And on top of everything else, Bismarck, at this particular moment as luck would have it, is alone, without allies: Russia (his entire hope) is now occupied in the East. Finally, if they manage to subdue Bismarck, even if only temporarily, then as quickly as possible and in good time they must lay down a foundation *for the future:* they must exploit the happy moment and once and for all shape France as a solid ally, obedient and ready for anything; and to do that they must bring about a revolution in her, a *serious*, radical, and enduring one. No doubt there is a lot of risk in all this, but let others hesitate—not the Jesuit fathers. The main thing is that at the present moment they have no choice but to take risks, again and again. . . . To limit themselves only to the clerical revolution that has taken place in France, without a war with Germany and without a *serious* revolution in France, is positively impossible. They have come to precisely such a stage. They must have all or nothing; if they take just a little and limit themselves to some bit of influence in the government over there, they will have made no gains at all, for their needs are now large ones! And so they must undertake a most obviously risky and audacious venture, for they must take the whole *va-banque*. If, by chance, the risk fails and the Germans, say, conquer and crush France once more, then it doesn't matter: they, the clericals, will be no worse off than they are now (that is, if they had sat peacefully and not begun a revolution): they will be left where they were before the beginning of the "adventure," that's to say, in a situation that is truly miserable but cannot get any worse. France is another matter: if she is conquered once more, she will surely perish. But are the Jesuits the sort to be stopped by something like that? They know that if France triumphs they will get *everything* and will become so strong in France that there'll be no way of getting rid of them. And for this they have their own special means that are still unprecedented in France.

All the other revolutionaries, even the most violent and reddest of them, take at least partly into account certain general things previously given and even lawful. The Jesuit revolutionaries cannot act lawfully, they act *singularly*. This black army stands outside of humanity, outside of citizenship, outside of civilization; they derive exclusively from themselves. This is a *status in statu*, this is the army of the pope; it needs nothing more than the triumph of *its own* idea—and then, let everything blocking its way perish; let all the other forces wither and perish; let everything that does not agree with them die—civilization, society, science! They will certainly find it necessary to give France a new and final shape, if luck should be with them, and to sweep all the *rubbish* out of it with a broom whose like we have never seen, so that there shouldn't be even a whiff of resistance any more, and to give the country a new system, under the strictest Jesuit supervision, forever and ever.

At first glance, all this might seem quite ridiculous. In the French newspapers (and in ours as well) all the right-thinking people are firmly convinced that the clericals will certainly fall on their faces in the next elections to the French Chamber. The French republicans, in the innocence of their hearts, are also completely convinced that all the *activité dévorante* of the newly appointed prefects and mayors will achieve absolutely nothing and that the former republicans will be reelected; they will constitute the majority as before and will quickly veto all of MacMahon's schemes; then the clericals will be thrown out, and perhaps MacMahon himself along with them. But there is very little basis for such confidence, and certainly the clericals are not particularly worried on this account. The fact, specifically, is that the naive and pure-hearted little old men, despite their long experience, still seem not to understand fully the kind of people they are dealing with. For if the elections should prove to be even a little unfavorable for the clericals, they will throw out the new chamber as well, despite all its legal and constitutional rights. Some may tell me that this will be illegal and therefore impossible. That's so, yet what do the laws matter to them, this black army? They will certainly (and there are already facts that bear witness to it) prompt the very obedient Marshal MacMahon to the desperate resolution to use here a remedy that has never once been used, even in France—namely, *military despotism*. People will shout that this is an old remedy, that the Napoleons, for instance, have used it several times already! However, I will venture to observe that all that was different: this remedy, *in all its manifestness, really* has not yet been used once in France. Marshal MacMahon, having enlisted the loyalty of the army, can simply clear out the future assembly of representatives of France at the point of a bayonet, *should it come out against him*, and then declare plainly to the whole country that *this was the will of the army*. Like a Roman emperor in the time of the empire's decline, he could then declare that henceforth "he would take into consideration only the opinion of the legions." There would then ensue a general state of siege and military despotism; and you'll see, you surely will, that awfully many people in France will be delighted by it! And believe me, if the need arises, there will also be plebiscites in which *a majority vote of the whole of France* would authorize war and allot the necessary funds for it. In his recent speech to the armed forces Marshal MacMahon spoke specifically in this tone, and he met with a very sympathetic reception from the army. There is no doubt that the army is largely on his side. Moreover, now he has already gone so far that he cannot stop for fear of losing his office, since his entire policy and his entire being are expressed in the single phrase: *J'y suis et j'y reste*, that's to say, "Here I am, and I'm not leaving." As we know, he's never gone beyond that phrase, and of course he's willing to risk perhaps even the existence of France to put that motto into practice. He showed his readiness for such risk once already during the Franco-Prussian War when, under the influence of the Bonapartists, he made a conscious decision to deprive France of her army out of loyalty to the Napoleonic dynasty. The clericals have certainly guaranteed him his *J'y suis et j'y reste*. Having united the parties—meaning the Bonapartists and the legitimists—under their banner, they certainly have managed cleverly *to point out* to MacMahon that if the need arises they can get by entirely without Chambord and Bonaparte and that there will be no need to summon them under any circumstances; he, Marshal MacMahon, should simply remain as dictator and permanent ruler, meaning not for seven years but forever. It is in this way that the motto *J'y suis et j'y reste* will be put into practice—all that's needed is the army's consent; the consent of France is inevitable, for a firm dictatorial hand at the fount of power will suit the taste of very many. Such flattering *suggestions* have certainly already been made. There may be doubts that a man like MacMahon could undertake and carry out all this. But in the first place, he has already undertaken and carried out the first half of the thing, and this half was certainly no easier, in terms of the resolve required, than the second one still to come. And in the second place, it is just such people as he who, though not at all enterprising on their own, can display immense and fateful resolve when they suddenly fall under the supreme and decisive influence of someone else, and this not because of any great genius but precisely for the opposite reason. The main thing here is not calculation but simply a push; and if they can be given a good push, they go on shoving in the same direction until they smash through the wall with their heads or break their horns.

5. A Rather Unpleasant Secret

All this is perfectly understood in Germany. At least all the semiofficial organs of the press that are under the influence of Prince Bismarck are thoroughly convinced of inevitable war. What they don't know is who will attack whom first, and exactly when, but war could very, very likely break out. Of course the storm may yet pass by. The entire hope lies in the chance that Marshal MacMahon might suddenly grow alarmed at everything he has taken on himself and, like Ajax once did, stop perplexed in the middle of the road. But then he would risk his own destruction, and it is unlikely that he doesn't realize that. And although there is a chance for a moment of perplexity in the middle of the road, one can scarcely put much hope in it. For the time being, Prince Bismarck is following all the developments in France with feverish attention; he watches and waits. As far as he is concerned, the real storm consists in the fact that this affair did not begin at the moment he expected. And now his hands are tied. What is most worrisome is that the weak spots, which to this point had been carefully kept hidden, have come to light. I have already spoken about the major weak spot of all the Germans—this is the fear that Russia will suddenly realize how powerful she is and what force her decisive word can have now, precisely at the present moment, and above all, that "*dependence on an alliance with Russia is, evidently, Germany's fated destiny, particularly since the Franco-Prussian War.*" This German secret may suddenly be disclosed, and this would be rather embarrassing for the Germans. Despite the sincere friendliness of Germany's policy toward us in recent years, all Germans have still kept the secret. The press, in particular, has been active in this regard. Until now the Germans have always had a calm and proud manner, quite appropriate to a power that needs no one's help. But now, of course, the weak point must come out into the open. For if clerical France resolves to enter the fatal struggle, then it will not be enough simply to conquer France or merely repel an invasion should France be the first to attack; it will be necessary to render her forever powerless, really to crush her by taking advantage of the opportunity—that's the task! And since France has, besides, an army of some million men, in order to finish the job properly it must be *guaranteed;* otherwise there's no point in even undertaking it. And there is no other guarantee than to enlist the decisive word of Russia. In short, the most unpleasant thing is that all this is emerging so suddenly. All the old calculations have been thrown off, and now it's the events that are already determining the calculations, not the calculations that are governing the events. France may begin today or tomorrow, just as soon as she manages to get her internal affairs in order. She has launched herself on a policy of adventures, which everyone can see; and if such is the case, then where will these adventures end? Where is their limit, their boundary line? This is very unpleasant: only so recently, and in the last year in particular, have the Germans had such an independent air. We recall that in this year Russia as well was trying to decide who her friends were in Europe, and the Germans knew of Russia's concerns and had a most triumphant air, appropriate to the occasion. Of course, any Slavic movement has always troubled Germany a bit, but one can plainly say that in Russia's declaration of war two months ago there was, perhaps, even something Germany found almost agreeable: "No," they were thinking in Germany two months ago, "now there's no way they will figure out that we need them; on the contrary—now that they're standing on the banks of the Danube, 'a German river,' they're completely convinced that they need us terribly and that at the end of the war they won't be able to get by without our weighty word. And it's a good thing the Russians think that way; that will be very handy in the days to come." There's no doubt that very many perceptive Germans certainly thought of us that way; all their newspapers thought and wrote that way and—suddenly this clerical state of mind turned everything upside down: "Oh, now they'll figure it out; now they'll figure everything out! And besides, Russia must get her job done in the East and free her hands. But to put pressure on her would be highly inexpedient. Maybe she'll take fright of England and Austria, but it's not likely. To join with England and Austria to put pressure on Russia isn't even worth thinking about: later on they'll be of no help to us, while Russia will get angry. A strange situation! Maybe we should help Russia get the job done quickly? That we could do, even without drawing our sword; it would only be a matter of political pressure, on Austria, for instance. . . ." That's how these same politicians are now thinking, and it is very, very likely that all this is exactly how it is in reality.

In short, I wanted only to express my conviction, my faith, that Russia is not only as strong and powerful as she has always been, but that now, and now in particular, she is the strongest of all the countries of Europe and that her decisive word could never be so highly valued in Europe as in the given moment. Russia herself may be busy in the East, but merely one decisive word from her on the scales of European politics now can tip those scales in whatever direction she wishes. Of course, even England herself realizes that in view of the *possibility* of some highly worrisome new events in the far western part of Europe—even she, perhaps, will lose two-thirds of her prestige in the eyes of Russians, and that even the most suspicious of Russians will at last realize that she will certainly not risk a war in the face of Russia's strong determination to continue her task, and that England will rather count upon dividing up the inheritance left by the "sick man" than venture to begin an open war for him at a moment which, apart from all this, is already so worrisome in Europe. In fact, should it happen that something unexpected and fateful does break out in western Europe, England will never venture to get thoroughly mixed up in such a troublesome business, so alien to the usual nature of her interests, and will certainly assume only an attitude of keen watchfulness, waiting, as is her wont, for a convenient moment when she catches the scent of the prey being divided up somewhere so as to join in at once. To start up something very serious with Russia now (meaning before the events in the far east of Europe have been clarified) would be much too imprudent for her. On the other hand, left *alone*, what can Austria do? And it's unlikely that the clerical complications of the affair in the far west of Europe haven't troubled her at least a little. And she, of course, is waiting like all the others for events to develop further, so that her hands are partly tied, as are those of all the others. Everyone's hands are tied; only Russia's are free. And so that means something *unforeseen* in our favor has come along. So how can one not count on the *unforeseen* in resolving human destinies?

The world is ruled by God and His laws, and if something new and complicated should indeed burst forth over Europe, it means that, sooner or later, it certainly had to happen. But God grant that I am mistaken; God grant that the new storm cloud that is approaching simply disperses and that all my premonitions prove to be only my "fervid" fantasies—the fantasies of a man who understands nothing of politics. The whole point is: are all the semiofficial organs of the press in Germany correct when they expect and predict a war? On the other hand, MacMahon's ministers are doing all they can, even before any accusations are made, to assure the French and the whole world that France will not begin a war. You must agree that all this is at least suspicious, and that a settling of doubts may follow, through the very course of events themselves, in a very, very short time. But what if so much depends on the "opinion of the legions"? It would be bad if things came to such a point; then we would see the end of France. However, this could happen only in France and nowhere else in the whole world. But God grant that it does not happen there either: it's a bad beginning, more of the same would be truly bad.

4

1. Those Who Love the Turks

Quite a few people who love the Turks have turned up among us of late—on account of the war, of course. Never before in all my life can I recall someone starting a conversation so as to express admiration for the Turks. But now I very often hear about those who defend them and have even met such people myself; and they even get quite excited. What we have here, of course, is the urge to show one's originality. But yet these people are scholars, teachers, and professors.

"The Moslem world brought science to the Christians. The Christian world was immersed in the darkness of ignorance while science was already casting its light over the Arabs."

Christianity, you see, is supposed to have been the cause of ignorance here. That's Buckle, and even Draper. Conversely, then, Islam is light, while Christianity is the principle of darkness. What a detached kind of logic! That's why, probably, Mohammedanism is now so enlightened when compared with Christianity. Why did they put out their torch so soon?

"Well, yes, but they have monotheism, while the Christians. . . ."

This glorification of the Moslems for monotheism, i.e., for the purity of their teachings of divine unity, which is supposed to be higher than that of the Christian teachings—this is a hobbyhorse of many of those lovers of the Turks. But the main thing here is that these Turk-lovers have split away from the People and do not understand them. Having split away from the People, they have managed to fabricate some amazing notions of what goes on in the head of the Russian common man. Meanwhile, the Russian common man, "who understands nothing in religious matters and who doesn't know any prayers"—as is often said about him—very often, if not always, still forms in his mind and in his soul a highly original but *true* and exacting conviction, which fully meets his needs, of the things he believes, even though only a rare person among the common People will be able to express his beliefs in an intelligible and consistent manner. This "cultured" Russian who has split away from the People would be astonished to hear that this illiterate muzhik believes completely and unshakeably in the oneness of God, that there is but one God and no other God than He. At the same time, the Russian peasant knows and piously believes (every Russian peasant knows this) that Christ is his true God; that He was begotten of God the Father and was born of the Virgin Mary. First of all, the cultured Russian who has split away from the People does not want to admit even the possibility that a Russian peasant who has never studied anything could have such knowledge: "He's so uncultivated, so ignorant; no one's teaching him anything. Where is his teacher?" He will never understand that the peasant's teacher "in matters of his faith" is the soil itself, the whole Russian land; that these beliefs are born with him, so to say, and are strengthened in his heart as he lives his life. But what some Russian thinkers find most difficult to believe is how the Russian common peasant cannot be led astray in his convictions! He himself, having long ago lost any concept of what the direct, great, warm faith of the People is, can no longer admit that the common man, piously believing in the great Christian mystery of the incarnation of the Son of God, can at the same time subscribe to the strictest monotheism. He will rather attribute this steadfastness of the Russian common man's *direct* convictions to his lack of habit of thinking, to his propensity to confuse abstract concepts because of laziness and dullness of mind and the absence of any critical sense; this "lamentable" state of mind he will attribute to the peasant's subjugation, his poverty, his dissipation, his enserfment, and so on. This is what the Russian scholar who *studies* the Russian People insists upon. Through exactly the same process, Orthodox Russians might be condemned for worshiping icons, for instance. Some Lutheran pastor would simply be unable to understand how, when one believes in the true God, one can at the same time worship a "wooden plank," the image of a saint, and still maintain that this is not idolatry. The cultured Russian is most often in agreement with this view of the pastor. And yet there is *not a single* Russian peasant man or woman who, in worshiping an icon, would at the same time confuse, *even a little,* this "plank" with God Himself, despite the fact that the Orthodox people at the same time believe in the miraculous powers of certain icons. But there is *not a single Russian* who would attribute the miraculous power of an icon to the icon itself and not to the will of God. And this is something quite different. It is this view of the Russian common man that neither the pastor nor the Russian who has split away from the People can ever admit; in fact, they can't even believe that it is so.

It would be better, however, if they were to recall Mohammed's paradise, so as to put the finishing touches to their conviction of the purity of Turkish conceptions of the oneness of God. Naturally, I'm not saying this to start a theological dispute with the admirers of Turkish monotheism; and, of course, I didn't start it. These admirers, after all, are more worried about *sound* conceptions of the People, while they themselves, perhaps, are indifferent as to who believes what. And that is why I limited this question only to the People's understanding of it.

2. Golden Tailcoats. Straight-Line People

Apart from those who love the Turks, a great many people have turned up who have a need for *opinions distinct from everyone else's:* "It's all nonsense; there isn't any Slavic movement; these declarations are nonsense, not the way the Russians do it; the field hospitals are nonsense, not the way the Russians do it. Sentimental rubbish. The Slavs were only an invention; the Bulgarians were an invention; the Turks are better than the Bulgarians; it's all nonsense. I love the Turks. . . ."

This isn't something that derives from some cunningly subtle considerations of higher politics. We do have "higher politics," it can't be denied, but this—this is simply vanity. It's vanity of two kinds: either one that has been suppressed to an extreme, the result being the urgent need to show one's originality so as to distinguish oneself and display oneself in some way; or a vanity that comes from exceptional self-aggrandizement. More often than not, the Russian "great man" is unable to bear his grandeur. It's true that were he able to put on some golden tailcoat made of brocade, for instance, so as to be unlike all the other, lower creatures, then he would do so quite candidly and wouldn't feel ashamed of it. I'm sure that if we haven't yet seen any of our "great men" in golden coats, it's probably because the tailors refuse to make them. "I am more intelligent than the others; I am great. They all think *that* about the war, so I refuse to think the way they do. I'll show them that I'm great. . . ."

Sometime I'd like to talk particularly about the golden tailcoat, about its characteristically Russian social and psychological origins, about some graphic examples, and so on; it's a lovely topic and I hope I won't forget about it later on. But now, having left the golden tailcoat in peace for a while, I'll say a word or two about "straight-line people." There are all sorts of straight-line people—good and bad ones, intelligent and stupid ones, honest and dishonest ones, etc. We've got a great many of them. These people just keep hammering away at the same thing and there's no way you can move them to anything else: *J'y suis et j'y reste*. They're our MacMahons.

News comes to us from the army of the heroism and self-sacrifice of the Russians, both common soldiers and officers. Those are our young people over there. Only so recently there was such a lack of faith in our young people, our hope; many saw in them only cynicism, accused them of mindless negation, coldness, indifference, mindless suicide; but now suddenly the air seems to have cleared: those same young people are displaying nobility, a longing for heroism, duty, honor, and sacrifice. They march in front of the soldiers and are the first to rush into danger. . . .

"Yes, but only a drunken man or a lunatic can rush to certain death so consciously. There's no other explanation to be found."

"What? You mean you don't believe they have any awareness of their noble aim of sacrificing themselves for Russia, of serving her. . . ."

"With their fists."

"What do you mean? In a war you have to fight. What else could he do to be useful?"

"Well, schools, for instance."

"Schools—in good time. Later he'll bring to the schools his awareness of a duty done, noble recollections, contact with the People."

"What do you mean, contact with the People?"

"In common solidarity for a common cause. The soldier and his officer are now living *over there* in a single spirit and with a single feeling. The intelligentsia feels its kinship with the People, comes back to them again, and this time in deed and not in theory; it learns to respect the People from whom this soldier has come and teaches the People to respect it, no longer as lord or master but as a human, to respect it in spirit. The recent story of the simple Russian who tearfully embraced Cherniaev in the Assumption Cathedral is significant. You want to educate the People, but you will do that more quickly by making them respect your ideas and your deeds and by winning the People's hearts. The more the People respect educated people *personally*, the more surely will the People's education be advanced. Thus, in earning the respect of the People you are already serving the cause of their education, the cause of those same schools you are so concerned about."

"Earning respect through the fist? Making the People respect the fist?"

"It's not only a matter of the fist; it's above all a matter of greatness of spirit, a matter of the sacrifice of one's own life for all to see. Even death, for all to see, can be beautiful. You're asking me, now, what is it that can compel a man in the flower of his years to go off and almost certainly sacrifice his life; and this must puzzle you, for there's no other explanation for your remark about the drunken man and the lunatic: that's just an allegory, a way of expressing yourself. But what can compel someone to sacrifice his life? A longing for glory, for an honorable deed; a longing to earn a good reputation and the praise of all his fellow citizens who are now watching his deed; to show what he can do; to glorify his name."

"Aha! To make a career!"

"But all these emotions and impulses are noble ones. There are thousands of them, and they're all mixed together. A person isn't made up of just one impulse; a person is a whole world, and we must hope that his basic impulse is noble. The shedding of his blood and the readiness to shed it ennoble even one who had hitherto been ignoble; these things impose on him the obligation of honor for the rest of his life. The press has already expressed some misgivings that these people will subsequently gain the upper hand; that they'll show complacency and pride and contempt for education and 'civvies'; that they'll run riot; that society will become imbued with these ideas. But these fears are pointless. We'll see a blue moon before that happens. There are bound to be some Kopeikins who have 'shed their blood, so to say,' that's true; but they will only make people laugh and damage their own reputations.

But the moral benefit will be incalculable. The misery of cynicism will fade away altogether; there will be new respect for a feat of honor. . . ."

"And for the fist."

"It's not a matter merely of those who know how to use their fists; here we have people who are almost still children, children who are pure in heart. A young man's only just got his commission; he rushes forward toward some great exploit thinking: 'What will my mother and sister back home say about me? I've only just said good-bye to them. . . .' Is this really only ridiculous and sentimental? Finally, why not acknowledge a superior awareness in these heroes? He understands that Russia has taken up a difficult task, that this task may grow even more complicated. They all see now that Russia isn't waging a war only with Turkey; that the Turkish armies are being advised by English generals; that English officers are setting up many fortifications paid for by English money; that the English fleet is encouraging Turkey to continue the war; that, finally, English forces have all but made their appearance (in Asiatic Turkey). . . . They know all this and rush virtually to their deaths, understanding that the time has come to render Russia a true service. I'm not talking now about the Bulgarians, about the oppressed 'Slavic brethren,' tortured and offended. To our shame, this topic has already become stale . . . but not in their hearts. Can you really not see in many of them a higher awareness that they are going off to serve humanity, the oppressed and the humiliated? . . .

"To serve humanity with the fist!"

"Permit me to tell you a little story that's relevant here. I've already told about one of the homes in Moscow where they take care of little Bulgarian orphan children who were brought to Russia after the destruction there; one of them is a girl of about ten, quite ill, who saw (and cannot forget) the Turks flaying the skin from her father while he was alive. Well, in that same home there is another Bulgarian girl, also ten and also ill, and I heard about her not long ago. She has a strange illness: a gradual, ever-increasing loss of strength and a constant desire to sleep. She's always sleeping, but her sleep doesn't make her stronger; just the opposite in fact. It's a very serious illness. By now this girl may have already died. She also has one unbearable memory. The Turks took her little brother, a child of two or three, and first poked his eyes out with a needle; then impaled him on a stake. The little child screamed long and terribly before he died. And that's an absolutely true fact.

Well, that's what the girl can't forget; they did all that in her presence, right before her eyes. Nature, perhaps, even sends sleep to such people who are afflicted in heart, because they could not remain awake for long with such continual memories. Now just imagine that you were there at the moment when they were poking the little child's eyes out. Tell me, would you really not rush to stop them, even if it meant using your fists?"

"Yes, but still—to use your fists. . . ."

"Well then, don't beat them, if that's what you want; but at least take away their sabers, their yataghans! Can't even that be done by force?"

By the way, can there really be such lovers of the Turks among us who would not wish to take their yataghans from them? I don't think and don't believe that there could be.

July and August

1

1. My Conversation with a Moscow Acquaintance. A Note Apropos of a New Booklet

After I had put out the belated May and June issue of my *Diary* and was on my way back to Kursk Province, I passed through Moscow and had a talk about this and that with one of my old Moscow acquaintances, a person I see rarely but whose opinion I value greatly. I won't quote the conversation in full, although in the course of it I learned some very interesting things about current matters, things I had never even suspected. But as I was leaving my acquaintance I happened to mention that I wanted to take advantage of the opportunity and make a small detour of some hundred miles in order to visit a place from my childhood and youth—the village that had once belonged to my parents but that long ago had become the property of another family member. I hadn't been there for forty years and had wanted to visit it so many times but had never been able to do so, despite the fact that this little, unremarkable spot had left a deep and strong impression on me for my whole life and that everything there was filled with the most cherished memories for me.

"So you have your memories and your favorite spots, and we have all had them. But I wonder what precious things today's young people, today's children and 'raw youths,' will have among their memories; in fact, will there be anything precious? Just what will it be? What sort of memories will they have?"

That today's children will also have their sacred memories is, of course, beyond doubt; otherwise there would be no more "living life." A person cannot even live without something sacred and precious from childhood to carry into life. There are some, apparently, who don't even think about it, yet they still preserve these memories unconsciously. These memories may even be painful or bitter, yet the suffering one has undergone can be later transformed into something sacred for the soul. People, in fact, are generally so created as to love the suffering they have undergone. Aside from that, people of necessity are inclined to mark off a point in their past, as it were, to orient themselves later in life and to derive from it something whole, to provide order and edification in their lives. And here the strongest and most influential memories are almost always those which remain from childhood. Therefore, there's no doubt that memories and impressions—perhaps the strongest and most sacred ones—are carried into life by today's children as well. But just what the content of these memories will be, just what the children will take with them into life, just how this precious stock of memories will be formed—all these things, of course, are interesting and serious questions. If we could make even a rough guess in answer to these questions, we could relieve many of today's deep anxieties, and perhaps many people would happily put their trust in today's Russian youth; above all, we could gain some vague sense of our future, our so enigmatic Russian future. But the problem is that never before has there been an era in our Russian life that has offered fewer facts that might be used to gain a sense and a knowledge of our always enigmatic future than the present era. And, indeed, never has the Russian family been more unsettled, more disintegrated, more disarranged and unformed than it is now. Where could you now find such *Childhood and Youths* as were recreated so harmoniously and distinctly by Count Leo Tolstoy, for instance, in depicting *his* era and his family or as he did in *War and Peace*? All these poems are now *no more than historical portraits of the distant past*. Oh, I certainly don't wish to say that these were only pretty pictures; by no means do I wish them to be reproduced in our day—that's not what I'm talking about at all. I'm speaking only of their *nature*, of their literary polish, their accuracy and the explicitness of their character—qualities thanks to which it was possible to have such a clear and distinct portrayal of an era like the one found in both these poems of Count Tolstoy. Nowadays we have none of this; there isn't the same explicitness and clarity. The contemporary Russian family is becoming more and more an *accidental* family. Specifically an *accidental family*—that's the definition of the contemporary Russian family. It seems to have suddenly lost its old features, unexpectedly even, while the new ones . . . will it be capable of creating for itself new, desirable features that satisfy the Russian heart? Some even very serious people say frankly that the Russian family of today "doesn't exist." Of course, all this is said only of the cultured Russian family, meaning that of the upper levels of society and not of the People. Yet isn't it also a question to be asked equally of the family among the People?

"What no one can dispute," said my acquaintance, "what no one can dispute is that in a very short time there will be new questions coming up among the People, and in fact they have already come up—a whole batch of questions, an awful mass of them, all new, which never existed or were heard of before, and all this is quite natural. But who will answer these questions for the People? Who among us is ready to answer them? Who'll be the first to seek out the answers? Who is waiting and preparing himself to do this? That's the question—our question, and it's one of foremost importance."

And of course it is of foremost importance. Such a sharp change in the direction of life as came from the reform of February 19th and as came with all the subsequent reforms, and, above all, literacy (even if only the slightest contact with it)—all these things, unquestionably, will give rise to—and have already given rise to—questions, and later they may give them some form, combine them, give them some stability; and who, in fact, is going to answer these questions? Well, who stands closest to the People? The clergy? But our clergy have not provided answers to the People's questions for a long time now. Apart from some priests who still burn with the fire of zeal for Christ, who are often inconspicuous and utterly unknown precisely because they seek nothing for themselves but live only for their flock—aside from these and, alas, a very few others apparently—the clergy, if pressed for answers, might well provide them in the form of a denunciation of the asker. Others so alienate their flocks by the disproportionate fees they charge that no one will go to them to seek answers. A great deal more could be added on this topic, but we shall do that later. Next, the rural schoolteachers are among those closest to the People. But what are our rural schoolteachers good for, and what are they prepared to do? What has this new profession, only in its infancy, to be sure, but of such great significance for the future—what has it shown so far, and what answers is it capable of giving? This question is best left unanswered. Accordingly, there remain answers that come by chance—in the towns, at railway stations, on the roads and streets, in the markets, from passersby, from tramps, and, finally, from former landowners (it goes without saying that I don't include the authorities here). Oh, of course there will be all kinds of answers, maybe even more than there are questions—good and bad answers, foolish and wise answers; but the principal character of the answers will be, I think, that each of them will give rise to three new questions, and it will go on and on crescendo. The result will be chaos, but chaos would not be so bad: halfbaked solutions are worse than chaos.

"Yet what's most important is that there's nothing to be said about it. The People will hold up."

Of course they will hold up, and they'll hold up without us, with or without people to give them answers. Russia is mighty, and she's stood up to worse things than this. And her mission and goal are not such that she should be diverted for naught from her age-old path; her scope is greater than that. He who believes in Russia knows that she will stand up resolutely to *everything,* even to these questions, and she will remain in essence as she has always been, our Holy Russia; and no matter how her features may change, there is nothing to fear in a change of features, and there is no need at all to delay or postpone the questions: he who believes in Russia is even ashamed to do this. Her mission is so lofty and her inner awareness of that mission so clear (especially now, in our era, and particularly at the present moment), that he who believes in this mission must stand above all doubts and trepidation. "Here is patience and the faith of saints," as it is said in Holy Scripture.

That same morning I had just seen for the first time the announcement in the newspapers of the separate publication of the eighth and final part of *Anna Karenina* that had been rejected by the editor of *The Russian Messenger,* the journal in which the novel had been appearing since its beginning. Everyone also knew that this final, eighth part had been rejected because of its disagreement with the journal's policy and the convictions of the editors, specifically in regard to the author's view on the Eastern Question and the war of last year. I resolved to buy this book at once, and as I was bidding farewell to my acquaintance I asked him about it, knowing that he had known its contents for a long time. He began to laugh.

"It's the most innocent thing there could ever be!" he replied. "I really can't understand why *The Russian Messenger* couldn't publish it. Besides, the author had given them the right to state any reservations they pleased and to make marginal notes about anything they disagreed with. And so they should have just made a footnote stating that the author. . . ."

However, I will not include here the contents of this footnote suggested by my acquaintance, the more so as he kept on laughing when he stated it. But finally he added, seriously:

"The author of *Anna Karenina,* despite his immense artistic talent, has one of those Russian intellects that sees clearly only that which is standing right before its eyes, and so it keeps pushing away at the same point. Such intellects don't have the ability, apparently, to turn to the right or to the left so as to make out what is standing beside them: to do that they have to turn the whole body. And then, perhaps, they'll start to talk about just the opposite thing, since on any one occasion they're always absolutely sincere. Such a turnabout may never happen at all, but it may happen within a month, and then the respected author will begin shouting with the very same passion that we have to send volunteers and make lint for bandages, and he'll be saying all the things we're saying. . . ."

I bought this little book and then read it and found it by no means so "innocent." And since I, despite all my distaste for making criticisms of contemporary literary figures and their works, have decided that I will certainly talk about it in in my *Diary* (even, perhaps, in this very issue), I thought it relevant also to include here my conversation with my acquaintance, whom I therefore ask to excuse my indiscretion. . . .

2. The Hunger for Rumors and for "What They Aren't Telling Us." The Expression "They Aren't Telling Us" May Have a Future, and So Some Advance Measures Should Be Taken. More about the Accidental Family

These "places of my childhood" I intended to visit were about a hundred miles from Moscow, all but six or seven of those miles on the railway, but it took me almost ten hours to travel those hundred miles. There were many stops and changes of train, and at one station I had to wait for three hours to change. And all this on top of the discomforts of Russian rail travel and the careless, almost contemptuous, attitude of the conductors and "management" toward you and your needs. Everyone has long known the motto of the Russian railways: "The railway wasn't made for the public, the public was made for the railway." There isn't a railway man, from conductor right up to the director, who would doubt this motto and would not look at you with mocking astonishment if you were to try to tell him that the railway was made for the public. First of all, he wouldn't even listen to you.

By the way, this summer I have traveled some twenty-five hundred miles, at least, and this time everywhere I went I was particularly struck by the People; everywhere the People were talking about the war. Nothing could compare with the interest and the eager curiosity with which common people asked about the war and listened to news about it. In railway carriages I noticed even a few peasants reading newspapers, reading them aloud for the most part. A few times I happened to take a seat next to some: a townsman would look you over carefully at first, and especially if he noticed you were holding a newspaper or had one beside you he would promptly and most politely inquire where you were from. And if you answered, "From Moscow" or "From Petersburg" (and he was even more interested if you were from the south, from Odessa, for instance), then he would certainly ask: "What's the news of the war?" Then, if you established his trust by your reply and readiness to answer his questions, he would at once, though still cautiously, change his curious expression to a mysterious one, draw close to you, and ask with lowered voice, "And haven't you heard—you know—anything special?"—meaning something a bit more special than what's in the newspapers, something "they aren't telling us." In this connection I'll add that there isn't anyone among the People who is dissatisfied with the government for declaring war, even among the types most given to malicious joy—and there are such types, but now they have a special kind of malicious joy. For instance, you walk along the station platform at some stop and suddenly you hear: "Seventeen thousand of our men have been killed—a telegram's just come!" You look, and it's some nasty young fellow making the speech; his face is filled with a kind of malicious rapture, and it's not at all because he is happy that seventeen thousand of our men were killed; no, there's something else here, something akin to when a man's possessions have gone up in flames and everything has been destroyed—his hut, his money, his livestock: "Just look at me, Orthodox Christians; everything's gone, I'm in rags with not a soul in the world!" At those moments the face of such a fellow also wears a kind of delighted expression of malicious self-intoxication. But as far as the "seventeen thousand" is concerned, there was something else as well, namely: "There is such a telegram, only they're holding it back, they're not telling us about it, they've not yet released it . . . we've seen it, we've read it ourselves . . ."—that's the meaning of it. I couldn't help myself and suddenly went up to the crowd and said that it was all nonsense, silly rumors, that seventeen thousand of our men could not have been killed, that all was well. The young fellow (apparently a townsman, but maybe even a peasant) was a little taken aback, but not much: "We're ignorant people; it's not our own words we're using, just the things we've heard." The crowd quickly dispersed as the station bell rang. I find this curious now because it happened on the nineteenth of July, at about five o'clock in the afternoon. The day before, the eighteenth, was the battle at Plevna. How could anyone, never mind someone in the middle of a railway train, have already received a telegram? Of course, it was just a coincidence. I don't think, however, that the young lad was spreading and inventing false rumors; most likely he really had heard this from someone else. One has to think that Russia this summer has produced a great many fabricators of false and, of course, malicious rumors about defeats and misfortunes, and of course they have a definite aim in mind, not just telling tall tales.

In view of the passionate, patriotic mood of the People in this war; in view of the *awareness* our People have displayed since last year of the significance and the aims of this war; in view of the ardent and pious faith of the People in their tsar—all this delay and secrecy in news from the theater of the war is not only unhelpful, it is positively harmful. Of course, no one can either demand or wish that strategic plans, the numbers of troops to be deployed in an action, military secrets, and so on, be made public; but at least there are some things our newspapers could be told before the Viennese newspapers find out about them.*

Sitting at the station, where I had to wait for three hours to transfer to a different train, I was in a very foul mood and annoyed at everything. For lack of anything to do, I suddenly got the idea of investigating why I was annoyed and whether there weren't, aside from the general causes, some accidental and more immediate

* Now this has been rectified for the most part: the public is left for scarcely a day without a communiqué from the commander-in-chief. [Dostoevsky's note]

cause. I thought about it for a little while and suddenly began to laugh when I discovered the reason. It was because of an encounter I had had not long before, in the railway carriage, two stations before this one. Into the carriage suddenly came a gentleman, an absolute gentleman, very like the type of Russian gentlemen who go wandering about abroad. He came in with his little son, a boy who could have been no more than eight, perhaps even younger. The boy was very nicely dressed in a most fashionable European child's suit with a charming little jacket; he had beautiful shoes and a batiste shirt. It was obvious that the father took good care of him. As soon as they had taken their seats the boy suddenly said to his father, "Papa, may I have a cigarette?" The father at once reached into his pocket, took out a mother-of-pearl cigarette case, took out two cigarettes, one for himself, the other for the boy, and both began to smoke with the most normal air, suggesting that they both had been used to doing this for a long time. The gentleman lost himself in his thoughts, whatever they were, and the boy looked out the window of the carriage, puffing away and inhaling. He finished his cigarette very quickly and then, after no more than a quarter-hour had passed, he asked again: "Papa, may I have a cigarette?"—and again they both lit up. And in the course of the two stations we passed while they were sitting in the carriage with me the boy smoked at least four cigarettes. I had never seen anything of the sort and was very astonished. The weak, tender, still quite undeveloped chest of such a small child had already been accustomed to such a horror. And where could such an unnaturally precocious habit come from? From watching his father, naturally: children are so given to imitation; but how could the father have allowed his youngster to use such poison? Consumption, catarrh of the respiratory tract and pulmonary cavity—that's what certainly awaits the unfortunate boy, the chances are nine in ten, that's clear and known to everybody; and it's just those things that the father is encouraging in his youngster through this unnaturally precocious habit! What this gentleman wanted to prove by so doing I really can't imagine: was it his scorn for prejudices? Was he following the new idea that everything that was formerly forbidden is nonsense and that, on the contrary, everything is permitted? I can't understand it. This occurrence is still something I can't explain; it's almost a marvel. Never in my life have I encountered such a father, and probably I never will again. Truly, we run across some amazing fathers in our day! However, I stopped laughing at once. I had laughed only because I had so quickly found the reason for my bad mood. At this point, though it had no direct connection with the event, I recalled the previous day's conversation with my acquaintance about those dear and sacred things from childhood that today's children might bring with them into life; then I was reminded of my idea about the *accidental nature* of today's family . . . and so I again sank into some very disagreeable ruminations.

People will ask what this *accidental nature* is and what I mean by these words. I reply that in my opinion the accidental nature of today's Russian family consists in the loss among contemporary fathers of any common idea about their families—an idea common to all fathers that binds them together, an idea in which they could believe and could teach their children to believe, passing on to them this faith for the rest of their lives. Please note as well that this idea, this faith, might even be a mistaken one, so that the best of the children would themselves later renounce it, or at least improve upon it, for their own children; but still, the very existence of this common idea that binds society and the family is already the beginning of an order—a moral order, I mean—which, of course, is subject to change, progress, and modification, I grant you, but which is still an order. Whereas in our day there is no such order, for there is nothing common and binding in which all fathers could believe; instead there is either, first, a wholesale and utter rejection of the things of the past (but this is merely rejection and contains nothing positive), or, second, attempts to say something positive but not general or binding, simply a matter of each expressing his own idea, attempts made by splinter groups and people lacking experience and practical knowledge, and who invent things which they do not even fully believe themselves. Such attempts sometimes even have an excellent rationale but are irresolute, unfinished, and sometimes even utterly grotesque, such as the indiscriminate license for all things formerly forbidden, based on the principle that everything old is stupid; and this taken even to the most absurd extreme of permitting seven-year-old children to smoke tobacco. Finally, a third feature: a lackadaisical attitude toward work; listless, lazy fathers; egoists: "Ah, who cares what happens; why should we worry? The children will make their way as we all do; they'll fit themselves in somewhere. But really, they're so tiresome; we'd have been better off without them!" Thus the result is disorder, fragmentation, and the *accidental nature* of the Russian family, while hope is virtually placed in God alone: "Maybe He'll send us some sort of general idea and we'll be united once more!"

Such an order of things gives rise to a cheerless outlook which, in turn, gives rise to even more indolence, while among passionate individuals it fosters cynical, spiteful indolence. But even now there are many who are not at all indolent; to the contrary, there are some even very conscientious fathers. For the most part they are fathers with ideas. One such fellow, let's say, has heard a good many things that are by no means silly in themselves; he reads two or three clever books and suddenly reduces the whole business of child rearing and all his duties to his family simply to beefsteak: "Beefsteak, very rare; and Liebig, of course . . . ," and so on. Another, intrinsically a most honorable man, a renowned wit in his day, has already dismissed three of this children's nurses: "Those sneaks are impossible. I strictly forbade it, but can you imagine: yesterday I came into the nursery unexpectedly and saw her putting Lizochka into her crib; she was teaching her the "Mother of God" and crossing her: 'Lord, have mercy on papa and mama. . . .' Why, I strictly forbade that! I've decided to engage an Englishwoman; but will she be any better?" A third one is looking for a mistress for his boy, who is barely fifteen: "Otherwise, you know, he'll develop those dreadful childish habits, or he'll go out on the street somewhere and pick up some nasty disease . . . no, it's much better to look after this business for him before that happens. . . ." A fourth fellow introduces his seventeen-year-old boy to the most advanced "ideas," and the lad quite naturally (for what can come from certain kinds of knowledge acquired before one has lived and had experience?) reduces all these advanced notions (often very good ones) to the motto: "If nothing is sacred, then it follows that one can commit any dirty deed." Granted, in these cases the fathers are passionate, but are there many of them whose passion is justified by anything serious, by real thought, by suffering? Are there many such fathers among us? For the most part, all they have is some liberal snickering based on other people's ideas and so, above all else, the child takes with him into life a laughable memory of his father, a laughable image of him.

But these are the "conscientious" fathers, and there are not all that many of them; there are incomparably more indolent ones. When any society is in a state of transition and disintegration, it gives rise to indolence and apathy, because in such eras only a very few can see clearly ahead of them and not lose their way. The majority of people get confused, lose the thread, and, at last, throw up their hands: "Ah, the hell with you all! What sort of obligations can there be when none of us is able to say anything that makes sense! As long as I can somehow get through myself; it's too much to try to think about obligations on top of it." And so these lazy fathers, so long as they have money, are even quite *proper* in carrying out all their duties: they dress their children well, feed them well, engage governesses and then tutors; their children, at last, may even enter university, but . . . they never had a father, they never had a family; the young fellow enters life utterly alone; he has never lived with his heart; his heart is not bound in any way to his past, to his family, to his childhood. And what's more, this is true only of the well-off ones; they never lacked for anything, but are there many such? The majority, the huge majority are poor, after all, and so, given the indolent attitude of their fathers toward the family, the little ones are abandoned almost entirely to chance! Poverty and the cares of their fathers are stamped on their hearts from childhood in gloomy images, in memories that sometimes have a most malignant character. Until old age these children recall the spinelessness of their fathers, the quarrels in the family, the arguments, the accusations, the bitter reproaches and even curses upon them for being extra mouths to feed; and, what is worst of all, they sometimes recall the servility of their fathers, the mean actions done to acquire a position or some money, the vile intrigues and repulsive cringing. And for many years thereafter, perhaps all life long, the young person is prone to make blind accusations against these people from his past; he has taken away nothing from childhood to help cleanse the filth of his memories and to give him a just, realistic, and, accordingly, *forgiving* view of those old people among whom his early years dragged out so drearily. But these are still the best of the children; the majority of them bring into life not only the filth of *memories* but the filth itself; they even deliberately provide themselves with a stock of it; they cram their pockets full of this filth for the road so as to use it later on in life, and not gritting their teeth painfully as their parents did, but with a light heart: "We're all up to our knees in filth; only a few dreamers rave about ideals; it's better with a bit of dirt. . . ."

"But what is it that you want? What sort of memories are they supposed to be taking away from childhood to clean away the filth of their families and to look *forgivingly,* as you say, at their fathers?"

I reply, "What can I, alone, say if our whole society has no answer to this?" Today's fathers hold nothing in common, I said; there is nothing that binds them together. There is no great idea (it has been lost); in their hearts they have no great faith in such an idea. And it is only a great faith of this kind that is capable of giving birth to *something beautiful* in the memories of children, and indeed it can: even despite the harshest childhood environment, poverty, and even that same moral filth that surrounded their cradles! Oh, there are cases where even one of the most fallen of fathers, who still managed to preserve in his soul perhaps only an obscure image of his former great idea and his great faith in it, has been able to transplant the seed of this great idea and great feeling in the impressionable and eager souls of his pitiable children and has later been wholeheartedly forgiven by them because of this good deed alone, despite all the other things. A person must not leave childhood and go into life without the rudiments of something positive and beautiful; one must not launch a generation on its journey into life without the rudiments of something positive and beautiful. Just look around you: don't the fathers of today—those who are passionate and conscientious—believe in this? Oh, they believe completely that without a binding, general, moral, and civic idea they cannot bring up a new generation and launch it into life! But they themselves have all lost the whole; they are bereft of anything common; they have become fragmented; they are united only in the negative, and even there only haphazardly, and they all disagree in the positive; moreover, in essence they themselves do not even believe in anything, for they speak with someone else's words, they have thrown in their lot with an alien life and an alien idea and have lost all links with their native Russian life.

I repeat, however, that there are few of these passionate ones; there are infinitely more of the indolent. By the way, do you recall the trial of the Dzhunkovskys? It's a very recent trial and was heard in the Kaluga circuit court only on June 10th of this year. Amid all the commotion of current events, very few people, perhaps, paid any attention to it. I read about it in the newspaper *New Times* and don't know whether the account has yet been reprinted anywhere else. It's the case of the Przremysl landowners, Major Alexander Afanasevich Dzhunkovsky, fifty, and his wife, Ekaterina Petrovna Dzhunkovsky, forty, who were accused of cruel treatment of their young children Nikolai, Alexander, and Olga.... It's appropriate to note here that the children involved were of the following ages: Nikolai, thirteen; Olga, twelve; and Alexander, eleven. I'll also add, running ahead of myself, that the court acquitted the defendants.

In my view, this trial brings out in very high relief many things that are typical of the real life around us, and yet what was most striking about it was how amazingly ordinary and commonplace it was. You feel that there are now an extraordinarily large number of just such Russian families—not exactly just like them, of course; one doesn't find everywhere such accidental features as *the massaging of feet*, of course (I'll say more about that later); but the essence of the case, the basic trait of many such families, is one and the same. This is specifically the type of "indolent family" I was just speaking about. If it's not a complete and utterly true type (particularly judging by certain very exceptional and characteristic details), then it is still a remarkable example of this type. But let the readers judge for themselves. The accused were committed to trial by order of the Moscow High Court Tribunal; let me remind you of the indictment. I am reprinting it from *New Times* as it appeared there, i.e., in condensed form.

3. The Case of the Dzhunkovsky Parents and Their Children

> The accused Dzhunkovskys, who are reasonably well-off and employ a suitable number of servants, treated three of their children, Nikolai, Alexander, and Olga, altogether differently from their other children. They did not include these three in their family circle and showed them no affection, they left them without supervision, failed to provide adequate support (housing, clothing, beds, and meals), forced them to do things such as massaging their feet and so on, thus arousing and maintaining in the children a sense of dissatisfaction and anger that led them to the commission of an act with their late sister which will be discussed below. All this could not fail to have an unfavorable influence upon the health of the children. Thus, for example, it is evident from the case that Olga suffers from epilepsy. Aside from that, in not fostering the supervision or ensuring the moral development of their children, the accused resorted to measures that cannot be regarded as mild corrective measures taken by parents against young children. Thus, the accused locked up their children in a toilet for extended periods, left them at home in an unheated room almost without food, or sent them to eat and sleep in the servants' room,

thus placing them in the society of people ill-suited to contribute to their improvement. Finally, they often beat them with whatever was at hand, and even with their fists; they beat them with birch rods, branches, and a horse whip, and with a ferocity that was terrible to see; according to the testimony of the boy Alexander, the back of one child ached for five days after one such flogging. Beatings of this kind were not always the result of some insignificant mischief but simply happened by chance, when the parents so desired. The soldier's wife Sergeeva, who worked as a laundress at the Dzhunkovskys', explained among other things that the accused did not like the children Nikolai, Alexander, and Olga, who slept apart from the other children, on a felt mat on the floor in a room downstairs; their bedding was whatever happened to be at hand (they had one ragged blanket); they were fed servants' meals so that they were always hungry. They were given shabby clothes: in summer they wore torn shirts, and in winter, short fur coats. Mrs. Dzhunkovsky was worse than a stepmother to these children; she beat them—Alexander in particular—with anything she could find or simply with her fists. It was terrible to watch her flogging Nikolai. The children were mischievous, but no more than children normally are. They were abused most of all in the evenings, when they had to massage their mother's feet, a procedure that lasted an hour or more until the mother fell asleep. This had formerly been done by the servants, including Sergeeva, who at last refused because her hand became swollen! Usachkova's testimony reveals that Alexander and Olga would lie about on the floor, on dirty pillows: "They were kept in a filthy state; a pigsty was cleaner than their room." Liubimov (a nobleman), who lived as a tutor with the Dzhunkovskys until August 1875, stated that Nikolai, Olga, and Alexander were poorly looked after and that there were times when they had to walk barefoot. The testimony of Miss Shishova, a graduate of the Nicholas Institute (she did not appear at the trial and her testimony was read), who was employed as a governess to the children of the defendants until August 1874, mentions that Mrs. Dzhunkovsky was an egotistical woman who, like her husband, never showed any affection to the children Alexander and Nikolai. Shishova explained the overall lack of order in the home of the defendants and the indifference toward the children by a certain carelessness of the accused toward everything, even toward themselves; their affairs were in a constant state of confusion and they lived with constant problems and had no ability to manage their household. Mrs. Dzhunkovsky, trying to ensure that nothing would disturb her, gave her husband the responsibility of punishing the children, which he in fact did; and although Shishova was not present to witness the floggings, she affirms that "there was no cruelty in the punishments." "It happened," the teacher Shishova continues, "that when the children got into mischief Mrs. Dzhunkovsky or even I might lock them up in the room where the water closet was located, but this room was no colder than the others in the apartment and it was heated." Shishova herself lashed the children with a belt, "but it was only a little one." She never witnessed the children being deprived of food for several days at a time.

Then the boys Nikolai and Alexander gave calm statements to the examining magistrate; however, it was evident from these statements that they had been flogged with birch rods, a lash used for horses, and also with a branch employed for that purpose by the teacher Liubimov. On one occasion Alexander's back was sore for five days after his mother beat him for bringing his sister Olga a potato from the kitchen for her breakfast.

In his defense Mr. Dzhunkovsky cited the fact that his children were totally spoiled and provided the following example to support his claim: when the eldest daughter, Ekaterina, died and her body was still lying on a table, the boys Nikolai and Alexander cut some switches in the garden and beat the dead girl across the face while saying, "Now we'll get you for telling on us."

At the trial the defendants pleaded not guilty.

The defendant Dzhunkovsky assured the court that he was spending more than his means allowed on the education of his children but that he unfortunately had not achieved his goal and that the children were becoming worse and worse.

The eldest son, Nikolai, had been a good boy until he was sent off to high school; but after a time in school he began to steal; before entering the school he knew his prayers, but subsequently he forgot them because he declared himself a Catholic and as a result took no religious instruction at all, even though his birth certificate, stating that he was of the Orthodox faith, had been produced.

In her final statement Mrs. Dzhunkovsky declared that she had engaged several governesses for the children but, unfortunately, had misjudged all of them, as she had the tutor; at present, however, the father himself was working with the children and she hoped that the children would be completely rehabilitated.

That was the trial. As I said earlier, the defendants were acquitted. And why not? What's remarkable is not that they were acquitted but that they were charged and brought to trial. Who—what court—could have found them guilty, and of what? Oh, of course there is a court that could find them guilty and show clearly of what, but it is not a criminal court with jurors who judge by written law.

And nowhere in written law is there any article that makes a father's laziness, incompetence, and heartlessless in raising his children a criminal offense. If so, we would have to condemn half of Russia—a lot more than half, in fact. And what do we mean by heartlessness? Now if there had been cruel torture, something terrible, inhuman. But I recall how the defense attorney in the trial of Kroneberg, who was accused of cruel treatment of his young child, opened the code of laws and read the article on cruel treatment, brutality, and so on, having in mind to prove that his client did not fall under any one of those articles in which it is clearly and exactly set out what must be considered as cruelty and brutality. And, I recall, these definitions of cruelty were themselves so cruel that they positively resembled the bashibazouks' torture of the Bulgarians; and if there were no impalings on a stake or cutting of strips of flesh from the back, then there were broken ribs, hands, legs, and I don't know what else, so that a lash of some sort, and a small one to boot, as Miss Shishova testified, positively cannot enter into the article of the code of laws and form grounds for indictment. "They were beaten with birch rods," they said. Well, who doesn't beat children with birch rods? Nine-tenths of Russia does. There's just no way you can make this subject to criminal law. "The children were beaten for no special reason," they said, "for a potato." "No, sir, not for a potato," Mr. Dzhunkovsky would reply, "it was for everything taken together—for their vices, for the fact that they, the little brutes, beat my deceased daughter Ekaterina on the face." "The children were locked up in a toilet," they said. "Yes, but it was a heated toilet, so what more do you want? A jail is always a jail." "But why did you feed them servants' food and send them to sleep in a virtual pigsty, on a mat of some kind with one ragged blanket?" "This is also for punishment, you see; and what does it matter if the blanket was ragged? Even so, I'm spending beyond my means for my children's education; the law has no business looking in my pockets to count my money." "Why, then," we say, "did you show no affection to your children?" "But come now, show me an article in the code of laws that would force me, under threat of punishment by criminal court, to show affection to my children, and especially to naughty, heartless, wretched little thieves and brutes. . . ." "Why, at last, did you choose the wrong system for raising your children?" "Well, what system of child-rearing does criminal law prescribe, under threat of punishment? This certainly isn't any concern of the law. . . ."

In short, I want to say that it was impossible to drag this Dzhunkovsky case into criminal court. And so it happened: they were acquitted; nothing came of the charge. And yet the reader feels that this case could give rise to, and perhaps there already has given rise to, a whole tragedy. Oh, this is a matter for another court, but which one?

Which one? Well, let's take Miss Shishova, the teacher, for instance; she gives her testimony and already pronounces the sentence in it. Let's note that although this Miss Shishova herself had lashed the children with a belt ("but it was only a little one"), it seems that she is still a very intelligent woman. One can't give any more exact and intelligent assessment of the character of the Dzhunkovskys than she does. Mrs. Dzhunkovsky is *an egotist,* she says. The Dzhunkovsky house is *disorderly . . . due to the indifference of the defendants toward everything and even toward themselves.* Their affairs are in a constant state of confusion and they live with constant problems; they have no ability to manage their household; they worry, yet more than anything they seek peace and quiet: Mrs. Dzhunkovsky, who continually *tried to ensure that nothing should trouble her,* even gave her husband the responsibility of punishing the children. . . . In short, Miss Shishova received from the Dzhunkovsky household the impression that these people were heartless egotists and, above all, indolent egotists. It all stems from indolence, and their hearts are indolent. It was indolence, of course, that caused the eternal disorder in the house, disorder in their affairs, and yet there is nothing they want more than peace and quiet: "Ah, to hell with you; just let me get on with my life!" What the cause of their indolence and apathy was, God only knows! Did they find it difficult to live amid the chaos of today's world in which it's so difficult to understand anything? Or did today's life provide so few answers to their spiritual needs, to their wishes and questions? Or was it, at last, because they could not understand what was happening all around them, so that their own conceptions of life fell apart and could not be put together again and they became disillusioned? I don't know, I really don't know; but evidently these are people with some education who once, perhaps—and maybe even now—cherished the beautiful and the sublime. The business we saw of massaging the feet wouldn't contradict that. Massaging the feet is just something in the nature of lazy, apathetic disillusionment, a lazy self-indulgence, a longing for seclusion, peace, warmth. It's a matter of nerves—and not so much laziness as this longing for peace and seclusion, for cutting oneself off from all duties and obligations. Yes, of course there's egotism here, and egotists are irresponsible and cowardly when it comes to duty: they have a permanent, cowardly aversion to saddling themselves with any duties. Note that this permanent and ardent wish to free oneself from all duties almost always gives rise to and develops in the egotist the conviction, conversely, that everyone he encounters is obligated to him in some way, is, as it were, charged with some duty to him, must pay him tribute, owes him something. However ridiculous this fantasy may seem, it finally takes root and is transformed into an irritable dissatisfaction with the whole world and a harsh, often embittered attitude toward everything and everyone. When these imagined debts are not fulfilled, the heart of the egotist often takes it as an insult, so that sometimes you can spend your whole life unable to imagine why such a person is always angry and spiteful toward you. This embittered feeling often extends even to their own children—oh, to the children most of all. Children are precisely the preordained victims of this capricious egotism, and besides, they are the nearest to hand; worst of all, there is no constraint here: "They're my children, my own and no one else's!" Don't be astonished that this odious feeling, this permanently irritating reminder of the children's unfulfilled obligations, the irritating, constant presence underfoot of these new little individuals who demand everything from you and who brazenly (alas, not brazenly, just childishly!) refuse to understand that you need peace and quiet and who put no value at all on that peace and quiet—don't be astonished, I say, that this odious feeling even toward one's own children can at last be transformed into a real feeling of vengeance and, encouraged and incited by the absence of any punishment, even into brutality. Indolence, indeed, always gives rise to brutality; it ends in brutality. And this brutality comes not from cruelty but precisely from laziness. These hearts are not cruel, they are just lazy.

And so this lady who was so fond of peace and quiet, who loved it so much she needed to have her feet massaged, who at last became embittered because only she, *she alone*, never had any peace and quiet because everything around her was in a muddle and demanded her constant presence and attention—this lady at last jumps up from her bed, picks up a branch, and beats her own child, beats him insatiably, voraciously, maliciously, so that "it was terrible to watch," as the servant testifies; and why, for what? Because the boy brought his hungry little sister (who suffered from epilepsy) a few potatoes from the kitchen; in other words, she beats him for a kindly feeling, for the fact that the child's heart has not yet become hardened and depraved. "It doesn't matter," she says. "I forbade it, but you did it. So I'll show you: you mustn't do your kindly deed, you must do my wicked deed." No, sir, this is a case of hysterics. The children sleep in filth, "worse than a pigsty," with one ragged blanket for the three of them. "Let them stay there, that's just what they need," thinks their own mother. "They never give me any peace and quiet!" And she thinks that, not because her heart is cruel; no, her heart, perhaps, is naturally very kind and good, but they just won't give her any peace and quiet; never in her life has she been able to find any peace, and as each day passes it gets worse; and here these children ("Why are they here? Why did they have to come along?") are growing up, playing pranks, and demanding more and more effort and attention as each day passes! No, if this is a case of hysterics it has been accumulating for years on end. At the side of this unhealthy (she's been reduced to a state of ill health) mother, the father, Mr. Dzhunkovsky, stands before the court. Well, perhaps he may even be a very good man; he seems an educated fellow, by no means without ideals; on the contrary, he is aware of his fatherly duty, aware of it to the point of being grieved at heart. Here he is in court, complaining almost in tears about his young children; he stretches out his hands: "I've done everything for them, everything; I've hired tutors and governesses; I've spent more on them than my means allow, but they're brutes; they've taken to stealing; they beat their deceased sister across the face!" In short, he considers himself completely in the right. The children stand there beside him; it's remarkable that they gave testimony that was "calm, guarded"; that's to say, they made few complaints and only barely tried to defend themselves, and I think that this was not only out of fear of their parents, to whom they will still have to return. On the contrary, it would seem that the fact their father is already being tried for abusing them would have made them bolder. They simply felt awkward at being involved in the trial of their father, at standing next to him and testifying against him; whereas he, with no regard for the future and for the kind of feelings this day will leave in the hearts of these children, not even suspecting what they will take with them into their future from this day—he accuses them and reveals all that was bad in them, all their shameful acts; he complains to the court, to the spectators, to society. But he believes that he is right, and Mrs. Dzhunkovsky even believes in the future as well, and believes in it totally! She declares to the court that *everything* has been caused by bad tutors and governesses, that she has become disillusioned with them and that now, when her husband himself undertakes to teach and rear the children, the children will be "completely rehabilitated" (Certainly! Certainly!). May God help them, however.

By the way, let me note a few things about the pranks of the young Dzhunkovskys.

The fact that they lashed their dead sister's face with birch rods because she had told on them is, of course, shocking and odious. But if we try to be more dispassionate, I swear that we shall see that even this is only a childish prank and, specifically, childish "fantasizing." Here we see something coming from a child's imagination, not from a depraved heart. The childish imagination by its very nature, particularly at a certain age, is remarkably impressionable and inclined to the fantastic. And this is especially true of those families which, though they live in crowded conditions with someone always underfoot, still keep the children apart in a separate group because of the worries and perpetual lack of time of the fathers: "Do your lessons! Read your book! Don't get into mischief!" That's all they hear, and they sit with their little books in their designated corners, not even daring to swing their feet. Going off to sleep at night in that pigsty of theirs, or sitting at their tedious lessons, or locked up in the toilet, the little Dzhunkovskys might get accustomed to harboring strange fantasies, kindly, heartfelt fantasies, spiteful fantasies, or, in simple childish fashion, fabulous, preposterous fantasies: "Now if I were bigger," the boy might think, "I'd go off to war; and then I'd come back here. That awful tutor would ask: 'Where have you been? How dare you leave the classroom!' And I'd take my St. George's Cross from my pocket and pin it to my buttonhole. And wouldn't he get frightened and fall on his knees!" And when the sister died, one of the three, trying to warm himself under a corner of his ragged blanket, might think up such a thing as he fell asleep: "Do you know what, Kolia? It's God Himself that's punished her for being mean and telling on us. She can see us from up there right now and she'd like to tell on us, but she can't. Let's beat her tomorrow with switches; let her look down and get angry because she can't tell on us!"

I would swear that just a few days later, perhaps, these little urchins repented in their hearts for doing such a disgustingly stupid thing. Children's hearts are soft. On that account I can tell you this little incident. A mother died, leaving seven children. One child, a girl of seven or eight, seeing her dead mama, began sobbing terribly. She cried so much that they took her into the nursery almost in hysterics and did not know how to comfort her. A silly fool of a hanger-on in the household, who happened to be there and was trying to comfort her, suddenly told her: "Don't cry. Why are you carrying on so? Why, she didn't even like you. Don't you remember how she punished you? You had to stand in the corner, remember?" The silly fool thought she would make things better; the child would stop crying, she thought, and calm down. And she did get what she was after: the little girl suddenly stopped crying. Moreover, the next day at the funeral the child had a kind of cold, composed, offended air, as if to say, "She didn't like me." She enjoyed the thought that she was offended, mistreated, unloved. I swear, this happened to a child in her eighth year. But this childish "fantasizing" did not last long: within a few days the child was again grieving so much for her mother that she fell ill, and never again in her whole life could this daughter recall her mother without a feeling of reverence. The little Dzhunkovskys should be punished for what they did to their dead sister, of this there is no doubt; but this act—childish, stupid, grotesque—is specifically something childish and certainly does not indicate depravity in their hearts. The boy Nikolai's prank in the high school—declaring himself a Catholic so as to avoid religious instruction—is very much a piece of childish mischief, a bit of outlandishness to show off before his school friends: "You see," he says, "all of you have to take religious instruction, but I've been able to drop it. I fooled them all, thanks to the fact that my last name sounds Polish." This is positively no more than a *school prank*—silly, nasty, and requiring severe punishment; but it does not mean one should despair of the boy; it does not mean one should believe he's so corrupted that he's become a real scoundrel. But the Dzhunkovsky father believes that, it seems: he would not have made such a sorrowful complaint in court had he not believed it.

In our courts it happens that when defendants are acquitted (and particularly when they are obviously guilty but are released only through the mercy of the court), the presiding judge, in making his statement discharging the defendant, will say a few edifying words to him on the subject of just how he should accept this acquittal, what he should learn from it to help him along in life, and how he might avoid getting into the same trouble in the future. In such a case the presiding judge is speaking for the whole of society and the state, as it were; these words are important, a supreme moral lesson. Perhaps the Dzhunkovskys were declared innocent without any particular admonition of this kind—that I don't know; but I am simply imagining what a presiding judge might have said in his dismissal. And this is what I think he could have said to them.

4. An Imaginary Speech by the Presiding Judge

"Defendants, you are acquitted; but remember that apart from this court there is another court—the court of your own conscience. You must act so that this court as well would acquit you, even if only in years to come. You have declared that you yourselves now intend to undertake the rearing and the teaching of your children: had you done so earlier, today's trial involving your children would probably not have taken place. But I must ask myself whether you have sufficient strength within you to put your good intentions into practice. It is insufficient merely to resolve to undertake such a deed; you must ask yourself: will I have sufficient dedication and patience to carry it out? I do not wish and do not dare to suggest that you are heartless parents who hate your own children. Indeed, to hate one's own children is something almost unnatural in essence and therefore impossible. To hate children who are still so young is something senseless and even ridiculous. But indolence, indifference, the lazy habit of not carrying out such a fundamentally natural and supremely civic duty as raising your own children truly can engender such a dislike for them, almost a hatred, almost a desire for some personal vengeance on them, particularly as they grow up and their natural demands upon you increase accordingly, as your awareness increases of how much you must do for them and how much you must work and, accordingly, how much of your own self-satisfied isolation and peace of mind you must sacrifice for them. Moreover, your neglected children's growing tendency to make mischief, their acquisition of bad habits, their evident, unhealthy inclinations of mind and heart can ultimately inspire an open aversion to them even in their parents' hearts. In your passionate, tearful complaints about your children's flaws we have all heard and seen your profound, genuine distress, the distress of an unfortunate father who has been hurt by his children. Yet think for a moment and consider: what did they have to make them better? It was disclosed in court, for example, that because of their laziness and mischief-making you shut them up sometimes for several hours in a toilet. Of course, a jail is a jail, and your toilet in fact was *heated*, and so there was no cruelty here; yet is that really true? Sitting there, feeling the humiliation and disgrace of his situation, the child could become embittered; the most fantastic, distorted, and cynical thoughts might pass through his head; he might lose his love once and for all—his love for his own nest and even for you, his parents, for it might seem to him that you place no value at all on his feelings for you or on his human dignity, while a child, even the smallest child, also has a completely formed sense of human dignity—that you must keep in mind. It seems that it has never even occurred to you that later he will take these thoughts—and above all, his strong yet childish impressions—with him into life and bear them in his heart, perhaps to his very grave. Did you yourself do anything previously to avoid the humiliating necessity of confining him in such a place, thereby shaming and ridiculing him? Later on in his life he will certainly raise that question and consider it. You maintain that you have done *everything* for your children and seem to be convinced of it yourself, but I do not believe that you have done everything; and when you, with such wounded feeling, made that remark I was convinced that you yourself had great doubt about that very point. You assure the court that you engaged tutors and spent money beyond your means. There is no doubt that a tutor is essential for children and that when you hired one, of course, you were acting as a diligent father; but to engage a tutor to teach your children does not mean, of course, to *surrender* the children to him and have done with it, to get rid of them so that they trouble you no further. And it seems that this is just what you did; and you thought that once you had paid out the money, you had done absolutely everything and even more than *everything*—'beyond your means.' Yet I assure you that you did only the very minimum of what you could have done for them; you merely bought yourself out of your duty and parental obligations with some money and thought that you had already done everything. You forgot that their small, childish souls demand uninterrupted and constant contact with your parental souls; they demand that spiritually you should always be on a pedestal for them, so to say, as an object of love, of great and genuine respect and beautiful imitation. Learning is one thing, but for his children a father should always be like a good, conspicuous example of all the moral conclusions their hearts and minds derive from their learning. Your heartfelt concern for them, a concern that they can always see, and your love for them would, like a friendly ray of sunshine, warm everything that had been planted in their souls; it would have borne fine and abundant fruit. But it seems that having sown nothing yourself and having given them up to a sower of seeds who was alien to your family, you have already demanded a harvest and, unaccustomed to these matters, you have demanded this harvest too soon; and when you did not get it you grew angry and embittered . . . at the little ones, your own children, and too soon, much too soon!

"All this happened because bringing up children is a labor and a duty, a sweet one to some parents, despite even the cares that oppress them, the lack of means, even poverty; but for others, and even for very many well-off parents, it is a most oppressive labor and a most difficult duty. That is why they strive to buy their way out of it with money, if they have money. If even money does not help or, as is the case with many, there is no money, they usually resort to strict measures, to cruelty, to abuse, to birch rods. Let me tell you what the birch rod is. In the family the birch rod is a product of parental indolence, the inevitable result of that indolence. All that could have been achieved by labor and by love, by ceaseless work on the children and with the children; all that could have been attained through good sense, explanation, admonition, patience, training, and example—all this the weak, lazy, but impatient fathers hope to achieve by the birch rod: "I'll not explain, I'll order; I'll not suggest, I'll compel." And what is the result? The sly, secretive child will certainly submit and deceive you, and your birch rod will not correct him but will only corrupt him. The weak, cowardly, and tender-hearted child you'll crush. Finally, the good, artless child with a frank and open heart will first suffer torments and then will become embittered, and you will lose his heart. It is difficult, often very difficult for a child's heart to tear itself away from those it loves; but once it has torn itself away, a terrible, unnaturally premature cynicism, an embitterment, is engendered in it, and its sense of justice becomes distorted. All this, of course, only happens in cases when the cruelty stems from the egotism of the parents and when the owner of the meadow, not having sown himself, demands a good harvest from it. In such cases, cruelty and injustice on the part of the fathers grow stronger, unrestrained;

and this is what most commonly happens. "Don't do your good deed, do my wicked one!" This is what at last becomes the motto, and the child is punished even for a good deed, for a few potatoes he has brought from the kitchen for his sister: how can the heart not grow embittered and how can the understanding not be distorted? Not being cruel and even loving them, you have punished them by your neglect, by your humiliation of them: they had to sleep in a dirty room, on a mat of some sort, and eat food that did not come not from your table, and eat with the servants. And of course you thought that they would at last sense their own guilt and be reformed. If that were not so, one would have to suppose that you did this out of hatred for them, to take revenge on them, to do them wrong. But the court refused to make such a conclusion and attributed your actions to your mistaken beliefs about bringing up children. But now you are planning to train and teach them yourself: this is a difficult task, even though your wife thinks it is a simple one.

"Your children are not in the court; I have asked that they be removed, and therefore I can touch upon the main point in this difficult task that faces you. The most important thing here is that both sides will have to forgive a great many things. They must forgive you the bitter, painful impressions left in their childish hearts, their embitterment, their vices. And you must ask them to forgive your egotism, your neglect of them, the distortion of your feelings for them, your cruelty, and the fact, finally, that you were here on trial because of them. I say that because you will not blame yourself for all this when you leave the courtroom, but will certainly blame them, of that I am certain! And so, as you begin the difficult task of bringing up your children, you must ask yourself: is it possible for you to blame all these misdemeanors and crimes of yours not on them but on yourself? And if that is possible, then—oh, you will succeed in your labor! That means that God has made you see clearly and has enlightened your conscience. If it is not possible, then it is better not to carry out your intention.

"The second difficult thing that faces you in your labor is to change their hearts, to overcome and efface so many of the former impressions and memories stored there. But here there is so much they must be made to forget and so many things to be created anew that I am at a loss to know how you will achieve it. Oh, if you learn to love them, of course you will achieve it all. But even love is a labor, after all; can you believe that even love must be learned?

Finally, can you believe, are you convinced that in your admirable undertaking you will not be stopped and defeated by some of the most trivial, most basic, most routine and ordinary concerns that, perhaps, do not even occur to you now but that still may create a major impediment to your good intentions? Every dedicated and sensible father knows, for instance, how important it is in daily family life not to indulge before his children in that sloppiness, so to say, which we often see in family relations, that lack of discipline and permissiveness; to abstain from bad and ugly habits and, above all, to avoid overlooking and neglecting their own, childish opinion of you; to be aware of the unpleasant, ugly, and comic impression that so often is made on them, considering how little attention we pay to everyday family life. Can you believe that a dedicated father sometimes even has to reeducate himself completely for his children? Oh, if the parents are kind, if their love for the children is fervent and ardent, the children can forgive them much and will later overlook many things, and not only things that were comic and ugly; moreover, they will not pass final sentence on them for some of their thoroughly bad deeds; on the contrary, their hearts will undoubtedly find extenuating circumstances. But something altogether different can happen in families where there is disharmony and harshness. Your wife, as was shown in court, has the unhealthy habit of making someone massage her feet before she goes to sleep. The maid servant testified that she found this duty a painful one, that "her hands swelled." Now can you imagine this boy, your son, being forced to do this instead of the servant? Oh, if her mother genuinely loved him with all her heart, and if he were certain of that, then even now, and indeed ever after, he would recall this weakness of a person he held dear with a fond smile even though, perhaps, he might have felt annoyed and angry during the moments he was made to massage his mother's feet. But I can imagine what he thought and what he felt and what came into his head while he sat there for an hour or more at this ridiculous task, before a creature who did not love him, who might jump up and begin beating him at any moment for no reason at all. Demanding such a service of him then must certainly have seemed a humiliation, an expression of disregard and contempt. He could not help but realize or—to put it better—to feel that his mother did not need him as a son, that she despised him as a son, ignoring him and sending him off to sleep on some sort of mat; and if she did think about him, then it was only in order to beat him; and so she needed him not as a son but only as some implement or other who was available to massage her feet! And yet, after all this, you complain that they have become corrupted, that they are heartless brutes, 'that they've begun to steal!' Strain your imagination a little; imagine your son in the future, at the age of thirty, let's say, and think of the disgust, the angry feeling, and the contempt with which he will recall this episode from his childhood. . . . He will take this memory with him to his very grave, of that there is no doubt. He will not forgive; he will develop hatred for his memories and his childhood; he will curse his former family nest and those who shared that nest with him! Now you are faced with the necessary task of wiping away these memories, transforming them; you must overpower them with new, different, powerful, and sacred impressions—what an enormous labor! It's terrible to think of it! No: the task you are undertaking is far more difficult than your wife imagines!

"Do not be angry, do not be offended at my words. In speaking to you I am carrying out a necessary duty. I am speaking in the name of society, the state, the fatherland. You are the fathers, they are your children; you are today's Russia, they are tomorrow's: what will happen to Russia if Russian fathers shy away from their civic duty and begin seeking seclusion or, to put it better, a secession, lazy and cynical, from society, from their People and their most basic duties toward them? What is most terrible is that this is so widespread: you are not the only such people, although others fall into the same errors as you under different formulas, perhaps. But what is most noteworthy here is that you are not only not the worst but in many ways are among the better of today's fathers, for the awareness of your duty has still not died out in your hearts, even though you did not fulfill that duty. You do not deny altogether that you had a duty. You are not cold egotists; to the contrary, you are angry—whether at yourselves or at your children I will not try to determine; but you have proven capable of taking your lack of success to heart and being deeply grieved by it!

"And so, may God help you in your decision to put right your failure. Seek out love and store it up in your hearts. Love is so all-powerful that it can regenerate even us. It is only through love that we buy the hearts of our children, not merely through some natural right over them. And indeed, among all our obligations, Nature herself helps us most in our obligations to our children, having so arranged it that we cannot help but love them. How can we not love them? If we cease loving children, then whom will we be able to love thereafter, and what will become of us? Remember also that it was only for children and their little golden heads that our Savior promised to shorten "the times and the seasons" for us. For their sake the torments of the regeneration of human society into a more perfect one shall be shortened. And may this perfection come to pass, and may the sufferings and perplexities of our civilization be brought to an end!

"And now, go; you are acquitted. . . ."

2

1. Dissociation Again. Part Eight of *Anna Karenina*

Many educated Russians these days have taken to saying: "What People? I am one of the People myself!" In part eight of *Anna Karenina,* Levin, beloved hero of the novel's author, says that *he is one of the People.* Speaking of *Anna Karenina* once some time ago, I called Levin "pure in heart." While I continue to believe as before in the purity of his heart, I do not believe that he is "one of the People"; on the contrary: I see now that he is aiming, with love, to dissociate himself. I became convinced of it when I finished that same part eight of *Anna Karenina* that I mentioned at the beginning of this July and August portion of my diary. The Levin we speak of is not a real person, of course, but merely the invention of a novelist. Nevertheless, this novelist—an enormous talent, a remarkable mind, and a man highly respected by educated Russia—this novelist depicts in part in this ideal, i.e., invented, character his own view of our contemporary Russian reality, something that is clear to anyone who reads this remarkable work. Thus, when we discuss the non-existent Levin, we shall also be discussing the actual view of one of our most remarkable contemporary Russians on current Russian reality. And this is already a serious topic for discussion, even amid the many rumblings of our age, filled as it is with enormous, shattering, and quickly changing events of real life. This view of so remarkable a Russian writer, and on a matter holding such interest to all Russians as does the general national movement of all Russian people over the last two years regarding the Eastern Question, is expressed precisely and decisively in this same eighth and final part of his work, the part rejected by the editors of *The Russian Messenger* because the author's convictions did not coincide with their own and that appeared only recently as a separate booklet. The essence of this view, as I understand it, consists mainly in the following: first, that the People by no means share the aims of this so-called national movement and do not even understand it; second, that it has all been deliberately fabricated, first by certain well-known people who were subsequently supported by journalists aiming to profit from it by increasing their readership; third, that all the volunteers were either desperate and drunken people or simply fools; fourth, that this whole so-called upsurge of Russian national feeling for the Slavs was not only fabricated by well-known people and supported by hired journalists but had been fabricated contrary to our most fundamental principles, so to speak.... And finally, fifth, that all the barbarities and unprecedented torture inflicted on the Slavs cannot arouse in us Russians any direct feeling of compassion and that "such direct feeling for the oppression of the Slavs *does not and cannot exist*." The last point is expressed finally and categorically.

So it is that the "pure-in-heart" Levin has set off to dissociate himself and has split away from the overwhelming majority of Russians. His view, however, is by no means new or original. It would have been all too useful and would have suited the taste of many (people who are by no means at the bottom of the social ladder) who were thinking almost the same thing here in Petersburg last winter; and so it's a pity that this little book appeared a bit too late. What caused Levin, in such gloom, to dissociate himself and "secede" in so morose a fashion I can't determine. It's true enough that he's an ardent, "restless" person who is given to analyzing everything and who, if you look closely, has nothing within him in which he can believe. But still, this man is "pure in heart," and I maintain this even though it is difficult to imagine by what mysterious and sometimes even ridiculous ways the most unnatural, most artificial, and most ugly things can enter into what is otherwise a heart of great sincerity and purity. However, I will also note that even though many insist—and even I can see clearly (as I said above)—that the author uses Levin to express many of his own views and convictions, putting them into Levin's mouth almost by force and even sometimes clearly sacrificing his artistry by doing so, I still refuse to confuse the author himself with the figure of Levin as his creator depicted him. As I say this I find myself in a certain painful quandary, because even though very much of what the author expresses through Levin evidently concerns only Levin himself as an artistically depicted character, I still did not expect this from such an author!

2. Confessions of a Slavophile

But that's not it. At this point I really must express some of my own feelings, even though, when I began publishing my *Diary* last year, I resolved to make no place in it for literary criticism. But feelings are not criticism, though I may express them about a work of literature. I am writing my "diary," in fact: that's to say, I'm recording my impressions of everything that most strikes me about current events, and so why should I deliberately impose on myself some artificial obligation always to conceal what may even be the strongest impressions I have simply because they pertain to Russian literature? Of course, the idea behind this decision was correct enough, but carrying it out literally, I can see, isn't right, if only because it means being literal-minded. Furthermore, the literary work on which I have refrained from commenting until now is much more than a literary work for me; it is a whole *fact* having significance of a different sort. Perhaps I am expressing myself in too naive a fashion, yet I am determined to say the following: this *fact* of my impression from the novel, from the fiction, from the "poem" coincided in my heart this spring with the enormous fact of the declaration of the war now in progress; both facts, both impressions, connected in my mind, and I found their point of contact striking. So instead of laughing at me, why not listen more closely?

In many respects my convictions are purely Slavophile ones, although I am perhaps not a complete Slavophile. The Slavophiles are still being interpreted in different ways. For some, the Slavophile doctrine even now means only kvass and radishes as it did in the old days for Belinsky, to take an example. Belinsky *really* went no further than that in his understanding of the Slavophile doctrine. For others (and, I'll note, for very many others, and for almost the majority of even the Slavophiles themselves), the Slavophile doctrine means striving for the liberation and union of all Slavs under the supreme leadership of Russia, a leadership that might not even be strictly political. And finally, for a third group, the Slavophile doctrine means, apart from this union of Slavs under Russian leadership, a spiritual union of all who believe that our great Russia, at the head of the united Slavs, will pronounce to the whole world, to the whole of European humanity and civilization, its own new, healthy word, a word that the world has not yet heard. This word will be uttered for the sake of a blessed and genuine union of all humanity in a new, fraternal, universal alliance whose fundamental principles are already found in the animating spirit of the Slavs and above all in the spirit of the great Russian People, who have suffered for so long, who have been condemned to silence for so many centuries, but who have always possessed mighty powers for the future clarification and solution of many painful and fateful misapprehensions of western European civilization. And it is to this latter group of the convinced and believing which I belong.

Here again there is no cause for mockery and laughter: these words are old and this faith is ancient; the very fact that this faith does not wither and these words do not cease to be uttered but, rather, grow ever more emphatic, expand their meaning, acquire new supporters and new stalwarts ready to advance them—this alone ought to make the opponents and mockers of this *doctrine* take it a bit more seriously, at last, and abandon their empty and ossified animosity toward it. But enough said of that for the moment. The fact is, in the spring our great war was launched for a great feat which, sooner or later, despite all the temporary setbacks that delay settlement of the issue, will nonetheless be brought to its conclusion, even though its complete and desired conclusion may not be reached in the present war. This feat is so great and the aim of the war so improbable from Europe's point of view that Europe, naturally, is bound to be indignant over our *cunning;* she is bound to disbelieve what we told her when we began the war; she is bound to try to harm us in every way, using every possible means; and by allying herself with our enemy—though not openly, in a formal, political alliance—Europe will be at odds with us and will struggle against us, behind the scenes, perhaps, in expectation of open war. And all this, of course, stems from our stated intentions and goals! "The great eagle of the East has soared up above the world, his two wings glittering on the summits of Christianity": he seeks neither to conquer nor to acquire or expand his boundaries, but to liberate and restore the oppressed and forgotten, to give them a new life, for their benefit and for humanity's. However you look at it, however skeptically you view this matter, that, in essence, is our very aim, that precisely; and that is precisely what Europe refuses to believe! Believe me, Europe is not frightened so much by the supposed growth of Russia's power as by the very fact of Russia's capacity to undertake such tasks and have such aims. Note that particularly. Undertaking something not for one's own direct benefit seems so bizarre to Europe, so at odds with international practice, that Europe naturally takes Russia's action not only as the barbarism of a "backward, bestial, and ignorant" nation capable, *through meanness and stupidity,* of embarking in our day on something like the crusades of the dark ages, but even as something immoral, dangerous to her, and supposedly a threat to her great civilization. Just take a look: who has any particular love for us in Europe these days? Even our *friends,* our bona fide, formally declared friends, so to say—even they openly announce that they are *happy at our setbacks.* A Russian defeat is dearer to them than some of their own victories; it delights and flatters them. When we do have a success, these friends of ours have long since agreed among themselves to use every power to derive more benefit from Russia's good fortune than Russia herself will. . . .

But I shall say more of this, as well, later on. I began speaking mainly of the impression that everyone who believes in Russia's great future and universal significance must have had this past spring after the declaration of war. This unprecedented war for the sake of the weak and oppressed, to give them life and liberty, not take it away—this is an aim of war that the world has not seen for a long time, and it appeared suddenly, for all our believers, as a fact that solemnly and significantly confirmed their faith. It was no longer a dream or simply the words of some soothsayer but a reality *that had begun to happen.* "If it has already begun to happen, then it will go on to the end, to that great new word that Russia, at the head of a Union of Slavs, will utter to Europe. And even the word itself has already begun to be uttered, although Europe is still far from understanding it and will refuse to believe it for a long time." That is how the "believers" thought. Indeed, the impression was solemn and significant, and of course the faith of believers ought to have been tempered and strengthened even more. However, what had begun was so grave that disturbing questions cropped up even in the minds of believers: "Russia and Europe! Russia draws her sword against the Turks, but who knows: she might yet come to blows with Europe. Isn't that premature? A clash with Europe isn't the same as one with the Turks, and it will surely take place with more than just the sword." That was how the believers always perceived it. But are we prepared for this other conflict? The word has already begun to be uttered, true enough, but never mind Europe—do we ourselves understand it? Here we are, the believers, who prophesy, for instance, that only Russia has within her the principles capable of solving the fateful all-European question of our smaller brethren, without battle and without blood, without hatred and malice; but we say that Russia will utter this word when Europe is already soaked in its own blood, because until then no one in Europe would hear our word, and even if they should hear it, they would utterly fail to understand it. Yes, we believers believe this, but what do our own Russians answer meanwhile? They answer that all this is nothing more than the frenzied talk of soothsayers, religious mania, mad dreams, fits; and they ask proof of us, solid evidence and established facts. And what shall we show them, meanwhile, to support our *prophecies*? Can it be the liberation of the peasants—a fact that is still so little understood among us as a measure of manifestation of Russian spiritual strength? Can it be the innateness and naturalness of our brotherhood, which in our time is emerging more and more distinctly from beneath everything that has been crushing it for ages despite the rubbish and filth that it now encounters, which besmirch and distort its features to the point of unrecognizability?

But suppose we do show them these things: they will again answer that these facts are another form of our religious mania, a crazy dream and not facts; that they can be interpreted variously and unsystematically and as yet are incapable of proving anything. That is what almost everyone will answer; and meanwhile we, who so poorly understand ourselves and have so little faith in ourselves, we are coming into conflict with Europe! Europe—why it's a terrible and a sacred thing, Europe is! Oh, gentlemen, do you know how dear Europe is to us Slavophile-dreamers who, as far as you're concerned, should only hate it, Europe, this "land of holy miracles"! Do you know how dear these "miracles" are to us and how we love and revere, with more than brotherly love and reverence, those great tribes that populate it, together with all the grand and beautiful things they have accomplished? Do you know the many tears we shed and the pangs of heart we suffer at the fate of this dear and *native* country, and how frightened we are by the storm clouds that are ever gathering on her horizon? Gentlemen, never did you, as Europeans and Westernizers, love Europe so much as we, Slavophile-dreamers who, as far as you are concerned, are her mortal enemies! No, this land is dear to us—dear is the future peaceful victory of the great Christian spirit that has been preserved in the East. . . . And in our dread of conflict with Europe in the current war we fear most of all that Europe will not understand us, and as before, as always, will meet us with arrogance, contempt, and her sword, as if we were still wild barbarians, unworthy of speaking in her presence. Yes, we have asked ourselves what we can tell her or show her so that she might understand us. Evidently we still have so little of anything that might be *intelligible* to her and earn us her respect. Our fundamental, main idea, our emerging "new word" she will not understand for a long, long time yet. She needs facts that are intelligible *now*, intelligible to her *present* point of view. She will ask us: "Where is your civilization? Is there any economic structure to be perceived amid that chaos we all see in Russia? Where is *your* science, *your* art, *your* literature?"

3. *Anna Karenina* as a Fact of Special Importance

And so, at that very time—one evening last spring, that is—I happened to meet one of my favorite writers on the street. We meet rarely, once every few months, and somehow always by chance on the street. He is one of the most prominent among those five or six writers who are usually called the "Pleiade," for some reason. The critics, at least, have followed the readers and have set them apart and placed them above all the other writers; this has been the case for some time now—still the same group of five, and the Pleiade's membership does not increase. I enjoy meeting this dear novelist of whom I am so fond; I enjoy showing him, among other things, that I think he is quite wrong in saying that he has become old-fashioned and will write nothing more. I always bring away some subtle and perceptive insight from our brief conversations. We had much to talk about this time, for the war had already begun. But he at once began speaking directly about *Anna Karenina*. I had also just finished reading part seven, with which the novel had concluded in *The Russian Messenger*. My interlocutor does not look like a man of strong enthusiasms. On this occasion, however, I was struck by the firmness and passionate insistence of his views on *Anna Karenina*.

"It's something unprecedented, a first. Are there any of our writers who could rival it? Could anyone imagine anything like it in Europe? Is there any work in all their literatures over the past years, and even much earlier, that could stand next to it?"

What struck me most in this verdict, which I myself shared completely, was that the mention of Europe was so relevant to those very questions and problems that were arising of their own accord in the minds of so many. The book at once took on, in my eyes, the dimensions of a fact that could give Europe an answer on our behalf, that long-sought-after fact we could show to Europe. Of course, people will howl and scoff that this is only a work of literature, some sort of novel, and that it's absurd to exaggerate this way and go off to Europe carrying only a novel. I know that people will howl and scoff, but don't worry: I'm not exaggerating and am looking at the matter soberly: I know very well that this is still only a novel and that it's but a tiny drop of what we need; but the main thing for me here is that this drop already exists, it is given, it really and truly does exist; and so, if we already have it, if the Russian genius could give birth to this *fact,* then it is not doomed to impotence and can create; it can provide something *of its own,* it can begin *its own* word and finish uttering it when the times and seasons come to pass. And besides, this is much more than a mere drop. Oh, I'm not exaggerating here either: I know very well that you won't find, either in any individual member of this Pleiade or in the whole Pleiade together, anything that can be called, strictly speaking, a creative force of true genius. In our entire literature there have been but three unquestioned geniuses who had an unquestionably "new word" to utter, and these three were Lomonosov, Pushkin, and, in part, Gogol. This whole Pleiade (including the author of *Anna Karenina*) emerged directly from Pushkin, one of the greatest of Russians who, however, is still far from being interpreted and understood properly. There are two principal ideas in Pushkin, and they both contain a model of the whole of Russia's future mission and goal, and therefore of our whole future destiny. The first is Russia's *universality,* her capacity to respond, and the genuine, unquestioned, profound kinship of her genius with the geniuses of all ages and all peoples of the world. Pushkin does not merely call our attention to this idea or convey it in the form of a doctrine or theory or as a cherished hope or prophecy; he carries it out *in practice,* embodies it, and proves it forever in his brilliant creations. He is a man of the ancient world; he is also a German and an Englishman, deeply aware of his own animating spirit and the anguish of his aspirations ("A Feast in Time of Plague"); he is a poet of the East. To all these peoples he stated and proclaimed that the Russian genius knew them, has understood them, has touched them like a brother, that it can fully *reincarnate* itself in them, that to the Russian spirit alone is given universality and the future mission to comprehend and to unify all the diverse nationalities and to eliminate all their contradictions. Pushkin's other idea was his turning to the People and investing his hopes in their strength alone, his pledge that in the People and in the People alone will we fully discover our whole Russian genius and our consciousness of its mission. And here, too, Pushkin did not merely point out a fact but was also the first to realize the fact in practice. It was only with him that we began our real, conscious turn to the People, something that had been inconceivable before him ever since Peter's reforms. The whole Pleiade of today have worked only along his lines; after Pushkin no one has said anything *new*. All their sources were in him, and he pointed them out. And besides, the Pleiade has elaborated only the tiniest part of what he pointed out. What they have done, however, has been done with such largess of talent, with such depth and distinction, that Pushkin would naturally have acknowledged them.

The idea behind *Anna Karenina*, of course, is nothing new or unheard of in Russia. Instead of this novel we could, of course, show Europe the source—Pushkin himself, that is—as the strongest, most vivid, and most incontestable proof of the independence of the Russian genius and its rights to a great, worldwide, pan-human and all-unifying significance in the future. (Alas, no matter how we tried to show them that, Europe will not read our writers for a long time yet; and if Europe does begin to read them, the Europeans will not be able to understand and appreciate them for a long time. Indeed, they are utterly unable to appreciate our writers, not because of insufficient capacity, but because for them we are an entirely different world, just as if we had come down from the moon, so that it is difficult for them even to admit the fact that we exist. All this I know, and I speak of "showing Europe" only in the sense of our own conviction of our right to independence vis-à-vis Europe.) Nevertheless, *Anna Karenina* is perfection as a work of art that appeared at just the right moment and as a work to which nothing in the European literatures of this era can compare; and, in the second place, the novel's idea also contains something of ours, something truly *our own*, namely that very thing which constitutes our distinctness from the European world, the thing which constitutes our "new word," or at least its beginnings—just the kind of word one cannot hear in Europe, yet one that Europe still so badly needs, despite all her pride.

I cannot embark upon literary criticism here and will say only a few things. *Anna Karenina* expresses a view of human guilt and transgression. People are shown living under abnormal conditions. Evil existed before they did. Caught up in a whirl of falsities, people transgress and are doomed to destruction. As you can see, it is one of the oldest and most popular of European themes. But how is such a problem solved in Europe? Generally in Europe there are two ways of solving it. Solution number one: the law has been given, recorded, formulated, and put together through the course of millennia. Good and evil have been defined and weighed, their extent and degree have been determined historically by humanity's wise men, by unceasing work on the human soul, and by working out, in a very scientific manner, the extent of the forces that unite people in a society. One is commanded to follow this elaborated code of laws blindly. He who does not follow it, he who transgresses, pays with his freedom, his property, or his life; he pays literally and cruelly. "I know," says their civilization, "that this is blind and cruel and impossible, since we are not able to work out the ultimate formula for humanity while we are still at the midpoint of its journey; but since we have no other solution, it follows that we must hold to that which is written, and hold to it literally and cruelly. Without it, things would be even worse. At the same time, despite all the abnormality and absurdity of the structure we call our great European civilization, let the forces of the human spirit remain healthy and intact; let society not be shaken in its faith that it is moving toward perfection; let no one dare think that the idea of the beautiful and sublime has been obscured, that the concepts of good and evil are being distorted and twisted, that convention is constantly taking the place of the healthy norm, that simplicity and naturalness are perishing as they are crushed by a constant accumulation of lies!"

The second solution is the reverse: "Since society is arranged in an abnormal manner, one cannot demand that human entities be responsible for the consequences of their actions. Therefore, the criminal is not responsible, and crime at present does not exist. In order to put an end to crime and human guilt we must put an end to the abnormality of society and its structure. Since curing the ills in the existing order of things is a long and hopeless process, and the medicines needed have not even been found, it follows that the whole society must be destroyed and the old order swept away with a broom, as it were. Then we can begin it all anew, on different principles as yet unknown but which, nevertheless, can be no worse than those of the present order; on the contrary, they offer many chances of success. Our main hope is in science." And so this is the second solution: they wait for the future ant heap and in the meantime will wet the earth with blood. The world of western Europe offers no other solutions for guilt and human transgression.

The Russian author's view of guilt and transgression recognizes that no ant heap, no triumph of the "fourth estate," no abolition of poverty, no organization of labor will save humanity from abnormality and, consequently, from guilt and transgression. This is expressed in a monumental psychological elaboration of the human soul, with awesome depth and force and with a realism of artistic portrayal unprecedented among us. It is clear and intelligible to the point of obviousness that evil lies deeper in human beings than our socialist-physicians suppose; that no social structure will eliminate evil; that the human soul will remain as it always has been; that abnormality and sin arise from that soul itself; and, finally, that the laws of the human soul are still so little known, so obscure to science, so undefined, and so mysterious, that there are not and cannot be either physicians or *final* judges; but there is He who says: "Vengeance is mine, I will repay." He alone knows *all* the mystery of this world and the final destiny of man. Humans themselves still cannot venture to decide anything with pride in infallibility; the times and the seasons for that have not yet arrived. The human judge himself ought to know that he is not the final judge; that he himself is a sinner; that the measure and the scales in his hands will be an absurdity *if* he, holding that measure and scales, does not himself submit to the law of the yet unsolved mystery and turn to the only solution—to Mercy and Love. And so that man might not perish in despair and ignorance of his path and destiny, of his conviction of evil's mysterious and fateful inevitability, he has been shown a way out. This the poet has brilliantly shown in a masterful scene in the novel's penultimate part, in the scene of the heroine's mortal illness, when the transgressors and enemies are suddenly transformed into higher beings, into brothers who have forgiven one another everything, into beings who, through mutual forgiveness, have cast off lies, guilt, and crime and thereby at once have absolved themselves with full awareness of their right to absolution. But later, at the end of the novel, we have a gloomy and terrible picture of the full degeneration of a human spirit; this we follow step by step through the depiction of that compelling state in which evil, having taken possession of a human being, trammels his every movement and paralyzes every effort toward resistance, every thought, every wish to struggle with the darkness that falls upon the soul; deliberately, eagerly, with a passion for vengeance, the soul accepts the darkness instead of the light. In this picture there is such a profound lesson for the human judge, for the one who holds the measure and the scales, that he will naturally exclaim in fear and perplexity, "No, vengeance is not always mine, and it is not always for me to repay." And the human judge will not cruelly charge the grievously fallen criminal with having scorned the light of the age-old solution and with having *deliberately* rejected it. He will not, at least, cling to the letter of the law. . . .

If we have literary works of such power of thought and execution, then why can we not *eventually* have *our own* science as well, and our own economic and social solutions? Why does Europe refuse us our independence, *our own* word? These are questions that cannot help but be asked. It would be absurd to suppose that nature has endowed us only with literary talents. All the other things are a matter of history, circumstances, and the conditions of the time. Our own homegrown Europeans, at least, ought to be thinking this way while they await the judgment of the European Europeans. . . .

4. A Landowner Who Gets Faith in God from a Peasant

Now that I have expressed my feelings, people may understand how I was affected by the defection of such an author, by his secession from the great Russian and general cause, and by the paradoxical untruth he tells about the People in the unfortunate eighth part of his novel, which he published separately. He simply takes away from the People all their most precious things and deprives them of what means most in their lives. He would have found it far more gratifying had our People's hearts not risen up everywhere for the sake of their brethren who suffer for their faith. In that sense alone, he denies this phenomenon, despite its obviousness. Of course, he does all this only through the fictional characters of his novel; but, I repeat, it's only too plain that the author himself shares their views. True enough, this little book is sincere, and the author speaks from his heart. Even the touchiest of things (and there are some *touchy* things there) have been fitted in as if quite casually, so that despite all their touchiness, you accept them quite literally and never admit the possibility of any underhandedness at all. Nevertheless, I still think this little book is not so innocent as all that. Now, of course, it does not and cannot have any influence, except maybe to give another nod of assent to some little group that has cut itself off from everyone else. But the fact that such an author can write this way is very sad. It's sad for the future. But I'd best get down to business: I'd like to voice my objections and point out the things that struck me particularly.

First, however, let me say something about Levin—obviously the main character of the novel: in him the positive side is expressed, as if in contrast to those abnormalities that have brought suffering and ruination to the other characters of the novel; Levin, apparently, was specifically destined by the author be the expression of all these things. And yet Levin is still not complete; he still lacks something, and this should have been taken up and solved so that there would be no more doubts and questions about what Levin represents. The reader will eventually understand the reason why I am dwelling on this and not moving directly to the main thing.

Levin is happy; the novel ends with his glorification, but his inner, spiritual world is still lacking something. He is tormented by the age-old questions of humanity: God, eternal life, good and evil, and so on. He is tormented by the fact that he is not a believer and that he cannot peacefully settle into the things that everyone else settles peacefully into, i.e., self-interest, worship of one's own self or one's own idols, vanity, and so on. That's a sign of a noble spirit, is it not? But one couldn't have expected less of Levin. It appears, by the way, that Levin has read a great deal: he's familiar with the works of philosophers and positivists and ordinary natural scientists. Yet none of this satisfies him; rather, it confuses him even more, so that in moments of freedom from his work on the estate he runs off into the woods and groves, gets angry, and even appreciates Kitty much less than she merits. And so, once, he suddenly meets a peasant who, in talking about two other peasants, Mitiukha and Fokanych, whose moral qualities are very different, expresses himself as follows:

> "... Mitiukha, now, he'll be sure to get his due! He'll lean on a person till he gets what's owing. He's got no pity for a fellow Christian; but take old Fokanych—do you think he'd try to strip a man's hide from his back? He'll give a fellow credit, and sometimes he'll just forget about it. And there's times when he won't ask for all of it back—he's a human being, you see."
>
> "But why would he let people off?"
>
> "Well, you see, folks are all different: one fellow lives only for his needs; take Mitiukha, here—all he thinks about is stuffing his belly.

But Fokanych is a righteous old man. He lives for his soul and remembers God."

"What do you mean, 'remembers God'? How does he live for his soul?" Levin almost shouted.

"Why, that's plain enough: he lives rightly, in God's way. Folks are all different, you see. Take you, now, you wouldn't harm a fellow either."

"Yes, yes! Good-bye, then!" said Levin, choking with emotion; and turning away he took up his stick and set off quickly for home.

However, he ran off to the forest once again, lay down under some aspen trees, and began thinking, almost in a kind of ecstasy. The word had been found, all the age-old riddles had been solved, and this through a few simple words from a peasant: "To live for one's soul, to remember God." The peasant, of course, had told him nothing new; he himself had known all that for a long time; but the peasant still suggested the idea and prompted him to a solution at the most critical moment. Thereafter follows a series of Levin's thoughts, very fitting and aptly expressed. Levin's idea is as follows: why should one seek with one's mind for something that has already been *given* by life itself, something with which every person is born and which (even involuntarily) every person should observe and does observe. Every person is born with a conscience, with a conception of good and evil, and so every person is also born with a direct aim in life: to live for good and not to love evil. Both peasant and master are born with this, as are the Frenchman, the Russian, and the Turk—they all cherish good (N.B.: Although many of them do so in a way that's very much their own). But, says Levin, I was trying to comprehend all this through mathematics, science, reason, or was expecting some miracle, whereas this was given to me as a gift; it was born along with me. And that it is given as a gift can be proven directly: everyone on earth understands or can understand that we must *love our neighbor as ourselves*. That knowledge, in essence, contains the entire *law* of humanity, as was also declared to us by Christ Himself. Yet this knowledge is innate, and so it has been sent as a gift, for reason could never ever have provided such knowledge. Why? Because "loving one's neighbor," when you look at it rationally, is something irrational.

"Where did I get this?" [asks Levin]. "Was it reason that proved I must love my neighbor and not strangle him? I was told that as a child, and I *believed it gladly*, because they told me something that was already in my soul. But who discovered this? Not reason. Reason discovered the struggle for survival and the law that demands I strangle everyone who stands in the way of my satisfying my desires. That's what reason deduces. But loving one's neighbor is something reason could never discover, because it's unreasonable."

Then Levin thought back to a recent scene with his children. The children had started cooking raspberries in a cup over a candle and squirting streams of milk into their mouths. When their mother caught them at their antics she began scolding them, saying that if they ruined the dishes and wasted the milk they would be left with neither dishes nor milk. But the children obviously didn't believe her because they could not imagine "the full scope of all the things they enjoyed, and so they could not imagine that what they were destroying was the very same thing by which they lived."

"This all happens by itself," they thought. "And there's nothing interesting or important about it because it's always been so and always will be. And it's always just the same. There's no point in our worrying about it, it's all done for us; but we want to think up something of our own, something new. And so we got the idea of putting some raspberries in a cup and cooking them over a candle, and squirting streams of milk into each other's mouths. That's fun, and it's new, and it's not a bit worse than drinking out of cups."

"Don't we do just the same thing, and didn't I do it in trying to use reason to discover the meaning of the forces of nature and the purpose of human life?" Levin continued thinking.

"And don't all the philosophical theories do the same thing, trying by an approach of thought that is odd and unnatural to humans to lead them to the knowledge of something they have known for a long time, and known so surely that they could not live without it? Isn't it clearly obvious in the development of the theory of every philosopher that he knows beforehand, and knows as certainly as the peasant Fedor and not a bit more clearly than he, the most important things about the meaning of life and is only trying through some dubious intellectual process to come back to something that everyone knows?

"Well, then, suppose we let the children fend for themselves, make their own dishes, milk the cows, and so on. Would they get up to such antics? They'd die of hunger. Well, then, suppose we were left to our own passions and thoughts, without any concept of the one God and Creator! Or without any concept of what is good, without any explanation of moral evil!

> "Well, then, just try to construct anything without these conceptions!
>
> "We only destroy, because we have had our fill spiritually. Just like the children!"

In short, his doubts are ended and Levin comes to believe—in what? He still has not strictly defined this, but he already believes. But is this a faith? He gladly poses this question to himself: "Can this be faith?" One must suppose that it is not yet faith. Moreover, it's hardly likely that people like Levin can have a conclusive faith. Levin likes to call himself "one of the People," but he's the son of a nobleman, the son of a Moscow nobleman of the upper-middle level whose foremost historian was Count L. Tolstoy. Although the peasant never told Levin anything new, he still nudged him toward the idea, and with this idea began a faith. In that very thing alone Levin should have seen that he is certainly not "one of the People" and that he cannot say, "I myself am one of the People." But I'll talk about that later. I only want to say that men like Levin, no matter how long they live with the People or near the People, will still never fully transform themselves into the People; moreover, there are many things about the People that they will never understand at all. It's not enough simply to think oneself one of the People or to try to become so through an act of will, and a very eccentric will at that. He may be a landowner, a landowner who works his land and who knows peasant work; he may go out mowing himself and know how to harness a horse and know that honey in the comb is served with fresh cucumbers. Still, no matter how he tries, his soul will still show the effects of what I think can be called *idling*—that same idling, physical and spiritual, which, no matter how much he tries to resist it, is still part of his inheritance and which, of course, the People see in every nobleman since they do not see with our eyes. However, I'll talk about that later as well. And he will destroy his faith again, destroy it himself; it will not last long: there will be some new hitch and everything will collapse at once. Kitty set off in life and she stumbled; so why did she stumble? If she stumbled, then she could not help but stumble; it's only too clear that she stumbled for this reason or for that reason. It's clear that everything here depended on laws that can be strictly defined. And if that's so, then science is everywhere. Where is Providence, then? What role does it play here? Where is human responsibility? And if there is no Providence, then how can

I believe in God? And so on, and so on. Take a straight line and project it into infinity. In short, this honest soul is a most idly chaotic soul, otherwise he would not be a contemporary Russian educated nobleman, and one from the upper-middle level besides.

He proves this brilliantly only an hour or so after the acquisition of his faith; he is trying to prove that the Russian People have no feeling at all for the things that people in general feel; he destroys the soul of the People in a most autocratic manner; moreover, he declares that he himself feels no pity at all for human suffering. He declares that "there is not and cannot be any immediate feeling of compassion for the oppression of the Slavs"—i.e., not only in him but in the Russians as a whole: "I myself am one of the People," he says. They put much too cheap a value on the Russian People. But they've been appraising them that way for a long time. Not more than an hour had passed since the acquisition of faith, and again raspberries started being cooked over a candle.

3

1. The Irritability of Vanity

The children came running and told Levin that guests had arrived: "One of them waves his arms around just like this." The guests, it turns out, are from Moscow. Levin seats them under the trees in the garden, serves them honey in the comb and fresh cucumbers, and the guests at once start in on the honey and the Eastern Question. All this happens last year, you see; you can remember: Cherniaev, the volunteers, collecting donations. A heated conversation quickly develops because everyone has an irrepressible urge to get to the major topic of the day. Those involved, apart from the ladies, are, first, some little professor from Moscow, a dear man but not awfully bright. Next is a man of enormous intellect and erudition (he's brought in for just this reason), Sergei Ivanovich Koznyshev, Levin's half-brother. This character is skillfully drawn in the novel, and eventually we understand him (he's a man of the 1840s). Sergei Ivanovich has only just plunged, completely and passionately, into work for the Slavs, and the Committee has given him so many responsibilities that it's difficult even to imagine, when you recall last summer, how he could drop everything and come to the country for two whole weeks. It's true that if he hadn't come there wouldn't have been any conversation by the apiary about the People's movement and, accordingly, no eighth part of the novel, which was written for this conversation alone. You see, this Sergei Ivanovich had published in Moscow a month or two before some scholarly book about Russia, a book he had been working on for a long time and for which he had high hopes; but the book was an unexpected failure, and not just a failure but a fiasco; no one made any comment about it and it passed without notice. And so at that point Sergei Ivanovich plunged into work for the Slavic cause, and with a passion one never expected from him. It appears, therefore, that this was an unnatural thing to do; all his passion for the Slavs is *ambition rentrée* and no more, and you sense clearly that Levin cannot help but emerge victorious over such a person. Sergei Ivanovich was very skillfully drawn in a comic light in the earlier parts as well; in part eight, however, it becomes completely clear that he was conceived only so that at the end of the novel he could serve as a pedestal for Levin's greatness. But he is a very successful character.

Among the most unsuccessful characters, however, is the old prince. He's also sitting there discussing the Eastern Question. He is unsuccessful throughout the whole novel, not just in regard to the Eastern Question. He is one of the positive figures in the novel, intended as an expression of positive beauty—though not without some sinning against realism, of course: he does have his weaknesses and almost has a touch of absurdity about him; yet he is ever so respectable. He's also the novel's kindhearted character, as well as a fountain of common sense, but not some Mr. Goodsense of the Fonvizin kind who, once he takes to something, just keeps on like a trained donkey: common sense and nothing more. No, he has humor and, in general, truly human traits. The amusing thing is that this old man was designed to illustrate wittiness. Having passed through the school of life, the father of many children (who are well established in life, however), he gazes at everything around him in his old age with the quiet smile of a wise man; his smile is far from being meek and inoffensive, though. He'll give you advice, but watch out for the play of his wit: it'll tell you what for. And so, suddenly, there's a mishap here: Mr. Goodsense, designed to illustrate wittiness, appears—God knows why—as not witty in the least; in fact he's even rather common. It's true that he makes a real effort, just as he does all through the novel, to say something witty, but all we see is the effort and nothing more. Out of consideration for him the reader is prepared at last to give him credit for trying and to accept these vain attempts at wit for real wit; but what's far worse is that this same character, in the eighth part of the novel that was published separately, is intended to express things that, granted, are again not witty (in this respect the old prince remains thoroughly in character), but which are cynical and slanderous toward a part of our society and our People. Instead of a Mr. Goodheart we have some sort of clubman who rejects both the Russian People and all that is good in them. One senses a clubman's irritability, an old man's bile. However, the political theory of the old prince is not new at all. It's the same thing, repeated for the hundred-thousandth time, that we're constantly hearing even without him:

> "My view as well," said the prince. "I was living abroad, reading the newspapers and, I confess, even before the Bulgarian atrocities I simply couldn't understand why all Russians developed such a sudden affection for their Slavic brethren, while I didn't feel any love for them at all. I was very grieved indeed and thought I must be a monster [he's being witty here, you see: just imagine, he thinks he must be a monster!] or that the waters of Karlsbad were having that effect on me [a particularly good quip]. But since I've come home I've stopped worrying [I should think so!]; I see that there are others besides me who are interested only in Russia, and not their Slavic brethren. . . ."

Now here we see real profundity! We must take an interest *only* in Russia. So that aid and comfort to the Slavs is flatly regarded as none of Russia's business; had he regarded it as Russia's business he would not have said that we must take an interest *only* in Russia, since taking an interest in the Slavs would then mean an interest in Russia herself and in her mission. The nature of the prince's views is, accordingly, a narrow conception of Russian interests. Of course we've heard that; we've heard it a thousand times, and there are some circles in which you hear nothing else. But here's something far more malignant, however; this is a conversation that took place a few minutes earlier. The old prince asks Sergei Ivanovich:

> ". . . for heaven's sake, Sergei Ivanovich, explain to me where all these volunteers are going and whom they're going to fight?"
>
> "Why, the Turks," answered Sergei Ivanovich, with a calm smile. . . .
>
> "But who has declared war on the Turks? Ivan Ivanovich Ragozov and Countess Lidia Ivanovna along with Mme. Stahl?"

Now here he's let the cat out of the bag. You understand that this was what he was getting at, and perhaps it was why he hurried back from Karlsbad. But this is a question of another sort, and the fact that the prince raised it seems not such a good thing. Of course, even this idea isn't new; but why, then, is it repeated once more? Last winter there were quite a number of people who, for their own reasons, kept saying that someone in Russia had declared war on the Turks. This idea was set forth; but this little idea made the rounds and came back to those who had invented it. Because absolutely no one in Russia last year declared war on the Turks; and to make such a claim is, at very least, an *exaggeration*. True, Sergei Ivanovich later dismisses it with a joke, but the naive and honest Levin, like a genuine enfant terrible, plainly expresses the thing that is on the prince's mind:

> "No one has declared war; but people sympathize with the sufferings of those close to them and want to help them," said Sergei Ivanovich.
>
> "But the prince isn't talking about help," said Levin, interceding for his father-in-law. "He's talking about war. The prince means that private individuals cannot take part in a war without permission of the government."

Now do you see what Levin is worrying about? The matter is put quite plainly; beyond that, it is clarified by Katavasov's silly remark. This is what Levin goes on to say:

> "Well, this is my theory: on the one hand, war is such a bestial, cruel, and terrible thing that no one—to say nothing of a Christian—can himself personally assume the responsibility of starting a war; this can be only be done by a government, instituted to do such things when they are inevitable. On the other hand, both science and common sense tell us that in matters of state, and in matters of war in particular, citizens have to renounce their personal will."
>
> Sergei Ivanovich and Katavasov, with ready objections, both began to speak at once.
>
> "But my dear fellow, the point is that there may be instances when the government is not expressing the will of the citizens, and then society expresses its will," said Katavasov.
>
> But Sergei Ivanovich evidently did not approve of this argument. . . .

In short, they advance and support the view that someone in Russia, behind the back of the government, really did declare war on the Turks last year. Given his intellect, Levin should be able to figure out that Katavasov is a fool, that Katavasovs are to be found everywhere, that last year's movement was precisely opposed to the ideas of the Katavasovs because it was something Russian, national, and genuinely ours, and not the game of some opposition. But Levin insists on his own view; he takes his accusation to its conclusion; what matters to him is not truth but the thing he has invented. Here are the arguments with which he concludes his ideas on this topic:

> . . . He [Levin] was speaking in the same spirit as Mikhailych and the People who expressed their idea in the legend of the summoning of the Varangians: 'Be our princes and rule over us. We gladly swear our complete submission. All the toil, all the humiliations, all the sacrifices we shall take on ourselves; but we do not wish to judge and make decisions.' And now, Sergei Ivanovich claimed, the People *had renounced this right they had purchased so dearly.*
>
> He wanted also to ask that if public opinion were such an infallible judge, then why were the revolution and the commune not as legitimate as the movement on behalf of the Slavs? . . .

Do you hear that? And no considerations can lead these gentlemen astray, and no facts, no matter how evident they are. I have already said that it would have been better had the prince and Levin never made such accusations; but who can't see that one of them suffers from injured vanity and the other is a paradoxicalist. However, perhaps Levin also suffers from injured vanity, because one never knows what may suddenly injure a man's vanity! And yet the issue is clear, the accusation is nonsensical; and besides, there can be no such accusation because it simply cannot exist. The facts were altogether different.

2. *Tout ce qui n'est pas expressément permis est défendu*

War on Turkey was declared last year not by Russia and not in Russia but in the Slavic lands, by the Slavic ruling princes, i.e., the sovereigns, Prince Milan of Serbia and Prince Nicholas of Montenegro, who took up arms against Turkey because of the unprecedented persecutions, atrocities, plunder, and massacres committed against the Slavs they ruled, including the Herzegovinians, who at last were driven by these atrocities to rise up against their oppressors. The unprecedented tortures and massacres to which the Herzegovinians were subjected became known to the whole of Europe. The news of these horrors reached us in Russia as well, first our educated public and then the People. Because of its unprecedented nature the news spread everywhere. Reports came that hundreds of thousands of people—old men, pregnant women, abandoned children—had fled their homes and were streaming out of Turkey into any neighboring country to which they could make their way, without food, shelter, or clothing, in an utter animal panic of self-preservation. The princes, the church, and the church's representatives raised their voices on behalf of these unfortunates and began collecting assistance for them. Our People as well began making donations to them; contributions flowed into specific points—editorial offices of magazines, branches of the former Slavic Committees—and there was absolutely nothing in this that was illegal, antigovernmental, or immoral. On the contrary, one can confidently say that it was nothing but good. As to the Slavic princes who began this war against Turkey, neither Russia nor anyone in Russia could be blamed for that. It is true that one of these rulers, namely Prince Milan of Serbia, was not a fully independent ruler; rather, he had a certain feudatory obligation to the Sultan, so that one Russian newspaper bitterly reproached him for being a rebel, as it were, and in order to embarrass and shame him utterly, wrote that he had risen up against his "sovereign lord." But, once again, this was still the personal business of Prince Milan, for which he alone will have to answer. But neither Russia nor anyone in Russia declared the war of last year; accordingly, we have committed no sin against the Sultan. The contributions, meanwhile, kept flowing in, but that is another matter entirely. But then, suddenly, one Russian general who held no active post at the time, a man not yet old and only a major-general but already having a certain reputation for his earlier and rather successful operations in Central Asia, set off to Serbia of his own volition and offered his services to Prince Milan. He was accepted and enlisted into service, but certainly not as commander-in-chief of the Serbian army, as the rumor in Russia then had it (and the rumor persisted for a long time). At this point, Russian volunteers began to step forward, although there certainly had been some volunteers even earlier, i.e., before Cherniaev; and at the same time the flow of contributions increased, and the whole of Russia rose up to make them. Over the last year there were not all that many volunteers—a few thousand, perhaps—but certainly the whole of Russia was with them on their way to Serbia, and the People in particular—the real People, not the idle trash, as the angry Levin particularly insists; he regards the volunteers as idle trash as well. But this was not so; this affair did not happen in some out-of-the-way corner, it was known to everyone; everyone could see it and be convinced, and everyone—the whole of Russia, that is—decided that this cause was a good one. The People displayed so much that was noble, touching, and knowing during their movement in support of the Slavs last year that it will unquestionably remain one of the finest pages in their history.

However, to defend the People against the Levins, to prove to the Levins that these were not idle trash and not malcontents but, rather, people well aware of their cause—to try to prove all this is, I think, entirely futile and unnecessary; moreover, it is even humiliating to the People. What matters most is that all this happened openly, in full view of everyone: facts came to light that were striking and characteristic, that were recorded and remembered, that will not be forgotten and that cannot be disputed. But I'll say more about the People later; as far as the volunteers are concerned, there were bound to be, along with those who made the supreme sacrifice for the sake of their neighbor (N.B.: Kireev), some who were concerned merely with showing some dash and verve, with carousing and so on. It all happened as these things happen everywhere and always. It's true that no one has yet counted the numbers of these drunken carousers and idlers, if, indeed, there were any such among the volunteers who gave their lives for a noble cause faraway over there, and so there is no reason to come out against them with such censure and abuse. But to maintain that the volunteers of last year were *all* carousers, drunkards, and desperate people is, at very least, senseless; for again, I repeat: this thing did not happen away off in a corner somewhere and everyone could witness it. But in any case, last year there certainly was no declaration of war on a neighboring power by some Russians behind the back of the government. Ivan Ivanovich Ragozov and Countess Lidia Ivanovna could not declare war on the Turks even if they had wanted to. Moreover, it was not they who caused the volunteers to step forward; they did not lure or hire anyone; each one went *absolutely voluntarily,* and that is certainly plain to everyone. But that they did help the volunteers and, beyond that, sent money to the Slavic lands to help the unfortunate, the beleaguered, and the injured and, beyond that, helped finance those who rose to defend the unfortunate—that did happen; oh, that did happen, and it happened with a most fervent wish that the bloodsucking Turks might be crushed—yes, that certainly did happen! But the whole question is: was this a declaration of war? If not, then was it or was it not prohibited by the government? That is, was it prohibited to help finance those who were fighting for Christians and to wish that the Turks should be crushed? Once more, I simply can't believe that it was prohibited, for the matter happened openly, everyone saw it, everyone participated in it, and the volunteers received their passports for abroad from the government itself. I don't know—perhaps there is a law that says "private individuals cannot *participate* in a war without permission of the government," that is, they cannot enlist in the service of a foreign sovereign without special permission from their government. Perhaps there really does exist some such law, a very old one that has still not been repealed; but the government itself could have invoked that law, so what's Levin worrying about? What's his concern with all this? Yet he's worried about this thing in particular. . . .

"*Pardon monsieur, mais il me semble que tout ce qui n'est pas expressément défendu est permis.*"

"*Au contraire, m-r: tout ce qui n'est pas expressément permis est défendu.*"

Which translated is:

"I beg your pardon, sir, but it seems to me that everything that is not expressly prohibited is permitted."

"On the contrary, sir: everything that is not expressly permitted is prohibited."

This is a brief comic dialogue between a man of disorder and a man of order which took place in France. But the one who explains the meaning of order has been placed there to keep order; he interprets and defends it, and that is his function. But what is Levin's concern? What kind of a specialist in this area is he? All the while he's afraid some right may be lost. And meanwhile the entire People, sympathizing with the oppressed Christians, knew very well that they were right, that they were doing nothing against the will of their tsar and that in their hearts they were at one with their tsar. Yes, they knew that. Those who helped equip the volunteers thought exactly the same thing. Not one of them consoled himself, even in secret, with the absurd notion that he was undertaking something against the will of the government. The tsar's word was awaited with patience and high hopes, and everyone could sense beforehand what it would be, and they were not mistaken. The accusation about the declaration of war is, in short, a preposterous accusation that falls apart by itself and is impossible to sustain.

But Levin and the prince themselves do not include the People in this accusation. They flatly deny the People's participation in last year's movement; instead they flatly assert that the People understood nothing and, indeed, could understand nothing, that it all was something artificially stirred up by journalists in order to win subscribers, that it was deliberately fabricated by the Ragozovs, and so on:

> "Personal opinions are of no significance here," said Sergei Ivanovich. "Personal opinions are irrelevant when the whole of Russia—the People—have expressed their will."
>
> "I must beg your pardon. I don't see that. The People *don't know a thing about it,*" said the prince.
>
> "But papa. . . . How can they not know? What about last Sunday in church?" said Dolly, who was following the conversation. . . .
>
> "Well, what about last Sunday in church? The priest *had been ordered* to read that. He read it. They *understood nothing*; they sighed, *as they do at every sermon,*" the prince continued. "And then they were told that a collection was being taken in church for some worthy Christian cause, and so *they each took out a kopeck* and gave it. But what it was for *they have no idea*."

This is a ridiculous opinion that goes directly contrary to the facts, and it is easily explained coming from the mouth of the prince: the opinion comes from one of the former guardians of the People, a former serf-owner who, no matter how kind he may be, cannot help but despise his slaves and consider himself immeasurably superior to them in understanding: "They heaved a sigh," he says, "and understood nothing." But here is Levin's opinion; it, at least, is set forth by one who is not a former serf-owner:

> "I don't need to ask," said Sergei Ivanovich. "We've seen and are still seeing hundreds and hundreds of people who give up everything to serve a just cause; they come from all corners of Russia and they announce their idea and their aim plainly and clearly. They bring their few pennies or go off to serve themselves, and they tell you plainly why. What does that mean?"
>
> "It means, I think," said Levin, beginning to get excited, "that among a nation of eighty million you can always find, not hundreds, as now, but tens of thousands of people *who have lost their station in society, a reckless lot always ready for anything—to join Pugachev's gang, to go to Khiva, to Serbia. . . .*
>
> "I tell you it's not hundreds and they are not 'a reckless lot' but the finest representatives of the People!" said Sergei Ivanovich, as

> excited as if he were defending the last thing he possessed. "And what about the donations? Here, at least, we have the entire People directly expressing their will."
>
> "This word 'People' has such a broad meaning," said Levin. "Parish clerks, teachers, and perhaps one peasant in a thousand may know what's going on. The other eighty million, like our Mikhailych here, not only do not express their will, they haven't the least idea what they can express their will about. What right do we have, then, to say that this is the will of the People?"

But in general here it should be noted, once and for all, that the phrase "the will of the People" is utterly inappropriate in connection with last year's movement and serves absolutely nothing because it means precisely nothing. It was not the will of the People that showed itself last year, it was their great compassion, in the first place; and in the second place, it was their zeal for Christ; and in the third place, it was their own repentance, as it were, something akin to fasting before a sacrament—truly, one could put it that way. I'll explain this further on, but will add now that I'm very glad to hear, coming from Levin, such things about last year's volunteers as "*going off to join Pugachev's gang,*" and so on. At least these notions I certainly can't attribute to the author, which makes me very pleased, for I can see clearly that the author has stepped in to exercise his rights as an artist: he sensed all too well that the excited hypochondriac Levin, as a literary character he has created, could not help but be completely true to his character at the given moment of the argument; that's to say, he could not but end his remarks with a most insulting bit of abuse about both the volunteers and the Russian People who wished them well. Nevertheless, since there really did circulate an accusation that the People were stupid and obtuse for their movement of last year, and the reference to Pugachev's gang really was made, I've decided that this is a good place to try to explain, as briefly as possible, how we should understand the riddle of the *consciousness* of our People's movement last year to help the Slavs. For this really did pose a riddle to certain circles: "How can it be," they said; "the People heard about the Slavs only yesterday; they know nothing—neither geography nor history; and here, suddenly, they get all worked up over the Slavs; all of a sudden they've developed such devotion to them!" Aside from specific circles, some gray-haired old fellows—clubmen like the old prince—also fastened onto this topic; and, as we see, it pleased Levin as well, since it gave him grounds to sustain the explanation he gives about certain people artificially fabricating the movement for certain purposes. It's true that Sergei Ivanovich is set up against Levin as a kind of defender of the conscious purpose of the People's movement; but he defends his cause poorly, also grows excited, and, as I said, is generally depicted in a comic light. And yet this matter of the consciousness and clarity of the People's feelings toward the oppressed Christians is so clear and can be so accurately defined that I could not help but succumb to the temptation to explain how, in my view, we must understand this matter in order to avoid confusion and, particularly, to avoid *riddles*.

3. On the Uneducated and Illiterate Russian People's Unerring Knowledge of the Real Essence of the Eastern Question

From the very beginnings of the Russian People and their state, from the very time of the baptism of the Russian land, our pilgrims began setting forth to the holy lands, to the Holy Sepulcher, to Mount Athos, and so on. As early as the time of the Crusades, a Russian abbot traveled to Jerusalem and was received kindly by the king of Jerusalem, Baldwin, an event the abbot described beautifully in the account of his travels. Since then, pilgrimages to the holy places in the East have continued right up to our day. In Russia even now there are many monks who have lived at Mount Athos. And so the backward and totally uneducated Russian People—I mean even the most simple village peasants—who know nothing at all of history and geography still know very well, and have known for a long time, that the holy places and all the Eastern Christians who live in them have long been under the rule of godless Agarians, Mohammedans, and Turks and that all over the East the lives of Christians are extremely hard and difficult. The Russian People know this and feel afflicted at heart; and the Russian People's nature, historically, has been such that they have long put high value on pilgrimages to holy places made as acts of contrition. Their hearts have always drawn them there—it is a historical trait. People without a penny, old men, retired soldiers, old peasant women knowing nothing of geography, would leave their villages carrying a beggarly bundle on their back and would, indeed—sometimes after countless misfortunes—reach the

Holy Land. When they returned to their native soil the stories of their travels were listened to reverently. And on the whole, the Russian People are very fond of stories about "Godly things." Peasants, their children, townspeople, and even merchants would listen to these stories eagerly, tenderly, and with sighs. Now, to take one example, answer me this: who has read the *Lives of the Saints*? In the monasteries, a few people; among laymen, some professor who does it as a matter of duty or some eccentric old fellow who fasts and goes to vespers. It's even difficult to get a copy: you have to buy one, and just try borrowing it from your parish church—they won't give it to you. But now, if you can believe it, knowledge of the *Lives of the Saints* is common all over Russia—oh, not of the whole book, of course, but at least a knowledge of its spirit is common. Why is that so? Because there are a great many storytellers, both men and women, who tell about the lives of the saints. They tell stories from the *Lives* beautifully and accurately, without putting in a single superfluous word of their own; and they are listened to with delight. In childhood I myself heard such stories even before I learned to read. Later I heard these stories told even in prisons among robbers, and the robbers listened and sighed. The stories are not handed down by books but are learned orally. The Russian People find in these stories and in tales of the holy places something penitent and cleansing, so to say. Even bad, good-for-nothing people, those who practice usury and exploitation, often have a strange and irresistible urge to go off on a pilgrimage, to purify themselves through labor and noble deed, to fulfill some vow made long ago. If not to the East or to Jerusalem, then they would set off to the holy places of Russia, to Kiev, to the Solovetsky miracle-workers. Nekrasov, creating his great "Vlas," being a great artist, could not conceive of his character other than on a pilgrimage of repentance, wearing chains to humiliate his flesh. This trait in the life of our People is a historical one impossible to ignore, even if only because it no longer exists among any other European people. What will come of it is difficult to say, the more so as enlightenment is coming to our People as well, through schools and literacy, and new questions that may change a great deal will certainly arise. But for the present it is this and only this—I mean only this trait—that can solve the whole *riddle of consciousness* of last year's movement of our People to help "the Slavic brethren," as it was officially called last year and is now called almost scornfully. Our People really did know scarcely anything about the Slavs, and not only just one in a thousand, as Levin puts it, but one in many thousands, perhaps, had happened to hear anything about some Serbs, Montenegrins, and Bulgarians over there who shared our Orthodox faith. Yet our People, almost entirely or *in their overwhelming majority,* have heard and know that there are Orthodox Christians under the Mohammedan yoke, that they suffer and are tormented, and that even the very holy places themselves—Jerusalem, Mount Athos—belong to people of another faith. Even twenty years ago or more they could have heard of the torments of the Eastern Christians and the holy places lying in bondage when our late emperor began his war with Turkey and then with Europe—a war that ended with Sevastopol. At that same time, when the war began, word was passed from above about the holy places, and the People could have kept it in their memories since then. Besides, the atrocities against the Balkan Slavs began long before last year's surge of support for them, and almost a year before it was talked and written about in Russia; I myself heard how the People even then were asking: "Is it true that the Turk is rising up again?"

Besides (although this is a rather unlikely opinion), it still seems to me that the times also helped foster all this—last year's movement, I mean. It has been a rather long time, relatively speaking, since the liberation of the peasants took place, and now those years have passed—but what have the People seen in their midst? Among other things they have seen the spread of drunkenness, the increase in number of solidly established kulaks, misery all around them, and, often, the stamp of bestiality on themselves. Many—oh, very many, perhaps—have been afflicted at heart by a kind of anguish, a penitent anguish, an anguish of self-accusation and a quest for something better, something sacred. . . . And then, suddenly, a voice calls out about the oppression of Christians, martyrdom for the church and the faith; about Christians who give up their lives for Christ and who ascend the cross (since if they agreed to renounce the cross and accept Islam they would have all been spared and rewarded—the People were aware of that fact, of course). Appeals were made for contributions; then the word spread of a Russian general who had gone off to help the Christians; then the volunteers began to step forward—all these things jolted the People. And it really was a jolt, as I said earlier, that came as *an appeal to repentance, to preparation for a sacrament.* He who could not go himself brought his few pennies; but the volunteers went off with the good wishes of everyone, of the whole of Russia. The old prince, sitting in Karlsbad, could not understand this movement and came back to Russia, a humorous smile on his lips, when the movement was at its very peak. But then, how could this old fellow, a habitué of Moscow clubs, understand anything of Russia and the Russians? The clever Levin could understand much more, but he was led astray by the view that the People know nothing of history and geography and, most of all, by his anger that some Ragozovs or other were declaring war without even asking him. But there was no declaration of war, while on the People's part there was a kind of universal, emotional repentance, a longing to take part in something holy, in the cause of Christ, for the sake of those who were zealously bearing His cross—all those things happened. And so this movement was at once both penitential and historical.

Please do note that when I speak of this historical trait of the Russian People—I mean of their zeal for "Godly things," for the holy places, for oppressed Christians and, on the whole, for everything that is *penitent and Godly*—I certainly don't mean to praise the Russian People for it: I neither praise them nor blame them, but simply state a fact *that can explain a great deal.* What can we do if we possess such a *historical trait?* I don't know what will result from it, but it's very possible that something will. In the lives of peoples all the most important things always take shape in accordance with their most important and characteristic national peculiarities. *Every time* Russia has fought the Sultan, the historical trait I pointed out above seems thus far to have produced in the People a consciously national attitude to the war; thus there is no cause for surprise at the People's ardent participation in such a war, even though they know nothing of history and geography. What they need to know, they know. Oh, our People are illiterate know-nothings, of that there's no doubt; and even in a moral sense there are many excellent and most enlightened things they could be taught about this deeply ingrained and ancient historical trait of theirs. They could be shown that all their wanderings and pilgrimages represent but a narrow understanding of their duty and obligations; that there is no need to travel so far to look for something good; that it would be better if they were to abandon their drunkenness and pay some attention to increasing their own well-being, build up some economic assets, not beat their wives, look after schools, highways, and so on—in short, that they should at least in some way help Russia, their fatherland, at last to begin to resemble other "enlightened European states."

Finally, one could explain to the pilgrim that God does not require him to travel to holy places because, above all, it benefits neither him nor his family nor anyone else but, rather, causes only damage, for when he travels and is absent for a long time he abandons his home and his homeland for what is in essence a selfish purpose—the salvation of his own soul—whereas God would be much more pleased were he to spend his free time doing something to benefit those around him: he might work in his garden, tend to his calves, and so on. In short, there are many fine things he might be told; however, what can be done if this historical trait has taken shape in precisely this manner and the quest for the good has assumed among our People *almost this form exclusively,* i.e., a *penitent* form, as pilgrimage or sacrifice? At least the clever Levin, while awaiting "enlightenment," might credit the People with this *historical trait of theirs.* He might realize, at least, that many volunteers and the People who sent them on their way were acting from worthy motives and were hoping to do something good (that cannot be disputed!); and so, in any case, these were fine representatives of the People—not "dazzlingly enlightened," of course, but also not desperate people, not reckless people, not idle trash, not windbags; on the contrary, they may even have been the best among the People. This cause was presented openly as the cause of Christ, and for many—for very many, in the deep recesses of their souls—it was specifically regarded as a matter of purification and penitence. And not a single one of them felt any guilt toward his tsar about this cause! On the contrary, he knew that the Tsar-Liberator's merciful heart was at one with his People. Everyone was waiting, with deep emotion and hope, to learn the will of the tsar and to hear his word, while we, sitting in our own corners, quietly rejoiced that the great Russian People had justified our great and eternal hope in them. And therefore, how can one, in any sense whatsoever, compare these people and their noble, humble movement with Pugachev's gang, the commune, and so on! It's only just such a hypochondriac as Levin, irritated to the point of agitation, who could make such a claim. That's what it means to be a touchy person!

4. Levin's Agitation. A Question: Does Distance Have an Influence on Love for Humanity? Can One Agree with the Opinion of One Turkish Prisoner on the Humaneness of Some of Our Ladies? So What, Then, Are Our Teachers Teaching Us?

But his agitation goes still further: Levin flatly and exasperatingly proclaims that there can be no compassion toward the torments of the Slavs, that "*there is no immediate feeling for the oppression of the Slavs, and there cannot be any.*" Sergei Ivanovich says:

> ". . . There is no declaration of war here, only an expression of humane, Christian feeling. Our brothers, of our blood and our faith, are being killed. Now suppose they were not our brothers and not of our faith but simply women, children, and old people; feeling is aroused and Russians run off to help put an end to these horrors. Just imagine if you were walking along the street and saw some drunken men beating a woman or a child; I think you wouldn't stop to ask whether or not a war had been declared on those men; you would simply rush at them and defend the victim."
>
> "But I wouldn't kill them," said Levin.
>
> "But you might."
>
> "I don't know. If I should see such a thing, I might yield to my immediate feeling; *but I can't say that beforehand*. But there is no such immediate feeling for the oppression of the Slavs, and there cannot be any."
>
> "Perhaps there isn't any for you. But it exists for others," said Sergei Ivanovich, frowning with displeasure. "Among the People there still survive the legends of Orthodox Christians suffering under the yoke of the 'godless Agarians.' The People have heard of the sufferings of their brethren and they have spoken."
>
> "That may be," said Levin evasively, "but I don't see it; *I'm one of the People myself,* and I don't feel it."

Again we have "I'm one of the People myself." I repeat once more: it's only been two hours since this Levin got his faith from a peasant—or at least the peasant gave him the idea of how to believe. I am not praising the peasant or disparaging Levin and, indeed, won't now undertake to decide which of them had the better faith and whose soul was in the higher and more developed state, etc., etc. But you have to agree, I repeat, that this very fact alone should have led Levin to realize that there is a certain *fundamental* difference between him and the People. And then he says: "I'm one of the People myself." But why is he so certain that he's one of the People himself? Because he knows how to harness a horse to a cart and knows that cucumbers with honey make tasty eating. Such people! And what vanity, what pride, what arrogance!

Yet this isn't the most important thing. Levin insists that *there is not and cannot be* any immediate feeling for the oppression of the Slavs. Sergei Ivanovich objects that "the People have heard of the sufferings of their brethren and they have spoken"; Levin replies: "That may be, but I don't see it; I'm one of the People myself, *and I don't feel it.*"

Does he mean he doesn't feel compassion? Note that Levin's argument with Sergei Ivanovich about compassion and immediate feeling for the oppression of the Slavs is developed with a bias, as if it were intended to end with Levin's victory. For instance, Sergei Ivanovich does his best to argue that, were Levin to be walking along and see some drunken men beating a woman, he would rush to save her. "But I wouldn't kill them!" Levin objects. "But you might," insists Sergei Ivanovich and, of course, he's talking nonsense, because would anyone helping out a woman being beaten by drunkards have to kill those drunkards? She could be rescued without any killing. But the main thing is that this certainly isn't a matter of some street brawl; the comparison is false and without basis. They are talking about the Slavs, about the torments, tortures, and massacres they suffer, and Levin knows full well they are talking about the Slavs. Accordingly, when he says that he doesn't know whether he would help, that he doesn't see anything and *doesn't feel anything,* etc., etc., he is stating plainly that he feels no compassion for the torments of the Slavs (and not for the torments of a woman beaten up by drunken men) and he insists that there is not, and cannot be, any immediate feeling for the sufferings of the Slavs. In fact that is literally what he says.

There is a rather interesting psychological fact here. The book came out only two and a half months ago, and two and a half months ago it was already very well known that all the countless stories of the countless torments and tortures of the Slavs were the absolute truth—a truth to which thousands of informants and eyewitnesses of all nations can now attest. What we have learned over the last year and a half about the tortures suffered by the Slavs goes beyond the fantasies of even the sickest and most frenzied imagination. We know, first, that these massacres are not incidental but systematic, instigated deliberately, and encouraged in every way. People are being exterminated by the thousands and tens of thousands. Tortures have been refined to such a degree as we have not read or heard of before. The skin is stripped from living people while their children watch; children are tossed in the air and caught on the point of a bayonet while their mothers watch; women are raped, and during the act the woman is stabbed with a dagger; worst of all, infants are tortured and abused. Levin says that he feels *nothing* and recklessly affirms that there is no immediate feeling for the oppression of the Slavs and there cannot be any. But I venture to assure Mr. Levin that there can be such a feeling and that I myself have witnessed it on more than one occasion. For instance, I saw one gentleman who does not like talking about his feelings but who, when he heard how one two-year-old boy had his eyes pierced with a needle while his sister watched and was then impaled on a stake so that he did not die quickly but screamed for a long time—when he heard that, this gentleman almost fell ill, did not sleep that night, and for two days thereafter was so depressed and worn-out that he could not work. In this regard, I venture to assure Mr. Levin that this gentleman is an honest person and is certainly a respectable one; he is certainly not "idle trash" and is far from being a member of Pugachev's gang. I wanted only to state that immediate feeling for the torments of the Slavs can exist, feeling of even the strongest kind, and even in all classes of society. But Levin insists that *there cannot even be* any feeling and that he himself feels *nothing*. For me, that is an enigma. Of course, there are people who are simply unfeeling, coarse, and perverted. But Levin, it seems, is not such a person; he is depicted as altogether a sensitive man. Is it simply the distance that influences the matter? In fact, does this *psychological* peculiarity exist in some characters: "I can't see it myself," they say; "it's happening far away, and so I don't feel a thing." Jokes aside, just imagine that there are people living on the planet Mars and that they are piercing the eyes of some infants there. Do you think we'd feel any pity here on earth, any great amount of pity, at least? The same thing happens on earth, perhaps, when very great distances are involved: "Ah, it's happening in another hemisphere, not right here!" I mean to say, he may not state that frankly but that's how he feels—he feels *nothing*, in other words. In that case, if distance really does have such an influence on humaneness, then a new question arises of itself: at what distance does love of humanity end? And Levin really does pose a great enigma in terms of love of humanity. He states flatly that *he does not know* whether he would kill: "If I should see such a thing, I might yield to my immediate feeling; but I can't say that beforehand."

So he doesn't know what he would do! And yet, he's a sensitive man, and so, as a sensitive man, he's afraid to kill . . . a Turk. Imagine such a scene: Levin is standing right there, with rifle and fixed bayonet, and two paces away a Turk is voluptuously holding a needle, ready to pierce the eyes of the child already in his arms. The boy's seven-year-old sister screams and rushes madly to tear him away from the Turk. And here stands Levin, thinking and hesitating: "I don't know what I'll do. I don't feel anything. I'm one of the People myself. There isn't any immediate feeling for the oppression of the Slavs and there cannot be any."

But, seriously, what would he have done after all the things he's told us? How could he not save the child? Would he really let the child be tortured? Would he really not snatch him from the hands of the villainous Turk?

"Well, yes, I'd snatch him away, but suppose I had to give the Turk a good hard push?"

"Then push him!"

"Push him, you say! And if he doesn't want to let the child go and draws his saber? Why, suppose I had to kill the Turk?"

"Well then, kill him!"

"But how can I kill him! No, I mustn't kill the Turk. No, it's better to let him pierce the child's eyes and torture him; I'll go home to Kitty."

That's what Levin would do; it emerges directly from his convictions and from all that he says. He says frankly that he *does not know* whether he would help the woman or the child if he had to kill a Turk to do so. And he's awfully sorry for the Turks.

> "Twenty years ago we would have kept silent" [says Sergei Ivanovich], but now we hear the voice of the Russian People, ready to rise up as one man, ready to sacrifice themselves for their oppressed brethren; that's a great step forward and a token of strength."
>
> "It's not only a matter of sacrificing themselves, though, but of killing Turks," Levin said meekly. "The People make their donations and are prepared to make more for the sake of their souls, but not for the sake of murder. . . ."

In other words: "Here you are, little girl, we donate this money for the sake of our souls; your little brother will just have to have his eyes pierced. We can't kill a Turk. . . ."

And then, later on, the author himself says of Levin: "He could not agree that a dozen people, including his brother, should have the right to say, on the basis of what they had been told by a couple of hundred volunteer rabble rousers who were swarming into the cities, that they and the newspapers were expressing the will and the ideas of the People, especially when it was an idea *that expressed itself through vengeance and murder*."

This is unjust: there is no *vengeance* involved here at all. We are now at war with these bloodthirsty Turks and we hear only of the the most humane actions on the Russian side. One can confidently say that there are not many European armies that would treat such an enemy the way our army is now treating them. Only recently two or three of our newspapers suggested that it might be more advantageous, specifically with a view to reducing the number of atrocities, to take reprisals against Turks who were clearly responsible for atrocities and torture. They murder prisoners and wounded after subjecting them to ghastly tortures such as cutting off noses and other organs. Specialists in the extermination of nursing infants have appeared among them, experts who seize the child by both legs and at once tear it in half, to the amusement and laughter of their comrades, the bashibazouks. This nation, steeped in lies and villainy, denies the atrocities it has committed. The Sultan's ministers assure us that there can be no slaughter of prisoners since "the Koran forbids it." Not long ago the humane German emperor indignantly rejected the official, sweeping, and false complaint of the Turks about the supposed savagery of the Russians and declared that he did not believe it. It would seem impossible to treat this contemptible nation in a humane manner, but we are treating them humanely. I'll even venture to express my personal view that it would be best not to resort to reprisals against Turks found guilty of murdering prisoners and wounded. This would hardly diminish their savagery. It's said that even now, when they are taken prisoner, they look frightened and suspicious, *firmly convinced* that their heads will be cut off at once. It would be better not to have the Russians' noble and humane conduct of this war besmirched by reprisals. But piercing the eyes of infants must not be allowed; and for this infamy to be stopped forever the oppressed peoples must be promptly liberated and the tyrants disarmed once and for all. Don't worry: once they've been disarmed they'll start making and selling dressing gowns and soap as our Kazan Tatars did—which I've spoken about already. But taking away their weapons means engaging them in battle. But battle is not vengeance; Levin need not worry about the Turk.

Even last year Levin would have had no need to worry about the Turk. Does he not know the Russian, the Russian soldier? Just now there are reports that though the soldier may stab the vicious Turk in battle, he has more than once shared his soldier's ration with a Turkish captive, fed him, and taken pity on him, as eyewitnesses have observed. And, believe me, our little soldier knew everything about the Turk; he knew that were he to fall into his hands, this same captive Turk would have cut off his head and used it, along with the other severed heads of prisoners, to fashion a crescent, and in its center would have made an obscene star out of other severed limbs. Our little soldier knows all this and he still feeds the captive Turk exhausted by the battle: "He's a human being, too, even if he's not a Christian." The correspondent of an English newspaper said, when he witnessed such incidents, "This is an army of gentlemen." And Levin, better than many others, ought to know that this truly is an army of gentlemen. When the Bulgarians in some towns asked His Highness, the Commander-in-Chief, what they were to do with the property of the Turks who had fled, he replied, "Collect the property and keep it until they return; harvest their fields and keep the grain, taking a third of it as recompense for your labor." These are the words of a gentleman and, I repeat, Levin need not worry about the Turk: is there any sign of vengeance here? Any reprisals? Moreover, Levin, who knows Russian society in such detail, might also consider that the Turk will be spared also through our false Europeanism and the absurd, artificial, and single-minded sentimentalism so common in our educated society. Has Levin heard about our ladies who throw flowers to Turkish prisoners being transported in railway carriages and bring them expensive tobacco and sweets? There was a report that as a train pulled out, one Turk loudly hawked and energetically spat into the very midst of a group of humane Russian ladies who were waving their handkerchiefs in farewell to the departing train. Of course, it's difficult to agree entirely with the opinion of this insensitive Turk, and Levin might consider that the kindness of ladies toward the Turks was merely hysterical sentimentalizing and pseudoliberal Europeanism: "Just look at how humane we are, and what advanced Europeans we are, and how well we can display it!" But what about Levin? Doesn't he expound and express the same single-mindedness and the same sentimental Europeanizing? Turks are being killed in war, in honorable battle, not for *vengeance* but only *because* there is no other way to wrest their dishonorable weapons from their hands. That was so last year as well. And if we do not take away their weapons and—so as to avoid killing them—simply go away, then they will at once begin again to cut off women's breasts and poke out children's eyes. What's to be done? To let them poke out eyes, just so we can avoid somehow killing a Turk? But that's surely a distorted understanding of things; that's the most obtuse and gross sentimentalizing; that's fanatical single-mindedness; that's utter and total perversion of nature. Furthermore, the soldier who is compelled to kill a Turk is himself bearing his own life in sacrifice and, besides, endures suffering and tribulation. Was it to seek vengeance, was it only to commit murders that the Russian People rose up? And when was it that helping whole provinces of those being massacred and exterminated, helping women and children who are being violated and who have no one else on earth to stand up for them—when was it that this was considered a crude, ridiculous, almost immoral action, a thirst for vengeance and blood? And what a lack of feeling, side by side with sentimentalism! Why, Levin himself has a child, a little boy; surely he loves him; and when this child is given a bath, why it's a regular event in the household; so why doesn't his heart bleed when he hears and reads about mass killings, about children with crushed heads crawling after their raped mothers, about murdered women with breasts cut off? This happened in one Bulgarian church, where two hundred such corpses were found after the city had been plundered. Levin reads all this and stands thinking: "Kitty is in fine spirits and had a good appetite today; we've given the boy a bath and he's begun to recognize me; what do I care what goes on over there in another hemisphere? *There is no immediate feeling for the oppression of the Slavs and there cannot be any,* because I don't feel *anything.*"

Is this how Levin ends his epic? Is he the one the author wants to set forth as an example of a righteous and honorable man? People like the author of *Anna Karenina* are the teachers of society, our teachers, while we are merely their pupils. So what is it, then, that they are teaching us?

September

1

1. The Unfortunate and Unsuccessful

It's hard to imagine anyone more unfortunate than the French republicans with their French republic. It will soon be a hundred years since this institution first appeared in the world, and during that period every time (it's the third time now) some cunning usurpers have taken over the republic and used it for their own ends, no one—aside from a few marginal groups—has made any serious effort to defend it. Never once was there any strong support from the whole population. Even in the periods when the republic did have a life there were few who regarded it as a final and not a transitory thing. Nevertheless, no one believes more strongly that the country supports them than do the French republicans.

However, in the first two attempts to create a republic in France—in the last century and in 1848—there still might have been some grounds for the republicans of the day to count on the country's support for them, especially in the early stages of their attempts. It would seem, though, that the republicans we see today—the very ones who, along with their republic, will be taken over and used by someone else—could have no hope for an assured future even if the country does show some support for them (a very shaky support, however, since they exist now only in a negative sense—as the proverb has it, when the fishing's poor, even crayfish count). And yet, virtually on the eve of their collapse, they are convinced they will win a complete victory. But what unfortunate people they are, and what an unfortunate thing this last, third republic was, a republic which, though it may have been accepted by the late Thiers, was accepted just the way a crayfish is when the fishing's poor!

We have only to remember how this third republic came into being. These republicans had been waiting almost twenty years for the "glorious" moment of the usurper's downfall, when they would again be "summoned by the country." And what happened? Having seized power after Sedan, these unfortunate fellows were compelled to take on their shoulders the burden of a terrible war they had not wanted but with which the usurper rewarded them before leaving to smoke cigarettes in the charming castle of Wilhelmshöhe. And if this cunning usurper, strolling along the paths of the gardens of the German castle, was furious at them for again seizing his power, then he must certainly also have had moments when he smiled a malicious smile to himself, thinking of the vengeance he had taken on them by heaping his guilt on their weak shoulders. Because, no matter what happened, France later blamed them rather than him (or at least they blamed them more than they did him) because they were the ones who carried on a hopeless war, they were not able to make a peace as soon as they assumed power, they gave away two large provinces and three billion francs, they devastated the country, they conducted the war incompetently, and they ran the country in a hit-and-miss, disorderly way lacking all control. The former dictator, Gambetta, is still accused of these things even though he is guilty of none of them; rather, he did all anyone could do under the terrible conditions of the time. In short, this accusation of the incompetence of the republicans and their ruining of the country persisted and persists very seriously and strongly even now. Everyone may realize that the Emperor Napoleon was the major cause of the calamity, "But what about them?" everyone says; "why weren't they able to patch things up once they had taken on the job? What's worse, they made a far bigger mess of things"—that's the accusation! But this accusation was not all: when people thought of the bind the republicans had gotten into at the very start when they seized power, they were seen as contemptible and ridiculous; yet what else could they have done? Not to accept this war, to make peace at the very beginning, after seizing power and after Sedan, was quite impossible: even then the Germans would have demanded territorial concessions and money, and what would have happened to the republicans had they made peace under such conditions? They would have been plainly accused of pusillanimity, of disgracing the country, of not fighting "while they still had an army" but surrendering disgracefully. That would have been a fine stamp to put on their new republic! And since the republic and its restoration in France meant everything to them and was much dearer than the salvation of the country, they were compelled to wage war while almost clearly sensing that they would come to even greater disgrace when the war ended. And so, disgrace lay ahead of them and disgrace lay behind them—a situation that was not only unfortunate, not only tragic, but, in a certain sense, even comic, for that was not at all the way they had imagined they would assume power after the "tyrant"!

The comic aspect of the situation was intensified even more by the fact that they still assumed power with light hearts, despite everything that was going on; I don't mean to say that they didn't grieve over France—oh, among them were some men of exquisite sensibility and even some genuine servants of their fatherland, so long as that fatherland is called a republic. There may even be some one or another among them who is willing to let the republic take second place so long as France is happy (although it's not likely there are such, apart from literally one or two—no more). But the fact is that no sooner had they come to terms with the Germans and settled down to run the country in peace when they at once got the notion that the country was hopelessly in love with them, to say the least. That's what was comical! Every French republican certainly holds the fateful and pernicious conviction that the word *republic* itself is enough, that it is enough merely to call the country a republic and it will at once live happily ever after. All the failures of the republic they always ascribe merely to adverse external circumstances, the presence of usurpers or evil people, and never once have they thought of the unbelievable weakness of the roots that hold the republic to the soil of France, roots that for a whole hundred years have been unable to grow stronger and penetrate more deeply. Furthermore, the republicans have never once in these six years realized that their comic situation, inherited from Napoleon III, continues even now, and that if the old disaster has passed, a new one is drawing near, similar to the old and which will certainly place them an a *most* comical position, such that they will no longer be able to hold on in France; and this may happen in the very near future. This new bit of drollery lies in the fact that the disaster to come, just as before, consists in their carrying out a lofty duty of service to the fatherland that *consciously* works to its ruination; furthermore, just as before, this disaster is utterly unavoidable and consists of almost exactly the same kind of bind as the one they got into in 1871; and finally, to cap it all, just as before they have received it as a legacy from that same Napoleon III whom they so hate and whose memory they so profane.

In fact, who is now the world's most zealous devotee of the French republic and the man most sympathetic to its institution? Without a doubt, Prince Bismarck. As long as a republic exists in France, a war of "revenge" is impossible. Just try to imagine the republicans daring to declare war on the Germans again! Prince Bismarck understands this. And meanwhile, it's as clear as day that the enormous, forty-million organism that is France cannot remain eternally under a disgraceful German trusteeship. The wounds will be healed; the shock will be forgotten; new forces will come on the scene; health will be regained; the means and the armies will be created—and can a country that has so long held first place politically among the nations fail to aspire to its former role and former position in Europe? This moment, perhaps, is now not very far away; the excess of inner strength must certainly prompt her to break away from Bismarck's trusteeship and restore all her former *independence* (France can still not be called independent in any way now). And so the whole of France, from the moment she takes her first new step, would hit her head against her republic. Once more I repeat: can you imagine the present republicans doing anything to insult Prince Bismarck and even going so far as to risk war with him? In the first place, who would follow them, even if France herself wanted a war? And in the second place, there comes an inescapable consideration: what if the Germans crush them once again? Why, then there would be an end to the republic in France once and for all, because France would blame them for the defeat and would drive them out for good, having forgotten that she herself wanted "revenge" and a return to her former dominance. . . . But should the republicans hold firm; should they not heed the new voices and cries; should they not declare war—this would mean going against the aspirations of the country, and then the country would again turn them out and surrender to the first artful leader who came along. In short, there is a Sedan behind them and a Sedan in front of them! And meanwhile, they certainly haven't even begun to think about this, despite the fact that a new upsurge of feeling in the country is, perhaps, very close at hand. They have never realized, either, that they are in essence no more than "protégés" of Prince Bismarck and that as each year passes, France must be becoming more and more aware of this, particularly as she restores herself and builds up her strength; accordingly, she must despise them more and more, silently at first and not so obviously, but then much more obviously and, at last, out loud and not merely silently.

But the republicans will not admit their comic aspect. These are pathetic people. Rather, it is at this very time that they have taken courage, after MacMahon, the president of the "republic," turned them out of office and locked the Chamber until the new elections in October. Now they are "persecuted," and so they think they are wearing halos; they're waiting for the whole of France suddenly to start singing the Marseillaise and shout: "*On assassine nos frères*" ("They're murdering our brothers!")—the well-known cry of all the former Paris street revolutions, after which the mobs usually rushed off to build barricades. In any case, they are waiting for "legality"; that's to say, they're waiting for the country, indignant with Marshal MacMahon, a newly hatched future usurper, to elect all the former republican majority to the Chamber again and add some new republican deputies besides; and then the newly assembled Chamber will pronounce its strict veto on the marshal and he, frightened of legality, will tuck in his tail and retire. They are unshakeably convinced of the force of this "legality"; and this is not because of any lack of mental capacity but because these good people are too much men of their own party; they've been fussing over the same thing for too long and have spent too much time sitting in the same corner. They have suffered too long for their beloved republic, and for that reason are confident of retribution. Astonishingly enough, many of our newspapers in Russia also believe that their triumph is near and that "legality" will inevitably win. But how is this legality guaranteed if MacMahon does not deign to submit to it, as he has already indicated to the country in his surprising manifesto? By the indignation and anger of the country? But the marshal will soon find many supporters in this same country, as has always been the case in similar situations in France. What's to be done then? Build barricades? But given the rifles and the artillery of today, the old barricades are of no use. And, indeed, France would refuse to build barricades even if she really did want a republic. Exhausted and worn-out by a century of political disarray, she will reckon most prosaically where the strength is and will submit to strength. The strength is now in the *legions*, and the country senses this. And so the whole question is: on whose side are the legions?

2. A Curious Character

The legions, as a new force coming to take its place in European civilization, I have already discussed in my May and June diary;

this was well before the manifesto of the marshal-president, and now it has all happened as I then thought it would. In this manifesto, which astonished everyone, the marshal did promise to observe legality and did promise peace, etc., yet at the same time, right there, he says plainly that if the country does not concur with his opinion and in the forthcoming elections sends him the same old republican majority as before, he, in turn, will be compelled not to concur with the opinion of the country and not to submit to its choices. The marshal must have some motive to act in such a surprising way. He could not speak to the country in that language and that tone (France isn't some village, after all) were he not firmly confident of his power and success. And so now it's already clear that all his hopes rest on the army, in which he has complete confidence. And in fact, during his summer travels through France the marshal met with a rather ambiguous reception in many towns and provinces—all too many, it seems; but the army and the navy everywhere showed their complete loyalty and greeted the marshal with shouts of support. There is no reason to doubt the marshal's good and even innocent, so to say, feelings. If he acted in a manner so contrary to his usual practice in plainly declaring in advance that he would not heed the legally expressed opinion of the country should the country not heed him, then of course it was only because he wished, in his own way, to promote the well-being of his country and was confident that he would promote it. And so it is not the marshal's moral qualities that should cause us doubt, but certain of his other ones. . . . And truly, it seems that the marshal is one of those characters who cannot help being under someone's supervision, and from this aspect his character shows certain remarkable peculiarities. Here's a question, for instance: for whom is he now working? For whom is he making such efforts and for whom is he taking such risks? There's no doubt that he is under complete supervision, and yet I am confident (this is still just my personal opinion, however) that he is the only one in all of Europe still completely convinced that he is not under anyone's supervision at all and is acting on his own. The adroit people who have taken hold of him no doubt encourage this conviction of his for the time being; they go to any lengths to appear to be yea-sayers, meanwhile turning him in any direction they choose. They can do all this, of course, because they have a very good knowledge of characters like his and their vanity. But adroit people like this can be found only in one party—in the immense and powerful clerical party, it's true.

None of the other political parties in France can boast such adroitness.

The question, then, is: if the marshal is under supervision, then under whose? It's common knowledge now that the Bonapartists are awfully excited, that they have nominated a lot of candidates, that those candidates are under the patronage of the marshal himself, that they are confident of victory in the elections and confident in the army, that the imperial prince has already gone to the Continent and people even say that he will go to Paris. Yet can one really believe that Marshal MacMahon, such a self-assured president of a "republic," will take on a load of troubles and dangers like this simply in order to enthrone the imperial prince? It seems to me (and once again this is entirely my personal opinion)—it seems to me that he will not. But maybe there are quite special schemes of some sort—for instance, a certain rumor that went around the newspapers about a month ago that the imperial prince was engaged to the marshal's daughter, and so on. But if there are no such special, secret schemes, if there exist no special agreements and treaties, then it seems to me that the marshal is rather inclined to oblige the country in *his* favor rather than anyone else's; and if he is supporting the Bonapartist candidates, then he is sure that they are more reliable than the others and that he will subsequently be able to turn them in whatever direction he pleases. God knows what thoughts might be born in a mind such as his. It's not for nothing that a certain bishop, in his speech introducing the marshal, told him that he was a descendant of Charlemagne on his maternal side. In short, a few years being president may actually have stirred up certain nagging and fantastic ideas in him. Besides, he is a military man. However, all these thoughts are only speculatory attempts to explain a puzzling character. For the moment, the truth is that the marshal is in the hands of the clericals and that they are directing him even though he, no doubt, goes on thinking that it's he who is directing them and they are in his hands and not he in theirs. But, of course, they are not in his hands, and the fate of France at the present moment seems certainly to depend on them and *on them alone.* There is no doubt that a terrible underground intrigue still continues, and though the whole of Europe has long known, and has known from the very beginning, that the clericals are playing a large role in the present western European movement, still it seems that they have managed until now to hide *the extent and the strength of this role;* they maneuver and hide behind others for the time being—behind the marshal, for instance, and behind the Bonapartists; and so the matter will continue until they achieve the goal they have in mind. In essence, it doesn't matter to them whether success goes to the marshal or to the imperial prince. They have no personal sympathies and must not have any. For them there is but one task: that France should draw her sword as soon as possible and fling herself on Germany. And so it was with this in mind that they crushed the republicans, who were incapable of standing up to support the pope. Now they are quietly and cleverly waiting to see who has the better prospects. If the imperial prince really does offer them greater prospects in terms of a declaration of war, then, perhaps, they will fasten onto him and accompany him to Paris with no more thought of MacMahon. But for the moment it seems that they are still hanging onto the marshal.

By the way, not long ago there was a report that the marshal observed in conversation, "Rumors are being spread that I want to destroy republican institutions, but people forget, of course, that when I accepted the presidency of the republic I gave my word to preserve these institutions." These words can serve as solid support for my supposition about the marshal's moral innocence, despite all the accusations of the republicans. As an honorable and military man, his word of honor is precious to him and, of course, he will not violate it. But if he preserves the republic and at the same time sends the republicans packing, then it means he intends to continue the republic without any republicans. One has to think that such really is his political program and that he has been assured that it is entirely possible. This program, along with the motto *J'y suis et j'y reste* ("I am here and I am staying"), evidently constitutes the whole cycle of his political convictions right up to the year 1880, when his term of presidency, and therefore his word of honor, runs out. But at that point a new vision arises: "A grateful country, seeing him step down from the presidency, offers him a new position to save it from the demagogues—the position of a Charlemagne, say; and then everything will again run as smoothly as silk." The inevitable result here is that the crafty people behind him will, should he in fact decide to fulfill his word of honor and preserve the republican institutions, immediately exchange him for Bonaparte if the preserved republic, even without republicans, stands in the way of their further plans. It seems they had that in mind when they induced him to support the Bonapartist candidates after assuring him that this would be good for him. In any case, he continues to be under supervision so strict that he will never be able to wriggle out of it. In short, the world is facing some momentous and utterly new events; one can foresee the appearance of the legions and the enormous Catholic movement. The reports are that the health of the pope is "satisfactory." But there will be a disaster if the pope's death coincides with the elections in France or happens immediately after them. Then the Eastern Question could at once be transformed into an all-European one. . . .

3. That's It, Yet It Isn't It. A Reference to What I Wrote Three Months Ago

I set forth this idea of mine in some detail in the May and June issue of the *Diary*, but no one, it seems, paid attention to the main thing in my article—i.e., that the whole key to the present and future events of all of Europe *lies in the Catholic conspiracy* and in the forthcoming, certain, and enormous Catholic movement that will come with the death of the pope, which in all likelihood is imminent, and the election of a new one; but no one paid attention to this and my article passed unnoticed (in the press).

Yet now I hold to that same opinion even more strongly and confidently than two months ago. Since then there have been so many events that have supported my hypothesis that now I can no longer doubt its validity. Since then even the newspapers, both our own and the foreign ones, have begun to make some references to this topic, but still without venturing to state a final conclusion. This is what the *Moscow News* said in its excellent editorial in issue No. 235. Among other things it quotes the view of some English newspaper correspondents:

> Correspondents of English newspapers are providing some very frank explanations. The key to European politics, in their understanding, is in the hands of Germany, and Germany is disposed to side with Russia even more firmly than before, for reasons that are quite understandable. In the first place, Berlin has seen that the failures of Russian strategy have inspired and encouraged Austria who, they suppose, still bears a certain grudge against Prussia. Furthermore, Germany's main enemies are France and Catholicism, and both these forces still bestow all their sympathy on the Turkish side. It is true that when the disturbances began in the East, France did engage

in a brief flirtation with Russia; but if she did have a certain sympathy for us then, it has now not only cooled but has shifted entirely to the side of the Turks. As far as militant Catholicism is concerned, everyone knows that not only now but from the very beginning it has decidedly and passionately taken Moslem Turkey rather than schismatic Russia under its protection. The indecency of zealous clericals reached the point where one of them spoke of the Koran with a certain tenderness, so that even ultramontane "Germania" found it necessary to curb such antics with the observation that though one must rejoice at the victories of the Turks over the hateful Russians, it was still rather gauche to express direct praise for Islam. Since the *mot d'ordre* of Catholicism coincides so remarkably with the shift in French public opinion in favor of the Turks, and since Austria, also a Catholic country, has interests opposed to Russian ones, Berlin naturally dreads the possibility of such a Catholic and anti-Prussian league into which ultramontane and separatist interests of southern Germany and "even England" might later be drawn. That is how English correspondents view it, but undoubtedly the leading role in these intrigues is being played by England.

And so, as before, we are left to confront Turkey alone.

All this is very fine, yet that's still not it; it's not the real and final word of explanation which, astonishingly enough, no one seems to want to say and which no one even seems to sense in all its fullness. However, this article did take up the issue of *militant Catholicism* and the significance of Catholicism in Bismarck's eyes; its current influence in France; and, finally, even the *league* and the fact that *Berlin naturally dreads the possibility of such a Catholic and anti-Prussian league into which ultramontane and separatist interests of Southern Germany and "even England" might later be drawn.* Now it was about such a league, about a Catholic *conspiracy,* that I spoke just over two months before others raised the topic; but then I did say my final and concluding word, i.e., that the whole point lies in the conspiracy, that everything in Europe now depends on it, and that the Eastern war itself may very soon be transformed into an all-European war solely as a result of this enormous conspiracy of dying Roman Catholicism. Meanwhile, in these "correspondents' opinions" and in the entire excellent article in the *Moscow News,* there still seems to be no wish to admit this idea; instead, the article maintains that "undoubtedly the leading role in these intrigues is being played by England" and that we "*as before, are left to confront Turkey alone.*" But is that so? Are we alone? Will we not, rather, in the very near future suddenly find ourselves alone confronting not just Turkey but the whole of Europe?

In fact, what is this "militant Catholicism" that everyone has already begun to notice and recognize in current events? What is the source of this militancy that causes Catholicism, even "passionately," to take Moslem Turkey rather than schismatic Russia under its "protection"? Is it all really only because "Russia is a schismatic country"? At the present moment, Catholicism has so many problems and immediate concerns that it has no time to think about all these ancient clerical altercations. And, most important, what is the origin of this "Catholic league" that is so feared in Berlin? Well, it was about all these things that I spoke in detail over two months ago when I tried to explain them. And my conclusion was that this league, whose existence other people as well now admit, is a solid and tightly organized Catholic *conspiracy* now existing all over Europe and aiming at the restoration of Rome's worldly dominance; that this conspiracy will have an immense influence on all current events in Europe; and that, accordingly, the key to all the contemporary *intrigues* lies neither there or here, nor only in England, but precisely in this undeniable, universal Catholic conspiracy!

Militant Catholicism intensely "and passionately" takes the side of the Turks against us. And even in England, even in Hungary, there is no one at the moment who hates Russia as intensely as these militant clericals. It was not some prelate but the pope himself who, loudly, in meetings at the Vatican, spoke joyously "of the victories of the Turks" and prophesied "a terrible future" for Russia. This dying old man who is, after all, "the head of Christianity," was not ashamed to say publicly that he is happy every time he hears of a Russian defeat. This passionate hatred becomes entirely comprehensible when one admits that Roman Catholicism is now actually "mobilized" and that, in deed—*by the sword*, I mean—it is now conducting a war in Europe against its dreaded and fatal enemies. But who in Europe is now the most dreaded enemy of Roman Catholicism, i.e., of the worldly monarchy of the pope? There is no disputing that it is Prince Bismarck. Rome itself was taken away from the pope at the very moment of the greatness of Germany and Bismarck, a moment when Germany crushed the main defender of the papacy at the time, France, and in so doing immediately freed the hands of the Italian king, who at once occupied Rome. Since then, the entire concern of Catholicism has been to seek out an enemy and rival for Germany and Prince Bismarck. Prince Bismarck, for his part, has long been keenly aware that Roman papal Catholicism is, besides, the eternal enemy of Protestant Germany, which for so many centuries has protested against Rome and its idea in all its forms and against all its allies, defenders, and followers; but beyond that he realizes that Catholicism, at *this* very moment—i.e., at the most important moment for a united Germany—is the most harmful element of all those standing in the way of unification, i.e., of the completion of the edifice on which Prince Bismarck has labored so industriously all his life. And besides, the fact that Berlin dreads the "possibility" of such a Catholic and anti-Prussian league into which ultramontane and separatist interests of southern Germany might later be attracted—besides that, in Berlin they dread and have long foreseen that Catholicism, sooner or later, will certainly serve as a pretext for the future rise of France against the Germany which has humiliated, conquered, and devastated her and that Roman Catholicism will present this pretext before anyone else, and that, accordingly, the most pressing danger to a united Germany rests precisely in Roman Catholicism and in nothing other than that. And Berlin's foresight has stemmed from the consideration, emerging naturally and necessarily, that, first, the papacy has no other defender in the whole world than this same France, that it can count only on France's sword *so long as it can manage to seize that sword firmly in its own hand;* and, second, that Roman Catholicism is far from being a vanquished enemy, that this enemy is a thousand years old, that this enemy passionately wants to live, that its vital powers are phenomenal, that it still retains a multitude of forces, and that such an enormous historical idea as secular papal power cannot die out in a single moment. In short, Berlin has not only recognized the enemy but has also recognized his strength. In Berlin they do not scorn their enemies before the battle.

But if Catholicism wants so much to live and must live, and if the sword that could defend it rests in the hands of France alone, then clearly it follows that Rome will not let France slip through its fingers, particularly if it finds the right moment. This right moment came in the spring; it was the Russian war with the Turks, the Eastern Question. In fact, who is Germany's most important ally? Russia, of course. Rome fully realizes this. That's why the pope was so happy about Russian "reverses": the most important ally of the most dreaded enemy of papal power had now been drawn away from its age-old ally, Germany, by a war; and so Germany was now alone; and so the very moment Catholicism had been awaiting so long had arrived: when, if not now, would there be a better time to ignite the age-old hatred and cast France into a war of revenge on Germany?

Besides, other fateful moments for Catholicism are drawing near right now, so that it cannot afford to tarry even a minute. The death of the pope and the election of a new one are inevitably approaching, and Rome knows full well that Prince Bismarck will use all his intelligence and all his strength to deal a final and most dreaded blow to papal power, exerting all the influence he has in the election of the new pope so as to transform him from a secular ruler and lord into nothing more than a simple patriarch; and, if possible, he will do this with the pope's own consent, so that having divided Catholicism into two hostile camps he can engineer the collapse and ruination of all its plans, claims, and hopes once and for all. And therefore how can Catholicism not hasten to take every measure it can against Bismarck? And here, once again, the Eastern Question is the answer! Oh, now France can go off looking for the allies she has been unable to find for so many years; now a whole coalition can be put together. Let all of Europe be soaked in blood, but in return let the pope triumph; and for the Roman confessors of Christ this means everything.

And so they have begun to work. First of all, of course, they had to manage to gain France's support. How could that be done? They have already done it. Now all of Europe's politicians and all the European press admit that the May coup in France was engineered by the clericals; but again I'll repeat that no one still seems to admit the fundamental significance contained in this fact. Everyone seems to have decided some four months ago that the clericals arranged this coup in France only so as to give themselves more scope, certain advantages and privileges, and an extension of rights. And at the same time, it is simply impossible to imagine that the coup was not planned for the most radical aims—i.e., to bring about (in view of the imminent strife that will break out in the Roman church after the death of the pope) as quickly as possible an inevitable war between France and Germany—a war, to be sure! And you will see that no matter how this affair ends, they will achieve their aim; they will get a war in which, should France be victorious, the pope may again gain worldly power.

They've done an amazingly clever thing; and what's most important, they've chosen a moment when everything seems to have come together to promote their success. They had to begin by getting rid of the republicans, who would never have supported the pope and never have agreed to a war with Germany. And they did get rid of them. Beyond that, they had to force Marshal MacMahon to make an irreparable mistake (precisely an irreparable one), so as to set him off on a course that was irrevocable; he did make that mistake: he got rid of the republicans and declared to the whole of France that they would never come back. And so, a solid beginning has already been made and the clericals are serene for the moment; they know that if France again sends a republican majority to the Chamber, the marshal will send them back. Gambetta has declared that the marshal either will have to submit to the country's decision or resign his post. All the republicans have come to the same conclusion, but they have forgotten that the marshal's motto is: *J'y suis et j'y reste* ("I'm here and I'm not leaving") and that he will not leave. It's clear that all the marshal's hopes rest on the loyalty of the legions. The clericals also want to exploit the legions' loyalty to the marshal, or to whomever. As long as they can achieve a conclusive coup d'état, they will maneuver it as they wish. Most likely, it will happen this way: they will be standing beside the usurper and will be maneuvering him. And even if they were not right there, the matter would proceed of its own accord without them, since they have arranged it all to happen as long as there is a coup d'état: they know what a colossal impression *any change in government in France* will produce on Prince Bismarck. Even in 1875 he was seeking to declare war on France, fearing her steady annual increase in strength. The republicans he favored would not under any pretext have dared to begin a war with him themselves, and to that point he had been largely undisturbed, seeing them heading a hostile state, even despite that state's steady annual increase in strength. But any new change of power in France will naturally make him extremely upset. And particularly at a moment when Germany is left without her natural ally, Russia; when Austria (also Germany's old rival), in which there are so many Catholic elements hostile to Germany, has suddenly become aware of her own value; and when England, with such irritated impatience, has been waiting and looking for an ally in Europe since the very beginning of the Eastern war! The thinking in Berlin must be as follows: what if France, headed by a new government with clericals scurrying all around maneuvering and controlling it—what if France suddenly realizes that if there is going to be a war of revenge, then she will never find a more opportune moment to begin it than now, and never find such important allies to support her as she can find now! And what if the pope should die right in the middle of all this (which is quite possible)? What if the clericals make the new French government declare to Prince Bismarck that his views on the election of the new pope do not coincide with the opinion of France (and this certainly will happen if the republicans are ousted)? What if the new French government at the same time realizes that, should it manage (given the possibility of finding powerful allies in Europe) to win back even one of the provinces taken away from France in 1871, it will thus strengthen its power and influence in the country for at least twenty years? No, indeed, how can he help but be upset now?

There is one other little thing here that is most important: the German is arrogant and proud; the German won't tolerate disobedience. Until now France has been utterly and submissively under Germany's guardianship; she has replied to Germany's inquiries about almost her every movement; she must explain and apologize for every division and every battery she adds to her forces; and now, suddenly, this France makes so bold as to raise her head! And so the clericals may be confidently counting even on Prince Bismarck himself to begin the war first. He did want to begin it in 1875, after all. Not to begin a war means to let France slip from his grasp forever. It's true that the situation in 1875 was not the same as the situation today; but if Austria should be on Germany's side, then. . . . In short, at the recent meeting of the first ministers of Germany and Austria the talk was likely not merely confined to the Eastern Question. And if there is now a state in the world that is in a most favorable situation as regards foreign policy, that state is Austria!

4. What Austria Is Now Thinking About

But people will say that there are disturbances in Austria, that half of Austria does not want what her government wants. There are demonstrations in Hungary. Hungary is avid to support the Turks against the Russians. Some sort of Anglo-Magyar-Polish conspiracy has even been uncovered. On the other hand, though the Slavic elements within Austria support the government at present, the government of Austria looks at them askance and suspiciously, even more so, perhaps, than it looks at the Hungarians. And if that is the case, then can one really say that Austria is presently in the most favorable political situation any European state can be in?

Indeed, that's true. It's true that the Catholics are certainly working in Austria as well. The clericals have a lot of foresight: it's unlikely they fail to understand the current importance of this country; it's unlikely they will miss an opportunity. And, of course, they aren't missing the opportunity to incite all sorts of disturbances in this Catholic and "most Christian" land, under every conceivable pretext, guise, and form. But here's something to think about: who knows, it could be that though Austria makes a show of being very angry over these disturbances, in essence she may really not be all that angry; and it may be quite the reverse: she is keeping these disturbances *just in case*, with a view to their utility in the very near future. . . . However, the most obvious thing is that though Austria may feel herself to be in a most fortunate political situation, still, in view of current events, she has perhaps not yet decided on her *long-term* and very specific policy but is only watching and waiting to learn what *prudence* will impel her to do. If she has decided on anything, then it is only on her *immediate* policy, and even that is only conditional. On the whole, Austria is in a real state of bliss; she can take her time to decide, she can wait, knowing that everyone else is waiting for her and that everyone needs her; she is fixing her sights on the quarry she herself can choose and sensuously licking her lips while thinking about the blessings that will inevitably soon be hers.

At the recent meetings of the chancellors of both German states a great many "conditional" things were perhaps brought up. At least the Austrian government declared for all to hear that nothing would happen or be resolved in the East without taking Austria's interests into account—a remarkably wide-ranging idea. In such a way, without even drawing her sword, Austria is already assured that she will have a significant share in Russian successes, should there be any, and perhaps an even more significant share if there shouldn't be any. And this will follow merely from her short-term policies! And in the long term? Even now everyone needs Austria so much; they seek her opinion, her neutrality; they make promises and perhaps are already giving away things to her; and this is only because she sits there and says, "Hmm." But this state, now so aware of her own value, cannot help but count on the chances of her long-term policy, which is still unknown even despite the chancellors' friendly meetings—of that I am certain. I am even certain that this policy will not be known until the last and most fateful moment, something that will be entirely in keeping with the customs and traditions of Austria's age-old policies. And how avidly, perhaps, is she now watching France, awaiting that country's fate, awaiting some new, fascinating developments and, most important, doing so in a mood of utmost self-satisfaction. However, she cannot help but be excited: perhaps she will very soon have to decide even on her very long-term policy, and do so irrevocably: this is an excitement which, in her situation, is pleasant yet intense. After all, she realizes, and may have a very delicate realization, that, given any coup in France (something so close and so possible), given even any new government in France (so long as it is not a republican one again), the chances of conflict between France and Germany are *absolutely certain;* and this would be so even in the event that France's new rulers themselves might not want a war but, rather, might strive with all their might to preserve the former peace. Oh, Austria, perhaps, can realize better than anyone that there are moments in the lives of nations when they are drawn to a certain action, not by will and not by calculation, but by fate itself.

I shall now permit myself to enter into a little fantasy (and of course it's only a fantasy). I'll permit myself to imagine what Austria, at the present critical and indefinite moment, is thinking in regard to this same *long-term* policy of hers, which of course she has still not decided upon since not all the facts have yet been clearly defined; yet someone is already knocking at the door; she sees that someone is certainly intending to come in and is already turning the door knob; but the door has not yet opened, and who will come in no one yet knows. France is faced with a riddle that will be solved there, while for the moment Austria is sitting and *thinking;* and how could she not be thinking? If swords are drawn, if Germany and France throw themselves upon one another in a real struggle, then whom will she support? Whose side will she be on? That's the very *long-term* question, and yet how soon, perhaps, will she have to find an answer to it!

And so how can she fail to realize her own value now? After all, the one for whom she draws her sword will triumph. No one knows what was said at the meeting of the chancellors of both German empires, but the two of them must certainly have exchanged some hints. How could they have failed to make hints? Perhaps there were not only hints but something more plain was stated and *proposed*. In short, Austria was promised a good many presents and treats, and of that there's no doubt, since she is absolutely certain that, should she remain in an alliance with Germany in the event of the latter's war with France, she will receive in return . . . *a good deal*. And all this only for some sort of *neutrality;* only for sitting peacefully at home for six months or so awaiting a reward for good behavior—why, that's the most pleasant thing of all! Because I think that no chancellor could get her to participate actively against France; Austria would never make a mistake like that: she will not go off to crush France to death; rather, perhaps, she will defend France at the final, fateful moment through diplomatic intercession and in so doing ensure herself of even more rewards. She could not be left *entirely without France* in the friendly embrace of the giant that Germany would become after a second victory over France. It could happen that the giant might later suddenly take her into his arms so enthusiastically that—unawares, of course—he would crush her like a fly. And then the other Eastern giant lying to her right might at last arise entirely from his age-old bed. . . .

"Good behavior is a fine thing," Austria may be thinking to herself now, "but. . . ." In short, another vision—a most fantastic one, though—cannot but flash through her mind:

"A coup in France may begin even this autumn and, perhaps, it will be over very, very quickly. If the republic falls, or if it remains in some nominal, absurd form, then perhaps strife with Germany will begin in the winter. The clericals are already trying to arrange this, the more so as the pope will certainly be dead by that time, and then the papal election will at once provide a pretext for dissension and conflict. But even if the pope does not die, the possibility of dissension and conflict remains as strong as ever. And if Germany makes the firm decision, the war will begin by spring. On the other edge of Europe, a winter campaign against Turkey is also inevitable, it seems, so Germany's ally will still be occupied in the spring. And so, if a war of revenge does break out, France will at once find two allies: England and Turkey.

"Germany, accordingly, will be alone . . . with Italy, which means almost the same as being alone. Oh, of course Germany is haughty and powerful. But France has managed to get on her feet, after all: she has a million troops, and England could offer her some help as well: the German cities on the coast would have to be protected from England's fleet, and so some troops, artillery, armaments, and supplies would have to be kept aside. All this would weaken Germany, at least to some extent. In short, France's chances of carrying on a successful war even without me are considerable," Austria thinks. "They are at least twice as good as in 1870, since France will now certainly not make the mistakes she made then. Moreover, whether France is crushed or not, I'll still get my due in the East: nothing in the East will be resolved contrary to the interests of Austria. That has already been decided and signed. But . . . what if I, at the very most decisive moment, having prudently reserved my complete freedom to decide, should just come out in support of France and even draw my sword!"

In fact, what would happen then?

Austria would at once find herself amid three enemies: Italy, Germany, and Russia. But Russia will be terribly busy with her own war and won't be able to attack. Italy, in any case, doesn't represent any great threat. There remains only Germany; but if she sends a force into Austria she would weaken herself; and of course it wouldn't be a very large force because she needs all the forces she has to fight France. In fact, Austria has only to decide on an alliance with France and France would launch an attack on Germany, perhaps, and would make the first move even if Germany did not want to fight. France, Austria, England, and Turkey against Germany and Italy—that's an awesome coalition. It's very, very possible it would be successful. And with success Austria could regain all that she had lost at Sadova and even a lot more. Then she would be in no danger at all of losing her advantages in the East and all the other things she has been promised. And most important, she would certainly win influence in Catholic Germany. Should Germany be defeated—and even not defeated but simply should she come back from war without a complete success—German unity would be powerfully and suddenly shaken. Separatist movements would appear in southern, Catholic Germany—movements which, moreover, the clericals are making every effort to encourage and which Austria, of course, will take advantage of . . . even to the point, perhaps, where there would then be two Germanies, two united German empires, one Catholic and one Protestant. Thereupon, having strengthened herself with a German element, Austria could take some liberties with her own "dualism," place Hungary in her former, ancient, and respectful relations to her; and then, of course, she could take her own Slavs in hand and do so in a way that would be final. In short, the benefits might be incalculable! Finally, even if Germany were victorious, it would not be such a calamity, as she could not defeat such a powerful coalition as *decisively* as she did in 1871; on the contrary, she would certainly have a few bruised ribs. Therefore a peace could be concluded with no terrible consequences. "And so, whose side should I choose? Which is better? Whose side would bring more benefits?"

In view of the present course of events in Europe, Austria must undoubtedly be asking herself such radical questions. . . .

5. Who's Knocking at the Door? Who Will Come In? Inescapable Fate

When I was beginning this chapter the facts and reports that are suddenly filling the entire European press had not yet appeared, so that everything I wrote here as speculation has now been borne out almost word for word. My *Diary* will come out next month, on October 7, while today is only September 29 and the "soothsayings," if I may call them that, on which I rather riskily embarked in this chapter will look somewhat dated, like established facts from which I merely copied my "soothsayings." But I will be so bold as to remind readers of the *Diary* of this summer's May and June issue. Almost everything I wrote in it about Europe's immediate future has already been confirmed or *is beginning to be confirmed*. And yet, at the time I heard views expressed about the article (the views of nonspecialists, it's true) that called it "frenzied raving" and preposterous exaggeration. People simply laughed at the strength and significance of the clerical conspiracy and, in fact, would not admit there was any conspiracy at all. However, even two weeks ago I heard a "competent" person's opinion to the effect that the pope's death and the election of a new pope were of absolutely no importance and would change nothing in Europe. But even now we know the importance Bismarck attributes to these things and what he said about it in Berlin to Crispi. In my May and June *Diary* I wrote that ever since the beginning of the Franco-Prussian War the genius of Prince Bismarck recognized that the most dreaded enemy of newly united Germany was Roman Catholicism, which, before anything else, would provide the pretext for a great war of "revenge" that would engulf the whole of Europe. People found that absurd, and so on. And that was all because I wrote it then, at a time when no one, either in the Russian or in the European press, even thought to worry about these things, despite the Eastern war, whose reverberations were already being felt and were causing worry to everyone. At that time, everyone imagined that the matter would be confined to the East. However, even now perhaps, no one yet fully believes in the *inevitability* of a European war in the very near future. On the contrary, not long ago people were still paying serious attention to the view of competent Englishmen (Northcote's speech) that it was still possible to settle things before winter. And so maybe I'm wrong in thinking this present chapter to be outdated in advance: even though the facts have come to light, even though their immense significance is already being revealed, even though something fateful, awesome, and—most important—near at hand is certainly looming over Europe; still, despite all these established facts, I am sure that very many people even now find my explanations of the facts to be erroneous and absurd, preposterous and exaggerated, because everyone now accepts what has happened as something incomparably smaller and more trivial than it in fact is. For example, the elections in France are just around the corner; France, say, will return the former republican majority to the Chamber, which could well happen; and then I am almost convinced that everyone will begin shouting that it's all ended happily, that the skies have cleared and there are no conflicts, that MacMahon has admitted his guilt, that the *impotent* clericals have faded away in disgrace, and that peace and "legality" reign in Europe once more. All my *fabrications* in this chapter will again seem merely the product of an idle imagination. People will say once more that I have ascribed the wrong meaning to facts—even established facts—and, above all, a meaning that *no one anywhere ascribes to them*. But again, let's wait for events to unfold, and then we shall see where the more correct and true road lay. But for the record, I shall try, in conclusion, once more to indicate the points and the signposts along the road that is already beginning to appear before us all, and on which, like it or not, it seems we are all destined to set forth. I do this for the record so that it may later be verified. However, this is only a simple and concluding summary of this chapter.

1. The road begins in Rome, in the Vatican, where a dying old man, the head of the crowd of Jesuits surrounding him, has traced

it long ago. When the Eastern Question flared up, the Jesuits realized that the most opportune moment had come. They burst into France, following the road that had been indicated, created a coup d'état there, and placed the country in such a position that a war with Germany in the near future was almost inevitable, even if France did not want to begin it. Prince Bismarck had foreseen and realized all this long before. It seems, at least, that he alone—and perhaps even several years before the present moment—was able to make out and comprehend who his principal enemy was, as well as the immense world significance of this last battle for survival that *papal Catholicism in its ultimate death throes* will certainly offer to the whole world in the very near future.

2. This fateful struggle is already assuming its ultimate shape at the present moment, and the final battle is drawing near with awesome speed. France was selected and designated as the terrible battleground, and there will be a battle. The battle is inevitable, that is certain. However, there is still a slight chance that it will be postponed, but merely for a very short time. In any case, it is *inevitable and near at hand.*

3. As soon as the battle begins, it will at once be transformed into an all-European one. The Eastern Question and the Eastern war, by the force of destiny, will also merge with this all-European war. One of the most remarkable episodes of this battle will be Austria's final decision: to which side will she lend her sword? But the most essential and important part of this final and fateful struggle will consist, on the one hand, in the fact that it will resolve the thousand-year question of Roman Catholicism and, on the other hand, that by the will of Providence a reborn Eastern Christianity will take its place. In such manner our Russian Eastern Question will expand into a worldwide, universal question with an extraordinary, preordained significance, even though this preordination may occur before eyes that are blind and do not recognize it, eyes that are incapable until the last minute of seeing the obvious and of comprehending the meaning of what has been preordained. Finally—

4. (And you may call this the most hypothetical and fantastic of all my predictions—I'll admit that beforehand.) I am certain that the battle will end in favor of the East, of the Eastern alliance; that Russia has nothing to fear if the Eastern war merges with the all-European one, and that it would even be better if the matter should broaden in this way. Oh, there's no denying that it will be a terrible thing if so much precious human blood is shed! But there

is at least consolation in the thought that the blood that has been shed will certainly spare Europe from ten times more bloodshed should the matter be postponed and drawn out even further. The more so that the great struggle will certainly end quickly. And, in return, so many problems will finally be solved (the Roman Catholic problem, along with the fate of France, the German, Eastern, and Mohammedan problems); so many matters that were utterly insolvable, given the former course of events, will now be settled; the face of Europe will be so altered; so many new and progressive things will begin in human relationships that, perhaps, there is no cause for spiritual anguish and excessive fear over this last convulsion of old Europe on the eve of its great and certain renewal. . . .

Finally, I'll add one more consideration: if you make it a rule to judge all world events, even those that the most superficial view can see as being of the greatest importance, according to the principle "Today as yesterday, and tomorrow as today"—then isn't it clear that this rule goes utterly contrary to the history of nations and of humanity? Meanwhile, this is just what is prescribed by so-called realistic and sober common sense, so that ridicule and scorn are heaped upon almost anyone who ventures to think that tomorrow everyone may see some matter in quite a different aspect from the one in which they saw it yesterday. Even now, for instance, when the facts are already at hand, does it not seem even to very many people that the clerical movement is a most insignificant little thing; that Gambetta will give a speech and everything will be restored to the way it was yesterday; that our war with Turkey, very, very possibly, will end by winter and thereupon the stock-exchange gambling and railroad business will resume, the ruble will rise, we'll happily go traveling to Europe, and so on? The inconceivability of continuing the old order of things was an evident truth for all the leading minds in Europe on the eve of the first European revolution that began in France at the end of the last century. Meanwhile, was there anyone in the whole world, even on the eve of the summoning of the Estates-General, who could have foreseen and foretold the form this event would assume virtually the day after it began? . . . And once it had assumed its form, who could have predicted the rise of Napoleon I, for instance, the one who, in essence, was virtually preordained to complete the first historical phase of this same event that began in 1789? Moreover, in the time of Napoleon I, perhaps, everyone in Europe thought that his rise was, without a doubt, an entirely external matter of chance in no way linked with that same universal law by which the former face of this world had been destined, at the end of the last century, to change its whole appearance....

Yes, indeed; and now again someone is knocking; someone, a new man, with a new word, wants to open the door and come in.... But who will come in? That's the question. Will it be an entirely new man, or will it once more be someone like all of us, the old homunculi?

2

1. A Lie Is Saved by a Lie

Once upon a time Don Quixote—that very well-known knight of the doleful countenance, the noblest of all the knights the world has ever seen, the simplest in soul and one of the greatest in heart—while wandering with his faithful attendant, Sancho, in search of adventure, was suddenly struck by a puzzle that gave him cause to think for a long while. The fact is that often the knights of old, beginning with Amadis da Gaula, whose stories have come down to us in the absolutely truthful books known as the romances of chivalry (for acquisition of which Don Quixote did not regret selling several of the best acres of his little estate)—often these knights, during their glorious peregrinations that were so beneficial to the whole world, would suddenly and unexpectedly encounter entire armies of even a hundred thousand warriors sent forth against them by some evil power, by evil sorcerers who envied them and prevented them in all sorts of ways from achieving their great goal and being united at last with their fair ladies. It usually happened that when a knight encountered such a monstrous and evil army he would draw his sword, invoke the name of his fair lady for spiritual succor, and then hack his way into the very midst of his enemies, whom he would annihilate to the last man. This would seem to be quite a simple matter, but Don Quixote suddenly fell to thinking, and on this problem: he suddenly found it impossible to believe that a single knight, no matter how strong he might be and no matter if he were to go on wielding his armipotent sword for a whole day without getting tired, could at once lay low a hundred thousand enemies, and this in only one battle. Killing each man would still take some time; killing a hundred thousand men would take a great deal of time; and no matter how he wielded his sword, a single person could not do this at once, in a few hours or so. And yet these trustworthy books told of such deeds being done in just a single battle. How could it happen?

"I have solved this puzzle, Sancho, my friend," Don Quixote said at last. "Inasmuch as all these giants, all these wicked sorcerers, were the evil spirit, their armies likewise possessed the same magical and evil nature. I presume that these armies were composed of men quite unlike you and me, for instance. These men were no more than an illusion, the product of magic, and in all probability their bodies were unlike our own but were more akin to those of slugs, worms, and spiders, for example. And thus in his powerful hand the knight's steadfast and sharp sword would, when it fell upon these bodies, pass through them in an instant, almost without resistance, as if through air. And if that is so, then truly with a single blow he could cut through three or four bodies, and even through ten if they were standing close together. Hence one can understand that the thing would be greatly expedited and a knight really could annihilate whole armies of such evil blackamoors and other monsters. . . ."

Here the great poet and seer of the human heart perceived one of the most profound and most mysterious aspects of the human spirit. Oh, this is a great book, not the sort that are written now; only one such book is sent to humanity in several hundred years. And such perceptions of the profoundest aspects of human nature you will find on every page of this book. Take only the fact that this Sancho, the personification of common sense, prudence, cunning, the golden mean, has chanced to become a friend and traveling companion to the maddest person on earth—he precisely, and no other! He deceives him the whole time, he cheats him like a child, and yet he has complete faith in his great intellect, is enchanted to the point of tenderness by the greatness of his heart, believes completely in all the preposterous dreams of the great knight, and the whole time he never once doubts that the Don will at last conquer the island for him! What a fine thing it would be if our young people were to become thoroughly steeped in these great works of world literature. I don't know what is now being taught in courses of literature, but a knowledge of this most splendid and sad of all books created by human genius would certainly elevate the soul of a young person with a great idea, give rise to profound questions in his heart, and work toward diverting his mind from worship of the eternal and foolish idol of mediocrity, self-satisfied conceit, and cheap prudence. Man will not forget to take this *saddest* of all books with him to God's last judgment. He will point to the most profound and fateful mystery of humans and humankind that the book conveys. He will point to the fact that humanity's most sublime beauty, its most sublime purity, chastity, forthrightness, gentleness, courage, and, finally, its most sublime intellect—all these often (alas, all too often) come to naught, pass without benefit to humanity, and even become an object of humanity's derision simply because all these most noble and precious gifts with which a person is often endowed lack but the very last gift—that of *genius* to put all this power to work and to direct it along a path of action that is truthful, not fantastic and insane, so as to work for the benefit of humanity! But genius, alas, is given out to the tribes and the peoples in such small quantities and so rarely that the spectacle of the malicious irony of fate that so often dooms the efforts of some of the noblest of people and the most ardent friends of humanity to scorn and laughter and to the casting of stones solely because these people, at the fateful moment, were unable to discern the true sense of things and so discover their *new word*—this spectacle of the needless ruination of such great and noble forces actually may reduce a friend of humanity to despair, evoke not laughter but bitter tears and sour his heart, hitherto pure and believing, with doubt. . . .

However, I wanted only to point out this most interesting feature which, along with hundreds of other such profound perceptions, Cervantes revealed in the human heart. The most preposterous of people, with a crackpot belief in the most preposterous fantasy anyone can conceive, suddenly falls into doubt and perplexity that almost shake his entire faith. What's curious is the thing that was able to shake it: not the absurdity of the crackpot notion itself, not the absurdity of wandering knights who exist for the benefit of humanity, not the absurdity of those magical wonders told of in those "absolutely truthful books"—no, on the contrary, it was something external and secondary, an altogether particular thing. The preposterous man suddenly *began yearning for realism!* It wasn't the appearance of sorcerers' armies that bothered him: oh, that's beyond any doubt; and how else could these great and splendid knights display all their valor if they were not visited by all these trials, if there were no envious giants and wicked sorcerers? The ideal of the wandering knight is so great, so beautiful and useful, and had so captivated the heart of the noble Don Quixote that it became utterly impossible for him to renounce his faith in it; that would have been the equivalent of betraying his ideal, his duty, his love for Dulcinea and for humanity. (When he did renounce his ideal, when he was cured of his madness and grew *wiser*, after returning from his second campaign in which he was defeated by the wise and commonsensical barber Carrasco, the skeptic and debunker, he promptly passed away, quietly, with a sad smile, consoling the weeping Sancho, loving the whole world with the mighty force of love contained in his sacred heart, and yet realizing that there was nothing more for him to do in this world.) No, it was not that; what troubled him was merely the very real, mathematical consideration that no matter how the knight might wield his sword and no matter how strong he might be, he still could not overcome an army of a hundred thousand in the course of a few hours, or even in a day, having killed all of them to the last man. And yet such things were written in these trustworthy books. Therefore, they must have lied. And if there is one lie, then it is all a lie. How, then, can *truth* be saved? And so, to save the truth he invents another fantasy; but this one is twice, thrice as fantastic as the first one, cruder and more absurd; he invents hundreds of thousands of imaginary men having the bodies of slugs, which the knight's keen blade can pass through ten times more easily and quickly than it can an ordinary human body. And thus *realism* is satisfied, *truth* is saved, and it's possible to believe in the first and most important dream with no more doubts—and all this, again, is solely thanks to the second, even more absurd fantasy, invented only to salvage the *realism* of the first one.

Ask yourselves: hasn't the same thing happened to you, perhaps, a hundred times in the course of your life? Say you've come to cherish a certain dream, an idea, a theory, a conviction, or some external fact that struck you, or, at last, a woman who has enchanted you. You rush off in pursuit of the object of your love with all the intensity your soul can muster. It's true that no matter how blinded you may be, no matter how well your heart bribes you, still, if in the object of your love there is a lie, a *delusion*, something that you yourself have exaggerated and distorted because of your passion and your initial rush of feeling—solely so that you can make it your idol and bow down to it—then, of course, you're aware of it in the depths of your being; doubt weighs upon your mind and teases it, ranges through your soul and prevents you from living peaceably with your beloved dream. Now, don't you remember, won't you admit even to yourself what it was that suddenly set your mind at rest? Didn't you invent a new dream, a new lie, even a terribly crude one, perhaps, but one that you were quick to embrace lovingly only because it resolved your initial doubt?

2. Slugs Taken for Human Beings. Which Is Better: When People Know the Truth about Us or When They Talk Nonsense about Us?

In our time almost the whole of Europe has fallen in love with the Turks, more or less. Formerly, for instance—even a year ago—though people in Europe tried to discover some sort of great national powers in the Turks, almost everyone still realized privately that they were doing this solely out of hatred for Russia. In fact, they could not help but realize that in Turkey there were not and could not be any forces befitting a sound and healthy national organism; that, moreover, there may be no organism left, so much has it been shaken and debilitated and become putrefied; that the Turks are an Asiatic horde and not a proper state. But now, ever since Turkey has been at war with Russia, in certain places in Europe there has gradually developed and become established even a real and serious conviction that this nation is not only an organism but is even one with great vitality and, accordingly, the capacity for development and further progress. This dream more and more captivates many European minds and, at last, has even reached us: here in Russia as well certain people have begun to talk about the unexpected national vitality Turkey has suddenly displayed. But in Europe this fantasy has taken hold, again, out of hatred of Russia, while among us it comes from pusillanimity and the terrible rush to pessimistic conclusions that have always been qualities of our society's educated classes whenever we began to suffer some "reverses" somewhere! The same thing happened in Europe as occurred in the deranged mind of Don Quixote, but in reverse, even though the essence of the thing is the same: to save the *truth*, he invented people with the bodies of slugs; to save the basic fantasy of Russia's insignificance and impotence, which gave them so much consolation, they have made from a real slug a human organism, endowing it with flesh and blood, spiritual vitality, and health. The most advanced countries in Europe are now spreading absolute absurdities about Russia. Even in times past Europe knew very little about us—so little, in fact, that one was always amazed that such educated peoples took so little interest in studying a people whom they so hated and whom they constantly feared. Europe's meager knowledge of us, and even her inability, in certain ways, to understand many things about us have worked partly to our advantage until now. And so even now no harm will come of it. Let them shout over there about "Russia's scandalous weakness as a military power," despite testimony from the very field of battle from dozens of their own correspondents who were amazed at the fighting capacity, chivalrous fortitude, and superb discipline of the Russian soldier and officer; let them regard the very understandable (though significant) errors of the Russian staff at the beginning of the war not only as irreparable but as organic and inherent defects of our army and our nation (having forgotten how many times we thrashed them on the field of battle over the last two hundred years). Finally, let their *very most serious* political publications inform Europe, as an absolute truth, that there was an enormous uprising of the People, led by nihilists, on the Vyborg Side in Petersburg and that the authorities brought in two regiments from Dinaburg by rail in order to save Petersburg—let them say all that in their blind rage. I repeat, this even works to our advantage, since they themselves do not know what they are perpetrating. Why, of course they would like to arouse hatred against us everywhere over there as "dangerous enemies of their civilization," and so they picture us in a state of collapse, in disgraceful impotence as a military power and a government. But how, then, can one so weak and insignificant arouse the fear of a coalition against him? And yet they feel it necessary to incite their society against us. Consequently, what they are saying does damage to themselves; and if that is so, then it does us no damage, it works to our advantage. As for us, we'll wait for the end.

But can you imagine what would happen were they to get the most complete, accurate, and true information about all the strength of our spirit and feeling and the unshakeable faith of the Russian People in the justness of their great cause, for which their emperor has drawn his sword, and in the certain triumph of this cause, sooner or later? Imagine that Europe at last realized that for Russia this war is a national war to the highest degree and that our People are no dead and soulless mass, as they always imagine them to be, but a mighty organism aware of its own might, united as one and inseparable in heart and will from their army—oh, what fear and what general alarm this news would cause among them! And, of course, this would encourage an actual, overt European coalition against us rather than the slanders, of which they are so fond, about our impotence and collapse. No, let them rather believe in the uprising on the Vyborg Side. It can only encourage us when they believe that.

When this happens in Europe it is understandable, and what causes it is understandable. But how is it that we can hesitate, worry, and even believe in some new, suddenly discovered vital force in the Turkish nation? How has she displayed this force? In fanaticism? But fanaticism is a cadaver and not a force; that has been preached here a hundred times by those same people who now believe in Turkish vitality. They talk about Turkish victories. But the Turks have merely repelled our attacks once or twice, and so these victories are negative, so to say, and not positive. When we were trapped in Sevastopol we once repelled an assault of the French and the English, who suffered terrible losses; but then Europe did not go shouting about our victory. For the last two months we have possessed far weaker forces than the Turks have, so why didn't they take advantage of this? Why didn't they push us beyond the Balkans and drive us back across the Danube? On the contrary, we held our main positions everywhere and repelled the Turks everywhere. There have been cases when seven or eight of our battalions have beaten twenty of theirs, as happened not long ago near Tserkovna. However, those convinced of Turkish strength point out their rifles, which are better than ours, and even their artillery, which supposedly is better than ours. But they don't care to recall that, in essence, we are waging war not with the Turks alone but with the European powers; that many Englishmen are serving as officers in the Turkish army; that the Turks have been armed using European money; that European diplomacy has in many ways stood in our way from the very beginning of the war by depriving us of the help of our natural allies and even depriving us of our real routes to Turkey. Besides, Europe's hatred of us has certainly encouraged the fanaticism of the Turks. Finally, a conspiracy of whole gangs has been discovered in Europe; they are already organized, with weapons and money, to make a sudden attack on the rear of our army. To top it all, not long ago they cooked up a loan over there for the Turks, at a huge cost to themselves; and this ridiculous loan went through solely because Europe has so fallen in love with the fantasy that Turkey is not a state composed of slugs but is really of the same flesh and blood as are the European state organisms. And this coming at a time when entire provinces of Turkey are soaked with blood, when even a proper conspiracy among the rulers of Turkey has been uncovered, a conspiracy whose aim was to annihilate the Bulgarians to the last one! The Turks wage war with us, feeding and maintaining their army with such requisitions of supplies, horses, and cattle as cannot but cause the utter ruination of this richest province of Turkey. And it is to these people, who would wreck and devastate their own country, that the enlightened English have loaned money, trusting in their economic solvency! But let that be, let it be over there; over there one can understand it. But how is it that we can regard the Turks as a force? The devastation of their own land and the complete annihilation of the Christian population of the country—does that constitute a force? They'll run out of that sort of force before the end of the war. The first turn of events in our favor and all this preposterous edifice of their military and national strength will collapse instantly, at one stroke, and will evaporate like a real phantom along with their fanaticism, which will blow out like steam through an opened valve.

Some intelligent people among us are now disparaging the Slavic question, both orally and in print: "We've become so wrapped up in these Slavs and all these fantasies about their unification! Who was it who saddled us with these Slavs, and why? To cause permanent disputes with Europe, to earn her permanent suspicion and hatred, now and in the future! Slavophiles, be damned!" And so on, and so on. But it seems that the intelligent people who shout these things are utterly misinformed, both about the Slavs and about the Eastern Question, while many of them never even took an interest in such things until the very last moment. And so one can't argue with them. And, in fact, they truly do not know that the Eastern Question (and that means the Slavic one as well) was certainly not invented by the Slavophiles; indeed, it wasn't invented by anyone but arose of itself, and long ago; it arose before the Slavophiles, before us, before you, even before Peter the Great and the Russian Empire. It arose with the first consolidation of the Great Russian tribe into a united Russian state, that's to say, at the same time as the Muscovite tsardom. The Eastern Question is the age-old idea of the Muscovite tsardom; Peter the Great was fully aware of that, and when he abandoned Moscow he did not abandon the Eastern Question but took it with him to Petersburg. Peter fully understood its organic link with the Russian state and the Russian soul. That is why the idea not only did not die out in Petersburg but was frankly acknowledged as a *Russian mission*, as it were, by all Peter's successors. That is why it cannot be abandoned and cannot be changed. To abandon the Slavic idea and to cast aside the problem of the fates of Eastern Christianity (N.B.: the essence of the Eastern Question) without solving it would be equivalent to smashing the whole of Russia to pieces and inventing something new to take its place; but that something would certainly not be Russia. That would not even be a revolution, but simply destruction; and therefore it would be utterly unthinkable because it would be impossible to destroy such a whole and restore it again within an entirely different organism.

Now perhaps only the very blindest of the Russian Europeans, and with them—to their shame—the stock-exchange gamblers, do not see and acknowledge this idea. I arbitrarily call stock-exchange gamblers all today's Russians generally who have no concern in Russia other than their own pockets and who therefore look upon Russia only from the viewpoint of the interests of their own pockets. They're now shouting out in chorus about the stagnation of trade, the crisis in the market, the fall of the ruble. But if these stock-exchange gamblers of ours were farsighted enough to understand anything beyond their own sphere, they would realize that if Russia had not begun the present war, they themselves would have been worse off. If "business," even stock-exchange business, is to proceed, the nation must live in the full sense of the word, i.e., it must have a genuine living life, fulfilling its natural mission, and not be merely a galvanized corpse in the hands of Yids and stock-exchange gamblers. If we had not begun the present war, after all the cynical and offensive challenges from our enemies, and if we had not helped the martyrs who were being tortured, then we would begin to despise ourselves. And self-contempt, moral collapse, and the cynicism that follows are obstacles even to "business." Nations live by great feelings and by great ideas that unite all and illuminate everything, by solidarity with the masses of their population when, at last, those masses spontaneously realize that they are at one with the upper levels of people; this generates the vigor of the nation. This is what nations live by, and not by mere stock-exchange speculation and concern for the value of the ruble. The wealthier a nation is spiritually, the wealthier it will also be materially. . . . And yet, what timeworn things am I saying here!

3. An Intimation of the Future Educated Russian Man. The Certain Lot of the Future Russian Woman

There are some strange perplexities and strange concerns these days. There truly are some Russian people who even *fear* Russian successes and Russian victories. They are not afraid because they wish the Russians ill; on the contrary, they genuinely grieve over every Russian reversal; they are good Russians, but they fear Russian successes and victories "because after a victorious war there'll be self-confidence, self-congratulation, chauvinism, and stagnation." But the whole error of these good people lies in the fact that they have always seen Russian progress exclusively in terms of self-abasement. But a little self-importance, perhaps, is just what we most need now! We need some self-respect, at last, and not self-abasement. Don't worry: there won't be any stagnation. The war will illuminate so much that is new and will compel a change in so much that is old that you could never achieve the same through the self-abasement and mockery that lately have become little more than a simple amusement. On the other hand, many things will also come to light that even our clever faultfinders used to regard as mere trifles, ridiculous frivolities, and lacking any importance, but which, however, constitute our real essence in every respect. Indeed, we are not ones to give way to chauvinism and self-admiration, certainly not! Where and when did this ever happen in Russian society! Those who make such claims simply do not know Russian history. After Sevastopol a good deal was said about our self-admiration: self-confidence, so they said, was our ruination then. But never had educated society been less self-confident and more in disarray than in the era before Sevastopol.

I'll note in passing: among those who wrote of our self-admiration and who taunted us with it after Sevastopol were a few new young writers who, at the time, had a great deal of attention paid to them by society and whose accusations aroused ardent sympathy. However, these accusatory writers, who truly wanted to do good, were at once joined by such a lot of brazen and disreputable people; real mayhem ensued; so many people stepped forth who understood nothing of the real essence of the matter but who still imagined that they were Russia's saviors; among them, moreover, were even some outright enemies of Russia, so that, at last, they damaged the cause to which they had rallied and which had originally been led by talented people. But at first they did have success, solely because Russian people who were pure in heart were then truly longing for a wholesale regeneration and for a new word; such people did not recognize the scoundrels, the untalented who lacked any convictions, and the outright corrupt among them. On the contrary, they thought that they were the ones who were supporting Russia, her interests, her regeneration, her People and her society. The result was that the huge majority of Russians at last grew disillusioned and forsook them; and then came the stock-exchange gamblers and railway concessionaires. . . . Now this mistake will not be repeated, it seems, because some new people certainly will come on the scene, people with new ideas and new energy.

These new people will have no fear of self-respect, but neither will they have any fear of charting their own, new course. Nor will they have any fear of our "wise men": they will be modest, but because of their experience and practical work they will know many things of which these wise men of ours have not even dreamed. Through experience and practical work they will learn to respect the Russian and the Russian People. It is this knowledge they will surely bring with them, and it will provide their principal support. They will not charge all our misfortunes and all our *incompetence* only to the qualities of the Russian man and the Russian character, something that has already become an officially accepted technique among our "wise men," because it is easy and needs no intelligence. They will be the first to provide living testimony, by their example, that the Russian spirit and the Russian man are in no way guilty of the hundreds of thousands of accusations that have been heaped upon them; they will show that so long as the Russian has the possibility of tackling a job, he will do it no worse than anyone else. Oh, these new people will at last realize, despite their modesty, how often our "wise men," even those who are the purest in heart and who truly have the common welfare at heart, have "sat between two stools," as we say, in their desire to seek out the root of the evil. These new people, who will certainly appear after the war, will be joined by many vital forces from the People and from Russian youth. These had made themselves known even before the war, but we were then still unable to recognize them; and while all of us here were expecting to see only a spectacle of cynicism and decay, they presented over there a spectacle of such conscious self-denial, such sincere feeling, such complete faith in the cause to which they had gone forth to give their lives that we, here, could merely wonder: what was the source of it all? Certain foreign correspondents of foreign newspapers reproached certain Russian officers for being vain, being careerists, longing to distinguish themselves, and forgetting their main aim: the love of their homeland and of the cause they had undertaken to serve. But even if we do have such officers, it would also not be a bad thing if these correspondents could also learn about the young people or the officers of inconspicuous rank who are humble servants of their fatherland and a just cause and who valiantly died along with their soldiers in complete self-denial, and certainly not for reward, for show, or for their careers but only because they had great hearts, were great Christians, and were *inconspicuous* Russian people, of whom there are so many—almost to the last man—in our army. Note also that when I speak of the new man who is to come, I by no means have in mind only our military men, in anticipation of their return. Countless others will appear—*all those who formerly so longed to believe in the Russian man* but who were unable to make themselves known and to go against the general pessimism and denial that prevailed around them. But now, seeing the degree of *faith* in his powers that the Russian has displayed *over there*, they cannot help but be encouraged and believe that genuine Russian powers exist here as well: where did the people over there come from if not from here? And having taken courage, they will rally and humbly but steadfastly take up a genuine cause without fear of anyone else's loud and pompous words. And they're all such old, old words! And yet these little old wise men of ours are still certain that it is they who are the newest and *youngest* people and that they are pronouncing the newest words!

But the most important and most beneficial role in the regeneration of Russian society will certainly fall to the Russian woman. After the present war, in which our Russian woman has displayed such lofty, radiant, and sacred qualities, it's impossible to doubt the lofty role that certainly awaits her among us. At last the age-old prejudices will fall away, and "barbaric" Russia will reveal the place she will give to the "little mother" and "little sister" of the Russian soldier, the self-renouncer and martyr for the Russian man. Can we really continue to deny her, that woman who has so graphically displayed her valor, full equality of rights with men in education, employment, and official positions, when it is upon her that all our hopes now rest, after her glorious feat in the spiritual regeneration and moral elevation of our society! That would be shameful and unreasonable, the more so that this will now not depend entirely on us, because the Russian woman herself has assumed her proper place, has herself climbed above those rungs that hitherto had been considered her limit. She has shown the heights she can attain and what she can achieve. In saying that, however, I am speaking about the *Russian woman* and not about those sentimental ladies who gave candies to the Turks. There's no harm in showing kindness to the Turks, of course, but still, this isn't what *those women* accomplished over there; and so *the former* are only *old* Russian ladies, while *the latter* are the *new* Russian women. But I am not talking only about the women who pursue God's cause and serve humanity; their appearance has shown us only that in the Russian land there are many women who are great of heart and who are prepared to work for the common good and to sacrifice themselves because, once again, where did they come from if not from here? But I would like to talk more and more specifically about the Russian woman and the certain lot that awaits her in our society in the immediate future; and so I shall return again to this topic in the subsequent, October, issue of my *Diary*.

October

1

1. To the Reader

Owing to the inadequate health that has presented a particular obstacle to publishing the *Diary* on strictly specified dates, I have decided to suspend publication for a year or two. I do this with singular regret, because when I began my *Diary* last year I had not expected to meet with so much support from my readers. This support has continued the whole time, until this day. I thank you sincerely for it. I particularly thank all those who have written me letters: I have learned a good many new things from these letters. And on the whole, publication of the *Diary* over the course of these two years has taught me a good deal and has further strengthened my beliefs in many things. But, unfortunately, I absolutely am compelled to pause. The publication will cease with the December issue. I trust that neither I nor the readers will forget one other until we meet again.

2. An Old, Customary Military Rule

People in both Europe and Russia have written about our military errors during the present campaign. The discussion continues even now. A true and complete assessment of our military operations belongs only to the future, of course; that's to say, it can only take place after the end of the war, at least. But certain facts even now have emerged fully enough to allow them to be evaluated more or less accurately. I shall not venture to pass judgment on our military errors, being a person with little competence in such matters (although it seems that those in Russia with little competence are the ones who now get most indignant). I merely want to point out one contemporary fact (and not an error) that has been little explained and observed in military science until now; it has not succeeded in being evaluated in its *contemporary* essence; it is a fact that could have been guessed at only in theory but has almost never been confirmed in practice right up until the present war. This fateful fact, unconfirmed in practice in military affairs until the present war, was destined, as if on purpose, to manifest itself in its full force and its ultimate precision during the present campaign because this purely military fact conformed exactly to the national military character of the Turks, or, to put it better, to the principal distinguishing quality of their military character. Moreover, one can even conclude that this fact would not have come to light, perhaps, without the Turks; at least in Europe, despite the recent wars (and such huge wars as the Franco-Prussian one), it would not have come to light and would not have managed to define itself. Now, after the fateful experience of the current war, it will naturally enter into the art of war and its significance will be appreciated. But in the current war, the *fateful* thing for us was that the Russian army, one might say, stumbled over this military fact whose full practical significance was still unexplained, a fact we Russians were destined to explain at enormous cost to ourselves, at least until its meaning became fully clear to us. Meanwhile, very many people, both in Russia and in Europe, are still inclined to regard the enormous price we paid because of this unexplained fact merely as our military error, whereas there was something fateful and inevitable here, and not a mistake; and even if the German army, say, had been in our place, it would have suffered some cuts and bruises from colliding with this fact . . . although, perhaps, it would have appreciated its significance more quickly and been swifter to take corrective measures. I want only to say that not all our mistakes in the present campaign are mistakes in essence and that the biggest of these mistakes would have been made by any European army in our position. I repeat, we stumbled over an unexplained military fact and paid the price until it was explained—and this cannot be considered an absolute error. But what, then, is this fact?

When, in the days of my youth, I studied higher military and engineering sciences in the Main School of Military Engineering, there existed among us one conviction that was considered indisputable; it was an engineering axiom. (However, I hasten to make this reservation in parentheses: I gave up engineering and military matters so long ago that I do not pretend to have the least competence here. I entered the Main School of Military Engineering and attended a six-year course there at the end of the thirties and the beginning of the forties; then, when I had finished my course and left the school, I served for merely a year as an engineer; I retired and took up literature. Totleben graduated three or four years ahead of me. I recall Kaufmann from our officer training. At one time I was a fellow specialist of the younger Kaufmann. Radetsky, Petrushevsky, and Iolshin were only one year ahead of me. From my own class, only three deviated from the straight path to a precarious and uncertain one: I, the writer Grigorovich, and the painter Trutovsky. In short, all this was long ago.) This engineering axiom stated that there is not and cannot be an impregnable fortress; that is to say, no matter how artfully fortified and defended a fortress may be, in the final analysis it must fall; accordingly, the military art of attacking a fortress is always superior to the means and the art of its defense. Of course, this is all generally and theoretically speaking: the axiom merely looks abstractly at the essential qualities of both engineering arts, the attack and the defense. It's also true, of course, that there is no rule without its exceptions, and even in those days we were given examples of certain existing fortresses said to be impregnable. Gibraltar, for example, though we knew it only by hearsay. But still, in the scientific sense there is no Gibraltar that can or should be considered impregnable, and the axiom that the art of attacking a fortress is always superior to the art of defending it remained unshaken.

Oh, the practice is another matter. A given fortress, for instance, may acquire the character of an impregnable strong point (without being such) only because it, for one reason or another, might hold back the main forces of the enemy for too long, exhaust those forces, and thus render the greatest service one could ask of it. Totleben, for instance, certainly knew that Sevastopol would be taken sooner or later and was bound to be taken no matter how he defended it. But when the allies began the siege they certainly never knew or suspected that Sevastopol would put such a strain on their resources. They probably supposed, rather, that Sevastopol would keep them busy for a month or two and would enter only as a passing episode in their broad plan for those countless blows which they were preparing to inflict on Russia aside from the taking of Sevastopol. And so Sevastopol was one such place that served as an impregnable strong point even though it was taken in the end. Totleben's long and brilliant defense, which the allies did not expect, so exhausted and shattered the allies' military and financial resources that after the taking of Sevastopol there was never a thought of any further blows, and our enemies sought peace at least no less than we did! And they would hardly have offered us the peace terms they did had they managed to take Sevastopol in two months! Thus there is *no need* for absolutely impregnable fortresses: given a skillful defense and valiant tenacity on the part of the defenders, a fortress that is by no means impregnable may shatter the enemy's forces. Nevertheless, no matter how brilliant the defense of Sevastopol was, I repeat that sooner or later it had to fall, because given equal forces of both opponents, the force of the attack always exceeds the force of the defense (i.e., speaking once again in a scientific and not in a practical sense; for there have been certain strong points from which the attacking forces have actually withdrawn even after a long siege, not because these positions were impregnable, but merely because the attackers decided to deliver another blow in another place and with fewer losses once they had the opportunity to do so).

3. The Same Rule, Only in a New Guise

And now this military fact, this military axiom, so to say, suddenly seems to have been shaken in our current war with the Turks—not by some "permanently" fortified defensive position, not by the impregnable strength of some formidable fortress, but by some hastily erected field defenses largely of a "temporary" nature. Defensive positions in the field were formerly not even taken into account; they were only field defenses. Field defenses only reinforced a zone of battle, but could never make it impregnable. We did put up redoubts at Borodino, and they helped us by strengthening the position, but they still were taken; and though the enemy suffered losses in doing so, they were taken on the day of the battle nevertheless.

And now something completely new has taken place at Plevna. A series of simple field defenses, largely *temporary* (not a very significant thing in the old days), have given the position the significance of an impregnable stronghold, one that is impossible to capture using the old means, one that has required us to use twice or thrice the effort initially anticipated, one that has still not been captured. Had this whole formidable series of fortifications been defended using the old techniques, could it have withstood an energetic, brilliant, unexcelled attack by the Russians? Of course not: it would have served its purpose; it would have impeded the attack; but of course fifty thousand Russians in such a reckless charge as they made on August 30 would have captured the redoubts and smashed the fifty-thousand-strong army of Osman Pasha, i.e., the task would have been accomplished, given the equality of forces, and no reinforcements would have been needed. But now, after two unsuccessful assaults, it has proved essential to double the size of our army, at the very least; and that is only the first step toward achieving our aim.

What is the matter here? Of course, it's the rifle that's now being used. The Turk, taking cover behind a hastily thrown up earthworks, can pour such a mass of bullets on the attackers that it is not unlikely the assaulting column will be wiped out to the last man before it even reaches the glacis. Oh, of course the whole of Plevna could be taken using the old methods entirely—that is to say, by the old frontal attack without putting up defenses, just as the redoubts were taken at Borodino. And *our Russians would have done it!* Perhaps there's not another army in Europe that would have dared to do it, but they would have done it. But here's the problem: experience has shown that this would certainly have cost tens of thousands of Russian lives, so that once the redoubts had been taken in a frontal attack, we, given an initial equality of our forces and Osman's, would have emerged so numerically weakened that we would not have been able to hold Osman back, since he, behind his earthworks, would have suffered losses only one-tenth of ours. And so, after two terrible, unsuccessful assaults it finally proved necessary, first, to double our forces; then, with Totleben's help, to undertake engineering works comparable even to those needed for attacking the strongest, most permanent fortress; and third, to encircle Plevna, occupy the roads, and cut off communications and supplies to the enemy. In short, a series of most ordinary temporary field defenses served the enemy as a first-class fortress. And although Plevna will be taken—that is certain—or, to put it more correctly, although Osman will be captured when he tries to force his way out so as to escape from his own trap and not starve to death inside it (and, when he attempts to break out, will *expose himself* and instead of being a defender *will shift to the role of attacker*—for us, that's the whole point—and in so doing will at once lose all the advantages of his deadly and invincible fire power from behind defensive cover), nevertheless, the result will still be that Plevna has already served its purpose for our enemy: it has halted the initial victorious march of the Russians; it has compelled them to double and triple their efforts, and has inflicted losses (of which even Europe considered Russia incapable). And, who knows, the final outcome for Osman may not be so terrible: he is still hoping to snatch at least half his army out of the hands of the Russians and retreat with it to dig in again somewhere and erect some new Plevna (at least if he is given an opportunity to do all this; yet everyone is allowed to hope, and Osman is a proud and energetic man).

One can even say that if the defending forces have entrenching tools and some twenty thousand soldiers armed with modern rifles, then a series of simple, old field defenses, any number of which can be thrown up over a chosen area in a single night, will the next day give those twenty thousand troops the strength equivalent to an army of fifty or sixty thousand; and if circumstances are unfavorable for maneuvering, this is an army you will be unable to deal with. And so this series of light defenses sometimes may prove even more useful for the defender than the most formidable and impregnable fortress, because when the defender retreats, he virtually carries it along with him wherever he goes, so long as he has entrenching tools. You capture his position at last, having sacrificed some thousands of soldiers in the attack, and on the next day the same sort of fortification sits across your path, at least if the enemy has managed to escape from you. There's not just one Plevna in Turkey now; every Turkish army, even every little detachment, is digging itself in, and on the next day its deadly rifles will be pointing out of the trenches at the Russians: "Just come up closer," they are saying, "with your doubled forces, and you'll take losses ten times as high as you thought you would when the war began." In order to achieve equality of force with the attacked, the attacker can do nothing but halt before him and dig in as well. But he mustn't do this, he's the attacker; he came to launch an attack and to advance. He can't be sitting behind fortifications, he's come to assault fortifications. . . . Knowledgeable people realize that I am speaking only theoretically; that I'm speaking about attack and defense in general, disregarding all the other accidents of war which moment by moment change the course of events, shifting it this way or that. I want only to express the theorem that, *given the rifle of today,* with the help of field defenses, any defending force *in any country in Europe* has suddenly acquired a terrible advantage over the attacking force. The strength of the defense now *exceeds* the strength of the attack, and the defender has unquestionably the greater advantage in waging war than does the attacker. This is the fact that, to this point, has not been sufficiently well explained in military science and that was even quite *unexpected;* this is the fact that we Russians were destined to stumble over and explain, at great injury to ourselves. And it is certainly not our *mistake,* but merely a new military fact that has suddenly emerged and suddenly made itself clear. . . .

4. The Most Enormous Military Errors May Sometimes Not Be Errors At All

Well, people will say, what new fact have you uncovered here? Didn't we know about this new rifle and its deadly power before the campaign began? And it's not a new rifle in any case, but quite an old one, so that even when we were in Petersburg we could and should have calculated and prepared for its terrible effect, especially when used from behind cover. But the point is that *in practice* things do not happen as they do in theory, and that we really *could not* have calculated and prepared ourselves. Such things seem easy only to those civilians who sit in their offices and now criticize our military operations. Please note that I'm not denying that mistakes were made; I recognize, after all, that they happen and must happen; but I want only to regard this single *fact* as being not an absolute error on our part; and I declare that until the present war it was a fact that had not been explained and whose *full, overwhelming force* was not even known. Oh, there's no doubt that we could have calculated and known beforehand that with the rifle of today the defending force, behind the lightest defenses, can inflict even twice as much damage on the attacker as previously; to find out and to calculate is an easy thing and doesn't even require any military science. But the thing that is incomparably more difficult to calculate and know in advance is this: that given the rifle of today the defending forces, under cover, will inflict not *twice* as much damage as before but at least *five times* as much; and with such an energetic defense as we encountered from the Turks (and which we can be fully excused for not considering), the damage would be *ten times* as much. The fact, we may assume, was known, but its effect and its dimensions were not known. It was not known that, though the rifle of today might have strengthened the hand of the attacker, it strengthened the defender *incomparably more.* This very *excess* of advantage was unknown to us, and it is this very *excess* that is the new, unexpected fact over which we stumbled.

It was not known, and could not have been known, because until the current war with the Turks it had not been revealed to its full extent. Believe me, if the German army had been in our place, then it would have *stumbled* over this fact and would have taken a substantial whipping. The German army, I repeat, might have appreciated the full significance of the fact sooner than our own, learned from it, and taken some corrective measures. But here the qualities of the national spirit come into play: the German is more cautious and circumspect, in some cases, than the Russian; but on the other hand the Russian soldier possesses such self-denying discipline, such a complete capacity for self-sacrifice, such a force of energy, steadfastness, and impetuosity that, in truth, it is hard to decide which of them is better in military matters. Naturally, our competent people, knowing the Russian soldier and prior to any experience with the modern rifle, even from behind defensive positions, might not have thought very long on the matter; and although it might be *not only twice, but even three times* as formidable as the old rifle, they might not have had much fear of it. But it turned out that the modern rifle, used from defensive positions, was *five* or *ten* times more deadly than the old rifle; but this could be proven *only* through practical experience. And in this case, there had not yet been any practical experience in European wars. Indeed, when the modern rifle appeared, there were still a good many facts that had not been spelled out, even some of the most basic ones, it seems. For instance, only now have we had our hopes raised with the arrival among our troops of the Berdan rifle; but in the beginning we issued the troops another rifle, slow and with limited range. There's no doubt that was a mistake. But the fact I am pointing out was not a mistake: it could not have been anticipated in all its ramifications, nor was it possible to make any exact calculations before the practical experience.

The Franco-Prussian War, a war between two such highly developed nations, so equal in terms of inventions and discoveries, so equal in terms of weaponry (the French had an even better rifle than the Germans, and the Germans had to accept it without delay at the very moment the war came)—this Franco-Prussian War, which introduced so much that was new into the military art and almost revolutionized it, still did not bring to light *our* fact *in any way*. And yet it could have done so. But special circumstances arose to prevent that, and the victor over France, until now, right until our war with the Turks, remained ignorant that the French he had conquered held a colossal weapon to stop the German advance in 1871; but the French never used this weapon simply because of particular circumstances under which its possibilities never even entered their heads. The German did not conquer the French, merely the French practices of that time, first of the Napoleonic regime and then of the republican chaos. At the beginning of the war, the French army, whose national trait is the frontal attack with hand-to-hand combat, was terribly astonished and morally crushed by the fact that, instead of crossing the Rhine and invading Germany, it was compelled to defend its own territory at home. Several battles occurred in which the Germans were victorious. But the thought that with their magnificent *Chassepot* they could have at once set up several most formidable Plevnas to stop the terrible onslaught of the enemy never even occurred to the French. They rushed ahead into hand-to-hand combat and right until Sedan would not believe that they had been beaten. Then came Sedan, and after that the majority of the regular army, for reasons that were by no means military, was left out of action. There remained the defense of Paris by the mad Trochu. Gambetta escaped from Paris in a balloon, *descendit du ciel* (descended from the heavens) in one *département* (as one historian writes about him), declared a dictatorship, and began recruiting a new army. This new army bore scant resemblance to a real fighting force and was composed of all sorts of rabble—though this was not Gambetta's fault. They themselves wrote at the time that the majority of their soldiers did not even know how to load a rifle and aim it and were not concerned about learning; they did not want to go to war, they wanted to be left in peace. Winter came, bringing cold and hunger. How could they guess that they could suddenly become three or four times as strong as the enemy with the *Chassepot* rifle and entrenching tools? And indeed, did they have any entrenching tools? Another obstacle was the siege of Paris, whose meaning was more political rather than military. In short, the French did not take advantage of a formidable *new* military fact, and, indeed, did not even recognize its power. In our present Turkish war the fact has been spelled out *with all its ramifications,* and of course Germany's political and military people have anxiously made a mental note of it. Indeed, if this fact enters into the science and tactics of all armies, then perhaps even the French will take advantage of it when Germany again attacks them. And if the French, having discarded their military prejudices (which is very difficult to do), fully pick up the conviction, derived from our Turkish war, that defense with the modern rifle and entrenching tools is incomparably more powerful now than the attack, and demands a doubling of forces on the part of the attacker, then this is what results: the French have a million troops, but there is a general military rule that the one attacked finds it incomparably easier to concentrate all his forces if he wages war at home, even if the military boundaries of the state are as unfavorable as Russia's; but the attacker, even if he were to have an army of two million (which never happens), can never invade the attacked country with more than six or seven hundred thousand troops. Just imagine now that the whole million of the defenders were to take up their entrenching tools with the same energy and scope as the Turks are now doing; imagine, besides, a talented military leader and excellent engineers—why, then Germany would have to send, not just a million, but even a million a half, minimum, into France! Someone in Germany is certainly thinking about this now.

5. We Have Only Stumbled Over a New Fact, but There Was No Error. Two Armies, Two Opposites. The Actual State of Affairs

And it was specifically the Turks who were destined to discover this new fact with all its ramifications! Other nations, other armies would have taken a long time to discover it *practically* and in *such* detail. For a very long time now the Turks have not attacked Europe themselves and have grown accustomed specifically to a defensive role. That is the principal national feature of the Turkish army. Behind fortifications the Turk shows endurance and energy; in the present war Europe, as if deliberately, encouraged him, supplied him with weapons, engineers, huge amounts of money, and, finally, encouraged his fanaticism by inciting him and setting him against us. There were people enough to remind him of the fact, even if he had not known it; but the fact exactly suited his national spirit. He realized at once what an entrenching tool meant when used along with a quick-firing rifle, and what an excessive advantage these would now give the defense over the attack. And as if fate had planned it, the ones to run up against it were the Russians—i.e., that very army which, by its age-old practice, had taken as its method of attack the breathless assault, hand-to-hand combat, with everyone in closed-up ranks that transformed a thousand suddenly into a single being. . . . Out of the clash of these two opposites the new axiom has made itself known in full detail. Once more, I repeat: one could still have foreseen and calculated that the power of the new rifle from the cover of a trench exceeds two and even three times the force of the attacker. Relying on the steadfastness and unparalleled energy of the Russian soldier, we might regard the *two* and *three times* with contempt (and we did so for a long time), but it turned out not to be two and three times but ten times. This fact could not have been foreseen and quickly assimilated, even with practical experience.

The civilian warrior, of course, will find all this absurd. And, indeed, he doesn't even recognize any fact here at all: "We should have figured it out in advance, and that's all. Everyone knows that the Peabody rifle can fire ten or twelve shots a minute, and so they should have known that with such a rifle, and sitting in a fortified position, the Turk would wipe out an attacking column to the last man." But I repeat that, in theory, before any experience, this could not have been fully and completely determined. There are amazingly simple things which even the most brilliant generals could not have figured out in advance. One French military historian bitterly reproaches Napoleon I because in 1815 he had an army of 170,000 men (only that many) and knew very well that he would not get a single soldier more from France—so exhausted was she from twenty years of wars—he nevertheless decided to attack his enemies himself, i.e., he undertook to fight a war outside the country rather than within it. This historian makes a great effort to prove that even a victory at Waterloo would in no way have saved him from ultimate defeat in that same campaign, in view of the overwhelming numerical superiority of the coalition forces. Napoleon's whole mistake, says this historian, was that he continued as before to regard one French soldier as being worth two German ones; and if this really had been true, then of course he would have been able to compensate for the lack of forces he had to wage war against the whole of Europe. But in 1815 this was no longer so, the historian says: in twenty years the Germans had learned to fight and had improved the quality of their troops to the point where the German soldier was absolutely equal to the French. And so even the brilliant Napoleon made a seemingly very simple mistake; he did not realize something he should have known for a long time, something that was so glaringly obvious to his critic. But it's easy to criticize and easy to be a great armchair general. It's noteworthy that both Napoleon and we *erred* on a very similar point, i.e., we erroneously attributed too much importance to certain national peculiarities of our troops.

In conclusion, I repeat still one more time: everything here has been said in only a general, scientific sense (and whether or not it is correct is for each to judge for himself). But in practice the results may change drastically. So it was, for example, that at the beginning of the war the Turks even let us cross the Danube and reach the Balkans; they surrendered their strong points and towns and retreated before us without even giving a thought to entrenching tools and the effect of their Peabody rifle. And it seems that, then, there was still no fanaticism among them either. *The fact of the matter* they themselves only discovered fully at Plevna. It was there that they first discovered all the tactical advantages the side being attacked now possessed. But it may happen that Plevna is taken within a week, and with it *the whole* of Osman's force; in other words, he may not manage to take a single soldier away with him if he attempts to break out. And then, to take one possibility, the morale of the Turks may suddenly fall to its former low point; they will forget about Adrianople and Sofia and throw down their entrenching tools as they flee in haste before the Russian onslaught—in short, many a thing could happen; but all this does not alter in the least the significance of the new axiom in its general sense, i.e., that given the current means, the force of the defense exceeds the force of the attack not in the degree to which it formerly did, but *excessively* so. Let's take one more example: a war is going on somewhere and a general has enclosed himself and his troops behind strong fortifications. Having considered all the factors, i.e., the quantity of supplies, the position and the strength of the fortifications, engineering science can (it seems to me) determine almost precisely how long this position can resist and thereby render a positive service to its state by tying up beneath its walls, at the most critical moment, an enemy attacking force twice as strong as its own. Let's suppose this period is six or seven months; and so, suddenly, the general who has shut himself up in this fortress surrenders it, for his own particular reasons, not after seven months but after two! Nevertheless, this does not alter in any way at all the original scientific calculation of the possibility of defending it for seven months. In short, practical experience may provide countless variants. Still, the axiom of the *excessive* advantage (such as no one anywhere even dreamed of prior to our current war with the Turks) of the strength of the defense over the strength of the attack, given the armaments presently in use, remains in full force. (I stress once more: it was not the advantage itself that we were unable to foresee, but its *excessive* degree.)

But now practical experience is on our side and we will no longer make *such* a mistake. Now Totleben is there; what he will do we do not precisely know, but the brilliant engineer will, perhaps, find the means (not only in this specific instance, but in general) to shake this *axiom*, to do away with the *excessiveness* and balance the two forces (the attack and the defense) by some brilliant new discovery. Europe is attentively, eagerly watching what he is doing and is expecting not only political results but scientific ones as well. In short, our military horizon has cleared, and once again there are many hopes. In Asia the matter has ended with a great victory. Our Balkan army is large and magnificent; its morale is equal to its great goal. The Russian people (I mean the People), united as one, all want to achieve the great aim of the war for Christianity. Mothers cannot help but weep over their children who go off to war: this is nature; but the conviction of the holiness of the cause remains in full force. Fathers and mothers know what they are sending their children to: the war is a People's war. There are some who deny this, who do not believe it, who select facts that would contradict it; yet news such as the following, which appears in the newspapers in fine print, remains almost unnoticed: "*The Odessa Messenger* has received a report from Birzula Station that on October 3 some 2,800 convalescent soldiers were transported through that station to the army in the field. It is remarkable that among the wounded *not a single one* expressed the wish to take advantage of his right and remain with the reserves. Everyone hastens to the front" (*The Moscow News,* No. 251).

How do you like that bit of news? Now facts like those, I think, testify to the nature of the cause! After that, how can anyone claim that the current war is not a Popular one and that the People are not involved? Yet there is not just one such fact but a multitude of them. They will all be collected, will cast their light, and will go into History. . . . Fortunately, the majority of these facts were attested to by many European eyewitnesses, and now it's no longer possible to change them, juggle them, and present them in a stock-exchange or a *Roman-clerical* light. . . .

2

1. Hartung's Suicide and Our Eternal Question: Who Is to Blame?

All the Russian newspapers have recently been discussing (and still are discussing) the suicide of General Hartung in Moscow during the session of the Circuit Court a quarter of an hour after he heard the jurors pronounce him guilty. And so I think that all the readers of the *Diary* already know more or less about this extraordinary and tragic event and that I need not describe it in detail. The overall gist of the case is that a man of substantial rank and from the upper levels of society gets involved with a former tailor, subsequently a moneylender and discounter, Sanftleben; and he does this not only because he had to borrow money from him but even as a friend, apparently taking on quite willingly, for instance, the duty of being Sanftleben's executor. Then, after Sanftleben's death, several heinous events took place: a ledger listing promissory notes disappears no one knows where; in complete violation of practices prescribed by law, Hartung removes various promissory notes, papers, and documents to his own apartment. Hartung, as it turns out, enters into an agreement with one group of the heirs, to the detriment of another group (although, perhaps, he does not realize this himself). Then one of the heirs bursts into his apartment and the poor executor gets a practical demonstration of the kind of people he's mixed up with. Then the direct accusations begin—the theft of promissory notes and the ledger, improper endorsement of notes, the disappearance of documents entailing a loss of property of at least a hundred or even two hundred thousand rubles. . . . Then the trial begins. The prosecutor is even happy about having a trial and a general sitting next to a common man, thus giving the Russian Themis an opportunity to proclaim the triumph of equality before the law of the powerful and exalted and the low and insignificant.

The trial, however, proceeds quite normally (whatever might have been said about it), and at last the jurors bring in the almost inevitable conviction which, for Hartung, means "guilty of embezzlement." The court retires to determine the sentence, but General Hartung did not choose to wait and hear it: the reports say that he withdrew to another room, sat down at a table, and clasped his poor head; then, suddenly, a shot rang out: he had shot himself in the heart with a revolver he brought with him and had loaded beforehand. On his body was found a note, also written previously, in which he swore by *Almighty God* that he had not stolen anything in this affair and that he forgave his enemies. And so he died, convinced of his innocence and his gentlemanly behavior.

And now this death has titillated everyone in Moscow and all the newspapers all over Russia. The reports are that both the judges and the prosecutor came out of their chambers deathly pale. The jurors, it is said, were also unnerved. The newspapers even bewailed the "obviously unjust verdict," and one of them noted that now Russian courts can no longer be accused of bringing in lenient verdicts that only encourage more criminality: "Here," they said, "is one example. An innocent person has perished." Others justly noted that it was almost impossible not to believe such solemn last words from a man, and so one could conclude, almost beyond doubt, that a lamentable miscarriage of justice had occurred. And a great deal has been said and written in the newspapers. One must admit that some of the newspapers' responses were strange: there was something false in them; it may have been ardent and sincere, yet it was false. One feels sorry for Hartung, but this is still a tragedy (a very deep one)—the destiny of Russian life—rather than a mistake on anyone's part. Or, to put it better, everyone is guilty here: the mores and the habits of our educated society; the characters that have been formed and created in this society; and finally, the mores and habits of our young courts that we have borrowed and have not sufficiently Russified. But if the whole lot of us are guilty, then separately no one is guilty. Of all the responses from the newspapers, the one that most appealed to me came from *New Times*. On the eve of the verdict I happened to be speaking with one of our most discerning lawyers, a man who knows Russian life very well, and it turned out that we both had come to the same conclusion about this case; my friend very aptly pointed out the "tragic nature" of this case and the reasons for that tragedy. The next day, in "Mr. X's" column, I read a great deal that was very similar to what we had been discussing the night before. And so, if I do say a few words now, they are only in particular and "apropos."

2. The Russian Gentleman. A Gentleman Cannot but Remain a Gentleman to the End

The fact is that the old character types have not yet disappeared and, it seems, will not disappear for a long while yet, because a certain time is needed for everything and nature is everywhere involved. I am speaking of character types in our educated society. Here, however, I must stubbornly and insistently note that it would not be a good thing were we to change suddenly like weather vanes, because the most abhorrent trait of our educated individuals is precisely this volatility and lack of content. There is something servile in it, something of the lackey dressed in his master's coat. One aspect of our gentlemanizing, for instance, is *making an impressive show*, the need to arrange our lives on a grand scale, and this is revealed when we somehow come into contact with the wealthy and prominent, and especially when we manage to enter their circle. Note that now I am saying not a single word about Hartung personally; I know nothing at all of his biography; I want only to register several traits of the universally known character of our educated person, speaking generally, a person to whom exactly the same thing might happen as did to General Hartung, given the appropriate circumstances.

Take an insignificant person of low rank, without a penny in his pocket, who suddenly finds himself in the highest society or at least comes into contact with it for some reason. And so this poor fellow, who possesses nothing apart from the ability to worm his way into high society, suddenly acquires his own carriage, an apartment in which he can live "appropriately," servants, suits, and gloves. Perhaps he wants to make a career for himself and become a somebody, but more often than not he simply wants to copy: "Everybody lives that way," he thinks, "so why shouldn't I?" He feels a certain shame which he simply cannot overcome; in short, he has rather peculiar notions of honor and decency, and he turns out to have no personal dignity at all. Parallel to this lack of understanding of such a fundamental thing as a sense of personal dignity there is, I think, merely a lack of understanding among almost everyone in this educated, European age, of freedom and what it consists of; but of that, later. The second, and again almost tragic quality of our Russian educated person is his tendency to give in, his readiness to agree. Oh, there are many kulaks, stock-exchange gamblers, repulsive but determined scoundrels: there are even some good, determined people as well, but there are awfully few of them; in the majority of decent Russian people there prevails specifically this quickness to yield, the need to concede, to come to terms. And this certainly is not due to good nature and not, by any means, cowardice; it is just there, due to some sort of politeness or goodness knows what. How often, for instance, in conversation with some stubborn fellow who presses you and insists that you express your opinion, have you agreed with him and given up your own opinion or even your vote at some meeting or other even though, inside yourself, you may not have wished to do so at all? The Russian is also very much enthralled by the word *everyone:* "I, like everyone"; "I agree with the general view"; "Everyone is going, hurrah!" But there is one other strange thing here: the Russian is very fond of seducing, charming, enthralling, and persuading himself. He really doesn't feel like doing this or that—becoming Sanftleben's executor, for instance—but he talks himself into it: "Well, why not? I'll do it. . . ."

Among this class of educated Russians there are types with some remarkably attractive features, but they have precisely these unfortunate qualities of Russian gentlemanliness which I just indicated. Some of them are almost innocent, virtual Schillers; their lack of knowledge of "business" adds something almost touching to their characters, but they have a strong sense of honor: such a person will shoot himself, like Hartung, if he thinks he has lost his honor. There may even be quite a number of such people. But they scarcely ever know the sum total of their own debts, for instance. And it's not that they're all spendthrifts; rather, they are excellent husbands and fathers, but money can be squandered by an excellent father just as quickly as by a spendthrift. Very many of them enter life with the paltry remnants of former family estates, which quickly disappear in the first days of their youth. Then comes marriage, and then rank and a nice little government job which is only fair-to-middlin' but which still provides a certain income and a basis in life, something solid, as opposed to the wandering in the world of high society that marked the former life. But the debts constantly pile up and, of course, he pays them because he is a gentleman; but he pays them with new debts. One can positively say that many of them, when they ponder their situation privately at certain moments, might state confidently and with great nobility, "We have misappropriated nothing and have no intention of misappropriating anything." And yet some little thing like this might come up: if the need arises (I mean a very great need), he's capable of borrowing even from his children's nurse some ten rubles that she's managed to save up. Well, indeed, why not? Besides, this old woman, more often than not, is someone who has lived on such close, intimate terms in his house. She's almost a member of the family; they are kind to her, and she's even entrusted with the most important keys of the household. The good general, her master, long ago has promised her a place in the almshouse in her old age, but now it's just that these business dealings always keep him from taking care of the matter, otherwise he would have long ago put in a word for her. And the nurse is simply afraid of reminding him of it; maybe she reminds him about the almshouse once a year, but she trembles at the thought of bothering such a constantly nervous and preoccupied man as her general. "They're good people, after all; they'll remember it on their own," she thinks sometimes, as she settles her old bones in her bed; and she's even ashamed to remind him about the ten rubles; she has her own conscience, she has. And then suddenly the general dies, and the old woman is left with neither a place nor her ten rubles. This is an awfully trivial thing, of course—a most inconsequential matter; yet if in the next world the general were suddenly reminded that the nurse never got her ten rubles back, he would be terribly embarrassed: "What ten rubles? Ah, yes, of course, four years ago! *Mais comment, comment*—how could this happen!" And this debt would torment him more than some other ten-thousand-ruble debt he had left unpaid! He would be so terribly ashamed: "Oh, believe me, I never intended that; believe me, I never even thought of it; I forgot to think!" But only the angels would be listening to the poor general (since he would certainly get to paradise), while the nurse would still be left on earth without her ten rubles, and sometimes the old woman would feel sorry for him: "Well, God be with him; it's a sin to remember such a thing about him; he was a priceless man, the most righteous master you'd ever find."

And here's one more thing: if this charming man somehow suddenly found himself back on earth as the general again, would he give back the ten rubles to the nurse?

But they don't just keep borrowing all the time. Here's his friend, that no-o-blest fellow, Ivan Petrovich, asking him to write him a promissory note for six thousand; "I'll put it in my bank," he says, "and discount it; and you, my dearest friend, shall have this counter note for six thousand." What is there to think about? The notes are exchanged. He often meets Ivan Petrovich afterwards in the club; of course they've both forgotten even to think about the notes they've given because they're both the very flower of respectability, so to say, in our society; and suddenly, six months later, the whole six thousand falls on the general's shoulders: "Would you be so good as to settle this, your excellency." And so at this point they rush off to people like Sanftleben and sign notes at a hundred percent interest.

Once more, please believe me when I say that in my description here I make no claim to accusing the late General Hartung in any way: I did not know him at all and have no personal information about him. I only ventured to make a rough character sketch of one member of this society; but were such a character to get into the same sort of scrape as General Hartung did with Sanftleben, then just the same thing might happen to him as did to Hartung, including the suicide. And so it seems to me that in the case of Hartung there is no reason to put the court to shame or for the court to feel any shame. This is a matter of fate, after all—a tragedy: General Hartung, until his final moment, felt himself to be innocent, and he left a note. . . .

"Yes, he did," some may say, "but let's look at that note. Surely it's not possible that at such a moment a person, and one who also believes in God, as it turns out, could lie. That means he didn't steal anything, if he so solemnly declared that he didn't. Indeed, he couldn't even have struck some sort of deal with his conscience here: no matter how shaky and befogged the man's reasoning was because of this whole mess, when he says 'I didn't steal,' he must surely have known whether he did or not. It's something one can tell, after all. The simple question here is this: did he fill his pockets or didn't he? If he had stolen something, how could he not know?"

That's absolutely true, but here is what could have happened and surely did happen: he was only referring to himself when he wrote,

"I stole nothing and had no thought of stealing"; but still, others could have stolen.

"Absolutely impossible," people will object. "If he allowed others to steal and, knowing this, said nothing in his capacity as trustee, then *he did steal* in collusion with the others! General Hartung must have known that there was no difference."

My answer, first, is that the argument "If he knew and allowed others to steal, then he stole as well" can still be disputed; and, second, there certainly is a difference here. And, third, General Hartung might well have written merely in the literal sense of which we are speaking, that is: "I personally took nothing and *never wanted* to take anything; others did so, and against my will. I am guilty only of weakness, but not of fraud because I had no intention of taking anything myself and even resisted it. It was done by others. . . ." He might have written his fateful words in precisely that spirit, but at the same time, being so honest and noble, could simply be unable to concede that "if he allowed others to steal, it means he stole himself." He was going to God, and he knew that he had had no intention of stealing or of tolerating stealing by others, but money just got stolen. And note as well that there was no way he could have explained the words in his note in more detail, i.e., to have said that he was guilty of leniency, but not of theft, and so on. As a gentleman he could not denounce other people, especially at such a solemn moment, in which he "forgave his enemies."

Finally, and most probably, in his heart he perhaps could not even admit his leniency, his weakness, his good-natured tolerance. Here, perhaps, there was such a network of circumstances that he was unable to understand it even at the very final moment, and thus he departed for the next world. "The notes ledger has disappeared"; and then the shrewd people whom he fully trusts convince him at first that this, after all, is only a minor thing, that it's simply been mislaid because, after all, no one needed it. They produce figures showing mathematically that the ledger would have been to the detriment and not the benefit of the heirs themselves. (Why, that same argument was later used in court by the defense, and it seems that it was correct.) All the rest could have been demonstrated and explained to Hartung in the same sense. He wasn't a businessman, after all, and he could be convinced of anything. "Believe us," they would say, "we're also honest people; we don't want to steal *anything* from the heirs any more than you do; but Sanftleben's affairs were left in such a ticklish state that if they (the heirs) now find out about that ledger and the other things, they might accuse us directly of fraud, and so we have to hide it from them." Of course, this "muddle" in Sanftleben's affairs was not revealed at once but only gradually, so that Hartung was learning the truth or, to put it better, was losing hold of the truth and being drawn into lies gradually, as each day passed. And then, suddenly, one of the heirs came bursting right into his apartment, and if he didn't shout that General Hartung was a thief, then he did virtually the same thing: he came in with a triumphant air, a victorious and malicious smile, and was already convinced that now he could venture to do any nasty thing he pleased in the general's apartment. And only then did the general fully realize what a den of thieves he'd got himself into. And then he lost his grip entirely; he began to suggest compromises and deals and, of course, became more and more entangled, while the accusing side avidly fastened on those compromises and deals as new facts to discredit him even more. The whole thing became part of the case. In short, Hartung died with the conviction of his absolute personal innocence; but even so, there was no mistake . . . no miscarriage of justice, in the strict sense. It was fate; there was a tragedy: a blind force for some reason picked out Hartung alone to punish him for the *vices* that are so widespread in his society. There may be ten thousand like him, but Hartung alone perished. With his tragic outcome this innocent and supremely honest man, of all those ten thousand, was able to arouse the greatest sympathy, though his trial had maximum publicity in Russia and served as a warning to those "steeped in vice"; but Fate, the blind goddess, could hardly have considered that when she struck him down.

3. Lies Are Indispensable for Truth. A Lie Times a Lie Equals Truth. Is That True?

And yet, an old impression of mine has come to life again in my mind, and even though it may be a very naive one, I would like to share it. It's about our courts in general. A public trial by jury is accepted all over the world as all but perfection achieved: "It's a triumph, so to say, the supreme fruit of reason." I believe that, along with everyone else, because if you're told, for instance, "Well, invent something better," you just can't do it. And so you have to agree, simply because it's impossible to invent anything better.

Meanwhile, the prosecutor mounts the stage . . . or rather, the podium. We'll imagine that he's an excellent man, intelligent, conscientious, educated, with Christian convictions, and a man who knows Russia and the Russians as few people in Russia do. And so this most conscientious man begins directly by saying that he is "even pleased that this crime has taken place because at last this villain—the accused over there—will be punished; because if you only knew, gentlemen of the jury, what a rapscallion he is!" I mean to say, of course, that he won't use the word "rapscallion," but that makes no difference: in the most polite, gentle, and humane fashion he at last makes him out to be even worse than a rapscallion, worse than any rapscallion could be. With grievous heart he tells them in a most delicate way that the accused's mother was also of the same stripe, that the accused, finally, could not help but steal because the lowest forms of vice drew him deeper and deeper into the abyss. But he did it all consciously and with the most complete premeditation. Just recall how well he was served by the fire in the next street that broke out while he was committing the crime, because when the fire caused an alarm it diverted the attention of the porters and the whole neighborhood.

"Oh, of course I'm in no way making any *direct* accusation of arson, but, gentlemen of the jury, you must agree that there is a strange coincidence of two events here which inevitably leads one to a certain thought; but I'll say no more. But, of course, you will send this thief, this murderer (because he certainly would have committed murder had he encountered anyone in the apartment), this arsonist—this inveterate, confirmed arsonist—you'll send him away for a good long time and thereby allow decent people to breathe freely, housewives to leave their apartments to buy groceries without having to worry, and landlords to rest easy about their property, even though it be insured by this or that insurance company. Yet the main thing is that I have no need to repeat all this: just look at him! There he sits, not daring to look honest people in the eyes; do you need more than a quick glance to see that he is a thief, a murderer, and an arsonist? There is only one thing I solemnly regret: that he did not manage to commit ten such thefts of linen, murder ten such housewives, and set fire to ten such buildings, because then the very immensity of the crime would have shaken our society, which ignores its civic duties, and would have compelled it to resort at last to self-defense and shake off its civic slumber. . . ."

Oh, we know that Mr. Prosecutor will speak in a much nobler fashion than that. Our words are a caricature and are suited merely for the little Sunday comic papers with their couplets and caricatures, let's say. Let's say we have even one of those cases that give rise to profound social and civic questions and, most important, one that has psychological aspects; and as we know, prosecutors even throughout Europe are exceptionally smart when it comes to psychology. Well, and even then the outcome would be the same, i.e., it's a pity that instead of just one there weren't ten, or thirty, or five hundred poisonings, because then your hearts would throb and you would rise up as one man, etc., etc.

But, people may object, what's all the fuss about? Granted, awfully few prosecutors are orators at all, but the prosecutor, in the first place, is a civil servant who is supposed to act in accordance with his office; and, in the second place, the fact that prosecutors always exaggerate the accusation is not at all reprehensible but, rather, is all to the good. For that is just as it should be. On the other side, opposing him, is the defendant's attorney who is given full scope to refute the prosecutor. Moreover, even throughout Europe it is permitted to prove—with the most absolute politeness, of course—that the prosecutor is stupid, foolish, rather despicable, and that "if anyone set fire to a house on the Third Line, Vasilevsky Island the other day, then it was none other than this very prosecutor, since at that very time he was on Vasilevsky Island at a name-day party for General Mikhailov, that most excellent and no-o-ble creature; that he set fire to the house is beyond doubt, for the sole reason (psychology again) that, had he not set fire to this house because of his animosity toward the owner, the merchant Ivan Borodaty, then he would never have taken it into his head to make such a stupid, inconceivable, and base accusation against the defendant of arson for the purpose of diverting the attention of the whole street while he committed this fictitious and preposterous crime. It was the prosecutor's own act of arson that gave him the idea of making this accusation." Finally, take into consideration as well that the defense attorney is permitted to make gestures, shed tears, gnash his teeth, tear his hair, knock the chairs about (but not threaten anyone with them), and, finally, fall into a faint if he is so truly noble and unable to tolerate injustice; these things, it seems, are not permitted to the prosecutor, no matter how noble he may be, because it would seem strange, somehow, for a civil servant in uniform suddenly to fall down flat in a faint. That isn't done at all.

Once again, everything I am saying is a caricature and only a caricature, and none of this happens; everything is done in a most noble fashion, I agree (although chairs have been knocked about and people have fallen into a faint)! But I'm only concerned about the essence of the thing, because one may achieve the same point by using the most gracious locutions as by the least gracious.

"Come now, what are you saying?" people may ask. "That's just what's needed; exaggeration is precisely what's needed, from both sides! The juror is often not such an educated man and, besides, he's busy; he has his own shop, his own affairs; sometimes he's preoccupied, and sometimes he's simply unable to get absorbed in the case. And so something is needed to arouse his attention, to show him all the angles of the case, even the most unlikely ones, so that he may be absolutely convinced that the prosecution has exhausted all the possibilities he can imagine and nothing more needs to be thought about it; and also that the defense, in the same way, has brought out everything possible and impossible to conceive in order to whitewash the defendant whiter than mountain snow. And so, when they're off in their own special room summing it up, they already know—mechanically, so to speak—what they have to conclude, plus or minus, so that at least their consciences may be absolutely at rest. As a result, it's clear that all this is absolutely indispensable to reveal the truth—that is, a furious attack and a furious defense; and it's even true that a furious attack by the prosecutor, in the strictest sense, is even more useful to the accused than to the prosecutor, so that, once more, we see that it's impossible to invent anything finer."

In short, the court of today is not only the triumph or the supreme fruit of reason but also full of the most subtle complexities. One can't help but agree with that. Moreover, the court is public; the public throngs there by the hundreds—and can you really suppose that they do so only from idleness, merely for the spectacle of it? Of course not: whatever brought them to the court, it is necessary that they depart with a lofty, powerful, edifying, and wholesome impression. Yet they all sit there and see that the whole thing is based on a kind of lie—oh, it's not in the trial, of course, and not in the significance of the sentence, but simply, say, in certain practices borrowed from Europe with such exuberant lack of discrimination and which have taken root in those responsible for the defense and the prosecution. And so I go home, where I think to myself: why, I know this Ivan Khristoforovich, the prosecutor, personally; he's a most intelligent and good man, and yet he lied and knew that he was lying. A case that should have required only some reprimand or a two-month jail sentence he stretched out to a twenty-year exile in a remote area. What he did may well have been necessary to elucidate the case, yet he lied, and lied deliberately; and the case involved a man's neck, after all. How can this be reconciled, particularly if he's a man with talent: *il en reste toujours quelque chose,* after all, particularly if the defense is not so good and only knows how to knock chairs about. Granted, Ivan Khristoforovich's vanity made its presence felt here, and that's a purely human trait; but can it be excused in a case as important as this? What's happened to the man himself, that higher, humane, civilized man?

Let's grant that, ultimately, the truth does emerge from all this and emerges even mechanically, so to say, through a most devious process; but the public who have gathered in the courtroom may then be gathering to watch a spectacle, to observe this mechanical and devious process; and, listening with delight as the talented defense attorney, say, lies so beautifully against his conscience, they are almost ready to applaud him and his chairs: "Just listen to the fellow; how he can lie!" Now this gives rise to cynicism and falsehood in the mass of that public, and these things imperceptibly take root. People no longer yearn for truth but for talent, so long as it can amuse and divert them. The humane instincts are dulled, and these cannot be restored by somersaulting into a faint. Well, just imagine, once more, what happens when the liar really does have great talent!

I know that all this is only idle whining on my part. But listen: the institution of public trial by jury is not a Russian one, after all; it was copied from a foreign model. Can one really not hope that the Russian nationality, the Russian spirit, will some day smooth out the rough spots and eliminate the falsity . . . of bad habits, and that the matter will proceed fully in accordance with truth and justice? It's true that now this is impossible: now, particularly, the defense and the prosecution flaunt these bad habits, for the former are looking to make money and the latter to make careers. But still, someday it will be possible for the prosecutor even to defend the accused instead of prosecuting him, so that if the defense attorneys should try to object that even the small bit of the accusation the prosecutor has left with the defendant should not be charged to him, they would not be believed by the jury.

I even think that such a technique would promote finding the truth more readily and more accurately than the former, mechanical means of exaggeration, consisting of extremism in the prosecution and utter fury in the defense. Of course, the reply will be that this is utterly impossible, and since this is the way things are done in Europe, then my way could not be implemented and that "*the more mechanical it is, the better*."

Now it is this very mechanism, this mechanical means of dragging the truth out into the open that may be replaced . . . simply by truth. Artificial exaggeration will disappear from both sides. Everything will appear sincere and just and not a game at seeking the truth. On stage there will be no spectacle, no game, but a lesson, for instance, an example, something edifying. It's true that lawyers will be paid much less. But all such utopias will be possible, maybe, only when we grow wings and are transformed into angels. But then there won't be any law courts either. . . .

3

1. Roman Clericals Here in Russia

Not long ago *The Moscow News*, No. 262, made the following observation in its editorial:

> A few days ago we drew attention to a certain party in Russia that is acting in accord with Russia's enemies and that is prepared to assist the Turks in their conflict with us—a party of Anglo-Magyars that hates every manifestation of our national spirit and every action of our government made in this spirit; it is a party that places Russian patriotism on the same level as nihilism and revolution, a party that feeds the foreign press, hostile to us, with the most disgusting information. Our article had scarcely been sent to press when a telegram from our Petersburg correspondent supplied us with the essence of the communiqué, made public in *The Government Messenger*, which provided ample evidence of new machinations of this party. At the same time our army was winning brilliant victories between Plevna and Orhanie, the conspirators, in an attempt to demoralize the public, spread rumors of the defeat these same victorious troops supposedly suffered; the efforts of the conspirators are so intense that the government considered it necessary to alert the public against such malicious rumors.

The very next day, *New Times* remarked in this connection—only in passing, however—that *The Moscow News* had overstated the matter somewhat and that *The Government Messenger* had in mind, perhaps, simply some idle talk among the public which had no such significance. (I am setting forth the idea of *New Times* in my own words, from memory.)

It's very possible that this is so and that *The Government Messenger* really was speaking only of some "idle talk." Nevertheless, the hypothesis of *The Moscow News* does have real foundation. Only who are these Anglo-Magyars *The Moscow News* refers to? In Russia, in the border areas as well as the interior, we do have our own Roman clericals. It's no longer May, however; now everyone knows and writes about the worldwide clerical conspiracy, and even the most liberal of our newspapers have agreed that this conspiracy does exert its influence. But it would be a strange thing if a Vatican conspiracy overlooked our Roman clericals and failed to use them in its cause. Disturbances in the rear of the Russian army would be extremely useful to the Vatican, especially at the present moment. Here is another excerpt, this time from *New Times*, No. 587. *New Times*, in its section "Survey of Our Newspapers and Magazines," cites the opinion *The Voice* expressed on several articles in the English *Morning Post* and in several Polish magazines published abroad. Here is the excerpt:

> *The Morning Post* of October 22 published an article, curious because of its unexpected nature, in which the Turkophile newspaper reported on talks that had supposedly begun between Russia and Germany over the ceding to Germany of the lands along the Vistula right up to the river itself! It goes without saying that in the eyes of *The Morning Post* this is the result of a deal in which Germany guarantees to support "Russia's acquisitions in the Balkan peninsula." The London newspaper insists further that the Poles of the lands along the Vistula now have no thought of rebellion, "not wishing to fall into an even more ruthless enslavement," i.e., under Prussian power, and that if there are any disorders in "Russian Poland," then they will be simply a result of "Russo-Prussian intrigues." . . . It is remarkable that a few days before this article appeared in *The Morning Post, Dziennik polski* spoke about the same thing, although in a rather different tone, reporting that the Russian government, when it withdrew its troops from the Vistula region, supposedly broadcast an appeal to the peasants there, inviting them to form their own rural guard to watch the landowners and put down any attempt at rebellion. In conveying the contents of these articles, *The Voice* expressed amazement as to why *Dziennik polski* and *The Morning Post* suddenly began to be so impassioned. Why did they find it necessary to publish this absurd tale of a Russian appeal to the peasants along the Vistula and of Russo-Prussian *agents-provocateurs* supposedly trying to rouse "an artificial rebellion" in Congress Poland?
>
> These surprising antics must have some purpose. The newspapers that published such things probably have information which leads

> them to fear the outbreak of disturbances in the region along the Vistula, and they are attempting to distort in advance the meaning of a movement whose consequences, evidently, they fear. This tactic is not new. It was used by the Poles and their Western friends in 1863. This recollection alone compels us to admit that the articles in *Dziennik polski* and *The Morning Post* are not without significance and have some mysterious link with the earlier talk in the Magyar press of the Poles' sympathy for the Turks and of their secret wish to add complications to Russia's situation through revolutionary agitation on our western frontier. It is interesting that these articles come at the same time as the news of Cardinal Ledochowski's candidacy for the papal throne. "We do not belong," says *The Voice,* "to those who are eager to give exaggerated significance to all the fantastic schemes seized upon by Russia's ill-wishers in the hope of preventing a favorable outcome to the present war. In the given instance, the matter seems to us to be sufficiently serious that the fact of the unexpected and, evidently, uncalled for appearance of the articles in *Dziennik polski* and *The Morning Post* cannot be left without being noted."

And so is there, perhaps, something resembling the tentacles of a clerical conspiracy here in Russia as well? The report of Ledochowski's candidacy certainly comes from Polish sources, for only the irresponsible mind of a Polish agitator abroad could seriously believe that the Roman conclave, replete with such subtle intellects, would blunder so badly as to elect Ledochowski: then the new pope would do little else but work for the restoration of his fatherland and not for the Roman and universal domain of the popes. But that's a side issue; the fact is that the tentacles of the clerical conspiracy are clearly visible in Russia. *New Times* adds: "the current persistent polemics of the *Journal de St.-Pétersbourg* with the Italian clerical newspapers over the supposed suppression of Catholicism in Poland suggests that there are signs of certain agitation on our western frontier."

Well, these certainly aren't merely "signs." They show that it is precisely the *party* that *Moscow News* says "is acting in accord with Russia's enemies . . . that hates every manifestation of our national spirit, *every action of our government made in this spirit;* it is a party that places Russian patriotism on the same level as nihilism and revolution, a party that feeds the press, hostile to us, with the most disgusting information. . . ."

Yes, indeed, it's very, very possible that dispatches to Europe from Russia are the work of this party. This delight in Russian reverses and the silly screams of joy that, supposedly, Russia has suddenly proved "weak, without financial resources, with her army in disarray, with a discontented, restive People, with a nihilism that has undermined her society"—all these fictions undoubtedly bear the stamp of such a well-known source. Oh, certainly there are also some Russian pens ready to write in unison with the clericals, but these dispatches abroad cannot, it seems, have been written by Russians: that would have been too base an act. Nevertheless, the clericals, perhaps without even exerting much effort, are certainly controlling even Russian pens right here at home. They may not be making any direct suggestions to them at all, and are not entering into any *direct* and *proper* relations with them because these ready liberal pens *sometimes* belong to the most principled people who, should they hear a direct proposal from a clerical, might well throw him out the door. Yet a clerical, particularly one who has lived among us for some time, knows very well that he does not need to approach this ready pen himself because the ready Russian pen will write everything he wants for free, solely because he imagines (oh, the dear people!) that this is honorable and liberal. The ready pen is indignant, for instance, at the clericals who have clung to MacMahon in France and writes threatening articles against them. But, at the same time, he not only fails to notice the Russian Roman clerical but sometimes sings in complete unison along with him. Such people exist, they truly do. And our crafty Roman clericals may even wonder at them: "How eager they are to play a double game and fall flat on their faces," they think, nodding their heads. "And how selfless they are! It's true that they have to be liberal to the end. Now they're shouting that Russia doesn't even have the right to liberate the Slavs: why, if we were to pay them a hundred thousand rubles for that it would be too little! And the whole time they're playing this double game. How is it they don't feel the strain? Or do they recover from it so quickly? . . ."

2. Old Poland's Summer Attempt at Reconciliation

At the beginning of the summer these clerical-agitators tried to make their presence felt among us even via Russian periodicals. The wolves dressed themselves in sheep's clothing and began speaking as if they represented the entire Polish "emigration" abroad. They began proposing a reconciliation: "Accept us," they said.

"We can also see that Slavic brotherhood certainly exists and we don't wish to be left out." They spoke with extraordinary tenderness and set forth their reasons:

> "We have engineers, chemists, technologists, tradesmen, bookkeepers, agronomists and so on," they say. There are many such people among the emigrés. Let them in! A resident of Lithuania, writing in *The St. Petersburg News*, No. 172, said: "Is there no work among you for people of the class that once produced a Tengoborski for Russia and a Wolowski for France? And in art, which does so much to refine manners and ennoble character, Brotzki the sculptor and Matejko the painter are now known all over the world as representatives of Polish society. Do you not need such people? And what do you say about the whole assembly of literary men, journalists, entrepreneurs, manufacturers, and every other kind of active person? Do you not need these people either?" (*New Times*, from Kostomarov's article)

Mr. Kostomarov gave a superb answer, in *New Times*, to all this currying of favor. I regret that I do not have space to include excerpts from this excellent article. Mr. Kostomarov proves, in clear and precise arguments, that all this is merely a trap laid for us, that they would send us traitors like Konrad Wallenrod; that the Pole of Old Poland instinctively, blindly hates Russia and the Russians. Mr. Kostomarov admits, however, that there are some very fine Polish people who can live even in friendship with a Russian, save him in times of misfortune, and lend him money. That's true, of course; but the moment this Russian, even after twenty years of friendship, expressed to this very fine Pole any truly Russian political convictions about Poland, this same Pole would at once become, openly or in secret, the enemy of his Russian friend, for the rest of his life, to the end—the implacable and perpetual enemy. Mr. Kostomarov forgot to add that point.

This whole summer attempt at "reconciliation," which found both Russian supporters and an opponent as powerful as Mr. Kostomarov, is unquestionably a covert act of the clericals in Europe, an offshoot of the all-European clerical conspiracy. Oh, these Poles of Old Poland assure us that they certainly aren't clericals or papists or Romans and that we should have realized this long ago. But can you really suppose that Old Poland, this Polish emigration, does not cling to the pope in the Jesuitical sense and is far from the wild imaginings of the clericals—oh, what an absurd notion! Aren't they the very ones who would cling to the Vatican when they are so fully aware of its strength and have always been aware of it? The Vatican never ever betrayed Old Poland, after all; on the contrary, the Vatican gave full support to Old Poland's every wild notion when other states would not even listen. No, they won't betray the Vatican, and the Vatican won't betray them. The summer foray to seek reconciliation was made precisely at the time the entire emigration came out against the Russians, when Polish legions were being formed, when the aristocrats of the emigration appeared in Constantinople with huge sums of money (not their own, of course). This whole attempt at reconciliation was no more than an act of perfidy, as Mr. Kostomarov defined it. By the way: they are offering us their scientists, technologists, and artists, and they tell us, "Take them; don't you need them?" One might add here that they probably regard us as a savage people and do not know that we have all the things they are offering us, perhaps even better ones than theirs. But there's no point in taking offense; the main thing is: why don't they come? We did have several Poles who showed their talents, and Russia honored them, respected them, gave them a place of distinction, and in no way treated them differently from the Russians. So why all these arrangements? Come! Be reconciled and accept the situation, but know that Old Poland will never exist again. There is New Poland, a Poland liberated by the tsar, a Poland that is being reborn and certainly may expect to have, in time to come, a fate equal to those of the other Slavic tribes when Slavdom is liberated and resurrected in Europe. But Old Poland will never exist again because she could never get along with Russia. Her ideal is to assume Russia's place in the Slavic world. Her motto, in regard to Russia, is: "*ôte-toi de là, que je m'y mette*" ("get out of the way so I can take your place"). It's curious that this Polish advance skirmisher speaks only of scientists and artists. Well, what of the leaders of the emigration, the aristocrats? Just picture the result were Russia to give in to these flattering words and declare that she wants to make peace; and there they would sit, asking haughtily: "What are your terms?"

Because if you suggest that we allow the emigrés back into Russia, and they don't come on their own, *it means they are waiting for terms*. And so, imagine that Russia suddenly acknowledges that they amount to something, accepts them as a belligerent party, and begins these talks! Then they would make their way back to Russia; the magnates would at once start to find fault and demand high positions and honors; and then they would at once shout to the whole of Europe that they had been deceived; and then they would begin a Polish rebellion. . . . And Russia would be drawn into such a catastrophe and would make such a stupid mistake! Of course, the Poles themselves could not have believed that such a crude trick would deceive Russia. But they were counting on their Russian partisans who are so pure in heart. That this is the work of the clericals, a clerical move into Russia—of this there can be no doubt. People will ask what the purpose of this move was. But don't the clericals need to put out some feelers, to sow confusion, to conceal their real intentions, to acquire some Russian pens, to arouse Russian Poland, and so on, and so on? There's many another such notion they could have had!

3. The Escapade of *The Stock-Exchange News*. Not Ready Pens, Malicious Ones

We were talking just now of "ready pens." But we have pens that are certainly not ready, they are disgusting. And they also whistle (and at full volume) in tune with the Polish nightingales; but the Poles do not even have to control them; they do it all idealistically, knowing not what they do. Here it's simply a matter of malice, betrayed hopes, and wounded vanity. Such is the article in *The Stock-Exchange News* (No. 257) about Mr. Ilovaisky; they should at least learn how to write, but they just make fools of themselves!

Everyone knows that our scholar, Mr. Ilovaisky, was arrested and maltreated in Galicia. Traveling through Galicia for scholarly purposes, he asked, by mistake, a Polish priest to show him some local antiquities. Later he found a Russian priest, but the malicious Pole immediately denounced him for being a Russian Panslavist, propagandist, and agitator. Mr. Ilovaisky was unceremoniously arrested, searched, taken from one prison to another; at last, after the intercession of a local scholar, he was escorted to the Russian border. This promptly gained publicity in Russia: *The Moscow News* published an article about it. Our newspapers spoke up, but many of them did so without much passion, simply as a matter of interest. The fact of the maltreatment of a Russian scholar, for no reason whatsoever, it seems, appeared to everyone as something normal. Mr. Ilovaisky himself also had a few lines published in *The Moscow News* to reply to the articles in hostile newspapers, but these were meek, lethargic, and drowsy. Yet our stock-exchange manipulators, who regard Russia only from the point of view of their own pocket and who have no concern at all for the country, did their country a marvelous service. Here is the article from *The Stock-Exchange News:*

> . . . What sort of strange tricks was Mr. Ilovaisky playing in Galicia? What kind of propaganda was he trying to spread there?
>
> Are not the misfortunes which Russia is now suffering enough to drive the nonsense from the heads of our grizzled Panslavists? After all that is happening before our very eyes, do they really still have the spirit to carry on with the foolishness and buffoonery of this Panslavist nonsense, which has caused incalculable disasters for our state and which we all have long been sick of?
>
> So long as our Panslavists, who had grown dull from lack of activity, limited themselves to sending off Panslavic church bells, no one was concerned and they could amuse themselves as much as they pleased; but when, along with the church bells, they begin sending off bell ringers to spread the word, the matter takes on another significance entirely.
>
> Who summoned and who authorized Mr. Ilovaisky to carry on his Panslavist propaganda?
>
> Does he or does he not realize the consequences this might entail, particularly now, at the present moment? You gentlemen heap abuse on Klapka for inciting the Magyars to support the Turks; but what are you doing yourselves? What is Mr. Ilovaisky doing, under the pretext of studying Slavic antiquities? Tell me, isn't the evil wrought by your foolishness of last year enough for you? What more do you want? What new mess are you trying to create? That you can throw a stone into the water and are capable of it, that much we know full well; but you ought also to remember that the stones you throw sometimes have to be dragged out by the efforts of the whole People at a cost of sacrifices in blood and national exhaustion.
>
> So stop playing the fool; to everything there is a season. If heretofore you have done nothing but arouse the laughter of sensible people, now their attitude will only be one of indignation.

These people talk of indignation! Listen, *how dare you,* without knowing the case, write so positively to the whole of Russia and the whole of Europe (for your article had *its own* significance in Europe)—how dare you write about Mr. Ilovaisky: "Who summoned and who authorized Mr. Ilovaisky to carry on his Panslavist propaganda?" And then, after the absurd comparison of Mr. Ilovaisky with Klapka: "And what are you doing yourselves? What is

Mr. Ilovaisky doing, *under the pretext of studying Slavic antiquities?*" How dare you write about that so *positively,* when you *know perfectly well* that all this is untrue? Do you really think that people will allow you to betray Russia? You ask about Mr. Ilovaisky, "Does he or does he not understand?" And I ask you, Mr. Publicist, "Do you or do you not understand what you have done?" Why, in Austria they won't ask: "What sort of man wrote this? Is he clever or not, educated or not? Does he know anything at all about Panslavism or does he know nothing? Has he ever read anything about it?" Why, in Austria they'll say straightaway: "So it must be true that Russia is sending out agitators. If it weren't true, then how could a major Petersburg daily independent newspaper point so *positively,* with such passion and with such reproach, to the Slavophiles and so corroborate the fact of sending out emissaries to carry on agitation? The one who wrote that is a Russian himself," they will say. "One would think his patriotism would have restrained him and led him to conceal the crime. But he was unable to conceal the truth because his indignation as a patriot boiled over onto the Panslavists; thus they must be planning to inflict some truly terrible calamities on Russia with their desperate propaganda and agitation in Austria and the Slavic lands. And so we have no reason to apologize for the arrest of some Ilovaisky fellow there; rather, we have to increase the number of arrests and from now on must keep all Russians in Austria under strict observation. It's not for us to apologize; the Russian government ought to apologize to us for so openly tolerating the activity of noxious, anti-Austrian political societies and constantly sending over hordes of propagandists and agitators to rouse the Austrian Slavs against their legal government."

That's certainly what they'll say in Austria, and your article will certainly be considered in that sense, Mr. Publicist. What do you think: isn't that treason? Are you not betraying the interests of Russia to the Poles and the Austrians? Are you not supporting political turmoil, are you not furthering it? Surely you know *for certain, completely, precisely,* that no one has ever sent out any emissaries whatever; so how dare you write that Mr. Ilovaisky was traveling to sow dissension *under the pretext of studying Slavic antiquities?* Is there anyone in Russia who believes you when you say that? Yet you express yourself so positively about this case, as if you know it like the back of your hand. So who is sowing dissension?

Now, about another point: once you have vented your spleen by writing a deliberate untruth, you still permit yourself to trust—after your act of blatant betrayal of Russian interests to the Old Poles, the Austrians, and the various European riffraff constantly agitating against us—in the sympathy of Russian readers. Do you really have such a low opinion of them?

And what a tone! And what trepidation, what abasement before Austria! "What if she should take offense?" you think. In Gogol an ataman says to the Cossacks: "The favor of some foreign king—and not even a king, but the favor of a Polish magnate who kicks them in the face with his yellow boot—is dearer to them than any brotherhood." This ataman is talking about traitors. Do you really want the Russians, quaking with animal fear over their interests and their money, to bow down the same way before some yellow boot? On the contrary, isn't our best policy toward Austria, at this moment and this moment in particular, one of supreme national dignity and not the one you would have? You see, the more we abase ourselves—which you so long for—the more we strengthen and augment her demands. And what do we have to fear from Austria in any case? She would never be able to draw her sword against us even if she wanted to. On the contrary, it is precisely now that the time has come for a direct and open policy, so that later, when the war ends, there should be no unfortunate misunderstandings. We have no need to sign any promissory note. We ought to regard England in just the same way. They must realize, at least, that we have no reason to fear them and that, to the contrary, we are capable of doing more harm to them than they are to us. This they must realize, yet they have false information about us which is reinforced by just such escapades as that of *The Stock-Exchange News*. Last summer did the Austrians not maintain a belief that Russia's strength was an illusion that had deceived everyone and that henceforth Russia could no longer be considered a strong military power? It was at that very point that Austria's tone grew harsher. Were the English, also in the highest circles, not convinced that ten thousand English troops landed at Trebizond could settle once and for all our *problem* in the East and in the Caucasus? We do know them, but it seems that they do not know us. But it's poor service to Russia to betray her interests to our opponents and to see her in a cowardly, humiliating role when this is not the case at all and the whole thing is a lie.

November

1

1. What Does the Word "Striutsky" Mean?

During the two years of publishing my *Diary* I have used the rather obscure word "striutsky" two or three times and have had several inquiries from Moscow and the provinces as to its meaning. I regret that I have not yet answered any of these inquiries: I always intended to answer them, in passing at least, in the *Diary*. Now, as I am finishing off the *Diary*, I shall devote a few lines to this incomprehensible little Petersburg term; and if I begin the first page of my November issue with such a trifling thing, then it is specifically because in putting it off to the last page as I always have before, I scarcely ever find any free space for the "striutskys" because of other topics and each time have to put off the explanation until the next issue.

The word "striutsky, striutskys" is not used in educated circles but exclusively by the common folk and, it seems, only in Petersburg. So, it seems, this word was also coined in Petersburg. I say "it seems," because no matter how many "experts" I asked, none could tell me where it came from, how it developed phonetically, whether it was used anywhere outside Petersburg, and, finally, whether it was actually coined in Petersburg. As far as I'm concerned, again "it seems" to me (I cannot say any more positively) that this word is a purely Petersburg one and was coined specifically by the common folk of Petersburg, but by whom, when, how long ago?—that I do not know. On the basis of many inquiries among the People, and as far as I can understand, I can say that it has the following meaning.

A "striutsky" is a shallow, worthless, and insignificant fellow. In the majority of cases, and perhaps always, he is a drunkard who squanders everything on drink, a lost fellow. It seems, however, that in some cases a person who is not a drunkard can be called a "striutsky." But the principal qualities of this shallow and worthless sot, which have earned him a special appellation and the invention of a whole new word, are, first, senselessness, a particular sort of foolishness, witlessness, superficiality. He's a conspicuous nonentity. On a holiday evening some drunken people are shouting on the street; one hears a quarrel, a frenzied cry for the police; from the midst of the tightly packed crowd one can clearly make out someone's protesting, imploring, complaining, and threatening voice. There's a lot of fake anger. You go up to find out what is going on. In reply, people wave their hands and walk away: "It's nothing; just the striutskys." The word "striutskys" is pronounced here with disdain, with contempt. Always with contempt, and if the man who is shouting really has been beaten or maltreated, then even so, it seems, he will find no sympathy but only scorn, since he's merely a "striutsky"—that's to say, there's nothing worthwhile about him, and the things he's shouting are rubbish, and the fact that he's been beaten is rubbish as well; he's "the most no-account fellow" there could be. I might add that "striutskys" for the most part are shabbily dressed in out-of-season clothes and worn-out shoes. I might also add that "it seems" only those wearing European ("German") clothes are called "striutskys." I can't guarantee that, but it seems to be so.

The second essential trait of the confirmed drunkard called a "striutsky," apart from his worthlessness and superficiality, is his insufficiently defined status in society. I should think that a man who has money, a house, or some property and, besides, has a job which is even a bit steady and fixed—a factory worker, say—could not be called a "striutsky." But if he has a business, a shop (however small) or some such, but manages it carelessly, thoughtlessly, any-which-way, then he may fall into the category of "striutsky." And so a "striutsky" is a worthless fellow who cannot get along and settle down anywhere; he's a superficial man with no understanding of himself who, when drunk, often brags and blusters, a loudmouth; he's often resentful, mostly because he likes feeling offended; he's the one who calls the police or the authorities and who shouts, "Help!" And when you put it all together, you have only some worthless rubbish, a soap bubble that evokes scornful laughter: "Ah, it's nothing; just a 'striutsky.'"

I repeat, it seems to me that this word is exclusively a Petersburg one. But whether it is used in other places in Russia, I don't know.

It's very widely used among the common folk of Petersburg. In Petersburg there are a great many people who have come from the provinces, and so it's rather likely that this little term might reach other provinces as well, if it has not already done so. It may even find its way into literature; I think that writers besides me have used it. For one whose business is words, the attraction of this word lies in the shade of contempt with which the People use it to designate precisely such worthless, senseless, loudmouthed, careless, trashy fellows showing off in their meaningless rage. There are a lot of creatures of that sort in educated circles as well, and also in the highest circles—isn't that so? They're not necessarily drunkards in worn-out shoes; but that is often the only difference. How can one resist sometimes calling these higher-ups "striutskys" as well, the more so that the word is right there, tempting you with that shade of contempt with which the People utter it?

2. The History of the Verb "Stushevatsia"

By the way, since I'm speaking of the origin and use of new words: in our literature there is a word "stushevatsia," which is used by everyone; and although it didn't originate yesterday, it is of rather recent origin and has existed for no more than three decades; in Pushkin's day it was entirely unknown and used by no one. Now you may find it used not only by literary people of all sorts, from the most comical to the most serious, you may also find it in scientific treatises, dissertations, and philosophical works; moreover, you may find it in official government papers, reports, proceedings of meetings, and even in official instructions: everyone knows it, everyone understands it, everyone uses it. However, in the whole of Russia there is only one person who knows the exact origin of this word, the time it was coined, and the time it first appeared in literature. That person is I, because it was I who introduced and used this word in literature for the first time. This word appeared in print for the first time on January 1, 1846, in *Notes of the Fatherland*, in my story "The Double: The Adventures of Mr. Goliadkin."

My first tale, *Poor People*, I began in 1844; the work was completed, was read by Belinsky, and was accepted by Nekrasov for his almanac, *Petersburg Anthology*, in 1845. This almanac appeared at the end of 1845. But in the summer of that same year I had begun—after meeting Belinsky—this second tale of mine, "The

Double: The Adventures of Mr. Goliadkin." From the very beginning of the autumn of 1845, Belinsky took a great interest in this new work of mine. Even before reading it he informed Andrei Aleksandrovich Kraevsky about it (Belinsky was then working for Kraevsky's magazine); he introduced me to Kraevsky, and he and I agreed that when this new tale, "The Double," was finished, I would submit it to his *Notes of the Fatherland;* it was to appear in the early months of 1846. This tale of mine did not turn out well at all, but the idea behind it was quite clear and logical, and I never expressed anything in my writing more serious than this idea. But I did not succeed at all with the form of the tale. Subsequently, some fifteen years later, I revised it thoroughly for the then *Complete Collection* of my works, but then, too, I came to the conclusion that the thing was a total failure; and if I now were to take up the idea and elaborate it once more, I would choose an entirely different form; but in 1846 I had not found this form and was unable to cope with the tale.

Nevertheless, at the beginning of December of 1845, I believe, Belinsky insisted that I read at his house at least two or three chapters of this work. He even arranged an evening party for this (something he scarcely ever did) and invited his close friends. I recall that Ivan Sergeevich Turgenev was at the party; he listened to only half of what I read, paid it some compliments, and left in a great hurry. Belinsky very much liked the three or four chapters that I read (although they were scarcely worth it). But Belinsky didn't know how the tale ended and was still enthralled by *Poor People*. Well, it was right then, at this reading, that the word "stushevatsia," which later was to become so popular, was used, by me, for the first time. Everyone forgot the tale, and rightly so, but they picked up the new word, used it, and made it acceptable in literature.

The word "stushevatsia" means to disappear, to perish, to be reduced *to naught,* so to say. But it means to perish not all at once, not by being wiped from the face of the earth with crashes of thunder, but delicately, so to say, gradually, sinking imperceptibly into nothingness. It's like a shadow on a pen-and-ink drawing that gradually shades from black ever more lightly until it's reduced completely to whiteness, *to naught*. I must have used this word aptly in those first three chapters I read at Belinsky's when I described how one annoying and sly little fellow managed to disappear from the scene at appropriate times (or something like that,

I forget). I say that because the new term did not cause any surprise among the listeners; on the contrary, it was at once understood and noted by everyone. Belinsky interrupted me specifically to compliment me on the expression. All those listening at the time (they are all still alive) also complimented me. I recall very clearly that Ivan Turgenev also complimented me (he's most likely forgotten it now). Later, Andrei Kraevsky also had much praise to give. Apart from them, there are still some people who, I think, might recall that they were also a bit intrigued by the new word. But it did not take root and enter literature all at once; it did so very gradually and imperceptibly. I recall that in 1854, when I left prison in Siberia, I began reading through everything that had appeared in literature over the five years I had been away (*A Hunter's Sketches* had only just begun to come out when I was still in Petersburg; this and Turgenev's first tales I read all together, at a sitting, and was entranced. It's true that the sun of the steppes was shining over me then; spring was beginning, and with it an entirely new life, the end of my forced labor, freedom!)—and so, having begun to read, I was even astonished how often I encountered the word "stushevatsia." Later on, in the 1860s, it became completely accepted in literature; and now, I repeat, I encounter it even in official documents published in newspapers and even in scholarly dissertations. And it's used in just the same sense as I used it for the first time.

However, though I was the one to use it first in literature, it was certainly not I who coined it. This term was invented when I was studying in the Main School of Military Engineering, and by my own classmates. Perhaps I also took part in its invention, I don't recall. It seemed to invent itself, of its own accord, and came into use by itself. In all six years of our study at the school we were required to draw various plans—of fortifications, structures, and military buildings. The ability to draw a good freehand plan was a strict requirement for all of us, so that even those who had no inclination for drawing still had to try to attain a certain level in this art, like it or not. The marks awarded for drawing plans were counted as part of the total marks and so affected one's overall average. You might graduate from the senior officer's class and enter the service as an excellent mathematician, a builder of fortifications, or an engineer, but if the drawings you produced were poor, the marks assigned, when taken into your overall marks, could lower your average to the extent that you might lose some very significant advantages on graduation, such as promotion to a higher rank; therefore, everyone tried hard to learn to draw. All the plans were drawn and shaded in India ink and, among other things, everyone tried to learn how to shade a given surface well, from dark to light to white—to naught; good shading gave the drawing a stylish look. And suddenly, people in class began to ask: "Where's so-and-so?" "Ah, he's disappeared ('stushesevalsia') somewhere." Or, say, two friends were talking and one would say that he had to get to work: "Well," the one would say to the other as he took up his books, "now you'd better disappear ('stushevaisia')." Or a senior student would say to a first-year newcomer, "I was calling you just now; where did you manage to disappear ('stushevatsia')?" "Stushevatsia" meant to remove oneself, to disappear, and the expression was borrowed from shading, that is, from the gradual fading of a shade, the transition from dark *to naught*. I clearly recall that this term was used only in our class and was never adopted by the others; and when our class left the school, it seems that the word disappeared as well. Some three years later I remembered it and used it in my tale.

I have written with such seriousness and at such length on the history of such an unimportant little word only for the sake of some future scholar compiling a Russian dictionary—some future Dahl; and if I have now bored my readers, the future Dahl will still thank me. So let's say that this was written only for him. But if you like, *for the sake of clarity*, I'll make a full confession: in the course of my literary career, what I've liked *most* is the fact that I managed to introduce an entirely new word into the Russian language; and whenever I encounter that word in print I'm always very pleased; and so now you'll understand why I thought it possible to devote a special chapter to describing such a trifle.

2

1. Servility or Good Manners?

As we know, all educated Russian people are extraordinarily well mannered—I mean in those cases when they are dealing with Europe or think that Europe is watching them, even though Europe is not watching them at all. Oh, at home, alone and amongst ourselves, we'll take our due; at home all this Europeanism is pushed aside, and we needn't look far for examples; they're easily found in our family relations and in our approach—in the vast majority of cases—to civic responsibilities, to honor, to duty. Indeed, who of those who propound "European" ideas among us seriously believes in them? Of course, it's only the honest people, and those who are good-hearted besides (so that they believe only out of the goodness of their hearts), but do we have many such people? Strictly speaking, then, we may not have even a single European among us because we are incapable of being Europeans. In Russia the most advanced intellects, the stock-exchange intellects and the intellects that are in every way leading us, are only extracting a quitrent from European ideas, and I think that is the case everywhere among us. I'm not speaking, of course, about people with a great deal of common sense; those don't believe in European ideas because there's nothing to believe in; for nothing on earth was ever marked by such obscurity, murkiness, lack of definition, and lack of definability as that "*cycle of ideas*" we have acquired over the two-century period of our Europeanization—and in essence it's not a cycle but a chaos of bits and pieces of sentiments; alien, imperfectly comprehended ideas; alien conclusions and alien habits; but particularly, words, words, and more words—highly European and liberal ones, of course, but for us they are still words and nothing more.

This cannot be explained as merely an urge to parrot someone else's ideas. Neither can it be explained by intellectual servility, by Russian intellectual servility before Europe. We do have a great deal of intellectual servility, even a very great deal; but the major cause of our European bondage is still not servility, but rather our Russian, inborn good manners where Europe is concerned. You may say that this, after all, is the same thing as servility. In many cases it is, but one can't say that it always is. (Of course, I'm not talking about the wretched people I mentioned earlier who supposedly lead the way: these Europeans don't give a hang about Europe and they never did. As clever people, they go fishing in troubled waters and have been doing so for two hundred years now).

Here is what the Englishman Gladstone, for instance, says about the current war with Turkey: "Whatever one might say about certain other chapters of Russian history, by the liberation of many millions of enslaved peoples from a cruel and humiliating yoke Russia renders humanity one of the most splendid services history can recall, a service which shall never be erased from the grateful memory of nations."

Now honestly, do you think a Russian European could utter such words? Never in his life! He'd swallow his tongue before saying that; his politeness, not only toward Europe but toward himself, would cause him to blush the moment he read or heard this in Russian and from a Russian. "For heaven's sake, how could we aspire to such a thing . . . our ugly mugs in a place of honor! . . . Rendering a service '*to the whole of humanity*'—we Russians! We're not cut out for that sort of work; we're far too repulsive ourselves to think of 'liberating humanity.' And what illiberal notions all these are: 'Russia liberating enslaved peoples'—what an illiberal notion!"

That is the sincere opinion of the pure-blooded Russian European, and he'd rather chop off all his fingers than write the things that Gladstone wrote. "It's all very well for Gladstone to compose such a speech; either he doesn't know anything about Russia, or he's got some private purpose, some future aim in mind"—that's what the European thinks. And some of them—the kinder and more ardent ones—may well add to themselves, not without pride: "Why, we Russian Europeans may be even more liberal than the European Europeans; we've gone further: who among our earnest intellects would now even dare suggest any 'liberation of nations'? What a retrograde notion! And Gladstone can say such things without shame!"

What can we call all this, gentlemen? Is is servility or good manners toward Europe?

I still maintain that in the European period of our history, good manners played a huge role. Why, these Europeans of ours include so many truly honest and courageous people; they are people of honor, though their honor is alien and acquired and may not be understood by the gallant knights themselves, since it's still a lot of European gibberish as far as they're concerned, but it's honor just the same; they are people who won't permit anyone to step on their toes. So how, then, can one plainly label them servile? No, it was good manners that corroded us, not servility. Once again, of course, it's good manners toward Europe: we make up for it with our behavior at home.

The ladies who enthusiastically brought candies and cigars to the Turks also did so out of good manners, of course: "Just look at how sweetly, tenderly, graciously, humanely, Europeanly enlightened we are!" Now certain coarse people have brought these ladies at least partly to their senses, but formerly, before that happened—let's say on the day after the ladies threw flowers and candies at that train full of Turks—what if another train of Turks had arrived carrying that very bashibazouk who, reportedly, has the special knack of tearing a nursing infant in half at one go by seizing both its legs and of cutting strips of flesh from its mother's back? Yes, I think that these ladies would have greeted him with screams of enthusiasm, ready to treat him not only to candies but to something even better; and then, perhaps, their ladies' committee would have taken up the question of creating a scholarship in his name at the local high school. Oh, believe me, good manners in Russia may lead to anything, and this hypothesis is by no means far-fetched. When these ladies looked at themselves in the mirror, I think they fell in love with what they saw: "How humane we are; what dear liberal creatures we are!" And do you really believe this preposterous little scene couldn't actually happen? That haughty glance which some Europeans now cast at our People and their movement, denying in our whole People any kind of thought and movement "aside from the stupid religious hysteria of one fool out of thousands of common folk"—doesn't such a view, the possibility of actually holding such a view, justify the preposterous little scene I described above?

Good manners toward Europe prevail everywhere among us. The Turkish prisoners demanded white bread, and white bread was given to them. The Turkish prisoners refused to work. Prince

Meshchersky, an eyewitness, describes a scene in his *Diary* from the Caucasus:

> The captive pashas left Tiflis. The intention was to transport them using relays of horses, but they rebelled and made so bold as to declare that they would not go since they were unaccustomed to Russian wagons. As a result, they were provided with postal coaches and carriages with springs, each being drawn by six horses. They graciously declared their satisfaction with this arrangement, and as a result of the enormous number of horses requisitioned for the Turks, the poor travelers on the Georgian Military Highway will have to wait for three days to get their horses. And the serving Russian officer who is accompanying them, who has been granted a per diem of fifty kopecks, does not ride in a carriage but in an omnibus, like a servant! This is humaneness! (*The Moscow News*, No. 273)

Not humaneness, that is, but the very same good manners as regards European opinion of us, susceptibility, oversensitivity: "Europe is looking at us, so we have to be in full uniform and give the pashas carriages."

Later on, in another issue (No. 282), *The Moscow News* reports on the huge outcry in Moscow when the Muscovite saw the unprecedented comfort in which we transported captured Turks:

> The prisoners who were private soldiers were comfortably placed in third-class carriages; officers in second class; and the pasha occupied a first-class carriage. "Why do they get such accommodation?" people asked. "Our own grenadiers were shipped out of Moscow in horse-carriages, but the Turks get a special passenger train."
>
> "Never mind the grenadiers," says some shopkeeper in the crowd. "Even our poor wounded soldiers were transported in freight cars, and they didn't manage to find any straw for them to lie on. That pasha's as fat as a hog; he ought to go in a freight car—that'd make him lose a few pounds."
>
> "They've been slaughtering our wounded over there, pulling out their tendons, roasting them over slow fires; and just look at the treatment we give them. . . ."
>
> These are not solitary voices [*The Moscow News* goes on], they express the People's general opinion that it is painful to watch the bashibazouks and all this Turkish riffraff, who have been robbed by their own pashas, enjoying comforts that cannot compare with those offered our own soldiers. . . .

In other words, we are not seeing anything special here: it's good manners or, so to say, a dress coat of good manners put on before

European opinion, that's all; but we've been doing that here for two centuries, so it's about time we got used to it.

We've come to anecdotes, so here's one more. I noticed it in *The Petersburg Gazette,* which took it from a letter Mr. V. Krestovsky wrote from the front, to whom I don't know. Neither do I know the source from which *The Petersburg Gazette* took it. It runs as follows:

> Mr. Krestovsky's letter mentions one comical fact: "Near the retinue appeared some Englishman in a pith helmet and a pea-green civilian overcoat. Some reports claim that he is a member of Parliament who is taking advantage of the parliamentary recess to write dispatches 'from the front' for one of the large London newspapers (*The Times*); others maintain that he's simply an amateur, and yet others that he is a friend of Russia. Whatever the case may be, one can't but notice that this 'friend of Russia' behaves rather eccentrically: for instance, he remains seated in the presence of the Grand Duke while everyone else, including His Highness, stands; at dinner he gets up from the table where the Grand Duke is seated whenever he pleases, and today he even asked one officer he knows to help him pull on his pea-green overcoat. The officer measured him from head to foot with a rather surprised glance, smiled slightly, shrugged his shoulders, and without demur helped him put on his overcoat. Of course, there was nothing else to be done. The Englishman acknowledged this by carelessly touching his hand to his pith helmet."

The Petersburg Gazette called this a comical fact. Unfortunately, I see absolutely nothing comical in it; on the contrary, I find it quite infuriating, enough to make one's blood boil. Besides, from childhood we've been inculcated with the belief (from novels and French farces, I suppose) that every Englishman is a queer fellow and an eccentric. But what is a queer fellow? He's not always a fool or so naive as to be unaware that practices elsewhere in the world are not just the same as they are over there in his own corner at home. Englishmen are, rather, a very intelligent and most broad-minded people. As people who have sailed the seven seas and who are well-educated besides, they have observed very many different peoples and customs in all countries of the world. They are very keen and talented observers. They discovered humor among themselves, gave it a special word, and explained it to humanity. Could such a man, and a member of Parliament besides, not know when to stand and when to sit? Indeed, there is no country in which etiquette is more strictly observed than England. English court etiquette, for instance, is the most complex and refined in the world. If this Englishman is a member of Parliament, then of course he should have learned some etiquette from the very way in which one Parliament—the lower house—deals with the other, the upper, and specifically in the sense of who may sit and who must stand in the presence of another. And if he is also a member of higher society, then again, nowhere is there such etiquette as at the receptions, dinners, and balls of the English aristocracy during their London season. No, there's something quite different going on here, at least if one judges from this anecdote. Here we have English pride, but not mere pride—it is pride with an *arrogant challenge*. This "friend of Russia" cannot be her great friend. He sits looking at the Russian officers and thinks: "Gentlemen, I know that you are lion-hearted; you undertake the impossible and you carry it out. You have no fear of the enemy; you are heroes, you are Bayards to the last man and you know full well what honor means. I cannot help but admit what I see with my own eyes. Nevertheless, I am an Englishman, and you are only Russians; I am a European, and you are obliged to show 'good manners' toward Europe. No matter how lion-hearted you may be, I am still a superior type. And I find that a very pleasant thought; it's particularly pleasant to study your 'good manners' toward me, *inborn* and *compelling*, without which a Russian cannot treat a foreigner, even more so such a foreigner as I. You think that all these things are mere trifles; but it is trifles that console me and amuse me so; I've come to ramble around; I've heard that you are heroes and have come to take a look at you; still, I'll return with the conviction that as a son of Old England (at this point his heart quivers with pride), I still hold first place on the earth, while you are merely second-rate. . . ."

What's most curious in the account I've cited are the last lines: "The officer measured him from head to foot with a rather surprised glance, smiled slightly, shrugged his shoulders, and without demur helped him put on his overcoat. *Of course, there was nothing else to be done*."

What does this "of course" mean? Why was there *nothing* else to be done? On the contrary, something quite different could have been done, just the reverse and just the opposite: he could have "measured him from head to foot with a rather surprised glance, smiled slightly, shrugged his shoulders" and—gone away, just like that, without touching the overcoat—that's what could have been done.

Could no one really realize that this educated traveler of the seven seas was playing a trick, that the most discriminating expert on etiquette was seizing a moment to satisfy his petty pride? But the whole point is that perhaps no one really could realize it at that instant; these very enlightened "good manners" of ours stood in the way—not good manners toward this Englishman, not toward this member of Parliament wearing some sort of pith helmet (just what is a pith helmet?), but good manners toward Europe, "good manners" toward the debt of European enlightenment in which we were raised, in which we've become mired to the point of losing our independent personality and from which we'll be a long time in breaking free.

There are colossal shipments of cartridges to the Turkish army from England and America; it's now been reliably established that the Turkish soldier at Plevna sometimes fires five hundred rounds per day; the Turks could have neither the means nor the money to equip their army in this way. There is no doubt of the presence of the English and their money in the current war. Their ships are delivering armaments and all the other essentials. And in Russia our newspapers are crying out, from "good manners": "Oh, don't say that; oh, please, don't raise that issue! Let's just assume we didn't see it and didn't hear about it, otherwise the well-educated travelers of the seven seas will get angry, and then. . . ."

Well, and then what? What are you afraid of? A lot more could be added on this topic of "good manners."

And even if we did issue Europe some tiny little promissory notes, in the form of various promises made before we even crossed the Barboshi bridge, then these, too, certainly must have been made because of our good manners toward Europe and our worship of her. But let's leave the topic of "good manners" for the moment. I will merely remind you that at the beginning of the chapter, when I spoke of good manners, I added: "But that's only in regard to Europe; we always make up for it by our behavior at home." I'd like to take the occasion to point out how we sometimes make up for it at home and extract our *revanche*. . . .

2. The Most Extreme Case of Servility There Could Be

Do you remember last summer, gentlemen, well before "Plevna," when we suddenly invaded Bulgaria and made our appearance beyond the Balkans, how we were stricken dumb with indignation?

Not everyone, I mean—that's the first thing that must be stated; not even half, but far fewer; still, there were significant numbers of indignant people, and voices were raised. Voices of correspondents with the army followed closely by voices in our press, particularly in the Petersburg press. These were passionate, convinced voices full of most righteous indignation. . . .

The whole matter arose because those to whom the voices belonged were going off—as the whole world knows, and as we in particular know—to save the oppressed, the humiliated, the downtrodden, and the suffering. Even before war was declared I recall reading in our most important newspapers that, as we considered the chances of war and the inevitable expenses to be borne, we should also realize that "when we entered Bulgaria we would have to feed not only our own army but also the starving Bulgarians." I read that myself and I can show you where I read it; and so, having such an idea of the Bulgarians—those oppressed and harassed people for whose sake we journeyed from the shores of the Gulf of Finland and all the rivers of Russia to shed our blood—suddenly we saw the charming little Bulgarian houses surrounded by delightful gardens, flowers, fruits, cattle, cultivated land yielding almost a hundredfold and, to top it all, three Orthodox churches for every mosque—this among people oppressed for their faith! "How dare they!" was the thought that was at once enkindled in the offended hearts of some of the liberators, and outrage colored their cheeks. "And besides, we've come to save them, so they ought to be welcoming us virtually on their knees. But they're not on their knees; they look askance at us, almost as if they weren't pleased to see us! Us, their liberators! They do welcome us with bread and salt, it's true, but how they look askance at us! . . ."

And voices were raised. But, gentlemen, think about this for a moment: suddenly you receive a false telegram, or one that you improperly understood, saying that someone close to you—a friend or a brother—is lying ill or has been robbed somewhere or has been run over by a train or some such thing. You drop everything you are doing and rush off to your unfortunate brother—and suddenly you find that nothing has happened: you encounter a man who is healthier than you, who's sitting at the table eating; he loudly calls you to join him and laughs about your false alarm and the *qui pro quo* that's happened. Whether you liked this person or not, would you really get angry at him because he had not been robbed or run over by a train? Above all, would you get angry at him because he has such rosy cheeks and is setting to his dinner and glass of wine with such appetite? Surely you wouldn't. On the contrary, you would rejoice that he's alive and healthier than you are. Well, of course, it's only human nature that you'd be a little angry, but surely not because his legs hadn't been cut off by the wheels of the train. You wouldn't get right up after dinner and start writing dispatches and anecdotes about him, blackening his character and seizing upon his negative traits. . . . Well, that was what was done to the Bulgarians. "Even a prosperous peasant in Russia doesn't eat as well as this oppressed Bulgarian." And later others came to the conclusion that it was the Russians who were the cause of all the Bulgarian misfortunes: that if we, not understanding the situation, had not threatened the Turk earlier over the oppressed Bulgarians and then had not come to liberate these prosperous folk who had been "plundered," then the Bulgarians would be living to this day as if in the very bosom of Christ. Some people claim this even now.

My point is only that we sometimes manage to make up for our "good manners" toward Europe and our enlightened Europeanism at home, in our own way, where Europe can't see us and isn't looking, and doesn't understand Russian in any case. And Bulgaria is "*at home,*" after all. We came to liberate them, which is the same thing as coming *home*, they are *our own*. He's got a garden and some land over there, and that land is the same as if it were mine; of course, I'm not going to take anything from him because I'm an honorable person and, indeed, I don't have the power to do it; still, he ought to *feel* and to be eternally grateful, because once I've come to help him out, everything he has is the same as if *I had given it to him*. I took it away from his Turkish oppressor and returned it to him. He ought to remember that. . . . And here, suddenly, we find that no one is oppressing him—how exasperating and how unpleasant, isn't it really?

And what servility instead of enlightened good manners, isn't it? And what a ridiculous situation! This is the most comical of all the cases when we, *among ourselves*, "at home," have made up for the tight fit of the awkward uniform coat of European good manners in which we flaunt ourselves before Europe. This extreme case of servility involved the most ardent gentlemen and caught *quite a number* of us completely unawares. This is a bit more serious than being caught unawares holding an overcoat for an Englishman.

Eventually all the facts came to light and the truth was revealed to many of the indignant people, although not to all—and even now not to all of them. We learned, first, that it was certainly not the Bulgarian's fault that he was industrious and his land returned a harvest of a hundredfold. Second, we learned that it was not his fault that he "looked askance." Just consider the fact that for four centuries he has been a slave, and when he encounters some new masters he can't believe they are his brothers; he believes only that they are new masters, and beyond that he still fears his former masters and thinks painfully: "And what's to happen if the other ones come back and find out that I've given a welcome to these?" Well, it was private questions like this that made him look askance—and he was right, after all; he had it figured out, the poor fellow: after we had made our first bold push beyond the Balkans, we suddenly withdrew; the Turks came back once more, and what they did to the Bulgarians is now a matter of world history! These pretty little houses, the well-tended fields, the gardens, the livestock—all this was plundered, reduced to ashes, and wiped from the face of the earth. It was not by tens nor by hundreds, but by thousands and tens of thousands that the Bulgarians were exterminated with fire and sword; their children were torn to bits and died in torment; their wives and daughters were violated and were either beaten after the act or taken away as captives to be sold; and their husbands—those same ones who welcomed the Russians, and even those who never welcomed the Russians but to whom the Russians *might* someday come—all of them paid for the Russians on the gallows or on bonfires. The beasts administering their tortures would nail their ears to a fence for the night and hang them all the next morning, forcing one of them to hang the others; and he, having hanged a score of the suspects, ended by having to hang himself to the general laughter of his torturers, those sadistic beasts called the Turkish nation, whom some of our best-mannered young ladies so greatly admire. . . .

N.B.: Incidentally, not long ago, in the middle of November, there were reports from Pirgos of these monsters' new barbarities. During a furious battle that took place there, the Turks temporarily pushed back our troops so that we did not manage to gather our wounded soldiers and officers; later, toward evening on the same day, when we recovered our former position, we found our wounded soldiers and officers robbed and naked, with noses, ears, and lips cut off, stomachs cut out, their bodies charred after having been burned on stacks of straw and hay to which the Turks had carried them, still alive, and then set afire. Reprisals are a cruel thing, of course, the more so that in essence they lead nowhere, as I have already said in one of the preceding issues of the *Diary;* but severe measures against the commanders of these beasts would not be out of place. We could state bluntly, aloud and to the whole of Europe (the Prussians would surely do so, because they dealt just so with the French, for reasons ten times less valid than we have against the beasts who are waging war with us), that if atrocities are committed, the immediate superiors of the Turks responsible will, if taken captive, be tried on the spot by a military court and placed before a firing squad. This would perhaps have some influence on the Turkish officers and pashas. (N.B.: I think it would always be possible to find out, either now or later, which of the Turkish commanders was leading the attack at Pirgos.) A surprise like that, rather than carriages with springs, might inspire some wisdom in many of them. But now this same "commander," if he should be taken prisoner and see how he is welcomed after his atrocities, would plainly imagine that he is immeasurably superior to the "infidel Russian." Believe me, this Turk will never put any faith in our European good manners and our awe of Europe; indeed, he won't understand it at all and won't be able to conceive what lies behind it. Polite awe of Europe is a purely Russian matter and invention and can never be understood by anyone else. And so the Turkish commander reasons that "if you bow and scrape before me this way after I, perhaps, allowed your own brother's nose to be cut off only yesterday, you must feel you are my inferior and I am your superior. But that is just as it should be, by the will of Allah, and it's nothing to be surprised at!" That is what the captive Turkish pasha must be, and certainly is, thinking to himself.

And so, when those who had become indignant over Bulgarian prosperity lived to see the sorrowful end of the matter, they could not but realize that Bulgarian life was in essence only a stage decoration; that all these little houses and gardens, and the wives, children, and little boys and girls in these houses—all of it, in essence, belongs to the Turk and will be taken by him whenever he wishes. And he does take it; he takes it also in times of peace and in times when it is flourishing; he takes money and livestock and wives and little girls; and if, in spite of it all, the country continued to flourish, it was only because the Turk did not want to destroy utterly such a fertile meadow, thinking to draw from it in the future. On the contrary, at times and in places he permitted it to flourish fully precisely so he could draw from it again and again. . . .

Now, of course, the Turks have shown their fury and are devastating Bulgaria utterly. They regret not having done this before. Should we take Plevna and not hasten to advance, the Turks will see that they may have to bid farewell to Bulgaria forever and will destroy everything in it that they can, while they still have time. There are two views that are remarkable: our wise men still maintain that without Russian intervention the Bulgarian would be living virtually in the very bosom of Christ and that the Russians are the cause of all his misfortunes. And now the Englishman Forbes, correspondent of the *Daily News* known for his excellent and comprehensive articles from our side of the battlefield, at last has frankly expressed all his English truth. He *sincerely* admits that the Turks had "full right" to exterminate the entire Bulgarian population north of the Balkans once the Russian army had crossed the Danube. Forbes almost regrets (politically, of course) that this has not happened and concludes that the Bulgarians ought to be eternally grateful to the Turks for not slaughtering them all like sheep at that time. If we recall our Russian opinion of "the Bulgarian living in the very bosom of Christ" and compare it with the opinion of Forbes, one might address the following admonition to the Bulgarians: "Now how could you not be living in the very bosom of Christ when they haven't slaughtered you all, to the last man?"

But there's one more thing that is strange here; it stands out and will remain on historical record: "Is it really possible that such an educated man as Forbes, a member of as great and enlightened a nation as England, could so calmly and imperturbably admit that the Turks have such a right? Are these the last fruits and flowers of English civilization?" But note, of course, that he would not have expressed himself in this way had the matter concerned the French or the Italians instead of the Bulgarians. He only expressed himself in this way because these were only Bulgarian Slavs. It shows you in what tribal, ancestral contempt people everywhere in Europe hold the Slavic tribe! They're considered to be no better than dogs! They admit the possibility and the legitimacy of slaughtering them all to the last man, the whole tribe, with women and children. And note as well (this is very important) that this is not Count Beaconsfield speaking: he could express such predatory and bestial convictions because he was compelled by politics, by "English interests"; but Forbes is a private individual, not a man of state, and he is not entrusted with the duty of maintaining the interests of England *whatever happens and whatever the cost;* and, indeed, what a man he is: talented, truthful, humane—judging by his previous dispatches. The cause here is precisely, precisely that western European loathing of everything bearing the name of Slavdom. These Bulgarians can be dropped in boiling water like nests of bugs in the wooden beds of old women! Is there not some sort of instinct at work here, a sense that when all these eastern Slavic tribes are liberated, they will someday play a huge role in the new humanity to come and take the place of the old civilization that has lost its way? Westerners cannot now consciously imagine or even admit that of course, just as they cannot imagine a nest of bedbugs as something superior that will replace them in the future. But Russia is involved here; it is obvious that an entirely new idea has been raised here, one that can seduce, anger, and astonish everyone; the banner of the future has appeared here; and since Russia is not a "nest of bedbugs" (as they consider the Bulgarians) but a giant and a power impossible to ignore, and since Russia is also a Slavic nation—then how these Western people must now hate Russia in their hearts, even instinctively, involuntarily, rejoicing in her every setback and her every misfortune! It truly is a matter of instinct; it is a presentiment of things to come....

3. Some Quite Special Remarks about the Slavs That I Intended to Make Long Ago

Incidentally, I'll make a few *special* remarks about the Slavs and the Slavic question. And I've been wanting to say this for a long time. It's just now that everyone in Russia has suddenly begun talking about the imminent possibility of peace, about the imminent possibility of somehow solving the Slavic question. Let's give our fantasy free rein and imagine suddenly that the whole matter is ended, that through Russia's insistence and blood the Slavs are already liberated and, moreover, that the Turkish Empire no longer exists and the Balkan peninsula is free and is living a new life. Of course, it's difficult to predict down to the last details just what form this Slavic freedom will assume at first—that is, will it be a kind of federation of the small liberated tribes (N.B.: it seems a federation will still be a very, very long way off) or will there be small separate domains in the form of tiny states with sovereigns who have been summoned from the various ruling houses? Neither can one imagine whether Serbia's boundaries will at last be expanded or whether Austria will stand in the way; the extent of territory Bulgaria will occupy; what will become of Herzegovina and Bosnia; what sort of relations will ensue between the small, newly liberated Slavic peoples and, say, the Romanians or even the Greeks—the Greeks of Constantinople and the others in Athens. Finally, will all these countries and tiny lands be completely independent, or will they find themselves under the protection and supervision of "the concert of European powers," including Russia? (I think that these little peoples themselves will all certainly request a European concert, even including Russia, but solely as a means of protecting them from Russia's territorial ambitions.) None of these issues can be precisely resolved ahead of time, and I won't venture to solve them. However, even now it's possible to know two things for certain: (1) that sooner or later all the Slavic tribes of the Balkan peninsula will ultimately be freed from the Turkish yoke and will begin to live a new, free, and, perhaps, independent life; and (2) . . . Well, it's this second thing, which will most certainly come to pass, that I intended to talk about long ago.

This second thing is my inner conviction, complete and overpowering, that Russia never will have and never has had anyone who can hate, envy, slander, and even display open enmity toward her as much as all these Slavic tribes will the moment Russia liberates them and Europe agrees to recognize their liberation! And you needn't raise objections, dispute my view, or shout that I am exaggerating and that I hate the Slavs! On the contrary, I have great love for the Slavs; but I am not going to defend myself because I know that everything will come to pass exactly the way I have said; and this is not due to the supposedly base and ungrateful nature of the Slavs, not at all—in this sense they are the same as everyone else; it is precisely because *such things* can happen on earth in no other way. I'm not going to enter into details here, but I know that we certainly must not expect any gratitude from the Slavs; we ought to prepare ourselves for this in advance. I repeat: after their liberation they will begin their new life by asking Europe—England and Germany, for instance—for guarantees and protection of their freedom, and even though Russia will also be part of the concert of European powers, they will do this precisely as a means of defense against *Russia*. They will certainly begin by announcing and convincing themselves—privately, if not aloud—that they owe not the slightest debt of gratitude to Russia; on the contrary, they will say that they barely managed to escape Russia's territorial ambitions when peace was concluded through the intervention of the European concert, and had Europe not intervened, then Russia, having taken them away from the Turks, would at once have swallowed them up, "with a view to expanding her frontiers and founding a great panslavic empire by enslaving the Slavs to the greedy, devious, and barbaric Great Russian tribe." Oh, it will be a long, long time yet before they will be capable of acknowledging Russia's selflessness and her great, sacred, unprecedented raising of the banner of a great idea, one of those ideas by which man lives and without which, should these ideas cease to live within him, will grow numb, become crippled and die, ulcerated and impotent.

Take this present war, a war of all the Russians and of the entire Russian People, headed by the tsar and initiated against monsters for the liberation of unhappy nationalities—do you think that the Slavs have now at last understood this war? But I won't speak of the present moment; besides, the Slavs still need us; we are liberating them; but later on, when we have liberated them and they have managed to get themselves on their feet—will they recognize this war as a great exploit undertaken for their liberation? Try and answer that question. Nothing in the world will make them recognize that! On the contrary, they will maintain, as a political and then as a scientific truth, that had there been no Russia to liberate them over these hundred years, they would long ago have managed to liberate themselves from the Turks on their own, through their own valiant efforts or with the help of Europe who, had Russia not existed, would not only have had nothing against their liberation but would herself have liberated them. This devious doctrine certainly exists among them even now, while in time to come it will inevitably develop into a scientific and political truism. Moreover, they will even begin to speak of the Turks with greater respect than of Russia. Perhaps for a whole century or more they will live in constant trepidation for their freedom and in fear of Russia's territorial ambitions; they will curry favor with European states, spread slander about Russia, gossip about her and plot against her. Oh, I'm not speaking about individuals here: there will be some who will understand what Russia meant, what she means, and what she always will mean for them. They will realize all the grandeur and all the sanctity of Russia's cause and of the great idea whose banner she raised among humanity. But those people, especially at the beginning, will be in such a pitiful minority that they will be subject to mockery, hatred, and even political persecution. It will be particularly pleasant for the liberated Slavs to announce and trumpet to the whole world that they are educated peoples capable of attaining the heights of European culture, while Russia is a barbaric country, a gloomy northern colossus) that she does not even have pure Slavic blood and is the oppressor and hater of European civilization. They will have a constitutional form of government from the very beginning, of course, with parliaments, responsible ministers, orators, and speeches. They will take tremendous comfort and delight in this. They'll be in raptures when they read reports about themselves in the Paris and London newspapers informing the whole world that after a lengthy storm in parliament the cabinet has finally fallen in Bulgaria and a new one has been formed from the liberal majority, and that some Ivan Chiftlik of theirs has at last agreed to accept the portfolio of president of the council of ministers. Russia must seriously prepare herself to watch all these liberated Slavs rushing rapturously off to Europe to be infected by European forms, both political and social, to the point where their own personalities are lost; and so they will have to undergo a whole long period of Europeanism before comprehending anything of their own significance as Slavs and their particular Slavic mission among humanity. These little countries will be eternally quarreling, eternally envying one another and plotting against one another. Of course, the moment there is any serious disaster they will certainly turn to Russia for help. No matter how much they may spread hatred, gossip, and slander against us in Europe as they flirt with her and assure her of their love, they will always instinctively feel (in a moment of disaster, of course, but not before) that Europe is the natural enemy of their unity, that she always was and always will be, and that if they exist in the world it is naturally because there is a gigantic magnet, Russia, irresistibly drawing them all to her and so maintaining their integrity and unity. There will even be moments when they will be capable almost consciously of agreeing that were it not for Russia, the great center of the East and the great attracting force, their unity would collapse in an instant and fly into fragments and their very nationality would disappear into the European ocean, just as a few drops of water disappear into the sea. Russia's lot for many years will be the heartache and the travail of making peace among them, bringing them to their senses, and on occasion, perhaps, even drawing her sword on their behalf. Of course, the question immediately arises: of what advantage is all this to Russia? Why did Russia struggle for them for a whole hundred years, sacrificing her blood, her forces, and her money? Was it really only to reap such petty, absurd hatred and ingratitude? Oh, of course, Russia will still always be aware that she is the center of Slavic unity; that if the Slavs are living free lives as nations, it is because she wished it and still wishes it; that she has accomplished and created it all. But what good will this realization bring her, apart from the efforts, the cares, and the endless travail?

It's difficult at present to give an answer to that question, and the answer cannot be precise.

In the first place, as we all know, Russia will have no thought—nor should she ever have any—of expanding her territory at the expense of the Slavs, of annexing them politically, of creating her own provinces out of their lands, and so on. Even now, all the Slavs suspect Russia of such ambitions, just as the whole of Europe does, and they will harbor such suspicions for another hundred years. But may God preserve Russia from such ambitions; and the more she shows her complete political disinterestedness in regard to the Slavs, the more likely her success in uniting them around her in the future, a hundred years or more from now. Rather, by providing the Slavs from the very beginning with as much political freedom as possible and by removing herself even from any sort of tutelage and supervision over them, declaring only that she will be prepared to draw her sword against those who encroach upon their freedom and national integrity, will Russia save herself from the terrible travails and concerns of supporting *by force* her tutelage and political influence over the Slavs, something that they, of course, find hateful and that Europe always finds suspicious. But by having shown her absolute disinterestedness, Russia will triumph and will at last draw the Slavs to her; at first they will look to her in times of trouble, and then, someday, they will all *cling* to her with complete, childish trust. They will all return to their own native nest. Oh, of course, even now many Russians hold different scholarly and even poetical views. These Russians are expecting that the new Slavic nations, liberated and resurrected into a new life, will take their first step by coming to cling to Russia as their own mother and liberator, and that they will certainly, and very quickly, bring many new and unprecedented elements into Russian life; that they will broaden Russia's Slavic nature and her very soul; that they will even have an influence on the Russian language, literature, and creative forces; that they will enrich Russia spiritually and show her new horizons. I confess that these notions have always seemed to me no more than academic overenthusiasm; the truth, of course, is that something of this sort will certainly take place, but it will not happen for another hundred years, say, and in the meantime, and perhaps for another century, Russia will have nothing at all to borrow from the Slavs, either from their ideas or from their literature; they have a lot of maturing to do before they can teach us anything. On the contrary: through this whole century, perhaps, Russia will have to struggle against the narrow outlook and stubbornness of the Slavs, against their bad habits, against their certain betrayal of Slavdom—which is not far-off—for the sake of the European forms of social and political organization they are so eager to embrace.

After the settlement of the Slavic question, Russia will obviously be faced with the final settlement of the Eastern Question. It will be a long time before the Slavs of today understand what the Eastern Question means! Indeed, it will also be a long time before they understand what Slavic unity, brotherhood, and harmony mean. To explain that to them, continually, by deed and by great example, will be Russia's ever-present task in the future. Once more, people will ask: "What's the purpose of all this? Why should Russia take on such a task?" The purpose of it is to live a higher life, a superior life; to illuminate the world with a great, selfless, and pure idea; to realize and ultimately create a great and mighty organism of a brotherly union of peoples; to create this organism, not by political force, not by the sword, but by conviction, example, love, selflessness, and light; to elevate, at last, all these little ones to her own level, to an understanding of her maternal mission—that is Russia's aim, and those, if you like, are also the benefits she will derive. If nations do not live by superior, selfless ideas and by the superior aims of serving humanity, but only to serve their own "interests," then these nations will certainly perish; they will lose feeling, grow impotent, and die. But there are no aims higher than those which Russia sets for herself in selflessly serving the Slavs and not demanding their gratitude, serving their moral (and not merely their political) unification into one great whole. Only then will the whole of Slavdom pronounce its curative word to humanity. . . . There are no aims on earth higher than these. Consequently, there can be nothing of more "benefit" to Russia than to keep these aims before her, to continue ever to clarify them to herself and to continue ever to elevate herself spiritually in this eternal, ceaseless, and valiant toil for humanity.

Let the present war come to a favorable end, and Russia will certainly enter a new and higher phase of her existence. . . .

3

1. Rumors of Peace. "Constantinople Must Be Ours"—Is That Possible? Various Opinions

And suddenly everyone's begun talking about the end of the war, not only in Europe but here as well. Everyone's started to argue over possible peace terms. It's pleasing to see that even the majority of our political newspapers now have a more or less proper appreciation of Russia's sacrifices of labor, blood, and effort and are suggesting peace terms that are as appropriate as possible to the scale of these efforts. It is particularly comforting to see the majority of those considering the question also beginning to acknowledge Russia's independence in the face of the certain, imminent European intervention once peace is concluded, and her right to conclude a separate, individual peace without calling in Europe and even without paying much attention to her, if this is possible. The lot of the Slavs is also being taken into account. There is talk of reparation and heated demands for the iron-clad Turkish monitors. Many have expressed their full support for our right to annex Kars and Erzerum.

There are people, however, who are still offended by the suggestion that we might make so bold as to annex something like Kars. On the other hand, there are those who talk even of Constantinople—never mind Kars—and who say that Constantinople must be ours. Such talk and discussions of peace and the terms of peace will come up continually, after every one of our major military actions. I'd like only to observe that among all (or almost all) these current opinions of our press there seems to lurk something that is not exactly a blunder but an oversight. It is that everyone considers Europe as . . . as Europe; that's to say, as the same Europe that has existed, with certain variations, throughout the century: there is an acceptance of almost the same great powers, the same political balance, and so on. Meanwhile, Europe hour by hour is now becoming something different from what she was even six months ago; and this has even reached the point where one can't now guarantee anything three months in advance—such is the degree to which her former aspect may change even by next spring. Colossal and fateful facts of the present time, which will likely need to be formulated and settled very soon, are still not being considered in the true dimensions in which the world must regard them. It is difficult to envisage correctly even the kind of Europe there will be to intervene, perhaps, in our affairs at the conclusion of peace. Therefore, to talk of peace terms on the basis of only the former facts—without fully appreciating that all these former facts have now shifted of themselves, are moving, slipping away, and awaiting new definition—seems to me also to be a mistake. . . . More about this later, however. But now, since the topic has turned to Constantinople, I would like to note in passing one very strange and, for me, unexpected opinion on the immediate "fate" of Constantinople; this was expressed by a man from whom one might have expected quite a different conclusion, in view of the events now taking place and the ones that certainly will take place. Nikolai Iakovlevich Danilevsky, who eight years ago wrote his excellent book *Russia and Europe* (which contains just one unclear and unsound chapter dealing with the future fate of Constantinople), recently published a series of articles in the newspaper *Russian World* on this same subject. His final conclusion about Constantinople is very original.

However, I am not going to analyze it in detail.

After some excellent and very sound arguments—for instance, that after the Turks have been driven out Constantinople can certainly not be made a free city such as Cracow once was, for instance, without the risk of it becoming a nest of every sort of abomination and intrigue, a refuge for all the conspirators of the world, the prey of Yids and speculators, and so on—Danilevsky concludes that Constantinople should someday become a common city for all the nationalities of the East. All these nations, he says, will own it on an equal basis with the Russians, who will be given ownership on equal terms with the Slavs. Such a conclusion is astonishing, in my view. What kind of comparison between the Russians and the

Slavs can there be here? And who will establish equality among them? How can Russia participate in the ownership of Constantinople on an *equal* basis with the Slavs if Russia in every respect is unequal to them—to each little nation separately and to all of them combined? Had he felt like it, the giant Gulliver might have assured the Liliputians that he was equal to them in all respects, but this would have been patently absurd, surely. Why assume an absurdity and then take it to the point of compelling oneself to believe it? Constantinople must be *ours,* conquered by *us,* the Russians, from the Turks, and it must remain ours forever. It must belong to us alone; and when we possess it, of course, we can admit all the Slavs and whomever we like, and do so, moreover, on the broadest possible terms; but this will not be a federative possession of the city together with the Slavs. Just consider the fact that a whole century's work still won't be enough to set up a federal union of Slavs. Russia will possess only Constantinople and the essential territory around it, as well as the Bosphorus and the Straits; she will maintain troops, fortifications, and a fleet there; and so it should remain for a long, long time. Oh, many people will take up this notion and begin shouting: "So, Russia's service to the Slavic cause was evidently not so selfless after all!" The reply to that is simple: Russia's service to the Slavs has still not ended and will continue for ages to come; it is only through Russia and her great centralized power that the Slavs can continue to live on earth; a service such as this can never ever be repaid; and if Russia now does occupy Constantinople, then it is only because within her mission and her destiny she has another question apart from the Slavic one—the greatest and most decisive one for her: this is the Eastern Question, and this question can be resolved only in Constantinople. A federative possession of Constantinople by various tiny nations might even kill the Eastern Question, whose solution we must insistently pursue, when the time is at hand, since it is closely liked with the fate and the destiny of Russia herself and can be solved only by Russia. I am not speaking now of the fact that in Constantinople all these tiny nations would merely be bickering among themselves over their influence in it and their terms of possession. The Greeks would set them at odds with one another. The western Slavs also would be envious that the others possessed such a magnificent part of Europe and the globe. . . . In short, Constantinople would then serve only to cause dissension throughout the Slavic and the Eastern world, and that would hinder the union of the Slavs and halt the course of their proper existence. In such a case, salvation lies in Russia's taking possession of Constantinople alone, for herself, on her own account. Russia can then say to the people of the East that she is taking Constantinople for herself because "not one of you, nor all of you together are mature enough to possess it, but Russia is mature." And she is. This new phase in Russia's life is beginning at this very time. Constantinople is the center of the Eastern world, and the spiritual center and head of the Eastern world is Russia. It is necessary and even *useful* now for Russia to forget Petersburg, at least for a little while, and spend some time in the East, in view of the changes in her fate and that of the whole of Europe, changes which are at hand and which are standing "at the door." However, let us leave for a time the analysis of all the problems of joint possession of Constantinople and even of the harm that can come of it, particularly for the Slavs; let us merely note, however briefly, something of the fate of Constantinople's Greeks and of Orthodoxy in such an event.

The Greeks would look enviously at the new Slavic component in Constantinople and would hate and fear the Slavs even more than they did the Mohammedans who had ruled formerly. The recent quarrel of the Bulgarians with the patriarchal throne may serve as an example of things to come in such an event. The representatives of Orthodoxy in Constantinople may lower themselves to indulge in intrigues, petty maledictions, excommunications, irregular ecclesiastical councils, and so on; perhaps they may even fall into heresy—and all this for reasons of nationalism, national affronts, and aggravations. "Why are the Slavs set above us?" all the Greeks may ask. "Why is their absolute right to Constantinople recognized, even though it may be held jointly with our own?" And now, please note at the same time that Russia, possessing Constantinople and having power and enormous, obvious authority, would eliminate the possibility of such questions. Even the Greeks would not be so envious of and angry at her for possessing Constantinople precisely because she is such an obvious power and such a clear sovereign of the fates of the East. Russia, possessing Constantinople, would guard the freedom of all the Slavs and *all the Eastern* peoples, making no distinctions between them and the Slavs. Moslem rule through all these centuries has not been a unifying but an oppressive force for all these peoples, and under it they did not dare to move; they did not live like people at all in other words. With the abolition of Moslem sovereignty, terrible chaos might ensue among these peoples who have so suddenly escaped from the yoke and into freedom. Thus, not only a proper federation but even basic accord among them is, doubtless, merely a dream of the future. And meanwhile, the new, unifying force for them will be Russia, in part precisely because she will establish herself firmly in Constantinople. She will save them from one another and will stand guard over their freedom. She will stand on guard for all of the East and for its future order. And finally, she and she alone, is able to raise in the East the banner of a new idea and to explain to the whole of the Eastern world its new mission. For what is the Eastern Question? The Eastern Question, in its essence, is the resolution of the fate of Orthodoxy. The fate of Orthodoxy is merged with the destiny of Russia. What do I mean by the fate of Orthodoxy? Roman Catholicism long ago sold out Christ for the sake of earthy dominion, forcing humanity to turn away from it and so being the principal cause of Europe's materialism and atheism; quite naturally, this Catholicism also engendered socialism in Europe. For socialism's goal is to resolve the fates of humanity not through Christ but without God and without Christ; and it had to be born in Europe in a natural process, replacing the fallen Christianity and its principles to the degree that these had been distorted and lost in the Catholic church itself. The lost image of Christ has been preserved in all the light of its purity in Orthodoxy. It is from the East that this new Word will be carried to the world to counter the future socialism; and it may be that this Word will again save European humanity. That is the mission of the East; that is what the Eastern Question means for Russia. I know that very many will call such a view "religious hysteria," but Danilevsky can well understand what I am saying. But to accomplish such a mission Russia needs Constantinople, since it is the center of the Eastern world. Russia, with the People and the tsar at their head, already has a tacit awareness that she is merely the bearer of the idea of Christ, that the word of Orthodoxy will be transformed within her into a great deed, that this deed has already begun with the current war, but ahead of her still lie centuries of labor, self-sacrifice, propagation of the brotherhood of peoples, and ardent maternal service to them, as to dear children.

Yes, this is a great Christian deed; this new endeavor of Christianity and Orthodoxy has already begun in the current war and because of the current war, but Danilevsky still cannot believe it . . . evidently because he still thinks that no one, not even Russia, is yet *worthy* of possessing Constantinople. That is difficult understand: is it because the Russians aren't mature enough for Constantinople? Of course, it is difficult to establish harmonious ownership of Constantinople, on the basis of *equal rights*, by all the Eastern peoples and tiny nations, yet the author of the article admits that Russia could rule Constantinople alone, temporarily, protecting the city rather than daring to rule it, but with the aim of later transferring it to the common ownership of small peoples. (Why? Why transfer it?) It seems that Danilevsky believes exclusive possession of Constantinople would be a temptation for Russia and would seduce her, so to say; it would arouse harmful, imperialistic instincts in her, and so on; but it seems that it is finally time to put some trust in Russia, particularly after her valiant feat of the current war. She has matured; she is even mature enough for Constantinople. . . .

And then, suddenly, the author shows reluctance to entrust Russia with Constantinople even *for the time being*. And just imagine how he ends his article: he concludes that *for the time being* Turkey's existence must be prolonged (having taken away from her all the Slavs, the Balkans, and so on) and for the time being Constantinople be left under Turkish control; and that this, supposedly, is even the most beneficial solution for Russia *now*, a solution virtually created by the hand of God. But why on earth the hand of God? Naturally, the author supposes that Russia would dominate this new Turkey and that Turkey would be dependent on Russia. But what is the point of such a masquerade? Judge for yourselves: Russia is the sovereign, yet the Turks must still be kept in place for a time. I might note that Europe would be less likely to consent to such a scheme than to the complete conquest of Turkey, for an actual fait accompli is better than something still contested, continuing, and threatening to cause new wars in the near future. Thus the author, ultimately, almost agrees with the political view of Lord Beaconsfield, i.e., that Turkey's existence is essential and that she must not be annihilated.

"Only a shadow of Turkey will remain," says Danilevsky, "but that shadow *must* (!) be cast on the shores of the Bosphorus and the Dardanelles for some time yet, for to replace it with a *living*—and not merely living, but healthy—organism is still impossible (!?). . . ."

Does he mean that Russia isn't a healthy organism, isn't yet even a living organism that can't even dare take the place of the Turkish rot in the capital of Orthodoxy? I find that astonishing (once again, after the *valiant feat* of the current war!). Surely there's something I don't understand here. Does the author not mean, plainly and simply, that Russia cannot yet be allowed into Constantinople (for exclusive rule or for transferring it later to various nations) because Europe would not consent to it? Perhaps the author doesn't believe that Russia is capable of achieving such a decisive result in the current war. In one place in his article he says specifically "that the *occupation* of Constantinople by the Russians would meet a most decisive resistance from the majority of European powers." If that is so, then his conclusion on the need to leave the Turks in Constantinople for a time is more readily understood; nevertheless, as far as "resistance from the majority of European powers" is concerned, two things should be noted: first, that Europe, as I said earlier, may see a more conciliatory outcome in our occupation of Constantinople than in the formula proposed by Mr. Danilevsky—i.e., a depersonalized Turkey under Russia's complete tutelage, without the Balkans, without the Slavs, with fortifications demolished, without a fleet—in short, "a shadow" of the former Turkey, as the author expresses it. Now, of course, that isn't the Turkey that "the majority of European powers" would like to see; and Europe could not be taken in if merely "the shadow of Turkey" remained on earth: "It makes no difference: if not today, then tomorrow you will enter Constantinople," Europe would say to the Russians. And so Europe would much prefer a final solution than a Turkey that would be a mere shadow. The second thing to be noted is that, *perhaps*, there really never yet has been (nor will there be) such an opportune moment for us to occupy Constantinople as now, precisely during this war, precisely at the given moment or a moment that is immediately at hand, in view of Europe's own political situation at the moment.

2. Once More, for the Last Time, Some "Soothsayings"

You keep saying that "the majority of European powers" will not permit it. But what is meant by "the majority of European powers" nowadays? Can that even be defined at the present moment? I repeat what I said earlier: hour by hour Europe is becoming different from what she was in earlier times, different, perhaps, from what she was only six months ago, so that at present one cannot guarantee that she will remain as she is even three months in the future. The fact is, we are certainly on the eve of the greatest and most stupendous changes and revolutions in Europe herself, and I say that *without the least exaggeration*. At the given moment, now, in November, this "majority of European powers" that could issue us an intimidating *veto* on anything once peace is concluded, amounts merely to England and, perhaps, Austria, although England will draw her into an alliance whatever the cost and even has hopes for an alliance with France. But we shall not be alone (that is already obvious). In Europe there is Germany, and she is on our side.

Indeed, Europe is awaiting enormous upheavals, of a sort that the human mind refuses to believe them, thinking that such things must be utterly preposterous. Meanwhile, many things that even this summer were regarded as preposterous, impossible, and exaggerated came to pass quite literally in Europe as the year was ending; and the view of the power of the worldwide Catholic conspiracy, for instance—a view that in the summer *everyone* was inclined to ridicule, or at least ignore—is now shared by *everyone* and has been borne out by facts. I bring this up only so that the readers may have some faith in my current "soothsaying" and not regard it as a preposterous and exaggerated picture, as many no doubt regarded my summer predictions of last May, June, July, and August—things which came to pass with literal exactitude.

The only politician in Europe whose brilliant insight has penetrated to the very bottom of events is, unquestionably, Prince Bismarck. Long ago he perceived the most sinister enemy of Germany, her unity, and her future revival to be Roman Catholicism and the monster to which Catholicism has given birth—socialism. (Germany has been corroded by socialism.) Bismarck must crush Catholicism at the time it is electing a new pope. Oh, he realizes that he will not crush it absolutely and that he will only put it into a particular new phase of the struggle. But so long as France is alive, the old phase of the struggle still continues for Catholicism. So long as France is alive, Catholicism has a powerful sword and hopes for a European coalition. As for France, her fate is sealed, in Prince Bismarck's eyes. For him there is but a single problem: who shall live—France or Germany? For if France falls, Catholicism, and socialism with it, will enter a new phase. And while the European politicians, who are following MacMahon's endless struggle with the republicans, long with all their hearts for a republican victory, *still accepting and believing* that in France a republic is a government of the people capable of uniting the country—Prince

Bismarck, meanwhile, understands full well that France has outlived her day, that this nation is divided against itself internally, finally, and forever, and will never have a stable, authoritative government capable of unifying everyone and never have a sound national and unifying center. And though France's weakness could thus merely encourage Germany, still—I repeat—Prince Bismarck can see that so long as France lives, Roman Catholicism is also alive politically and holds a naked sword; moreover, he sees that Catholicism itself, perhaps, might once more provide this disintegrated country, *temporarily,* with a unifying idea, even if only in terms of foreign policy. For it is quite impossible that France, though she be led by republicans, would *not, sooner or later,* draw her sword to defend the pope and the fate of Catholicism. Even the republicans themselves would see that if they were to abandon the pope and Catholicism, their own existence in France would become impossible. It's true that they themselves, maybe, will be incapable of understanding every last detail of this and so will remain to the end, not only the favorites—the protégés—of Prince Bismarck, despite the fact that he has already condemned them to death, along with sundry other French parties having pretensions to unite France once more into a single, indivisible whole; but they will also remain Germany's slaves who hand over the whole of France to her, not only into political bondage but into an inward, fundamental spiritual bondage as well; they do this by depriving France of the most distinct of her *political and historical* ideas, by tearing away the banner she has held high for so many centuries as champion of the Roman element among the people of Europe. Yet those who will drive the incompetent and useless republicans from office will certainly be concerned to raise the Catholic banner against Germany for the last time (Bismarck knows this); it is a banner in which—I repeat—France no longer has any faith, which she rejects *almost completely,* but which can still serve her *politically* as a last point of support against the fatal (and also final) assault of Protestant Germany, which has eternally protested against the western European principles, inherited from ancient Rome, of fully half the European peoples.

And so it's most likely that Prince Bismarck has already predetermined the fate of France. The fate of Poland awaits France, and she will not live politically; either that, or Germany will cease to exist. Having achieved this, Bismarck will then force militant Roman Catholicism (whose militancy will continue to the end of the world) to enter a new phase of existence and struggle for existence—a phase of underground, reptilian, and conspiratorial war. And he is awaiting this new phase of Catholicism. The sooner it arrives, the better, since for him it means the alliance of both enemies of Germany and of humanity; thus he is hoping to crush them both more easily, at once. . . .

3. The Moment Must Be Seized

The alliance of both enemies will certainly take place just as soon as France collapses politically. Both these enemies have always had an organic connection with France. Catholicism, until almost recently, was her unifying and fundamental idea. Socialism was also engendered within it. Having deprived France of a political life, Prince Bismarck plans to deal a blow to socialism as well. Socialism as the legacy of Catholicism and France are the things most hateful to a true German, and one can excuse Germany's leaders for thinking they can deal with socialism so easily, by the mere political destruction of France, its source and its cradle. But this is what will happen, in all likelihood, should France collapse politically: Catholicism will lose its sword and will turn for the first time to the people, whom it has scorned for so many centuries while paying court to the kings and emperors of the world. But now it will turn to the people, for it has nowhere else to go; it will turn specifically to the leaders of the most volatile and restive element among the people—the socialists. It will tell the people that everything the socialists are preaching to them has also been preached by Christ. It will distort Christ and sell Him to them once more, as it sold Him so many times before for the sake of earthly dominion, upholding the rights of the Inquisition, torturing people for freedom of conscience in the name of a loving Christ—a Christ who valued only those disciples who came freely to him, not those who had been bribed or frightened. It has sold Christ, giving its blessing to the Jesuits and justifying "any means for the cause of Christ." From time immemorial it has transformed the cause of Christ into mere concern for its earthly possessions and its future political domination of the whole world. When the Catholic peoples turned away from the monstrous image in which Christ was finally presented to them, after several centuries of protests, reformations, and so on, there at last appeared, at the beginning of the present century, some attempts to arrange life without God and without

Christ. Lacking the instincts of the bee or the ant, which flawlessly and accurately construct their hives and anthills, people sought to construct something in the nature of a flawless human anthill. They rejected the single formula for their salvation that came from God and was proclaimed through revelation to humanity, "Thou shalt love thy neighbor as thyself," and replaced it with practical conclusions such as, "*Chacun pour soi et Dieu pour tous*" (Every man for himself and God for all), or scientific slogans such as "the struggle for survival." Lacking the instincts by which animals live and flawlessly arrange their lives, people proudly placed their hopes in science, having forgotten that, in regard to matters such as constructing a society, science is still in its swaddling clothes. Wonderful visions appeared. The future tower of Babel became the ideal and, at the same time, the dread of all humanity. But in the wake of the visionaries there soon came other doctrines, simple and comprehensible to all, such as: "Rob the rich, pour blood over the earth, and then *somehow everything will come to right by itself.*" Finally, things went even beyond what these teachers were saying: the doctrine of anarchy appeared, after which, should it be realized, would certainly ensue a new period of cannibalism, and people would be compelled to begin everything from the beginning, as they did some ten thousand years ago.

Catholicism realizes all this very well and will manage to seduce the leaders of an underground war. It will tell them: "You have no center, no orderly way of managing your work; you are a force that is fragmented all over the world; and now, with the collapse of France, you are also oppressed. I shall provide your unity and shall also bring you all who still believe in me." One way or another, the alliance will come into being. Catholicism does not want to die; a social revolution and a new, social period in Europe is also certain: two forces, doubtlessly, must come to an accord, two currents must merge. Naturally, Catholicism will find slaughter, blood, pillage, and perhaps even cannibalism to be advantageous. It is just in such circumstances—in troubled waters—that it can hope to hook its fish once more, sensing the moment when at last a humanity worn out by chaos and lawlessness will rush into its embrace; and it will once more find itself, now totally, exclusively, and in reality, "sovereign of the earth and authority in this world," sharing its power with none; and thus will it achieve its ultimate goal. This picture, alas, is no fantasy. I avow positively that many, many people in the West can already foresee this. And no doubt the lords of Germany also foresee it. But the leaders of the German people are wrong in one thing: the ease with which these two fearsome and already united enemies can be conquered and crushed. They rely on the might of a renewed Germany, on her Protestant spirit protesting against the ancient and the new Rome, its principles and its *consequences*. But they will not stop the monster: it will be stopped and vanquished by a reunited East and the new Word it will utter to humanity. . . .

In any case, one thing seems clear: Germany *needs* us even more than we think. And she needs us not for a temporary political alliance, *but forever*. The idea of a reunited Germany is a broad, majestic one with roots in ages gone by. What can Germany share with us? Her object is the whole of Western humanity. She has assigned herself the Western world of Europe, to instill there her principles in place of the Roman and Romanic ones and eventually to become its leader, leaving the East to Russia. Two great peoples, thus, have been destined to change the face of this world. These are not some fanciful inventions of the mind or of ambition: this is the way the world is composing itself. There are new and strange facts and they are appearing every day. While we in Russia, scarcely more than a few days ago, were considering it preposterous to speak and dream of Constantinople, many people in the German newspapers spoke of our occupation of Constantinople as of a most ordinary thing. This is almost strange when compared with Germany's former attitudes toward us. One has to think that the friendship of Russia and Germany is not hypocritical but solid and will become more solid as time passes, that it will spread and gradually take root in the consciousness of the peoples of both nations; and so, perhaps, there was never a moment more favorable than now for Russia for the ultimate solution of the Eastern Question. People in Germany, perhaps, await the end of our war even more impatiently than we do. Meanwhile, now one really cannot guarantee what will transpire even three months hence. Shall we end this war before the final and fateful cataclysms begin in Europe? This we do not know. But whether or not we manage it in time to help Germany, Germany still is relying on us not as *temporary* allies but as *eternal* ones. As far as the present moment is concerned, once again the whole key to the thing is in France and in the election of the pope. Here we can expect a collision between France and Germany; this is already assured, the more so that there are people trying to provoke it. England will make special efforts in this regard, and then, perhaps, Austria will move as well. But we spoke about all these things not long ago. Nothing has changed since then to alter our former opinions; on the contrary, they have been strengthened. . . .

In any case, Russia must seize the moment. But will this favorable European moment of ours last for long? So long as Germany's current great leaders are acting, this moment is *most surely* guaranteed for us. . . .

December

1

1. The Concluding Explanation of an Old Fact

As I conclude the two-year publication of my *Diary* with this final, December issue, I find it necessary once more to say a few words about a matter I have spoken about at very great length already. I had decided to say something about it as long ago as May, but for particular reasons I had to postpone it until this final issue. Once more, it concerns that stepmother Kornilova who, in a fit of anger at her husband, threw her six-year-old stepdaughter out of a window; the girl, who fell from a height of nearly forty feet, survived. As we know, the perpetrator was tried and found guilty; then the sentence was appealed; and finally she was acquitted at a second trial on April 22 of this year. (See *A Writer's Diary,* October 1876 and April 1877.)

I happened to play a certain role in this case. The president of the court, and subsequently the prosecutor as well, declared publicly in the court room that the initial guilty verdict on Kornilova was quashed precisely as a result of the idea set forth in the *Diary* that "the pregnant condition of the perpetrator may have had an influence on her act." I set forth and developed this idea as a result of the extraordinary and strange psychic peculiarities that were so compellingly obvious and that arrested one's attention on reading the details of the crime. My readers know all this already, however. They may also know that after a most rigorous investigation and the most stubborn and insistent arguments by the prosecutor, the jury still deliberated for no more than ten minutes before acquitting Kornilova, and the spectators left the court with wholehearted approval of the acquittal. Yet even so, at the time and on that same day, it occurred to me that in a case as important as this, involving the very highest questions of civic and spiritual life, it is useful for everything to be explained as thoroughly as possible so that no doubts, hesitations, or regrets remain, either in society or in the hearts of the jurors who acquitted Kornilova, that a woman who had undoubtedly committed a crime had been let off unpunished. Children are involved here, the fate of a child (often a terrible thing, especially among the poor) is involved, as is the whole question of children—and now one who would have murdered a child is acquitted, and with the approval of the public! And here I myself was partly responsible for it (according to the statement of the court itself)! I was acting out of conviction, yet after the verdict was brought in I suddenly began to be tormented by doubt: had the public not been left dissatisfied, puzzled, mistrustful of the court, even angry? Our press said little about Kornilova's acquittal—people had other things to think about at the time; they sensed the coming of war. But in *The Northern Messenger,* a newly opened newspaper at that time, I did read an article full of indignation over the acquittal and even of anger at me for my part in the case. This article was written in an unworthy tone; and indeed, I was not the only one to suffer the indignation of *The Northern Messenger:* Leo Tolstoy also suffered it for *Anna Karenina* and was subjected to malicious and unworthy mockery. I would not have responded personally to the author, but in this article I saw the very thing I had dreaded seeing in a certain part of our society, i.e., a confused impression, puzzlement, indignation at the verdict. And so I decided to wait a whole eight months so as to convince myself in that time, as best and as thoroughly as possible, that the verdict had had no ill effect on the accused; that, rather, the mercy of the court had fallen like a good seed on fertile soil; that the accused *truly had been worthy* of compassion and mercy; that the fits of incomprehensible and almost fantastic fury, in one of which she had committed her evil deed, had not returned and *could not* ever return to her again; that she really was a kind and meek soul and not a ravager and murderess (of which I was convinced all through the trial); and that the crime of this unfortunate woman truly had to be explained by some special, accidental circumstance, pathological condition, or "affect"—by just those pathological fits which occur rather often among pregnant women (given a whole range of other adverse conditions and circumstances, of course) during a particular period of their pregnancy; and that, at last, it followed that neither the jurors, nor society, nor the people present in the court who greeted the verdict with wholehearted approval had any more reason to doubt the appropriateness of the verdict and regret their mercy.

And so now, after these eight months, I am able to report something and say more about this case of which, perhaps, everyone may have already grown weary. I shall address my reply to society, as it were—I mean, to that portion of society which, I suppose, may not agree with the verdict rendered, has doubts about it, and is indignant over it—at least if there has been such a portion of the dissatisfied within our society. And since, of all these dissatisfied people, I know (not personally, however) only the one "Observer" who wrote the intimidating article in *The Northern Messenger,* I shall direct my answer to this Observer. It's most likely that my conclusions will in no way change his mind, but perhaps my readers will understand me.

The Observer, in dealing with Kornilova's case in his article, attributed the highest importance to this *case* from his very first line: he indignantly referred to the fate of children, defenseless children, and regretted that the accused had not been sentenced to the strictest punishment. It was thus a matter of Siberia, of the exile of a twenty-year-old woman with the infant child she had borne while in prison (and who also would be exiled to Siberia along with her), of the destruction of a family. In such a case, it seems, the first thing would have been to deal carefully, seriously, and dispassionately with the facts that had been brought forward. And yet (can you believe it?) this Observer *does not know* the case on which he is pronouncing judgment; he says the first thing that comes into his head; he himself invents things that never happened and throws them right in the face of the former accused; he *obviously* had not been present in the courtroom, had not heard the speeches, and was not present at the verdict—and given all this, he callously and angrily demands that the person be punished! But this is a matter of the fate of a human being, after all—even of several human beings at once; it's a matter of tearing a human life in two, mercilessly, bloodily. Granted, the unfortunate woman had already been acquitted when the Observer came out with his article; yet such attacks have an influence on society, on the courts, on public opinion; they reflect on those accused of similar things in the future; finally, they offend the acquitted—well, to be sure, she is one of the ignorant, common people and so she is defenseless. However, here is that article—at least the whole part of it dealing with Kornilova's case; I am quoting the most essential parts and am making some very minor deletions.

2. The Excerpt

. . . .

. . . It is much more difficult for the jury to put themselves in the state of mind of a pregnant woman, and even more difficult to put themselves in the state of mind of the six-year-old girl this woman has thrown out of a fourth-floor window. One must have all the power of imagination in which, as we know, Mr. Dostoevsky so excels in order to capture fully the state of mind of the woman and reach an awareness of all the compelling affects of pregnancy.

He truly has captured that state of mind; he has visited the lady in question in prison, been struck by her humility, and over several issues of his *Diary* has come out as her ardent defender. But Mr. Dostoevsky is too impressionable, and besides, "the pathological manifestations of the will" are right in his line as author of *The Devils, The Idiot,* and so on; so he may be excused for having a weakness for such things. I take a simpler view of the matter and maintain that, after such instances exonerating the physical abuse of children—and they happen not infrequently in Russia, as they do in England—we are left without even a shadow of a deterrent to such crimes. And how many cases of child abuse are there for each one that happens to be scrutinized in court? There are children whose entire lives—morning, noon, and night of every day—are nothing more than one torment after another. These are innocent creatures whose hard lot makes the labor of parricides in Siberian mines seem sheer bliss; the latter have time to rest, they are not burdened with everlasting fear that can never be overcome, they have complete peace of mind, insofar as it is not disturbed by conscience. Of ten thousand, and probably of a hundred thousand cases of child abuse, only one finds its way into the courts; one which for some reason manages to attract more attention. For instance, a stepmother continually beats (?) an unfortunate little six-year-old and at last throws her out of a fourth-floor window; when she discovers that this child she so hated has not been killed, she exclaims, "She's got more lives than a cat." We find here neither a sudden display of hatred for the child nor any repentance after committing the murderous act; it is all consistent and logical in its display of one and the same evil will. And this woman is acquitted. If we acquit people in such obviously clear cases of child abuse, then what may we expect in other cases that are less sharply defined and more complex? Acquittals, of course; acquittals and more acquittals. In England, among the uncultured classes of "roughs" in the cities, cases of child abuse are not infrequent, as I noted earlier. But I would like someone to show me a single example of such an acquittal by English jurors. Oh, when some dissenter is brought before our jurors for making an insulting remark about the dome of a church, that's a different matter. In England such a person would never even be brought to trial; in Russia he would never be let off. But for abusing a little girl—well, is it worth ruining a young woman's life for that? She is still a stepmother, after all, which is almost the same as being the victim's mother; she is the one who feeds her, in any case, and she goes on beating her more and more. But you won't surprise a Russian with this latter fact. A friend of mine told me the other day that he was riding in a cab whose driver was continually lashing his horse. When questioned about this, the cabbie answered, "That's her lot in life! You've got to be beat her all the time, beat her with no mercy."

And you, the Russian—such has been your lot over the course of centuries! It may well have been that the stepmother was also beaten in childhood; and so you take that into account and say: leave her alone! But you must not do that. You must have pity on the little ones; you will not be beaten now, and you should not excuse the cruelty of one who, now, is not born a slave.

People will say: "You are attacking the institution of the jury, when, without it . . ." and so on. I am not attacking the institution and have no intention of doing so; it is a good thing; it is immeasurably better than that court in which social conscience played no part. But I am addressing that conscience about one or another of its manifestations. . . .

. . . But to go on beating a child for a year or so and then throw it out a window to certain death—that's another matter. "The husband of the acquitted woman," writes Mr. Dostoevsky in his *Diary* that came out just recently, "took her home that same evening sometime after ten o'clock, and she entered her own home again, happy." How touching. But woe to the poor child, if she remained in that home to which the "happy woman" came back; woe to her should she ever find herself in her father's home again.

"The affect of pregnancy"—well, a touching new phrase has been invented. However powerful that affect may have been, the woman under its influence still did not attack her husband or the tenants next door. The entire affect was exclusively directed toward this defenseless little girl whom she had tyrannized for a whole year even without any affect. On what did the jurors base their acquittal? On the fact that one psychiatrist admitted "the pathological emotional state" of the accused at the time the crime was committed; three other psychiatrists declared only that a pathological condition of the pregnant woman could have influenced the commission of the crime; and one obstetrician, Professor Florinsky, who likely knows all the symptoms of pregnancy just as well, expressed his outright disagreement with these views. Thus, four out of five experts did not admit that in the given instance the crime was definitely committed under an "affect of pregnancy" and subsequent irresponsibility. Yet the jurors acquitted her. Well, what does it matter? The child wasn't killed, after all; and as far as her being beaten is concerned, well, "such is her lot in life."

3. Distortions and Manipulation of the Evidence—These Cost Us Nothing

That's the excerpt, that's the accusation; there's a good deal of hostility directed at me as well. But now I would like to ask Mr. Observer: "How could you, in an accusation as serious as this, so distort the facts and present them all in such a false and fanciful manner? Tell me, when was there any beating, systematic beating *by the stepmother*? You write plainly and precisely: "A stepmother *continually beats* (?) an unfortunate little six-year-old and at last throws her out of a fourth-floor window. . . ." And then: "But to go on beating a child *for a year or so* and then throw it out a window to certain death. . . ." Referring to the child, you exclaim: "Woe to her should she ever find herself in her father's home again." And finally, you put this brutal remark in the jurors' mouths: "Well, what does it matter? The child wasn't killed, after all; and as far as her being beaten is concerned, well, 'such is her lot in life.'"

In short, you have refashioned all the facts and presented the whole case in such a way that, in your view, it happened supposedly only because of the stepmother's hatred for the child whom she tormented and beat for a year and finally threw out of a window. You deliberately portrayed the accused as a beast, a stepmother filled with endless hate, solely in order to justify your own article and arouse society's indignation toward the merciful verdict of the jurors. And we are justified in concluding that you refashioned the facts of the case solely for the purpose I have just indicated; we are justified in doing this because you should not (you had no right to do so) have failed to learn the most minute details of a case in which you assumed the right to pronounce a verdict and demand a punishment.

Meanwhile, this beast, this brutal stepmother who hated the child and who was insatiable in her desire to torment it, *never* existed *at all*. And the investigation definitely established this. Initially the notion really was advanced that the stepmother had tormented the child and had decided to kill the girl because she hated her. But subsequently the prosecution abandoned this notion altogether: it became all to clear that the crime had been committed from motives entirely other than hatred of the child, motives that were thoroughly explained in court and in which the child did not figure at all. Moreover, there were not even any witnesses in court who could have confirmed the stepmother's cruelty and the *stepmother's* beatings. There was only one testimony of only one woman who lived down the corridor from them (a lot of people were living there) to the effect that Kornilova did give the child some very painful thrashings, but even this testimony was later shown by the defense to be "hallway gossip" and nothing more. There was something that usually happens in families of this sort, given their level of education and development, namely, that both the father and the stepmother actually did punish the child when she misbehaved; but this was done only at times, i.e., very rarely, and not cruelly but "in a fatherly way," as they both expressed it; and that is exactly what still happens, unfortunately, in all such Russian families all over Holy Russia, even though the parents have an intense love for their children and (this is very often the case) a greater and deeper concern for them than do some educated, wealthy, "advanced" European-style families. In Kornilova's case there was only a lack of competence, not cruelty. Kornilova, in fact, was a very good stepmother; she cared for the child and watched over her. Only once did the child receive *severe* punishment: the stepmother thrashed her once on awakening in the morning *because she had failed to get up to relieve herself during the night*. There was no hatred of the child shown here. When I pointed out to Kornilova that this was not a matter for punishment, that the nature and physical constitutions of children differ, that a six-year-old child is still too small to know how to ask to be taken to the toilet each time, Kornilova replied, "But I was told that I had to beat her so as to break the habit, and that otherwise she'd never learn." On that occasion she struck the child with a rope "six times," but in such a way that welts were raised—and it was these welts that were seen by the woman down the hall, the only witness to the only incident of cruelty, and it was about them that she testified in court. It was also because of the welts that the husband, when he came home from work, promptly punished his wife, i.e., he gave her a beating. He is a stern, straightforward, honest man who, above all, is inflexible, although, as you will see, he holds to some of the customs of olden times. He beat his wife rarely and not cruelly (this she herself says), and only to assert the principle of the husband's authority—this is a result of his nature. He loves his child (although he punished her for misbehavior more frequently than did the stepmother), but he is not the kind of man who would allow the child to be mistreated, even by his wife. And so the only instance of a cruel punishment (to the point of raising welts) that was disclosed in court is transformed by the prosecutor of *The Northern Messenger* into a stepmother's systematic, brutal beatings for a whole year, into a stepmother's hatred which, growing ever stronger, ended with the child being thrown out of a window. Yet Kornilova was not even thinking about the child five minutes before she committed her horrible crime.

You will laugh, Mr. Observer, and say to me, "Isn't punishment with switches that raise welts an example of cruelty, an example of beating *by the stepmother*?" Yes, punishment that raises welts is brutal, that's true, but this incident (the only one of its kind, a fact that was established in court, and as far as I am concerned it has now been established positively), I repeat, is still not constant, brutal beating by the stepmother for a whole year, this is only an *accident* that arose from her incompetence in child-rearing, from a false conception of how the child must be taught, and certainly not because she hated her or felt that "such is her lot." Thus, your depiction of this woman as an evil stepmother and the personality that emerged in court on the basis of actual facts are two entirely different things. Yes, she threw the child out of the window; that is a terrible and brutal crime, but she did not commit it as a spiteful stepmother—that is the first reply to your unsubstantiated accusation. Why do you persist in making such a cruel accusation if you know yourself that it cannot be proven, that it was set aside in court, and that there were no witnesses at all to corroborate it? Was it really only for literary effect? When you try to prove that this was done by a *stepmother* who brought a whole year of tormenting the child (which was altogether untrue) to a conclusion in this murderous act, you thereby distort the impressions of a reader who knows little in this case; as he reads your article, you banish any of his involuntary feelings of compassion and mercy for the monstrous stepmother; and yet, had you not shown him this stepmother as a torturer of the child, she might have earned at least a little indulgence in his heart as a sick person, as one unnerved by a pathological condition, as an aggravated pregnant woman, as emerges from the fantastic, violent, and puzzling details of the event. Is it fair for a public figure to act this way? Is it humane?

But you go on to say more wrong things. You have written, once again firmly and precisely as an observer who has studied the whole case down to the smallest details: "'The affect of pregnancy'—well, a touching new phrase has been invented. However powerful that affect may have been, the woman under its influence still did not attack her husband or the tenants next door. The entire affect was exclusively fixed on this defenseless little girl whom she had tyrannized for a whole year without any affect. On what did the jurors base their acquittal?"

On what did you base yourself, Mr. Observer, to construct such an absolute distortion of the case? "She did not attack her husband!" But that was the one thing that was disclosed at the trial: that her quarrels with her husband at last reached the point (only during the final few days, however) of madness and frenzy, something which led to the crime. The quarrels were certainly not over the child, because the child had literally nothing to do with them; *Kornilova was not thinking about the child at all on those days*. "I didn't need the girl at all then," was how Kornilova herself expressed it.

It is not for you but for my readers that I shall attempt to delineate both these characters, the quarreling husband and wife, as I understood them even before the verdict and as they revealed themselves to me even more, under my most careful observation, after the verdict. In discussing these two people I am committing no great indiscretion; a good deal more was said about them in court. In any case, I am doing this specifically to vindicate them. And so the point is this. The husband, first and foremost, is a steady, frank, utterly honest and kind man (there is even some nobility about him, as he later showed); but he is rather too puritanical, too naive, and given strictly to following a view and conviction he has accepted once and for all. There is also a certain difference in age between him and his wife, he being a good deal older than she and a widower besides. He works all day, and though he wears

European ("German") clothes and looks as if he were an "educated" person, he has never had any particular education. I might also note that his overall appearance conveys his real sense of his own dignity. I can add that he is not very talkative, not very cheerful or humorous; his disposition is perhaps rather gloomy. He married Kornilova while she was still very young. She was an honest girl, a seamstress by trade, who earns a decent wage through her work.

I don't know how they met. She married him by choice, "out of love." But disagreements quickly began, and though they did not go to extremes for a long time, misunderstanding, estrangement, and, at last, even malice grew on both sides—slowly, yet steadily and surely. The fact is—and it may be the whole reason—that both, despite their growing malice, loved one another even too passionately and continued to do so to the very end. It was love that hardened the demands on both sides, strengthened them, further aggravated them. And at this point her character came into play. Hers is a character rather reserved and somewhat proud. Among both men and women there are such characters who, though they may cherish even the most ardent feelings in their hearts, are always somehow ashamed to display them; they show little affection, have few affectionate words, few embraces, and little open display of emotion. If they are called heartless and unfeeling because of this, then they become even more aloof. If accused of something, they rarely try to explain the matter themselves; rather, they leave this task to the accuser: "Figure it out yourself; if you love me, you ought to know that I'm right." And if he does not understand and grows more and more aggravated, her response is to become more and more aggravated as well. And so, from the very beginning this husband began severely (although by no means cruelly) reproaching her, admonishing her, teaching her, holding up the example of his first wife, something she found particularly painful. Things did not go that badly, however; yet it happened that when he reproached and accused her, she would begin quarreling and making spiteful remarks instead of seeking to clear things up and end the misunderstanding by offering some final explanation or indication of its cause. At last, even this was abandoned. It ended with morose disillusionment, not love, filling her heart (it happened first to her, not her husband). And all these things developed rather unconsciously: this is the life of working people, a hard life in which there's not a lot of time to think about feelings. He leaves for work, she is busy with the housework, the cooking, and even washing the floors. On each side of the long corridor in the government building where they live are tiny rooms, one for each married worker employed by that government establishment. It happened that she had gone, with her husband's permission, to a name-day party at the family of the tradesman with whom she had learned to sew in her childhood and youth and with whom she and her husband had kept up an acquaintance. The husband, busy with his work, stayed at home this time. The party turned out to be a very happy one; there were many guests, refreshments, and people started dancing. The celebration went on until morning. The young woman was accustomed to a rather dull life at home with her husband, living in one cramped room and always toiling; evidently, she recalled the years of her youth and went on enjoying herself "at the ball" so long that she forgot the curfew her husband had imposed on her. At last, she was persuaded to spend the night at her hosts', since she was a long way from home. It was at this point that the husband, who for the first time had spent a night apart from his wife, grew angry. He grew very angry: the next day, not going to work, he set off to fetch her; he found her and, right there in the presence of the guests, he *punished* her. They returned home in silence and for two days and nights thereafter did not speak to one another and did not eat together. I learned all this in bits and pieces; despite my questions, she herself revealed little to me about her state of mind at that time. "I can't recall what I was thinking about then, over those two days, but I just kept on thinking. *I didn't even look at her* (meaning the little girl) at all. I remember everything about how it happened, but just how I did it I can't explain." And so, on the morning of the third day, the husband left for work early and the girl was still asleep. The stepmother is busy at the stove. Finally, the girl wakes up; the stepmother mechanically washes and dresses her as usual, puts on her shoes and seats her at the table to have breakfast . . . "and I wasn't thinking about her at all." The child sits there, sipping from her cup and eating—"and all of a sudden I looked at her. . . ."

4. Malicious Psychologists. Obstetrician-Psychiatrists

Listen now, Mr. Observer, you state positively and precisely that the whole thing was done with no hesitation, deliberately and calmly; you say that she had been beating the child for a whole year and at last thought it over, calmly made the decision, and threw the infant out of the window: "*There is neither a sudden display of hatred* for the child," you write indignantly, "nor any repentance after committing the murderous act; it is all consistent and logical in the display *of one and the same* evil will. And this woman is acquitted." Those are your own words. But yet, the prosecutor himself withdrew the charge of a premeditated crime, do you realize that, Mr. Observer? He withdrew it publicly, solemnly, in an open court, at the most critical moment of the trial. Yet the prosecutor's accusation against Kornilova had been one of persistent cruelty. Now, after the prosecutor's withdrawal of the charge, how can you, Mr. Observer, assert that there was no sudden display of hatred but, rather, that it was all the consistent and logical manifestation of the same evil will? Consistent and logical! Therefore it was deliberate, and therefore it was premeditated. Let me quickly refresh your memory once more: she told the girl to get up on the window sill and look out of the window, and when the girl did so, she picked her up by the legs and threw her from a height of some forty feet. Then she closed the window, got dressed, and went off to the police station to confess what she had done. Tell me, is this really consistent and logical? Is it not fantastic? And in the first place, why give the child breakfast if the deed had long been planned in her mind; why wait while the child drinks her coffee and eats her bread? How could she (it's natural, after all) not even look out the window after she had thrown out the child? And tell me, please, why would she go and confess? If it was all caused by malice, by hatred for the girl "whom she had been beating for a whole year," then why, after having killed this girl, having conceived and at last carried out this murder she had calmly planned long ago—why should she at once go off and confess? Let the girl she so hated die, but why should she ruin herself? Besides, if there was another motive for murder beyond hatred of the child—I mean, hatred of her husband, a desire to take revenge on her husband through the death of his child—then she could have simply told her husband that the naughty girl herself had crawled onto the window sill and had fallen out herself; her aim would have been achieved, after all; the father would have been shocked and shaken, and no one in the world would then have been able to accuse her of premeditated murder even though she might have been suspected of it. What evidence would there be? Even if the girl had survived, who would have believed her childish babblings? Had she done this instead, the murderess would have more readily and more fully achieved everything she was striving for—that's to say, she would have taken a much more cruel and painful revenge on her husband who, even if he did suspect her of murder, would thus have been tormented all the more by her going unpunished and by seeing that punishing her—bringing her to justice, that is—would be impossible. But by punishing herself at that very time, by ruining her life in prison, in Siberia, at hard labor, she would thereby be giving satisfaction to her husband. What would be the point of that? And in such a case who on earth would get smartly dressed to go off and ruin her life? Oh, people will tell me that she did not want merely to take revenge on the child and her husband; she wanted to end the marriage with her husband: "They'll send me off to hard labor and the marriage will be annulled!" But, setting aside the fact that there are ways and means of ending a marriage other than by destroying one's life and freedom at the age of nineteen—setting that aside, you must agree that a person who consciously decided to destroy himself, to throw himself into the abyss yawning at his feet without a second's thought or a moment's hesitation—you must agree that at such a moment there would be a terrible sensation within the person's soul, a black despair, an irresistible urge to perish, an urge to cast himself into the abyss and destroy himself. And if such is the case, then can one possibly say, while preserving one's common sense, that "there was neither a sudden display of hatred nor any sign of repentance in her soul"! If there was no repentance, there was blackness, damnation, madness. At the very least, one can't say that it was all consistent, all logical, all premeditated, with no sudden impulse. One must himself be in the grip of an "affect" to maintain that. Had she not gone off to confess but remained home, lied to her husband and to others that the child had caused her own death, that would have truly been logical and consistent and without any sudden display of evil will; but causing her own ruination at that very time, not under compulsion but voluntarily, certainly bears witness, at least, to the awful and disturbed emotional state of the murderess. This dismal condition continued for a long time, for several days. The expression "She's got more lives than a cat" was used by the expert witness for the defense (not the prosecution) when he described to the court that dismal, cold, seemingly numb emotional state of the accused after she committed her crime, and not to show any spiteful, cold, moral insensitivity on her part. My own whole problem was that, having read of the court's initial sentence at the time and being struck specifically by the strangeness and fantasticality of all the details of the case, and having taken into consideration the fact of the fifth month of her pregnancy when she committed the crime (this was mentioned in the newspapers), I—quite involuntarily—could not help but wonder if her pregnancy had not had an influence here; I mean to say, as I wrote at the time, that perhaps it happened as follows: "She took a look at the child and thought, in her anger: 'What if I threw her out of the window?' Were she not pregnant, she might have thought it, in her anger, but she would not have done it; she would not have thrown the child out; but being pregnant, she simply did it." Well, that was my whole problem: that was what I thought and what I wrote at the time. But could these words alone really have led to the quashing of the verdict and the subsequent acquittal of the murderess? You ridicule the experts, Mr. Observer! You maintain that merely one of the five said that Kornilova actually was under the affect of pregnancy and that three others only stated that pregnancy might have had an influence but did not positively say that it actually did. From this you conclude that merely one expert *positively* absolved the defendant, while four did not. But, you see, your reasoning is unsound: you demand too much from the human conscience. It's sufficient that three experts obviously did not want to absolve the defendant *positively*—meaning that they did not want to take that on their consciences; yet the facts were still clear and evident enough to make these experts hesitate and conclude by being unable to say *no*, simply and directly, but were *compelled* to say that "there actually could have been some pathological influence at the moment of the crime." Well, so far as the jurors were concerned, this amounted to a verdict: if they could not help but admit that "there might have been," then maybe there really had been. Such strong doubts in the minds of the jurors naturally could not but influence their decision as well, and this is absolutely as it should have been from the standpoint of higher justice: could they really pass a sentence to kill a woman whose complete guilt was doubted by three experts, while a fourth, Diukov, an expert specifically in mental disorders, directly and firmly attributed the entire misdeed to the disturbed emotional state of the accused at the time? But "The Observer" seized particularly on Mr. Florinsky, the fifth expert, who did not concur with the opinions of the first four experts: he's an obstetrician, the Observer suggests, and so he ought to know about women's ailments more than anyone. But why should he know more about emotional disorders than the expert psychiatrists themselves? Because he's an obstetrician and does not practice psychiatry but something else entirely? That isn't quite logical either.

5. One Incident That Explains a Good Deal, in My View

Now let me tell you about one incident that, in my view, can provide a final explanation for certain things in this case and that can directly serve the purpose for which I undertook this article. On the morning of the third day after the acquittal of the defendant Kornilova (April 22, 1877), the husband and the wife came to see me. The previous day they had been at the children's home where the victim, the little girl who had been thrown out of the window, had been placed; now, the next day, they were going there once more. Incidentally, the fate of the child has now been assured and there is no need to exclaim, "Woe to the child, now! . . ." and so on. When his wife was taken to prison, the father himself placed the child in this children's home because he had no possibility of looking after her himself, being away at work from morning till night. And after his wife returned they decided to leave her at the home because she was being so well looked after there. But on holidays they often take her home with them. She had spent Christmas with them. Despite her own work, which lasts from morning till night, and despite another nursing infant (the one born in prison) on her hands, the stepmother even now sometimes finds time to tear herself away and run off to see the little girl at the children's home, to bring her some little treat, and so on. When she was still in prison, recalling the sin she had committed against the child, she often dreamed of finding some way to see her and of doing something to make the little girl forget what had happened. These fantasies seemed strange somehow, coming from a woman as reserved and as wary as Kornilova was during her trial. But her fantasies were destined to become real. About a month ago, just before Christmas, not having seen the Kornilovs for some six months, I dropped in at their apartment; Kornilova's first words to me were that the little girl "comes running joyously to her and hugs her each time she visits her in the children's home." And as I was leaving Kornilova suddenly told me, "She'll forget. . . ."

And so they came to see me that morning, the third day after her acquittal. . . . But I keep getting off the topic and will do so once more, just for a minute. In his article "The Observer" makes some malicious jokes about these visits of mine to Kornilova when she was in prison. "He truly has captured that state of mind" (meaning the state of mind of a pregnant woman), he says about me; "he has visited the lady in question in prison, been struck by her humility, and over several issues of his *Diary* has come out as her ardent defender." In the first place, what is the point of the word *lady* here? What is the point of this nasty tone? "The Observer" knows very well that she is not a lady but a simple peasant woman, one who toils from morning till night; she cooks, scrubs floors, and sells her sewing, if she can find time to do any. I visited her in prison precisely once a month, spent no more than ten or at most fifteen minutes with her each time, for the most part in a cell she shared with other women awaiting trial and who had nursing infants. If I did examine this woman with curiosity and tried to comprehend her character, then what was the harm in that? Did it deserve mockery and humor? But let's return to my story.

And so they came to visit me; they sat there, both in a thoughtful, serious mood. Until then I had known the husband only slightly. And suddenly he said to me, "The other day, when we came back home"—(this was after her acquittal and so was after eleven o'clock, and he gets up at five)—"we sat right down at the table, and I took out the Gospel and began reading to her." I confess, when he told me this it suddenly occurred to me as I looked at him: "Yes, he couldn't have done anything else; he's a type, a thoroughly consistent type; I could have guessed it." In short, he's a puritan, a most honest and serious fellow, kind and noble, to be sure, but one who will never make any compromises and never surrender any of his convictions. This husband, with total faith, regards marriage as a sacrament. He is one of those husbands we still can find in Holy Russia, who, following old Russian tradition and custom, on returning from the wedding and retiring to the bedroom with his new bride, would first cast himself down on his knees before the icon and pray for a long time, asking God's blessing on his future. In this case he acted in a similar fashion: bringing his wife into his house once more and renewing the marriage that had been sundered by her terrible crime, he first opened the Gospel and began to read it to her, his manly and serious resolve not restrained in the least even by the consideration that this woman was almost ready to collapse from exhaustion, that she had been under terrible strain even while preparing for the trial, while on this last crucial day of her judgment she had endured so many overwhelming impressions, both moral and physical, that it would naturally now be no sin even for such a strict puritan as he to let her have just a moment to rest and collect herself first, something that would have been even more in keeping with the aim he had when he opened the Gospel in front of her. And so this act of his struck me as almost clumsy—too single-minded, meaning that this very thing might cause him to fail to achieve his aim. A very guilty soul—and particularly one such as hers, all too aware of its own guilt and already having endured much torment because of it, should not be too plainly and *hastily* reproached for its guilt, for the result may be just the opposite, particularly when the soul is already repentant. Here is the man on whom she depends, raising himself above her, wearing the halo of a judge; she sees something merciless in him; he autocratically intrudes into her soul and sternly casts aside her repentance and the good feelings that have been born within her: "One such as you needs no rest, or food, or drink; just sit and listen to how you must live." As they were leaving, I managed to remark in passing that he should undertake *this business* again with somewhat less severity or, to put it better, that he should not be in such a hurry, not forge ahead so directly, and that such an approach might prove better. I spoke briefly and clearly, yet I thought that he still might not understand. And suddenly he said in reply, "But right then, as soon as we came into the house and started to read, she told me everything—how on your last visit you taught her the right way to behave if they exiled her to Siberia, and gave her some advice about getting on there. . . ."

And this is what had happened: I had, in fact, gone to visit her in prison on the very eve of the trial. No one, neither I nor her lawyer, had any firm hopes for an acquittal. Nor did she. I found her looking rather resolute; she was sitting sewing something; her baby was fretful. It wasn't that she was downcast, yet she seemed somehow oppressed. Several gloomy thoughts about her kept running through my mind, and I had dropped in specifically to give her some friendly advice. We had firm hopes that she would be exiled only to a settlement, and so a woman barely the age of maturity would set off to Siberia with a baby in her arms. The marriage would be annulled; I was thinking that out there, alone, defenseless, pretty as well, and so young—how could she resist the temptations she would face? Fate was truly pushing her into debauchery, for I know Siberia: there are a good many people there eager to corrupt a young woman; very many unmarried men—some in service, some after easy money—go there from Russia. It is easy to fall, but the Siberians—both the simple peasants and the townsfolk—are utterly merciless toward a fallen woman. No one would think to stand in her way, but once a woman has tarnished her reputation she can never restore it: she will face endless scorn, words of criticism and reproach, mockery; and so it will remain until her old age, to her very grave. They will give her a special nickname. And her child (a girl) will at once be *compelled* to follow her mother's career: coming from a bad home, she will not find a good and honest husband. But it's another thing if the exiled mother conducts herself honorably and strictly in Siberia: a young woman who leads a chaste life enjoys enormous respect. Everyone defends her, everyone wants to do her favors, everyone takes his hat off to her. She will certainly be able to set her daughter on the right path in life. With time, once people have managed to come to know her and trust her, even she herself may enter into an honorable marriage and an honorable family. (In Siberia, neither in the prisons nor in any place of exile, no one asks about one's past, meaning the reason for one's exile, nor do they show any curiosity about it. That may be because virtually everyone in Siberia, over the course of these three centuries, is descended from exiles, and the country has been populated by them.) And so this was what I had in mind to tell this young woman, barely the age of maturity. I even deliberately chose to tell her this precisely on this last day before her trial: it would remain more graphic in her mind and be stamped more surely on her soul, I thought. After listening to me tell her how to get on in Siberia should she be exiled, she thanked me, gloomily and seriously, scarcely raising her eyes. And so, tired, worn-out, shaken by this whole terrible impression of the many hours of her trial, and then at home, where her husband sternly made her sit and listen to the Gospel, she did not think to herself, "He could at least have had some pity on me; he could at least have put it off until tomorrow, and given me something to eat and let me rest now." Neither was she offended by the fact that *he so elevated himself above her*. (N.B.: The most dreadful criminal, fully aware of his own crime, and even the most repentant one, can still feel offended that others *elevate themselves above him*.) But on the contrary: she could find nothing better to say to her husband than *promptly* to tell him that in prison people had also taught her the right way to behave, that they had taught her something about living in an alien land, honorably and chastely. And clearly she did this because she knew the story would please her husband, would fit in with his tone and cheer him: "So, she is truly repenting, she does truly want to live rightly," he would think. And that is just what he did think; and as to my advice not to frighten her by too much hasty severity, he told me plainly and, of course, with joy in his heart, "There's no need to fear for her and be suspicious; she herself is glad to be honest. . . ."

I'm not sure, but it seems to me that all this is clear. The readers will understand why I am revealing all this. At least one may now hope that the court's great mercy did not spoil the guilty woman even more; rather, it is very possible that this mercy fell on good soil. After all, even before, and while she was in prison, and even now she considered and considers herself clearly guilty and attributes her acquittal only to the great mercy of the court. She herself does not understand this "affect of pregnancy." And, truly, she certainly is guilty; she was fully aware while committing the crime, she remembers every moment and every detail of it; the only thing she does not know and even now cannot explain to herself is: "*How could she have done such a thing then; how could she have brought herself to it?*" Yes, Mr. Observer, the court has pardoned an actual criminal, despite the now indubitable and fateful "affect of pregnancy" which you so ridicule, sir, and of which I am now deeply and surely convinced. Now then, decide for yourself: had the marriage been dissolved; had she been torn away from a man whom she certainly loved and still loves, and who represents her entire family; had she, alone, twenty years old, with a baby in her arms, been exiled, helpless, to Siberia to shame and corruption (she would certainly have fallen in Siberia)—tell me, what sense would there be in her ruination, in reducing her life to ashes, a life which now, it seems, has been regenerated, returned to the truth through a severe process of purging and repentance, and with a heart that has been renewed? Is it not better to reform, to find, and to restore a human being than simply to cut off his head? Cutting off heads is easy if one follows the letter of the law, but it is always much more difficult to settle a matter in accordance with the truth, in a humane and paternal fashion. Finally, you surely knew that along with this young, twenty-year-old mother—an inexperienced woman who certainly would become a victim of want and debauchery—her infant child was also being exiled. . . . But permit me to say a few words to you about infant children in particular.

6. Am I an Enemy of Children? On What the Word "Happy" Sometimes Means

Your entire article, Mr. Observer, is a protest "against condoning the of abuse of children." The fact that you stand up for children does you credit, of course, but you behave much too haughtily toward me. You say about me:

> One must have all the power of imagination in which, as we know, Mr. Dostoevsky so excels in order to capture fully the state of mind of the woman and reach an awareness of all the compelling affects of pregnancy. . . . But Mr. Dostoevsky is too impressionable, and besides "the pathological manifestations of the will" are right in his line as author of *The Devils, The Idiot,* etc., so he may be excused for having a weakness for such things. I take a simpler view of the matter and maintain that after such instances exonerating the physical abuse of children—and they happen not infrequently in Russia, as they do in England—we are left without even a shadow of a deterrent to such crimes.

And so on, and so on. In the first place, as far as my "weakness for the pathological manifestations of the will" is concerned, I will say merely that it seems I actually did sometimes manage, in my novels and tales, to *reveal* certain people who considered themselves healthy and to prove to them that they were ill. Do you know that there are very many people whose illness is precisely their good health; that's to say, their excessive confidence in their own normalcy infects them with a terrible conceit, a shameless narcissism that sometimes reaches the point of a virtual conviction of their own infallibility? Well, it was people such as these whom I managed many times to point out to my readers and even, perhaps, to show that these healthy fellows were by no means as healthy as they thought but, on the contrary, were very ill and needed to go for treatment. I don't see anything wrong in this, but Mr. Observer is too harsh with me because his phrase about "acquittal for physical abuse of children" refers directly to me; he only tempers it "a wee bit" by saying, "He may be excused for that." His entire article was written directly to prove that because of my predilection for "the pathological manifestations of the will," my common sense has been so distorted that I would rather take pity on the torturer of a child, the bestial stepmother and murderess, than on the tortured victim—the weak, pitiful little girl who was beaten, abused and, finally, nearly murdered. I find that offensive. In contrast to my pathological condition, "The Observer" directly, hastily, and candidly points to himself and flaunts his own good health: "I take a simpler view of the matter" (than does Mr. Dostoevsky) "and maintain that after such instances exonerating the physical abuse of children . . ." etc., etc.

And so I am condoning physical abuse of children—a terrible accusation! In that case, then, permit me to defend myself. I shall not point to my past thirty years of literary work to settle the question of whether I am a great enemy of children and a proponent of abusing them; but I will merely recall the two last years of my writing, i.e., the publication of *A Writer's Diary*. When Kroneberg's trial was going on, despite my penchant for "the pathological manifestations of the will," I happened to stand up for the child, the victim, and not for the torturer. And so, even I *sometimes* take the side of common sense, Mr. Observer. Now I even regret that you did not then also step forward to defend the child, Mr. Observer; surely you would have written a most passionate article. But somehow I can't seem to recall even a single passionate article on behalf of the child. And so it never occurred to you, then, to stand up for the child. Subsequently, and not long ago—last summer—I happened to stand up for the young children of the Dzhunkovskys, who had also been tortured in their parents' home. You did not write anything about the Dzhunkovskys either; however, no one wrote about them, and that's understandable: everyone was busy with such important political questions. Finally, I could point out not merely one but several instances when I, over these two years, have spoken up about children in my *Diary*—about their education, about their wretched fate in our families, about young delinquents in our correctional institutions; I even mentioned one little boy at Christ's Christmas party—not an actual occurrence, of course, but still, one that provides no direct evidence of indifference and heartlessness toward children. Let me tell you this, Mr. Observer: when I first read in the newspaper about Kornilova's crime, about the irrevocable verdict on her, and when I was involuntarily struck by the idea that, perhaps, this guilty woman was not nearly as guilty as it seemed (please note, Mr. Observer, that even then almost nothing was said about "the *stepmother's* beatings" in the newspaper accounts of the trial and that even then this charge was not pressed)—then I, having decided to write something on Kornilova's behalf, realized full well what I was taking on. I now frankly admit that to you. I knew very well that I was writing an article that would find little sympathy, that I was standing up for one who had inflicted suffering and on whom?—on a little child. I foresaw that *some people* would accuse me of being heartless, self-important, even diseased: "He's standing up for a stepmother who tried to murder her child!" I could clearly foresee such a "straight-and-narrow" accusation from certain arbiters—from you, for instance, Mr. Observer; and so I even hesitated for some time, but ended by deciding to do it just the same: "If I believe that I have a truth here, then is it worth serving a lie in order to court popularity?" That was what I came to in the final analysis. Besides, I was also encouraged by faith in my readers: "They will understand, at last, that I can't be accused of wishing to condone the abuse of children, and if I stand up for a murderess, setting forth my suspicion of her pathological and deranged state of mind while she was committing the crime, thereby I'm surely not supporting the crime itself and am not pleased at the fact that a child was beaten and nearly killed; on the contrary, I perhaps have the utmost compassion for the child, and no less than anyone else. . . ."

You ridiculed me maliciously, Mr. Observer, for one sentence in my article about the acquittal of the defendant Kornilova. You say: "'The husband of the acquitted woman,' writes Mr. Dostoevsky in his *Diary* that came out just recently, 'took her home that same evening sometime after ten o'clock and she came back to her own home again, happy.' How touching. But woe to the poor child," etc., etc.

I think I could not have written such stupid things. It's true that you quote my sentence accurately, but this is what you did: you have cut it in half and inserted a period where there was none. This gave it the particular sense that you wanted it to have. In my article there is no period there; the sentence continues to its second half; I think that, taken together with this other half which you threw out, the sentence is by no means as inane and "touching" as it seems. Here is my sentence, but the entire sentence with nothing left out: "The husband of the acquitted woman took her home that same evening sometime after ten o'clock and she came back into her own home again, happy, after a year's absence, *with the impression of an enormous lesson learned for the rest of her life and a clear sense of the hand of God at work in this case—even if only beginning with the miraculous survival of the child. . . .*"

You see, Mr. Observer, I am even prepared to qualify my remarks here and apologize for reproaching you just now for cutting my sentence in half. In fact, I can now see that this sentence may certainly not have come out as clearly as I had hoped and that one might interpret it incorrectly. It needs a little clarification, and that I shall now make. The whole point here is in my understanding of the word "happy." I saw the happiness of the acquitted woman not only in the fact that she had been freed, but in the fact that "she came back into her own home with the impression of an enormous lesson learned *for the rest of her life* and a clear sense of the hand of God stretched over her." There is no greater happiness, after all, than to be assured of people's mercy and love for one another. This is faith, a whole faith, for an entire life! And what happiness is superior to faith? Can this former transgressor now ever doubt people at all? Can she doubt people or humanity as a whole, in their lofty, sensible, and sacred substance? For one who was about to perish and be ruined, to enter her own home bearing such a powerful impression of a great new faith is the greatest happiness there could be. We know that some very noble and superior minds have often suffered their whole lives from lack of faith in the soundness of the lofty purpose of humanity, in its goodness and ideals, in its godly origin; and they have died in bleak disillusionment. Of course, you will smile at what I am saying and tell me, perhaps, that here too I am letting my imagination run wild; that the ignorant and coarse Kornilova, who has emerged from the common rabble and has no education, can experience neither any such disillusionment nor any such tender feelings. Ah, but that's untrue! These "dark people" simply don't know the names we would give to all these things and how to explain them in our language; but they do feel, completely and utterly, just as deeply as we "educated people" do; and they experience their feelings with just the same happiness or just the same sorrow and pain as we do.

They become disillusioned with people and lose faith in them just the same way as we do. Had Kornilova been exiled to Siberia and had she fallen and perished there, do you really think she would not have felt, at some bitter moment in her life, the full horror of her fall? And would she not have carried in her heart, perhaps to her very grave, a malice that was all the more bitter because it would have been aimless? For apart from herself she would have no one to blame because, I repeat, she is completely convinced even now that she is *truly guilty* and merely does not know how it all happened to her at the time. But now, feeling that she is guilty and considering herself such, and suddenly having been forgiven by people, showered with mercy and blessings, how could she not feel restored and reborn into a new life, higher than her old one? It was not just one person who forgave her; *everyone*—the court, the jurors, and therefore society as a whole—showed mercy to her. After that, how could she not take with her a sense of the enormous debt that would last all her life—a debt to all who had shown mercy to her, meaning all people on the earth. Every *great* happiness bears a certain suffering within it, for it arouses in us a higher consciousness. Such a clarity of consciousness within is aroused more rarely by grief than by great happiness. Great—meaning sublime—happiness places an *obligation* on the soul. (I'll repeat: there is no greater happiness than to come to believe in the goodness of people and their love for one another.) When the woman taken in adultery and condemned to stoning was told, "Go, thou, and sin no more," do you really think that she returned home to commit more sins?

And so the whole question in the Kornilova case amounts merely to the kind of soil in which the seed fell. And that is why it seemed necessary for me to write this article now. After reading your attack on me seven months ago, Mr. Observer, I specifically decided to delay my reply to you so as to expand my knowledge of the case. And so, I think, on the basis of some of the particulars I have gathered, I would not err now in stating that the seed has fallen on good soil; that a person has been restored to life; that this has caused no wrong to anyone; that the soul of the guilty woman has been crushed both by repentance and by an eternal, beneficent impression of the boundless mercy of people; and that now, after experiencing such goodness and love, it would be difficult for her heart to go wrong again. She certainly does not think herself justified because of the incontestable "affect of pregnancy" that so troubles you, Mr. Observer. In short, it seemed to me not at all futile to pass on this information, not only to you, Mr. Observer, but to all my readers as well, and to all those merciful people who acquitted her. And as far as the little girl is concerned, Mr. Observer, you needn't worry about her or exclaim, "Woe to the child!" Her fate now has also been rather well settled, and "she will forget"—there is real hope of that.

2

1. The Death of Nekrasov. On What Was Said at His Grave

Nekrasov is dead. I saw him for the last time a month before his death. At that time he already looked almost like a corpse, so that it even seemed odd to see him move his lips and speak. Yet he not only spoke but preserved all the clarity of his mind. It seems that he still did not believe in the possibility of his imminent death. A week before his death he suffered paralysis of the right side of his body, and then on the twenty-eight, in the morning, I learned that Nekrasov had died the evening before, at eight o'clock. That same day I went to pay my respects. His face, terribly emaciated and distorted by suffering, somehow struck me particularly. As I left I could hear the psalm-reader's clear, drawn-out tones over the deceased: "There is no man who has not sinned." When I came home I could not get down to work; I picked up all three volumes of Nekrasov and began reading from the first page. I sat up the whole night, till six o'clock in the morning, and it was as if I had relived those whole thirty years once more. Those first four verses that begin the first volume of his poetry appeared in the *Petersburg Anthology* in which my first tale also appeared. And then, as I went on reading (I read one poem after another), it seemed as if my whole life were passing before me. I recognized and recalled those of his poems I had first read in Siberia when, after being released from four years of imprisonment in the labor camp, I at last acquired the right to put my hands on a book. I also recalled the impression the poems had made on me at the time. In short, that night I reread almost two-thirds of everything Nekrasov had written and literally for the first time realized how large a place Nekrasov, as a poet, has occupied in my life over all those thirty years! As a poet, of course. We met infrequently and only once with wholehearted, ardent feeling: this was at the very beginning of our acquaintance, in 1845, during the time of *Poor People*. But I have already talked about that. We shared several moments then in which the most fundamental and private aspects of the spirit of this mysterious man stood out clearly before me. As I at once sensed at the time, his was a heart that had been wounded at the very beginning of its life, and it was this *never-healing* wound that provided the foundation and the source of all the passionate, suffering poetry he produced over the rest of his career. He told me then, in tears, of his childhood, of the pain he had suffered from the ugliness of life in his parents' home, of his mother; and the way he spoke of his mother, the deep tenderness with which he recalled her, suggested even then that if anything were to be sacred in his life, anything that might save him and serve him as a beacon, a guiding star in the darkest and most critical moments of his fate, then it would certainly be only this first childhood impression of childish tears, childish sobs shared with his martyred mother, this creature who loved him so, as they stole an embrace somewhere in secret (these things he told me). I think that no subsequent attachment could have had such an influence and powerful effect on his will and on those dark, irresistible impulses that pursued him throughout his life as did his devotion to his mother. And those dark impulses made their presence felt even at that time.

Not long thereafter, I recall, we somehow went our separate ways; our close relationship lasted no more than a few months. Misunderstandings, external circumstances, and some good people also contributed to this. Then, many years thereafter, when I had already come back from Siberia, we would meet (though not often); and despite the differences in our convictions that were already becoming evident, when we met we sometimes even said rather strange things to one another—just as if something that had begun in our youth, back in 1845, really was continuing in our lives and seemed unwilling and unable to end, even though we might not meet one another for years at a time. So it was that once in 1863, I think, in presenting me with a little volume of his verses, he pointed to one, "The Unfortunates," and said significantly, "I was thinking of you when I wrote that" (meaning my life in Siberia). "It was written about you." And finally, in recent times, we again would sometimes see one another while my novel *A Raw Youth* was being published in his magazine. . . .

Several thousand admirers gathered for Nekrasov's funeral. There were a good many students. The procession with the coffin began at nine o'clock in the morning and dispersed from the cemetery when it was already beginning to grow dark. Many speeches were made over his coffin, but few literary people spoke. A beautiful poem by someone was read, among other things. Feeling deeply moved, I made my way to his open grave, strewn with flowers and wreaths, and following the others I said a few words in my weak voice. I began by saying that his was a wounded heart, wounded once for his whole life, and that this unhealed wound was at the same time the source of all his poetry, all this man's love—passionate to the point of torment—for everyone who suffers from violence, from the cruelty of unbridled will, from all that oppresses our Russian woman, our child in the Russian family, our common man in his lot, which is often so bitter. I also expressed my conviction that in our poetry Nekrasov was the last of that series of poets who came to us with their "new word." In fact (leaving aside any question of the artistic power of his poetry and of its general dimensions), Nekrasov truly was an original to the highest degree and truly did come to us with his "new word." In days gone by, for instance, there had been the poet Tiutchev, a poet who was broader and more artistic than Nekrasov; yet Tiutchev will never have such a prominent and memorable place in our literature as Nekrasov unquestionably will be given. In that sense, among our poets (I mean those who came with a "new word") he should stand directly after Pushkin and Lermontov. When I expressed that thought aloud, a little incident occurred: a voice from the crowd cried out that Nekrasov was *greater* than Pushkin and Lermontov and that the latter were merely "Byronists." Several voices took up this refrain and shouted, "Yes, greater!" I, however, had no intention of saying anything about greatness and the comparative merits of the three poets. But this is what happened later: in *The Stock-Exchange News* Mr. Skabichevsky, in his epistle to young people on Nekrasov's significance, noted that when *someone* (that is, me) at Nekrasov's grave "took it into his head to compare his name with those of Pushkin and Lermontov, you all" (i.e., all the students) "*in one voice, in chorus,* shouted, 'He was greater, greater than they.'" I venture to assure Mr. Skabichevsky that he has been misinformed and that I recall clearly (I trust that I'm not mistaken) that at first there was only one voice that shouted, "Greater, greater than they" and added at once that Pushkin and Lermontov were

"Byronists"—a little footnote that is much more characteristic and natural for one voice and one opinion than for *everyone* at one and the same time, in a thousand-voice chorus; this fact, then, tends to support my account of what happened. Only after the first voice had shouted were there a few other voices raised, but only a few; I heard no thousand-voice chorus, I repeat, and I trust that I am not mistaken.

I am being so insistent about this because I would have been pained to see *all* our young people falling into such error. Gratitude to the great names of the past should be inherent in any young heart. No doubt, the ironical shout about Byronists and the exclamations of "Greater, greater!" happened not from any desire to start a literary debate over the open grave of a dear departed, something that would have been out of place; it was simply an ardent impulse to express as strongly as possible all the feelings of emotion, gratitude, and passion roused by a great poet who moved us so strongly and who, though in his grave, still remains close to us (and as for those other great old men of the past, well, they're so far away from us!). But this whole episode aroused in me, right there on the spot, the desire to explain my view more clearly in some future issue of the *Diary* and to express in more detail my view of such a remarkable and extraordinary phenomenon in our life and our poetry as was Nekrasov and what I believe to be the essence and the meaning of this phenomenon.

2. Pushkin, Lermontov, and Nekrasov

And in the first place, the word "Byronist" mustn't be used as a term of abuse. Although Byronism was a passing phenomenon, it was still a great, sacred, and necessary phenomenon in the life of the peoples of Europe, if not in the life of humanity as a whole. Byronism appeared at a moment when people were suffering terrible anguish, disillusionment, and almost despair. In the wake of the frenzied raptures of the new faith and the new ideals proclaimed at the end of the last century in France, the most advanced nation in Europe at the time, there came something so different from what had been expected, something that so betrayed people's faith, that never, perhaps, had there been such a sad moment in the history of western Europe. And it was not only because of external (political) reasons that the idols, raised up for only a moment, fell once more; it was also because of their internal shortcomings, something that all perceptive hearts and leading intellects could see. The new *outcome* had not yet made itself known, the new valve had not yet opened, and everyone was stifling within the terribly cramped and shrunken limits of the old world. The old idols lay smashed. And so, at that very moment, there appeared a great and mighty genius, a passionate poet. The strains of his verse echoed the anguish of people at the time, their gloomy disenchantment with their mission, their betrayed ideals. His was a new muse, one that had never been heard before, a muse of vengeance and sorrow, execration and despair. The spirit of Byronism suddenly seemed to sweep over the whole of humanity, and the whole of humanity responded to it. It was just like an opened valve; at least, amid the general, incoherent groans—unconscious ones, for the most part—this was a mighty outcry in which all the outcries and groans of humanity joined in chorus. How could we, too, not fail to respond to it, and through such a great, brilliant, and guiding mind as Pushkin? At that time in Russia as well, no powerful intellect and no noble heart could avoid Byronism. And this was not merely because of sympathy from afar for Europe and the European peoples; it was because we in Russia, at that very same time, were also faced with so many new, unsolved, and tormenting questions, and with all too many old disillusionments. . . .

But the greatness of Pushkin as a guiding genius lay precisely in the fact that he, surrounded almost entirely by people who did not understand him, so quickly found a sure path, *a great solution which we Russians had been longing for, and showed it to us*. This solution was nationality, turning to the People and *bowing down to the truth of the Russian People*. "Pushkin was a great and an extraordinary phenomenon." Pushkin was "not only a Russian but also the first Russian." A Russian who fails to understand Pushkin has no right to call himself a Russian. Pushkin understood the Russian People and perceived their mission with a degree of profundity and breadth that no one else has ever surpassed. I speak not only of the fact that, through the universality of his genius and his capacity to respond to all the diverse spiritual concerns of the peoples of Europe and almost to reincarnate himself into the genius of other peoples and nationalities, he testified to the universality and the all-embracing nature of the Russian spirit, thereby divining the future mission of the Russian genius within humanity as a whole as an all-unifying, all-reconciling and all-regenerating principle. I will not even speak of the fact that Pushkin was the first among us, in his anguish and prophetic foresight, to exclaim, "Shall I behold a People liberated, / And slavery overthrown at the tsar's behest!"

I shall speak now merely of Pushkin's love for the Russian People. This was an all-embracing love, a love such as no one before him had manifested. "Do not love me, love the things that are *mine*"—that is what the People will always tell you when they want to be assured of the sincerity of your love for them.

To love—that is, to pity the People for their want, their poverty, and their sufferings—is something any nobleman can do, especially one who is humane and enlightened in the European fashion. But the People *need* to be loved not for their sufferings alone but *for themselves*. What does it mean *to love them for themselves?* "You must love the things that I love, cherish the things that I cherish"—that is what it means, and that is how the People will answer you; and in no other way will they ever acknowledge you as one of their own, no matter how many tears you may shed for them. They will also always recognize falseness, no matter how many tender words you use to try to seduce them. Pushkin loved the People in just the way that the People require; he did not make conjectures about how to love the People; he did not prepare himself for it; he did not study: he himself suddenly became one of the People. He bowed down before the truth of the People; he accepted the People's truth as his own truth. Despite all their vices and many foul habits, he was able to discern the mighty essence of their spirit at a time when almost no one regarded the People in this way; and he took this essence of the People into his own soul as his ideal. And this was at a time when the most humane lovers of the Russian People, those having European enlightenment, openly regretted that our People were so base that they were simply unable to rise to the level of a Parisian street mob. In essence, these lovers of the People always despised the People. They believed, above all, that the People were slaves. They used slavery to excuse their degradation; but a slave could not be loved, after all; a slave was still a disgusting creature. Pushkin was the first to declare that the Russian *was not a slave* and never had been one, despite many centuries of slavery. There was slavery, but there were no slaves (on the whole, of course, and in general, not in exceptional individual cases)—that was Pushkin's thesis. Even the appearance and bearing of the Russian peasant led him to conclude that this was not a slave and could not be a slave (even though he remained in slavery)—a trait testifying to Pushkin's profound, direct love for the People. He recognized as well the high sense of personal dignity among our People (once again, on the whole, aside from the customary and inevitable exceptions); he foresaw the calm dignity with which our People would accept their liberation from serfdom—a thing that even many years after Pushkin was not understood by those like our most prominent, educated Russian Europeans, who expected something quite different from our People. Oh, they loved the People sincerely and passionately, but in their own fashion, in European fashion, that is. They shouted about the bestial state of the People, about their bestial condition in the slavery of serfdom, but they also believed in their hearts that our People actually were beasts. And suddenly the People acquired their freedom with such manly dignity, without the least inclination to cause offense to their former owners: "You live your way, I'll live mine; come and see me, if you like. You'll always have my respect for the good within you." Indeed, our peasant after his liberation posed a strange puzzlement for many people. Many even decided that his reaction to freedom came from his lack of development and obtuseness, remnants of his former slavery. And that's now; what must it have been like in Pushkin's day? Did I myself not hear, in my youth, the view of leading and "competent" people that, in *The Captain's Daughter,* Pushkin's Savelich, the slave of the landowning Grinevs, who fell at Pugachev's feet imploring him to spare the young master and "hang him, an old man instead, to make an example and instill fear"—that this Savelich is not only the image of a slave but the very apotheosis of Russian slavery!

Pushkin loved the People not for their sufferings alone. Suffering inspires pity, and pity so often goes along with contempt. Pushkin loved everything that this People loved, cherished everything that they cherished. He loved the Russian landscape passionately, tenderly; he loved the Russian countryside. He was not a nobleman serf-owner, merciful and humane, pitying the peasant for his hard lot; he was a man whose heart was reincarnated into the common man, into his essence, almost into his image. To belittle Pushkin as a poet whose devotion to the People was historical and archaic rather than actual is erroneous and does not even make sense. In these historical and archaic motifs there is a love and an *appreciation of the People* that belongs to them *eternally,* always, both now and in the future, and not merely to some historical People of the distant past. Our People love their history above all because in it they encounter, fully preserved, that very same sense of sanctity with which they have preserved their faith even to this day, despite all their sufferings and ordeals. From the majestic, immense figure of the chronicler in *Boris Godunov* to the depiction of Pugachev's henchmen—in Pushkin they are all the People in their most profound manifestations; and the People understand them as their very own essence. But is that the only thing? The Russian spirit infuses Pushkin's creations; a Russian pulse is felt everywhere. The great, inimitable, incomparable songs, supposedly of the western Slavs but whose essence was clearly engendered by the great Russian spirit, convey the Russian's entire conception of his Slavic brethren; they express the whole of the Russian heart; they reveal the whole outlook of the People, preserved even now in their songs, epic poems, traditions, and legends; everything the People love and cherish is expressed here—their heroic ideals, the tsars, those who stepped forth to defend the People or express sorrow for them, images of courage, humility, love, and sacrifice. And such charmingly whimsical pieces as the banter of two drunken peasants or the "Tale of the Bear" whose mate has been killed—these are something loving, touching, and tender in his observations of the People. Had Pushkin lived longer, he would have left us artistic treasures for understanding the People which, through their influence, would certainly have shortened the times and the seasons for our whole intelligentsia—whose pride in their Europeanism still leads them to elevate themselves above the People—to move to the People's truth, the People's strength, and an awareness of the People's mission. It is this same bowing down to the truth of the People that I see, sometimes (and, alas, I may be the only one of his admirers who sees it) in Nekrasov as well, at least in his best works. I very much value the fact that he "grieved o'er the sorrows of the People" and that he spoke so often and so passionately about the People's grief; but I value even more the fact that in the sublime, painful, and rapturous moments of his life, despite all the opposing influences and even despite his very own convictions, he bowed down before the People's truth with his whole being and showed this in his best creations. So it was in this sense that I placed him as one who came after Pushkin and Lermontov, having, in part, the same new word as they (because Pushkin's "word" is still a new word for us even now. Indeed, it is not only new but still unrecognized and uninterpreted, regarded as the oldest sort of rubbish).

Before turning to Nekrasov, I will say a few words about Lermontov as well, in order to justify why I also placed him among the believers in the People's truth. Lermontov, of course, was a Byronist, but his great, original poetic power made him a Byronist of a particular kind—a kind of mocking, capricious, and fastidious Byronist, eternally disbelieving even in his own inspiration and in his own Byronism. But had he stopped fussing over the bruised personality of the educated Russian man tormented by his own Europeanism, he would certainly have ended by finding the same solution as did Pushkin, in bowing down before the truth of the People; and there are some very obvious and accurate indications of that. But death again stopped him short. In fact, in all of his poetry he is gloomy and capricious; he wants to speak the truth but more often lies and realizes it himself and is tormented by his lies; but as soon as he concerns himself with the People, he is serene and lucid. He loves the Russian soldier, the cossack; he cherishes the People. And so once he wrote an immortal song about the young merchant Kalashnikov, who killed the sovereign's bodyguard, Kiribeevich, for committing a dishonorable act; summoned to appear before the fearsome Tsar Ivan, he tells him that he killed the tsar's servant Kiribeevich "of his own free will, and not by chance."

Do you recall, gentlemen, "the slave Shibanov"? He was the slave of Prince Kurbsky, the Russian emigré of the sixteenth century who kept writing critical and almost abusive letters from abroad, where he had taken refuge, to that same Tsar Ivan. Having written one letter, he summoned his slave Shibanov and ordered him to deliver the letter to Moscow and hand it personally to the tsar. So the slave Shibanov did. In the Kremlin Square he stopped the tsar, who was coming out of the cathedral and was surrounded by his minions, and handed him the epistle from his master, Prince Kurbsky. The tsar raised his sharply pointed staff and plunged it into Shibanov's foot; then, resting on the staff, he began to read the letter. Shibanov, with his foot pierced through, did not stir. And the tsar, writing his reply to Prince Kurbsky later, stated in passing, "Thy slave, Shibanov, has put thee to shame." This meant that he himself had been put to shame by the slave Shibanov. This image of a Russian "slave" must have moved Lermontov's soul. His Kalashnikov speaks to the tsar without rebuke or reproach for

Kiribeevich; he speaks, knowing the certain execution that awaits him; he tells the tsar "the truth, entire and sincere"—that he has killed the tsar's favorite "of his own free will, and not by chance." I repeat, had Lermontov lived longer we would have had a great poet who also acknowledged the People's truth; perhaps we would have had one who genuinely "*grieved o'er the sorrows of the People*." But it was Nekrasov who earned this title. . . .

Once again, I am not comparing Nekrasov with Pushkin; I am not applying a measure to see who is greater and who is lesser, because there can be no comparison here, or even any question of one. Pushkin, through the breadth and depth of his Russian genius, still shines like a sun over the worldview of all our educated Russians. He is a great prophet, still not understood. Nekrasov is but a small dot in comparison with him, a lesser planet that, nonetheless, emerged from that same great sun. And aside from any attempts to measure who is greater, Nekrasov will have the immortality he fully deserves, and I have already explained why: for his bowing down before the truth of the People, which happened not because of some sort of imitation and not even fully consciously; it happened because of a need, an irresistibly compelling force. And Nekrasov's case is all the more remarkable in that all his life he was under the influence of people who, though they may have loved the People, though they may have grieved for them quite sincerely, still never recognized the People's truth and always placed their European enlightenment immeasurably higher than the reality of the People's spirit. With no understanding of the Russian soul and no knowledge of what it expected and craved, it often happened that they, with all their love for our People, wished them things that could only have harmed them. Was it not they who, in the movement of the Russian People of the last two years, scarcely recognized the lofty upsurge of spirit the People were expressing for the first time, perhaps, in such fullness and force, thereby showing their sound, powerful, still unshaken, vital unity in the same lofty idea and virtually showing prescience of their future mission? And besides refusing to acknowledge the truth of the People's movement, they even consider it something almost retrograde, something that reveals the People's utter lack of consciousness, the deep-rooted, centuries-old backwardness of the Russian People.

Despite his remarkable, extraordinarily powerful intellect, however, Nekrasov was still without any real education; his education, at any rate, was very limited. Never in his life did he escape certain well-known influences and, indeed, did not have the strength to escape. But he had his own, unique strength in his soul, a strength that never left him—this was his genuine, passionate and, above all, direct love of the People. He agonized over their sufferings with all his soul, but saw in them more than just the image of creatures humiliated by slavery, a bestial image; through the strength of his love he was able, almost unconsciously, to comprehend the beauty of the People, their power, their intellect, their suffering humility, and even to have some faith in their future mission. Oh, when he relied on his consciousness he could err in many a thing. Regarding with alarmed reproach the People now liberated from their serfdom, he could exclaim, in an impromptu recently published for the first time: "... But are the People happy?" His heart's great intuition suggested a sense of the People's sorrows, but were you to ask him what the People needed and how that might be achieved, his solution might be a highly mistaken and even fatal one. And, of course, he cannot be blamed for that: political sense is a real rarity among us, while Nekrasov, I repeat, spent his whole life under the influences of others. But in his heart, in his great poetical inspiration, in some of his great poems, he attached himself irresistibly to the very essence of the People. In this sense he was a Popular poet. Anyone who comes from the People, though he may have the scantiest of education, will understand a great deal in Nekrasov. But only if he has some education. The question of whether the Russian People as a whole can understand him is clearly a senseless one. What would the "simple People" understand in his masterpieces "The Knight for an Hour," "Silence," or "Russian Women"? Even in his great "Vlas," which the People may understand (although it would not inspire them at all, for this is all poetry that has long departed from real life), they would certainly pick out a few false touches. What would the People make of one of his most powerful and most appealing poems, "On the Volga"? Here we have the real spirit and tone of Byron. No, Nekrasov still is merely a poet of the Russian intelligentsia, speaking of the People and their sufferings with love and with passion, but to that same intelligentsia. I am not speaking of the future—in the future the People will become aware of Nekrasov. They will realize then that once there lived a good Russian nobleman who shed bitter tears over the People's grief and could think of nothing better to do, when fleeing from his wealth and the sinful temptations of his nobleman's life, than come to them in his most painful moments, come to the People and, in his irresistible love for them, cleanse his tormented heart—for Nekrasov's love for the People was merely *a solution for his own personal grief for himself*....

But before I explain what I mean by the dear, departed poet's "personal grief for himself," I must devote some attention to one characteristic and curious circumstance that was noted by almost all our newspapers immediately after Nekrasov's death, in almost every article that mentioned him.

3. Poet and Citizen. General Views of Nekrasov as a Man

As soon as all the newspapers began writing about Nekrasov after his death and funeral, and as soon as they began to define his significance, they at once added—every one, without exception—some remarks about a certain "practicality" in his nature; about certain failings of his, even vices; about a certain duplicity in the image he left to us. Some newspapers merely dropped faint hints about this in a line or two, but what matters is that they still did hint at it, evidently because of some necessity they could not escape. In other publications that spoke of Nekrasov at greater length, what emerged was even more strange. In fact, without making any detailed accusations and seeming to avoid such things out of profound and sincere respect for the deceased, they still set forth . . . to apologize for him, so that the result was even less comprehensible. "Why do you have to apologize for him?"—that was the question one couldn't help asking. "If you know something, then why hide it? But we want to know if he really needs your apologies." That was the question that arose in one's mind. But they did not want to develop any accusation and hastened to apologize and express qualifications, as if wanting, rather, to forewarn someone; and the main thing, again, was that they seemed utterly unable to avoid doing this even though, perhaps, they wanted to. On the whole, it was a most curious case; yet if you think deeply about it, then you and anyone else will certainly come to the conclusion, as soon as you have pondered it for a while, that this case is an absolutely normal one, that once you begin to speak of Nekrasov as a poet, you really cannot escape talking about him as an individual as well, because in Nekrasov the poet and the citizen are so bound together, are each so inexplicable without the other and, taken together, explain one another so clearly, that once you have begun to speak of him as a poet, you cannot help but go on to speak of him as a citizen; and you sense that somehow you are compelled to do this and simply cannot avoid it.

But what can we say, then, and just what do we see? The word "practicality" is uttered—meaning the ability to look after one's own affairs and no more; but then people hasten to make apologies: "The sufferings he underwent," they say. "He was corroded by his environment since childhood." Even as a youth in Petersburg—homeless and abandoned—he endured so much hardship, and as a result he became "practical" (meaning, apparently, that he could not help but do so). Others go still further and hint that without this very "practicality" Nekrasov perhaps would not have accomplished so many clearly useful things for the common good—for instance, taking over the publication of a magazine, and so on. So does that mean that good aims justify bad means? And this is in speaking of Nekrasov, a man who made hearts throb, who, with his poems, evoked delight and tender feeling for the good. Of course, all this is said as an apology, but it seems to me that Nekrasov is not in need of such apologies. Apologies for things like these always seem to contain something humiliating, and the image of the one for whom the apologies are offered seems to be obscured and diminished almost to the level of triviality. In fact, as soon as I begin to apologize for his "duplicity and practicality," I thereby am insisting, as it were, that this duplicity is even a natural product of certain circumstances and is all but inevitable. If that is so, then one has to reconcile oneself completely with the image of a man who is battering himself against the floor of his own church, repentant and crying: "I have fallen! I have fallen!" And we find this in the immortal beauty of the poetry he will write that very same night, while on the next day, as soon as the night has ended and the tears have dried, he will again set about his "practicality," because apart from everything else, they claim, *it is necessary*. Well, then, what is the significance of the groans and cries expressed in the poetry? Art for art's sake and no more, and this even in the most trivial sense, because he himself praises this poetry; he himself admires it and is utterly pleased with it; he publishes it and relies on it: it will add splendor to his periodical and stir young hearts. No, if apologies are to be offered for all this without giving any full explanation, then we risk falling into even greater error and we give rise to misunderstanding; and then, in answer to the question "Who is being buried?" those of us who accompanied his coffin to the cemetery would be compelled to answer that we are burying "the most brilliant representative there could ever be of art for art's sake." Well, was this really so? No, *in truth it was not so;* in truth, we were burying "one who grieved o'er the sorrows of the People," one who always suffered for himself, one who was never able to set his mind at rest and who rejected cheap reconciliation with disgust and self-reproach.

The matter must be clarified, with sincerity and impartiality, and whatever does emerge should be taken for what it is, setting aside any questions of personality and any further considerations. What is needed here is a clarification of the whole essence of the matter, as far as is possible, so as to provide the most accurate image of the personality, the character, of the deceased; our hearts insist on it so that not the slightest misunderstanding of him remain, a misunderstanding that could not but tarnish the memory and leave, as is often the case, an unworthy shadow on a lofty image.

I myself knew little of the "practical life" of the deceased, and so I cannot set about providing the anecdotal portion of the matter; but even if I could, I would not want to because I should be plunging into something that I myself regard as gossip. For I am firmly convinced (and was convinced before) that of all the things being said about the deceased, at least half, and perhaps three-quarters, are pure lies. Lies, nonsense, and gossip. Such an original and remarkable man as Nekrasov could not help but have enemies. And as for the things that were true and actually happened, these too must sometimes have been exaggerated. Yet, even when we take all this into account, we can see that something still remains. What is it? Something dismal, dark, and unquestionably painful, since what, then, is the point of those groans, those cries, those tears, those admissions that "he has fallen," that passionate confession before the shade of his mother? What of the self-flagellation here, the punishment? Once more, I do not intend to go into the anecdotal side of this, but I think the essence of that dismal and painful half of our poet's life was foretold, as it were, by himself at the dawn of his days, in one of his very first poems, jotted down even before his acquaintance with Belinsky, I think (and then later polished and given the form in which it appeared in print). Here are those verses:

The cold wind howled and drove the rain,
The evening fires burned on the grates,

When I, from fair Poltava's plain,
First trudged through the city's gates.
  My worldly goods—a traveler's staff,
  An empty bundle at its end,
  The sheepskin coat upon my back,
  And fifteen kopecks left to spend.
I had no prospects, no good name,
No social grace, no handsome brow,
But in forty years I made my fame:
I've a million in my pocket now.

A million—that was Nekrasov's demon! Well, was he so fond of gold, luxury, enjoyments that he took to "practicality" in order to have them? No, his was a demon of a different kind; it was a most dismal and degrading devil. His was the demon of pride, a longing for security, a need to isolate himself from people behind a solid wall and look calmly out at their anger and their threats. I think that this demon had already attached itself to the heart of the child, the child of fifteen who found himself on the pavement of Petersburg after having almost fled from his father. The shy and proud young soul was struck and afflicted; it did not want to seek out patrons and enter into an arrangement with this alien mob. It is not that a distrust of people crept into his heart at such an early age; rather, it was a skeptical and premature (and so also a mistaken) attitude toward them. They may not be evil, they may not be so terrible as people say (he must certainly have thought), but still, they are all a weak and spineless rabble and therefore they will destroy him, even without any ill will, the moment he infringes on their interests. It was then, perhaps, that Nekrasov's dreaming began; perhaps it was then that he composed, right on the street, the line: "I've a million in my pocket now."

It was a longing for gloomy, morose, isolated security so as not to be dependent on anyone. I think that I am not mistaken; I can recall a few things from my own very first acquaintance with him. At least, that is the way it seemed to me all my life. But this demon was still a menial demon. Was this the kind of *security* that Nekrasov's soul could have longed for, this soul that had such capacity to respond to all that was holy and never lose faith in it? Do such gifted souls reward themselves with this kind of security? Such people set off on their journey barefoot and with empty hands, and their hearts are serene and bright. Their security is not in gold. Gold is crudeness, violence, despotism! Gold might seem to represent security to that same weak and spineless mob Nekrasov so despised. Is it possible that pictures of violence, and subsequently of sensuality and debauch, could persist within such a heart, within the heart of a man who himself could appeal to another: "Abandon all, take up thy staff and follow me"? "Take me away to the camp of the perishing, / For the glorious cause of love of mankind."

But the demon overcame him and the man remained where he was and went nowhere.

For this he paid with suffering, suffering his whole life long. In fact, we know only the verses, but what do we know of his inner struggle with his demon, a struggle that was undoubtedly painful and that lasted all his life? I am not speaking now of Nekrasov's good deeds: he did not publicize them, but they certainly existed; people are already beginning to testify to the humaneness and tenderness of this "practical" soul. Mr. Suvorin has already published something along this line; I am certain much more favorable evidence will come to light; it cannot be otherwise. "Oh," people will say, "but you're also apologizing for him, and your apologies are even cheaper than ours." No, I am not apologizing for him; I am only explaining, and I have now come to the point where I can pose the question—the final and decisive question.

4. A Witness in Nekrasov's Favor

Even Hamlet marveled at the tears of the actor reciting his part and weeping over some Hecuba: "What's Hecuba to him?" asked Hamlet. We must face the same question: Was our Nekrasov just such an actor, capable of weeping *sincerely* over himself and that sacred spiritual treasure which he had lost, and then of pouring his grief (real grief!) into the immortal beauty of his poetry; and was he capable the next day of truly consoling himself . . . with the beauty of this poetry? With the beauty of the poetry and nothing more? Moreover: was he able to regard the beauty of this poetry as something "practical," capable of earning profits, money, fame, and of exploiting it in that sense? Or, on the contrary, did the poet's grief not pass away even after he had written his poetry; was his grief unrelieved by the poetry? Did the beauty and power expressed in it oppress and torment him, and if, unable to cope with his ever-present demon, with the passions that dominated him all his life, he fell once again, then did he calmly come to terms with his fall? Did his groans and cries not sound forth once more, even more strongly, during the private, sacred moments of repentance? Did they, perhaps, echo and grow stronger in his heart each time, so that he himself, at last, could clearly see the price his demon extracted from him and how dearly he had paid for those boons he received from that demon? In short, if he was able to *come to terms* instantly with his demon and could even begin to justify his "practicality" when speaking to others, was this coming to terms and attaining peace of mind something that endured or was it, rather, something that instantly vanished from his heart, leaving after it only a more burning pain, shame, and pangs of conscience? Then—if only this question could be resolved—what would we be left with? We would be left with merely having to condemn him for the fact that, being unable to resist his temptations, he did not put an end to his life as did, for example, the ancient martyr of Pechersk who, also being unable to resist the serpent of passion that tormented him, buried himself to the waist in the earth and died, unable to cast out his demon but at least having conquered it. In such a case, we ourselves—every one of us—would be placed in a humiliating and ridiculous situation, were we to take on the role of judges rendering such verdicts. Nevertheless, the poet who wrote about himself: "A poet thou needst not to be, / But a citizen—thou must," thereby acknowledged that people might judge him as a "citizen." We as individuals should be ashamed of judging him. Who are we to judge, any one of us? We merely do not speak of ourselves aloud, we hide our nastiness with which, inwardly, we fully come to terms. The poet wept, perhaps, over such of his deeds as would not give us a moment's pause had we committed them. It is from his own poetry, after all, that we know of his failings and his demon. Were it not for this poetry, which he, in his repentant sincerity, had no qualms about publishing, then everything that has been said about him as a person, about his "practicality" and so on, would have died along with him and would have been effaced from people's memories, reduced directly to the level of gossip, so that there would have been no need at all to make apologies for him. I might note, by the way, that for a practical man who was so good at managing his own affairs, it was truly impractical to make public his repentant groans and wailings; and so, perhaps, he was by no means as practical as some people maintain. Nevertheless, I repeat, he should be tried in the court of citizens, for he himself recognized this court. And so, if the question posed above—was the poet content with his poems filled with his own tears, and did he come to terms with himself to gain the peace of mind that allowed him once more to undertake his "practical dealings" with a light heart? Or, rather, were these reconciliations merely passing, so that the shame of them led him to despise himself, perhaps, and caused more and more bitter suffering, and so for the rest of his life—if, I repeat, the latter part of this question could be answered positively, then, of course, we would at once be reconciled with the "citizen" Nekrasov, for his own sufferings would have fully purified his memory for us. Of course, there is at once an objection here: if such a question cannot be resolved (and who can resolve it?), then there was no point in posing it. But the whole point is that it can be resolved. There is a witness who can resolve it. That witness is the People.

I mean his love for the People! In the first place, why would such a "practical" man be so stirred by love for the People? Everyone looks after his own affairs: one is concerned with practical matters, another grieves over the People. Well, suppose it was no more than a passing fancy, and so he toyed with it and then abandoned it. But through his whole life Nekrasov never abandoned it. People may say that for him the People were the same as "Hecuba," a subject for some tears to fill his verses and give him an income. But I am not speaking of the difficulty of feigning such sincere love as can be sensed in Nekrasov's poetry (the dispute over this could be endless); I am only saying that it is clear to me why Nekrasov so loved the People, why he was so drawn to them in the painful moments of his life, why he went to them, and what he found among them. Because, as I said above, love for the People in Nekrasov was *an outlet for his own grief for himself,* as it were. If you grant that and accept that, then all of Nekrasov is clear to you, both as poet and as citizen. In placing his heart and his talent at the service of the People he found the means to purify his own self. He had a genuine inner need for the People, and not for poetry alone. He found his own justification in love for them. Through his feelings for the People he elevated his own spirit. But what is most important is that he did not find an object for his love among the people around him or in the things that these people revered and worshiped. When he was overcome by disgust for that life to which he succumbed in moments of weakness and wickedness, he broke away, rather, from these people and went off to those who were dishonored and who suffered, to the simple-hearted and the humiliated; he went and he battered himself against the stone floor of his own poor village church, and he was restored. He would have not chosen such an outlet *had he not believed in it*. In love for the People he found something constant, a kind of constant and sacred outlet for all that tormented him. And if that is so, then it follows that he found nothing more sacred, more constant, and more genuine to worship. He could not have thought to find all his self-justification merely in little verses about the People, however. And if that is so, then it follows that he worshiped *the truth of the People*. If he found nothing in his life more worthy of love than the People, then it follows that he recognized *the truth of the People* and *the truth in the People;* he recognized that truth exists and is preserved only in the People. If he did not acknowledge this fully consciously, on the level of convictions, then he acknowledged it in his heart, as something irrepressible and compelling. In this corrupt peasant, whose humiliated and humiliating image so tormented him, he thus found something genuine and sacred that he could not help but honor, to which he could not help but respond with his whole heart. It was in that sense, when I spoke above of his literary significance, that I placed him among those who recognized the People's truth. The eternal quest for this truth, the eternal longing and eternal striving for it, bear clear witness to the fact that, I repeat, it was an inner need that drew him to the People, a supreme need, and that therefore this need must bear witness to his inner, constant, endless anguish, an anguish that never ceased, was never assuaged by any subtle rationalizings of temptation, by any paradoxes, by any practical justifications. And if that is so, then it follows that he suffered all his life. . . . And who are we to judge him after that? And if we are judges, then we are not accusers.

Nekrasov is a historical Russian type, one of the most significant examples of the many contradictions and duplicities in the realm of morality and convictions that the Russian can contain in our sorry, transitional age. But this man has remained in our hearts. This poet's outpourings of love were so often sincere, pure, and genuine! His longing for the People was so lofty that it places him in the highest ranks as a poet. As for the man, the citizen, once again through his love for the People and his suffering for them he has justified himself and has redeemed much—if, in fact, there was anything to redeem. . . .

5. To the Readers

The December and final issue of the *Diary* appears after such a delay for two reasons: because of my very poor health throughout the whole month of December and as a result of the unforeseen move to a different printer after the former one closed down his business. There were inevitable delays in this new, unfamiliar place. In any case, I assume the responsibility and beg the indulgence of my readers.

To the many questions of my subscribers and readers as to whether I might publish issues of the *Diary* from time to time in the next year, 1878, without restricting myself to monthly publication, I hasten to reply that I find this impossible for many reasons. Perhaps I shall venture to put out one issue and speak with my readers once more. I have been putting out my little periodical for myself as much as for others, after all, from a compelling need to express myself in our curious and most peculiar age. If I do put out one more issue, I shall make an announcement in the newspapers. I do not think I shall be writing for other publications. I might publish only a tale or a novel in some other publication. In this year of rest from the *deadlines* of publication I truly intend to devote all my time to a literary work that has imperceptibly and involuntarily been taking shape within me over these two years of publishing the *Diary*. But I have firm hopes of renewing the *Diary* a year from now. With my whole heart I thank all those who have so warmly declared their support. To those who wrote to tell me that I am abandoning my publication at a most exciting time, I would reply that a year from now there may ensue a time that may be even more exciting and more distinctive, and then we shall serve the good cause together once more.

I write *together*, because I plainly regard my many correspondents as my coworkers. Their letters, remarks, advice, and the sincerity with which they all treated me have helped me a good deal. How I regret that I was unable to reply to so many of them, owing to lack of time and poor health. I ask the kind, good-hearted indulgence of all those to whom I have still not replied. I feel particularly guilty toward the many who wrote to me in the last three months. To the person who wrote of "the anguish of poor young boys and that she does not know what to tell them" (the one who wrote that will probably recognize herself from those words)—I now take the final opportunity to say that I was profoundly and wholeheartedly interested in her letter. Had it only been possible, I would have printed my answer to her letter in the *Diary;* I had to give up this idea only because I found it impossible to print her whole letter. And yet it testifies so graphically to the ardent, noble frame of mind among the larger part of our young people, to their so sincere wish to serve every good cause for the common weal. I shall say but one thing to this correspondent: perhaps it is just the Russian woman who will save us all, our whole society, through the new energy she has generated and through the most noble urge *to serve the cause,* even to the point of sacrifice and heroic deed. She will cast shame on the inactivity of others and draw them after her, while those who have strayed she will return to true path. But enough: I am replying to my most worthy correspondent here in the *Diary,* as I suspect that the former address she gave me may no longer be valid.

I was unable to answer the questions of many correspondents because such important and vital issues as now absorb them cannot be answered in letters. To do this one must write articles or even whole books, but not letters. A letter cannot help but leave out some things and lead to a certain confusion. There are some issues that are certainly not matters for correspondence.

To the person who asked me to announce in the *Diary* that I had received her letter about her brother who was killed in the current war, I hasten to say that I was sincerely touched and moved both by her grief over her lost friend and brother and, at the same time, by her joy that her brother had served an admirable cause. I hasten, with pleasure, to tell this person that I have met here one young man who knew her late brother personally and who confirms everything she wrote me about him.

I give a hearty handshake to the correspondent who wrote me a long letter (five pages) about the Red Cross; I thank him sincerely and ask him to continue to write to me in the future. I shall certainly send him what he requested.

To those several correspondents who recently asked questions *point by point,* I shall certainly reply individually, just as I shall to the one who asked "Who is a striutsky?" (I trust that the correspondent will recognize himself from these words.) I apologize particularly to the correspondents from Minsk and Vitebsk for my tardiness in answering them. Once I have had a rest, I shall set about my replies and will answer everyone as best I can. And so please do not complain, and please wait.

My address will remain as before, but I ask that you indicate the house number and the street and not address your letters to the office of *A Writer's Diary*.

Once more, my thanks to you all. I hope we may look forward to a happy meeting in the near future. We now live in a glorious but difficult and critical time. How much now hangs by a thread at this very moment, and somehow we shall manage to speak about it all a year from now!

P.S. The publisher of a new book that has just appeared—*The Eastern Question in Its Past and Present. A Defense of Russia,* by Sir T. Sinclair, Baronet, member of the English Parliament, translated from the English—has asked me to insert an advertisement about it in this issue of the *Diary*. But having looked at the book and learned something about it, I wanted to recommend it personally to the readers instead of placing the usual advertisement. It would be difficult to write a more popular, more interesting, and more judicious book than this. We are so much in need of such a book now, and we have so few people competent in the history of the Eastern Question. And yet *everyone* now must be informed on this question. This is absolutely essential. Sinclair is a defender of Russian interests. He has long been known in Europe as a writer on political matters. This compact little volume of 350 pages costs only one ruble (one ruble, twenty kopecks with postage); it is sold in all the bookstores.

A Writer's Diary
A Monthly Publication

YEAR III
Single Issue for 1880

August

1

Explanatory Note Concerning the Speech on Pushkin Printed Below

My speech on Pushkin and his significance, which follows and which comprises the basic content of this issue of *A Writer's Diary* (the only issue for the year 1880),* was delivered on June 8 of this year at a ceremony held by the Society of Lovers of Russian Literature, before a large audience, and it created a substantial impression. Ivan Sergeevich Aksakov, who said of himself on this occasion that he was regarded virtually as the leader of the Slavophiles, stated from the tribune that my speech "was a significant event." I mention this now not in order to boast but to make the following point: if my speech was "a significant event," then it was only from one point of view alone, a view I shall outline below. It is for this reason I write this foreword. In my speech itself I wanted to make the following four points about Pushkin's significance for Russia.

1. That Pushkin, with his profoundly perceptive and brilliant mind and his purely Russian heart, was the first to uncover and indicate the essential, pathological actuality of our educated society, historically detached from its native soil and elevating itself above the People. He captured and graphically set before us our negative type: a restless and alienated man, lacking faith in his native soil and its native strength, rejecting Russia and, ultimately, himself (that is to say, his own society, his own educated class that had arisen over our native soil), wanting no dealings with others and genuinely suffering. Aleko and Onegin subsequently gave birth to

*If health permits, I hope to resume publication of *A Writer's Diary* in the coming year, 1881. [Dostoevsky's note]

many others like themselves in our literature. They were followed by the Pechorins, the Chichikovs, the Rudins and Lavretskys, the Bolkonskys (in Leo Tolstoy's *War and Peace*), and a host of others whose appearance itself testified to the truth of the idea first set forth by Pushkin. We owe a great tribute to him, to his immense intellect and genius, for recording the most painful sore of the society that arose here after the great reforms of Peter I. His skillful diagnosis identified and explained our disease, and it was also he who first gave us comfort: for it was he who gave us the great hope that this disease was not fatal and that Russian society could be cured, could again be renewed and resurrected, if it embraced the truth of the People; for,

2. He was the first (specifically the first, and there was no one before him) who gave us artistic types of Russian beauty that came directly from the Russian spirit that dwells in the People's truth, in our native soil; and it was he who discovered these types there. This is affirmed in the character of Tatiana, a completely Russian woman who preserved herself from the falsity around her; in historical characters such as the Monk and others in *Boris Godunov;* in genre types like those of *The Captain's Daughter;* and in a host of other images that shine through his poems, stories, and notes, and even in his *History of the Pugachev Rebellion*. The most important thing, which must be particularly stressed, is that all these types of positive Russian beauty, the beauty of the Russian soul, were derived entirely from the spirit of the People. Here one must admit the whole truth: it was not in our present civilization, not amid the so-called European culture (something which, I might note, we never ever had), not in the grotesque, superficially absorbed European ideas and forms that Pushkin showed us this beauty; it was only in the spirit of the People that he found it, *and exclusively there*. And so, I repeat, having diagnosed the ailment, he also gave us great hope: "Trust in the spirit of the People and expect salvation from it alone, and you shall be saved." If one truly understands Pushkin, one cannot help but draw such a conclusion.

The *third* point I wished to make about Pushkin's significance concerns that special and most characteristic trait of his artistic genius, found nowhere else and in no one else—the capacity to respond to the entire world and to assume completely the form of the genius of other nations in a reincarnation that is almost total. I said in my speech that Europe has claimed the world's greatest geniuses in art: the Shakespeares, the Cervanteses, the Schillers;

but in none of them do we find this capacity; we find it only in Pushkin. The point is not only in his capacity to respond, but in the amazing completeness with which he assumes alien forms. In my evaluation of Pushkin I could not help but note this capacity as the very most characteristic feature of his genius, one that belonged to him alone among all the geniuses of the world and that distinguishes him from all of them. But I said this not to belittle the greatness of European geniuses such as Shakespeare and Schiller; only a fool could draw such a silly conclusion from my words. I have no doubt at all about the universality, *the universal comprehensibility*, and the unexplored depths of the universal types of people of the Aryan race found in Shakespeare's immortal creations. And had Shakespeare created his Othello as an actual *Venetian* Moor rather than as an Englishman, then he simply would have given him an aura of local, national character; but the broader significance of this type would have remained the same, for he would have expressed the very same things through his Italian, with the very same force. I repeat, in explaining Pushkin's brilliant capacity to assume the form of the genius of other nations I did not intend to attack the universal significance of the Shakespeares and Schillers; I wanted merely to note the great and prophetic message this capacity and its completeness has for us, for;

4. This capacity is an altogether Russian one, a national one, and Pushkin merely shares it with our entire People; and, like a perfect artist, he is also the most perfect expression of this capacity, at least in his work, the work of an artist. Our People do bear in their souls this aptitude for responding to the entire world and for universal reconciliation, and they have already displayed it more than once during the two centuries since Peter's reform. In explaining this capacity of our People I also could not help but adduce from it the great consolation it provides for our future and, perhaps, the great hope that shines ahead of us. Most important here was my showing that our striving toward Europe, even with all its fervor and its excesses, was *fundamentally* not only legitimate and sensible but was also in the spirit of the People, that it coincided completely with the strivings of the Popular spirit itself and that in the last analysis it has, unquestionably, a higher purpose as well. In my brief, all too brief, speech, I was naturally unable to develop my idea fully, but at least the things I did say were clear, I think. And there is no need at all to be indignant over my remark that "our impoverished land, perhaps, will at last say a new word to the

world." It is also ridiculous to assert that before saying a new word to the world "we ourselves must develop economically, scientifically, and civically, and only then dream about 'new words' to such exemplary (supposedly) organisms as the peoples of Europe." I specifically stress in my speech that I am not attempting to equate the Russian People with the Western peoples in terms of economic or scientific renown. I am simply saying that the Russian soul, the genius of the Russian People may have a greater capacity than other nations to embrace the idea of the universal fellowship of humans, of brotherly love, the sober view that forgives enmity, distinguishes and excuses that which is dissimilar, eliminates contradictions. This is not an economic trait or any other such; it is only a *moral* trait, and can anyone deny or dispute it in the Russian People? Can anyone say that the Russian People are no more than an inert mass, condemned merely to serve *economically* the betterment and development of our Europeanized intelligentsia, an intelligentsia that has elevated itself above our People, that itself bears within only fatal inertia from which nothing can be expected and which gives no cause whatever for hope? Alas, many people maintain this, but I ventured to state something else. I repeat: I cannot, of course, provide any complete and detailed proof of "this fanciful notion of mine," as I myself put it, but neither can I refrain from explaining it. To maintain that our impoverished and disordered land cannot hold such lofty aspirations until it becomes like the West in economic and civic terms is simply absurd. The fundamental moral treasures of the spirit, in their basic essence at least, do not depend on economic power. Apart from its upper level, our impoverished, disordered land lives entirely as one person. All eighty million of its population represent a spiritual unity of a kind that, of course, cannot be found anywhere in Europe and could not exist there; and so, by this one fact alone one cannot say that our land is disordered or even, strictly speaking, that it is impoverished. On the contrary, in Europe, this Europe where so much wealth has been accumulated, the entire civic foundation of every nation has been entirely undermined and tomorrow, perhaps, will collapse once and for all, leaving not a trace behind, while in its place will ensue something new, unprecedented, and utterly unlike what existed before. And all the wealth that Europe has accumulated will not save her from collapse, for "wealth, too, shall pass away in an instant." And yet it is this—this same undermined and contaminated civic order of theirs—that our People are shown as an ideal they must strive toward, and only when they have achieved this ideal are they to make so bold as to shyly pronounce their word to Europe. We, on the other hand, affirm that it is possible to contain and embody the force of a loving and all-unifying spirit even given our current economic impoverishment, and even given a worse one. Such things can be preserved and embodied even amid the kind of impoverishment that existed after the invasion of Batu or after the devastation of the Time of Troubles, when it was only through the all-unifying spirit of the People that Russia was saved.

And, finally: if, in order to have the right to love humanity and to bear within oneself an all-unifying soul; in order to have the capacity not to hate other nations for being different; in order to have the desire not to wall ourselves off from other nationalities behind our own nationality so that we alone may acquire everything while regarding other nationalities as merely lemons to be squeezed dry (and there really are peoples in Europe who feel this way!)—if, in order to attain all this it truly is necessary, I repeat, first to become a wealthy people and to haul back from Europe the European civic order, then must we still slavishly copy this European order (which is going to collapse in Europe tomorrow)? Can it be, even then, that the Russian organism will not be permitted to develop along national lines by its own organic forces, but must necessarily lose its personality in slavish imitation of Europe? What are we to do, then, with the Russian organism? Do these gentlemen understand what an organism is? And yet they talk about the natural sciences! "The People will never tolerate that," said one man a couple of years ago to another, a fervent Westernizer, apropos of something. "Then do away with the People!"—answered the Westernizer calmly and regally. And he was not just anybody, but one of the representatives of our intelligentsia. It's a true story.

Using these four points I indicated Pushkin's significance for us, and my speech, I repeat, produced an impression. It did not produce this impression because of its merits (this I stress), not because of the talent with which it was delivered (I agree with all my opponents on this and am not boasting); it was because of its sincerity and—I make so bold as to say—because of a certain irrefutability of the facts I presented, despite all the brevity and incompleteness of my speech. But what made it an "event," as Ivan Aksakov expressed it? It was precisely because the Slavophiles, or the so-called Russian party (good God, we have a "Russian party"!) took an immense and, perhaps, a final step toward reconciliation with the Westernizers; for the Slavophiles declared the complete legitimacy of the Westernizers' striving toward Europe, the complete legitimacy even of their most extreme enthusiasm and conclusions, and explained this legitimacy by our purely Russian, Popular striving that coincides with the very spirit of the People. This enthusiasm was justified by historical necessity, historical fate, so that in the final analysis—if there is ever to be such a final analysis—it will appear that the Westernizers served the Russian land and the strivings of its spirit every bit as much as did all those purely Russian people who sincerely loved their native land and, too zealously, perhaps, tried to guard it from all the enthusiasms of "the Russian outlanders." Finally, I stated that all the misunderstandings between both parties and all the bitter altercations between them hitherto had been no more than one great misunderstanding. So that, perhaps, might have constituted the "event," for the representatives of Slavophilism right there, immediately after my speech, fully agreed with all the points I made. I now can state—and indeed, I stated it in my speech—that the honor of this new step (if a most sincere desire for reconciliation does constitute honor) and the merit of this new (if you wish to call it so) word by no means belong to me alone but to the whole of Slavophilism, to the entire spirit and direction of our "party"; that this has always been clear to those who dispassionately tried to grasp Slavophilism; that the idea I expressed has more than once been, if not been expressed, then suggested by the Slavophiles. All I did was to manage to catch the right moment.

So now my conclusion: if the Westernizers accept our point and agree with it, then all the misunderstandings between both parties will naturally be eliminated, so that "the Westernizers and the Slavophiles will have nothing to argue about," as Ivan Aksakov expressed it, "since henceforth everything will be cleared up." From this point of view, of course, my speech would have been "an event." But alas, the word "event" was spoken merely with sincere enthusiasm on the one side; whether it will be accepted by the other side and not remain merely as an ideal is another question entirely. Along with the Slavophiles who embraced me and shook my hand right there on the stage almost as soon as I stepped down from the tribune, there were Westernizers as well who came up to shake my hand; and these were not merely the nobodies among them but the leading representatives of their movement who, now particularly, are playing leading roles within it. They shook my hand with just the same ardent and sincere enthusiasm as did the Slavophiles, and called my speech a brilliant one; and they did this several times, stressing this word "brilliant." But I'm afraid; I'm truly afraid that this may have been said in the first hot flush of enthusiasm! Oh, I'm not afraid that they might renounce their view that my speech was brilliant; I know very well that it was not brilliant and was not a bit taken in by their praise, so that I wholeheartedly forgive them for any disappointment in my brilliance; but this is what might happen, this is what the Westernizers might say after they've had a bit of time to think about things (*Nota bene:* I am not talking about those who shook my hand, I'll merely speak in general about the Westernizers now, and I stress this): "Yet," the Westernizers perhaps will say (note that: only "perhaps" and no more), "yet you have at long last agreed, after lengthy disputes and altercations, that our striving toward Europe was legitimate and normal; you have acknowledged that there was truth on our side as well and have lowered your banners; well, we accept your acknowledgment cordially and hasten to tell you that this was not a bad thing at all on your part: it shows, at least, that you have a certain intelligence, something we never denied, however, aside from the very dullest among us, for whom we decline to take responsibility; but . . . at this point, you see, there once more appears a new obstacle of sorts, and it needs to be spelled out as quickly as possible. The fact is that your proposition, your conclusion that in our enthusiasms we supposedly coincided with the spirit of the People and were secretly guided by it—this proposition of yours still remains more than dubious to us, and so an accord between us once more becomes impossible. You must know that we were guided by Europe, by its science and by the reforms of Peter the Great, but certainly not by the spirit of our People, for we never encountered this spirit or had any inkling of it along the road we traveled; on the contrary, we left it behind and fled from it as quickly as we could. From the very beginning we proceeded independently, certainly not following some instinct that supposedly drew the Russian People toward universal responsiveness and the fellowship of all humanity—in short, toward all those things you've spoken so much about just now. Since the time has come to express ourselves with complete frankness, we can say that, as before, we see the Russian People as no more than an inert mass from which we have nothing to learn, a mass which, rather, holds back Russia's progressive development and which must be entirely reshaped and recreated; and if this is impossible to do organically, then it must be done at least mechanically, that is, by simply making them obey us once and for all, and for all time to come. And in order to achieve such obedience it's essential for us to acquire a civic order identical to those in European countries, as was just said. Our People themselves are impoverished and foul, as they always were, and they are incapable of having either a personality or ideas. The entire history of our People is an absurdity from which you have been drawing the devil only knows what conclusions; we are the only ones with a sober view of things. A People such as ours must have no history; and what they have had under the guise of history they must forget in disgust—every last detail of it. Only our educated society must have a history, one the People must serve merely through their labor and their strength.

"Please, don't be upset and don't shout: when we speak of their obedience, we have no intention of enslaving the People, of course not! Please don't draw such a conclusion: we are humane, we are Europeans, you know that very well. On the contrary, we intend to educate our People little by little, in good order, and to crown our edifice by raising the People to our own level and remaking their nationality in another form, something that will happen of itself after they have been educated. Their education will be founded on and begun with the things we began with, that is, on the rejection of everything from their past and on the denunciation they themselves must pronounce upon their past. As soon as we have taught someone from the People to read and write, we shall at once make him take a whiff of Europe; we shall at once begin to seduce him with Europe—even if only with the refinement of life there, good manners, clothes, drinks, dances—in short, we shall make him ashamed of his old bast shoes and kvass, ashamed of his ancient songs, and even though there are several quite lovely and musical ones, still we shall make him sing only rhymed music-hall songs, no matter how much this may anger him. In short, for the sake of a good cause we shall act first of all on the weak points in his nature, using many and varied means, just as happened to us; and then the People will be ours. He will be ashamed of his past and will curse it. He who curses his past is already ours—that's our motto! We shall apply it completely when we set about raising the People to our level. If the People prove incapable of education, then "do away with the People." For then it will already be clear that our People are no more than an unworthy, barbaric mass that must be compelled merely to obey. For what can be done here: truth resides only in the intelligentsia and in Europe, and even though you may have eighty million People (something you boast of, it seems), all these millions must first serve this European truth, since there is not and cannot be any other. You'll not frighten us with your millions. This is our perennial conclusion, only now it is exposed in all its nakedness, and we remain true to it. Were we to accept your conclusion, we could not discuss such odd things with you as, say, *le Pravoslavié* (Orthodoxy) and whatever special significance it is supposed to have. We hope that you will not expect that of us, at least, particularly now when the last word of Europe and European science, in its overall conclusion, is atheism, enlightened and humane; and we cannot help but follow after Europe.

"And so that half of the speech you gave, in which you praise us, we shall, perhaps, consent to accept within some specific limits—so be it, we'll pay you that courtesy. But as for the half that relates to you and to all your 'principles'—well, you must excuse us, but that we cannot accept. . . ."

That's the sort of sad conclusion that might be made. I repeat: not only do I dare not put this conclusion into the mouths of those Westernizers who shook my hand, I don't wish to put it into the mouths of many, very many, of the most enlightened among them, active Russians and completely Russian people who, despite their theories, are honorable and respected Russian citizens. But the mass, the mass of those who have split themselves off and live apart, the mass of your Westernizers, the mediocre ones, the street along which the idea is dragged—all these slaves to "the proper tendency" (as numerous as the sand on the shore), oh, they will certainly say something of this sort and, perhaps, have even said it already. (*Nota bene*. As far as religion is concerned, for instance, one publication has already declared, with the wit that is typical of it, that the goal of the Slavophiles is to convert the whole of Europe to Orthodoxy). But let us cast aside gloomy thoughts and rest our hopes on the leading representatives of our Europeanism. And if they accept only half our conclusion and our hopes in them, then they deserve the highest accolades even for that, and we shall greet them with joy in our hearts. If they accept even one half—that is, if they acknowledge even the independence and the personality of the Russian spirit, the legitimacy of its existence and its love of humanity, its striving for the unity of all—then there will already be scarcely anything to argue about, at least nothing fundamental and principal. Then my speech really would have served as the basis for a new event. It is not the speech itself, I repeat for the last time, that would have constituted the event (it is not worthy of being so designated); it is the great Pushkin celebrations that have served as the event of our unity—the unity of all educated and sincere Russians for the sake of a most beautiful purpose for the future.

2

Pushkin (A Sketch)

Delivered on June 8 at a Meeting of the Society of Lovers of Russian Literature

"Pushkin is an extraordinary and, perhaps, unique manifestation of the Russian spirit," said Gogol. I would add that he is a prophetic one as well. Indeed, for all us Russians there is something unquestionably prophetic in his appearing. Pushkin arrived just as we were beginning to be truly conscious of ourselves, a self-consciousness that had barely begun and that developed in our society after the whole century that followed the reforms of Peter the Great, and his appearance did so much to cast a guiding light along the shadowy path we traveled. It is in this sense that Pushkin is prophetic and revelatory. I divide the work of our great poet into three periods. I am speaking now not as a literary critic: in discussing Pushkin's creative work I wish merely to explain my idea of his prophetic significance for us and what I mean by those words. I might note in passing, however, that I see no firm boundaries between these periods of Pushkin's work. For example, it seems to me that the beginning of *Onegin* is still a part of the first period of the poet's work, but *Onegin* ends in the second period, when Pushkin had already found his ideals in his native land, had fully taken them into his loving and perceptive soul, and had come to cherish them. The accepted view is also that during the first period of his work Pushkin imitated the European poets—Parny, André Chenier and others, particularly Byron. Yes, there is no doubt that the poets of Europe had a great influence on the development of his genius and that they continued to exert an influence on him for the rest of his life. Nevertheless, even Pushkin's first narrative poems were no mere imitations, so that even they express the extraordinary independence of his genius. Imitations never contain the kind of personal suffering and depth of self-consciousness that Pushkin displayed, for example, in "The Gypsies"—a poem I place entirely within the first period of his creative work. And I am not taking into account the creative power and energy that would not have been so evident had he been merely an imitator. In the character of Aleko, the hero of "The Gypsies," one already finds a powerful, profound, and completely Russian idea, subsequently expressed in such harmonious fullness in *Onegin*, where we see almost this same Aleko, no longer as an outlandish figure but as someone palpably real and comprehensible. In Aleko, Pushkin had already found and brilliantly rendered that unhappy wanderer in his native land, that historical, suffering Russian who appeared with such historical inevitability in our educated society after it had broken away from the People. Such a character Pushkin derived not only from Byron, of course. This is a genuine and flawlessly conceived character, a type that has long become a permanent fixture in our Russian land. These homeless Russian wanderers continue their wandering even now and, it seems, are unlikely to disappear for a long time yet. And if in our day they no longer frequent the camps of the gypsies to look for universal ideals in their wild and distinctive way of life and to seek in the bosom of nature some respite from our confused and ridiculous Russian life—the life of educated society—then, still, they go running off to socialism, which did not yet exist in Aleko's time; they take their new faith to a different field and work it zealously, believing, as did Aleko, that through their bizarre labors they will achieve their goals and find happiness not only for themselves but for the whole world. For what the Russian wanderer needs is the happiness of the whole world in order to find his own peace of mind: he will not settle for less—so long as matters are confined to theory, of course. This is still the same Russian, only belonging to a different era. This person, I repeat, came into being in our educated society, detached from the People and the People's strength, just at the beginning of the second century after the great Petrine reforms. Oh, the vast majority of educated Russians even then, in Pushkin's day just as in our own time, served and serve peacefully as functionaries, for the state, the railways, the banks, or simply made a living by other means; some even took up scholarly work, giving lectures, and they did all these things in a regular, leisurely, peaceful fashion, receiving their salaries and playing cards, with never the slightest notion of running off to the gypsy camps or whatever their equivalent might be in our time. At most they might flirt with liberalism "with a tinge of European socialism" but with a certain Russian softheartedness about it—but this is only a question of the age, after all. What does it matter that one fellow still hasn't begun to be troubled, while another has already managed to get as far as the locked door and painfully knocked his head against it? The same thing awaits them all in due time if they do not take the road to salvation through humble communion with the People. Granted, the same fate does not await every one of them; still, it is enough if it happens merely to "the chosen few," merely to a tenth of those who began to be troubled, since through them the remaining vast majority will be deprived of their peace of mind.

Of course, Aleko still does not know how to express his anguish properly: for him it is still all some kind of abstraction; he has merely a longing for nature, a grievance against fashionable society, universal aspirations, a lament for the truth which someone, somewhere, has lost and which he simply cannot find. There is a bit of Jean-Jacques Rousseau here. Of course, he himself cannot say what this truth is, where and in what it might appear, and just when it was lost, yet he is genuinely suffering. This bizarre and impatient character still seeks salvation from external things first of all, and so he must: "The truth," he imagines, "is somewhere outside him, perhaps in some other land, in Europe, for instance, with her stable historical order and well-established social and civic life." And he will never understand that the truth is to be found, first of all, within himself; indeed, how could he understand that? He is a stranger in his own land, after all; for a whole century he has been unaccustomed to work; he has no culture; he has grown up behind solid walls like a boarding-school miss; he has carried out some odd, unaccountable duties associated with one or another of the fourteen classes into which Russian educated society is divided. He is still no more than a blade of grass, torn from its stem and carried off by the wind. And he can sense that and suffer for it, and often suffer so painfully! So what does it matter if he, who perhaps belongs to the hereditary nobility and very likely owns serfs, took advantage of the freedoms of the nobility and indulged in a little fantasy to fall in with people who live "outside the law" and lead a trained bear in a gypsy camp? One can understand that a woman, a "wild woman" as one poet has called her, would be most likely to give him hope of relieving his anguish; and so, with frivolous yet passionate faith, he throws himself at Zemfira: "Here," he says, "is my way out; here I may find happiness, in the bosom of nature, far from society, here, among people who have no laws or civilization!" And what happens? In his first encounter with this wild nature he cannot restrain himself and reddens his hands with blood. The unhappy dreamer is not only unsuited to universal harmony, he is even unsuited to the gypsies, and they drive him away—without vengeance, without malice, in a dignified, simple-hearted fashion: "Depart from us, O haughty man; / Savages are we, not bound by law, / We neither punish nor chastise."

This is all rather farfetched, of course, but "the haughty man" is real, and Pushkin's perception here is apt. Pushkin was the first among us to perceive him, and we must remember that. The very moment Aleko finds something not to his liking, he angrily attacks his opponent and punishes him for the offense or—what he finds even handier—he remembers that he belongs to one of the fourteen classes and may appeal (for this also happened) to the law to attack and punish; and he will resort to the law, so long as his personal grievance can be redressed. No, this is not an imitation, this is a brilliant poem! Here we already find a suggestion of the Russian solution to the question, the "accursed question," in accordance with the People's faith and truth: "Humble thyself, O haughty man; first curb thy pride. Humble thyself, O idle man; first labor on thy native soil." That is the solution in accord with the People's truth and the People's wisdom. "The truth is not outside you but within; find yourself within yourself; submit yourself to yourself; master yourself, and you shall see the truth. This truth is not to be found in things; it is not outside you or somewhere beyond the sea but is to be found first in your own work to better yourself. Conquer yourself, humble yourself, and you shall be freer than ever you imagined; you will embark on a great task and make others free, and you will find happiness, for your life will be made complete and you will at last understand your People and their sacred truth. Universal harmony is not to be found among the gypsies or anywhere else so long as you yourself are still unworthy of it, if you are spiteful and proud and expect life as a gift, not even supposing that it must be paid for." This solution to the question is already strongly suggested in Pushkin's poem. It is still more clearly expressed in *Eugene Onegin*, a poem that is not far-fetched but palpably realistic, a poem in which actual Russian life is embodied with a creative power and accomplishment such as had never been seen before Pushkin or, perhaps, after him.

Onegin arrives from Petersburg—it had to be from Petersburg; this was absolutely essential to the poem, and Pushkin could not have omitted such a major, realistic feature of his hero's biography. I repeat once more: he is the same Aleko, particularly later in the poem, when he exclaims in anguish: "Oh, why, like some poor Tula assessor, / Am I not lying paralyzed?"

But at the beginning of the poem he is still half a dandy and socialite and has not yet lived enough to be completely disillusioned with life. But even he begins to be visited and troubled by "The noble demon of secret ennui."

Deep in the provinces, in the heartland of his native country, he naturally feels out of place and not at home. He does not know what to do and feels as if he were a guest in his own home. Subsequently, when he wanders in anguish through his native land and through foreign parts among strangers, he, as an undoubtedly intelligent and sincere man, feels even more a stranger to himself. It's true that he loves his native land, but he has no faith in it. Of course, he's also heard of the ideals of his native land, but he doesn't believe in them. He believes merely in the utter impossibility of any sort of labor on his native soil, while—then, as now—he regards those who do believe in this with sad mockery. He killed Lensky simply out of spleen; and who knows?—his spleen may have been caused by his longing for a universal ideal; this is very much in our style, this is very probable.

Tatiana is another matter: she is a strong character who stands solidly on her own native soil. She is deeper than Onegin and, of course, more intelligent than he. Her noble instinct alone tells her where and in what the truth is to be found, and this is expressed in the poem's ending. Pushkin might have done even better to name his poem after Tatiana rather than Onegin, for she is unquestionably its protagonist. She is a positive, not a negative character, a type of positive beauty; she is the apotheosis of Russian womanhood, and the poet has given her the task of expressing the poem's idea in the remarkable scene of her last meeting with Onegin. One might even say that a positive type of Russian woman of such beauty has almost never been repeated in our literature except, perhaps, in the character of Liza in Turgenev's *A Nest of Gentlefolk*. But Onegin's manner of looking down on people caused him to disregard Tatiana entirely when he met her the first time, in a provincial backwater and in the humble image of a pure, innocent girl who was so timid in his presence. He was unable to see the accomplishment and perfection in this poor girl and perhaps really did take her for a "moral embryo." She, an embryo, and this after her letter to Onegin! If there is anyone who is a moral embryo in the poem, then of course it is he, Onegin himself: there is no disputing that. Indeed, he was utterly incapable of recognizing her: what did he know of the human soul? He is a man of abstractions, he is a restless dreamer, and has been so all his life. He did not recognize her later either, as a grand lady in Petersburg, when, in the words of his letter to Tatiana, "his soul perceived all her perfections." But these are merely words: she has passed through his life unrecognized and unappreciated by him; herein lies the tragedy of their romance. Oh, had Childe Harold or, somehow, even Lord Byron himself come from England to Onegin's first meeting with her in the country, and had one of them noticed her shy, humble charm and pointed her out to him—oh, Onegin would at once have been amazed and astonished, for these people afflicted by Weltschmerz often have such servility of spirit! But this did not happen, and once the seeker after world harmony had given her a lecture and had, still, treated her honorably, he set off with his Weltschmerz, his hands stained with blood spilled in a foolish fit of anger, to wander over his native land without ever perceiving it, brimming with health and strength, exclaiming with curses: "I am young and full of life, But what awaits me? / Inner strife."

Tatiana understood this. In some of the novel's immortal stanzas the poet has shown her visiting the home of this man she finds so fascinating and mysterious. I need not speak of the artistry, the matchless beauty, and the profundity of these stanzas. We see her in his study, examining his books, his possessions, his trinkets, trying through them to comprehend his soul and solve her riddle; the "moral embryo" stops at last, deep in thought, with a strange smile on her face, sensing that she has solved the riddle; and she gently whispers, "Is he a parody, perchance?"

Yes, she had to whisper that; she has solved the riddle. Much later, when they meet again in Petersburg, she understands him completely. Incidentally, who said that society and court life had a pernicious effect on her soul and that it was precisely her standing as a society lady and her new ideas inspired by society that were part of her reason for refusing Onegin? No, that was not what happened. No, this is the same Tanya, the same country girl as before! She has not been corrupted; rather, she is depressed by this ostentatious Petersburg life; her heart aches and she suffers; she despises her position as a society lady, and anyone who sees her differently does not understand anything Pushkin was trying to say. She tells Onegin firmly: "But now I am another's wife, / And will be true to him for life."

She said this specifically as a Russian woman; this is her apotheosis. She expresses the truth of the poem. Oh, I shall say not a word about her religious convictions, about her view of the sacrament of marriage—no, I shall not mention that. But still, why did she refuse to follow him even though she admitted she loved him? Was it because she, "as a Russian woman" (and not a southern woman or some Frenchwoman), was incapable of taking such a bold step, unable to break her shackles, unable to overcome her worship of honors, wealth, and social standing, to break with conventional virtue? No, the Russian woman is bold. The Russian woman will boldly follow one in whom she believes, and she has proved that. But she "is now another's wife, and will be true to him for life." To whom, then, and to what is she being true? To what obligations? To this old general, whom she cannot love because she loves Onegin, and whom she married only because "in tears her mother begged, implored," while in her aggrieved and lacerated soul there was only despair and no hope, no glimmer of light? Yes, she is faithful to this general, her husband, an honorable man who loves her, respects her, and is proud of her. Her mother may have "implored her," but still it was she and no one else who gave her consent; it was she, after all, who swore to be a faithful wife to him. She may have married him in despair, but now he is her husband, and betrayal would cast shame and disgrace upon him and would mean his death. And can one person found his happiness on the unhappiness of another? Happiness is found not only in the pleasures of love, but also in the higher harmony of the spirit. How can one's spirit be set at rest if in one's past there is a dishonorable, merciless, inhumane act? Is she to run off simply because the one who represents her happiness is here? But what kind of happiness can it be if it is founded on the unhappiness of another? Can you imagine that you are erecting the edifice of human destiny with the goal of making people happy in the end, of giving them peace and rest at last? And now imagine as well that to do this it is essential and unavoidable to torture to death just one human creature; moreover, let that creature be not an entirely worthy one, a person some may find even ridiculous—not some Shakespeare, but simply an honorable old man, the husband of a young wife whose love he blindly believes in; even though he knows nothing of her heart, he respects her, is proud of her, happy with her, and is at peace. And so you need only to disgrace, dishonor, and torment him and build your edifice on the tears of this dishonored old man! Will you consent on those terms to be the architect of such an edifice? That is the question. And can you admit, even for a moment, the idea that the people for whom you were building this edifice would themselves agree to accept such happiness from you if its foundations rested on the suffering of, say, even one insignificant creature, but one who had been mercilessly and unjustly tortured—and, having accepted this happiness, would they remain happy ever after? Tell me, could Tatiana, with her noble soul and her heart that had suffered so much, have settled the matter in any other way? No; this is how a pure Russian soul settles it: "Let it be that I alone have no happiness; let my unhappiness be immeasurably greater than the unhappiness of this old man; finally, let no one, not even this old man, ever learn of my sacrifice and appreciate it; but I do not want to be happy after having destroyed another!"

This is the tragedy: it unfolds, and the line cannot be crossed; it is already too late, and so Tatiana sends Onegin away. People will say that Onegin is also unhappy, after all; she has saved one and ruined another! That may well be, but that is another question, perhaps even the most important one in the poem. Incidentally, the question of why Tatiana did not go off with Onegin has, at least in our literature, a very characteristic history of its own, and so that is why I allowed myself to go on at such length about it. What is most characteristic is that for such a long time we cast doubt on the moral solution to this question. This is what I think: even if Tatiana had become free, if her old husband had died and she had become a widow, even then she would not have gone off with Onegin. One must understand the whole essence of this character! She can see what he is, after all: the eternal wanderer has suddenly seen a woman, whom he formerly spurned, in a new, dazzling, unattainable setting; and it is the setting, perhaps, that is the entire essence of the thing. This girl, whom he all but despised, is now the one to whom society pays homage—society, this awesome authority for Onegin, despite all his universal strivings; and surely that is why he rushes blindly to her! "This is my ideal!" he exclaims, "this is my salvation, this is the solution to my anguish; I overlooked it, yet 'happiness was so possible, so near!'" And just as Aleko rushed to Zemfira, so he rushes off to Tatiana, seeking all his solutions in some odd new fantasy. Does Tatiana really not see this? Has she not seen through him long ago? She knows very well that in essence he loves only his new fantasy and not her, the Tatiana who is as humble as before! She knows that he takes her for something other than what she is, that it is not even her he loves, that, perhaps, he does not love anyone and is incapable of loving anyone, despite the fact that he suffers such torment! He loves his fantasy; indeed, he himself is a fantasy. Should she follow him, he would grow disenchanted the very next day and look mockingly at his infatuation. He has no soil under his feet, this blade of grass borne by the wind. She is altogether different: in her despair and her agonized awareness that her life has been ruined, she still has something solid and unshakeable on which her soul can rely. These are her memories of childhood, her memories of her native home deep in the provinces where her humble, pure life began; it is the "cross and the shade of boughs o'er the grave of her poor nurse." Oh, these memories and images from her past are what she treasures most now; these images are all she has left, but it is they which save her soul from ultimate despair. And they are no small thing; no, they mean a great deal, because they provide a complete foundation, something unshakeable and indestructible. They represent contact with her native land, her native People and their sacred values. But what does he have, and who is he? She cannot follow him out of compassion, simply in order to console him, to use her infinite loving pity to provide him, at least temporarily, with an illusion of happiness, knowing full well that the very next day he would ridicule that happiness. No, there are profound and steadfast souls that cannot consciously give up their most sacred values to be defiled, even though it may be from infinite compassion. No, Tatiana could not have followed Onegin.

And so in *Onegin*, in this immortal and unsurpassable poem, Pushkin appeared as a great Popular writer, as no one before him ever had. At one stroke, in a most apt, perceptive manner, he identified the innermost essence of the upper levels of our society that stand above the People. Having identified the type of the Russian wanderer, who continues his wandering even in our days; having been the first to divine, through his brilliant instinct, that wanderer's historical fate and his enormous significance in our future destiny; having placed beside him the type of positive, indisputable beauty of the Russian woman, Pushkin, in his other works of this period (first among Russian writers once again, of course), showed us a whole series of positively beautiful Russian types he found among the Russian People. The beauty of these types lies above all in their truth, an unquestionable and palpable truth that makes them impossible to disavow; they stand before us as if carved in stone. Let me remind you once more that I am not speaking as a literary critic and so I shall not try to explain my idea through a detailed literary analysis of these brilliant creations of our poet. One could write a whole book, for instance, about the type of Russian chronicler-monk, pointing out all the importance and significance there is for us in this majestic Russian image Pushkin found in the Russian land, brought forth and sculpted, and whose indisputable, humble, and majestic spiritual beauty has now been placed before us forever as testimony to the powerful spirit of Popular life capable of producing images of such unquestioned beauty. The type has been provided; it exists; it cannot be denied by saying it is a mere invention, merely the poet's fantasy and idealization. Think well about it and you must agree: yes, it does exist, and so, within the spirit of the People who created it the vital force of this spirit also exists; and it is great and limitless. Everywhere in Pushkin we perceive a faith in the Russian character, a faith in its spiritual power; and if there is faith, then there must be hope as well, a great hope for the Russian: "With hopes for glory and for good, / I look ahead and have no fear," said the poet himself when speaking of another subject; but these words of his can be applied directly to the whole of his creative activity drawn from his nation. And never has any Russian writer, before him or since, been so akin in spirit to his People as was Pushkin. Oh, we have many experts on the People among our writers, ones who write with such talent, so aptly and so lovingly about the People; and yet if one compares them with Pushkin, they are, truly (with perhaps two exceptions from his latest followers), merely "gentlemen" who write about the People. The most talented of these, even these two exceptions I just mentioned, will now and then suddenly show a haughty attitude, something from another world and another way of life, something that shows a wish to raise the People to their own level and make them happy by doing so. In Pushkin there is precisely something that *truly* makes him akin to the People, something that reaches almost the level of simple-hearted tenderness. Take his "Tale of the Bear" and the peasant who killed his "lady bear," or recall the verses "Brother Ivan, when you and I start drinking," and you will see what I mean.

Our great poet left all these treasures of art and artistic vision as signposts for the artists who came after him and for those who would toil in the same fields as he. One can positively state that had Pushkin not existed neither would the talented people who came after him. At least they, despite their great gifts, would not have made their presence felt with such power and clarity of expression as they did later, in our time. But the point is not merely in poetry and not merely in creative work: had Pushkin not existed, it might well be that our faith in our Russian individuality, our now conscious hope in the strength of our People, and with it our faith in our future independent mission in the family of European peoples would not have been formulated with such unshakeable force (this did happen later, but was by no means universal and was felt by merely a few). This feat of Pushkin's becomes particularly evident if one studies what I call the third period of his creative work.

Once more, I repeat: these periods do not have such firm boundaries. Some of the works of even this third period could have appeared at the very beginning of our poet's career, because Pushkin was always a complete, integrated organism, so to say, an organism bearing all its beginnings within itself and not acquiring them from without. The outside world only aroused in him those things already stored in the depths of his soul. But this organism did develop, and the particular nature of each of the periods of this development actually can be shown and the gradual progression from one period to the next indicated. Thus, to the third period belongs the series of works in which universal ideas shine forth most brightly, which reflect the poetic images of other nations and which incarnate their genius. Some of these works appeared only posthumously. And in this period of his career our poet stands forth as an almost miraculous and unprecedented phenomenon, never before seen anywhere else. In fact, the European literatures had creative geniuses of immense magnitude—the Shakespeares, Cervanteses, and Schillers. But show me even one of these great geniuses who possessed the capacity to respond to the whole world that our Pushkin had. And it is this capacity, the principal capacity of our nationality, that he shares with our People; and it is this, above all, that makes him a national poet. The very greatest of these European poets could never exemplify as intensely as Pushkin the genius of another people—even a people that might be near at hand—the spirit of that people, all the hidden depths of that spirit and all its longing to fulfill its destiny. On the contrary, when the European poets dealt with other nationalities they most often instilled in them their own nationality and interpreted them from their own national standpoint. Even Shakespeare's Italians, for instance, are almost to a man the same as Englishmen. Pushkin alone, of all the poets of the world, possesses the quality of embodying himself fully within another nationality. Take his "Scenes from Faust," his "Covetous Knight," his ballad "Once There Lived a Poor Knight." Read "Don Juan" once more, and were it not for Pushkin's name on it you would never guess that it had not been written by a Spaniard. What profound, fantastic images there are in the poem "A Feast in Time of Plague!" But in these fantastic images you hear the genius of England; this marvelous song sung by the poem's hero about the plague, this song of Mary with the verses, "Once the noisy school rang out, / With the voices of our children," these English songs, this longing of the British genius, this lament, this agonizing presentiment of the future. Just recall the strange verses: "Once, wandering 'midst a valley wild. . . ."

This is almost a literal reworking of the first three pages of a strange, mystical book written in prose by one ancient English religious sectarian—but is it merely a reworking? In the melancholy and rapturous music of these verses one senses the very soul of northern Protestantism, of an English heresiarch whose mysticism knows no bounds, with his dull, gloomy, and compelling strivings and with all the unchecked force of mystical visions. Reading these strange verses, you seem to sense the spirit of the age of the Reformation; you begin to understand this militant fire of incipient Protestantism; you begin to understand, finally, the history itself, and understand it not only rationally but as though you had been there yourself, had passed through the armed camp of sectarians, sung hymns with them, wept with them in their mystical ecstasies, and shared their beliefs. Incidentally, right next to this religious mysticism we find other religious stanzas from the Koran, or "Imitations of the Koran": do we not find a real Moslem here? Is this not the very spirit of the Koran and its sword, the simple-hearted majesty of the faith and its awesome, bloody power? And here, too, we find the ancient world—"The Egyptian Nights"; here we see these earthly gods, who have been enthroned as divinities over their people, who despise the very spirit of their people and its aspirations, who no longer believe in it, who have become solitary gods in truth and who have gone mad in their isolation, who in their anguish and weariness while waiting to die seek diversion in outrageous brutalities, in insectlike voluptuousness, the voluptuousness of a female spider devouring her mate. No, I will say positively that there has not been a poet so able to respond to the whole world as Pushkin; and the point is not only in this ability to respond but in its astounding depth and in his ability to infuse his spirit into the spirit of other nations, something that was almost complete and so was marvelous as well, because nowhere in any other poet anywhere in the world has such a phenomenon been repeated. This we find only in Pushkin, and in this sense, I repeat, he is unprecedented and, in my view, prophetic, for . . . for it was just here that his national Russian strength was most fully expressed, that the national spirit of his poetry was expressed, the national spirit as it will develop in the future, the national spirit of our future, already concealed within our present and expressed prophetically. For what is the strength of the spirit of Russianness if not its ultimate aspirations toward universality and the universal brotherhood of peoples? Having become completely a national poet, Pushkin at once, as soon as he came in contact with the force of the People, at once senses the great future mission of this force. Here he is a visionary; here he is a prophet.

In fact, what did Peter's reform mean for us, not only in terms of the future but even in terms of what has already happened and already is evident to all? What was the significance of this reform for us? It meant not only our adopting European clothing, customs, inventions, and European science. Let us try to understand what happened and look into it more closely. Indeed, it is quite possible that Peter first began to carry out his reform in just this sense, that is to say, in an immediately utilitarian sense; but subsequently, in his further development of his idea, Peter undoubtedly followed a certain secret instinct that led him to work toward future goals that certainly were immensely broader than mere immediate utilitarianism. The Russian People as well accepted the reforms in just the same spirit—not merely one of utilitarianism but having certainly sensed almost at once some further and incomparably more elevated goal than immediate utilitarianism; I must repeat, of course, that they sensed that goal unconsciously, yet also directly and as something absolutely vital. It was then that we at once began to strive toward a truly vital reunification, toward the universal brotherhood of peoples! It was not with hostility (as should have been the case, it would seem) but with friendship and complete love that we accepted the genius of other nations into our soul, all of them together, making no discriminations by race, knowing instinctively almost from our very first step where the distinctions lay, knowing how to eliminate contradictions, to excuse and reconcile differences; and in so doing we revealed the quality that had only just been made manifest—our readiness and our inclination for the general reunification of all people of all the tribes of the great Aryan race. Indeed, the mission of the Russian is unquestionably pan-European and universal. To become a real Russian, to become completely Russian, perhaps, means just (in the final analysis—please bear that in mind) to become a brother to all people, *a panhuman,* if you like. Oh, all our Slavophilism and Westernizing is no more than one great misunderstanding between us, although it was historically necessary. To a real Russian, Europe and the lot of all the great Aryan tribe are just as dear as is Russia herself, as is the lot of our own native land, because our lot is universality, achieved not through the sword but through the strength of brotherhood and our brotherly aspirations toward the unity of people. If you care to look closely into our history after the Petrine reforms, you will already find traces and indications of this idea—this vision of mine, if you wish to call it that—in the way we dealt with the peoples of Europe, even in our official policy. For what was Russia doing in her policy over these whole two centuries if not serving Europe, far more, perhaps, than she was serving herself? I do not think that this happened merely through the ineptness of our politicians. Oh, the nations of Europe simply do not know how dear they are to us! And subsequently, I am certain, we (I mean not we, of course, but Russian people to come) will realize to the very last man that to become a genuine Russian will mean specifically: to strive to bring an ultimate reconciliation to Europe's contradictions, to indicate that the solution to Europe's anguish is to be found in the panhuman and all-unifying Russian soul, to enfold all our brethren within it with brotherly love, and at last, perhaps, to utter the ultimate word of great, general harmony, ultimate brotherly accord of all tribes through the law of Christ's Gospel!

I know, I know full well that my words may seem ecstatic, exaggerated, and fantastic. So be it: but I do not regret having said them. This had to be said, and particularly now, at the moment of our celebration, at the moment we pay honor to our great genius who embodied this very idea in his artistic power. And, indeed, this idea has been expressed more than once; I have said nothing new. What is most important is that all this might seem conceited: "Is it for us," some may say, "for our impoverished, crude land to have such a destiny? Can it be we who are ordained to utter a new word to humanity?" But, after all, am I speaking about economic prominence, about the glory of the sword or science? I am speaking merely of the brotherhood of people and of the fact that, perhaps, the Russian heart is most plainly destined, among all the peoples, for universally human and brotherly unity; I see traces of this in our history, in our gifted people, in the artistic genius of Pushkin. Our land may be impoverished, but this impoverished land "Christ Himself, in slavish garb, traversed and gave His blessing." Why can we not accommodate His ultimate word? Was He not born in a manger Himself? I repeat: at the very least we can now point to Pushkin and to the universality and panhumanness of his genius. He could accommodate the geniuses of other nations within his soul as if they were his own. In art, in his artistic work, at least, he showed beyond dispute this universal striving of the Russian spirit, and that in itself reveals something important. If my idea is a fantasy, then in Pushkin, at least, there is something on which this fantasy can be founded. Had he lived longer, perhaps, he would have shown us immortal and grand images of the Russian soul that could have been understood by our European brethren and might have attracted them to us much more and much more closely than now; he might have managed to explain to them the whole truth of our aspirations, and they would have understood us more clearly than they do now; they would have begun to divine our purpose; they would have ceased to regard us as mistrustfully and haughtily as they do now. Had Pushkin lived longer, perhaps there would be fewer misunderstandings and disputes among us than we see now. But God did not will it so. Pushkin died in the full flower of his creative development, and unquestionably he took some great secret with him to his grave. And so now we must puzzle out this secret without him.

3

Taking Advantage of an Opportunity. Four Lectures on Various Topics Apropos of One Lecture Given to Me by Mr. A. Gradovsky. With an Address to Mr. Gradovsky

1. On One Most Basic Point

I was already about to conclude my *Diary*, having limited it to the speech I gave in Moscow on June 8 and the foreword I wrote to it, foreseeing the row that was, in fact, raised later in our press after my speech appeared in *The Moscow News*. But after reading your criticism, Mr. Gradovsky, I stopped the printing of the *Diary* so as to append to it a reply to your attacks. Oh, my apprehensions came true; a fearsome row was raised. I was full of pride, I was a coward, I was a Manilov, I was a poet, and the police should have been summoned to restrain outbursts from the public—the moral police, the liberal police, of course. But why not the real police, after all? And nowadays our real police are liberal as well, no less liberal than the liberals who raised the howl against me. In truth, the latter haven't far to go to become the former! But let us leave this for the moment; I shall proceed directly to reply to your points. I frankly admit from the very beginning that I have no personal grounds for quarreling with you or anything to discuss with you. You and I will never come to an agreement; and so I have no intention whatsoever of trying to persuade or dissuade you. When reading some of your articles in the past I have naturally always been astonished at your train of thought. And so why do I reply to you now? I do it solely having in mind some other people who will settle our dispute, i.e., the readers. It is for these others that I write. I hear, I sense, I even see the rise of new elements who are longing for a new word, who have grown weary of the old liberal snickering over any word of hope for Russia, who are tired of the former old toothless liberal skepticism, tired of the old corpses that people have forgotten to bury, and who still see themselves as the young generation, tired of the old liberal, the leader and savior of Russia who, for the entire twenty-five years he's been present among us, has at last shown himself to be "a fellow raising a senseless ruckus in the marketplace," as the People say. In short, I wanted to say *a great deal* beyond replying to your remarks, so that in replying now I am merely taking advantage of an opportunity.

First of all, you raise the following question and even reproach me for not answering it more clearly: where did these "wanderers" I spoke of in my speech come from? Well, this is a long story, and one has to begin a long way back. Besides, whatever I might reply, you would still not agree, because your own opinion about where they came from and how they emerged is already preconceived and prepared: "They were sick at heart," you would say, "from living with the Skvoznik-Dmukhanovskys and from the civic grief they felt over the peasants who had then not yet been liberated." It's a conclusion worthy of a contemporary liberal person, generally speaking, for whom everything concerning Russia has already long been signed and sealed with the exceptional ease characteristic only of the Russian liberal. Nevertheless, this question is more complex than you imagine, much more so, despite your very conclusive answer. I shall talk about "Skvozniks and grief" in good time; but first of all, permit me to bring up a most characteristic little remark made, again, with an ease that has become almost frivolity, a remark I cannot overlook. You say:

> For two centuries now, in one way or another, we have found ourselves under the influence of European enlightenment, an enlightenment that has had an exceptionally strong effect on us, thanks to the Russian's "capacity to respond to the whole world," which Mr. Dostoevsky recognizes as our national characteristic. We have no way to escape this enlightenment, and no reason to try to escape it. It is a fact we can do nothing about, for the simple reason that every Russian person who wishes to enlighten himself *necessarily* acquires his enlightenment from a west European source, owing to the complete absence of any Russian sources.

This is said in a playful manner, of course; still, you have uttered an important word: "enlightenment." Let me ask you what you mean by it: the sciences of the West, practical knowledge, trades, or spiritual enlightenment? The first ones—sciences and trades, that is—we truly must not pass over, and we truly do have no way to escape them, and no reason to try. I also agree fully that we have nowhere to acquire them except from European sources, for which we owe Europe our praise and eternal gratitude. But by enlightenment I mean (and I think that no one can use the term in any other way) that which is literally expressed by the very word "enlightenment," that is, spiritual light that illuminates the soul, enlightens the heart, guides the mind, and shows it a path in life. If that is so, then permit me to observe that there is no reason for us to take up such enlightenment from west European sources owing to the complete availability (and not absence) of Russian sources. Are you surprised? You see, when I argue I like to begin with the very essence of the thing, to raise the most disputed point at once.

I maintain that our People were enlightened long ago, when they took Christ and His teachings as their very essence. I will be told that the People do not know Christ's teachings and that no sermons are preached to them; but that objection is hollow: they know it all, all they really need to know, even though they would not pass an examination on the catechism. They learned in the churches, where for centuries they listened to prayers and hymns that are better than sermons. They repeated and sang these prayers while still living in the forests, trying to save themselves from their enemies; perhaps even during Batu's invasion they were singing, "O Lord of Hosts, be with us!" And at that time, perhaps, they learned this hymn by heart, because apart from Christ they had nothing left, while this hymn alone contains the whole of Christ's truth. And what does it matter that sermons are rarely preached to the People and that the deacons may mutter unintelligibly? This is the most colossal accusation the liberals have thought up against our Church—along with the unsuitability of the Church Slavonic language, which is supposedly not understood by common folk (and what of the Old Believers? Good Lord!). Yet the priest comes out and reads, "O Lord, ruler of my being,"—and this prayer contains *the whole essence of Christianity*, its entire catechism, and the People know this prayer by heart. They also know by heart many of the lives of the saints; they retell them and listen to them with tender emotion. Still, the main school of Christianity they have passed through is the centuries of innumerable and endless sufferings they have undergone in their history when they, abandoned by everyone, scorned by everyone, laboring for everyone, remained with only Christ the Consoler, whom they then took into their souls for all time and who, in exchange, saved their souls from despair! However, why am I telling you all this? Do you think I'm trying to persuade you? Of course, my words will seem childish babble to you, almost indecent. But for the third time I repeat: I am not writing for you. And besides, it's an important topic; it needs to be discussed specifically and at length, and I will speak about it so long as I can hold a pen in my hands; but now I shall express my idea only in its most basic form: if our People have long been enlightened, having taken Christ and His teaching as their essence, then along with Him, with Christ, they of course also took *genuine* enlightenment. Given this fundamental store of enlightenment, the sciences of the West, of course, will become a true boon to them. They will not darken the image of Christ as in the West, where it was not darkened because of science, however, as the liberals maintain; this happened even before science, when the Western church itself distorted Christ's image, transforming the church into a Roman state by embodying that state anew in the papacy. Indeed, in the West there truly is no Christianity and no church, although there still are many Christians, and they will never disappear. Catholicism, in truth, is no longer Christianity and is transforming itself into idolatry, while Protestantism is taking giant steps toward atheism and toward inconstant, fashionable, changeable (and not eternal) morality.

Oh, of course you'll at once object that the whole range of enlightenment is by no means confined only to Christianity and the worship of Christ; that this is but one stage; that we need, rather, sciences, civic ideas, progress, and so on. I have no reply to make to you on that score; indeed, it would be unseemly to do so, for although you are right in part—concerning the sciences, for instance still, you will never concede that the Christianity of the People is, *and must always remain*, the principal and vital foundation of their enlightenment! I did say in my speech that when Tatiana refused to follow Onegin she acted in Russian fashion, in accord with the truth of the Russian People; but one of my critics, who was offended to hear that the Russian People have their truth, suddenly objected with a question: "What about their wholesale transgressions?" Now, can one really reply to such critics? What offends them most is that the Russian People could have their own truth and therefore could actually be enlightened. And are transgressions really so widespread everywhere among the People? Do they exist *as a truth*? Do the entire People accept them as truth? Yes, our People are coarse, although not all of them by any means—certainly not; and I can solemnly attest to this as a witness, because I have seen our People and know them; I have lived with them for some years, shared meals with them, slept alongside them, and was myself "numbered among the transgressors"; I worked with them at real, backbreaking labor at a time when others, who had "dipped their hands in blood" and were playing at liberalism and snickering about the People, were concluding, in their lectures and newspaper columns, that our People "bore the image and the stamp of the beast." So don't tell me that I don't know the People! I know them: it was from them I accepted Christ into my soul again, Christ, whom I had known while still a child in my parents' home and whom I was about to lose when I, in my turn, transformed myself into a "European liberal."

But still, let us grant that our People are sinful and coarse, that they do bear the image of the beast: "The son rode on his mother's back; he's put his young wife in harness"—well, don't you suppose this song had some basis? All Russian songs are based on some real event—have you noticed that? But you liberal people must be fair at least once: just think how much the People have endured over so many centuries! Just think who is most to blame for their "image of the beast" and don't condemn them! Isn't it absurd to condemn a peasant because his hair hasn't been trimmed in some French barber shop on the Bolshaia Morskaia? Yet that's almost the level reached when our European liberals begin to accuse and disparage the Russian People and start *rejecting* them: they claim the People have acquired no real individuality and have no sense of nationality! Good Lord! Do you think that in the West—anywhere you choose, among any people you like—there is less drunkenness and thievery, there is not the same brutality, and real cruelty with it (which is not the case among our People), and genuine, honest-to-God ignorance, a real lack of enlightenment, because often it is compounded by such lawlessness that people there no longer think of it as sin but have begun to accept it as truth. Still, let's grant that brutality and sin exist among our People; but this is what cannot be disputed: that as a whole, at least (and not merely as an ideal, but in actual, honest-to-God real life), they never accept, never will accept, and have no wish to accept their sin as truth! They will commit sins, but will always say, sooner or later, "I have done a wrong." If the one who has sinned does not say it, then another will say it for him, and the balance of truth will be restored. Sin is stench, and the stench will pass when the sun shines on it in full force. Sin is a passing thing, while Christ is eternal. The People sin and commit abominations every day, but in their best moments, in their Christly moments, they will never err about the truth. What is truly important is what the People accept as their truth, where they find their truth and how they conceive it, what they set up as their finest aspiration, what they love, what they ask of God, what they lament in their prayers. And the People's ideal is Christ. And with Christ, of course, comes enlightenment; and in their most sublime, critical moments our People always resolve every issue that concerns all of them in a Christian manner; they have always done so.

You will say with a sneer: "Weeping isn't enough, and neither is sighing; they must do something, they must prevail." But what about you, gentlemen—you enlightened Europeans: are there a lot of righteous men among you? Show me the righteous men you would set up in Christ's place. But you must know that the among the People there are righteous men. There are positive characters of unimaginable beauty and strength, ones that have still not come within your purview. These righteous ones and sufferers for truth do exist, but do we really see them? I don't know; he who has the gift of seeing will, of course, see them and understand; but he who sees merely the image of the beast will, of course, perceive nothing. But the People, at least, know that the righteous exist among them; they believe that such exist, they are steadfast in this thought, and they hope that when a fateful moment comes for all, such people will always save them. And how many times have our People saved their fatherland? And even so recently, having been befouled by sin, drunkenness, and lawlessness, the People as a whole were spiritually uplifted by the last war for Christ's faith, which the Moslems had trodden down among the Slavs. The People accepted the war, they seized upon it as an expiatory sacrifice for their sins and unjust ways; they sent their sons to die for a sacred cause and did not shout that the ruble was falling and that the price of beef had gone up. They listened avidly, asked questions avidly, they themselves read about the war, and we all witnessed it; there are many of us who are witnesses. I know: the upsurge of our People's spirit during the last war, and even more, the reasons for this upsurge, are not acknowledged by the liberals; they laugh at this idea: "These filthy vassals have a collective view, some civic sense, some political idea," they say. "Can this really be permitted?" And why, oh why is our European liberal so often the enemy of the Russian People? Why is it that in Europe those who call themselves democrats always stand up for their people, or at least rely on them, while our democrats are often aristocrats and ultimately almost always serve the aims of those who suppress the energies of the People and end with authoritarianism? Oh, I'm not maintaining that they are conscious enemies of the People, but it is their lack of consciousness that causes the tragedy. Do these questions make you angry? Well, so be it. For me they are all axioms, and of course I will not cease to explain and expound them as long as I can write and speak.

And so, let us end: sciences are one thing, but we have no need to draw "enlightenment" from west European sources. If we do, maybe we will draw such social formulas as "Chacun pour soi et Dieu pour tous" or "Après moi le déluge." Oh, people will at once begin to shout: "Don't we have just the same sayings? Don't we say things like 'Hospitality is soon forgotten,' along with hundreds of other aphorisms of this sort?" Yes, indeed, the People have many sayings of all sorts: the People's mind is broad, as is their humor; a developing consciousness is always aware of the negative side; but these are all merely *sayings,* and the People do not believe in their moral truth; they themselves make jokes about them and laugh at them; and as a whole, at least, the People reject them. But would you dare claim that "Chacun pour soi et Dieu pour tous" is only a saying and not a social motto accepted by everyone in the West, one that *everyone* there serves and believes in? At least all those who stand above the people, who keep them in check, who own the land and the proletariat, and who stand on guard for "European enlightenment." Why do we need that kind of enlightenment? We will find another sort here at home. Science is one thing, enlightenment is another. With hope in the People and their strength, perhaps we will someday develop in its fullness, in its complete radiance and brightness, this Christly enlightenment of ours.

You will tell me, of course, that this whole long peroration is still not a reply to your criticism. Well, so be it. I regard this as merely an introduction, but a necessary one. In the same way that you find and note in my speech certain points of disagreement which, in your view, are the most important, so I, too, have first noted and set forth a point in your article which I see as most fundamental to our disagreement and which presents the greatest obstacle toward our reaching an accord. But the introduction is finished; we shall turn to your criticism, this time with no digressions.

2. Aleko and Derzhimorda. Aleko's Sufferings for a Peasant Serf. Anecdotes

In criticizing my speech you write: "But when Pushkin portrayed Aleko and Onegin, with their negative attitude, he did not show just what they were 'negating;' and it would be most reckless to assert that they were rejecting specifically 'the People's truth,' the fundamental principles of the Russian view of the world. This is nowhere evident."

Well, whether it is evident or not, reckless or not to assert it, we shall soon return to it; but first, let us see what you say about the Dmukhanovskys, from whom Aleko supposedly fled to the Gypsies:

> But the world of the wanderers of those days truly was one that had rejected the other world. In order to explain these characters, it is essential to provide other characters, which Pushkin did not do, although at times he did refer to them with bitter indignation. The nature of his talent prevented him from descending to those murky depths and raising up as "the pearl of creation" all those owls and bats that filled the cellars [*and maybe the upper storeys?*] of the Russian dwelling. This was done by Gogol—the great reverse side of Pushkin. He informed the world why Aleko fled to the Gypsies, why Onegin was bored, why the "superfluous people" immortalized by Turgenev came into being. Korobochka, Sobakevich, the Skvoznik-Dmukhanovskys, Derzhimordas, Tiapkin Lapkins—they are the shadowy side of Aleko, Beltov, Rudin and many others. They are the background without which the latter figures cannot be understood. Yet these Gogolian characters were Russians—and, oh, what real Russians they were! Korobochka suffered no Weltschmerz, Skvoznik-Dmukhanovsky could deal superbly with the shopkeepers, Sobakevich knew all there was to know about his peasants, and they knew all there was to know about him. Of course, Aleko and the Rudins could never see all that completely and never understood it; they simply fled wherever they could—Aleko to the

> Gypsies, Rudin to Paris to die for a cause in which he was not the least involved.

They *simply* fled, you see. Oh, how easy to solve things in a newspaper column! And how simply it all comes out, how prepared and predetermined you have it all! The words you speak are truly ready-made. Incidentally, why did you mention that Gogol's heroes were Russians—"oh, what real Russians they were!" This has nothing at all to do with our argument. In any case, who doesn't know that they were Russians? Aleko and Onegin were Russians too; you and I are Russians; even Rudin was Russian, completely Russian, when he fled to Paris to die for a cause in which, supposedly, he was not the least involved, as you maintain. He was Russian to the highest degree precisely because the cause for which he died in Paris was by no means as alien to him as it would have been to an Englishman or a German, since Europe's cause, the universal, all-human cause, has long ceased to be alien to the Russian. This is Rudin's distinguishing trait, surely. Rudin's tragedy, specifically, was that he found no work to do on his native soil and died on foreign soil; but this soil was by no means as alien to him as you maintain.

But still, the point is this: all these Skvozniks and Sobakeviches may have been Russians, but they were spoiled Russians torn away from their native soil; and although they knew the life of the People from one side, they knew nothing of the other side and did not even suspect this other side existed—that is the whole point. They did not even suspect the existence of the People's soul, the things the People longed for and prayed for; they did not even suspect it because they had a terrible disdain for the People. They even denied that the People possessed a soul, apart from the "soul" that was registered in the census. "Sobakevich knew all there was to know about his peasants," you maintain. That's impossible. Sobakevich saw his Proshka merely as brute force he could sell to Chichikov. You maintain that Skvoznik-Dmukhanovsky could deal superbly with the shopkeepers. For heaven's sake! Just reread the mayor's monologue to those shopkeepers in act five: it's only dogs who are spoken to in that manner, not people. Is that what dealing "superbly" with Russians means? Is this what you are praising? It would have been better if he had just punched them in the face or pulled their hair. When I was a child I once saw a courier on the highway, wearing a uniform tailcoat and a three-cornered, plumed hat; he was brutally smashing his fist down on the back of the driver, while the driver was furiously lashing the steaming troika, galloping at full speed. This courier was Russian by birth, of course, but he was so blinded and detached from the People that he could deal with a Russian only by using his immense fist, not by conversing with him. And yet he had spent his whole life with coachmen and Russian people of all sorts. But the flaps of his tailcoat, his plumed hat, his officer's rank, his polished Petersburg boots he found dearer and more spiritually akin, not only than a Russian peasant, but perhaps than the whole of Russia, a country he had crossed from one end to another and in which, in all likelihood, he had found nothing remarkable or noteworthy beyond his own fist or the kick of his polished boot. For him the whole of Russia was represented only by his superiors, and everything apart from his superiors was scarcely worthy of existence. How could such a person comprehend the essence of the People and their soul! Although he was a Russian, he was already a "European" Russian whose Europeanism was just beginning, not with enlightenment, but with corruption, as all too many others began it. Yes, sir, this corruption was more than once accepted among us as the surest means of remaking Russians into Europeans. The son of such a courier may be a professor, perhaps—meaning a patented European. And so, don't talk about their understanding of the essence of the People. We needed the Pushkins, the Khomiakovs, the Samarins, and the Aksakovs before we could begin to talk about the real essence of the People. (Before these men appeared there was talk of this subject, but it was all pseudoclassical and theatrical.) And when they began speaking of "the truth of the People," everyone looked at them as if they were epileptics and idiots whose ideal was "eating radishes and writing denunciations." Yes, denunciations! At first their arrival and their opinions so astonished everyone that the liberals even began to wonder whether these men wanted to write denunciations of them. But I shall let you decide how far many contemporary liberals have departed from this ridiculous opinion of the Slavophiles.

But now, to the point. You maintain that Aleko fled to the Gypsies to get away from the Derzhimordas. Let's suppose this is so. But the worst thing is that you yourself, Mr. Gradovsky, recognize with complete conviction Aleko's right to feel such disgust: "He couldn't help but run off to the Gypsies," you say, "because Derzhimorda was just too despicable." But I maintain that Aleko, and Onegin too, were Derzhimordas in their own way, and in some respects were even worse. The only difference is that I am making no accusations against them at all, completely admitting the tragic nature of their fates, while you praise them for running away: "How could such great and interesting people settle down to live with monsters like that?" you ask. You're terribly mistaken. You yourself come to the conclusion that Aleko and Onegin had not lost touch with their native soil and had not rejected the People's truth at all. Moreover, you even maintain that "they were not haughty people at all." But their haughtiness here is the direct, logical, and inevitable result of their abstraction and their loss of touch with the soil. Surely you can't deny that they had no knowledge of the soil, that they had been raised and educated like girls in a finishing school, that they learned about Russia only through government service in Petersburg, that their relations with the People were those of a master to a serf. They may well have lived in the country with the peasant. My courier had rubbed shoulders all his life with coachmen and saw in them no more than objects worthy of his huge fist. Aleko and Onegin had a proud and impatient attitude to Russia, as do all those who live apart from the People in a separate little group, board and lodging provided—meaning provided by the labor of the peasant—and having a European education, which they also received as a gift. It is precisely this fact—that for almost the entire period of our history all our educated people, owing to historical design, have been transformed into mere idle "gentlemen of leisure"—that explains their abstractness and loss of touch with their native soil. It was not Derzhimorda who caused their ruin, but the fact that they were unable to explain Derzhimorda and his origins to themselves. They were much to haughty for that. Unable to find an explanation, they could find no way of working on their native earth. Those who did believe in the possibility of working they regarded as simpletons or as other Derzhimordas. And our wanderer was haughty not only toward Derzhimorda but toward the whole of Russia; for Russia, according to his decisive conclusion, contained only slaves and Derzhimordas. If Russia did have anything a bit more noble, it was they, the Alekos and Onegins, and nothing more. With such a view, haughtiness comes of itself: as they went on living their abstract lives, they naturally began to marvel at their own nobility and superiority over the vile Derzhimordas, whom they were unable to understand. Had they not been so haughty, they would have seen that they themselves were also Derzhimordas; and having realized that, they might then have found a way toward reconciliation. Their feelings toward the People were not so much haughtiness as disgust, and this was the case everywhere.

You will not believe any of this; rather, having said that certain traits of the Alekos and Onegins were truly unattractive, you haughtily begin scolding me for the narrowness of my view, for "treating the symptoms and discreetly passing over the root cause of the malady." You maintain that when I say, "Humble thyself, o haughty man," I am accusing Aleko only of personal failings and overlooking the root of the matter, "as if the whole essence of the matter lay merely in the personal qualities of those who put on haughty airs and refused to humble themselves." "What has not been answered," you say, "is over what the wanderers are exalting themselves; another question remains unanswered as well: before what are the wanderers to humble themselves?" This is all very arrogant on your part: I think I came to the direct conclusion that "the wanderers" are the products of the historical process of our society; thus I do not heap all the blame on them alone *personally* and on their *personal* qualities. You read that in my speech; it was written down and published; so why, then, do you distort my views? When you quote my tirade "Humble thyself," you write: "In these words Mr. Dostoevsky has expressed the 'holy of holies' of his convictions, that which at once represents the strength and the weakness of the author of *The Brothers Karamazov*. These words contain a great *religious* ideal, a powerful homily on *personal* morality, but they bear not even a hint of *social* ideals."

And after saying this you at once begin to criticize the idea of "personal betterment in the spirit of Christian love." I shall turn to your view of "personal betterment" in a moment, but first I wish to expose to you the whole implicit content of your article which, it seems, you wanted to conceal: you did not get so angry at me only because of my accusations against "the wanderer," but, rather, because I do not acknowledge him as an ideal of moral perfection, as a healthy Russian person, which he can and must be! When you admit that Aleko and Onegin do have some "unattractive traits," you are merely dodging the issue. Your own private view, which for some reason you do not wish to reveal fully, is that "the wanderers" are normal and admirable, admirable by the mere fact that they fled from the Derzhimordas. You look with indignation on anyone who dares to find even the slightest flaw in them. You state frankly, "It would be absurd to maintain that they perished from their pride and refused to humble themselves before the truth of the People." Finally, you passionately maintain and insist that it was they who liberated the peasants. You write:

> I will say further: if the souls of the best of these "wanderers" of the first half of our century did harbor any intention, then it was precisely an intention toward the People; the bitterest of their hatreds was focused specifically on the slavery that oppressed the People. Granted, they loved the People and hated serfdom in their own way, "in a European way," if you like. But who, if not they, prepared our society for the abolition of serfdom? They, too, served their "native soil" as best they could, first as proponents of liberation and later as some of the first mediators.

That's precisely the point: "the wanderers" hated serfdom "in their own way, in a European way"; that's the whole essence of the matter. The point is precisely that they hated serfdom not for the sake of the Russian peasant who worked for them and fed them and who, accordingly, was oppressed by them as well as by others. Who prevented them, if they were so overcome by civic sorrow that they had to run off to the Gypsies or the barricades in Paris—who prevented them from simply liberating at least their own peasants and giving them land, thus eliminating the cause of their civic sorrow, or at least the portion of it that was their own responsibility? But somehow we heard very little about such liberations, yet we heard a good deal of civic wailing. "Corrupted by his environment," was the verdict, "and besides, how could he give up his capital?" But why shouldn't he give it up when his sorrow for the peasants was so profound that he had to run off to the barricades? That's precisely the point: one still needs money to live in "gay Paree," even if one is busy on the barricades, and so the peasants still had to send off their quitrent. Some made it even easier: they mortgaged, sold, or exchanged (is there any difference?) their peasants and, taking the money thus raised, went off to Paris to support the publication of radical French newspapers and magazines for the salvation of the whole of humanity, not merely the Russian peasant. Are you trying to tell us that they all were consumed with sorrow over the peasant serf? Not so much for the peasant serf as a generalized, abstract sorrow over the slavery that existed in humanity: "This should not be; it's unenlightened; we must have *liberté, égalité et fraternité*." As for the Russian peasant personally, perhaps these noble hearts were not so terribly oppressed by sorrow for him at all. I know and can recall many things said privately even by some of the most "enlightened" people of the good old days gone by. "There's no doubt that slavery is a great evil," they would agree during intimate conversations among themselves. "But, all things considered, are our People really a People? Are they at all like the people of Paris in 1793? Why, they've grown used to slavery; their faces, their demeanor are those of the slave; or take flogging, for instance: of course it's a vile thing, generally speaking, but, good heavens, when you're dealing with the Russian you can't do without flogging: 'Our dear little peasant has got to be flogged; he'll start grieving if he isn't; that's the sort of nation we have.'" I tell you that I did hear things like that in days gone by, even from highly enlightened people. That's the "sober truth," ladies and gentlemen. Perhaps Onegin did not flog his servants, although, truly, it's hard to say that positively; but as to Aleko, I'm certain that he did—and not out of any cruelty in his nature but almost even from pity, almost for some good purpose: "Why, he needs it; he can't get by without a little flogging; why, he'll come on his own and ask: 'Flog me, master; make a man of me! I've gone altogether soft!' Now I ask you, what can you do with a nature like that? So you grant his wish and have him flogged!" I repeat, their feelings toward the peasant often reached the point of loathing. And how many contemptuous anecdotes about the Russian peasant made the rounds among them—contemptuous and obscene anecdotes about his slavish soul, about his "idol worship," about his priest, about his wife; and such stories were told, with complete insouciance at times, by those whose own family lives were frequently reminiscent of houses of ill repute—oh, of course this was not always due to some sort of wickedness but at times merely to the excessive passion with which the latest European ideas were accepted, in the fashion of Lucrezia Floriani, for instance, with all our Russian impetuous rush to understand and take in. They were Russians in every respect!

Oh, these grieving Russian wanderers were sometimes great scoundrels, Mr. Gradovsky, and it was precisely such little anecdotes about the Russian peasant and the scornful view of him that almost always helped soothe in their hearts the pain of civic sorrow over serfdom, giving it thus merely an abstractly universal character. And, after all, one can all to easily learn to live with an abstractly universal sorrow, nourishing oneself spiritually on the contemplation of one's own moral beauty and the flight of one's civic thought, while still nourishing oneself bodily on the quitrents of those same peasants—and nourishing oneself very well indeed! In fact, one doesn't have to look far for evidence: just recently one venerable old fellow, an observer of that time, cited in a magazine a story of one encounter between the most important Russian liberal and universal intellects of the day and a Russian peasant woman. These were dyed-in-the wool wanderers, so to say, who had historically declared their patent as such. It was right in the summer of 1845, you see, at a lovely suburban Moscow dacha where, in the words of this venerable observer, "colossal dinner parties" were given; many guests attended: some most humane professors, celebrated lovers and connoisseurs of the arts and all that sort of thing, renowned democrats who subsequently became prominent political figures of worldwide importance, critics, writers, and charmingly learned ladies. And suddenly the whole company, no doubt after a dinner with champagne, fish pies, and choice viands almost beyond imagining (there was a reason for calling these dinners "colossal," after all), set off for a stroll in the fields. In a far corner of the rye field they met a woman reaper. We all know what harvesttime means: the peasant men and women get up at four o'clock and go off to harvest the grain, working until late at night. It is hard work to reap, standing bent over for twelve hours with the sun burning on your back. Usually when a reaper gets in among the rye she can't be seen. And so it was here, in the rye field, that our company found the reaper—and, just imagine, she was wearing a "primitive costume" (only an undershirt, perhaps?). How terrible! Universal, humane feelings were aroused and an offended voice immediately rang out, "The Russian woman is the only one in the world who feels no shame in front of anyone!" Well, of course the inference that follows at once is, "Of all the women in the world it is only the Russian before whom no one feels ashamed about anything" (did he mean, perhaps, that one has no need to feel shame?). A controversy ensued. There were some who defended the woman, but what kind of defenders were they, and what objections did they have to contend with! Think of the views and opinions that could come out of a crowd of landowning wanderers drunk with champagne and full of oysters—purchased with whose money? Why, on the labor of that same woman reaper! Why, it was for you, the universal wanderers, that she was working; it was her labor that let you eat your fill. The fact that amidst the rye, where no one could see her, tormented by the sun and sweat, she took off her wool skirt and remained only in her undershirt—because of that your sense of shame was violated and you call her shameless: "The most shameless of all women," you call her—ah, you chaste people! And what of your "little diversions" in Paris? What of your kicking up your heels in "gay Paree"? What of the can-can at the Bal-Mabille, which made Russian fellows melt from the mere description of it? And the charming little song "Ma commère quand je danse, Comment va mon cotillon?" with its graceful lifting of the skirts and twitching of the posterior—does this not trouble our chaste Russians? Quite the contrary: it charms them. "Come now, why they do it all so gracefully, that little can-can; and the twitching of the posterior, why, that's a most refined *article de Paris* in its own way; but here, what do we have? We have a peasant woman, a Russian peasant woman, a beast of burden, homely as a mud fence!"

No, sir, what we have here is not even a matter of conviction of the loathsomeness of our peasant and our People; here the conviction has become a feeling; here we can see a feeling of personal repugnance toward the peasant—oh, of course it's involuntary, almost unconscious, a feeling they aren't even aware of. I confess, I am quite unable to agree with your most important point, Mr. Gradovsky: "Who, if not they, prepared our society for the abolition of serfdom?" Did they serve the cause through chattering about abstractions, shedding tears of civic sorrow according to all the rules? Oh, naturally, all this entered into the overall total and was of some use. But those who promoted the liberation of the peasants and who helped others who worked for it were, rather, people like, say, Samarin, and not your wanderers. The great work of those days was done by more than a few people like Samarin, a type utterly unlike the wanderers, and naturally we hear not a word about them from you, Mr. Gradovsky. All signs indicate that this cause very quickly bored the wanderers, and once more they began to sulk squeamishly. Had they acted differently they would not have been wanderers. When they received their redemption payments they began selling their remaining lands and forests to merchants and kulaks to be cut down and destroyed; the wanderers resettled abroad, beginning our practice of absenteeism. . . . You will not agree with my view, of course, Mr. Professor, but what can I do? I, in turn, simply cannot consent to accept this image, so dear to you, of the superior and liberal Russian person as the ideal of the real, normal Russian, as, supposedly, he actually was, is now, and ought to be even in the future. Over the last decades these people have done very few sensible things on their native soil. This is a more accurate view than your dithyramb in praise of these gentlemen whose time has passed.

3. Two Halves

And now I shall turn to your views on "personal betterment in the spirit of Christian love" and its complete inadequacy—supposedly—as compared with "social ideals" and, above all, with "social institutions." Oh, you yourself begin by saying that this is the most important point of our disagreement. You write:

> Now we have come to the most important point of my disagreement with Mr. Dostoevsky. In demanding humility before the truth of the People and their ideals, he accepts this "truth" and these ideals as something given, unshakeable, and eternal. We venture to tell him—no! The *social* ideals of our People are still in a process of *formation and development*. They still have a great deal of work to do on themselves before being worthy of the name of a great People.

In the first section of my article I already replied to you in part on the "truth" and the ideals of the People. You find this truth and these ideals of the People to be plainly inadequate to develop Russia's social ideals. Religion, you suggest, is one thing, while social matters are another. Your scholarly scalpel cuts a living, homogeneous organism into two separate halves, and you maintain that these two halves ought to be entirely independent of one another. Let's look a little more closely, analyze each of these halves separately, and perhaps we shall be able to come to some conclusion. Let's first analyze the half that deals with "personal betterment in the spirit of Christian love." You write:

> Mr. Dostoevsky urges us to work on ourselves and humble ourselves. Personal betterment in the spirit of Christian love is, of course, the first prerequisite for any activity, large or small. But it does not follow that people *who have personally perfected themselves in a Christian sense* would necessarily form a perfect society [?!]. Let me give an example.
>
> The Apostle Paul instructed masters and slaves about their mutual relationships. Both the former and the latter may have heeded and usually did heed the words of the apostle; *personally* they were good

> Christians, but because of this *slavery* became enshrined and remained as an immoral institution. In just the same way, Mr. Dostoevsky, along with every one of us, has known both landowners and peasants who were excellent Christians. Yet *serfdom* remained an abomination in the eyes of the Lord, and the Russian Tsar-Liberator came as one who expressed the demands of not only a *personal* but also a *social* morality, the latter being a thing of which there were no proper conceptions in times of old, despite the fact that there were no fewer "good people" then perhaps, than there are now.
>
> Personal and social morality are not the same. From this it follows that no *social* betterment can be realized *only* through improvement of the personal qualities of the people who comprise that society. Let me cite another example. Let us suppose that beginning in the year 1800 a series of proponents of Christian love and humility had undertaken to improve the morals of the Korobochkas and Sobakeviches. Could one suppose that they would have managed to abolish serfdom, that this "phenomenon" could have been eliminated without *the tsar's* word? On the contrary: Korobochka would have begun to demonstrate that she was a genuine Christian and a real "mother" to her peasants, and she would have held to this conviction, despite all the efforts of the preachers to prove otherwise. . . .
>
> The betterment of people in a *social* sense cannot be done only through work "on oneself" and through "humbling oneself." One can work on oneself and curb one's passions in a wilderness or on an uninhabited island. But as *social* creatures, people develop and improve in working *alongside one another, for one another, and with one another*. That is why people's social betterment depends in such a large measure on the betterment of *social institutions* that develop, if not their Christian, then their civic virtues.

Just look at how much I've quoted you! This is all terribly aughty, and "personal betterment in a spirit of Christian love" has certainly been raked over the coals: it's scarcely good for anything where civic matters are concerned, you suggest. Yet what a strange conception of Christianity you have! Imagine if Korobochka and Sobakevich were to become genuine Christians, already *perfect* (you yourself speak about perfection)—could they then be convinced to renounce serfdom? That's a sly question you're posing, and, naturally, you answer it: "No, one could not convince Korobochka to do that, even if she were a perfect Christian." But to that I shall answer directly: had Korobochka only become, or could she have become, a *genuine*, perfect Christian, then serfdom on her estate would have disappeared altogether, so that there would be nothing to worry about, despite the fact that all the deeds and bills of sale would have remained in her trunk as before. One more thing, if you please: was Korobochka not a Christian even before and was she not born such? Thus, when you speak of new proponents of Christianity, even though you speak of a Christianity that was in essence the same as before, do you mean a Christianity that has already attained its ideal, an intensified, *perfected* one, so to say? If that's the case, then for heaven's sake what slaves and masters could there be? You should at least have some basic acquaintance with Christianity! And what difference would it then make to Korobochka, a *perfect* Christian, whether her peasants were serfs or not? She would be a "mother" to them, a real mother, and the "mother" would at once have done away with the former "mistress." This would have happened of its own accord. The erstwhile mistress and erstwhile slave would have vanished like mist before the sun and entirely new people would have appeared, with entirely new and unprecedented relationships among them. Indeed, the thing itself would have been unprecedented: perfect Christians would have appeared *everywhere*, people who had formerly existed in such scant numbers that they were scarcely perceptible. You were the one who put forth such a fantastic proposition, Mr. Gradovsky; you yourself began this amazing fantasy, and once you've begun it, you must accept the consequences. I assure you, Mr. Gradovsky, that if this had been so, Korobochka's peasants would not have left her, for the simple reason that everyone looks for the place where he can be better off. Do you think they would have been better off with those institutions of yours than they would living with their own mother-landowner who loved them?

I also make so bold as to assure you that if slavery was maintained in the time of the Apostle Paul, it was simply because the churches that had arisen at the time were not yet *perfect* (something that is evident from Paul's Epistles). Those members of the churches who had attained personal perfection no longer owned and could not own slaves because the slaves had become brothers; and a brother, a true brother, cannot keep his brother as a slave. The way you describe it, it would appear that the preaching of Christianity had no effect at all. At least you do acknowledge that slavery was not enshrined by the apostle's preaching. Yet there are other scholars, European historians in particular, who have heaped many reproaches on Christianity for its alleged enshrinement of slavery. This is to misunderstand the essence of the matter. Can you imagine Mary of Egypt having peasant serfs and not wanting to set them free? What an absurdity! In Christianity, in genuine Christianity, there are and will be masters and servants, but a slave is inconceivable. I am speaking of genuine, perfect Christianity. Servants, though, are not slaves. The disciple Timothy served Paul when they traveled together, but read Paul's Epistles to Timothy: do you really think he is writing to a slave, or even to a servant? Indeed, he writes to his "son in the faith," his beloved son. Now those are just the kind of relations there would be between masters and servants should both become perfect Christians! There will be servants and masters, but the masters will no longer be masters, nor will the servants be slaves. Imagine that Kepler, Kant, and Shakespeare are living in the future society: they are carrying out a great labor for all, and everyone is aware of it and reveres them. But Shakespeare has no time to leave his work to tidy up, clean his room, and carry out the rubbish. And believe me, some other citizen will certainly come to work for him; he himself will want to do this, and he will come of his own free will and will carry out Shakespeare's rubbish. Will he be humiliated by this, or made a slave? Certainly not. He knows that Shakespeare is infinitely more useful than he: "Honor and glory be thine," he will tell him; "I am glad to serve thee; in so doing I contribute to the general good, though it be but a drop, for I shall save thee time for thy great work; but I am not a slave. By my conscious admission that thy genius, Shakespeare, makes thee superior to me, and by coming to serve thee, I have shown that I am in no way beneath thee in moral worth and that, *as a person*, I am equal to thee." In fact, he would not say such things for the sole reason that if this were to happen, such questions would never arise and, indeed, would be unthinkable. For, in truth, all would be new people, the children of Christ, and the former animal in man would be conquered. You will say, of course, that this is just another fantasy. But it was not I who first began to spin fantasies, after all, it was you: you were the one who tried to show Korobochka as a *perfect* Christian with "serf *children*" whom she did not want to set free; that's much more of a fantasy than mine.

At this point clever people will laugh and say: "So what's the point of advocating personal betterment in the spirit of Christian love when it seems that genuine Christianity doesn't exist on earth, or exists in such small measure that it's difficult to find? If it did exist (according to what I said, that is), everything would be settled instantly—all forms of slavery would be abolished, the Korobochkas would be reborn as bright spirits, and there would be nothing left for people to do but sing hymns to God." Well, of course (I reply to the gentlemen who are scoffing), there are still terribly few genuine Christians (although they do exist). But how do you know precisely how many are needed to keep the ideal of Christianity alive among the People and, with it, their great hope? Apply this to social conceptions: how many genuine citizens are needed to keep the ideal of civic virtue alive in society? You can't supply an answer to that, either. There's a political economy of its own at work here, one of a special kind which we do not know and which even you do not know, Mr. Gradovsky. People will say, again, "If there are so few who profess this great idea, then what benefit does it bring?" But how do you know what benefit it will bring, when all is said and done? Until now, evidently, all that was needed was that the great idea should not die out. But now, when something new is transpiring all over the world, we have a different situation and we must be prepared. . . . And, indeed, the point here is not at all one of benefit but of truth. If I believe that the truth is here, in those very things in which I put my faith, then what does it matter to me if the whole world rejects my truth, mocks me, and travels a different road? Indeed, that is the strength of a great moral idea, and that is the way in which it joins people into the surest union: that it is not measured in terms of immediate benefit but is directed toward the future, toward eternal ends and absolute joy. How can you unite people to accomplish your civic goals if you have no basis in a fundamental, great, moral idea? And moral ideas are all alike: they are all based on the idea of absolute personal betterment in the future, on an ideal; for this idea contains all within it, all aspirations and all longings; accordingly, all your civic ideals emerge from it. Do you think you could unite people in some civic association with "saving one's neck" as the only goal? Nothing would be achieved, save for the moral motto *Chacun pour soi et Dieu pour tous*. No civic institution will last long with a motto like that, Mr. Gradovsky.

But let me go on; I intend to surprise you: please be aware, my learned professor, that there are no social, civic ideals as such, ones that are not linked organically with moral ideals but exist independently as separate halves sliced off from the whole by your scholarly scalpel; there are no such ideals that, at last, can be taken from outside and transplanted successfully into the spot of your choosing in the form of distinct "institutions"; such ideals, I say, do not exist, never did exist, and cannot exist! Besides, what is a social ideal? What do we mean by this term? Of course, its essence lies in people's strivings to find a formula for social organization, one that, if possible, would be without flaws and would satisfy everyone—isn't that so? But people do not know this formula; people have been looking for it for the whole six thousand years of their history, and they cannot find it. The ants know the formula for their ant heap; the bee knows the formula for his hive (they may not know it in human terms, but they know it in their own way, and that is enough); but humans do not know their formula. If that is so, then where is the source of the ideal of civic organization in human society? If you follow it historically you will see at once where the source is. You will see that it is solely and exclusively the product of the moral betterment of individuals; this is where it begins, and so it has been from time immemorial, and so it shall remain for all time to come. In the origin of every people and every nationality the moral idea always preceded the genesis of the nationality itself, *for the idea was the force that created the nationality*. This moral idea always arose from some mystical ideas, from convictions that humans were eternal, that they were not simply animals roaming the earth but were linked with other worlds and with eternity. Always and everywhere these convictions were formulated in religion, in the confession of some new idea; and always, as soon as a new religion came into being, a new nationality was at once created on the civic level. Look at the Jews and the Moslems: the idea of nationality among the Jews took shape only after the law of Moses, although its beginning goes back to the law of Abraham, while the Moslem nationalities appeared only after the Koran. In order to preserve the spiritual treasure they have received, people are at once drawn to one another; and only then, zealously and anxiously, "working *alongside one another, for one another and with one another*" (as you put it so expressively)—only then do people begin to seek out ways to organize themselves so as to preserve the treasure they have received and not lose anything from it, to find some *civic* formula for living in common, one that would help them advance throughout the world the full glory of that moral treasure they have received. And note that, with the passage of centuries and ages (because such a process also has a law of its own, one we do not know), as soon as the spiritual idea of any nationality began to be shaken and weakened, the nationality itself also began to decline, and with it all their civic precepts; and all the civic ideas they managed to establish within their nationality faded away. The forms a religion have assumed among a people determine the way in which their civic system took shape and expressed itself. Thus, civic ideals are always directly and organically linked with moral ideals; what is most important, the former are always derived exclusively from the latter. Civic ideals never come about *of their own accord*, for when they do appear their sole purpose is to satisfy the moral aspirations of a given nationality in the manner and degree in which those moral aspirations have taken shape within it. And thus, "personal betterment in a religious spirit" is the basis for everything in the lives of nations, for personal betterment in fact *is the confession of the acquired religion*, while "civic ideals" themselves, without this aspiration toward personal betterment, can never appear and, indeed, can never even be born.

You will say, perhaps, that you yourself have stated that "personal betterment is the basis of everything" and that you have not made any divisions with your scalpel. The point, however, is precisely that you did make such a division and cut a living organism into two halves. Personal betterment is not merely "the *beginning* of everything," it is also the continuation and the outcome of everything. It embraces, provides the foundation for, and preserves the organism of nationality; and only it can do this. The civic formula of the nation exists for the sake of personal betterment, for the nation was created only for the purpose of preserving it as the treasure originally acquired. When a nationality loses the urge for general individual self-betterment *in that spirit in which it originated*, then all "social institutions" begin to die out, for there is nothing more to preserve. Thus one simply cannot say what you have said in your last sentence: "That is why people's social betterment depends in such a large measure on the betterment of *social institutions* that develop, if not their Christian, then their civic virtues."

"If not their Christian, then their civic virtues!" Don't you see here the scholarly scalpel that tries to sever what cannot be severed, that cuts the homogeneous, living organism into two separate, lifeless halves—a moral one and a civic one? You say that the most sublime moral idea can be found both "in social institutions" and in the dignity of "a citizen," that a "civic idea" within nations that are already mature and developed always takes the place of the original religious idea, which degenerates into a civic idea and which it legitimately inherits. Yes, many people maintain such things, but we have never yet seen such a fantasy in real life. Whenever the moral-religious idea within a nationality has worn itself out, there has always ensued a panicky, cowardly urge to unite for the sole purpose of "saving one's neck"—there are no other goals for civic union in such cases. Take the French bourgeoisie now, which unites for this very purpose of "saving its neck" from the fourth estate that is trying to break down its door. But "saving one's neck" is the very weakest and last of all the ideas that unite humanity. This is already the beginning of the end, a presentiment of the end. They unite, but keep their eyes peeled so that at the first sign of danger they can break apart all the more quickly. And what, here, can an "institution" as such, taken on its own, save? If there were brothers, then there would be brotherhood. If there are no brothers, then you will not achieve brotherhood through any sort of "institution." What sense is there in setting up an institution and inscribing on it: *Liberté, égalité, fraternité*? You will achieve nothing at all worthwhile here through an "institution," so that it will be necessary—absolutely, inescapably necessary—to add to these three "institutional" words a fourth *ou la mort*, *fraternité ou la mort*—and brother will set forth to chop the head off brother so as to achieve brotherhood by means of this "civic institution." That's only an example, but it's a good one. You, Mr. Gradovsky, seek salvation in external things just as Aleko did: we may have nothing but fools and scoundrels everywhere in Russia (and some feel that this is really so), but we need merely to transplant here some sort of "institution" from Europe and, in your view, all will be saved. Mechanically importing European forms (which will collapse over there tomorrow) that are alien to our People and not suited to their will is, as we know, the most important concept of Russian Europeanism. Incidentally, Mr. Gradovsky, when you condemn our lack of order and cast shame on Russia because of it while pointing out the example of Europe, you say the following: "And meanwhile, we are unable to settle the kind of disagreements and contradictions that Europe has settled long ago. . . ."

Europe, you think, has settled these things? Now who could have given you that idea? Why, your Europe is everywhere on the eve of collapse, a general, terrible collapse. The ant heap they have long been building there, without the church and without Christ (for the church, which has obscured its own ideal, has long been reincarnated everywhere there in the state), with moral principles that have been shaken to their foundation, with all that is general and all that is absolute now lost—this ant heap they have been building is, I say, completely undermined. The fourth estate is coming; it is knocking and hammering at the door; and if the door is not opened it will break it down. It does not want the old ideals; it rejects every existing law. It will not agree to compromises or concessions; the edifice cannot be saved by shoring it up. Concessions will only inflame the fourth estate; it wants everything. Something will come to pass that no one can even conceive. All this parliamentarianism, all the civic theories now being expounded, all the accumulated wealth, the banks, the sciences, the Yids—all of it will collapse in a moment, without a trace—except for the Yids, who will then find ways to carry on, so that this work will even be to their advantage. All of this is "at hand, at the door." You laugh? Blessed are they that laugh. If God grants you the time, you will see for yourself. Then you will be amazed. You will tell me, laughing: "You must love Europe a good deal if you forecast such a future for her." But am I rejoicing? I merely have a sense that the sums have been added. The final accounting and payment of the balance may happen even much sooner than the most potent fantasy can envision. The symptoms are frightful. The long-standing, unnatural political situation of the European states may serve as the beginning of it all. Indeed, how could it be natural when something unnatural has been laid in their very foundation and has been building up for centuries? One small part of humanity cannot possess all the rest as slaves, yet it was exclusively for this purpose that, until now, *all* the civic (which have long ceased to be Christian and are now thoroughly pagan) institutions of Europe were created. This unnaturalness and these "insoluble" political questions (known to everyone, however) must certainly lead to an enormous, final, political war of partition in which everyone will be involved and which will break out in this century, perhaps even in the coming decade.

What do you think: would society there *even now* withstand a lengthy political war? The factory owner is frightened and cowardly, the Yid as well; all the factories and banks will close the moment a war begins to drag on or threaten to drag on, and millions of hungry mouths, the outcast proletarians, will be driven onto the streets. Do you really pin your hopes on the prudence of politicians and the chance that they will not undertake a war? But when, indeed, was it possible to rely on such prudence? Do you really pin your hopes on the chance that the houses of legislature, foreseeing the consequences, will not appropriate funds for a war? But when, indeed, did the houses of legislature over there ever foresee the consequences and refuse money to any leader who pressed them even a little? And so the proletarians are out on the streets. What do you think: will they now wait patiently as before, dying from hunger? This, after we have had political socialism, after the Internationale, the social congresses, and the Paris Commune? No, now things will no longer be as before: the proletarians will throw themselves on Europe and the entire old order will collapse once and for all. The waves will merely break harmlessly against our shore, for only then, plainly and for all to see, will come the full revelation of how distinct our national organism is from Europe's. Then, even you, the doctrinaire thinkers, will perhaps come to your senses and begin to seek here at home "the principles of the People," at which you now only laugh. Yet now you gentlemen point to Europe and call on us to transplant here those very same institutions that will collapse there tomorrow as absurdities that have outlived their time, institutions in which, even there, many clever people have long ceased to believe, institutions that hang on and exist there only through the force of inertia. And who, apart from an abstract doctrinaire, could accept the comedy of bourgeois unity that we see in Europe as the normal formula for uniting all humans on earth? "They have settled their problems long ago," you say—and this after twenty constitutions in less than a century and nearly ten revolutions! Oh, perhaps only then, freed from Europe for a moment, we ourselves, without European tutclage, will take up our own social ideals, ones that unequivocally derive from Christ and personal betterment, Mr. Gradovsky. You will ask: what social and civic ideals of our own can we have apart from European ones? Well, we do have our own social and civic ideals, and our social ideals are better than your European ones, stronger than yours, and even—oh, horrors!—more liberal than yours! Yes, more liberal, because they derive directly from the organism of our People and are not some servile, impersonal transplant from the West.

I cannot enlarge upon this now, of course, if only because the article has turned out to be lengthy as it is. Incidentally, just recall: what was the ancient Christian church, and what did it strive to be? It came into being immediately after Christ and was formed by only a few people; and at once, virtually in the first days after

Christ, the church began to seek out its own "civic formula," one founded on the moral hope of satisfying the spirit through principles of personal betterment. Christian communes—churches—came into being; then a new nationality, hitherto unheard of, began to be formed; this was an all-fraternal, panhuman one in the form of a common, ecumenical church. But it was persecuted; the ideal was shaped underground, while above it, on the surface of the earth, an enormous edifice, a massive ant heap, also took shape—the ancient Roman Empire, also an ideal of sorts and an outlet for the moral aspirations of the entire ancient world: the man-god appeared; the empire itself incarnated the religious idea, providing within itself and through itself an outlet for all the moral strivings of the ancient world. But the final touches were never made to the ant heap; it had been undermined by the church. There was a collision between the two most completely opposed ideas that could exist on earth: the man-god encountered the God-man; Apollo Belvedere encountered Christ. A compromise ensued: the empire accepted Christianity, while the church accepted the Roman state and law. A small part of the church withdrew to the wilderness and continued its former work: once again Christian communes came into being, and then monasteries—but all were merely experiments; and so it continued to our time. The remaining, dominant part of the church was subsequently divided into two halves, as we all know. In the Western half the state at last entirely overcame the church. The church was wiped out and reincarnated once and for all as the state. The papacy appeared—the continuation of the ancient Roman Empire in a new incarnation. In the Eastern half, however, the state was conquered and destroyed by the sword of Mohammed, and only Christ remained, detached from the state. But the state that accepted and again elevated Christ has undergone terrible, centuries-long sufferings from its enemies, from the Tatars, from its own disorders, from serfdom, from Europe and Europeanism; and to this day it still endures so much suffering that a genuine social formula, in the sense of the spirit of love and Christian personal betterment, has not yet really been elaborated within it. But it is not for you, Mr. Gradovsky, to reproach Russia for this. Our People, for the moment, are only the bearers of Christ, and they rest their hopes in Him alone. They have called themselves "krestianin" (peasants), meaning "khristianin" (Christians), and this is not a matter of words alone: this is the idea of their whole future. You, Mr. Gradovsky, mercilessly reproach Russia for her lack of order. But who, over the past two centuries, and especially over the last fifty years, has been standing in the way of her establishing an order? Why, the whole body of Russian Europeans like yourself, Mr. Gradovsky; such people have never been lacking among us over these two whole centuries, and they have been pressing us particularly of late. Who is the enemy of Russian organic and independent development on her own, Popular principles? Who contemptuously refuses to admit that these principles even exist and will not take note of them? Who wanted to remake our People, with some preposterous notion of "raising them up to our level," simply to make them all liberal European creatures like yourself, from time to time plucking one little fellow out of the mass of People and corrupting him into a European, if only by giving him flaps for his uniform tailcoat? By this I don't mean that the European is corrupt; I am only saying that transforming a Russian into a European as the liberals do it is often a real process of corruption. Yet this is just what constitutes the whole ideal of their program of activity: pulling one little fellow at a time from the common mass—how absurd! Is this how they intended to pick apart the whole eighty-million body of our People and remake them? Can you seriously believe that our whole People, in their entire mass, would consent to become such a depersonalized nonentity as these Russian European gentlemen?

4. To One—"Humble Thyself"; To Another—"Exalt Thyself." A Tempest in a Teapot

Until now I've only been squabbling with you, Mr. Gradovsky, but at this point I want to reproach you for deliberately distorting my idea, the most important point in my speech.

You write:

> There is still far too much untruth—the remnants of centuries of slavery—lodged in them [in our People, he means] for them to *demand that we bow down before them* and, even more, for them to have pretensions to set the whole of Europe on the true path, as Mr. Dostoevsky predicts.
>
> It's a strange thing! A man who damns haughtiness in the person of individual wanderers calls upon an entire People, whom he regards as some kind of universal apostle, to be proud of themselves. To the former he says, "Humble yourselves!" To the latter he says, "Exalt yourselves!"

And further:

> And now, without having created a proper sense of nationality, suddenly to have visions of some universal role! Isn't this a bit premature? Mr. Dostoevsky takes pride in the fact that we have served Europe for two centuries. I must admit that this "service" does not evoke any joyous feeling in me. Can the time of the Congress of Vienna and the whole era of congresses generally be seen as an object of our "pride"? Or the time when we, in the service of Metternich, suppressed the national movement in Italy and Germany and even looked askance at the Greeks, our fellow Orthodox? What hatred we earned ourselves in Europe for just such "service"!

Let me pause first on the latter, small, almost innocent paraphrase of my views: in saying that "over the past two centuries we have served Europe even more, perhaps, than ourselves," was I praising *the manner* in which we served? I wanted only to register the fact of our service, and this fact is real. But the fact of our service and of *the manner* in which we served are two quite different things. We may have made very many political errors—and, indeed, the Europeans constantly make all kinds of them—but it was not our blunders I was praising; I was merely noting the fact of our service (which was almost always selfless). Can you really not understand that these are two different things? "Mr. Dostoevsky takes pride in the fact that we have served Europe," you say. In fact, I said that with no pride at all; I merely noted a trait of our national spirit, a very significant trait. Does finding a beautiful, wholesome trait in the national spirit in that way necessarily mean taking pride in it? And what are you saying about Metternich and the congresses? Is it you who are trying to teach me something here? While you were still a student I was speaking about our service to Metternich and speaking out even more strongly than you; and it was precisely for those words about our misguided service to Metternich (among other words, of course) that thirty years ago I paid in the usual manner. Why did you have to distort that? Well, it was so that you could show people: "You see what a liberal I am! And look at that poet, the ardent lover of the People—just listen to the reactionary things he's spouting, taking pride in our service to Metternich." Vanity, Mr. Gradovsky.

These things are trifles, of course; but what follows is not a trifle.

And so, when I say to the People: "Lift up your spirit!" does it mean I am saying: "Exalt yourselves!" Does it mean I am trying to make them haughty, to teach them pride? Just imagine, Mr. Gradovsky, that you are telling your own children: "Children, lift up your spirit! Children, be noble!" Does that really mean that you are teaching them to be haughty or that you yourself, in teaching them, are exalting yourself? And what did I say? I spoke of our hope "to become a brother to all people at last," asking that the phrase "at last" be particularly stressed. Can it be that the bright hope that someday, at least, brotherhood will become a fact in our suffering world and that we too, perhaps, *shall be allowed to become brothers* to all people—can it be that this hope is pride and an appeal to exalt ourselves? I did, after all, state frankly and plainly at the end of my speech: "But, after all, am I speaking about economic prominence, about the glory of the sword or science? I am speaking merely of the brotherhood of people and of the fact that, perhaps, the Russian heart is most plainly destined, among all the peoples, for universally human and brotherly unity. . . ." Those were my words. And do they really contain an appeal to self-exaltation? Immediately after the words I cited, I added in my speech: "Our land may be impoverished, but this impoverished land 'Christ Himself, in slavish garb, traversed and gave his blessing.' Why can we not accommodate His ultimate word?" Is it Christ's word that means an appeal to self-exaltation, and is the hope that we can accommodate his word self-exaltation? You write indignantly "that it is premature to demand that others bow down to us." Come now—was any demand made to do that? This desire to serve all, to become servants and brothers to everyone and to serve them with our love—does this mean demanding that they all bow down to us? If, indeed, there is any demand here to bow down, then the sacred, selfless wish to serve all immediately becomes an absurdity. People do not bow down to servants, and a brother does not expect a brother to get on his knees before him.

Imagine, Mr. Gradovsky, that you have done some good deed or are only on your way to do one; and so, along the way, filled with tender emotion, you reflect: "How happy this unfortunate fellow will be to get the unexpected help I'm about to give him! How he'll take heart; why, he'll be a new man. He'll tell his family, his children, of his joy and shed tears with them. . . ." As you think about this and imagine it you will naturally be moved yourself, sometimes even to the point of tears (has this really never happened to you?); and then a knowing voice says right in your ear: "Ah, but you are exalting yourself in imagining all this! It's your pride that makes you shed tears!" For heaven's sake, it's only the hope that we Russians can have some significance in humanity as a whole and, eventually, be worthy of serving it in a brotherly way—it is only this hope that evoked the delight and tears of delight among the thousand who heard my speech. I'm not recalling this to earn praise, and not out of pride; I'm merely noting the seriousness of the moment. We were offered only the bright hope that we, too, can amount to something in humanity as a whole, though it might be *merely* as brothers to other people; and so this single, ardent suggestion united everyone in a single thought and a single feeling. Strangers embraced each other and swore to be better in the future. Two old men came up to me and said: "We have been enemies for twenty years and have done much harm to one another, but hearing your words we have made our peace." One newspaper was quick to note that all this rapture proved nothing, that it was merely the mood of the moment, "with some hand kissing," and that there was little need for the speakers to take the rostrum and make their speeches. "No matter what they had said, there would have been the same outpouring of rapture, for such was the benevolent mood in Moscow." Yet had that journalist gone there himself and said something of his own, would they have rushed to him as they did to me? Why was it that, for the previous three days, speeches had been made and huge ovations given to the speakers, yet the things that happened after my speech happened to no one else? It was a unique moment at the Pushkin celebrations, and it was not repeated. God knows, I say this not for my own glorification; but the moment was too serious a one to allow me to pass over it in silence. Its seriousness consisted specifically in the fact that our society clearly and vividly manifested some new elements; people appeared who long for some noble feat, for a consoling idea, for the promise of a cause. This means that our society does not want to be content merely with our liberal snickering about Russia; it means that the doctrine of Russia's eternal impotence is becoming loathsome! They needed but a single hope, a single suggestion, and their hearts caught fire with sacred longing for a panhuman cause, for service to all people in universal fellowship, for a noble deed. Do you think it was pride that caused their hearts to take fire? Do you think it was pride that caused their tears to flow? Do you think it was pride that I was urging them to feel? What kind of person are you?

You see, Mr. Gradovsky, the seriousness of this moment threw many of those who dwell in our little liberal teacup into a panic, the more so that this happened so unexpectedly. "How can this be? Until now it's been so pleasant and advantageous to snicker and look down our noses at everything, and now, suddenly. . . . Can this be a rebellion? Help! Police!" Several panic-stricken gentlemen jumped up: "What's going to happen to us now? We've written a few things as well. . . . Where will they put us now? We have to wipe this whole thing out as quickly as possible so there's not a trace of it left; we have to explain quickly to all Russia that this was nothing more than the benevolent mood that happened to prevail in hospitable old Moscow, a delightful little moment that came after a series of dinners, and nothing more. And as for the rebellion, well, the police can stamp it out!" And they got down to work: I was a coward; I was a poet; I was a nonentity; my speech had no significance whatsoever—in short, in the heat of the moment some people abandoned restraint. The public, however, might not believe what they said. They should have done the thing, rather, with some skill and approached it with cooler heads; they might even have praised a few things in my speech: "There is, nevertheless, a certain train of thought at work here"; and then, little by little, they could have poured out their contempt for it all and wiped away every trace of it to general satisfaction. In short, they did not act very skillfully. There was a gap here and it had to be filled quickly; and so they at once found a reliable, experienced critic who had both the ability to make irresponsible attacks and the appropriate comme il faut. That critic was you, Mr. Gradovsky: you wrote your article, you were read, and everyone settled down again. You have served a common and an admirable cause; at least your article was reprinted everywhere: "The poet's speech cannot stand up to rigorous criticism; poets are poets, but here we have intelligent people standing on guard, always ready when needed to throw cold water on the dreamer." At the very end of your article you ask me to excuse any remarks I might consider to be harsh. As I end my article, I do not ask you to excuse me for any harsh expressions, if there be such in my article, Mr. Gradovsky. My reply was directed not to A. D. Gradovsky personally but to the publicist A. Gradovsky. I haven't the slightest reason not to respect you personally. But if I do not respect your opinions and continue to hold to my own, then how could I moderate anything by asking your forgiveness? But I found it painful to see a very serious and portentous moment in the life of our society portrayed in a distorted way and interpreted wrongly. It was painful to see the idea I serve dragged through the streets. And you were the one who was dragging it.

I realize that people on every side will tell me that it was ridiculous and pointless to write such a long reply to your article, which was rather brief in comparison with mine. But, I repeat, your article served only as a pretext: I wanted to make a general statement about certain things. I intend to resume publishing *A Writer's Diary* beginning next year. And so this present issue of the *Diary* may serve as my *profession de foi* for the future, a "trial" issue, so to say.

People may also say that in my reply to you I invalidated the whole meaning of the speech I delivered in Moscow, where I myself called upon both Russian parties to join together and to be reconciled and acknowledged the legitimacy of each one. No, not at all: the meaning of the speech has not been invalidated; it has, rather, been reinforced even more, for I make the specific point in my reply to you that both parties, in their alienation from one another, in their mutual enmity, place themselves and their activity in an abnormal position, whereas in unity and accord with one another they might be able to lift up all our spirits, save everything, rouse limitless energies, and mobilize Russia for a new, healthy, grand life such as has not been seen before!

A Writer's Diary

1881

January

1

1. Finances. A Citizen as an Offended Thersites. Crowning from Below and the Musicians. A Refuge for Windbags and the Windbags

Good Lord! Can it be that after three years of silence I now resume my *Diary* with an article on economics? What sort of economist and financial expert am I? I've never been either of those things. Despite the current epidemic, I have not been infected with the virus of economism, yet here I am, following all the others and coming out with an article on economics. That there is a regular epidemic of economism these days is beyond doubt. Everyone is an economist these days. Every new magazine looks as if it is specializing in economic issues and announces itself as such. Indeed, how can one not be an economist, and who can avoid it nowadays? The fall of the ruble! The deficit! This general concern over economics appeared among us in recent years, after our Turkish campaign. Oh, even before we had a good deal of discussion about finances, but during the war and after it, everyone plunged headlong into financial matters—and, of course, all this was quite a natural development: the ruble had fallen, there had been loans to cover the costs of the war, and so on. Aside from the ruble itself, though, we also saw a certain urge (and we still see it today) to get even—to get even for the war, specifically. "We told you so," they say. "We predicted it." Those who particularly took up economism were the ones who were saying then, in 1876 and 1877, that cold cash was better than noble deeds; that the Eastern Question was just a bit of naughtiness and a fiction; that not only was there no upsurge of Popular feeling, not only was the war not a

Popular and a national one, but, in essence, that there were no People as such, there was, as before, the same inert, deaf and dumb mass organized to pay taxes and support the intelligentsia, a mass which, if it did contribute its pennies through the churches, did so only because the priest and the authorities commanded them to do so. All the Russian Thersites (and there are a good many of them among our intelligentsia) found their finest sentiments terribly offended at the time. The citizen, as a Thersites, was offended. And so they began to get even by blaming the financial problems on the war. Little by little their ranks were increased by some who were not Thersites; even some former "heroes" joined them. They all pouted a bit, and some even more than a bit. It's true that the unprofitable peace and the Berlin Conference contributed to this. (N.B.: Speaking of this Berlin Conference: at the time, on a back road in a remote area in the provinces, an old peasant woman who kept a small inn once asked me, "Can you tell me, good sir, how they decided our case over there in Europe? Have you heard anything?" I was surprised at the old woman. But this—i.e., the upsurge of Popular feeling at that time—I shall discuss later). Now I wish only to say that everyone is now writing about the ruble and the deficit and, of course, this is partly due to the herd instinct: everyone else is writing about it and worrying about it, so how can I not worry as well? People will think that I'm not a real citizen, that I'm not taking an interest.

However, here and there we see the genuine concern of a good citizen; there is pain, there are painful doubts about the future—I can't pretend that this isn't happening. But still, even though this distress is very real, it almost everywhere revolves around the question Why is everything in Russia so different from Europe? "In Europe the taler is strong everywhere, while our ruble is low. So why aren't we Europe? Tell me, why aren't we Europe?" Clever people have at last answered this question of why we're not Europe and why things in Russia aren't the same as in Europe: "It is because our edifice has not been crowned." And so everyone started shouting about "crowning our edifice," having forgotten that the edifice itself hasn't even been erected yet and that, accordingly, there isn't anything there to be crowned; that instead of an edifice we have only a few white waistcoats who imagine that they already are the edifice; that the crowning, if it is to happen at all, would be much better begun from below, from the peasant's coat and bast shoes, not from the white waistcoat.

Let me make one necessary qualification here: at first glance, crowning the edifice from below seems to be absurd, of course, if only in an architectural sense, and it contradicts everything that has happened and is happening along these lines in Europe. But since everything in Russia is distinctive, utterly unlike Europe and sometimes even quite the opposite, then such an important matter as the crowning of the edifice can be done opposite to the European way, to the amazement and indignation of our Russian European thinkers. For, to Europe's amazement, our lower orders, our peasant coat and bast shoes, in fact are already an edifice in their own way—not merely a foundation but precisely an edifice—though incomplete yet sound and unshakeable, erected over centuries and, indeed and in truth, anticipating the whole real and genuine idea, though still not fully developed, of our future and architecturally complete edifice. However, all this shouting on the part of our Europeans about crowning the edifice, if one is to tell the whole truth, has just the sort of character I spoke of above: it is more a product of the herd mentality and more mechanically soothing than rational and truly civic, morally civic. And the reason why everyone has so latched on to this new soothing notion is that all these external, specifically *mechanically* soothing consolations are always easy and pleasant, and so readily available: "All we need is the European formula and everything will be saved at once; we just apply it, take it ready-made out of the box, and Russia will at once become Europe, and the ruble will become the taler." What is especially pleasant about these mechanically soothing notions is that one need not think at all, never mind suffer or be perplexed. I'm speaking about the herd, not the righteous people. There are righteous people everywhere, even among the Russian Europeans, and I respect them. But you must agree that among us, in the majority of cases, this all proceeds as if it were a ballroom dance of some sort. Why think, why rack one's brain, why get a headache? Take the ready-made stuff from someone else, and right away the music will begin, a whole harmonious concert: "We'll surely get it right seated neatly in a row."

Well, gentlemen, what if you're no good as musicians, and what if this is true of the overwhelming, colossal majority of you? What if the only thing that comes out of the white waistcoats is an endless stream of chatter? What if the colossal majority of the white waistcoats isn't admitted into the edifice at all (in the first instance, of course), if it should someday happen to be crowned? I mean to say that they could and should be allowed in, because they are still Russian people, after all (and many of them are good people), so long as they are willing, jointly with the entire land, to give their advice humbly in some great common cause. But, you see, they won't want to give their advice jointly with the rest of the Russian land; they'll begin to exalt themselves above it. Until now, for two whole centuries, they've kept themselves apart, and now, suddenly, they want to join in! This isn't some little farce, you know; this demands a sense of history and culture, and we have no culture and never have. Take a careful look at the fervor of some Russian European, one who might even have the most innocent and kindly nature; take a careful look at the absurd, venomous, and criminal fervor—to the point of foaming at the mouth and spreading slander—with which he argues about his cherished ideas, specifically about those most alien to the Russian People's view of the world, most alien to their truly sacred hopes and beliefs! How much does such a gentleman, with his soft, white hands, have to give up to attach himself to the Russian land, stinking of the peasant's coat and bast shoes? Which of his most sacred books and European convictions must he give up? He will not give up anything, for in spite of himself he turns up his nose at the People and is contemptuous toward the Russian land. "We are the only ones who can give advice," they will say, "and as for the rest (the whole of the Russian land, that is), let them be satisfied for the moment with the fact that in educating them we will be gradually raising them up to our own level, and will teach the People their rights and obligations." (And these are the ones who are planning to teach the People their rights and, most of all, their obligations! Ah, what a pack of rogues!) "Russian society," they will say, "cannot remain in some backwoods jail along with a raggedy People wearing their native bast shoes." And so, when they begin in such a frame of mind, it's possible (and even inevitable) again to reach the point of turning the People, the peasant coat and the bast shoe, into serfs once more, not by way of the former bondage, though, but through a cultured tutelage and its political consequences: "And again we shall forge chains for the People!"

Well, of course, they'll end by setting up their own refuge for windbags here in Russia. They'll set it up, but from the very first step they won't understand and recognize themselves and each other—and it will certainly happen this way. They'll only bump heads with each other in the darkness. Don't be offended, gentlemen: it isn't just to a society such as yours, detached from any meaningful work for two whole centuries and lacking any kind of original culture, that this has happened when its turn has come to utter its words of advice for the first time; it's happened also among the most cultured peoples. But since the latter have still had centuries of culture behind them and, above all, have always more or less relied on their people, they have set themselves quickly aright and started on a secure path, though not, of course, without some preliminary bumps on the head. But as for you, our Europeans—what are you relying on, and how are you going to reach an accord? Only by seating yourselves neatly in a row. And what a lot of windbags have multiplied in our midst of late! It's just as if they are really getting ready to do something. Some advanced gentleman who gives advice sits down in front of you and begins to talk: there's no end, no beginning, everything is mixed together and rolled up into a lump. He talks for an hour and a half, and he talks so smoothly and sweetly, just like the singing of a bird. You ask yourself what he is: a clever fellow, or what? And you can't make up your mind. Every word, it seems, is clear and comprehensible, but when you put them together you can't make anything out. Is it that, from now on, the eggs are going to teach the hen, or is the hen going to sit on the eggs as she used to? You can't make out any of it; you see only that the eloquent hen is laying rubbish instead of eggs. At last your eyes begin to bulge and your brain goes numb. This is a new type who has come into being recently; he's not yet been reflected in our literature. There's a good deal in our contemporary, current life that hasn't yet been touched upon in our literature; it has overlooked a good deal and is terribly behind the times. What we see most are types from the 1840s or, at best, the 1850s. Maybe writers have taken up the historical novel because they've lost the sense of the current moment.

2. Can We Expect European Finances in Russia?

"So what about finances? Where's your article on finances?" I'll be asked. But, again, what sort of economist am I? What kind of expert on financial matters? In fact, I don't think I even have the nerve to write about finances. So why, then, did I embark on such a venture and start writing such an article? I did so precisely because I'm sure that once I've begun to talk of finances I'll change the subject to something else entirely and the result will be an article not about finances but something altogether different. That's the only thing that encourages me. I am entirely unworthy of writing about finances since I know that I regard our finances from a quite un-European viewpoint and, in fact, don't even believe Europe's experience is applicable to us—for the very reason that we are not Europe at all and that everything in Russia is so distinct that, compared with Europe, we might as well be dwelling on the moon. In Europe, for instance, the slavish, feudal relationship of the lower classes to the upper was abolished over the course of centuries, and, at last, came the revolution; in short, everything happened historically and in accord with their culture. In Russia, however, serfdom, with all its consequences, collapsed in a single instant and, thank God, without even the slightest revolution. And so, it would seem, what could cause a cataclysm here—I mean a major, very great cataclysm? It is true, though, that everything that collapses suddenly always collapses in a very dangerous fashion, meaning with a great shock. Of course, I don't regret that the collapse was a sudden one. On the contrary, it's an awfully good thing that this whole vile historical sin of ours was done away with at once through the mighty word of the Tsar-Liberator. Nevertheless, one cannot escape the law of nature, and there was a mighty shock. It was, to be sure, a mighty concussion, but why was it so immense? Of course, history has laws for everything and, no doubt, there are many who even now can clearly perceive why it all happened as it did.

But without developing this topic any further—(it is a great and immense topic, with which, perhaps, only a historian of the next century will be able to contend)—without adding a single word more, I will point out only some particulars that especially stand out and give rise to confusion. Take one instance: serfdom, which stood in the way of everything, even the proper development of agriculture, collapsed; now it would seem that at this point the peasant ought to start flourishing and grow rich. That didn't happen: in his working of the land the peasant sank to the very minimum of what the land was capable of providing. And the main problem is that we still don't know whether even in the future some force will be found (and if so, just what that force consists of) to move the peasant to rise above the minimum that the land now provides and to ask for its maximum. Clever people will say that this is an idle question, understood by everyone; but I am firmly convinced that it is far from being solved and is incomparably more immense, incomparably more far-reaching in its content than people suppose it to be. Then take another instance: the whole former system of land tenure by the nobility broke down and was reduced to a lamentable level; yet at the same time there is an evident beginning of a rebirth of the whole former landowning class into something other than it was before—into a People, an educated People—for how else, it would seem, could it be reborn? Now that would seem to be a fine thing; nothing, it would seem, could be better, for the People are in dire need of an intelligentsia to lead them; they themselves long for and seek one. But, unfortunately, this too we still think of as an ideal and see it merely as some delightful stork winging its way across the sky; in actuality it is far from this. Does this class, the former landowners, want to become an educated *People*? That is the question, and, you know, it is the most important, the most fundamental question we now face, one on which our entire future depends, perhaps! Yet this question is a long way from being answered, and one can't even imagine how the answer to it can be found. Will this same class, rather, once more exalt itself and once more become a power over the People—not via the old route of serfdom, of course; but will it not, instead of uniting with the People, want to use its education to create a new authoritative and disruptive force and become an aristocratic intelligentsia, standing above the People and supervising them? Will it genuinely want to acknowledge the People as its brother in blood and in spirit, for all time to come? Will it revere the things our People revere? Will it consent to love the things our People have loved even more than themselves? And yet without that no one will ever merge with our People, for the things the People love and revere are matters of their firm conviction, and they will never renounce them for any intelligentsia, no matter how much they long for one.

This is a terribly vital question for us, and yet it is terribly far from being settled. On the whole, everything in Russia now exists in the form of questions. And what's most important is that it all demands time, history, culture, generations, yet we have to solve it in an instant. That in itself constitutes our main difference from

Europe: that so many things happen here, not via a historical, cultural process, but suddenly and somehow altogether unexpectedly, sometimes even through completely unanticipated instructions from the authorities. Of course, no one can be blamed for the way everything has happened and does happen, and so, perhaps, there is even a kind of historical process here; still, you have to agree that Europe has never experienced such a history. So how, then, can one expect us to be Europe and to have a European system of finances as well? For instance, I believe as an axiom of economics that the land is *possessed,* not by the railway magnates, not by the industrialists, not by the millionaires, not by the banks, and not by the Yids, but only by those who cultivate it; that those who work the land lead everything else; and that the tillers of the soil are themselves the state, its nucleus, its vital core. But is this true of Russia? Are things not inside out at the moment? Where is our nucleus, and in whom? Is it not the railway magnate and the Yid who own our economic assets? Railways are being built in Russia now, and again we see something that exists in no other country: it has taken Europe nearly half a century to cover herself with a network of railways, even given all her wealth. But in Russia the last ten thousand or so miles of railways have been built in ten years, and this given our poverty, and in a time of such economic disruption, immediately after the abolition of serfdom! And of course the railways attracted all the capital at the very time when the land was most in need of it. The railways were built at the cost of destroying our agriculture. And have we yet managed to settle the question of individual, private ownership of land? Will it carry on side by side with peasant ownership, with an established labor force that is solid and sound and not a tavern proletariat? Yet without sound solutions to such questions, what sound results can follow? It is truly essential to find sound solutions; until then there will be no serenity, and it is only serenity, after all, that provides the source of every great power. So how can people now expect us to have European budgets and proper finances? Here the question is not why we have no European economic system and solid finances; the question is merely: how have we managed to keep on our feet until now? Once more: we have managed to keep on our feet because of the steadfast, unifying strength of the whole People.

But there is little serenity among us, particularly spiritual serenity, i.e., the very most important kind, for without spiritual serenity there will be no other kind. People particularly neglect this matter and seek mere temporary, material repose. There is no serenity in their minds, and this is the case among all classes of people; there is no serenity in our convictions, in our views, in our nerves, and in our appetites. Work, and an awareness that only through work "shalt thou be saved"—these things do not exist at all. There is no sense of duty, and, indeed, where would it come from? There has been no proper culture for a century and a half—no culture at all, perhaps. "Why should I work when my culture itself has led me to the point where I reject everything around me? And if there do exist some simple souls who think they can save our edifice by European contrivances, then I reject those simple souls as well and believe only in the slogan 'the worse, the better'; that's the whole extent of my philosophy." I assure you that a good many people among us are saying that now, saying it to themselves at least, while others are saying it right out loud. However, the person who utters such aphorisms is himself made of flesh and blood, after all. "The worse, the better," he says, "but this is only in regard to everyone else; as for me, I'd like the best that's possible." That's how he understands his philosophy. He has the appetite of a wolf. A man the size of a bear but with a woman's nerves, distraught and pampered; he is cruel and sensual, unable to put up with anything: "Why on earth should I take the trouble and put up with this?" No more dinners in restaurants, no more cocottes—what's the point of living? And he puts a bullet through his head. It's all very well if he puts a bullet through his own head, but what if he goes out and robs someone else, observing all the proper legal formalities? And the course of events does not wait; poverty is growing everywhere. Shopkeepers are all complaining that no one buys anything. Factories are reducing production to a minimum. Just go into a store and ask about business: "There was a time when a fellow would buy at least half a dozen shirts for the holiday," you'll be told, "but now he just buys one at a time." Ask even in the fashionable restaurants, since this is the last place poverty would show up. "No," you'll be told, "nowadays they don't make the same big splash they used to; everyone's holding tight to his wallet; at best, a fellow will come in and order an ordinary dinner." And this is the former man about town and carouser. They've run through their redemption money. They're still chopping down the last of their forests now, but once that's done there'll be nothing more. And what sort of forests do we have left? When you're traveling by train just take a look at the firewood at the stations: formerly they would at least cut logs, but now it's not at all rare to see some sort of skinny sticks instead of real firewood; now they're not cutting trees but bushes and saplings. Of course, this point will seem trivial to you in view of the other immense questions of our time. But still, our financial experts have absolutely ignored our forests, just as if they didn't want to know about them, on principle, it would seem. Yet if you consider all this and go into it deeply, you'll realize that the loss of our forests will have a most damaging effect on our finances. But everyone seems to have given his word merely to skim the surface of the question of forests, so long as the catastrophe has not yet come. It will come suddenly, for everyone is still lulled by the fact that timber still fetches a decent price on the market; and they don't want to know that this is an artificial price, as it were, that comes from the intense selling by those who are cutting the forests and even the bushes because they have already run through all their other sources of income. They'll cut them down and suddenly find they have nothing; there will be nothing to put on the market. But I'll say more of this later. I began talking about the poverty everywhere and its reverse side, the growth of appetites.

I only want to observe in passing that a terrific number of Captain Kopeikins have come on the scene, in innumerable shapes and forms, from the genuine ones to those of the high-society, perfumed set. And they've all got their eyes greedily fixed on the treasury and public funds. Of course, they'll all be quickly transformed, if not into highway robbers like the real Captain Kopeikin, then into industrialist-pickpockets, some of whom will operate quite legally, while others won't even bother to cover themselves with the cloak of the law. A few of these fellows will even say proudly, "I am the way I am because I reject everything and am promoting rejection." Do you think there aren't any Kopeikin-liberals? They've realized full well that liberalism is in fashion and that they can cash in on it. Who hasn't seen them?—the cosmopolitan liberal, the cheap atheist who flaunts his five-kopeck education before the People! He's the most vulgar of all the vulgar manifestations of our pseudo-liberalism, but still he has an insatiable appetite and therefore he is dangerous. And it's just these people who are the first to cling to any idea of transplanting things from somewhere else to effect a mechanical cure; they group together and constitute a crowd led very often by very honorable people who, in essence, are not to blame for attracting such a following: "Let there be change of any sort, only so long as it happens without effort and is ready-made," says the liberal Kopeikin; "I'll still be better off with some superficial change, whatever it may be, because I'll certainly find a way to profit from it at first." And so from that aspect he's very dangerous, although he's no more than a Kopeikin. But let's leave Kopeikin. All that's now been said is still just the tiniest bit on the subject of our lack of serenity. I can see myself that my introduction has come out far too long. So let me get right down to finances at once!

3. Forget Immediate Problems So That the Roots Can Be Restored. Through Lack of Ability I Enter into Something Spiritual

My nature is such that I shall begin at the end and not at the beginning and set forth my whole idea at once. I've never had the knack of writing in measured fashion, of approaching a thing from the proper approaches and setting forth an idea only after doing all the preliminary ruminations and proving the point as best I can. I've never had the patience, my character stood in the way; and this, of course, harmed me, because some final conclusion, stated plainly, with no preparations and no preliminary supporting arguments, sometimes does nothing more than astonish and confuse people and maybe even make them laugh; but I have precisely the kind of conclusion—and I can sense it—that might at once cause the reader to burst out laughing if I haven't prepared him for it in advance. My idea, my formula, is as follows: "In order to establish sound finances in a state that has experienced certain upheavals, don't think too much about immediate needs, no matter how urgent they may seem; think only about restoring the roots, and you'll get sound finances."

Well, of course, there'll be a burst of laughter at once: "Everyone knows that," I'll be told. "There's absolutely nothing new in your formula; who doesn't know that you mustn't let the roots wither and that once the roots have dried out, you won't get any fruit?" And so on. But, still, let me qualify what I said; I haven't yet explained my whole idea, and, alas, my problem is that if I were to write even a whole book elaborating this idea of mine, even then (oh, I can sense this, too), I wouldn't manage to explain it sufficiently for it to be understood *in its entirety*. For this idea contains an element of predestination.

You see, it's obvious that everyone knows about making the roots healthy; everyone knows it, and what minister of finance hasn't concerned himself with it, more or less—especially the present minister: he's gone straight to the roots and now he's already abolished the salt tax. Still more reforms are expected—extraordinary, fundamental, "radical" ones. Moreover, a whole range of measures was always used in the past, and ten years ago, to keep the roots healthy: audits were set up, commissions were appointed to study the economic health of the Russian peasant and the things he produced, his courts, his local government, his physical ailments, his habits and customs, and so forth. These commissions spawned subcommittees to collect statistical data, and the matter proceeded like clockwork, meaning in the best possible administrative way. But that's certainly not the subject I'm taking up here. Moreover, not merely the subcommittees but even such fundamental reforms as the abolition of the salt tax or the anticipated great reform of the poll-tax system are, in my opinion, merely palliatives, something external that does not begin with the roots themselves—that is my point. We shall begin with the roots themselves when we forget—if not completely, then at least halfway—about immediate problems, about the issues of the day, about the pressing needs of our budget, our debts from foreign loans, the deficit, the ruble, even bankruptcy (the latter will never happen, despite the malicious prophecies of our foreign friends). In short, when we forget about all this, about all these immediate problems, and turn our attention exclusively to making the roots healthy, only then will we have truly abundant and healthy fruit. At that point we can again turn to immediate problems or, to put it better, to what will then be the immediate problems, because during this intermission one may expect that the former situation (meaning our contemporary situation of today) will all radically change and its character be transformed to the point that we ourselves will not recognize it.

Well, of course I realize that everything I've just said will seem fantastic, that it's impossible not to think about the ruble, paying off our loans, bankruptcy, and the armed forces, that these matters need to be seen to and, obviously, seen to at once. But I assure you that I, too, realize this. You see, I'm admitting to you that I deliberately set forth my idea point blank and took my heart's desires almost to the point of an impossible ideal. I thought that if I began with an absurdity I might make myself clearer. What I said was: "What if we could make ourselves forget, if only *halfway*, our immediate problems and direct our attention toward something completely different, into the very depths where, to be truthful, we have never looked before because we were searching for the depths on the surface?" But now I'm prepared to make some concessions to my formula, and so in its place I'll propose the following: we needn't forget immediate problems *halfway*—I'll drop the halfway—but only by a twentieth part; yet we must do so with the stipulation (and absolutely with that stipulation) that having begun by forgetting immediate problems by one-twentieth, we add another twentieth to that with each year that passes and so reach the point where we forget three-quarters of our immediate problems. What's important is not the amount; *what's important here is the principle* to be taken, kept before us, and then followed without deviation. Oh, of course we are still left with the same question: what are we to do about immediate problems? Doesn't this mean wiping them out as if they weren't real? But I'm not saying we should wipe them out; I know myself that you can't turn something real into something unreal; and yet, you know, gentlemen, sometimes you can. You see, if every year we could reduce our frantic concern for immediate problems by just one-twentieth and direct that same portion of frantic concern to something else, then the matter would seem hardly fanciful at all, but quite a plausible thing to undertake, the more so that (I repeat), neglecting immediate problems by one-twentieth is no cause for concern simply because they will certainly not be lost or wiped out but will, I repeat, be quite naturally transformed into something other than what they are now; they will acquiesce to a new principle and enter into its meaning and spirit; they will certainly change to something better, to the very best. I'll be told that I'm speaking in riddles, but this isn't the case at all. To give an example, I shall say a thing or two first, by way of a tiny word of preface, on the topic of how it's possible at once to begin the transition from immediate problems to "making the roots healthy."

What would happen, say, if Petersburg should suddenly agree, through some miracle, to take a less haughty attitude toward Russia—oh, what a glorious and sound first step this would be toward "making the roots healthy!" Because just look at Petersburg: she's reached the point where she believes absolutely that she is the whole of Russia, and this notion grows stronger with every new generation. In this sense Petersburg seems to be following the example of Paris, despite the fact that she is utterly unlike Paris!

Paris has shaped herself through a natural, historical process so that she has swallowed up the whole of France and all its political and social life, its entire meaning; and were you to take Paris from France, what would remain?—nothing more than a geographical designation. And so, some people here imagine that things are almost the same as they are in Paris, that Petersburg has absorbed the whole of Russia. But Petersburg is not Russia at all. The overwhelming majority of the Russian People see Petersburg's significance only in the fact that their tsar lives there. Meanwhile—and we know this—with each generation that passes, our Petersburg intelligentsia understands Russia less and less, simply because they, isolated from Russia in their Finnish swamp, change their view of Russia more and more, so that among some of them this view has been narrowed to the microscopic dimensions of some Karlsruhe. But just take a peep outside Petersburg and you'll see the broad ocean of the Russian land, a boundless and bottomless ocean. And yet the sons of Petersburg fathers can, with complete equanimity, deny that there is any ocean of the Russian People and accept it as something immutable and unconscious, insignificant in any spiritual sense and retrograde to an extreme. "It's a huge country," they say, "but it's stupid; it's only good for supporting us so that we can teach it a bit of sense and give it an idea of government." The future sons of the fatherland are created in Petersburg as they twirl across the polished parquet of the ballroom, while the "rats who do the dirty work," as Khlestakov called them, study their fatherland in government offices; and, naturally, they do learn something, but it isn't Russia; it's something quite different, sometimes something very strange. This strange something they superimpose upon Russia.

Meanwhile, the broad ocean goes on living its own special life and with every generation grows more and more spiritually detached from Petersburg. And don't tell me that though the life of the People is a vigorous one, it is still unconscious, as is believed not only by Petersburgers but even by some few Russians who do understand Russia. Oh, if you only knew how untrue this is, and how much consciousness already has grown among the Russian People, even during the present reign! Indeed, consciousness is already growing; it grows, and already there is so much that the People have realized and understood that Petersburg people would not believe it. This can be seen by those who know how to see; this can be sensed but is not yet making itself manifest as a whole, although it is evident in places, in far corners, in individual houses and peasant huts. In fact, where could it be made manifest as a whole?—this is an ocean, a real ocean, after all! But if this consciousness someday does manifest itself, or only begins to do so, then what a sudden shock it will be for the educated gentleman of Petersburg! It's true that he'll deny it for a long time and won't believe his five senses; this little European creature won't give in for a long time—some of them will die without giving in. But, so as to avoid the great misunderstandings of the future, how useful it would be, I repeat, if Petersburg, even in the person of her best representatives, were to tone down even a bit her haughty view of Russia! Just a bit more astuteness and understanding, a bit more humility before the great Russian land, before this broad ocean—that's what we need. And what a sound first step this would be toward "making the roots healthy. . . . "

"But wait," someone will interrupt. "All this is still only old, worn-out Slavophile ravings; there's nothing substantial in it at all; it's something spiritual, even. But what does this 'making the roots healthy' mean? You still haven't explained that. And what are these roots? What do you mean by this?"

"You're right, gentlemen, absolutely right; let's begin with the 'roots.'"

4. The First Root. Instead of an Authoritative Financial Tone I Lapse into Old Words. The Broad Ocean. The Longing for Truth and the Necessity for Serenity, So Useful in Financial Matters

The first root, the first and most essential root that we must certainly make healthy is, without a doubt, those same Russian People, that same broad ocean I just spoke about. I'm speaking now of our simple Russian People, the common man and peasant, the source of tax money, the calloused working hands, the broad ocean. Oh, how can I fail to know what our government has done and is continually doing for them in the current reign, beginning with their liberation from serfdom? Yes, the government is concerned about their needs, their education, their health; sometimes it even forgives their arrears—in short, it is concerned and does a good deal; how could one not know that? But that's not what I want to talk about: I have in mind only the spiritual recuperation of this great root, which is the beginning of everything else. Yes, it is spiritually sick, but not mortally sick: the main, sturdy core of their soul is healthy, yet the illness is a severe one. What sort of illness is it, and what is it called? That's difficult to express in a single word. One could put it this way: "the unsatisfied longing for truth." The People are continually seeking the truth, some outlet to it, and they cannot find it. I would like to limit myself here only to the financial aspect of this illness, but I have to add a few well-worn words as well. From the very time of their liberation from serfdom, a need and a longing for something new appeared among the People; this was a longing for something unlike the past, a longing for truth, but now for the full truth, for their complete civic resurrection into a new life after their great liberation. There came an urge for a new word; there began a ferment of new feelings; there began a profound belief in a new order. After the initial period of mediators of the first instance, there suddenly ensued something other than what the People had anticipated. There ensued an order in which the People were eager to put their trust but which they understood only poorly. They could not understand it; they felt they were losing their way in it and so could not put their trust in it. It was something external, something that seemed alien to them and their very own.

There's no point ruminating on this topic that has already been rehashed long ago: others will tell this story better than I—read about it in the magazine *Rus*, for instance. Then there appeared wanton drunkenness; it was as if a sea of drunkenness washed over Russia, and even though this continues to wreak havoc even now, the People, sodden with drink though they may be, have not lost their longing for something new, for the truth, for a new truth, for a complete truth. And never, perhaps, have they been more vulnerable to certain influences and tendencies and less protected from them than at present. Take even something like the *Stunde* and look at its success among the People: what does that signify? A quest for truth and a restless desire for it. And it is precisely a restless desire; the People are now morally "restive." I am even convinced that if nihilist propaganda has not yet managed to make inroads among the People, it is entirely due to the lack of ability, stupidity, and lack of preparation of the propagandists, who do not even know how to approach the People. Otherwise, given even the slightest ability, they would have found their way to the People just as the *Stunde* has found its way. Oh, we must take care of the

People. It is said: "The time will come when ye shall be told: here is Christ, or yonder. Do not believe it." Even now it seems that something of this sort is happening, and not only among the People but even, perhaps, among our upper strata. Aren't the People disturbed by various strange rumors of partitions of land and allotments, for instance, and of some new "golden charters?" Not long ago announcements were made in churches that they were not to believe these things, that this would not happen; yet—can you believe it?—in some places precisely after these announcements the idea grew even stronger that this would come to pass: "It's not for nothing they made those announcements; and if they've started announcing, then something's going to happen." That's what they began to say right after the announcements, in some places at least. I know of one specific instance: some peasants were buying land from a neighboring landowner and had almost agreed on a price, but after this announcement they pulled back: "We'll get it anyway, without paying." They just chuckle and wait. I'm speaking here only of rumors, about the readiness with which they are heeded, which testifies specifically to the moral restlessness of the People. And here is what is most important: our People are alone, in isolation; they have been abandoned entirely to their own resources, and no one gives them any spiritual support. There is the zemstvo, but the zemstvo are "the authorities." There are the courts, but they too are "authorities"; there is, finally, the peasant commune, but now even that seems to be moving toward becoming a kind of authority. The newspapers are full of accounts of how the People elect their deputies—in the presence of "the authorities," of some government official or other—and of the results. But there are thousands of such stories, and I won't recount them all. Some simple fellow looks around him and suddenly concludes that it's only the kulak and the bloodsucker who lives well, that everything is being done for them, it would seem. "So I'll become a bloodsucker too," he thinks. And he does. Another fellow, who's a bit more timid, simply takes to drink, not because his poverty has gotten the best of him but because he's been sickened by his lack of rights.

What's to be done here? It's fate. The People have been given an administration, after all, and there are authorities in place; it would seem that the problem is solved, yet for some reason it is quite the opposite. Just now someone has calculated that at this very moment the People have nearly twenty government officials standing over them, protecting and looking after them. Even without that, everybody is the poor man's boss, and here are twenty more of them, specially appointed! The peasant has about as much freedom of movement as a fly caught on a plate of molasses. And this is harmful not only from the moral but also from the financial point of view—such lack of freedom of movement, I mean. But the main thing is that the People are alone, with no one to advise them. They have only God and the tsar; it is these two mighty hopes that provide their support. But the other advisers all pass them by without influencing them at all. The entire progressive intelligentsia, for instance, pass by the People completely, for although there are many sensible people among our intelligentsia, there are few who have any understanding of the Russian People. We know only how to reject and continually complain: "Why doesn't society 'come to life,' and why can't we manage to revive it? What's the problem here?"

Society cannot be revived because you aren't relying on the People and because the People are not at one with you in spirit and are alien to you. You seem to think that you are some upper realm, above the People, directing the Russian land, and that it was for you—at least according to what you yourselves write and say—that Peter the Great, who transformed Russia, left the People enserfed so that they could serve you through their labor and thus give you the means to acquire a European education. And so, over two centuries, you have become educated, while the People have drawn away from you, and you from them. "But," you will say, "are we not the ones who agonize over the People; are we not the ones who write so much about them; are we not the ones who summon them to education?" Indeed, you do all these things, but for some reason the Russian People are convinced that it is not they over whom you agonize but someone else, some people who have settled into your brains and who are unlike the Russian People, whom you actually despise. This scornful attitude of some of you toward the People is even quite unconscious and, one can say, positively involuntary. It is a remnant of serfdom. It began from the time our People were killed off, in a civic sense, for the sake of your European enlightenment, and it certainly remains within you even now, when the People have come to life. And, you know, it is now even impossible to come together with the People unless some miracle occurs in the Russian land. Here I shall repeat my own very old words: the overwhelming majority of the Russian People are Orthodox and live completely by the idea of Orthodoxy, although they do not understand this idea in a fully responsible and scientific sense. *In essence* there is nothing at all in our People apart from this "idea," and everything stems from it alone; at least this is what our People desire, with all their hearts and with deep conviction. They want everything they have and are given to stem from this idea alone. And this despite the fact that many things happening among the People and taken to the point of absurdity come not from this idea but from things that are foul, vile, criminal, barbaric, and sinful. But though the criminal and the barbarian do commit sins, they still pray to God, in the higher moments of their spiritual lives, that their sins and abominations may cease and that everything may derive from their beloved "idea" once more. I know that our educated people have laughed at me: they do not even want to admit the existence of "that idea" among the People, pointing to their sins, their abominations (for which they themselves, who oppressed the People for two centuries, are responsible); they point to their prejudices, to the People's supposed indifference to religion, and some of them even imagine that the Russian People are atheists, pure and simple. Their great error lies in the fact that they do not recognize the existence of the church among the Russian People. I am speaking now not about church buildings and not about sermons; I am speaking about our Russian "socialism" (and however strange it may seem, I am taking this word, which is quite the opposite of all that the church represents, to explain my idea), whose purpose and final outcome is the establishment of the universal church on earth, insofar as the earth is capable of containing it. I am speaking of the ceaseless longing, which has always been inherent in the Russian People, for a great, general, universal union of fellowship in the name of Christ. And if this union does not yet exist, if the church has not yet been fully established—not merely in prayers alone, but in fact—then the instinct for this church and the ceaseless longing for it—sometimes even quite unconscious—is still certainly to be found in the hearts of the millions of our People. It is not in communism, not in mechanical forms that we find the socialism of the Russian People: they believe that salvation is ultimately to be found only in *worldwide union in the name of Christ.* That is our Russian socialism! So, you European gentlemen, you are laughing at the presence of this higher, unifying, "ecclesiastical" idea among the Russian People.

Oh, the People have many other "ideas" as well, ideas you will never accept and that you, with your European outlook, regard as coming directly from the Tatars. At this point I am not going to mention those other ideas, whose truth you utterly fail to understand, although they are extraordinarily important. At this point I am speaking only of this principal idea of our People, about their hope for a future universal church which, by the grace of God, is being established within them. And here one may set down a formula: he who does not understand our People's Orthodoxy and its final goals will never understand our People themselves. Moreover, such a person cannot even love the Russian People (and yet many of them, these Europeans of ours, have pure hearts, and long for justice, long to love), but will love them only in the form in which he would like to see them and as he imagines them to be. And since the People will never be transformed in the way our wise men would like but will remain themselves, one can foresee in the future an inevitable and dangerous collision. For the aforementioned formula can also be reversed, i.e., that the People will never accept such a Russian European as one of their own: "First love the things I hold sacred; revere the things I revere; and then you shall be just as I am, my brother, despite the fact that you are dressed differently, that you are a gentleman, that you are one of the bosses, and even that sometimes you don't know how to express yourself properly in Russian"—that is what the People will tell you, for our People have a broad outlook and are intelligent. Sometimes they will honor and love a good person who does not believe in the things they hold sacred; they will listen to such a person, if he is intelligent, will thank him for his advice and follow that advice. The Russian People can live on good terms with anyone, for they have seen many a thing, have taken note of much, and have remembered much from their long, difficult life over the past two centuries. (But you won't even agree with my statement that they have learned and remembered much, and so have an awareness of things, and so are by no means just an inert mass and a source of tax money, as you have defined them.) But to live on good terms with a person, and even to live lovingly with a person—that is one thing, but to acknowledge that person as one of *their own*—that is something altogether different. And without such acknowledgment there will be no union.

I want merely to express that the forces that estrange us from the People are extremely strong and that the People have been left alone, in their great isolation, and that apart from their tsar, in whom they believe unshakeably, they now cannot see and cannot hope for support from anyone anywhere. They would be glad for a glimpse of some support, but it is difficult to find any. And yet—what an awesome, constructive, blessed, and new—entirely new—force would appear in Holy Russia with the union of the educated classes and the People! I mean a spiritual union. Oh, gentlemen, you ministers of finance, you would then not be drawing up the kind of annual budgets you are drawing up today! Rivers of milk would flow in our kingdom; all your ideals would be realized at once! "Indeed, but how is this to be done, and does the blame really lie in our European enlightenment?" Oh, it's not enlightenment at all and, in truth, we have no enlightenment and have never had any; yet the disunity still remains and really did come about as if in the name of European enlightenment, which we do not have. But genuine enlightenment is not to blame here. I even think that had we had genuine, real enlightenment, there would have been no disunity among us at all, because it is enlightenment that the People are longing for. But when we became enlightened we flew away from our People, off to the moon, and we lost our way back. So how are we, who have flown away, to assume to responsibility for bringing health to the People? What can we do so that the People's spirit, which everywhere is languishing and disturbed, takes heart and is placated? Even capital itself and its movement seek a *moral* serenity, and without moral serenity capital either hides itself or remains unproductive. What can we do so that the People's spirit may be placated with truth, with perceiving the truth? Perhaps the truth exists even now, but it is necessary that the People believe it. How are we to instill in their souls the idea that truth exists in the Russian land and that its banner flies high? What can we do, for instance, to ensure that the People trust their own courts, believe that they represent their interests, and acknowledge them as flesh of their flesh and bone of their bone? Oh, I am not getting into details—how could I?—and even to begin to explain and describe it all would, I think, create more books "than even the world itself could contain." But even if the People could be assured of truth in the future so that they could fully believe it is coming for certain, if the fly could crawl even a little way out of the plate of molasses, even then a great thing of inestimable value would have been achieved. I shall say plainly that the whole trouble lies in the long-standing alienation of our upper, educated class from the lower class, our People. How, then, can the upper stratum be reconciled with the broad ocean, and how can the broad ocean be calmed so that no great disturbance arise within it?

5. Let Them Speak First, and for the Moment Let Us Stand Aside Simply to Acquire Some Good Sense

For this there are magic words—namely, "Trust them." Yes, we can trust our People, for they are worthy of trust. Summon those gray peasant coats and ask them what they lack and what they need and they will tell you the truth, and all of us, for the first time, perhaps, will hear the real truth. And there need be no great ceremony or assemblies; the People can be asked where they are, in their rural districts and peasant huts. For our People, asked individually, will say exactly the same thing as they would were they gathered together, for they are one. When they are dispersed they are one, and when they are together they are one, for their spirit is one. Each locality would only add something of its local distinctiveness, but on the whole and in general the result would be something harmonious and unified. We need only ensure that for the moment only the peasant express his views, only the real, dyed-in-the-wool peasant. It's true that along with the peasant the kulak and the bloodsucker would slip in, but even they are peasants, after all, and in such an important matter even the kulak and the bloodsucker will not betray the land and will say a true word—such is the quality of our People.

So how is this to be done? Oh, those who have power can decide that better than I; for my part, I believe only in one thing—that no special formulas are needed here. Our People don't bother much about forms, particularly about ready-made, foreign ones, which they don't need at all, for that's not what's on their minds; they have never been concerned about forms and never will be, because they have a different view of this matter, one that is distinct and entirely their own. Yes, in this instance our People—the sort of People ours are—can be seen as fully worthy of trust. For who has not seen them around the tsar, near the tsar, in his presence? They are the tsar's children, his own real, true children, and the tsar is their father. Is it only a phrase, only a sound, only an expression when we say "the tsar is their father?" He who thinks that understands nothing of Russia! No, there is an idea here, a profound and most original idea; here we have an organism, vital and powerful, the organism of the People merged with their tsar as one. This idea is a force. This force has been created over the centuries, especially over the last two centuries that have been terrible for the People, centuries that we so exalt for our European enlightenment, having forgotten that this enlightenment was provided for us two centuries ago by the bondage of serfdom and the Calvary of the Russian People who have been serving us. And so the People awaited their liberator, and he came—why, then, are they not his real, true children? For the People the tsar is not an external power, not the power of some conqueror (as happened, for instance, with the dynasties of the former French kings) but a power of all the People, an all-unifying power the People themselves desired, one they have nurtured in their hearts and have come to love, one for which they have suffered, because it was only through that power they expected their deliverance from the land of Egypt. For the People the tsar is the incarnation of themselves, of their whole idea, their hopes and their beliefs. These hopes were realized in such a monumental fashion only so recently; how, then, can the People give up their further hopes? How, rather, can they not be strengthened and made more steadfast, since after the peasant reform the tsar has become their father, not merely as an idea and not merely as a hope, but in reality. The People's attitude toward the tsar as their father is the genuine, adamantine foundation on which every reform in Russia can and will be based. One can say that in Russia we have no other constructing, preserving, and guiding power apart from this organic, vital link between the People and their tsar, and everything else we have derives from it.

For instance, how could anyone have imagined undertaking that same peasant reform had they not known and believed beforehand that the tsar was the father of the People and that it was precisely the People's faith in the tsar as their father that would save everything, protect everything, and avert a calamity? Alas, it is a poor economist-reformer who overlooks the actual and truly vital forces of the People because of some prejudices and alien beliefs. Indeed, we are not with the People and cannot understand them, because even though we may know and understand their attitude toward the tsar, we cannot fully accept the principal and essential point in our destiny: that the Russian People's attitude toward their tsar is the most distinctive point differentiating them from all the other peoples of Europe and the entire world; that this is not only some temporary, passing thing in Russia; that it is not a sign of the childlike nature of our People or a stage in their growth, and so on, as some wise man might conclude, but an age-old, perpetual fact, and it will never—or at least for a very, very long time—change. And so, considering this (and even this alone), can you not see that our People are distinct from all other peoples and have their own special idea? Is it not clear, rather, that our People bear within them the organic embryo of an idea distinct from all others in the world? This idea holds such great power for us that it is bound to influence the whole future course of our history; and since it is distinct from anything encountered anywhere else, then our history *cannot be like the history of other European peoples,* and even less can it be a slavish copy of someone else's history. Now this is just what our wise men do not understand; they believe that everything in Russia will be refashioned into a Europe with no distinctive features of its own, and they hate such distinctive features. Such thinking, of course, might even lead to a catastrophe. Here's the first example to show you that all our most fundamental things are different from those anywhere in Europe: liberty (in our future, when we have lived through our period of pseudo Europeanism, this will certainly be the case)—civic liberty can be established in Russia on a most extensive scale, more extensive than anywhere else in the world, in Europe, or even in North America, and it will be built precisely on this same adamantine foundation. It will not be based on some writing on a piece of paper but will be built exclusively on the childlike love of the People for the tsar as for a father, for children may be permitted many things that are unthinkable among other nations where relationships are based on contract; children can be entrusted with so much and permitted to do things unheard of anywhere else, for children will not betray their own father and, as children, will lovingly accept from him any correction of their errors and misdeeds.

And so, are we to refuse to trust such a People? Let them tell us themselves of their needs; let them tell us the full truth about themselves. But, I'll repeat, first let them tell us on their own; we, "the People's intelligentsia," shall stand meekly aside for the moment and at first merely look on while they speak and we listen. Oh, it's not for any political purposes that I would suggest our intelligentsia be kept aside for a time—please don't attribute such motives to me; but I would suggest this be done, if you'll pardon me, for purely *pedagogical* purposes. Indeed, let us for the moment stand aside and listen how clearly and sensibly the People will tell us their truth, with no help from us at all; and where their cause—their real cause—is concerned, they will hit the mark exactly and will not offend us, should we be mentioned. Let us stand aside and learn from the People how the truth must be told. And while we are at it, let us also learn the People's humility, their businesslike approach, the seriousness and down-to-earth nature of their mind. You may say: "But you yourself have just been saying how ready the People are to listen to ridiculous rumors—what sort of wisdom can we expect from them?" True enough, but rumors are one thing, while joining together in a common cause is something else. There will be a single whole, and the influence of the whole will bring reason. Yes, this truly will be a school for all of us, and a most productive school. When we see such a serious, businesslike attitude among the People we shall be taken aback and, of course, there will be some among us who will not believe their own eyes; but there will be very few such people, for all who are really sincere, all who genuinely long for the truth and, above all, for a genuine cause for the common good—all such people will join their voices with the wise expressions of the People; but all those who are insincere will at once reveal themselves and all their inner content. And if there should remain some sincere ones who even then do not put their trust in the People, they will be the old believers and doctrinaires of the forties and fifties, old, incorrigible children, and they will be merely ridiculous and harmless. But everyone else, for the first time, will have their eyes cleared and their understanding purified. This action might bear remarkably important consequences, for . . . for it is here, in this very form, perhaps, that it is possible to make a beginning and take a first step toward the spiritual bonding of our entire educated class, which has looked down so haughtily on the People, and our People themselves. I am speaking merely of a spiritual bonding—that is all we need, for it will be a tremendous help for everything else; everything will be born anew; it will provide a new idea.

It is our radiant and fresh young generation, I think, that will be the first to give up their hearts to the People and will be the first to understand them spiritually. My hopes rest above all on the young generation because they are the ones among us who also suffer in "seeking the truth" and whose hearts ache for it; and therefore they are most akin to the People and will at once understand that the People are also seeking the truth. And once they get to know the People better they will cast aside that extremist nonsense that nearly captured so many of them who imagined that they had found the truth in extremist European doctrines. Oh, I believe that I'm not fantasizing and not exaggerating the beneficial consequences that could come from such a fine thing. Haughtiness would disappear and respect for the land would be born. An entirely new idea would suddenly enter our souls and would illuminate everything within them that hitherto had been in darkness; its light would expose the lies and drive them out. And who knows, perhaps this would be the beginning of a reform whose significance might be even greater than that of the peasant reform: here there would also be a "liberation," a liberation of our minds and our hearts from the kind of serfdom in which Europe held us for two whole centuries, in the same way that we held the peasant, our erstwhile slave. And if this second reform could begin and be completed, it would be merely the consequence of the first great reform at the beginning of the reign. For it was then that the wall that for two centuries had separated the People from the intelligentsia collapsed physically, while now this wall would collapse spiritually.

What is greater, what can be more beneficial for Russia than this spiritual bonding of classes? For the first time kith would come to learn of their kin. Those who, until now, have been ashamed of our People as barbarians retarding our development would be ashamed of their former shame; they would humble themselves before many things and would revere many things they had formerly not revered and had despised. And when the People give their answer, when they give a full account of themselves and their humble word has been uttered, then try asking our intelligentsia their opinion of what the People have said, and you will at once see the consequences. Oh, then their word will also be beneficial, for they are educated people, after all, and the last word belongs to them. But the example of the People, who said their word first in any case, would save us from many slips and from much foolishness were we to speak our word before the People did. And you will see that our intelligentsia will then say nothing that contradicts what the People have said; they will merely put their truth into a scientific form and develop it to the full breadth of their education, for they still have science, or at least the rudiments of it, and the People are terribly in need of science. And if someone from the intelligentsia did want to contradict the People, if there were some disagreements with our People's basic principles, then they would still not venture to stand up strongly against the People's spirit—that's to say, against the People's views on the matter; that is what is important, and it is very important.

Indeed, it's quite possible that with this very step we would begin to have spiritual serenity. There would be hope—general hope, not divided, and our goals would reveal themselves to us clearly. And this is very important, because all our conscious strength, all our educated people either have no idea or only a very shaky and confused idea of what our goals are and what they can be in the future—I mean national, state goals. That is a very weak point among us, particularly now, at the present moment. This confusion, this lack of knowledge is, without a doubt, the source of great distress and lack of order; that is the case now, and it will be incomparably worse in the future. All this could be explained or illuminated, or at least some initial indication could be given of how it is to be illuminated and explained; we could learn something. . . . However, that's enough on this topic; I expressed myself as best I could. If I could not express myself well enough, not everything may be clear, and if so, the fault is mine; but what is understood should be taken in an benign and peaceful spirit. I simply would like it understood impartially that I am for the People above all, for their soul, for their great strength, whose full extent and greatness none of us yet knows; and above all I hold as sacrosanct their mission of salvation, their great preserving and creating spirit; and I long for but one thing: that everyone might perceive this. And as soon as they do perceive it, they will at once begin to comprehend everything else.

And why should all this be merely a dream? I'm not speaking about the whole immensity of the task, after all. I'm speaking only of the peasant, of his own immediate affairs that concern only him. Does he not have concerns that are particularly and exclusively his own, concerns we should be aware of when it comes to taking the initiative, so to speak, and as a preface to any subsequent reform which might be much more extensive? Yet great benefits would come from this: we would have facts; we would learn the truth about many things; we would gain valuable material that would preserve many of us from unrealistic hopes, distortions along Western lines, and exaggerations. And the most important thing is—and I repeat this once more—that we would have a proper tone and spirit; we would have that very spirit in which alone it is possible to achieve anything further and more extensive. It is as if there were a seal upon this matter, a national and profoundly conservative seal. In the future no one will be able to avoid this seal, not even the most speculative minds; and even these will succumb and voluntarily accept it.

2

1. A Witty Bureaucrat. His Opinion of Our Liberals and Europeans

But having finished my first chapter, I shall now break off my article on finance since I feel that what I'm writing is very dull. But I'm breaking off only for a time. I would still like to say something about the other roots and basic elements which, it seems to me, could be made healthy. I'm also ending my article because I couldn't manage to fit the whole thing into the thirty-two pages of my *Diary* and so, like it or not, would have to put off some of it to subsequent issues....

"There's no point in that; you needn't bother to write any more, even in subsequent issues," some fussy voices interrupt (I knew I'd be hearing those voices). "None of this is about finances, it's just . . . self indulgence. None of it is realistic" (although I don't see why it isn't); "it's all some sort of mysticism, and there's nothing essential in it, nothing that deals with immediate problems! Give us a story in your subsequent issues."

Strange voices these! You see, I am specifically arguing that we have to turn aside from many things we now see as essential and immediate and create for ourselves a different set of essential and immediate problems, ones even much more actual than those in which we've now become involved and are sticking—if you'll excuse the expression—like a fly in molasses. That was my whole idea. I mean specifically that we have to turn our heads and our eyes in another direction altogether—that's my idea. Those in power could start such a thing, and in that respect my fancies are not that fanciful at all, since if the authorities were to begin it, we could achieve a good deal even now. It is principles—some of our principles—that must be changed completely, the flies must be pulled out of the molasses and set free. This idea isn't a popular one, I suppose: we've long grown accustomed to our inability to move, and we've even begun to taste the sweetness of sitting in molasses.

It's true that I've gone off the topic again, and I might be reminded at this point that, despite all I've written so far, I still haven't managed to explain just what contemporary and immediate things I have in mind and just what immediate things I would prefer in the future. Now this is just what I want to devote my energies to explaining in future issues of my *Diary*. But to finish things now, let me tell you of one encounter I had with a rather witty bureaucrat who told me one rather interesting thing about some of those very principles relating to changes in our contemporary "immediate problems." In a certain gathering the talk turned to financial matters and the economy, but specifically to frugality in respect of our financial resources, building up those resources, and using them so that not a single kopeck should be lost or spent extravagantly. People are always talking about our economy in that respect now, and in fact the government as well is constantly occupied with the same thing. Controls have been set up, and every year there are reductions in the civil service. Lately there has also even been talk of cuts to the army; the newspapers have suggested specific figures, namely fifty thousand troops, while others have assured us our army could be cut by half: no harm would come of it, they said. That might be all very well, yet one can't help thinking: suppose we do cut the army by, say, fifty thousand in the first instance; still, the money saved would slip through our fingers once more, here and there—for the needs of the state, of course, but for needs which, perhaps, don't merit such a radical sacrifice. The fifty thousand troops cut will never be restored, or only with great effort, because once we have removed them they will be difficult to replace; but we really and truly need an army, especially now, when everyone's nursing a grudge against us. It's dangerous to set off on such a road, at least *now*, given the contemporary, immediate situation that gives rise to our expenditures. We could only be assured that this precious money was really being spent on a worthy cause if we were to embark, for instance, on an irrevocable, severe, gloomy policy of economizing such as Peter the Great might have instituted had he decided to cut expenditures. But are we capable of this, given the "crying" needs of the current reality in which we have become so enmeshed? I might note that were we to do this, or begin it, it would be one of the first steps toward turning away from our former, fantastic "immediate problems" toward something new, actual and appropriate. We quite often make cuts in the civil service, yet the result is that the number of government employees seems somehow to go on increasing. Are we capable of making the kind of cut that would at once reduce every forty functionaries to, say, four? That four functionaries can quite often accomplish the same as forty—that, of course, is beyond anyone's doubt, especially if official paperwork were to be cut down and present bureaucratic methods radically reformed. It was just such a topic that our group began discussing. Someone observed that this would mean a major shake-up. Others objected that we have had far more fundamental reforms than this one. Still others added that the new functionaries—meaning the four who had replaced the forty—could even have their salaries tripled, and that they would work very happily and not complain a bit. But if we were to triple their salaries and spend as much on those four as we now do for twelve, even so we would be reducing our expenditures by almost three-quarters.

At this point my bureaucrat interrupted me. I should note first that, to my great astonishment, even he made no objection whatever to the possibility of replacing forty functionaries by four, agreeing, apparently, that things would get done even with four people; and so he did not see this as an impossibility. But he did object to something else, namely to the principle, to the erroneousness and criminality of the principle that had been stated. I am not citing his objections word for word, and have even edited them extensively. I repeat: I am citing them specifically because his ideas seemed interesting in their fashion and even contained an almost piquant idea. Of course, he didn't consider it worthwhile replying to me in detail, since I'm not a specialist in such matters and "understand little" (something which, of course, I'm quick to admit); still, he hoped that I would understand the principle.

"Cutting the number of functionaries from forty to four," he began sternly and with feeling, "not only fails to help the cause but in essence is even harmful, despite the fact that state expenditures would be significantly reduced. A reduction of that scale is harmful and impossible, but so is one even from forty to thirty-eight, and this is why: because in so doing you would be making a vicious attack on a fundamental principle. For almost two hundred years now, since the time of Peter the Great himself, we, the bureaucrats, have constituted *everything* within the state; in essence, it is we who are the state and are *everything*—the rest is merely excess baggage. At least this was so until recent times, until the liberation of the peasants. All the former elective offices—the nobility's, for instance—automatically took on our spirit and sense simply by force of gravity, so to say. And we weren't the least troubled when we saw this because the principle set forth two hundred years ago was in no way violated. But after the peasant reform something new really began to be felt: self-government appeared, the zemstvo, and so on. . . . It's clear now that all these new things automatically and immediately began to take on our image, our body and soul, and to be embodied in our form. And it certainly wasn't our pressure that caused this (that's a mistaken notion)—it happened strictly of itself, since it's difficult to drop centuries-old habits and, perhaps, that's as it should be, particularly in such a great and fundamental national matter. You may not believe me, but if you're able truly to analyze the matter, you'll understand what I mean. For what are we? We are *everything*, *everything*, and to this day we continue to be everything; and, once again, it's happened without much effort on our part, without any particular strain; it's happened automatically, through the natural course of events. People have long complained that all we do is office work, nothing living, only dead paperwork, and that Russia has outgrown this sort of thing. Perhaps she has, but for the moment we are still the only ones who support her, build her up, and keep her from falling to pieces! For what you call bureaucratic deadweight—meaning we ourselves, as an institution, and all the things we do—is, to use a simile, the skeleton in a living organism. If the skeleton is taken apart, if the bones are scattered, the living body will perish as well. Our work may be done in a lifeless way, to be sure, yet it proceeds by a system, a principle, a great principle, if I may say so. The work may be done in tired, bureaucratic fashion; it may even be done badly and incompletely, yet in one way or another it is done; and the most important thing is that everything still stands and does not collapse—that's precisely the main point, that it still hasn't collapsed.

"I agree and am ready to concede to you that, perhaps, we aren't *everything*, in fact—oh, we're clever enough to realize that we don't constitute everything in Russia, these days in particular; and so

I'll grant that we are not everything, yet we are still *something*, meaning something real and actually existing, although, of course, we may be partly lacking a body. Now, tell me, what do you have? What would you replace us with so that we could depart knowing that you could also provide *something* to keep it all from collapsing? You see, all those self-governments and zemstvos of yours are still nothing more than the proverbial birds in the bush: they might be beautiful, but you don't have one in your hand yet. And therefore, no matter how lovely they may be, they don't mean a thing; we, on the other hand, are not lovely; you're fed up with us, yet we are *something* and aren't meaningless. You keep blaming us for the birds in the bush: why is it, you say, that we still haven't caught one? You say that it's our fault, that we are supposedly trying to shape those beautiful birds to our image and spirit. Now, it would be a very fine thing if it really were only our fault, since we could thereby prove that we stand for a centuries-old, fundamental, and most noble principle and can transform a useless nonentity into a useful something. But believe me, it's not our fault at all, or at least it's only a very little fault of ours; the fact is that the beautiful birds themselves can't make up their minds and don't know what they'll finally be: will they be like us, or will they be something independent? They're hesitating; they have no faith in themselves and are almost at a loss. I assure you that they came to us of their own free will and not because of our pressure. It turns out that we are, so to say, like a natural magnet to which everything even now is still drawn and will be drawn for a long time to come.

"You're still not convinced? You're amused? Well, I'm willing to make a bet for whatever you'd like: just try unfolding the wings of your beautiful little birds, give them full scope to fly; send your zemstvo a proper decree, in stern language and with a file number: 'Henceforth you are independent and no longer a bureaucratic bird in the bush.' Believe me, all of them, every single bird that's there, will start begging even more to come to us, and they'll end by becoming full-blooded bureaucrats, taking on our spirit and image and copying everything from us. Even the peasant deputy would ask to be admitted; that would flatter him immensely. Not for nothing have tastes been cultivated for two centuries. And now you want us—something solid and standing on its own feet—to be exchanged for this riddle, this charade, your beautiful birds in the bush? No, I think it's better to hold on to the one modest little bird in our hand. Better that we ourselves sort things out somehow, tidy things up, introduce something new and more progressive, so to speak, in keeping with the spirit of the age; and then, why, we may even become more virtuous. But we're not going to exchange our actual, real *something* for a mirage, for some suddenly dreamt dream, since there is nothing and no one to replace us, that's for certain! It's through inertia, so to say, that we resist being abolished. This inertia of ours is something precious because, to tell the truth, these days it's only thing holding everything together.

"And so cutting our staff even to thirty-eight from forty (never mind from forty to four) would be a most harmful and even immoral measure. You'd save a few pennies and destroy a principle. So go ahead and abolish or change our formula, if your conscience permits you to make such a threatening move: but don't you see that this would be a betrayal of all our Russian Europeanism and enlightenment? It would be a denial of the fact that we are also a state, that we are also Europeans; it would be a betrayal of Peter the Great! And, you know, your liberals (and ours, too, for that matter), who in the newspapers so zealously support the zemstvos against the bureaucracy, are essentially contradicting themselves. After all, the zemstvos and, indeed, all these new things set up in the spirit of populism, are those very same 'principles of the People,' or at least the rudimentary expression of those 'principles,' that our 'Russian party' (you may have heard that it was given that name in Berlin), which is so hated in Europe, is shouting about; these are the same 'principles' that our Russian liberalism and Europeanism so furiously deny and ridicule; they refuse even to acknowledge that these principles exist! Oh, liberalism truly fears those principles: what if they actually do exist and come to be realized? Why, that would be a real surprise! That means that all your Europeans are actually on our side, and we on theirs, and they should have understood this long ago and committed it to memory. If you like, we are not only at one with them, we are entirely one and the same thing: those Europeans of yours have our spirit within them; they even bear our very image, and that's the truth!

"Let me add just this: Europe—meaning Russian Europe, Europe and Russia—consists exclusively of us, and us alone. It is we; we are the incarnation of the entire formula of Russian Europeanism, and we contain it all within ourselves. We alone are its interpreters. And I can't understand why they shouldn't be given proper medals for their Europeanism when we are so flawlessly merging with them. They would be pleased to wear them, and they might even find us more attractive thereby. But we don't know how to do such things. And they abuse us—truly a case of kith not recognizing kin! So as to put an end to all your zemstvos and all these other innovations, let me tell you once and for all: no, sir! This is a lengthy matter, not a brief one. It requires its own culture beforehand, its own history—perhaps one that is also two centuries' long. Well, let's say a century, or even half a century, since we now live in the age of telegraphs and railways and all relationships are speeded up and made easier. Yet this is still a matter for half a century, it can't happen at once. 'At once,' 'right now'—these are nasty little Russian phrases. Nothing comes into being 'right now,' except for people like us. And such will be the case for a long time."

At this point my bureaucrat fell silent, with a proud and dignified air, and, you know, I didn't even argue with him because there really did seem to be a "something" in his words, a kind of melancholy truth that actually exists. Of course, inwardly I didn't agree with him. Besides, it is only people who are on their way out who speak in such a tone. But still, there was "something" in his words. . . .

2. Krylov's Old Fable about a Certain Pig

And so as to make an end to all this at last, let me cite a very fine little fable of Krylov which, probably, everyone has now forgotten, since what does our busy and frantic age have to do with Krylov? I couldn't help recalling this little fable when I began preparing my article on finances and how to make the roots healthy. It has a fine moral, but on another topic, about other roots. But that makes no difference, it's appropriate to us. Here's the fable:

One day beneath an ancient oak a boar
Was eating acorns; he ate his fill, and more,
Then fell asleep. He presently awoke
And, eyes still filled with sleep, began to poke
His snout among the roots to dig up more.
A raven sitting on a branch then said,
"You're damaging the oak; best use your head.
If you lay bare the roots you'll kill the tree."
The pig replied, "It's all the same to me;
It brings no benefit that I can see,

And if it dies, what does it really matter?
It's acorns that I want; they make me fatter."
"Ungrateful wretch!" the ancient oak then said,
"If you could only raise your head
Above the ground, you'd see
That acorns only grow on oaks like me."

Isn't that a good fable? Do we really want to be like this picture?

3. Geok-Tepe. What Does Asia Mean to Us?

Geok-Tepe has been taken; the Turkomans have been defeated, and although they have not yet been fully pacified, our victory is beyond doubt. Both society and the press have been jubilant. Yet it was not long ago that society, and the press as well, in part, were remarkably indifferent to this affair, particularly after General Lomakin's failure and at the beginning of the preparations for a second offensive. "Why do we have to go there? Why all this fuss about Asia? How much money it costs us, while we have famine, diphtheria, no schools, and so on." Yes, such opinions were common, and we heard them. Not everyone held this view—oh, not by any means; still, one has to admit that very many people of late began to take a hostile attitude toward our militant policy in Asia. It's true that lack of knowledge about the expedition undertaken contributed to this attitude. Only very recently did we have bits of news slipping in from foreign newspapers, and only toward the very end were Skobelev's dispatches printed all over Russia. Nevertheless, it is still difficult to say that our society has gained a clear awareness of our mission in Asia and of what, specifically, Asia means to us and could mean in the future. Indeed, speaking generally, our whole Russian Asia, including Siberia, still exists as a kind of appendage, as it were, in which our European Russia seems reluctant to take any interest. "We are Europe," is the notion, "so what business have we in Asia?" There were even some very harsh voices raised: "Never mind this Asia of ours, we can't manage to achieve any order and settle things properly even in Europe; and now we're getting mixed up in Asia. This Asia is something we don't need at all; if we could only get rid of her!" Even now we sometimes hear such views expressed by our wise men, coming from their great wisdom, of course.

Skobelev's victory will cause a furor all over Asia, even in her most isolated corners: "Here we have one more fierce and proud people, also belonging to the faithful, who have bowed down before the white tsar." But let there be a furor. Let the conviction grow among all these millions of people, to the very borders of India, and even within India, if you like, of the invincibility of the white tsar and the omnipotence of his sword. After General Lomakin's failure, doubt must have spread throughout Asia as to the invincibility of our sword, and Russian prestige was certainly shaken. That is why we cannot pause along this road. These peoples may have their own khans and emirs; in their minds and imaginations England, whose might amazes them, may stand as a threat; but the name of the white tsar should stand far above those of the khans and emirs, far above that of the empress of India, far above that of the caliph himself. He may be a caliph, but the white tsar is both a tsar and a caliph. That is the conviction that should take root! And it is taking root and growing every year, and it is essential to us, for it prepares them for the future.

"For what, and for what future? What need is there for some future annexation of Asia? What are we going to do there?"

There is a need because Russia is not only in Europe but in Asia as well; because the Russian is not only a European but an Asian as well. Moreover, we have more hopes in Asia, perhaps, than in Europe. Moreover, it is Asia, perhaps, that provides the main outlet for our future destiny!

I can anticipate the indignation with which some people will read this reactionary proposition of mine (but for me it is axiomatic). Yes, if there is one most important root we must make healthy, then it is precisely our view of Asia. We must cast aside this servile fear that Europe will call us Asiatic barbarians and say that we are more Asian than European. This shame that Europe will consider us Asians has been hanging over us for almost two centuries now. But the shame has become particularly strong in us during the present nineteenth century and has almost reached the point of panic, almost the kind of fear that the new words "metal and brimstone" once aroused in Moscow merchants' wives. This mistaken shame of ours, this mistaken view of ourselves as exclusively Europeans and not Asians (and we have never ceased to be the latter)—this shame and this mistaken view has cost us dearly, very dearly, over these two centuries, and we have paid for it by the loss of our spiritual independence, by the failures of our European policies, and, at last, by money—by God knows how much money we have spent proving to Europe that we are only Europeans and not Asians. But the jolt Peter the Great provided to push us into Europe, necessary and salutary as it was in the beginning, was still too powerful, and for this we cannot be blamed completely. And what didn't we do so that Europe would acknowledge us as *her own*, as Europeans, as Europeans and only Europeans and not Tatars! We were forever pestering Europe, forcing ourselves on her and meddling in her affairs, whether they were important or not. Sometimes we frightened her with our strength and sent her our armies "to save the kings"; sometimes we bowed down before Europe—which we shouldn't have done—and assured her that we had been created for nothing more than to serve her and make her happy. In 1812, having driven Napoleon out of our country, we did not make peace with him as a few perceptive Russians at the time wanted and advised us to do; instead, we advanced into Europe in a solid wall in order to please her by liberating her from the plunderer. This made a pretty picture, of course: on the one side was the despot and usurper, on the other the peacemaker and restorer. But our political fortune then lay not in some picture but in the fact that for the first time in his career, the usurper had been put in a position where he would have made a very solid, sincere, and lasting, perhaps permanent, peace with us. On the condition that we would not stand in his way in Europe, he would have given us the East; and the current Eastern Question of ours—the threat and the misfortune of our present and our future—would have been resolved long ago. The usurper himself admitted this later, and surely he was not lying, for he could have done nothing better than join us in an alliance so that we would have the East and he would have the West. And then he certainly would have been able to cope with the European peoples. They, in turn—even England—would have been much too weak to stand in our way in the East. Napoleon, perhaps, would have fallen later on, or his dynasty would have fallen after his death; but the East would still have been ours. (Then we would have had access to the sea, and we could have met even England at sea.)

But we gave all that away for the sake of a pretty picture. And what happened?—all these peoples we liberated immediately, before they had even finished off Napoleon, began looking at us with the most obvious malevolence and the most intense suspicion. At the congresses they all immediately united against us in a solid bloc, taking everything for themselves; and not only did they leave nothing for us, they even extracted certain obligations from us—voluntary ones, it's true, but which later proved to be very costly. And subsequently, despite the lesson we learned, what have we been doing for all the remaining years of the century and even to this very day? Was it not we who promoted the consolidation of the German states? Was it not we who provided them with power to the point where today they have become even stronger than we, perhaps? In fact, it's no exaggeration at all to say that we contributed to their growth and their strength. Was it not we who, in answer to their summons, went off to quell their civil strife? Was it not we who protected their rear when they were faced with disaster? And now, on the other hand, was it not they who threatened our rear when we were faced with disaster, or who threatened to invade our rear when we were faced with another disaster? The result is that now everyone in Europe, every group and tribe over there, has long been secretly nursing malice against us, ready to bring it into the open at the first conflict. So what have we gained by serving Europe in so many ways? Only her hatred! We've played the role of Repetilov who, in pursuit of fortune, "Got a fig for his dowry and no promotion."

But why is there this hatred for us? Why can't they all trust us, once and for all, believe that we are harmless, believe that we are their friends and servants—good servants—and that our entire mission in Europe is to serve Europe and its welfare? (Because is that not so? Is that not just what we have been doing through the entire century? Did we really accomplish anything for ourselves? Did we acquire anything for ourselves? Everything went to Europe!) No, they cannot put their trust in us! The main reason is that they are absolutely unable acknowledge us as *their own*.

They will never ever believe that we can truly participate, on an equal basis with them, in the future destinies of their civilizations. They have regarded us as alien to their civilization, as newcomers and impostors. They regard us as thieves who have stolen enlightenment from them, who are masquerading in their clothes. The Turks and Semites are closer to them in spirit than we Aryans. There is one outstanding reason for this: the idea we bear to humanity is entirely different from theirs—that's the reason! And this despite the fact that our "Russian Europeans" assure Europe with all their might that we do not have any idea and cannot have one in the future, that Russia isn't even capable of having an idea but can only copy, that all we ever will do is copy, and that we are certainly not Asians, not barbarians, but just the same as they—Europeans. But this time, at least, Europe didn't believe our Russian Europeans. In this case, rather, Europe's views coincided with those of our Slavophiles, even though Europe knows nothing about the Slavophiles and may only have heard some mere mention of them. There is a coincidence specifically, in that, like the Slavophiles, Europe also believes that we do have our own "idea," distinctive and non-European, that Russia can and is capable of having an idea. Of course, Europe still knows nothing of the essence of this idea of ours, since if she did know she would at once be pacified and even heartened. But she will certainly learn some day, and specifically when the most critical moment of her destiny arrives. But now she does not believe; recognizing that we have an idea, she fears it. And finally, we inspire disgust in her, even on a personal level, although at times she treats us politely. For example, the Europeans are prepared to admit that Russian science can now boast a few noteworthy figures and that it has produced a few good works which have been of some benefit to their European science. But Europe now will certainly not believe that here in Russia we can produce not merely workers in science (as talented as they may be) but geniuses as well, people like Bacon, Kant, and Aristotle, who can be leaders of humanity. That they will never believe, since they do not believe in our civilization and do not know the idea of our future. In actual fact, they are right, since we surely will have no Bacon, no Newton, no Aristotle until we set off on our own road and become spiritually independent. It's the same everywhere else—in our arts and in our industry: Europe is ready to praise us, pat us on the head, but will not acknowledge us as her own, secretly despises us, and openly considers us as people beneath her, as a lower species; and at times we inspire such disgust in them, real disgust, especially when we throw ourselves on them in a brotherly embrace.

But it's hard for us to turn away from our window on Europe; it's a matter of destiny here. Yet Asia might truly serve as an outlet to our future—this I shout out once more! And if, even in part, we could accept this idea and make it our own—oh, then what a root could be made healthy! Asia—our Asiatic Russia—why, this is also our ailing root that must not merely be refreshed but completely restored and reformed! A principle, a new principle, a new view on the matter—this is what we need!

4. Questions and Answers

"But why, why!"—I hear irritated voices asking. "Even now our affairs in Asia continually demand troops and unproductive expenditures. Do they have any industry there? What goods to they have, and where will you find people to buy our goods? And now you're suggesting that we, for reasons unknown, turn away from Europe forever!"

"Not forever," I continue to insist, "but temporarily, and not completely; we wouldn't be able to turn away entirely, no matter how hard we tried. We can't abandon Europe entirely, nor do we need to. It's 'the land of holy miracles,' and that was said by the most ardent Slavophile. Europe is also our mother, just as Russia is; she is our second mother; we have taken much from her, and we will take still more; we don't wish to be ungrateful to her. At the Pushkin celebration in Moscow last year I tried to say a word or two about our the Russian People's future great mission in Europe (in which I believe), and everyone heaped mud and abuse on me, even some of those who embraced me at the time because of what I had said, just as if I had done some vile, disgusting thing in expressing my opinion.

"But perhaps my word will not be forgotten. However, that's enough about it now. Yet we still have a right to be concerned about our reeducation and our exodus from the land of Egypt. For it is we who have created from Europe a kind of spiritual Egypt for ourselves."

"Come now," someone will interrupt, "how can Asia help us become independent? We'll just fall into an Asiatic slumber there and won't become independent!"

"But you see," I continue, "when we turn to Asia, with our new view of her, something of the same sort may happen to us as happened to Europe when America was discovered. For, in truth, Asia for us is that same America which we still have not discovered. With our push toward Asia we will have a renewed upsurge of spirit and strength. Just as soon as we become more independent we'll at once find out what we have to do; but living with Europe for two centuries we've become unaccustomed to any kind of activity and have become windbags and idlers."

"Well, then, how are you going to rouse us up to go to Asia if we are idlers? And who among us is going to rise up first, even if you do prove to everyone, as clearly as twice two is four, that it is there we shall find our happiness?"

"In Europe we were hangers-on and slaves, while in Asia we shall be the masters. In Europe we were Tatars, while in Asia we are the Europeans. Our mission, our civilizing mission in Asia will encourage our spirit and draw us on; the movement needs only to be started. Just build two railways and begin with that—one railway to Siberia, another to Central Asia, and you shall see the results at once."

"You don't ask for much!"—I'll be told, with a laugh. "Where do we find the means, and what shall we get in return? Losses, and nothing more."

"In the first place, had we, over the past twenty-five years, set aside only three million a year for these railways (and three million often just slips through our fingers), then we would have already built seventy-five million rubles' worth of railways in Asia, i.e., nearly seven hundred miles, however you choose to calculate it. Then you talk about losses. Oh, if the English or the Americans were living in Russia instead of us, they would show you losses! They would certainly have discovered our America. Do you know there are lands there we know less about than the interior of Africa? And do we know what riches are to be found in the bosom of these boundless lands? Oh, they would get at all of it—the metals, the minerals, the countless coal fields; they would find all of it, and they would learn how to use all this material. They would summon science to help them and would make the earth yield fiftyfold—that same earth that we, here, still think of as a steppe, bare as the palm of your hand. People would be drawn to such a harvest; production and industry would be set up. Don't worry, there would be consumers and ways to find them; they would be found in the depths of Asia, where they slumber now in the millions, and new roads would be built to reach them!"

"Well, you've made a lot of exclamations about science, yet you're pushing us to betray science and enlightenment in asking us to become Asians."

"But we'll need even more science over there!" I exclaim, "since what are we in science now? Merely semieducated dilettantes. But there we'll become real workers; we'll be forced into it by necessity itself the moment an independent, enterprising spirit arises; we'll at once become masters in science as well, not hangers-on as we so often are now. And the most important thing is that we shall understand and accept our civilizing mission in Asia from its very first steps (and this is beyond doubt). Our mission will elevate our spirits; it will help give us dignity and self-awareness—and these are things we lack altogether now, or at least have in very small quantity. Beyond that, our push to Asia, if it begins, would serve as an outlet for many restless minds, for all who are fraught with anguish, for all who have grown lazy, for all who have grown tired of idleness. Give water an outlet and the scum and stench will vanish. And once people are drawn into work they will be bored no longer; everyone will be reborn. Even some fellow without talent, whose vanity is badly bruised and aching, would find his outlet there, since often an untalented fellow in one place will be reborn as a virtual genius somewhere else. This often happens in the European colonies. And Russia won't be emptied, don't worry: it will begin gradually; first a few will set off, but soon there'll be news of them that will attract others. And yet, this won't even be noticed in the broad ocean of Russia. Free the fly from the molasses; set his wings aright as best you can; still, only a most insignificant portion of the population will go there, so change won't even be noticeable. But over there—there it truly will be noticeable. Every place the 'Russ' settles in Asia will at once become Russian land. A new Russia will be created that will also restore and resurrect the old one in time and will clearly show her the path to follow.

"But for all this to happen we need a new principle and change of direction. And such a thing requires a minimum of disruption and upheaval. Just let people begin to understand (and they will understand) that our outlet is in the Asia of the future; that our riches are there; that our ocean is there. Let people understand that when Europe, because of her overcrowding alone, establishes the inevitable and humiliating communism, which she herself will loathe, when whole crowds of people will have to press around a single hearth and, little by little, individual households will be destroyed and families will abandon their own homes and start living collectively in communes; when children (three-quarters of them foundlings) are raised in institutions, then—then we shall still have broad expanses, fields and forests, and our children will grow up with their own fathers, not in cramped stone prisons, but amid orchards and cultivated fields, seeing the pure, blue sky above them. Yes, many of our hopes are contained there, and many possibilities whose full extent we, here, cannot yet conceive! It's not merely gold that's hidden in the soil there. But we need a new principle.

A new principle will generate the money needed for the work. To be quite frank about it, why do we need (particularly at the present moment)—why do we need to keep so many embassies over in Europe, embassies with all their costly glitter, their subtle wit and banquets, their superb but costly staffs? And what do we need (particularly now) with all these Gambettas and these popes and their future fates, even though Bismarck might be oppressing them? Isn't it better, rather, to play the beggar before Europe for a time, to sit by the road, put our cap in front of us and collect pennies: Europe would say, '*la Russie se recueille* once more.' At home, meanwhile, we could organize things and shape ourselves inwardly! People might ask why we should humiliate ourselves this way. But we wouldn't be humiliating ourselves at all! I only brought in the beggar's cap as a kind of allegory. We shall not humiliate ourselves, we shall at once exalt ourselves, that's what will happen! Europe is crafty and clever; she'll guess what we're up to at once and, believe me, she'll begin to respect us immediately! Oh, our independent attitude will give her pause at first, of course, yet it will also appeal to her in part. When she sees that we have embarked on a policy of "gloomy economics" and have decided to live within our means, that we, too, have become frugal and are the first to save and value our ruble and not merely manufacture it out of paper, then Europe will immediately begin to value our ruble on her markets as well. Indeed, when the Europeans see that we're not afraid even of deficits and bankruptcies but are working busily toward our goal, they themselves will come to offer us money—and now they'll offer it to people they regard as serious, to people who have learned their business and know how to do things properly. . . ."

"Wait a moment," says a voice; "you mentioned Gambetta just now; but we can't simply drop everything over there. To begin with, take the Eastern Question: it's still open, after all; how can we just walk away from it?"

"On the Eastern Question at the moment I would say the following: in political circles in Russia at the moment we could probably find not a single political mind that would consider it a sound proposition that Constantinople should be ours (except, perhaps, in some distant and still enigmatic future). And if that's so, then why should we wait any longer? The whole essence of the Eastern Question at this moment lies in the alliance of Germany and Austria and in the Austrian annexations of Turkish territory, which Prince

Bismarck encourages. We can and will protest only in extreme cases, of course, but so long as these two nations are united, what can we do now without disrupting our lives enormously? Keep in mind that the allies, perhaps, would like nothing better than for us finally to get angry. Still, we can encourage and love the Slavic peoples as before and even offer them some help should they need it. In any case, they are certainly not going to perish in the short term. And that term may be very short indeed. Were we merely to make it appear that we have no intention of meddling in European affairs as much as we used to, then they, left without us, might quarrel among themselves all the sooner. Austria, after all, will never believe that Germany conceived such love for her simply because of her beautiful eyes. On the contrary, she knows full well that Germany, sooner or later, must still bring all her Austrian Germans into the German union. But Austria will not give up her Germans for any price—not even in exchange for Constantinople—so much does she value them! Thus the potential for discord is already there. Besides that, right on Germany's flank there is still the same unresolved French question that now has become an eternal question for her. And besides that, the very unification of Germany suddenly appears to be not only incomplete but even in danger of being shaken. And now it also appears that European socialism not only has not died, it continues to be a very serious threat. In short, we should merely wait and not meddle, even when they start appealing to us; and the moment something explodes over there—when strife commences and their "political equilibrium" is destroyed—we should at once put an end to the Eastern Question by choosing the moment, as we did in the Franco-Prussian War, to declare suddenly, as we declared then regarding the Black Sea, that "we do not intend to respect any Austrian annexations of Turkish territory"; and all these annexations would vanish at once, perhaps along with Austria herself.

"And so we shall make up for all the distance that, it might appear, we had temporarily lost. . . ."

"Well, what about England? You've forgotten England. When she sees our push into Asia, she'll panic immediately."

"'If you're afraid of England, then don't leave your house.' That's my reply, to recast an old proverb in modern terms. She'll have nothing new to cause her panic in any case, since she's in panic over the same old things even now. On the contrary, it is now that we can keep her confused and ignorant about the future, and she's expecting only the worst from us. When she does realize the real nature of all our movements in Asia, then, perhaps, a lot of her fears will be alleviated. . . . However, I have to concede that her fears won't be alleviated; she has a long way to go before that happens. But, I repeat, if you're afraid of England, then don't leave your house! And so, once more, long live the victory at Geok-Tepe! Long live Skobelev and his good lads, and eternal memory to the heroes who were 'struck off the roll!' We shall inscribe their names in our roll."

Notes

The following notes are intended to provide the English-speaking reader with at least minimal background information about references in the text. The most important source is provided by the voluminous and quite excellent annotations included in the USSR Academy of Sciences' thirty-volume edition of Dostoevsky's *Complete Works*, F. M. Dostoevsky, *Polnoe sobranie sochinenii v tridstati tomakh* (Leningrad: Nauka, 1972–88), abbreviated hereafter as *PSS*. These notes are based on a set of assumptions that are not always applicable to nonspecialist readers in the West, however: Soviet readers need not be told about Belinsky or Nekrasov, for example, whereas the Western reader might. Thus, I have not provided a complete translation of the notes in *PSS* but have used them, rather, as a guide. I have attempted to check independently each reference derived from this source, but this has not always been possible: many of the nineteenth-century Russian newspapers Dostoevsky read so avidly are not available in North America and are difficult to access even in the Soviet Union. Additional material was derived from specific works cited in the notes themselves, and from the works of individual writers whom Dostoevsky mentions in the *Diary*. The sources listed below were repeatedly consulted.

All dates mentioned in the notes are old style (o.s.), i.e., twelve days behind the Gregorian calendar, unless otherwise indicated.

Sources

Baedeker, Karl. *Russia, with Teheran, Port Arthur, and Peking: Handbook for Travellers*. Leipzig: Karl Baedeker, 1914.

Bol'shaia entsiklopediia [Great encyclopedia]. Ed. S. N. Iuzhakov. 22 vols. St. Petersburg: Prosveshchenie, 1896.

Bol'shaia sovetskaia entsiklopediia [Great Soviet encyclopedia]. Ed. O. Iu. Shmidt. 65 vols. Moscow: Sovetskaia entsiklopediia, 1926–47.

Bol'shaia sovetskaia entsiklopediia [Great Soviet encyclopedia]. 3d ed. Ed. A. M. Prokorov. 30 vols. Moscow: Sovetskaia entsiklopediia, 1970–78.

Dostoevskaia, A. G. *Vospominaniia* [Memoirs]. Moscow: Khudozhestvennaia literatura, 1971.

Encyclopaedia Britannica. 11th ed. 29 vols. Cambridge: Cambridge University Press, 1910–11.

Encyclopaedia Britannica. 14th ed. 24 vols. Chicago, London, and Toronto: William Benton, 1958.

New Encyclopaedia Britannica. 15th ed. 32 vols. Chicago: Encyclopaedia Britannica, 1987.

Entsiklopedicheskii slovar' [Encyclopedic dictionary]. 82 vols. St. Petersburg: Brokgauz and Efron, 1890–1904.

Entsiklopedicheskii slovar' [Encyclopedic dictionary]. 58 vols. St. Petersburg and Moscow: Granat, 1910–40.

Frank, Joseph. *Dostoevsky: The Seeds of Revolt, 1821–1849*. Princeton, NJ: Princeton University Press, 1976.

———. *Dostoevsky: The Years of Ordeal, 1850–1859*. Princeton, NJ: Princeton University Press, 1983.

———. *Dostoevsky: The Stir of Liberation, 1860–1865*. Princeton, NJ: Princeton University Press, 1986.

Der Grosse Brockhaus. 15 vols. Wiesbaden: F.A. Brockhaus, 1977–81.

Grossman, Leonid. *Seminarii po Dostoevskomu: Materialy, bibliografiia i kommentarii* [Seminars on Dostoevsky: Source materials, bibliography, commentaries]. Moscow and Petrograd: Gos. Izdatel'stvo, 1922.

———. *Zhizn' i trudy F. M. Dostoevskogo: biografiia v datakh i dokumentakh* [The life and works of F. M. Dostoevsky: A biography in dates and documents]. Moscow and Leningrad: Academia, 1935.

Guedalla, Philip. *The Second Empire*. London: Hodder and Stoughton, 1932.

Istoriia Moskvy [The history of Moscow]. 6 vols. Moscow: AN SSSR, 1952–59.

Istoriia russkoi literatury XIX veka [A history of Russian literature of the nineteenth century]. Ed. D. N. Ovsianiko-Kulikovsky. 5 vols. Moscow: Mir, 1908–10.

Kratkaia literaturnaia entsiklopediia [Short literary encyclopedia]. Ed. A. A. Surkov. 9 vols. Moscow: 1926–78.

Mochulsky, Konstantin. *Dostoevsky: His Life and Work*. Trans. and intro. by Michael Minihan. Princeton, NJ: Princeton University Press, 1967.

Modern Encyclopedia of Russian and Soviet History. Ed. Joseph L. Wieczynski. Gulf Breeze, Fla.: Academic International Press, 1976–.

Modern Encyclopedia of Russian and Soviet Literature. Ed. Harry B. Weber. Gulf Breeze, Fla.: Academic International Press, 1977–.

Nechaeva, V. S. *Zhurnal M. M. i F. M. Dostoevskikh "Vremia," 1861–*

1863 [M. and F. M. Dostoevsky's journal "Time," 1861–1863]. Moscow: Nauka, 1972.

———. *Zhurnal M. M. i F. M. Dostoevskikh "Epokha," 1864–1865* [M. M. and F. M. Dostoevsky's journal "Epoch," 1864–1865]. Moscow: Nauka, 1975.

Ocherki istorii Leningrada [Outlines of the history of Leningrad]. Ed. M. P. Viatkin. 7 vols. Moscow and Leningrad: AN SSSR, 1955–89.

Petrovich, Michael Boro. *A History of Modern Serbia, 1804*–1918. 2 vols. New York: Harcourt, Brace, Jovanovich, 1976.

Abbreviations

BV *Birzhevye vedomosti* [The Stock Exchange News]—liberal daily
D *Delo* [The Cause]—radical monthly
DP *Dnevnik pisatelia* [A Writer's Diary]
E *Epokha* [The Epoch]—St. Petersburg monthly edited by Dostoevsky (1864–65)
G *Golos* [The Voice]—St. Petersburg daily, moderately liberal
Gr *Grazhdanin* [The Citizen]—conservative weekly edited by Dostoevsky (1873)
MV *Moskovskie vedomosti* [Moscow News]—conservative daily
NV *Novoe vremia* [New Times]—leading St. Petersburg daily
OZ *Otechestvennye zapiski* [Notes of the Fatherland]—monthly, edited by N. N. Nekrasov and M. Saltykov-Shchedrin (1868–84)
PG *Peterburgskaia gazeta* [The Petersburg Gazette]—popular daily
RM *Russkii mir* [The Russian World]—conservative daily
RV *Russkii vestnik* [The Russian Messenger]—conservative monthly; a leading literary journal of the nineteenth century
S *Sovremennik* [The Contemporary]—radical monthly, edited by N. Chernyshevsky and N. Dobroliubov (1856—62)
SV *Sankt-Peterburgskie vedomosti* [St. Petersburg News]—conservative daily
V *Vremia* [Time]—monthly, edited by F. M. and M. M. Dostoevsky (1861–63)
VE *Vestnik Evropy* [The European Messenger]—liberal monthly
Z *Zaria* [Dawn]—neo-Slavophile monthly

January 1877, 1.1: Three Ideas

Dostoevsky does not quote himself accurately here; notably, the word "almost" does not appear in the *Diary* of December 1876.

vote in the Assembly: Dostoevsky refers to the attacks made on religion in revolutionary France in 1793 and the concomitant attempt to institute the worship of reason. Robespierre, however, came to the conclusion that outright atheism was having a negative effect on the populace. Friedrich Schlosser, Dostoevsky's source here, notes: "On the 7th of May 1794, Robespierre delivered a tedious and pompous speech in the convention respecting the connexion of religion and morality with republican principles; which in his mouth was in the highest degree ridiculous . . . and proposed a decree which was accepted and passed by the convention, and was to the following effect: 'The national convention acknowledges the truth of the existence of God and the immortality of the soul'" (F. C. Schlosser, *History of the Eighteenth Century and of the Nineteenth till the Overthrow of the French Empire* [London: Chapman & Hall, 1846], 6:510). Schlosser's work appeared in Russian translation in 1868.

Arminius: Latinized form of Hermann or Armin (17 B.C.–A.D. 21), German chieftain and national hero. In the year A.D. 9 he led a rebellion against Roman rule, inflicting a major defeat on a Roman army in the Teutoburger Wald.

The Eastern Question: See notes to April 1876, 2.1, June 1876, 2.3, September 1876, 1.2, October 1876, 2.1, and February 1877, 1.2.

"Pondering Peters": See December 1876, 2.4.

January 1877, 1.2: Mirages. Stundism and the Radstockists

February 19: The Act of Emancipation, liberating Russia's serfs, was signed by Alexander II on February 19, 1861.

Stundism: A Protestant religious movement that appeared in southern Russia in the late 1860s, its origins were linked to German settlers in that area.

Templars: A religious and military order of knighthood established during the Crusades. The Templars were later accused of heresy, and in 1312 the order was suppressed by Pope Clement V. The grand master of the order, Jacques de Molay, was burned at the stake in 1314.

Pythia: The name of the medium at the oracle of Apollo at Delphi.

Tatarinova's group: See notes to March 1876, 2.2.

Radstockists: See March 1876, 2.2.

January 1877, 1.3: Foma Danilov, a Russian Hero Tortured to Death

Foma Danilov: *MV*, no. 105, April 29, 1876, carried a report, which had been published in the newspaper *Russkii invalid* [Russian veteran] two days previously, describing how Danilov had been taken prisoner by tribesmen in Turkestan. After his captors had twice offered him wealth and a position of power if he would renounce Orthodoxy and accept Islam, Danilov is quoted as having replied, "The faith into which I was born is the one in which I shall die; I have given an oath not to betray my tsar, and I shall remain faithful to it." The newspaper account continues: "On orders of Khan Pulat, Abdul-Murmyn tried a third time to tempt Danilov, at the same time making a renewed threat to execute him if he refused. At this point Danilov lost his temper and, cursing all who were present, declared: 'You are wasting your time, you dogs, you'll get nothing from me; if you want to kill me, then get on with it.'" Danilov was then executed. Dostoevsky later used this episode in *The Brothers Karamazov*, pt. 1, bk. 3, chap. 7.

Kipchaks: Name loosely applied to a number of Turkic-speaking peoples of Central Asia.

Granovsky: See notes to July and August 1876, 2.1.

"Knowledge is light . . ." A Russian proverb.

January 1877, 2.1: A Conciliatory Dream beyond the Scope of Science

"happiness is better than heroism": Schast'e dorozhe bogatyrstva, Russian proverb.

three whales: In Russian folk belief the world is supported on the backs of three whales.

January 1877, 2.2: We Are but Useless Wretches in Europe

Useless Wretches: The word Dostoevsky uses here, *striutsky*, is discussed in detail in November 1877, 1.1.

Karamzin, N. M. (1766–1826), Russian writer and historian. In 1789–90 he made a "grand tour" of Europe, which he described in his *Pis'ma russkogo puteshestvennika* [Letters of a Russian traveler], 1791. His comments on the French Revolution show his abhorrence of mob violence as well as some sympathy toward the revolution's potential to put the ideals of the Enlightenment into practice. He expressed more enthusiasm for the revolution in an article "Neskol'ko slov o russkoi literature" [A few words on Russian literature] (1797), originally published in French, in Paris.

Rudins: The protagonist of Turgenev's novel of the same name, Rudin is an idealist, a man of fine talk but little practical ability; he dies a valiant but useless death on the barricades in Paris in 1848.

Potugin: In chapter 14 of Turgenev's novel *Smoke* [Dym] (1867) he expresses the Westernizer viewpoint and is sharply critical of Russia.

January 1877, 2.3: An Old Story about the Petrashevsky Circle

Petrashevsky Circle: Dostoevsky's involvement with this group of young men led to his arrest and imprisonment.

Kazan Square: On December 6, 1876, a group of radical students, inspired by the revolutionary group Land and Freedom (Zemlia i volia) demonstrated on Kazan Square in St. Petersburg. Their trial began on January 18, 1877. (See notes to December 1876, 1.4.)

Stronin, A. I. (1827–89), Russian sociologist and political thinker; his book *Politics as Science* [Politika kak nauka] was published in St. Petersburg in 1872.

"to the People": In the summer of 1876 Russian populists organized a "movement to the people." Groups of revolutionaries, mainly students, went to live among the peasants, in an attempt to gain their acceptance and then convert them to the cause of revolution.

Chernyshevsky's group: Literary critics and writers such as Nikolai Dobroliubov (1836–61), Mikhail Mikhailov (1829–65), and Nikolai Shelgunov (1824–91), who were grouped around the magazine *The Contemporary* [Sovremennik] and were leading members of the radical intelligentsia on the eve of the Emancipation.

Nechaev, Sergei (1847–82), Russian revolutionary and conspirator. (See also notes to 1873.16.)

Dolgushin affair: Dolgushin, Alexander Vasilevich (1848–85), revolutionary conspirator. His methods and aims were influenced by Nechaev's program. Arrested in September 1873, he was sentenced to ten years of hard labor.

raznochintsy: Literally, people of various classes, meaning those who left the class to which their parents had belonged. In the mid-nineteenth century, these sons (and a few daughters) of priests, doctors, etc., began to form an important part of the intelligentsia.

Alexander Lycée: The exclusive school at Tsarskoe Selo, south of Petersburg, whose most famous graduate was Alexander Pushkin. In 1844 it was renamed the Imperial Alexander Lycée.

School of Jurisprudence: An elite law school founded in 1835 with the aim of training young noblemen for high judicial posts and government service. See Richard S. Wortman, *The Development of a Russian Legal Consciousness* (Chicago and London: University of Chicago Press, 1976), p. 49.

January 1877, 2.4: Russian Satire. *Virgin Soil. Last Songs.* Old Reminiscences

views of one foreigner about Russian satire: Dostoevsky refers to a discussion, in *MV*, no. 314, December 6, 1876, of a review of a French translation of Chernyshevsky's *What Is to Be Done?* [Chto delat'?]

Turgenev's novel *Virgin Soil* [Nov'] appeared in *VE*, nos. 1 and 2, 1877.

Solomin: The passage, which appears in chap. 16 of the novel, is as follows: "It appeared that Solomin did not believe in the imminent approach of a revolution in Russia; but not wishing to force his views on others, he did not stand in the way of their efforts and kept an eye on them, not from a distance but by their side. He knew the Petersburg revolutionaries very well and he sympathized with them up to a point, for he himself was one of the people; but he understood the instinctive aloofness of those same peasants, without whom 'nothing could be done' and who need a long course of preparation, and not in the manner and by the means of these men. And so he kept aloof—not in any hypocritical or shifty way, but as a young fellow with some sense who did not want to ruin his own life, or anyone else's, in vain."

Nekrasov's *Last Songs*: A cycle of poems written during his final illness, in 1876–77; nine were published in *OZ*, no. 1, 1877.
difficult to diagnose: See notes to December 1877, 2. Nekrasov suffered from cancer of the bowel.
Grigorovich: See notes to 1873.14. His sketch, "Organ Grinders of Petersburg" [Peterburgskie sharmanshchiki], appeared in 1844 in an anthology, *The Physiology of Petersburg, Comprising Works of Russian Writers and Edited by N. Nekrasov* [Fiziologiia Peterburga, sostavlennaia iz trudov russkikh literatorov pod redaktsieiiu N. Nekrasova].
Fatherland Notes party: In the 1840s *OZ* was the leading journal of the Westernizers; Turgenev, Nekrasov, and Herzen published their writings in it. From 1839, Belinsky was the journal's principal literary critic.
completely alone: See notes to December 1877, 2. Nekrasov arrived in St. Petersburg in late July 1838.
The verse is from Nekrasov's "The Unfortunates" [Neshchastnye] (1856), an unfinished narrative poem centering on a revolutionary in exile; its hero is probably modeled on Belinsky.

January 1877, 2.5: The Boy Celebrating His Saint's Day

Tolstoy's *Childhood, Boyhood, Youth,* which is its full title, appeared in *S*, no. 9, 1852; no. 10, 1854; and no. 1, 1857.
a letter from K——v: The letter came from M. A. Iurkevich, deputy inspector of the Kishinev Seminary.

January 1877: Editor's Note

the new magazine *Light*: see December 1876, 2.2.
Miss O. A. An——ova: The letter came from O. A. Antipova, a seventeen-year-old girl. Portions of several of her letters to Dostoevsky, in which she pours out her unhappiness, can be found in F. M. Dostoevsky, *Pis'ma* [Letters], ed. A. S. Dolinin (Moscow and Leningrad: Academia, 1934), p. 387.

February 1877, 1.1: Self-Appointed Prophets and Lame Coopers Who Continue to Manufacture the Moon on Gorokhovaia Street. One of Russia's Least-Known Great Men

Jack of Hearts: See notes to May 1876, 1.3. Preparations were being made for the trial of forty-eight gang members in February 1877. *MV*, no. 33, February 9, 1877, published a special supplement containing the indictment against those apprehended. The description of the offenses committed by members of the gang over a period of years in five cities ran to eight pages in the newspaper.
this be ended: The verse is unidentified and may be Dostoevsky's own.
fiery land of Colchis: Line from Pushkin's poem "To the Slanderers of

Russia [Klevetnikam Rossii] (1831); here he describes the extent of Russian dominion. (See also notes to November 1877, 2.2.)

cooper is making on Gorokhovaia Street: In Gogol's "Notes of a Madman" the protagonist, Poprishchin, says, as he sinks more deeply into madness: "You see, they usually make the moon in Hamburg, and a very bad job they do of it too. I am surprised that England hasn't taken note of it. It's made by a lame cooper, and it's obvious that the poor fool has no idea of what a moon should be."

lame to boot: Probably a veiled allusion to Turgenev, whose Westernizing views and fondness for Germany offended Dostoevsky. In a letter of August 16, 1867, describing his visit to Turgenev, Dostoevsky quoted him as follows: "You should know that I have settled in [Germany] permanently, that I consider myself a German, not a Russian, and I'm proud of it!" The "lameness" may refer to the fact that Turgenev suffered from gout.

Pokrov Community: *MV*, no. 2, January 4, 1877, reported that twenty-five Bulgarian girls and one boy had arrived in Moscow on December 23 and were being cared for by the Pokrov Community of the Sisters of Charity.

Pushkin's "Songs of the West Slavs": Most of Pushkin's cycle of sixteen poems, "Pesni zapadnykh slavian" [Songs of the West Slavs], were drawn from Prosper Mérimées's forgery of Illyrian folk songs, *La Guzla* (1829); several are translations of genuine Serbian songs, and two were probably Pushkin's own creations.

relative of Napoleon III: Mérimée was a good friend of the Countess de Montijo, whose daughter later became Empress Eugénie, wife of Napoléon III; Empress Eugénie was instrumental in Mérimée being appointed a senator in 1854 (A. W. Raitt, *Prosper Mérimée* [London: Eyre & Spottiswoode, 1970]).

"The Captive of the Caucasus": Kavkazskii plennik (1822); The Gypsies [Tsygany] (1827).

a monument to him: The idea of collecting funds for a monument to Pushkin was first proposed in 1862; the monument itself was unveiled on June 6, 1880; Dostoevsky delivered one of the keynote speeches at the celebrations (see 1880.1 and 1880.2).

February 1877, 1.2: Home-grown Giants and a Humiliated Son of a Mountain Village. An Anecdote about Skin Flayed from the Back. The Higher Interests of Civilization, and "May They Be Damned If They Must Be Purchased at Such a Price!"

Skupshtina: The Serbian parliament. After the collapse of Serbian resistance in October 1876, an armistice, eventually extended to February 16, was arranged between Serbia and Turkey. Despite some official

Russian attempts to help reorganize the Serbian army, the Serbs decided that they could not resume the war and concluded a peace with Turkey, accepting a return to the conditions that had prevailed before the outbreak of hostilities. Serbia remained officially neutral during Russia's subsequent war with Turkey, although Montenegro continued to fight. See K. L. Struzhkova and N. I. Khitrova, "Serbiia i Chernogoriia v voine s Turtsiei: 1876–1878 gg." [Serbia and Montenegro in the war with Turkey, 1876–1878], *Balkanskie issledovaniia* [Balkan studies] (Moscow: Nauka, 1978), 4:43–71.

letter from a young Russian: The letter, dated December 26, 1876, came from A. P. Khitrov, a Russian student who had gone to Serbia as a volunteer. He argues that the Serbs were not cowardly fighters; they simply had little real hatred for the Turks and were homesick for their peaceful villages. *Dostoevskii: materialy i issledovaniia* [Dostoevsky: Source materials and studies] (Leningrad: Nauka, 1976), 2:312–13.

Cherniaev: See notes to April 1876, 2.1. Contemporary commentators have observed: "As commander-in-chief of the Serbian army, Cherniaev justified the hopes of neither the Serbs nor the Russians. His inability to command large operational units, which earlier had been noted only by a few, quickly became obvious" (Struzhkova and Khitrova, "Serbiia i Chernogoriia v voine s Turtsiei," 4:63).

Novoselov, Semen Kornilovich (1812–77), Major-General. In 1876, as a Russian volunteer, he commanded a Serbian army.

Horvatović, Djura (1835–95), Serbian colonel who commanded an army corps that was forced back from the Djuniz Heights in the last major battle of the 1876 war. In October 1876 he headed a Serbian mission to Russia.

Marinović, Jovan: leader of the Serbian conservatives, he opposed the 1876 war with Turkey. In November 1876 he headed a Serbian mission to St. Petersburg to try to determine Russian intentions in waging a war against Turkey; because of his outspoken criticisms of Russia's war preparations, he was expelled from Russia by Alexander II.

The Moscow News: Dostoevsky quotes an editorial from *MV,* no. 33, February 9, 1880, which condemned the Western powers for supporting Turkey and tolerating Turkish outrages against the Balkan Christians.

February 1877, 1.3: On Flaying of Skins Generally and Various Aberrations in Particular. Hatred of Authority with Toadyism of Thought

"Jack of Hearts": See notes to February 1877, 1.1. Many of the members of the gang came from landowning families.

"Virgin Soil": Dostoevsky refers here to the peasantry as a whole, as is suggested by the title of Turgenev's novel, which was then appearing. The epigraph to the novel reads: "Virgin soil should be turned up not by a harrow skimming over the surface but by a plough biting deep into the earth."

February 1877, 1.4: Metternichs and Don Quixotes

manifesto from the Russian emperor: On October 18, 1876, Alexander II threatened to break off diplomatic relations with Turkey unless she agreed to a cease-fire against the insurgent Slavs.

February 1877, 2.1: One of Today's Most Important Questions

Anna Karenina: Chapters 1 to 12 of part 6 of the novel, describing Dolly's visit to Levin and Kitty in the country, appeared in *RV,* no. 1 (1877).

agents of progress: The conversation among Levin, Oblonsky, and Vasenka Veslovsky, excerpts of which Dostoevsky quotes, takes place in *Anna Karenina,* pt. 6, chap. 11.

February 1877, 2.2: The Issue of the Day

Vlas: See 1873.5.

February 1877, 2.3: The Issue of the Day in Europe

Fourier, François Marie Charles (1772–1837), French socialist writer whose theories sought ways to achieve social harmony and the free development of the individual; his ideas had considerable influence on a generation of Russian radicals. Cabet, Etienne (1788–1856), French utopian socialist.

hundred million heads: The motif of "a hundred million heads" as the revolutionaries' price for instituting a new order in Europe is also found in *The Devils,* pt. 2, chap. 7.

February 1877, 2.4: The Russian Solution to the Problem

"where they neither hoard nor covet": "You will receive . . . :" Mark 10:21: "Then Jesus . . . said unto him, One thing thou lackest; go thy way, sell whatsoever thou hast, and give to the poor, and thou shalt have treasure in heaven: and come, take up the cross, and follow me."

March 1877, 1.1: Once More on the Subject That, Sooner or Later, Constantinople Must Be Ours

Tsargrad: See notes to June 1876, 2.4.

as some people envisage: Dostoevsky no doubt has in mind Danilevsky (see notes to June 1876, 2.4).

March 1877, 1.2: The Russian People Have Completely Matured to a Sane Conception of the Eastern Question from Their Own Standpoint

Dostoevsky uses the same two words (*khristianstvo, krest'ianstvo*) in September 1876, 2.3.

Stundism: See notes to January 1877, 1.2.
wooden plank: An icon.
fool in Christ (*iurodivyi*): Ascetic wanderers who often behaved eccentrically and were revered for their prophetic pronouncements.
Ilya Muromets: Hero of many of the traditional Russian epic songs, the *byliny*.
Vlases: See 1873.5.

March 1877, 1.3: The Most Appropriate Thoughts for the Present Time

the Greek and the Bulgarian churches: Bulgaria's Orthodox church had been independent of the Greek church for long periods, but in 1767 the ancient patriarchate of Ohrid was abolished and the Bulgarian church subjected to the ecumenical patriarch in Constantinople. In 1870 the Turkish sultan allowed the Bulgarians once again to form their own exarchate; this created a schism between the Greek and Bulgarian churches that did not end until 1945.
The article appeared in *MV*, no. 63, March 15, 1877.
sobor: In the Russian Orthodox church, a council consisting of the patriarch, the metropolitans, the bishops, and the abbots of the most important monasteries.

March 1877, 2.1: "The Jewish Question"

beautiful letter: The four articles in chapter 2 are largely a response to three letters Dostoevsky received from Arkady Grigorevich Kovner (1842–1909), in January and February 1877. Kovner, a journalist and writer, had been a fervent disciple of the radical Dmitry Pisarev in the 1860s. Although a Jew himself, Kovner had attacked traditional Judaism, seeing it as a barrier to the full integration of the Jews into Russian life. In the 1870s, however, he was alarmed by the upsurge of anti-Semitism and took Dostoevsky to task for his remarks about the Jews as exploiters. Kovner's letter to Dostoevsky of January 26, 1877, which Dostoevsky answers here, can be found in F. M. Dostoevsky, *Pis'ma* [Letters], ed. A. S. Dolinin (Moscow and Leningrad: Academia, 1934), pp. 377–82. See also David I. Goldstein, *Dostoevsky and the Jews* (Austin and London: University of Texas Press, 1981), pp. 106–16.
D. A. Goldstein, a teacher in a Moscow or Petersburg high school, had gone to Serbia as a volunteer and had been singled out by General Cherniaev as an example of courage and sangfroid in battle.
Disraeli, Benjamin (Earl of Beaconsfield) (1804–81), British statesman and man of letters, prime minister of Great Britain 1874–80.
Shchedrin: In chapter 1 of his *Contemporary Idyll* [Sovremennaia idilliia] (1877–78), the narrator says of a St. Petersburg restaurant: "And I had such a sudden urge to go there, into those low-ceilinged rooms in the back, into that stinking, raw atmosphere, to one of those cheap oilcloth

sofas whose entire expanse, without a doubt, contains not a single spot that hasn't been spat upon."

March 1877, 2.2: Pro and Contra

Lord Beaconsfield: Benjamin Disraeli.

restrictions for the whole mass of the Jews: As a result of the three partitions of Poland (1772, 1793, 1795), over a million Jews became subjects of the Russian Empire. Catherine II imposed restrictions limiting Jewish settlement to an area of western Russia, which became known as the Pale of Settlement (Cherta osedlosti). The Pale was expanded over the years to include underpopulated areas around the Black Sea that had been annexed from Turkey. By the 1860s, the Pale included all of Russian Poland, Lithuania, Belorussia, most of the Ukraine, the Crimea, and Bessarabia. Some loosening of restrictions on Jewish rights of residence occurred over the nineteenth century, so that certain merchants and artisans, those with higher education and those having completed military service, were permitted to reside anywhere within the empire except Finland.

the *European Messenger:* The article, "Iuzhnye shtaty severoamerikanskoi respubliki i ikh nastoiashchee" [The southern states of the North American republic and their present condition], appeared in *VE,* no. 3, 1877, and was by Iu. A. Rossel.

New Times (no. 371): The report in fact appeared in *NV,* no. 375, March 15, 1877.

March 1877, 2.3: *Status in Statu.* Forty Centuries of Existence

Status in statu: A state within a state (Latin). The ideas expressed in this chapter were taken in part from *Kniga Kagala. Materialy dlia izucheniia evreiskogo byta. Sobral i perevel Iakov Bravman* [The book of the kahal: Materials for the study of Jewish life. Collected and translated by Iakov Bravman] (Vilnius: Izd. Vilenskogo gubernskogo pravleniia, 1869). Dostoevsky's library contained three editions of this book. It is the work of a convert from Judaism and was used to help fuel the anti-Semitic movement in the later nineteenth century. Bravman maintained that the Jews recognized only Talmudic laws, not the laws of the Russian Empire; they thus formed "a state within a state" that exploited their non-Jewish neighbors. See David I. Goldstein, *Dostoevsky and the Jews* (Austin and London: University of Texas Press, 1981), pp. 96ff.

The verses are paraphrased from act 2, scene 2 of *Prince Daniel Vasilevich Kholmsky* [Kniaz' Daniil Vasil'evich Kholmskii] (1840), a play by Nestor Kukolnik (1809–68). The same play is probably the source of the "legend" Dostoevsky describes.

Rothschild, Jacob (James), baron (1792–1868). Banker and founder of the Rothschild family's business interests in France.

March 1877, 2.4: But Long Live Brotherhood!

The girl was Sofia Efimovna Lurye; Dostoevsky discusses an earlier meeting with her in June 1876, 2.5.

In *Crime and Punishment*, pt. 6, chap. 6, immediately before Svidrigailov shoots himself, he encounters a Jewish soldier. The narrator describes the soldier's face as wearing "the eternal expression of resentful affliction which is so sharply etched on every Jewish face, without exception."

March 1877, 3.1: The Funeral of "The Universal Man"

Rossi, Ernesto (1827–96), Italian writer, actor, translator, playwright, and critic. Rossi toured Russia in 1877 and played Hamlet in St. Petersburg in February of that year. Dostoevsky apparently found his performance somewhat overdone; *NV*, no. 350, February 18, 1877, gave Rossi a rather positive review, however.

Semiradsky, Genrikh Ippolitovich (1843–1902), Russian painter. Dostoevsky has in mind Semiradsky's massive painting *The Lamps of Christianity* (later renamed *The Lamps of Nero* [Svetochi Nerona]), which was shown at the Academy of Arts exhibition in March 1877 and aroused much comment.

Miss L.: Sofia Efimovna Lurye (see notes to March 1877, 2.4), who was living in Minsk at the time.

March 1877, 3.2: An Isolated Case

one mighty poet: Probably Apollon Nikolaevich Maikov (1821–97).

mother-of-pearl: One detail in Semiradsky's painting is the mother-of-pearl on Nero's sedan chair.

April 1877, 1.1: War. We Are Stronger Than the Others

Alexander II declared war on Turkey on April 12, 1877. The immediate cause of the war was Turkey's refusal to implement the reforms for its Christian population that had been set forth by the Constantinople Conference of 1876, as well as Turkish atrocities committed against Bulgarian civilians in response to a Bulgarian uprising in May 1876. Pan-Slavist sentiments, Russian rivalry with Austro-Hungary in the Balkans, and Russia's desire for free and safe egress from the Black Sea were other causes.

all over the Russian land: Dostoevsky's wife notes that when he learned of the declaration of war, he went directly to Kazan Cathedral and spent half an hour in fervent prayer. A. G. Dostoevskaia, *Vospominaniia* [Memoirs] (Moscow: Khudozhestvennaia literatura, 1971), pp. 315–16.

will of Napoleon: Alexander I is quoted as saying this in N. V. Putiata, "Obozrenie zhizni i tsarstvovaniia imperatora Aleksandra I" [Survey of the life and reign of the emperor Alexander I], in *Deviatnadtsatyi vek* [The nineteenth century] (Moscow: P. Vartenev, 1872), 1:456–57.

April 1877, 1.3: Does Shed Blood Save Us?

"the time is at hand": Matthew 26:18: "And he said, Go into the city to such a man, and say unto him, The Master saith, My time is at hand; I will keep the passover at thy house with my disciples."

April 1877, 1.4: The Opinion of the "Most Serene" Tsar on the Eastern Question

Tsar Alexis [Aleksei] reigned from 1645 to 1676. His reign was not as serene as Dostoevsky suggests here but was marked by frequent popular uprisings and the Great Schism in the Orthodox church. Alexis was the first Russian tsar to begin adopting, though in small measure, elements of Western culture. He earned the sobriquet "most serene" (*tishaishii*) because of his pleasant disposition, warmth, and humility.

April 1877, 2: The Dream of a Ridiculous Man

"Voltaire" one: A low-seated, high-backed armchair.

April 1877, 2: The Defendant Kornilova Is Freed

new judges and jurors: Dostoevsky discusses Kornilova's case in October 1876, 1.1, December 1876, 1.1, and again in December 1877, 1.1–1.6.

Florinsky, Vasily Markovich (1833–99), physician; in the late 1870s and 1880s, professor of obstetrics and gynecology at Kazan University; author of a number of books on obstetrics.

Diukov, Petr Andreevich (1834–99), psychiatrist and author of many articles on mental illness. Lustig, Vilgelm Iosifovich (1843–1915), prominent St. Petersburg lawyer.

April 1877, 2: To My Readers

nature of my illness: During the early spring of 1877 Dostoevsky had a renewed series of attacks of epilepsy and was advised by doctors to spend the summer in quieter surroundings in the country. He also suffered from bronchial problems, which were growing increasingly severe. He and his family spent the summer in Kursk Province, southwest of Moscow, at the country estate of his brother-in-law, I. G. Snitkin.

May and June 1877, 1.1: From the Book of Predictions of Johann Lichtenberger, 1528

The book in question is *Prognosticatio Johannis Lichtenbergers, quam olim scripsit super magna illa Saturni ac Jovis conjunctione, quae fuit anno MCCCCLXXXIIII, praeterea ad eclypsim solis anni sequentis videlicet LXXXV, durans in annum usque MDLXVII, jam denuo sublatis mendis, quibus scatebat, pluribus, quam diligentissime excussa. [Coloniae]*, 1528 [The predictions of Johann Lichtenberger, which he once wrote in connection with the great conjunction of Saturn and Jupiter, which took place in the year 1484 and lasting to the year 1567, carefully purged once more from the many major errors with which it abounded. (Cologne), 1528]. Lichtenberger (?–1503) was court astrologer to Frederick II; little is known about him, although some details may be found in Dietrich Kurze, *Johannes Lichtenberger: Eine Studie zur Geschichte der Prophetie und Astrologie* (Lübeck and Hamburg: Matthiesen, 1960). The book itself is an astrological forecast. It first appeared in Latin in Strasbourg in 1488 and was subsequently republished many times in Latin, German, and Italian.

one of our young scholars: In all likelihood, the Russian philosopher Vladimir Solovev, who worked in the British Museum in 1875–76. See *Literaturnoe nasledstvo, 86: F. M. Dostoevskii: novye materialy i issledovaniia* [Literary legacy, vol. 86: F. M. Dostoevsky: new material and research] (Moscow: Nauka, 1973), pp. 61–62.

war with Europe twenty-two years ago: Dostoevsky refers to the Crimean War, 1854–55.

lost her virginity: In his memoirs the Russian general P. A. Tuchkov (1775–1858) writes that, while he was a prisoner of the French at Smolensk in 1812, Napoleon told him: "A conquered province or a city occupied by the enemy is like a maid who has lost her honor. She may do what she likes thereafter, but she can never regain her honor." "P. A. Tuchkov. Moi vospominaniia o 1812 gode" [P. A. Tuchkov. My memoirs of 1812], *Russkii arkhiv*, no. 10, 1873, col. 1963.

"They can lay there a bit . . .": A. A. Panaev, in his "Kniaz' Aleksandr Sergeevich Menshikov v rasskazakh byvshego ego ad iutanta Arkadiia Aleksandrovicha Panaeva" [Prince Aleksandr Sergeevich Menshikov, in accounts by his former adjutant Arakdy Aleksandrovich Panaev], *Russkaia starina*, no. 5, 1877, p. 69, tells this story. Other Russian and French sources confirm that Russian soldiers in the Crimean campaign often took pity on their enemies. Similar stories were told of Russian soldiers in the war of 1877, at least during its early stages. *MV*, no. 214, August 18, 1877, quoted a correspondent from the French newspaper *XIX Siècle* who was amazed at the kindness with which the Russians treated Turkish wounded, even those accused of murdering Russian prisoners: "As far as the wounded are concerned, they care for them as if they were their own; often, while they are being transported, they lie on a wagon next to Russian soldiers, who treat them with complete good nature."

four centuries: I.e., from about the time of the fall of Constantinople to the Turks (1453); since then, Dostoevsky maintains, the Russian People have understood the essence of Russia's conflict with Turkey.

twenty years ago: Dostoevsky probably refers to the response of a secret committee, set up by Alexander II, to discuss means for the emancipation of the serfs. The committee's response to a proposal from the governor-general of Grodno, Minsk, and Kovno, V. I. Nazimov, for emancipating serfs in the western provinces (the Nazimov Rescript) was presented on

November 20, 1857. This rescript was the first public acknowledgment that serfdom could be ended in Russia and the peasants emancipated with land.

the pope: Pius IX (1792–1878), pope from 1846 to his death. Dostoevsky also refers to the dogma of papal infallibility, proclaimed in July 1870. *MV*, no. 104, April 30, 1877, quoting Austrian sources, reported that Pius IX, in an audience with a group of pilgrims from Savoy, had made the following comment about the Russo-Turkish War: "I do not know which of these two states will win, but I know that the hand of a just God hangs over one of these states, which calls itself orthodox but is, in fact, schismatic, because of its inhuman persecution of Catholics, which it began many years ago and which still has not ceased."

May and June 1877, 1.2: On Anonymous Abusive Letters

province of Kursk: Where Dostoevsky and his family were spending the summer of 1877. (See notes to April 1877, 2.)

Essentuki water: Name given to a variety of mineral waters originating in springs around the southern resort town of Essentuki.

sprang up suddenly: Dostoevsky probably has in mind the newspaper *New Times* [Novoe vremia], published in St. Petersburg since February 1876 by A. S. Suvorin. In his "Notebooks" of 1876–77 Dostoevsky remarked: "*New Times* is a newspaper which I do not always read with the greatest of pleasure but whose success shows the extent to which we have become tired of *The Voice*" (*PSS*, 24:274). *NV* actually began publishing in 1868; Dostoevsky's remark that it "sprang up suddenly" probably refers to the newspaper's shift to a more conservative line under Suvorin's guidance.

Masquerade: Drama by Mikhail Lermontov. The "mysterious stranger" lost all his possessions to the play's protagonist, Arbenin, in a card game and spent seven years plotting his revenge.

I witnessed this personally: Dostoevsky no doubt refers here to the five years of enforced military service that followed his prison term: from 1854 to 1859 he served in the army in Siberia, first as a private soldier and then as an officer.

the sort of words to use: In his *Selected Passages from Correspondence with Friends* [Vybrannye mesta iz perepiska s druz'iami] (1847), chapter 22, Gogol advises a Russian landowner on how to deal with a peasant who failed to show due respect to "exemplary masters": "You must give such a one a public going over; tell him, 'Ah, you unwashed mug.'... Don't beat the peasant! There is no great art to smashing him in the face. The police officer and the overseer and even the peasant elder can do that; the peasant is already accustomed to this and will only scratch his head a bit. But you must know how to reach his heart skillfully with a word; you are a master of the apt phrase, after all. Heap abuse on him before everyone, but in such a way that all the people would laugh at him then and there. This will be several times more beneficial to him than any blows on the head or punches in the mouth."

May and June 1877, 1.3: A Plan for a Satirical Novel of Contemporary Life

redemption money: As part of the arrangements for the abolition of serfdom in 1862, the government advanced landowners interest-bearing bonds to the amount of 80 percent of the total value of the land they had deeded to their former serfs. Some landowners were thus provided with a substantial yearly income.

Poprishchin: Protagonist of Gogol's story, "Notes of a Madman" [Zapiski sumashedshego] (1835).

"only pharmacists are afraid of disgrace": An echo of Gogol's Poprishchin, who says: "Letters are even written by pharmacists. . . ."

as Shchedrin's policeman expresses it: In chapter 3 of Saltykov-Shchedrin's "Contemporary Idyll" [Sovremennaia idilliia], which appeared in April, 1877.

May and June 1877, 2.1: Former Farmers—Future Diplomats

in one of his letters: Viktor Petrovich Burenin (1841–1926), Russian critic, poet, playwright, and publicist. In the 1860s Burenin had been a stalwart of the radical press, but he broke with the left in the mid-1870s and became a regular contributor to the conservative *NV*. In *NV*, no. 456, June 7, 1877, he told of meeting in a railway carriage a Russian, "the last Mohican among the incorrigible Westernizers," who lived abroad constantly because he felt that nothing worthwhile could be done in Russia. The man made a number of mocking references to the resurgence of Slavophile ideas, exemplified in Russia's policy in the Balkans, and joked about bringing Khomiakov's ghost to Bulgaria. Burenin was not amused.

Khomiakov, Aleksei Stepanovich (1804–60), Russian poet, philosopher, theologian; one of the founders of the Slavophile movement.

redemption money: See note to May and June 1877, 1.3.

foreign passports: In 1851 the regime of Nicholas I limited the stay abroad of Russian citizens of noble status to two years; each passport holder was required to pay a levy of 250 rubles for each six months of residence abroad; in 1856 this levy was lowered to five rubles for each six months.

Lucius Licinius Lucullus (ca. 110–56 B.C.), Roman general who, in retirement, led a life of elegant leisure and luxury.

last year: See July and August 1876, 3.2.

Mr. Turgenev's works written in French: Several of Turgenev's stories appeared in French translation before they were published in Russian. A. S. Suvorin, without Turgenev's knowledge, translated one of these, "Father Alexei's Story" [Rasskaz ottsa Alekseiia] from French into Russian and published it in *NV* (nos. 395 and 396, April 6 and 7, 1877). When Turgenev objected, Suvorin published an "Open Letter" to him, comparing a writer who published in a foreign language to a courtesan eager to acquire the latest fashionable dress (see I. S. Turgenev, *Polnoe sobranie sochinenii i pisem* [Complete collected works and letters] [Moscow and Leningrad: Nauka, 1968], 15:381). Turgenev replied that he had always written his literary works only in Russian.

Count Cavour: Camillo Benso, Count of Cavour (1810-61), Italian statesman. His efforts to transform Italy into a united, modern state were admired by Russian liberals.

"a mighty beast for petty deeds": From Krylov's fable "The Lion's Education" [Vospitanie l'va].

May and June 1877, 2.2: Diplomacy Facing World Problems

a war going on somewhere now: Although Russia declared war on Turkey in April, Russian forces were slow to mobilize and little serious fighting began until June.

fog that was spread a hundred years ago: Dostoevsky probably has in mind the Treaty of Kuchuk Kainardji (1774), under which Turkey acknowledged Russia's interest in the fate of the Christian population of the Balkans and undertook to protect the Christian religion there.

MacMahon, Marie Edmé Patrice Maurice de, duke of Magenta (1808–93), French marshal and president of France, 1873–79. MacMahon, a conservative, found it frustrating to work with a cabinet that represented the republican majority in the Chamber of Deputies and with a prime minister, Jules Simon, whom he felt was too much under the influence of leftist, anticlerical forces. Pope Pius IX, angry at a new Italian law restricting the activities of the clergy, had called upon Catholics to pressure their governments to support the independence of the papacy. Some militant French Catholics obliged, alarming and irritating the republicans; the French Chamber then passed a resolution condemning such "ultramontane activities." On May 16, MacMahon in essence forced the resignation of Jules Simon and on the following day formed a new ministry of conservatives. *NV*, no. 425, May 6, 1877, described the events as follows: "Paris is again seething. A coalition of clericals, Bonapartists, and monarchists has taken hold of Marshal MacMahon and forced him to write a sharp letter to Jules Simon over his subservience to the republican majority in the Chamber of Deputies; the prime minister has tendered his resignation. The crisis at once manifested itself on the streets."

lost almost all his battles: The army led by MacMahon suffered a serious defeat at Wörth, Alsace, during the Franco-Prussian War.

"J'y suis et j'y reste": (Here I am, and here I will stay), phrase attributed to MacMahon. (See notes to February 1876, 1.1.)

May and June 1877, 2.3: Never Has Russia Been as Powerful as Now—A Nondiplomatic Judgment

Kaidanov, Ivan Kuzmich (1782–1843), professor at the Tsarskoe Selo Lycée and author of a number of widely used textbooks of Russian and world history. The sentence Dostoevsky quotes from Kaidanov's *Rukovodstvo k poznaniiu vseobshchei politicheskoi istorii* [Handbook for the study of world political history], 3d ed., pt. 3: *Istoriia novaiia, ili trekh poslednikh vekov, prodolzhennaia do 1818 goda* [Modern history, or the three last centuries, to the year 1818] (St. Petersburg, 1827), p. 279, in fact reads as follows: "A most profound silence reigned in Europe when Frederick the Great closed his eyes forever; but never had a similar silence preceded such a mighty political storm as soon descended over the whole of Europe."

a dithyramb on the opening of the National Assembly: I have been unable to find any such work. Although Schiller was made an honorary citizen of the French Republic in 1792, his attitude toward the Revolution was hostile; he was particularly horrified by the execution of Louis XVI and the Terror. See Friedrich Burschell, *Schiller* (Hamburg: Rohwohlt, 1968), pp. 309–18.

Karamzin: See notes to January 1877, 2.2.

crossed the Danube: Russian forces crossed the Danube into Bulgaria on June 9/10, 1877.

isolation: Britain suspected Russia of having designs on India and was apprehensive of Russian movement southward and westward; British policy under Disraeli was to maintain the integrity of Turkey for as long as possible as a means of checking Russian expansion. Austria-Hungary, fearful of Slavic nationalism, also preferred to see Turkey remain intact but had signed secret treaties with Russia in which she agreed to remain neutral should Russia clash with Turkey; as a reward for her neutrality, Austria would obtain Bosnia-Herzegovina after any Russo-Turkish conflict ended. France, defeated in 1870, played little active role in the Balkans. The main players in the area were thus England, Russia, and Turkey.

May and June 1877, 3.1: The German World Problem. Germany—A Protesting Country

Arminius: See notes to January 1877, 1.1.

International: The International Working Men's Association, known as the First International, was founded in 1864 under the theoretical guidance of Marx and Engels.

May and June 1877, 3.2: One Brilliantly Suspicious Man

the sudden clerical upset in France: See notes to May and June 1877, 2.2. The fall of Simon's cabinet caused alarm in Europe and even led to talk of war. Many in Russia saw the crisis as caused specifically by clerical intrigues inspired by the Vatican. *MV,* no. 119, May 18, 1877, reported that the Italian government viewed the new French cabinet with "extreme suspicion," seeing it as composed of people who could be manipulated by ultramontanists who were plotting to destroy Italy's political unity and restore the worldly power of the pope. In its issue no.

125, May 24, 1877, the same newspaper's Paris correspondent called the cabinet crisis a veritable coup d'état "whose motto had come from the Vatican." The same correspondent quoted a "well-known statesman": "In order to understand contemporary events in western Europe, it is essential to keep in mind that there exist there two almost equal forces, both possessing the most powerful organizations the world has ever produced, forces which are engaged in a struggle to the death. One of these forces is the Prussian army, and the other is the Jesuits. Bismarck and Pater Beckx [Pierre-Jean Beckx (1795–1887), twenty-second general of the Society of Jesus, 1853–87] pull the strings of almost all the events occurring in western Europe. . . ."

king of Prussia: In late August 1870, Marshal MacMahon, commanding the French army of Châlons, made a suicidal attempt to relieve the army of Marshal Bazaine, which the Germans had blockaded in the fortress of Metz. MacMahon had to fall back to the town of Sedan; here, on September 2 (n.s.), his army surrendered to the Germans, who took as prisoners the emperor Napoleon III and some 80,000 French troops. Napoleon III remained a prisoner of the Germans until the end of the war; when freed, he lived out his days as an exile in England. The empire fell on September 4.

Bazaine, François-Achille (1811–88), marshal of France; commander of the Army of the Rhine in the Franco-Prussian War. After the surrender of MacMahon's army at Sedan, Bazaine was left to command France's only remaining organized army. Blockaded in the fortress of Metz, he opened negotiations with the Germans on terms of surrender and on October 29 (n.s.) capitulated, his 140,000-man army still intact. For this he was sentenced to death in 1873; the sentence was later commuted to twenty years' imprisonment.

three billions in reparations at once: Under the terms of the Treaty of Frankfurt (1871), France had to pay Germany an indemnity of five billion francs and maintain the cost of German forces of occupation until the indemnity was paid. In June 1871 the French government floated a loan, which was oversubscribed two and a half times, to pay the first installments of the indemnity; a year later, a second loan for the remaining installment of three billion was oversubscribed thirteen times. France was completely liberated by September 1873.

the latest unexpected escapade in France: I.e., the "clerical crisis" and collapse of the French cabinet on May 16.

hatred for Catholicism: In the 1870s Bismarck took a series of measures aimed at limiting the power of the Catholic church in Germany. See also notes to January 1876, 3.2.

the support of an Italian *alliance:* As part of his scheme to undermine Austria's dominance in Germany, Bismarck signed a treaty of alliance with Italy on April 8 (n.s.), 1866. In the subsequent war with Austria, Italy was unable to exploit the Prussian success at Sadowa and was defeated by the Austrians at Custozza.

May and June 1877, 3.3: Both Angry and Strong

He will very soon pass away: Pope Pius IX in fact died on February 7 (n.s.), 1878.

proclaimed his infallibility: Italian troops occupied Rome on September 20 (n.s.), 1870; a plebiscite in October resulted in an overwhelming majority of votes for the incorporation of Rome into the kingdom of Italy. Pius IX refused to accept this fait accompli and withdrew into the Vatican, where he remained for the rest of his days, regarding himself as a prisoner. The doctrine of papal infallibility was proclaimed by the Vatican council on July 18 (n.s.), 1870.

Khlestakov's brother: The inspired liar Khlestakov is the central character in Gogol's play *The Inspector-General* [Revizor].

allocutions and syllabuses: An allocution is a formal address given by the pope to the College of Cardinals and through them to the church; allocutions deal with some important ecclesiastical or political question and are published by being affixed to the door of St. Peter's church. "Syllabus" was the name given to the supplement to Pius IX's encyclical *Quanta cura* of December 8 (n.s.), 1864, in which were listed eighty of the "principal errors of our times" and which reverted to the absolutist doctrines of the Middle Ages. The church was declared superior to the state; it claimed a monopoly in education; freedom of the press was not admitted. The eightieth point condemned as erroneous the view that "the Roman Pontiff can and should reconcile himself to and agree with progress, liberalism, and modern civilization." The Syllabus did much damage to the church among liberal Catholics.

receiving pilgrims, damning and dying: Throughout most of the first half of 1877, Pius IX regularly received pilgrims who had come to mark the fiftieth anniversary of his election as pope; his remarks to these groups were often stern condemnations of what he saw as the errors of modern life; gravely ill, on a number of occasions he lost consciousness during these audiences.

one of the most enormous ideas in the world: Satan's temptation of Christ with worldly power, as described in Luke 4:5–8. The ideas expressed here are more fully developed in *The Brothers Karamazov*.

for a thousand years now: I.e., since the rise of the medieval papacy and the establishment of the papal state in the eighth century.

useful for the government of Napoleon III: Following the Revolution of 1848, the French government decided to give all Frenchmen over the age of twenty-one the right to vote. Prince Louis Napoleon (later Napoleon III) was elected president in December 1848. The assembly limited the franchise under the law of May 31 (n.s.), 1850. Louis Napoleon, unable to retain power constitutionally, staged a coup in December 1851 and then promptly restored full suffrage.

agreement with the socialists: Dostoevsky probably has in mind the efforts of Napoleon II to promote social welfare in France through labor legislation, improvements in workers' housing, and acknowledgment of workers' rights to form associations and to strike. See J. M. Thompson, *Louis Napoleon and the Second Empire* (New York: W. W. Norton, 1955), pp. 241–42.

May and June 1877, 3.4: The Black Army. The Opinion of the Legions as a New Element of Civilization

va-banque: In the games of chemin-de-fer and baccarat, to take a bet against the whole of the bank's stake.

to the French Chamber: *NV,* no. 452, June 3, 1877 wrote: "*République Française* outlines the present situation as follows: 'MacMahon's independent policy has reached its end. If MacMahon has really renounced power in favor of those responsible for the 16th of May, and if the revolution of the 16th of May truly was the work of the Vatican, then it will be an interesting spectacle if the result of the upcoming elections proves to be just as republican and, perhaps, even more liberal.'"

newly appointed prefects and mayors: After the crisis of May 16, MacMahon replaced republican prefects with people who had monarchist or Bonapartist sympathies. In so doing he hoped to minimize republican influence in the provinces in the period before the elections to the Chamber of Deputies, set for the autumn of 1877. Despite this and other pressures, the election of October 1877 resulted in a sizable republican majority in the Chamber of Deputies.

MacMahon himself with them: The influence of the republicans did continue to grow in the years following the 1877 election, and in January 1879 MacMahon retired.

reception from the army: On July 1 (n.s.), 1877, speaking to French troops at a military review in Paris, MacMahon stated: "You are aware of your obligations; you realize that the country has entrusted you with preserving its most precious interests. I have complete trust that you will defend them in any case. I am certain that you will assist me in maintaining respect for authority and the laws as I fulfill the mission entrusted to me, which I will carry out to the end" (*MV,* no. 158, June 26, 1877).

loyalty to the Napoleonic dynasty: During the Franco-Prussian War, in August 1870, MacMahon was torn between withdrawing his shattered army to defend Paris, a logical move from the military point of view, and attempting to relieve Marshal Bazaine's army, which was trapped at Metz. Empress Eugénie, acting as regent, informed MacMahon that if he abandoned Bazaine, revolution would follow. MacMahon reluctantly chose the latter course and lost his army. See André Maurois, *A History of France* (London: Jonathan Cape, 1957), pp. 418–19.

without Chambord and Bonaparte: Henri Charles Ferdinand Marie Dieudonne, Comte de Chambord (1820–83), regarded as King Henry V by French legitimists; his claim to the throne was advanced particularly in the early 1870s when monarchy seemed a credible alternative to republican government. Napoleon, Eugene Louis Jean Joseph Bonaparte

(1856–79), Prince Imperial, only son of Napoleon III and the empress Eugénie; on his father's death in 1873, he was proclaimed Napoleon IV by the Imperialists and became official pretender to the throne.

May and June 1877, 3.5: A Rather Unpleasant Secret

inevitable war: *MV*, no. 155, June 23, 1877, reported: "A dispatch from Berlin states . . . that the newspaper *Post* wrote in an editorial: 'With rifle in hand we await what will emerge from the French volcano. This country is on the eve of a plebiscite. A republic in France means peace for Europe; a monarchy guided by ultramontanes will inevitably lead to war.'"

middle of the road: In The *Iliad*, book 11, Zeus causes Ajax to retreat: "But Zeus father who sits on high drove fear upon Aias. He stood stunned, and swung the sevenfold ox-hide shield behind him and drew back, throwing his eyes round the crowd of men, like a wild beast." *The Iliad of Homer*, trans. Richmond Lattimore (Chicago: University of Chicago Press, 1962), p. 249.

"a German river": By late June, Russian forces had crossed the Danube and were advancing into northern Bulgaria. Many German and Austrian politicians were concerned that Russia would occupy the mouth of the Danube and transform it into a "Slavic river." *MV*, no. 131, May 30, 1877, stated that if Austro-Hungary were asked what would happen should the Russians defeat Turkey, occupy the mouth of the Danube, and transform it into a "Slavic river," the reply would be: "We would begin a war with Russia, since the Danube must remain an Austro-Hungarian and German river."

May and June 1877, 4.1: Those Who Love the Turks

Buckle, and even Draper: Henry Thomas Buckle (1821–62), English historian. His *History of Civilization in England* (1857–61) attempted to formulate the general laws that govern human progress and to show how those laws were exemplified in the histories of certain characteristic nations; the book enjoyed great popularity and influence in Russia, particularly in the 1860s. John William Draper (1811–82), American scientist and historian. His *History of the Intellectual Development in Europe* appeared in Russian translation in 1864.

May and June 1877, 4.2: Golden Tailcoats. Straight-Line People

declarations are nonsense: During the Russo-Turkish War of 1877–78 many public and private bodies published statements in newspapers declaring their patriotism and support for the war.

embraced Cherniaev: Mikhail Grigorevich Cherniaev (1828–98), lieutenant-general, publisher, Pan-Slavist. During the summer of 1876 he commanded, without official Russian approval, Serbian forces and Russian volunteers fighting the Turks in the Balkans. *RM*, no. 163, June 19, 1877, carried an item describing how Cherniaev and Ivan Aksakov had been cheered by the crowd at Kazan Cathedral, where they had come to attend a service of thanksgiving for a Montenegrin victory over the Turks. One old man emerged from the crowd and tearfully embraced Cherniaev.

Kopeikins who have "shed their blood, so to say": In the section of Gogol's *Dead Souls* entitled "The Tale of Captain Kopeikin," Kopeikin says, "I have, in a way, so to speak, sacrificed my life and shed my blood."

Russia isn't waging a war only with Turkey: Britain supplied considerable aid to Turkey, in the form of armaments, provisions, and military advisors. *MV*, no. 134, June 2, 1877, reported that a British general, Campbell, had been stationed in Erzerum, Turkey, and that nineteen British officers had been sent to locations in Bulgaria which were being threatened by the enemy. *MV*, no. 112, May 9, 1877, reported the arrival in Turkey of a group of British officers who were preparing to receive a British army corps; no. 133, June 1, 1877, carried reports of British naval preparations for a possible landing of forces in Turkey.

little Bulgarian orphan children: See February 1877, 1.2.

July and August 1877, 1.1: My Conversation with a Moscow Acquaintance. A Note Apropos of a New Booklet

back to Kursk Province: Where Dostoevsky was spending the summer. See note to May and June 1877, 1.2.

one of my old Moscow acquaintances: The acquaintance may have been I. S. Aksakov. In a letter to his wife of July 16, 1877, Dostoevsky mentions his wish to meet Aksakov in Moscow.

property of another family member: In 1831 Dostoevsky's father purchased an estate, Darovoe, situated some hundred miles southwest of Moscow. When Dostoevsky was a child his family spent a number of summers there. Dostoevsky recalls it fondly in "The Peasant Marey" (February 1876, 1.3). After his father's death the estate passed into the hands of his sister, Vera.

February 19th: The date in 1861 on which Alexander II signed the Act of Emancipation of the peasants. A subsequent series of reforms in education, finance, local government, and other areas radically changed Russian life.

this new profession: The Public School Statute of July 14, 1864, in effect created the profession of country schoolteacher. Facilities to train professional elementary schoolteachers developed only in the 1870s. See Patrick L. Alston, *Education and the State in Tsarist Russia* (Stanford, Calif.: Stanford University Press, 1969), p. 111.

best remains unanswered: Many village schoolteachers were influenced by the materialist and revolutionary doctrines of the 1860s.

"Here is patience and the faith of saints": Revelation 13:10.

rejected by the editor of *The Russian Messenger:* M. N. Katkov, editor of *RV,* had serialized *Anna Karenina* from 1875 to April 1877, when part 7 appeared. Katkov, an ardent supporter of Russia's involvement in the liberation movement of the Balkan Slavs, refused to publish the final part of the novel because of the criticism of the Russian volunteers which the hero, Levin, expresses in it. Tolstoy published it separately; announcements to that effect appeared in various Moscow newspapers between July 14 and 31, 1877.

any reservations they pleased: In a letter to the editor of *NV,* no. 463, June 14, 1877, Tolstoy's wife noted that "the editor [of *The Russian Messenger*] . . . would not agree to publish the ending of the novel without cuts even though the author had suggested the editor set forth any reservations he found necessary."

July and August 1877, 1.2: The Hunger for Rumors and for "What They Aren't Telling Us." The Expression "They Aren't Telling Us" May Have a Future, and So Some Advance Measures Should Be Taken. More about the Accidental Family

"a telegram's just come": *MV,* no. 169, July 8, 1877 (i.e., eleven days before Dostoevsky visited Darovoe), reported that on May 9 a telegram had arrived in the Ukrainian city of Poltava describing a fierce battle in Dobrudja, Bulgaria, that had resulted in a Russian victory but in which 4,700 Russians had been killed and 17,000 wounded. This news quickly spread through the city, but the telegram was soon found to have been a fabrication.

Plevna: The overall Russian plan in the Balkan campaign was to clear out the Turks from northern Bulgaria, seize the Balkan passes, and then push southward to drive the Turks from the Balkan peninsula. The initial stage of the plan went well, and a Russian-Bulgarian force led by General I. V. Gurko rapidly advanced to the Shipka Pass, a major route through the Balkans, and beyond. At this point it seemed that the path to Constantinople was clear and a Russian victory assured. However, a Turkish force, led by Osman Pasha, managed hastily to reinforce the town of Plevna, a crucial road junction. On July 8 a rash Russian attack on Plevna was repulsed with heavy losses. Two subsequent assaults failed to dislodge the Turks. The Russian advance was dramatically halted, since Plevna represented a major threat to the Russian flank and could not be bypassed.

Liebig, Justus von (1803–73), German chemist. His work on the chemistry of life processes was influential in Russia, particularly among the radicals of the 1860s.

trial of the Dzhunkovskys: An account of the trial was carried in *NV,* no. 472, June 23, 1877.

July and August 1877, 1.3: The Case of the Dzhunkovsky Parents and Their Children

massaging their feet: A traditional Russian means of relaxing and inducing sleep.
trial of Kroneberg: See February 1876, 2.
St. George's Cross: Russian decoration for military valor.

July and August 1877, 1.4: An Imaginary Speech by the Presiding Judge

"the times and the seasons": Acts 1:7: ". . . It is not for you to know the times or the seasons, which the Father hath put in his own power."

July and August 1877, 2.1: Dissociation Again. Part Eight of *Anna Karenina*

he is one of the People: Levin says this in *Anna Karenina,* part 8, chapter 15.
speaking of *Anna Karenina* once some time ago: See February 1877, 2.
"such direct feeling for the oppression of the Slavs *does not and cannot exist*": Levin says this in part 8, chapter 15. The italics are Dostoevsky's.

July and August 1877, 2.2: Confessions of a Slavophile

"poem": The word has a broader meaning in Russian than in English, signifying a work of epic sweep, whether poetry or prose. Dostoevsky frequently uses it.
launched for a great feat: Russia declared war on Turkey on April 12, 1877. The "great feat," of course, is the liberation of the Balkan Slavs from Turkish rule and their eventual union, to which Dostoevsky refers above.
temporary setbacks: I.e., the unsuccessful attempts to seize Plevna in July.
when we began the war: The manifesto of April 12 stated: "The keen sympathy with which we have always viewed the fates of the oppressed Christian population of Turkey is . . . widely known. Our desire to ameliorate and safeguard their position was shared by the entire Russian People, who now express their readiness for new sacrifices for the sake of easing the lot of the Christians of the Balkan peninsula. . . . Our forbearance at last exhausted, the disdainful intractability of the Porte has impelled us to resort to more decisive measures" (*MV,* no. 87, April 13, 1877).
"summits of Christianity": Paraphrased from Johann Lichtenberger's *Predictions,* which Dostoevsky discusses in May and June 1877, 1.1.
"backward, bestial, and ignorant" nation: A correspondent of *MV,* reporting in no. 182, July 21, 1877, on anti-Russian feeling among the Germans of Trieste, noted that they regarded Russia as "a savage, barbaric country posing a serious threat to European civilization."

the crusades of the dark ages: An anonymous writer in *D*, no. 6, 1877, commenting on Dostoevsky's view of the war in the Balkans, stated that Dostoevsky "still believes in the possibility of crusades, while Europe has long since outlived its period of religious fervor, and Russia has never had such a period."

formally declared friends: Dostoevsky has in mind Germany and Austro-Hungary, with whom Russia concluded the "Alliance of the Three Emperors" in 1873. *NV*, no. 514, August 4, 1877, reported that there was rejoicing among the German population of Hungary over Russia's setbacks in the summer of 1877. On August 10 the same newspaper quoted a German press source, which stated that although Germany was in favor of an ultimate Russian victory in the Balkans, she was pleased that the victory would not come easily.

"land of holy miracles": From A. S. Khomiakov's poem "Mechta" [A Dream] (1835). Khomiakov, considered the founder of the Slavophile movement, praises Europe's achievements in the poem, but ends with a statement that the West has been covered by a deathly pall and calls upon the East to awaken from its slumbers.

July and August 1877, 2.3: *Anna Karenina* as a Fact of Special Importance

one of my favorite writers on the street: Probably I. S. Goncharov.

"Pleiade": Tolstoy, Goncharov, Turgenev, Nekrasov, and Ostrovsky. Lomonosov, Mikhail Vasilevich (ca. 1711–65), Russian scientist, poet, grammarian, founder of Moscow University; Russia's first great linguistic reformer.

"A Feast in Time of Plague": *Pir vo vremia chumy* (1830), Pushkin's "little tragedy," a verse translation and adaptation of a scene from John Wilson's play, *The City of the Plague*.

"Vengeance is mine, I will repay": Deuteronomy 32:35, Romans 12:19 and, of course, the epigraph to *Anna Karenina*.

penultimate part: Dostoevsky errs here. The scene in which Karenin and Vronsky are reconciled at Anna's sickbed occurs, not in part 7, but in part 4, chapter 17.

darkness instead of the light: The scene leading up to and including Anna's suicide, part 7, chapters 23 through 31.

July and August 1877, 2.4: A Landowner Who Gets Faith in God from a Peasant

some *touchy* things there: Dostoevsky may have in mind Levin's doubts about religion and the Orthodox church, expressed in part 8, chapters 12 and 13 of *Anna Karenina*.

expresses himself as follows: The sections quoted here, and following, are from part 8, chapters 11 through 13. There are some omissions, and the italics are Dostoevsky's.

July and August 1877, 3.1: The Irritability of Vanity

"waves his arms around just like this": In part 8, chapter 14, of *Anna Karenina*, Dolly's children tell Levin: "Uncle Kostia! Mama's coming, and grandpapa, and Sergei Ivanych, and another man. . . . An awfully dreadful man! And he waves his arms just like this! . . ."

honey and the Eastern Question: The scene occurs in part 8, chapters 15 and 16.

Committee: The Slavic Committee. See notes to February 1876, 1.2.

passed without notice: Only one mention was made of Sergei Koznyshev's book, *An Outline of a Survey of the Principles and Forms of Government in Europe and Russia. The Northern Beetle* "suggested in a few contemptuous words that everyone had seen through it long ago and consigned it to general ridicule" (*Anna Karenina*, part 8, chapter 1).

in the earlier parts as well: Dostoevsky probably has in mind the scenes of Koznyshev's abortive courtship of Varenka (*Anna Karenina*, part 6, chapters 4 and 5).

the old prince: I.e., Prince Shcherbatsky, Kitty's father.

Fonvizin, Denis Ivanovich (1744–92), Russian dramatist. The characters in his plays are often "humors," whose names suggest the qualities or vices they personify—e.g., Prostakov (Mr. Simpleton), Pravdin (Mr. Truthful), Starodum (Mr. Oldsense).

even without him: The passage quoted here, as well as those that follow, are taken from part 8, chapters 15 and 16. There are minor omissions and errors, and the italics are Dostoevsky's.

Mikhailych: A peasant character, Levin's beekeeper.

summoning of the Varangians: The Russian *Primary Chronicle* [Povest' vremennykh let] (ca. 1040–1118) begins its account of the origin of the Russian state with the tale of the summoning of the Varangians, or Norsemen, who were invited to come and rule over the city of Novgorod and end the strife between tribes. Their leader, Rurik, founded a dynasty that ruled Russia until 1598.

July and August 1877, 3.2: *Tout ce qui n'est pas expressément permis est défendu*

Milan of Serbia (Milan Obrenović IV) (1854–1901), Grand Duke of Serbia, 1868–82; king of Serbia (as Milan I), 1882–89. Nicholas of Montenegro (1841–1921), Grand Duke of Montenegro, king of Montenegro, 1910–18.

against his "sovereign lord": *G*, no. 167, June 18, 1877, wrote (two days before Serbia's declaration of war on Turkey) that Serbia was a "vassal principality" that had acknowledged Turkey's rule over it and that Prince Milan, as a subject of Sultan Murad IV, might rebel against Turkey but, in a strictly legal sense, could not declare war; in such a case, the European powers would be obliged to refuse aid and sympathy to the Serbs.

operations in Central Asia: Between 1863 and 1865, M. G. Cherniaev was involved in a number of operations that formed part of Russia's campaign of conquest in Central Asia. He conquered Tashkent in June 1865, though his forces were outnumbered almost fifteen to one. He served as military governor of Turkestan in 1865–66.

commander-in-chief of the Serbian army: Cherniaev took command of the main Serbian force, the Army of Timoko-Moravia, in May 1876. Prince Milan remained nominally the commander-in-chief, although Cherniaev was the most important field commander and the real power behind the throne.

a few thousand, perhaps: Estimates vary, but most sources place the number of volunteers in 1876 at about three thousand.

Kireev, Nikolai Alekseevich (1841–76). A former soldier, Kireev was an active member of St. Petersburg's Slavic Committee. He traveled to the Balkans on behalf of the committee to assess the prospects for an uprising against the Turks. He took command of a detachment of Bulgarian volunteers in Serbia and, conspicuously dressed in a white uniform, led them into an attack on a Turkish position. He was killed by Turkish fire on July 6, 1876.

to join Pugachev's gang, to go to Khiva: Emelian Ivanovich Pugachev (1742?–75) leader of a massive uprising against the government of Empress Catherine II in 1773–75. Russia launched campaigns to conquer the Central Asian khanates of Khiva and Bukhara in 1839 and 1859; Bukhara was subdued in 1868; Khiva became a Russian protectorate in 1873.

July and August 1877, 3.3: On the Uneducated and Illiterate Russian People's Unerring Knowledge of the Real Essence of the Eastern Question

Mount Athos: A complex of monasteries at the western end of the Khalkidikí peninsula in northern Greece and popular destination of religious pilgrims; the monasteries on Mount Athos had had close links with Russian monasteries since the twelfth century.

account of his travels: The Russian abbot Daniil (d. 1122) described his pilgrimage from Constantinople to Palestine between 1106 and 1108 in a work known under various titles: *The Life and Travels of Daniil, Abbot of Russia* [Zhitie i khozhdenie Daniila, russkiia zemli igumena]; *The Pilgrimage of the Abbot Daniil* [Palomnik Danila igumena]; *The Pilgrim* [Strannik]. Daniil spent sixteen months in Jerusalem and was received by the crusader Baldwin I, known as the king of Jerusalem.

Agarians: In Russian folklore, the name given to Arabs or Saracens, who were seen as mortal foes of Christendom.

Lives of the Saints: [Chet'i-Minei], a collection of saints' lives and material about religious holidays, arranged by month and date and intended for daily reading.

Solovetsky: Kiev had many holy sites, including the Saint Sophia Cathedral and the Kiev-Pechersk Monastery and Crypt. The Solovetsky Monastery, located on one of the Solovetsky Islands in the White Sea, was noted for the rigorous regime observed by many monks there. Saints Zosima and Sabbatius founded the monastery in the fifteenth century; their relics were widely believed to have miraculous powers.

"Vlas": Dostoevsky discusses Nekrasov's poem "Vlas" in *DP*, 1873.5.

war that ended with Sevastopol: In his manifestos of June 14 and October 22, 1853, Nicholas I expressed his concern about the safety of the Orthodox church within the Turkish empire. The defense of Sevastopol (September 1854 to September 1855) was the last major campaign of the war.

about the holy places: Among the causes of the Crimean War was the question of who should control the keys to the Church of the Nativity in Bethlehem. Nicholas I was indignant at French Catholics who managed to acquire control of the church from the Turkish Sultan.

a Russian general: M. G. Cherniaev.

the Tsar-Liberator: Alexander II, in whose reign serfdom was abolished.

July and August 1877, 3.4: Levin's Agitation. A Question: Does Distance Have an Influence on Love for Humanity? Can One Agree with the Opinion of One Turkish Prisoner on the Humaneness of Some of Our Ladies? So What, Then, Are Our Teachers Teaching Us?

two and a half months ago: Dostoevsky errs here; part 8 appeared in July 1877 (see notes to July and August 1877, 1.1).

eyewitnesses of all nations can now attest: Among the first accounts of Turkish atrocities in the Balkans was William Gladstone's pamphlet "The Bulgarian Horrors and the Question of the East" (September 1876). A portion of this appeared in a supplement to *Gr* entitled *Russkii sbornik* [Russian anthology], vol. 1 (January 1877), together with accounts of Turkish atrocities witnessed by an English colonel, MacIver, who served as a volunteer with Serbian forces, and by the correspondent of the London *Daily News*, J. A. MacGachan (1844–78). MacGachan's vivid accounts of the Bulgarian massacres of 1876 did much to rouse public opinion in Europe and Russia against the Turks; Dostoevsky's evidence of Turkish atrocities derives mainly from this source.

screamed for a long time: Dostoevsky discusses this event in *DP*, May and June 1877, 4.2.

bashibazouks: Turkish irregular troops, noted for their ferocity and cruelty.

"the Koran forbids it": *NV*, no. 534, August 24, 1877, carried a report from a Viennese newspaper that, in answer to an enquiry from a major foreign embassy in Constantinple about rumors of killing Russian wounded, a Turkish cabinet minister replied that such rumors must be false, since the Koran forbids Moslems to murder captives.

he did not believe it: Several reports in *MV* in the summer of 1877 indicated that the Turkish embassy in Berlin was a major source of rumors of

Russian atrocities perpetrated against the Turks. These accusations were refuted by both Russian and European official sources. *NV,* no. 522, August 12, 1877, reported that the German government had sent an official protest to the Turkish government that included a reminder of the provisions of the Geneva Convention, of which Turkey was a signatory, regarding the guarantee of the safety of prisoners.

that their heads will be cut off at once: The correspondent of *NV* (no. 489, July 10, 1877) reported that Turks taken prisoner were terrified, as they had been told the Russians would torture and execute them.

I've spoken about already: See *DP,* September 1876, 1.4.

"an army of gentlemen": Correspondents of both the London *Times* and *The Daily News,* whose comments were reprinted in Russian newspapers, noted the civilized behavior of Russian troops.

"as recompense for your labor": *NV,* no. 508, July 29, 1877, reported that these measures were being taken but did not attribute the words to the commander-in-chief of the Russian forces in the Balkans, Grand Duke Nikolai Nikolaevich, brother of Tsar Alexander II.

expensive tobacco and sweets: *SV,* no. 158, June 10, 1877, reported that a group of Turkish prisoners being transported through the south Russian town of Novocherkassk quickly became a center of attention; some townspeople brought the prisoners bouquets of flowers. The same newspaper (no. 144, June 20, 1877) reported that Turkish prisoners in Tver walked freely about the town and that some "sentimental misses" gave them money, tea, and tobacco. *MV,* no. 137, June 10, 1877, stated that crowds gathered to look at a group of Turkish prisoners passing through Moscow: "Very many people bought cigarettes and gave them to the Turks, who did not refuse the gifts offered them." Later in the summer, when reports came of heavy Russian losses and Turkish atrocities, Russian newspapers such as *MV* began taking a much harsher view of such treatment of prisoners.

after the city had been plundered: J. A. MacGachan accompanied members of an official British inquiry into the massacres on a tour of the area during the summer of 1876. Of the town of Batak he wrote: "The town had 9,000 inhabitants. There now remain 1,200. . . ." In the *London Daily News,* August 7, 1876, he wrote: "The whole churchyard for three feet deep was festering with dead bodies partly covered—hands, legs, arms, and heads projected in ghastly confusion. . . . The church was still worse. . . ." Quoted in Mercia MacDermott, *A History of Bulgaria, 1393–1885* (New York: Praeger, 1962), p. 276.

September 1877, 1.1: The Unfortunate and Unsuccessful

(it's the third time now): I.e., Napoleon, who first seized power as consul in 1799; his nephew, Louis Napoleon who, after becoming president of the republic in the wake of the 1848 revolution, seized sole power in 1851 and a year later was proclaimed emperor; and Marshal MacMahon, who dissolved the Chamber of Deputies in May 1877.

convinced they will win a complete victory: Dostoevsky forecasts a defeat for the republicans, but they did in fact win an overwhelming majority of votes in the October elections.

Thiers, Louis Adolphe (1797–1877), French statesman and historian, president of the Republic from August 30 (n.s.), 1871, to May 24, 1873. In a speech published in *MV,* no. 207, August 20, 1877, several days before his death, Thiers, a conservative republican, declared that a republic was the only form of government possible in France.

Wilhelmshöhe: After Napoleon III ordered the surrender of the French fortress of Sedan to the Prussians, a republic with a Government of National Defense was proclaimed in Paris (September 4, 1870 [n.s.]). From September 5 to March 19, 1871, Napoleon III lived as a prisoner in the German castle of Wilhelmshöhe, near Kassel.

lacking all control: Under the leadership of the republican Government of National Defense, the French abandoned a number of smaller fortresses in late September, surrendered the fortress of Metz (October 27 [n.s.], 1870), and were forced to yield Paris after a four-month siege (January 18 [n.s.], 1871). A number of attempts by this government to sue for peace were unsuccessful. Peace was concluded only after Thiers was made president and humiliating terms were imposed on France. The terms included the loss of Alsace and Lorraine and the payment of an indemnity of five billion francs to the Germans (not three billion, as Dostoevsky states).

Gambetta, Léon (1838–82), French statesman. After Sedan he proclaimed the fall of the emperor and the establishment of the Republic; he became minister of the interior in the new government. In October 1870 he escaped besieged Paris in a balloon; at Tours he created a virtual personal dictatorship in his attempts to organize French resistance. He had some success in rallying and reequipping French troops, but to do so had to resort to high-handed measures that earned him the enmity of many highly placed people. When Paris fell, Gambetta submitted to the German terms of surrender.

German trusteeship: Although Germany closely watched France's recovery from the war, there was no formal "trusteeship" under the terms of the Treaty of Frankfurt (1871) that ended the war.

turned them out of office: Dostoevsky refers to the "coup d'état" of May 16 (n.s.) (see notes to May and June 1877, 3.2).

tuck in his tail and retire: After the republican victory of October, the Bonapartist MacMahon continued as president after reluctantly accepting a republican ministry. He did resign in January 1879, before the expiration of his term.

his surprising manifesto: *NV,* no. 549, September 8, 1877, carried a summary of MacMahon's manifesto of September 19 (n.s.) (on the eve of the French elections): "The marshal will not submit to the demands of demagogues and will remain in his post. Elections whose result might be damaging to his policies would (in the words of the manifesto) cause more confrontations and result in turbulence that would be harmful to the interests of all."

September 1877, 1.2: A Curious Character

summer travels through France: In the summer of 1877, Marshal MacMahon traveled to Normandy and through central and southern France; one purpose of the tour was to attempt to sway the French electorate away from republican candidates. The *Journal de St. Pétersbourg*, no. 211, August 11, 1877, reported that the voters generally gave him a cool and restrained reception; a similar report was carried in *NV*, no. 520, August 10, 1877.

he will go to Paris: *NV*, no. 563, September 22, 1877, quoted Belgian reports that the son of Napoleon III, one of the pretenders to the French throne, had left his exile in England and, after spending several weeks in a Belgian town near the French border, had gone on to Paris incognito. However, this report was later shown to be erroneous.

a descendant of Charlemagne: *MV*, no. 228, September 14, 1877, reported on MacMahon's reception in Poitiers: "There were a number of cries from the crowd, 'Vive le descendant de Charlemagne!' There were also more than a few shouts of 'Vive le roi!'"

"I gave my word to preserve these institutions": Dostoevsky paraphrases a report that appeared in *NV*, no. 571, September 30, 1877, which stated that MacMahon had "declared that the threats of radicals would only serve to strengthen his unshakeable intention not to give up his supreme authority under any circumstances or under any pretext before 1880."

if the pope's death coincides with the elections in France or happens immediately after them: Elections to the Chamber of Deputies took place on October 14 (n.s.); Pope Pius IX died on February 7 (n.s.), 1878. Neither the outcome of the French elections nor the death of the pope had any significant influence on the Eastern Question.

September 1877, 1.3: That's It, Yet It Isn't It. A Reference to What I Wrote Three Months Ago

the election of a new one: Pope Pius's successor, Leo XIII, was elected on February 20 (n.s.), 1878. He, too, was reluctant to admit the loss of temporal power, but was forced to remain only as a spiritual leader. Taking an approach considerably more conciliatory than that of his predecessor, he managed to improve relations with Germany and stem the rise of anticlericalism in at least some parts of Europe.

issue No. 235: The article appeared in *MV* on September 22.

"a terrible future" for Russia: See notes to May and June 1877, 1.1. *NV*, no. 535, August 25, 1877, carried a report from a Polish newspaper that quoted Pius IX as follows: "I experience real delight whenever I hear that the Russians have suffered a defeat and hope that with God's help they will at last be vanquished. I pray to the Most High that this may happen. . . ."

the Italian king, who at once occupied Rome: The forces of Victor Emmanuel II occupied Rome and declared it the capital of the Kingdom of Italy in September 1870. The French garrison stationed in Rome to defend the pope had been withdrawn the previous month, when the Franco-Prussian War began.

the May coup in France: See notes to May and June 1877, 3.2.

resign his post: in a preelection speech delivered in Lille on August 15 (n.s.), 1877, Gambetta expressed his confidence in a republican victory and stated that in that event MacMahon would not dare ignore the will of the electorate and would not attempt a Bonapartist coup. *NV,* no. 520, August 10, 1877, carried an account of the speech.

to declare war on France: Relations between France and Germany grew extremely tense in the spring of 1875, when France passed a new law that meant abandonment of Napoleon III's idea of a professional army in favor of the Prussian principle of a mass levy. France could thus raise an army much closer in strength to that of Germany. There was talk in Germany of a preventive war to maintain German supremacy. The diplomatic efforts of England and Russia helped defuse the crisis.

Germany's guardianship: Germany grew concerned about the possibility of a French war of revenge after MacMahon dissolved the Chamber of Deputies following the crisis of May 1877; the ultramontane cabinet that was subsequently installed in France was regarded as more bellicose than that of the former prime minister, Jules Simon.

first ministers of Germany and Austria: Prince Bismarck met with the Austro-Hungarian prime minister, Count Andrássy in Salzburg on September 19 (n.s.), 1877. *NV,* no. 552, September 11, 1877, reported that each party had agreed to carry on its former policy but that Germany had discouraged Austria from standing in Russia's way in her war with Turkey; German policy would be one of helping Russia, in small ways at least, against Turcophile Austria.

September 1877, 1.4: What Austria Is Now Thinking About

what her government wants: Austro-Hungary's position in the Russo-Turkish War was one of neutrality, although a substantial portion of the country's population, the Hungarians in particular, were anti-Russian and pro-Turkish. See Arthur J. May, *The Hapsburg Monarchy, 1867–1914* (Cambridge: Harvard University Press, 1951), pp. 125–26.

to support the Turks against the Russians: The nationalist Magyar movement was fiercely anti-Russian; a number of anti-Russian demonstrations took place after the unsuccessful Russian assault on Plevna on August 30, 1877. *NV,* no. 560, September 19, 1877, carried an account of bands of armed Hungarians gathering on the border with Russia with the aim of harassing the Russian rear in Rumania.

without taking Austria's interests into account: An Austrian communiqué, reprinted in *MV,* no. 228, September 14, 1877, stated that Austria's policy in the Russo-Turkish War was to preserve the interests of the monarchy.

Sadova: Austria was badly defeated at Sadova (Königgrätz) during her war with Italy and Prussia in 1866. The battle marked a decisive turn in the war, as a result of which Austria was expelled from the German Union and was forced to surrender Venetia and Holstein, won during the Austro-Prussian war with Denmark in 1864.

her own "dualism": Austria's defeat in her war with Prussia forced her to accept a Hungarian plan for the transformation of the Austrian Empire into a dual, Austro-Hungarian state. From May 1867, central authority in the empire was confined to matters of finance, the military, and foreign affairs; the government of each of state was responsible for its own internal matters. Prior to this, and since 1699, Hungary had been in a more or less subservient position vis-à-vis Austria.

September 1877, 1.5: Who's Knocking at the Door? Who Will Come In? Inescapable Fate

almost word for word: During the summer of 1877 the European press carried many items dealing with the political crisis in France and the growing possibility of war between France and Germany, matters which Dostoevsky had discussed in his May and June *Diary*. One of Dostoevsky's "speculations" that appeared to be borne out by reports in the Russian press was the influence of the Catholic church on French politics. *NV*, no. 565, September 24, 1877, called the French government of the day "a genuine *gouvernement des curés*."

what he said about it in Berlin to Crispi: Bismarck held talks in Berlin with the president of the Italian Chamber, Francesco Crispi (1819–1901) on September 24 (n.s.), 1877. According to reports of the *London Daily Telegraph* (reprinted in *NV*, no. 555, September 14, 1877), the talks concerned the successor to Pope Pius IX and Franco-German relations. In regard to the latter question, Bismarck was reported to have gained Italian support in any coming conflict with France.

Northcote's speech: Stafford Henry Northcote (1846–1911), chancellor of the exchequer in Disraeli's government in 1877. *NV*, no. 569, September 28, 1877, quoted Northcote as saying that Russia and Turkey should take advantage of an opportunity to settle their dispute peacefully. *NV* scorned this advice, which it interpreted as Britain's attempt to interfere in Russia's affairs so as to further British trade interests.

the Estates-General: The representatives of the three estates in France (nobility, clergy, and bourgeoisie) were summoned on May 5 (n.s.), 1789—i.e., on the eve of the French Revolution.

September 1877, 2.1: A Lie Is Saved by a Lie

Amadis de Gaula: Romance of chivalry dating probably from the thirteenth century; Cervantes pronounced it "the best of all the books of this kind that have ever been written."

"Sancho, my friend": As first noted by the Spanish scholar M. de Guevara, no such episode occurs in *Don Quixote* (see V. E. Vagno, "Dostoevskii o 'Don-Kikhote' Servantesa" [Dostoevsky on Cervantes's *Don Quixote*], *Dostoevskii: materialy i issledovaniia* [Dostoevsky: Source materials and studies], [Leningrad: Nauka, 1978], 3:126–35). Vagno shows, however, that many of the elements of the scene Dostoevsky created were taken from Cervantes.

September 1877, 2.2: Slugs Taken for Human Beings. Which Is Better: When People Know the Truth about Us or When They Talk Nonsense about Us?

absolute absurdities about Russia: *MV,* no. 198, August 10, 1877, surveyed anti-Russian opinion in the European press and noted that the Austro-Hungarian newspapers were particularly virulent in their Russophobia. The Russian setbacks at Plevna in July and August suggested to these newspapers that Russia's forces were extremely weak.

the Russian soldier and officer: In the late summer of 1877 several Russian newspapers, including *G* and *NV,* quoted Western correspondents' praise of Russian troops.

the last two hundred years: Russian victories over European armies include Peter the Great's defeat of the Swedes at Poltava in 1709, Suvorov's victories over the French in northern Italy in 1799, the victory over Napoleon in 1812, and the Russian role in the defeat of Napoleon's armies at Leipzig in 1814.

an enormous uprising of the People: The French-language Russian newspaper *Journal de St. Pétersbourg,* no. 253, September 25, 1877, carried a report from the Paris newspaper *Estafette* concerning a supposed major clash on the "Petersburg Side" (a predominantly industrial area on the right bank of the River Neva) between workers and police in St. Petersburg; the city's governor was reported to have summoned two infantry regiments from Dinaburg (now Daugavpils, Lithuania) to restore order. *Journal de St. Pétersbourg* commented sarcastically on the sensationalism of the French Turcophile press in magnifying a minor disturbance into a popular uprising.

an assault of the French and the English: The Russians repelled a number of assaults on the heavily defended fortress of Sevastopol during the Crimean War, notably a combined attack by 44,000 French and British troops on June 8, 1855.

near Tserkovna: A communiqué from the commander-in-chief of the Russian forces, published in *MV,* no. 228, September 14, 1877, stated that twelve Russian battalions had beaten off an attack by twenty thousand Turks in an encounter near the Bulgarian town of Tserkovna on September 9. The Turks were reported to have lost some two thousand men, the Russians, 66 killed and 220 wounded.

their rifles, which are better than ours: Most of the Turkish forces were equipped with German or American weapons (Henry-Martini, Schneider, and Winchester rifles, Krupp artillery) that was superior to Russian equipment. (See also notes to October 1877, 1.3.)

with the European powers: Dostoevsky discussed British aid to the Turkish forces in his *Diary* of May and June, 1877. 4.2. *NV*, no. 574, October 3, 1877, quoted an Austrian war correspondent's figure of as many as fourteen thousand British officers officially attached to the Turkish army, as well as uncounted numbers of unofficial British volunteers.

our real routes to Turkey: Dostoevsky has in mind mainly the diplomatic efforts of Austro-Hungary, which feared a Russian alliance with Serbia, Rumania, and Montenegro. In the summer of 1877 the war had been confined to the territory of present-day Bulgaria; Austro-Hungary was officially neutral, as was Serbia, but *NV*, no. 486, July 7, 1877, reported that Austria had allowed Turkish arms to be shipped through her territory, thus violating her neutrality; Russia, the newspaper argued, should therefore be allowed to move her troops through the Timok valley in Serbia. Somewhat earlier (no. 480, July 1, 1877), the same newspaper reported that Austria had become convinced of Serbia's decision to enter the war on Russia's side and had therefore decided to occupy Serbia.

a conspiracy of whole gangs has been discovered in Europe: See notes to September 1877, 1.4.

at a huge cost to themselves: *NV*, no. 513, August 3, 1877, quoting the (London) *Times*, reported that Disraeli's government had arranged a secret loan of £2,500,000 to the Turks. Later reports enlarged the figure to ten to twenty million pounds.

to annihilate the Bulgarians to the last one: *MV*, no. 166, July 5, 1877, reported rumors that the Turks had prepared lists of Bulgarians to be executed; women and children were to be carried off to Turkey; the rapid Russian advance did not allow the Turks to carry out these plans, the paper reported.

the fall of the ruble: One of the economic consequences of the Russo-Turkish War was a sharp drop in the value of the ruble. Russian currency was discounted by 20 to 50 percent on foreign exchanges. *NV*, no. 566, September 26, 1877, stated that because of the war the ruble had only 65 percent of its prewar value, but interest on foreign loans had to be paid at full value, putting great strain on Russia's finances.

September 1877, 2.3: An Intimation of the Future Educated Russian Man. The Certain Lot of the Future Russian Woman

chauvinism and stagnation: Dostoevsky probably has in mind the newspaper *G*, whose policy was essentially Anglophile and which expressed some concerns about Russian chauvinism aroused by the war. *MV*, no. 137, July 5, 1877, strongly criticized this view.

railway concessionaires: Railway construction in Russia had its first boom period in the decade following 1865. Most construction was undertaken by private, and often foreign, companies. The Main Society of Russian Railways, established in 1857 and made up mainly of European bankers, was given a concession, with profits guaranteed by the Russian government, to construct four major lines. Costs of building the lines were far higher than planned, and the Russian government was forced to indemnify the concessionaires the sum of forty-six million rubles.

the cause they had undertaken to serve: *NV,* no. 481, July 2, 1877, reprinted a report from the (London) *Times* stating that the confidence of Russian officers, coupled with their desire to distinguish themselves, might lead them to foolhardy ventures and needless losses of troops.

the lofty role that certainly awaits her among us: The bravery and selfless behavior of the many women who served as nurses in field hospitals during the war was frequently mentioned in the Russian press (e.g., *MV,* no. 214, August 28, 1877; *NV,* no. 533, August 23, 1877; *NV,* no. 559, September 18, 1877).

sentimental ladies who gave candies to the Turks: See July and August 1877, 3.4.

October 1877, 1.1: To the Reader

to suspend my publication for a year or two: Dostoevsky's emphysema worsened, despite his summer's rest in the country (see notes to April 1877, 2). He was advised by his doctor to reduce his work load.

October 1877, 1.2: An Old, Customary Military Rule

Main School of Military Engineering: Dostoevsky was a cadet at the school in St. Petersburg from 1838 to 1843.

Totleben, Eduard Ivanovich (1818–84), count, military engineer, and chief planner of the defense of Sevastopol during the Crimean War. Totleben completed his studies at the School of Military Engineering in 1838. Dostoevsky for a time shared an apartment with Totleben's younger brother and fellow engineer, Adolf; it was through him that he made the acquaintance of Eduard Totleben.

Kaufmann, Konstantin Petrovich (1818–82), general of engineers; he served with distinction in the Caucasus, the Crimean War, and the conquest of Central Asia.

Radetsky, Fedor Fedorovich (1820–90), lieutenant-general; he served in the Caucasus and in the Russo-Turkish War of 1877–78), distinguishing himself in the defense of the Shipka Pass.

Petrushevsky, Mikhail Fomich (1832–93), major-general; he served with distinction in the Russo-Turkish War of 1877–78.

Iolshin: Possibly Major-General Mikhail Aleksandrovich Iolshin (1830–83), who was decorated as commander of the first brigade of Russian troops to cross the Danube on July 14, 1877. Iolshin was not a graduate of the School of Military Engineering, however.

Grigorovich: See notes to 1873.14.

Trutovsky, Konstantin Aleksandrovich (1826–93), landscape and genre painter.

October 1877, 1.3: The Same Rule, Only in a New Guise

redoubts at Borodino: At the Battle of Borodino (August 26, 1812), Russian field engineers hastily erected earth redoubts and flèches to protect their artillery against Napoleon's army.

still not been captured: Prior to the second attack on Plevna, on July 18, 1877, Russian forces numbered 32,000; by the time of the third attack, on August 30, the Russian and Rumanian troops involved had been reinforced to total 96,000.

Osman Pasha: Planner of the defense of Plevna and commander of the Turkish forces there.

the rifle that's now being used: The rifle used by the Turks, which Dostoevsky calls the Peabody, was also known as the Peabody-Martini, the Henry-Martini, and the Henry. The Peabody-Martini was a single-shot, breech-loading weapon of American manufacture, accurate to distances as far as 3,000 yards. The Turks were also armed with American Winchester rifles, which had multi-shot capacity but shorter range. Using such weapons and occupying the heights on which they dug trenches and tunnels and erected earthworks, the Turks were able to pour very damaging fire on the Russian attackers.

glacis: An earthwork, sloping toward the enemy, in front of a ditch that formed part of a fortification; the glacis was intended to absorb artillery projectiles, preventing them from reaching the defenders beyond.

with Totleben's help: Totleben joined the Russian army in the Balkans only in mid-September 1877 and took charge of the Russo-Rumanian military engineers organizing the siege of Plevna. It was the Russian blockade rather than military engineering that ultimately led to the taking of Plevna, however. Running short of provisions and ammunition, Osman Pasha attempted to break out of the siege on the night of November 27/28, but was forced to surrender along with his forty thousand troops. Some weeks later, Totleben was named commander-in-chief of the Russian forces in the Balkans.

October 1877, 1.4: The Most Enormous Military Errors May Sometimes Not Be Errors At All

the Berdan rifle: At the onset of the Russo-Turkish War, nearly half the Russian troops were still equipped with the obsolescent, single-shot Krnka rifle; after the unsuccessful attempt to take Plevna on August 30, the Russian troops were reinforced by units of the Guards equipped with Berdan rifles. The Berdan was capable of fire twice as rapid as the Krnka.

an even better rifle than the Germans: When the Franco-Prussian War began, the French infantry was using the quick-firing Chassepot rifle; the German von Dreyse breech-loading rifle was of similar design to the Chassepot but was a much older weapon with some serious defects. The French in 1870 also used a cartridge that was far superior to the German one.

compelled to defend its own territory at home: The French were slow to mobilize their reserves when the war began and were hindered by chaotic supply services; thus they were unable to take the offensive.

the Germans were victorious: German armies won encounters at Weissenburg on August 4 (n.s.) and at Wörth and Spicheren on August 6 (n.s.).

the mad Trochu: The siege of Paris lasted from September 19, 1870, to January 28 (n.s.), 1871. Its defense was the responsibility of General Louis-Jules Trochu (1815–96), who had largely untrained and ill-equipped troops at his disposal. Nevertheless, he sent them on a number of unsuccessful raids on German positions and suffered heavy losses as a consequence.

Gambetta escaped from Paris in a balloon: See notes to September 1877, 1.2.

October 1877, 1.5: We Have Only Stumbled Over a New Fact, but There Was No Error. Two Armies, Two Opposites. The Actual State of Affairs

one French military historian: J-B. A. Charras, *Histoire de la campagne de 1815*. Waterloo. Par le colonel Charras (Brussels, 1863). Dostoevsky's library contained the fourth edition of this work. L. P. Desiatkin and G. M. Fridlender, "Biblioteka Dostoevskogo (novye materialy)" [Dostoevsky's library: new materials], in *Dostoevskii: materialy i issledovaniia* [Dostoevsky: source materials and studies], 4:267.

cross the Danube and reach the Balkans: Russian troops crossed the Danube June 12 to 15, 1877, generally taking the Turks by surprise and meeting with light resistance. By mid-July the Russians had already seized important passes through the Balkans.

flee in haste before the Russian onslaught: Dostoevsky's prognosis generally proved true: after the fall of Plevna there was little more serious resistance from the Turks in the Balkans.

a great victory: Russian forces had also been doing battle with the Turks in Transcaucasia. In October 1877 the Turkish army of Mukhtar Pasha was defeated at Avliar, near Kars, Turkey. This victory in Transcaucasia was as significant for the war there as the taking of Plevna was to be for the conflict in Bulgaria.

remains almost unnoticed: The article appeared in *MV*, no. 251, October 11, 1877.

October 1877, 2.1: Hartung's Suicide and Our Eternal Question: Who Is to Blame?

after he heard the jurors pronounce him guilty: The trial of Major-General Leonid Nikolaevich Hartung (1834–77), and a number of others, for theft of various financial documents, took place from October 7 to October 13, 1877. Hartung committed suicide on the last day of the trial. The speech of Hartung's lawyer had some influence on the account of Dmitry's trial in *The Brothers Karamazov*. See V. Ia. Kirpotin, *Mir Dostoevskogo* [Dostoevsky's world], 2d ed. (Moscow: Sovetskii pisatel', 1983), pp. 345–49.

a general sitting next to a common man: On trial with Hartung were Count S. S. Lanskoi and the servant of the "discounter" Sanftleben, the peasant Egor Myshakov. The prosecutor, N. V. Muravev, noted: "The very fact, the very possibility that *General* Hartung, *Count* Lanskoi and their companions can appear in the dock cannot but be seen as a certain *preliminary*, so to say, victory of justice" (*MV*, no. 252, October 12, 1877).

a lamentable miscarriage of justice had occurred: *MV*, no. 255, October 15, 1877, noted that Hartung's manner of death strongly suggested that he was innocent; *NV*, no. 587, October 16, 1877, raised the possibility of a miscarriage of justice.

one of our most discerning lawyers: Possibly A. F. Koni, prominent lawyer and writer.

in "Mr. X's" column: "Mr. X." (Neznakomets) was the pen name under which A. S. Suvorin wrote his column in *NV*. Like Dostoevsky, Suvorin blamed Russian laxity in business and legal matters for the misfortune. Such attitudes, Suvorin suggested, could have led Hartung to believe that he was doing no wrong.

October 1877, 2.3: Lies Are Indispensable for Truth. A Lie Times a Lie Equals Truth. Is That True?

copied from a foreign model: The Russian legal system was thoroughly reformed in 1864, instituting for the first time public trials and the jury system; Western (particularly French) jurisprudence was used as a model.

October 1877, 3.1: Roman Clericals Here in Russia

in its editorial: The quotation comes from *MV*, no. 262, October 22, 1877.

New Times remarked in this connection: The article to which Dostoevsky refers in fact appeared in *NV* three days later, in no. 596, October 25, 1877. *NV* did dismiss the "conspiracy" as merely the product of rumors, inevitable in time of war. The original article, in *The Government Messenger* [Pravitel'stvennyi vestnik], merely noted the prevalence of false information about the war and cautioned its readers about accepting wild rumors as truth; certain reports appearing in foreign newspapers should likewise be viewed skeptically, the newspaper added.

this conspiracy does exert its influence: Dostoevsky refers to the May "coup d'état" in France (see notes to May and June, 1877, 3.2); several Russian newspapers carried stories of the efforts of the Catholic church to influence the outcome of the French elections, which were imminent.

As "the most liberal of our newspapers" Dostoevsky has in mind *G*, which he refers to below.

Here is the excerpt: The item appeared in *NV*, no. 587, October 16, 1877.

candidacy for the papal throne: Ledochowski, Mieczyslaw Halka (1822–1902), count, archbishop of Poznan. Ledochowski was an ardent Polish nationalist who came into conflict with the German government over his insistence on the use of Polish for religious instruction in Polish schools. According to a report in *NV*, no. 520, August 10, 1877, Ledochowski had links with groups of his countrymen working for Polish independence.

October 1877, 3.2: Old Poland's Summer Attempt at Reconciliation

Old Poland: Dostoevsky has in mind the Polish aristocrats and intelligentsia who emigrated to France after the uprising of 1863 and who hoped for a restoration of an independent Poland.

via Russian periodicals: Over the summer of 1877 the Russian press carried several articles by Polish emigrés calling for reconciliation and economic cooperation between Russia and Poland (e.g., in *SPV*, no. 148, May 31, 1877).

Tengoborski, Liudvig Valerianovich (1793–1857), Russian-Polish economist and statistician, author of a number of works on trade and finance. He began his career in Poland and continued as an active participant in Russian financial and tariff negotiations with various European countries.

Wolowski, Louis-François-Michel-Raymond (1810–76), political economist, born in Warsaw, who emigrated to France in 1831 and spent the remainder of his life there. His economic views influenced Napoleon III.

Brotski: Wiktor Brodzki (1817–1904), sculptor, born in Volynia, he settled in Rome in 1855 but became a professor at the St. Petersburg Academy of Arts in 1868.

Matejko, Jan (1838–93), Polish artist. His paintings of subjects from Polish history were very popular in Europe in the 1870s.

from Kostomarov's article: Nikolai Ivanovich Kostomarov (1817–1885), noted Russian historian, writer, and ethnographer. Kostomarov's article, a response to a letter from "A Resident of Lithuania" (*SPV*, no. 172, June 24, 1877), appeared in *NV*, no. 478, June 29, 1877. The "quotation" cited here is actually a combination of Kostomarov's remarks and Dostoevsky's own commentary.

Konrad Wallenrod: Central character in the narrative poem of the same name, written by the Polish poet Adam Mickiewicz in 1828. In the poem, Wallenrod, a legendary character from fourteenth-century Lithuania, entered the Teutonic Order with the aim of undermining it in revenge for the Order's ravaging of his homeland.

(not their own, of course): *NV*, no. 487, July 8, 1877, carried a note about a Polish legion being assembled in Constantinople to fight against the Russians. *NV*, no. 573, October 2, 1877, reported that Count Wladyslaw

Plater, one of the leaders of the Polish emigrés, had arrived in Constantinople with four million francs to support the legion.

October 1877, 3.3: The Escapade of *The Stock-Exchange News*. Not Ready Pens, Malicious Ones

about Mr. Ilovaisky: The anonymous editorial that Dostoevsky subsequently cites appeared in *BV*, no. 257, October 11, 1877. The same issue of *BV* also carried a detailed account of the arrest of the historian D. I. Ilovaisky accusing him and the leaders of the Pan-Slavist movement of spreading propaganda among the Slavs under Austro-Hungarian rule, thereby damaging relations between Russia and Austro-Hungary.

he was escorted to the Russian border: Ilovaisky was arrested in Galicia and held for three days in prison in Lviv (Lemberg), ostensibly because his passport lacked an Austrian visa. He had been denounced by a Polish priest, Marion Matkowski. The editor of a local Galician-Russian newspaper interceded with the authorities to have Ilovaisky freed.

The Moscow News published an article about it: *MV*, no. 244, October 4, 1877.

a few lines published in *The Moscow News*: *MV*, no. 254, October 14, 1877, carried Ilovaisky's "Letter to the Editor" in which he denied charges that he had traveled as an emissary of the Pan-Slavists and had attempted to spread Pan-Slavist propaganda through a Polish priest. The letter is not "a few lines" but a full column and contains Ilovaisky's strong attack on the Russophobia of the European press as well as on Russian newspapers that accepted the charges against him as being true.

Klapka, György (1820–92), Hungarian general, hero of the revolution of 1848–49. According to reports in some Russian newspapers in the autumn of 1877, he was helping organize Hungarian soldiers to invade Rumania and cut Russian supply lines. Klapka denied this.

an ataman says to the cossacks: Dostoevsky paraphrases a speech made by Taras Bulba from chapter 9 of Gogol's novel of the same name.

Russia could no longer be considered a strong military power: I.e., after Russia's initial reverses at Plevna.

ten thousand English troops landed at Trebizond: *NV*, no. 594, October 23, 1877, noted that the pro-Turkish British press had exaggerated Turkey's military strength and underestimated Russia's, "to the point that they thought the landing of ten thousand English troops at Trebizond would be enough to defeat totally our Transcaucasian army and end the campaign in Asia Minor in accord with England's interests."

November 1877, 1.1: What Does the Word "Striutsky" Mean?

the rather obscure word "striutsky": Dostoevsky uses the word in the title of his *Diary* for January 1877, 2.2, and on several other occasions (e.g., April 1877, 2.1 and July and August 1877, 3.2). Vladimir Dahl's *Tolkovyi slovar' zhivogo velikorusskogo iazyka* [Explanatory dictionary of the living Great-Russian language] defines "striutskii" or "striutskoi" as a "base, worthless, contemptible person"; Dahl labels this definition as dubious, however.

November 1877, 1.2: The History of the Verb "Stushevatsia"

entirely unknown and used by no one: As has been pointed out by Solomon Reiser (in his *Sovremennaia russkaia leksikografiia.* 1977 [Contemporary Russian lexicography, 1977], [Leningrad: Nauka, 1979], pp. 147–50), the word was used in Pushkin's day with the meaning provided by Dostoevsky, although the latter's use of the word probably popularized it; it does appear in Dahl's dictionary.

"The Double" appeared in *OZ*, no. 2, on February 1, 1846.

accepted by Nekrasov for his almanac, *Petersburg Anthology*, in 1845: Dostoevsky describes the reception of his first work in his *Diary* of January 1877, 2.3.

Kraevsky, Andrei Alexandrovich: (1810–89), Russian journalist and publisher. Kraevsky approached publishing as a business and sometimes exploited the writers who contributed to his journals. He published many of Dostoevsky's early writings, including "The Double." Dostoevsky's letters and journalism of the 1860s and early 1870s contain many unflattering references to Kraevsky.

I revised it thoroughly for the then *Complete Collection* of my works: A revised version of the story appeared in Dostoevsky's *Polnoe sobranie sochinenii* [Complete collected works] (St. Petersburg: F. Stellovsky, 1866).

still enthralled by *Poor People*: The first four chapters of "The Double" deal more or less conventionally with the world of the bureaucracy and the petty clerk, subjects that were very common in Russian literature of the 1840s. Only in chapter 5 does Goliadkin's "double" appear and the story begin to take a turn toward the bizarre.

everything that had appeared in literature over the five years I had been away: During the four years he had spent at a forced labor prison (January 1850 to February 1854), Dostoevsky had very little reading matter apart from the New Testament he had been given on the way to Siberia. Letters written to his friends after his release are filled with requests for books and journals.

A Hunter's Sketches had only just begun to come out when I was still in Petersburg: The first version of Turgenev's collection of stories entitled *Zapiski okhotnika* [A sportsman's sketches; a hunter's notebook] was published in 1852. Individual stories included in the cycle appeared from 1847 to 1851; others were added after 1852.

some future Dahl: Vladimir Ivanovich Dahl [Dal'] (1801–72), Russian lexicographer, writer, and folklorist, compiler of the *Tolkovyi slovar' zhivogo velikorusskogo iazyka* (see notes to November 1877, 1.1).

November 1877, 2.1: Servility or Good Manners?

about the current war with Turkey: William Ewart Gladstone (1809–98), British statesman, four times prime minister of Great Britain. He had given up leadership of the Liberal party in 1875, but took a very active part in trying to rally British opinion against Turkey. The passage Dostoevsky quotes comes from a lecture Gladstone gave on the Eastern Question in November 1877 and was reported in *NV*, no. 619, November 17, 1877. Elsewhere in his speech, however, Gladstone expressed his concern for the possible threat to British interests that new Russian influence in the Balkans might pose.

candies and cigars to the Turks: See July and August 1877, 3.4.

in his *Diary* from the Caucasus: Vladimir Petrovich Meshchersky, prince (1839–1914), conservative Russian writer, journalist, and publisher. The passage quoted comes from Meshchersky's *Putevoi dnevnik* [Travel diary], an account of his trip to the Balkan front in 1877, and appeared in *MV*, no. 273, November 4, 1877.

we transported captured Turks: The passage appeared in *MV*, no. 282, November 13, 1877.

to whom I don't know: Vsevolod Vladimirovich Krestovsky (1840–95), Russian writer. In 1877 he was a correspondent with the Russian forces in the Balkans. *PG*, no. 205, November 10, 1877, quotes Krestovsky's letter.

discovered humor among themselves, gave it a special word, and explained it to humanity: The English sense of the word *humor* displaced the earlier French sense (*humeur*, or temperament) in many European languages, including Russian.

sometimes fires five hundred rounds per day: *SV*, no. 203, November 20, 1877, estimated that some Turkish troops were firing four to five hundred rounds per day and noted that this meant their supply of ammunition, from Britain and the United States, must be massive.

issued to Europe in the form of various promises: The manifesto of Alexander II of April 13, 1877, in which he declared war on Turkey, stressed that the aim of the war was the liberation of the Balkan Slavs and not territorial gain. Prince A. I. Vasilchikov, president of the St. Petersburg branch of the Slavic Committee, wrote in *Severnyi vestnik* [The Northern Messenger], no. 183, October 31, 1877, about terms for a possible peace: "We undertook this war with a clearly expressed but imprecisely defined goal: the liberation of the Balkan Slavs; and with that, to reassure European cabinets, we made a pledge to take not a scrap of Turkish territory in Europe." But Russia should receive some compensation for her efforts and for the losses she had suffered, Vasilchikov continued. This should take the form of free Russian access to the Black Sea, and to ensure it Russia should be given Turkey's fleet.

the Barboshi bridge: One of the earliest operations in the war was the securing and crossing of the Barboshi bridge across the river Siret, a vital link between Rumania and Austro-Hungary.

November 1877, 2.2: The Most Extreme Case of Servility There Could Be

well before "Plevna": Russian forces finally took Plevna on November 28, 1877. This brought northern Bulgaria under their control and allowed them to begin a general offensive toward Constantinople.

full of most righteous indignation. . . . : One of the articles Dostoevsky probably had in mind was A. N. Pypin's "Nasha pechat' i bolgarskie dela" [Our press and Bulgarian affairs], *VE*, no. 10, 1877, which criticizes Russian press coverage of the war. Pypin notes: "The naive correspondents, who evidently had never read a single book on Bulgaria, were expecting to encounter the Bulgarians as downtrodden beggars, and they were amazed when they saw the 'oppressed' Bulgarian living in a manner that would be greatly envied not only by the poor Russian peasant but even by a Western one. . . . They suddenly wondered if the Bulgarians really were in need of liberation" (pp. 886–87).

the starving Bulgarians: Several Russian newspapers and magazines touched on the financial burden Russia might have to assume in liberating Bulgaria (e.g., "Voevat' ili ne voevat'" [To go to war or not to go], *OZ*, no. 6, 1876, pp. 358–76).

all the rivers of Russia: an echo of Pushkin's poem "To the Slanderers of Russia" [Klevetnikam Rossii] (1831). The poem was addressed to the deputies of the French Chamber who had expressed support for the Polish rebellion of 1830–31 and is an ardent defense of Russian dominion over Poland, along with a strong suggestion that Europe should mind its own business.

we suddenly withdrew: Russian and Bulgarian forces under the command of Lieutenant-General I. V. Gurko liberated Bulgaria's ancient capital, Tyrnovo, on June 25; shortly thereafter, on July 7, the same forces made a very rapid advance to the Shipka Pass and beyond it. The Turks quickly reinforced their troops in the area, and after engagements at Stara Zagora and Eski Zagora (July 19), General Gurko's force had to withdraw to the Shipka Pass. When the Turks regained control of this area in the Tundzha valley that had been under Russian occupation, they slaughtered ten thousand Bulgarians for welcoming the Russians. *VE*, no. 10, 1877, wrote: "In every place that had been occupied and then abandoned by the Russians there occurred the most terrible, inhumanly vile repressions, carried out by the Turks in revenge for actual or supposed sympathy toward the Russians."

these monsters' new barbarities: *NV*, no. 613, November 11, 1877, reported that Russian forces had been pushed out of the town of Pirgos on November 7, after fierce fighting; a Russian counterattack soon retook the town, but many of the Russian dead who were recovered had been mutilated by the Turks.

in one of the preceding issues of the *Diary*: See July and August, 1877.

the Englishman Forbes: *MV*, no. 267, October 29, 1877, discussed comments on the war by Archibald Forbes (1838–1900), correspondent of the

London Daily News. Forbes paid tribute to the bravery of Russian soldiers but argued that the Bulgarians were incapable of self-government, were exploiting the Russians, and were committing atrocities against the Turks; the Bulgarians, Forbes maintained, had lived rather well under Turkish rule. *NV*, no. 617, November 15, 1877, carried portions of Forbes's article in which he stated that the Turks erred in not carrying out a scorched-earth policy: "In not attempting to offer strong resistance to the Russian crossing of the Danube and in withdrawing before their enemy's push into Bulgaria, the Turks committed a major military blunder; they should have devastated the territories they were leaving open to invasion. . . . The Turks should have driven every last Bulgarian into the interior of the country and should not have left a single ear of wheat standing in the fields."

November 1877, 2.3: Some Quite Special Remarks about the Slavs That I Intended to Make Long Ago

the imminent possibility of peace: Talk of peace intensified in the Russian newspapers after the publication of Vasilchikov's article (see notes to November 1877, 2.1), which discussed conditions Russia might demand of Turkey in the event of peace talks.

"the concert of European powers": I.e., the great powers, including Britain, Austro-Hungary, Germany, France, Italy, and Russia.

Ivan Chiftlik: The name of a Bulgarian village (properly, Iovan Chiftlik) near Rushchuk, mentioned in Russian newspapers in the autumn of 1877 as the site of Russian military operations (e.g., *MV*, no. 241, September 28, 1877).

different scholarly and even poetical views: Dostoevsky has in mind, for instance, the book of N. Ia. Danilevsky (1822–85) *Russia and Europe* [Rossiia i Evropa]. Danilevsky, proceeding from ideas of the Russian Slavophiles and adding an element of Social Darwinism, regarded the Slavs as a single organism, each element of which enriched the others as it developed. Among the "poetical views" on the question are those expressed by A. S. Khomiakov (1804–60), F. I. Tituchev (1803–73), and A. N. Maikov (1821–97).

November 1877, 3.1: Rumors of Peace. "Constantinople Must Be Ours"—Is That Possible? Various Opinions

not only in Europe but here as well: As the war began to turn in Russia's favor, the European press began discussing possible terms of a peace treaty. Britain and Austro-Hungary, whose policies had been pro-Turkish, expressed some apprehension at the possibility of a Russian victory. A number of Russian writers, including Danilevsky (in his article "O nastoiashchei voine" [On the current war], *RM*, no. 207, August 2, 1877, and no. 279, October 13, 1877, which Dostoevsky discusses below), wrote of the "rewards" to be claimed by Russia for her efforts in liberating the Balkan Slavs.

demands for the iron-clad Turkish monitors: Danilevsky, in his August article noted above, stated: "As a compensation for her military expenditures Russia should be given the fleet of Turkish ironclads, which will become a useless burden for Turkey, as well as a part of Asia—at least Kars and Batumi."

annex Kars and Erzerum: *NV,* no. 613, November 23, 1877, and in subsequent issues, also demanded Turkish territory.

the future fate of Constantinople: Dostoevsky had followed Danilevsky's work very closely from the time of his book's first appearance in the journal *Zaria* [Dawn] in 1869. Although basically sympathetic to his ideas, Dostoevsky felt that Danilevsky did not sufficiently appreciate Russia's mission in conveying Orthodoxy to the rest of humanity. In chapter 14 of his book, Danilevsky proposes "an all-Slavic federation, with Russia at its head, with a capital in Tsargrad [Constantinople]—that is the only sensible solution to the great historical problem which in recent times has been called the Eastern Question." N. Ia. Danilevsky, *Rossiia i Evropa* [Russia and Europe] (St. Petersburg: Obshchestvennaia pol'za, 1871), p. 409.

on this same subject: Danilevsky published four articles, under various titles but generally on the Eastern Question, in *RM,* nos. 207, 279, 289–90, and 308–9; the articles can also be found in *Sbornik politicheskikh i ekonomicheskikh statei N. Ia. Danilevskogo* [A collection of political and economic articles by N. Ia. Danilevsky], ed. N. Strakhov (St. Petersburg, 1890), pp. 31–84. The final article was entitled "Constantinople" and argued that, with the collapse of the Turkish Empire, its capital should become a free city, the center of the Eastern Christian Union, to be held jointly by Russia and the rest of the Orthodox and Slavic world.

standing "at the door": Matthew 24:33: "So likewise ye, when ye shall see all these things, know that it is near, even at the doors."

quarrel of the Bulgarians with the patriarchal throne: See notes to March 1877, 1.3. In his fourth article, "Constantinople," Danilevsky had discussed this dispute. The Greeks, he argued, had tried to Hellenize the Bulgarian Orthodox church because of "their fears of all-consuming Pan-Slavism," fears that led significant numbers of the Greek intelligentsia to call for an alliance with Turkey against Russia and the Slavs.

transferring it to the common ownership of small peoples: Danilevsky wrote: "Constantinople should be placed temporarily in the hands of Russia with the intent that, in due time, the city be handed over to all those who have a right to it" (*RM,* no. 308, November 12, 1877).

"a most decisive resistance from the majority of European powers": Danilevsky said: "[Constantinople] might perhaps be recognized as a free city, but under Russia's exclusive protectorate . . . i.e., with a Russian garrison and under general Russian administrative supervision. Such a solution would be highly desirable and highly satisfactory; but there is no doubt that it would meet with the most decisive resistance on the part of the majority of European powers" (*RM,* no. 309, November 12, 1877).

November 1877, 3.2: Once More, For the Last Time, Some "Soothsayings"

the power of the worldwide Catholic conspiracy: Dostoevsky discussed this in May and June 1877, September 1877, and October 1877.

November 1877, 3.3: The Moment Must Be Seized

everything the socialists are preaching to them has also been preached by Christ: The ideas that follow are, of course, developed further in *The Brothers Karamazov,* "The Legend of the Grand Inquisitor."

December 1877, 1.1: The Concluding Explanation of an Old Fact

stepmother Kornilova: Dostoevsky wrote of the Kornilova affair in October 1876, 1.1, and December 1876, 1.1.

malicious and unworthy mockery: *The Northern Messenger* [Severnyi vestnik], no. 8, May 8, 1877, carried an article, "Beseda" [A conversation], signed by "Nabliudatel'" [An observer]. The reviewer maintained that Anna Karenina's death occured, not because Vronsky ceased to love her, but because readers of the novel had grown bored with her.

December 1877, 1.4: Malicious Psychologists. Obstetrician-Psychiatrists

Diukov and Mr. Florinsky: See notes to April 1877, 2.

December 1877, 1.5: One Incident That Explains a Good Deal, in My View

only to a settlement: Exile to Siberia could take the form of hard labor, settlement in a penal colony, or simple exile for a specific term. The second category was considerably less harsh than the first. See George Kennan, *Siberia and the Exile System,* abridged ed. (Chicago: University of Chicago Press, 1958), p. 26.

December 1877, 1.6: Am I an Enemy of Children? On What the Word "Happy" Sometimes Means

Kroneberg's trial: See February 1876, 2.
Dzhunkovskys: See July and August 1877, 1.2–1.4.
Christ's Christmas party: See January 1876, 2.2.
woman taken in adultery: John 8:11.

December 1877, 2.1: The Death of Nekrasov. On What Was Said at His Grave

a month before his death: Dostoevsky's wife notes that her husband visited Nekrasov frequently during the latter's last months of life. See A. G.

Dostoevskaia, *Vospominaniia* [Memoirs] (Moscow: Khudozhestvennaia literatura, 1971), pp. 316–17.

"There is no man . . .": "For there is not a just man upon earth, that doeth good, and sinneth not" (Eccclesiastes 7:20).

I have already talked about that: see January 1877, 2.3.

this mysterious man: Nekrasov's father, a retired army officer, was a bully and a drunkard who abused both his family and his serfs; his mother was a cultivated, sensitive, and compassionate woman. His father wanted him to follow a military career, but he chose to enroll as an auditor at St. Petersburg University; his father then cut off his financial support and left Nekrasov to his own devices. He eked out a precarious living for several years, then turned to journalism and publishing. In 1846 he managed to acquire a literary journal, *The Contemporary* [Sovremennik], which he soon transformed into an organ of the radical left and the leading literary periodical for the next twenty years. In purchasing this journal, and in later business dealings, Nekrasov showed a streak of ruthlessness and made a number of enemies in the literary world; stories (some of which had factual basis) of his greed and lack of principle in business dealings circulated for the remainder of his life. Nekrasov's poetry often takes up the cause of social reform (as far as censorship allowed), and its mood is one of compassion or anger toward the sufferings of the common people; he has a number of semiautobiographical poems filled with bitter self-reproach. His private life, however, was marked by some shabby financial dealings and a fondness for gambling, lavish entertainments, and mistresses.

back from Siberia: Dostoevsky returned to St. Petersburg from his term of forced labor and military service in late December 1859.

1863: Nekrasov's poem "Neschastnye" [The unfortunates] was published in part in 1856; the edition Dostoevsky refers to here appeared in 1863. Dostoevsky also discusses the poem in *DP*, January 1877, 2.3. "The Unfortunates" deals with a man exiled for his revolutionary activities.

A Raw Youth: published in Nekrasov's *OZ* in 1875.

I said a few words in my weak voice: Dostoevsky's wife recalls: "Fedor Mikhailovich, deeply moved, gave a brief speech in a deeply agitated and breaking voice; he rated the talent of the late poet very highly and explained why Russian literature had suffered a great loss with his passing. In the opinion of many, it was the most sincere statement made over Nekrasov's open grave." A. G. Dostoevskaia, *Vospominaniia* [Memoirs] (Moscow: Khudozhestvennaia literatura, 1971), p. 318.

Tiutchev, Fedor Ivanovich (1803–73), Russian lyric poet.

Skabichevsky, A. M. (1838–1910), critic and journalist. His article appeared in *BV*, no. 6, January 6, 1878, and may also be found in his *Sochineniia* [Works] (St. Petersburg: Novosti, 1890), 2:331–404.

he has been misinformed: Skabichevsky in fact did not attend Nekrasov's funeral. The memoirs of several other witnesses generally confirm Dostoevsky's version of this incident.

December 1877, 2.2: Pushkin, Lermontov, and Nekrasov

muse of vengeance and sorrow: From Nekrasov's poem "Be silent, muse of vengeance and sorrow!" [Zamolkni, muza mesti i pechali] (1856). The poem is elegaic in mood and was written during a period of serious illness from which Nekrasov did not expect to recover.

greatness of Pushkin: Dostoevsky develops the ideas that follow in his "Pushkin Speech," *DP,* 1880, 2.

"Shall I behold. . . .": Inaccurate quotation from Pushkin's poem "Derevnia" [The village] (1819): "Shall I, dear friends, behold a people free from all oppression, / And slavery fallen at the tsar's behest . . . ?"

Pushkin's love for the Russian People: Dostoevsky's remarks here are partly aimed at Skabichevsky, who, in his article noted above, argued that Pushkin and Lermontov were exclusively poets of their own aristocratic milieu whereas Nekrasov was a genuine poet of the People.

"to make an example and instill fear": The episode occurs in chap. 7 of *The Captain's Daughter* [Kapitanskaia dochka] (1836). Savelich is a serf assigned to look after the young hero of the novel; when he sees the rebel Pugachev about to hang his master, he offers himself in the latter's stead.

songs, supposedly of the western Slavs: Most of Pushkin's cycle of sixteen poems, "Pesni zapadnykh slavian" [Songs of the West Slavs], were drawn from Prosper Mérimées's forgery of Illyrian folk songs, *La Guzla* (1829); several are translations of genuine Serbian songs; and two are probably Pushkin's own creations.

two drunken peasants: In Pushkin's poem "Svat Ivan, kak pit' my stanem . . ." [Brother Ivan, when we start drinking] (1833), a poem written in playful folk language about peasants drinking in memory of those deceased.

"Tale of the Bear": "Skazka o medvedikhe" (1830), a narrative verse, written in the style of a folktale, in which a peasant kills a bear and captures her three cubs; it ends with the lament of the bear's mate.

Kalashnikov: Lermontov's "Pesnia pro tsaria Ivana Vasil'evicha, molodogo oprichnika i udalogo kuptsa Kalashnikova" (1838) [The song of tsar Ivan Vasilevich, the tsar's young bodyguard, and the bold merchant Kalashnikov]. Kalashnikov, a merchant, killed Kirbeevich, one of Ivan IV's bodyguards, in a fistfight that had been arranged as a public entertainment; Kirbeevich had previously offended Kalashnikov's wife. When asked by the tsar whether he had deliberately killed Kirbeevich, Kalashnikov answers truthfully and is executed.

the slave Shibanov: Andrei Mikhailovich Kurbsky (1528–83), one of Ivan IV's military commanders, lost the tsar's favor and fled to Lithuania, Russia's enemy. A correspondence between the two followed, in which each bitterly denounced the other. Kurbsky sent his companion and faithful servant, Vasily Shibanov, to deliver a letter to Tsar Ivan; the tsar impaled Shibanov's foot with his staff, but Shibanov stood motionless while the tsar read the letter. Ivan, impressed by Shibanov's willingness to suffer and die for his master, tried to shame Kurbsky by Shibanov's example: "Thou shouldst be shamed by thy slave, Shibanov: he has preserved his honor before tsar and People; having given his lord a vow of fealty, he did not betray it even before the gates of death." The story is told in Karamzin's *Istoriia gosudarstva Rossiiskogo* [History of the Russian state] (St. Petersburg, 1843), 9:65.

upsurge of spirit the People were expressing for the first time: Nekrasov's journal *OZ*, unlike the conservative and Pan-Slavist press, made scant mention of the excitement over the uprising and war in the Balkans.

without any real education: Nekrasov was educated first at home and then spent five years at a high school in Yaroslavl; he failed to pass the entrance examinations for St. Petersburg University, although he attended some classes as an auditor.

certain well-known influences: Dostoevsky has in mind, initially, the influence of Belinsky, and then that of Chernyshevsky, Dobroliubov, Saltykov-Shchedrin, and other radicals with whom Nekrasov worked in publishing *S* and *OZ*.

"happy": Line from Nekrasov's "Elegy" [Elegiia] (1874): "The People have been liberated, but are they happy?"

masterpieces: The poems "Rytsar' na chas" (1862), "Tishina" (1857), "Russkie zhenshchiny" (1871–72), and "Vlas" (1854). "Knight for an Hour" is a largely autobiographical poem, full of self-reproach, in which the narrator feels he has been a "knight" or champion of the cause of reform for far too short a portion of his life. See also 1873.5.

"On the Volga" [Na Volge] (1860), a cycle of four poems, originally planned as a larger autobiographical work with the general title "A Knight for an Hour."

December 1877, 2.3: Poet and Citizen. General Views of Nekrasov as a Man

duplicity in the image he left to us: See notes to December 1877, 2.1. Skabichevsky, in particular, makes excuses for Nekrasov.

battering himself against the floor of his own church: Dostoevsky here combines motifs from two of Nekrasov's poems, "Silence" and "A Knight for an Hour."

art for art's sake and no more: Again, a thrust at Skabichevsky, who had argued that Nekrasov's place of honor in literature came not from his devotion to the idea of art for art's sake but from his concern for social justice.

Here are those verses: Dostoevsky cites the first three stanzas of the second part of Nekrasov's "The Secret: An Attempt at a Contemporary Ballad" [Sekret: opyt sovremennoi ballady]. The poem in fact was not written before Nekrasov's acquaintance with Belinsky, but in 1846. The poem as a whole concerns a wealthy miser who is dying; the section Dostoevsky quotes is in quotation marks in the original and forms part of the millionaire's deathbed confession to his children of the shady dealings to which he has resorted in order to make his fortune. There is no suggestion in the poem that it refers to Nekrasov himself.

"love of mankind": Lines from Nekrasov's "A Knight for an Hour."

Mr. Suvorin: In *NV*, no. 662, January 1, 1878, Suvorin recalled with gratitude the help and advice Nekrasov had given him when he was beginning his career as a publisher and journalist.

December 1877, 2.4: A Witness in Nekrasov's Favor

Hecuba: *Hamlet,* act 2, scene 2: "What's Hecuba to him, or he to Hecuba, / That he should weep for her?"

ancient martyr of Pechersk: The *Paterik* [Book of the holy fathers] of the Kievan Caves Monastery, an eleventh- and twelfth-century collection of stories of monks who lived in the monastery, contains the story of Ioann the Solitary, who spent thirty years confined in a cave. In order to conquer his passions, he once buried himself up to his waist in the earth. He did not die while thus buried, but did conquer his passion. *Kyevo-Pecher'skyi paterik* (Kyiv: Akademii nauk, 1931), pp. 138–41.

"a citizen—thou must": From Nekrasov's "Poet and Citizen" [Poet i grazhdanin] (1856).

December 1877, 2.5: To the Readers

a literary work: Dostoevsky refers to his plans for *The Brothers Karamazov*, a work that was to engage him for most of the next three years.

Red Cross: The letter came from V. V. Mikhailov (1832–95), a writer and teacher. Mikhailov's letter has not survived, but probably dealt with the activities of the Russian Red Cross during the Russo-Turkish War.

striutsky: See November 1877, 1.1.

Sinclair: The book is Sir John George Tollemache Sinclair, *A Defence of Russia and the Christians of Turkey; including a sketch of the Eastern Question from* 1686 to September, 1877 (London, 1877). Sinclair's work appeared in Russian in 1878.

1880, 1: Explanatory Note Concerning the Speech on Pushkin Printed Below

created a substantial impression: The idea of erecting a monument to Pushkin was first proposed in 1862 by a group of graduates of the school at Tsarskoe Selo, where Pushkin had received his education. Funds for the monument were raised by public subscription. One of the highlights of the commemorative celebrations during the first week of June was a two-day public session of the Society of Lovers of Russian Literature, attended by Russia's leading writers; notably absent was Tolstoy, who declined the society's invitation to participate. The evening after he delivered his speech, Dostoevsky wrote to tell his wife how it was received by the audience: "The hall was packed to the rafters. No, Anya, you can never conceive or imagine the effect it had! What are my successes in Petersburg! Nothing, nil, in comparison with this! When I made my appearance there was thunderous applause in the hall and for a long, very long time they would not let me begin. I took my bows and made gestures, asking them to let me begin, but nothing worked: rapture, enthusiasm (and all from the Karamazovs)! Finally, I began to read: I was interrupted at absolutely every page, and sometimes at every sentence, by a thunder of applause. I read loudly, with passion. Everything I wrote about Tatiana was accepted with enthusiasm. . . . When I proclaimed at the end the idea of *universal unity* of people, the hall was as if in hysterics; when I finished—I won't tell you about the howl, the wail of rapture: strangers among the audience wept and sobbed, embraced one another *and swore to one another that they would be better, that they would not hate each other in the future, but would love*. The order of the meeting was disrupted: everyone rushed to me on the stage: *grand-dames*, female students, state secretaries, male students—all of them embracing and kissing me. All the members of our society who were on the stage; all of them, literally all of them, were weeping with rapture. For half an hour afterward I was called out to take bows; they were waving handkerchiefs; for example, two old men I didn't know stopped me: 'We've been enemies for twenty years and haven't spoken to one another, but now we've embraced and made up. It's you who has reconciled us. You are our saint, our prophet!' 'A prophet! A prophet!' came the cry from the crowd. Turgenev, about whom I put in a kind word in my speech, rushed to embrace me in tears; Annenkov ran up to shake my hand and kiss my shoulder. 'You are a genius, you are more than a genius!' they both told me. Aksakov (Ivan) ran on to the stage and declared to the audience that my speech *was not simply a speech but a historical event*!" (*F. M. Dostoevskii—A. G. Dostoevskaia: Perepiska* [F. M. Dostoevsky—A. G. Dostoevskaia: Correspondence] [Leningrad: Nauka, 1976], p. 346). Many other witnesses confirm the very profound effect Dostoevsky's speech had on the audience.

Aleko and Onegin: The central characters, respectively, of Pushkin's "The Gypsies" [Tsygany] and his *Eugene Onegin*.

Pechorin: Hero of Lermontov's *A Hero of Our Time* [Geroi nashego vremeni] (1840); Chichikov, hero of Gogol's *Dead Souls* [Mertvye dushi] (1842); Rudin: hero of Turgenev's novel of the same name (1856); Lavretsky: hero of Turgenev's *Nest of Gentlefolk* [Dvorianskoe gnezdo] (1859). All these characters are flawed, and most were considered by nineteenth-century Russian critics to be "superfluous men." Such fictional characters were seen as having an awareness of social and ethical problems but being unwilling or unable to do anything to remedy the ills of their society.

Tatiana: Heroine of Pushkin's *Eugene Onegin*.

History of the Pugachev Rebellion: [Istoriia Pugacheva] (1834), Pushkin's historical study of the peasant uprising of 1773–74, led by Emelian Pugachev.

eighty million: As one contemporary pointed out (V. P. Vorontsov, in *VE*, no. 10, 1880, p. 818), the population of the Russian Empire at the time was over ninety million, of which only thirty-five million were Russians.

"shall pass away in an instant": An echo of the prophecy of the fall of Babylon made in the book of Revelation 18:17: "For in one hour so great riches is come to naught."

Batu (1208?–55), Mongol khan, grandson of Genghis Khan; conqueror of northeast and south Russia. He headed a major invasion, launched in 1236; by 1241–42, his forces had reached the Adriatic coast. The invasion devastated many areas of the country and marked the beginning of a century of Tatar domination.

Time of Troubles: Name given to the period in Russian history from 1598 to 1613, from the demise of the Rurik dynasty to the accession of the Romanov dynasty. The period was marked by internal strife, peasant uprisings, the appearance of false pretenders to the throne, and invasions by Poles and Swedes. The Poles were driven out of Moscow by a national militia raised by Minin and Pozharsky.

convert the whole of Europe to Orthodoxy: A. N. Pypin, in his "Pol'skii vopros v russkoi literature" [The Polish question in Russian literature], *VE*, nos. 2 and 4, 1880, discussing an article by the Slavophile Samarin, suggests that Samarin's solution to the Polish problem was to convert the Poles to Orthodoxy.

1880, 2: Pushkin

said Gogol: The quotation is from Gogol's essay "Neskol'ko slov o Pushkine" [A few words about Pushkin], which appeared in his collection, *Arabesques* (1835).

Parny, André Chénier and others: Evariste-Désiré de Parny (1753–1814), French poet. Parny had profound influence on the verse of the young Pushkin. André de Chénier (1762–1794), French poet, the greatest French lyricist of the eighteenth century. Chénier influenced Pushkin in the 1820s, in his "Byronic" period.

"The Gypsies": [Tsygany] (1827), narrative poem by Pushkin. Its central figure, Aleko, is a weak but vicious character who, disgusted with civilization, flees the city to seek freedom among the "primitive" gypsies in southern Russia. He wants freedom only for himself, however; eventually he murders a gypsy girl and her lover and is banished from their community.

fourteen classes: See notes to October 1876, 2.3.

"Depart from us. . . .": At the end of the poem, an old man dismisses Aleko with these words.

"Oh, why. . . .": From *Eugene Onegin*, "The Travels of Onegin."

"Noble demon. . . .": From Nekrasov's poem "Otradno videt', chto nakhodit. . . ." [A joy to see. . . .] (1845).

"moral embryo": Belinsky, in his ninth article on Pushkin, thus describes Tatiana. V. G. Belinsky, *Sobranie sochinenii* [Collected works] (Moscow: Khudozhestvennaia literature, 1981), 6:422.

"all her perfections": Paraphrase of Onegin's remarks in his letter to Tatiana, chap. 8, stanza 32.

exclaiming with curses: In chap. 8, stanzas 12 and 13, after Onegin has killed his friend Lensky and has been rejected by Tatiana, he travels aimlessly through Russia. The couplet quoted is from the uncompleted "Fragments from Onegin's Travels."

"a parody, perchance": From chap. 7, stanza 24.

reason for refusing Onegin: Belinsky, like Dostoevsky, regarded Tatiana as the essence of Russian womanhood, but he said: "Tatiana does not like society and for the sake of happiness would leave it forever to live in the country; but while she is in society, its opinion will always be her idol, and fear of its judgment will always be the basis of her morals." V. G. Belinsky, *Sobranie sochinenii* [Collected works] (Moscow: Khudozhestvennaia literature, 1981), 6:423.

". . . true to him for life": Chap. 8, stanza 47.

old general: As N. O. Lerner has shown, Tatiana's husband is probably about thirty-five, hardly an old man. See "Muzh Tatiany" [Tatiana's husband], *Rasskazy o Pushkine* [Stories about Pushkin] (Leningrad: Priboi, 1929), p. 215.

"her mother begged, implored": Chap. 8, stanza 47.

peace and rest at last: The ideas that follow were developed by Ivan in *The Brothers Karamazov,* book 4 ("The Grand Inquisitor").

"'happiness was possible, so near'": Chap. 8, stanza 47.

"the grave of her poor nurse": Chap. 8, stanza 46.

"I look ahead and have no fear": The opening lines of Pushkin's "Stanzas" [Stansy] (1826).

"Tale of the Bear," "Brother Ivan": See December 1877, 2.2.

"Scenes from Faust" [Stsena iz Fausta] (1825) involves characters from Goethe's *Faust,* although the remainder is Pushkin's own creation. "Once There Lived a Poor Young Knight" [Zhil na svete rytsar' bednyi] (1829), set in Europe during the Crusades, is in the form of a legend or ballad and describes a knight who dedicates himself utterly to an ideal of purity.

"Don Juan": Pushkin's "Stone Guest" [Kamennyi gost'] (1830), in which he treats the Don Juan legend.

"A Feast in Time of Plague" [Pir vo vremia chumy] (1830), one of Pushkin's "Little Tragedies"; it is an adaptation of a scene from John Wilson's *City of the Plague*; "Mary's Song," sung by one of the characters, laments the fact that the plague has emptied the once noisy village school.

"Once, wandering. . . .": From Pushkin's poem "The Pilgrim" [Strannik] (1835), a free adaptation, in verse, of motifs from chapter 1 of John Bunyan's *Pilgrim's Progress.*

"Imitations of the Koran": Pushkin's "Podrazhaniia Koranu" (1824), verses in the style of the Koran.

"Egyptian Nights": [Egipeteskie nochi] (1837), a fragment of a proposed novel, it deals with Cleopatra.

"gave His blessing": From F. I. Tituchev's poem, "These Poor Villages. . . ." [Eti bednye seleniia] (1855).

1880, 3.1: On One Most Basic Point

The Moscow News: Dostoevsky's speech was first published in *MV*, no. 162, June 13, 1877. Liberal newspapers such as *Strana* and *Molva* were quick to challenge the ideas Dostoevsky expressed and argued that the speech's initial impact came more from the emotionally charged atmosphere surrounding it than from its content. *VE*, no. 7, 1880, dismissed it as a rehash of old Slavophile ideas.

Gradovsky, Aleksandr Dmitrievich (1841–89), professor, writer, historian of law. His article taking issue with Dostoevsky appeared in *G*, no. 174, June 25, 1880, and can also be found in his *Sobranie sochinenii* [Collected works] (St. Petersburg: M. M. Stasiulevich, 1901), 6:375–83.

a fearsome row was raised: The newspaper *Strana*, no. 64, August 17, 1880, for example, accused Dostoevsky of attacking liberalism without making his own position clear or fully expressing his own ideals. The newspaper's columnist A. Vvedensky accused Dostoevsky of fantasizing and of distorting the facts of Russian life.

Manilov: obsequious and shallowly sentimental character in Gogol's *Dead Souls*.

Skvoznik-Dmukhanovskys: The mayor in Gogol's play *The Inspector-General*, who personifies crude Russianness.

Batu's invasion: See notes to 1880, 1.

"O Lord of Hosts, be with us!": Prayer said in Orthodox churches during the first week of Lent.

Old Believers: Church Slavonic, a language distinct from but closely related to Russian in which Russian Orthodox services are conducted; Dostoevsky takes issue with those who charged that Church Slavonic would be imperfectly understood by poorly educated people. The Old Believers preserved, in large measure, the rites, language, icons, and books dating from before the Great Schism of 1667.

"O Lord, ruler of my being": Beginning of a prayer composed by Ephraim the Syrian (d. 373), a saint noted for his poetry and his commentaries on the Gospels.

"dipped their hands in blood": Inaccurate quotation from Nekrasov's "Knight for an Hour." In that poem the poet prays that he be led away from the "smug, idly chattering throng whose hands are stained with blood." (See also notes to December 1877, 2.2.)

"European liberal": I.e., in the late 1840s, when Dostoevsky participated in the Petrashevsky Circle and was under the influence of the ideas of French utopian socialists.

"The son rode. . . .": lines from the refrain found in a number of Russian folk songs in which a woman is used as a beast of burden, i.e., a grown son is being carried by his mother or a wife is harnessed to the plow. See A. N. Sobolevsky, *Velikorusskie narodnye pesni* [Great Russian folksongs] (St. Petersburg, 1895–1902), 7:94–95.

Bolshaia Morskaia: (Later Herzen Street), a fashionable shopping street in St. Petersburg.

the last war: The Russo-Turkish War of 1877–78.

1880, 3.2: Aleko and Derzhimorda. Aleko's Sufferings for a Peasant Serf. Anecdotes

Korobochka, Sobakevich: Characters from Gogol's *Dead Souls*; Skvoznik-Dmukhanovsky, Derzhimorda, Tiapkin-Lapkin: characters from Gogol's play *The Inspector General.*

Beltov, Rudin: Beltov is the protagonist of Alexander Herzen's short novel *Who Is to Blame?* [Kto vinovat?] (1841–46); Rudin, central character in Turgenev's novel of the same name, leaves Russia and dies heroically but uselessly on the barricades in Paris during the revolution of 1848.

a courier on the highway: Dostoevsky tells this story in more detail in January 1876, 3.1.

Khomiakov, Aleksei (1804–60); Samarin, Iu. F. (1819–76); Aksakov, Konstantin (1817–60), founders of the Slavophile movement.

"eating radishes and writing denunciations": From Turgenev's poem "Pomeshchik" [The landowner] (1846).

mediators: In the years following the emancipation of 1862, mediators [*miryovye posredniki*] were officials appointed to investigate disputes and complaints arising between peasants and landowners during the implementation of the emancipation edict.

Lucrezia Floriani: George Sand's novel of 1846.

venerable old fellow: P. V. Annenkov. In his memoirs, *An Extraordinary Decade* [Zamechateln'noe desiatiletie], he tells of how the Granovsky and Herzen families and Ketcher spent the summer of 1845 in the village of Sokolovo, near Moscow: "In all likelihood, Sokolovo never had before or has since presented so astounding a scene of noise and commotion as it did in the summer of 1845. Visiting the vacationers was done on a fabulous, massive scale. The lawn fronting the mansion was the site of almost colossal dinners. . . ." Annenkov notes that someone in the party did remark, on seeing the peasant woman harvesting grain, "that, of all women, the Russian woman was the only one who felt no embarrassment in front of anyone and in front of whom no one had any cause to feel embarrassed." He adds, however, that Granovsky objected to the joke: "The shame [is] not of the Russian peasant woman but of those who brought her to it and who are accustomed to treat her cynically." P. V. Annenkov, *An Extraordinary Decade*, trans. Irwin Titunik, ed. Arthur P. Mendel, (Ann Arbor: University of Michigan Press, 1968), pp. 129–30.

1880, 3.3: Two Halves

mutual relationships: "Servants, be obedient to them that are your masters . . ." (Ephesians 6:5); "Exhort servants to be obedient unto their own masters . . ." (Titus 2:9).

Mary of Egypt: early saint who, after her conversion to Christianity, lived for forty-seven years in the desert praying for forgiveness of her sins.

"at hand, at the door": "So likewise ye, when ye shall see all these things, know that it is very near, even at the doors" (Matthew 24:33).

1880, 3.4: To One—"Humble Thyself"; To Another—"Exalt Thyself." A Tempest in a Teapot

our fellow Orthodox: In 1821, at the Congress of Laibach, Metternich managed to sway Alexander I away from some of his more liberal intentions; when he learned of the Greek revolt against Turkish rule, Alexander disavowed any Russian sympathy for the movement and later refused to meet a Greek delegation.

about our service to Metternich: Dostoevsky refers to the reactionary policies of Nicholas I. Together with the monarchs of Prussia and Austria, Nicholas worked to stop the spread of revolution and the growth of nationalism among the peoples of eastern and central Europe. Nicholas I, with an army of one million, became the policeman of Europe, at least east of the Rhine. Dostoevsky is quoted as saying, apropos of his prison sentence that followed the trial of members of the Petrashevsky Circle: "Among other things . . . I suffered for my remarks that Russia had served Metternich's policies" (F. M. Dostoevsky, *PSS*, 18:316).

1881, 1.1: Finances. A Citizen as an Offended Thersites. Crowning from Below and the Musicians. A Refuge for Windbags and the Windbags

I now resume my *Diary* with an article on economics?: Dostoevsky's wife notes that at the beginning of 1881 "he decided to take up the publication of *A Writer's Diary* once more, since during the troubled years preceding he had gathered a good many disquieting ideas about Russia's political situation and he could only express them freely in his own magazine. In addition, the rousing success of the single issue of *A Writer's Diary* for 1880 led us to hope that the renewed publication would find a wide circle of readers, and Fedor Mikhailovich truly valued the opportunity to make his heartfelt ideas known. He planned to publish *A Writer's Diary* for two years and then hoped to write the second part of *The Brothers Karamazov* . . ." (A. G. Dostoevskaia, *Vospominaniia* [Memoirs] [Moscow: Khudozhestvennaia literatura, 1971], p. 370). Dostoevsky suffered a pulmonary hemorrhage on January 26, however, and died on January 28, the day the censor passed the final issue of the *Diary* for publication.

the current epidemic: Russian newspapers through the latter part of 1880 abounded in articles on economics offering a wide range of advice in dealing with the financial crisis in the country. A state budget, published on January 1, 1881, showed an anticipated deficit of over five hundred million rubles. A feuilleton in the newspaper *Novosti i birzhevaia gazeta*

[The News and Stock-Exchange Gazette], no. 263, October 5, 1880, complained: "At today's rate of exchange, the value of the paper ruble is sixty-three silver kopecks, i.e., nearly half. . . . We complain of the terrible rise in prices of all consumer goods, from bread and meat to 'regal' drinks and ladies' fashionable garments; we blame the elements, we blame the producers and the retailers, we criticize the government; but at the same time we do not notice that in fact it is not the prices of goods that have risen so much as it is the value of our money that has fallen." Many of these financial problems were results of the expense of the 1877–78 war with Turkey.

Thersites: In The *Iliad,* book 2, an ugly and foul-mouthed officer in the Greek army besieging Troy. Thersites heaped abuse on Agamemnon, accusing him of greed, and urged the Acheans to abandon their attempts to take Troy and return home. Here he personifies irresponsible and malevolent criticism.

Berlin Conference: More correctly, the Berlin Congress, which met in June and July 1878 and signed, as its final act, the Treaty of Berlin. The aim of the congress was to revise the terms of the Treaty of San Stefano (March 2, 1878 [n.s.]), which had ended the Russo-Turkish War and which, in the opinion of most European powers, left Russia with too much influence in the Balkan peninsula. The Treaty of Berlin made Bulgaria an autonomous principality under Turkish suzerainty; Bosnia and Herzegovina were to be occupied and administered by Austro-Hungary; the independence of Serbia, Montenegro, and Rumania was recognized. Russia received territory around Kars and Batumi in Asiatic Turkey, small reward for the sacrifices made during the war.

"crowning our edifice": The phrase is a translation of the French *couronner l'édifice* and was used frequently in nineteenth-century France to mean the granting of democratic rights and political freedom. E.g.: "'Freedom,' as Louis Napoleon put it, 'has never helped in the establishment of a lasting political structure; freedom crowns such a structure when time has made it strong.'" André Maurois, *A History of France* (London: Jonathan Cape, 1956), p. 400.

white waistcoats: I.e., liberals. The expression probably came from revolutionary France, where white waistcoats "à la Robespierre" were popular among the Jacobins. See *Grand dictionnaire universel du XIX siècle* (Paris: Larousse, 1865), 8:1256.

"seated neatly in a row": From Krylov's fable "The Quartet" [Kvartet] (1811), in which four animals attempt to play a quartet but cannot manage to produce pleasing sounds from their instruments. They decide the problem is in their seating arrangements, but, the fable concludes, without skill and taste they will not succeed even if seated neatly in a row.

"native bast shoes": The liberal journalist G. K. Gradovsky made this remark in attacking I. S. Aksakov's Slavophile newspaper *Rus*; Aksakov quotes Gradovsky's remark in his editorial in *Rus,* no. 8, January 2, 1881.

"forge chains for the People": A quotation from a poem, "Gentlemen's Rule" [Gospodchina], by an unknown author. The poem expresses the fear that the introduction of constitutional government (of which there were rumors in the late 1870s) would lead to reenslavement of the peasants. A. S. Suvorin remarks, in his reminiscences of Dostoevsky: "[Dostoevsky] called a constitution 'gentlemen's rule' and maintained that peasants in the various parts of Russia where he had spoken to them had given it that name. Even at the Pushkin celebrations he recited to me a little verse about this 'gentlemen's rule,' one stanza of which he included in his *Diary* that came out today. . . . He believed that first we had to ask only the People, not all the classes at once, not the representatives of all the classes, but only the peasants specifically." A. S. Suvorin, "O pokoinom" [On the deceased], in *F. M. Dostoevskii v vospominaniniakh sovremennikov* [Dostoevsky remembered by his contemporaries] (Moscow: Khudozhestvennaia literatura, 1964), 2:420.

1881, 1.2: Can We Expect European Finances in Russia?

built in ten years: The major boom in railway construction occurred between 1865 and 1875; about a thousand miles of track was laid in each of those ten years, increasing the length of the rail system fivefold.

redemption money: See notes to May and June 1877, 1.3.

Captain Kopeikins: A character from Gogol's *Dead Souls*. Dostoevsky uses him here as a personification of mindless greed, which is not the way he is portrayed in Gogol's novel. A disabled veteran of the 1812 war, his efforts to obtain a pension are thwarted by bureaucrats and he turns to robbery.

1881, 1.3: Forget Immediate Problems So That the Roots Can Be Restored. Through Lack of Ability I Enter into Something Spiritual

the present minister: A new minister of finance, A. A. Abaza (1821–95), was appointed on October 27, 1880.

salt tax: On November 23, 1877, Alexander II signed the *ukaz* abolishing the salt tax, a long-standing source of revenue for the Russian government. The salt tax was based on the number of persons in a household and thus imposed a relatively heavier burden on lower-income families. The idea of instituting an income tax to replace the poll tax was discussed but not implemented.

Karlsruhe: Quite likely a reference to Turgenev, who lived in Karlsruhe in 1868–69 and who spent much time in nearby Baden-Baden during the 1860s. (See also notes to February 1877, 1.1.)

Khlestakov: In act 3, scene 6 of Gogol's *Inspector General*, his hero, Khlestakov, boasting of his exalted position in the St. Petersburg bureaucracy, talks of the "poor rat of a copying clerk" who does all the work.

1881, 1.4: The First Root. Instead of an Authoritative Financial Tone I Lapse into Old Words. The Broad Ocean. The Longing for Truth and the Necessity for Serenity, So Useful in Financial Matters

arrears: Poorly organized tax collection in the countryside, coupled with a shortage of land, led to massive tax arrears on the part of Russian peasants in the years following the Russo-Turkish War. See W. Bruce Lincoln, *The Great Reforms: Autocracy, Bureaucracy and the Politics of Change in Imperial Russia* (DeKalb, Ill.: Northern Illinois University Press, 1990), p. 181.

mediators of the first instance: The mediator (*mirovoi posrednik*) was an official appointed to investigate disputes and complaints arising between peasants and landowners during the implementation of the emancipation edict. If disputes could not be resolved at this level, a higher body (the second instance), the District Congress, would try to resolve the dispute.

in the magazine *Rus*: A series of articles by I. S. Aksakov and N. M. Pavlov in the weekly *Rus* in late November 1880, argued that the full intent of the Act of Emancipation of 1861 had never been carried out and that institutions such as the mediator were never fully accepted by the peasantry. Bureaucracy had fought against rural self-government and limited the effectiveness of the reforms.

Stunde: See notes to January 1877, 1.2.

"Do not believe it": A paraphrase of Christ's warning to his disciples against false prophets, Matthew 24:23: "Then if any man shall say unto you, Lo, here is Christ, or there; believe it not."

"golden charters": A number of Russian folk legends told of the tsar's decrees printed in letters of gold. In the period following the announcement of the Emancipation, for example, rumors circulated that the publicized terms were false and that the actual and much more favorable terms of Emancipation, printed in gold, had been kept secret from the peasants.

zemstvo: An institution of local self-government and economic administration, existing in Russia from 1864 to 1918.

twenty government officials: A letter to the editor of *Rus*, no. 5, December 13, 1881, listed thirty-four officials in a typical district who had some authority over the local peasants.

"than even the world itself could contain": A paraphrase of John 21:25: "And there are also many other things which Jesus did, the which, if they should be written every one, I suppose that even the world itself could not contain the books that should be written."

1881, 2.1: A Witty Bureaucrat. His Opinion of Our Liberals and Europeans

cut by half: *NV*, no. 1741, January 2, 1881, suggested that Russian finances might be repaired by cutting fifty thousand troops from the army and that reducing it even by half would weaken the country less than chronic budgetary deficits. Earlier, an editorial in the liberal newspaper *Strana*, no. 87, November 6, 1887, had stated: "We will state plainly that the best minister of finance for Russia will be the one who could manage energetically to restrain the growth of expenditures in the ministries of war and the navy."

given that name in Berlin: *Novosti i birzhevaia gazeta* [The News and Stock-Exchange Gazette], no. 309, November 20, 1880, quoted an article from the Berlin *National Zeitung* written by an anonymous German statesman who knew Russia well. The article stated: "The *greatest* event in Russian history to our day was the decision of Peter the Great to bring Russia into the life of Europe by *drawing in forces which were not present within the country itself*. All the *great* rulers of Russia, beginning from the sixteenth century, acted in this spirit. But at the beginning of each new reign there arose a Russo-Slavic reaction to such a movement. This reaction was regularly suppressed (the last time in 1855). Now the strongest process of rejection is taking shape, a rejection in principle. Meanwhile, practical experience and the facts that have always followed from it shows the necessity for *help from the Germans* if the Russians actually want to emerge from their present disorder and negligent attitude toward work."

1881, 2.2: Krylov's Old Fable about a Certain Pig

fable of Krylov: The fable quoted here in part is entitled "The Pig Beneath the Oak" [Svin'ia pod dubom] (1825).

on another topic: The moral of the fable, which Dostoevsky does not quote, is that the pig belittles science and scholarship while feeding on their fruits.

1881, 2.3: Geok-Tepe. What Does Asia Mean to Us?

Geok-Tepe has been taken: Since 1879 Russian forces had been waging a war of conquest of the Akhal-Tekin oasis in Turkmenia. After an unsuccessful attempt by General N. P. Lomakin, in August 1879, to seize the Turkoman stronghold of Geok-Tepe, a second expedition, commanded by General M. D. Skobelev, took the town on January 12, 1881, after a three-week siege.

foreign newspapers: Russian newspaper correspondents had been forbidden to accompany Skobelev's expedition; until the fall of the Geok-Tepe the major source of information on the campaign was the *London Daily News*, whose correspondent managed to reach the town in time to witness its capture and hear survivors' accounts of the plunder and massacre ordered by Skobelev. Portions of the reports of the *Daily News* were reprinted in the Russian press. Only after January 1, 1881, did regular Russian newspaper reports begin to appear. See Peter Hopkirk, *The Great Game: On Secret Service in High Asia* (London: John Murray, 1990), pp. 404–6.

"metal and brimstone": In act 2, scene 2 of his comedy *Hard Times* [Tiazhelye dni] (1863), Ostrovsky ridicules the backwardness and fear of progress common among Moscow merchants. Two merchants' wives talk of the danger of reading modern, secular books and express their fear of unfamiliar (to them) words such as "metal" and "brimstone."

"to save the kings": At the request of Austria, Russian tsar Paul I sent troops to northern Italy to aid Austrian forces battling the French; in 1813–14 Russian troops participated in the anti-Napoleonic coalition whose actions eventually resulted in the restoration of the Bourbons to the thrones of France and Spain; finally, in 1849, Nicholas I sent troops to help put down an uprising in Hungary and so preserve the integrity of the Hapsburg Empire.

a few perceptive Russians: Among those opposed to carrying the war against Napoleon into Europe were A. S. Shishkov, the governor-general of Moscow, F. V. Rostopchin, and the minister of foreign affairs, Count N. P. Rumiantsev. See N. M. Druzhinin, "Osvoboditel'naia voina 1813 i russkoe obshchestvo" [The war of liberation of 1813 and Russian society], in *Osvoboditel'naia voina* 1813 g. [The war of liberation of 1813] (Moscow: Nauka, 1965), pp. 57–58.

The usurper himself admitted this later: Barry O'Meara, Napoleon's physician on St. Helena, quoted the ex-emperor as saying that Russia would eventually possess Constantinople, most of Turkey, and Greece: "Once mistress of Constantinople, Russia gets all the commerce of the Mediterranean, becomes a great naval power, and God knows what may happen." His plan was to erect a barrier against Russia so that the "northern barbarians" could not overrun Europe (Barry O'Meara, *Napoleon in Exile or, A Voice from St. Helena* [1853; rpt. New York: AMS Press, 1969], 2:31–32). M. A. Thiers describes French proposals to conclude a separate peace with Russia in January 1813 in his *Histoire du Consulat et de l'Empire* (Paris: Paulin, 1857), 15:219–30.

At the congresses: At the Congress of Vienna in 1815, England, France, and Austria opposed Russia's demands for territorial expansion into Poland; at the Congress of Berlin in 1878, the European powers again united to limit Russian influence in the Balkans.

to quell their civil strife: Dostoevsky possibly has in mind the Olmütz agreement of 1850. The two principal allies of Nicholas I, Austria and Prussia, came to the brink of military conflict in 1850 over their rivalry for dominance in the proposed German union. Nicholas I pressured his German allies into an agreement at Olmütz.

faced with another disaster: Dostoevsky may be referring here to Austria's behavior in the years preceding the Crimean War. Although the emperor of Austria owed his throne to the intervention of Nicholas I in Hungary in 1849, Austria was prepared to side with Britain and France to check Russia's advance into the Balkans. In 1854, Austria and Prussia, nominally Russia's allies, signed a defensive alliance to prevent Russia from moving westward.

Repetilov: A character from Griboedov's *Woe from Wit*. He tried to advance his career by marrying the daughter of the influential Baron von Klotz; but in act 4, scene 5 he complains that the marriage brought no dowry and has not helped his career in any way.

1881, 2.4: Questions and Answers

"land of holy miracles": From A. S. Khomiakov's poem "A Dream" [Mechta]. (See also notes to July and August 1877, 2.2.)

Gambetta, Léon (1838–82), French statesman, president of the Chamber of Deputies 1879–81. In early 1881, Russian newspapers commented on his growing influence, and some suggested he might become a dictator.

Bismarck might be oppressing them: Pope Leo XIII managed to regain many of the losses to ecclesiastical authority that had been made in Germany under Bismarck's *Kulturkampf* (see notes to January 1876, 3.2).

"*la Russie se recueille* once more": In 1856, after Russia's defeat in the Crimean War, her foreign minister, A. M. Gorchakov, summed up Russia's foreign policy as one of noninterference in European affairs so as to allow the country to recover from the ravages of the war. "La Russie ne boude pas, elle se recueille [Russia isn't sulking, she is collecting her wits]," he wrote. The phrase became widely quoted.

alliance of Germany and Austria: On October 7 (n.s.), 1879, Bismarck signed a defensive alliance with Austria under which each party agreed to come to the aid of the other in the event of an attack by Russia.

Turkish territory: Article 25 of the Treaty of Berlin, July 13 (n.s.), 1878, stated that Austria would occupy Bosnia and Herzegovina, formerly possessions of Turkey. (See also notes to 1881, 1.1.)

regarding the Black Sea: On October 19, 1870, taking advantage of the collapse of France, Russia announced that she would no longer abide by the provisions of the Treaty of Paris (1856) forbidding her from maintaining a naval presence in the Black Sea.

"don't leave your house": Dostoevsky's variation on the Russian proverb "If you're afraid of wolves, don't go into the forest."

Index